THE DIVISION OF LIGHT AND POWER

DENNIS J. KUCINICH

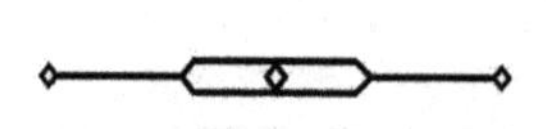

Supervising editor: Lizabeth Rogers, Finney Avenue Books.
Text, layout and Cover Design by Lizabeth Rogers, Finney Avenue Books.

Cover photograph "Sunset Lightning No. 6" by Kurt Shaffer Photographs - Licensed for use and copyright protected.
Back cover photo of Mayor Dennis Kucinich by Frank Aleksandrowicz.
Back cover photo of Dennis Kucinich, property of Dennis Kucinich.

Author's Note:
The dialogues in the book have been verified by and/or are authenticated by public records detailed in the end notes at the conclusion of the book.

A CIP record for this book is available from the Library of Congress - Cataloging in Publication Data

Published by Finney Avenue Books, LLC
PO Box 110145
Cleveland, OH 44111

www.FinneyAvenueBooks.com

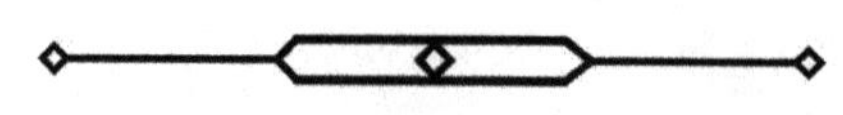

DEDICATION

This book is for my wife, Elizabeth.
I dedicate this book and all the years that went into writing it,
every effort poured into making it come alive,
every life experience reflected in it,
to you, to your heart and your soul,
to your great spirit,
to us.
Dearest Darling, to you, Wife, Life, my All.

Dennis

Greatest Love on Valentine's Day, 2021

"I believe in public ownership of all public service monopolies for the same reason that I believe in the municipal ownership of waterworks, of parks, of schools. I believe in the municipal ownership of these monopolies because if you do not own them, they will in time own you. They will corrupt your politics, rule your institutions and finally destroy your liberties."

Tom L. Johnson,
Founder of Muny Light
Mayor of Cleveland, 1901–1909

From his autobiography, "My Story" by Tom L. Johnson
Published by B.W. Huebsch, New York, 1911 • Page 194

Photo by Tibor Gasparik, City of Cleveland

TABLE OF CONTENTS

PART TWO - THE MAYOR WHO SAID "NO!"

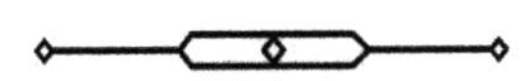

ACKNOWLEDGMENTS

There are so many friends to thank for their thoughtful suggestions, reviews, and edits over many years, all of which resulted in the production of this book. Thanks to:

Liz Rogers, editor extraordinaire, for her wisdom, her diligence, her attention to detail, her stellar work ethic, her counsel and her constant love and support.

To Mayor Tom Johnson who inspired our stand to save Muny Light. His legacy endures; and to the generations of Muny Light workers who kept alive his vision.

To the people of Cleveland, for their generosity and their determination to protect public power.

To all those men and women who served in City Hall when I was Mayor of Cleveland, your integrity in action was a great gift to our city.

To Sister Leona Neiberding, the lessons you taught an attentive sixth grader engraved the spiritual power of the moment into my heart and soul.

To Bob Weissman, for his dedication to the rights of working men and women; whose fearless guidance taught me how to challenge the status quo; whose unsurpassed intellect and vision understood the urgency of "challenging power which seems omnipotent," and the ever-present necessity of standing up for what one believes.

To Esther Weissman, for her brilliance, her gentle, powerful counsel and her caring support throughout.

To the UAW for always leading the way to protect Muny Light and the economic rights of its members; and for the leadership of Bill Casstevens and the intellect, the vision and the strength of Warren Davis.

To Carl and Louis Stokes who were central to our success. Your friendship and steadfast support were treasures. Carl, you were my brother, always there for me.

To Bob Scheer and Narda Zacchino for their encouragement to tell this story. Bob told me early on not to talk about the book, write it. Here it is Bob. Now can I talk about it?

To Gore Vidal, my dear friend, who believed I could write before I believed it. You are dearly missed.

To Shirley MacLaine, for her love and support in providing me with an opportunity to write the first full draft of the story and for teaching me about those things which really matter in life.

To Jack Schulman for his patient guidance, legal advice and editing through various drafts and for an enduring friendship.

To Milt Schulman, who with his wife Agnes, produced Jack and Howard. Milt figured prominently in my understanding of the actual workings of government so that I was unafraid to venture into unfamiliar territory.

To Al Grisanti and to everyone the Cleveland establishment ever scoffed at. I have always carried the awareness of your struggle forward. Your redemption was in your refusal to submit to selfish consensus.

To Blanche Nofel, who watched over me every day to make sure that I was sustained, rested and prepared to serve Cleveland.

To Joe Garry and David Frazier, who were there at the beginning of the story, for their friendship, guidance and love.

To Andy Juniewicz who has been a guiding light in my life, a constant source of laughter, an island of sanity in a topsy-turvy world, a place where I could breathe, and someone with whom I can play basketball.

To Amy Vossbrinck, for her unselfish service, constant encouragement and perseverance through proofreading one draft after another.

To Rich Barton, who helped me save Muny Light and continues to serve public power.

To Joe Tegreene, for fifty years of advice and friendship and his cogent editing of the financial narrative.

To Mark Daniels for his down-to-earth insight and helpful suggestions about content.

To Christopher Scheer, for his help in skillfully editing early drafts of the book.

To Chris Griscom, for her spiritual guidance which was essential to the daily unfolding of my path and the completion this book.

To George Forbes, one of the most gifted and cunning politicians who ever lived, for challenging me in so many ways. He remains one of my greatest teachers. When you read this book and understand that today George and I are good friends, you can understand why I believe world peace is possible.

To the attorneys who pursued the antitrust case on behalf of the people of Cleveland, lead counsel Brad Norris for his exceptional legal mind, James B. Davis for dedication to the people of Cleveland as city law director and his assistant, Robert Hart.

To Henry W. Eckhart, former chair of the Public Utilities Commission of Ohio, for his lifetime of commitment to the people and his long-time personal assistance.

To the journalists who demonstrated self-sacrificing courage in risking their careers to stand for the truth: Steve Clark, Jim Cox, Bob Franken and Bob Holden, the seer who helped turn the news tide in favor of Muny Light; and to Roldo Bartimole, the conscience of the Cleveland media.

To the Cleveland Police, and to Chief Fox, Inspector Nagorski, Detective Dustin Plank, Lt. Ed Kovacic and the Police Intelligence Unit, to Detectives Jim Benedict, John Zajac, Dan Mahon and Lucy Krause and all those who kept watch under dangerous conditions so that Sandy and I were able to safely complete our mission, 1977–1979.

To Ralph Nader, the Great Consumer Champion for coming to Cleveland's assistance at a crucial hour and alerting the nation about the significance of Cleveland's struggle.

To the Western Reserve Historical Society, Cleveland History Center, one of Cleveland's important legacy institutions and Margaret Roulett, for their safekeeping of the thousands of files needed for research for the Courage to Survive, Prayer for America and, The Division of Light and Power.

To members of the Kucinich Family, my mother and father, Virginia and Frank, my brothers Frank, Jr., Gary, Perry, Larry; my sisters Beth Ann and Terrie, who had to endure real hardship as a result of my being Mayor of Cleveland. My endless love, too, to Aunt Betty and Aunt Helen, who typed the first drafts of the manuscript.

To Judy, who provided me with a safe harbor and a place to protect the records which were invaluable in the writing of this book.

To Yelena, for helping me rediscover a new approach to health and diet so that I was up to the rigors of writing long hours.

To Dr. Donald Pensiero, his wife Marcine, and Dr. Mario Kamionkowski, for saving my life. (See Chapter 35.)

To Dr. Javier Lopez, whose dedication and selflessness in service to humanity has been one of the great inspirations in my life and whose personal assistance and attention enabled me to have the strength to follow the book through to completion.

Special thanks to Helen, who was with me at the very beginning of this journey, who brought fresh air and love to every day we were together, and who deserved, and found a better husband. "A million tomorrows shall all pass away…"

To Sandy, this book is our story. It is about the power of love to help survive even the most difficult circumstances. This book is also about your courage, your generosity, your insight, your faith, your great love which made the journey into the Division of Light and Power bearable and eventually a shared triumph. Thanks Sandy, to you and Ed, for your life-long love and friendship and sharing the miracle of our daughter.

INTRODUCTION

The following towns and cities had their municipal electric systems taken over by larger, investor-owned utilities prior to 1977. These takeovers resulted in higher utility rates for consumers and increased power costs to local governments, all of which were passed on to citizens in the form of higher taxes.

- Alaska: Craig.
- Arizona: Tombstone, Williams.
- California: Avalon.
- Colorado: Erie.
- Illinois: Bloomington, Woodstock, Cowden, Heyworth, Hopedale, Fithian, Sawyerville, Armington, Minier, Ogden, Jacksonville.
- Indiana: Decatur, Goshen, Portland, Crothersville, Albion, Oxford.
- Iowa: Grimes, Milo, Randolph, Imogene, Dunkerton.
- Kansas: Alton.
- Louisiana: Lake Providence, Thibodaux.
- Maine: Squirrel Island.
- Michigan: Grayling, Republic, Constantine, Allegan.
- Minnesota: St. Croix, Fall Lake, Wilton, Winton, Bayport, Mazeppa, Perley, Kelliher.
- Mississippi: Centerville, Fayette, Woodville, Shaw.
- Missouri: Canton.
- Nebraska: Burr, Ceresco, Mead, Peru, Cook.
- Nevada: Carlin.
- New Hampshire: Erroll, Wentworth Location, New Ipswich.
- New Jersey: Patterson.
- New Mexico: Carrizozo.
- North Carolina: Elm City.
- Ohio: Anna, Bellefountain, Caldwell, Clyde, East Palestine, Eatonville, Greenfield, Hiram, Huntsville, Liberty Center, Lowellville, Martins Ferry, Minerva, Norwalk, Paulding, Pioneer,

Reading, Stryker, Troy, Waterville, Wellston, Willard.

- Oklahoma: Ingersoll, Weleetka, Cashion, Crescent, Dacoma.
- Pennsylvania: Etna, Ford City, Sharpsburg, Tarentum, Brackenridge, Aspinwall.
- South Carolina: Ninety-six municipal utilities were privatized.
- Texas: Mansfield, Wake Village, Teague.
- Utah: Mantua.
- Washington: Grand Coulee.
- Wisconsin: Oliver, Commonwealth, Kewaunee, Readstown.
- Wyoming: Elmo, Sinclair, South Superior.

Privatizations proceeded in town after town, city after city, with few questions asked.

In 1969, at the age of twenty-three, I had just been elected to the City Council in Cleveland, Ohio, and began to ask questions when a monopoly utility worked with city officials to undermine the city's electric system, Muny Light.

This culminated in City Hall's decision to sell Cleveland's municipal electric system. I blocked the sale with a petition drive and was elected Mayor on a promise to save public power, unknowingly setting off a series of events that were at that time, unprecedented in U.S. history.

PROLOGUE

People who say, 'You can't fight City Hall,' don't know where it is. You have to find it before you can fight it. City Hall was not only the Doric gray stone temple on East Sixth and Lakeside Avenue in downtown Cleveland. City Hall was the boardroom of Cleveland's banks, its investor-owned utilities, its real estate combines - and the mob.

In Cleveland, City Hall was in the shadows, a giant specter invisible to the people of the city. I brought the invisible City Hall to light, with great consequences for my city, my family, my friends and myself. I was the Mayor and I fought City Hall.

Dennis J. Kucinich
Mayor of Cleveland
1977–1979

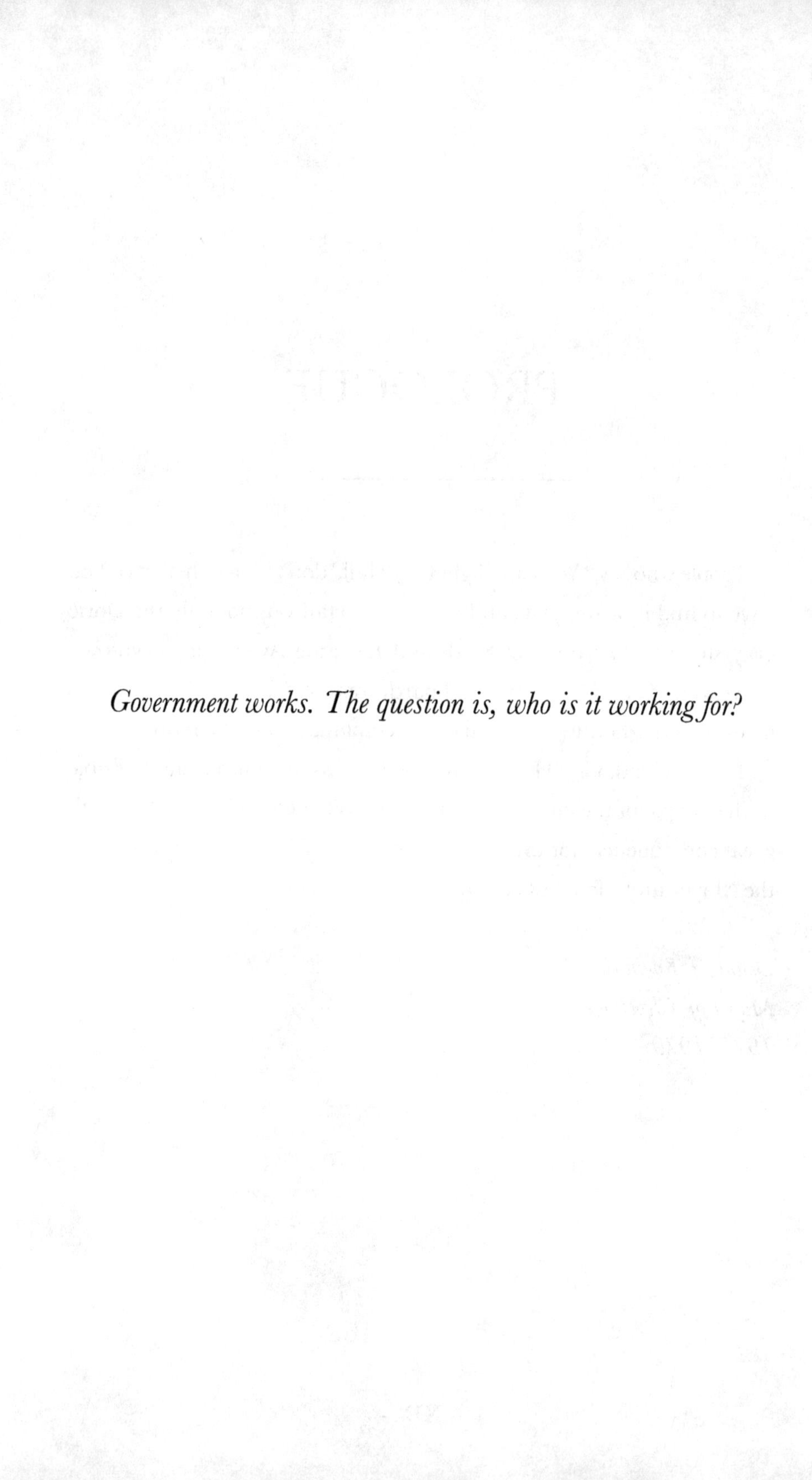

Government works. The question is, who is it working for?

PART ONE

A CITY IN THE DARK

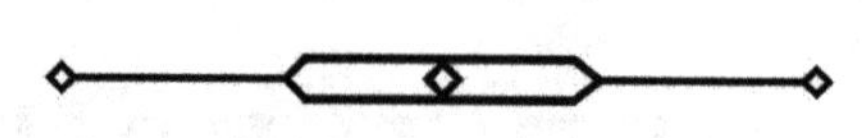

CHAPTER 1

Christmas Blackout

"Jeeee-sus loves you!" The words swirled in the crisp air of the glistening snow globe known as Cleveland, Ohio. If, in these wintry mists, it was redemption you sought, you found it in the Ministry of the Streets with Reverend Orris Price, a living, breathing holy card version of Jesus Christ, with dark olive skin, reddish beard, piercing blue eyes and a baritone voice which rose above the surging Christmas holiday crowd.

He called out randomly to the weary shoppers. Their interest wasn't salvation, but consumption, the search for tokens of affection. They were preoccupied with dazzling holiday lights, distracted by the elegant display windows of The May Company and entranced by the angelic carolers singing above the recorded music coming from the department stores.

Undaunted, the Reverend Price looked upwards, a pale yellow streetlight casting a touch of glory upon his face. He extended his arms toward the heavens in exultation, "Jeeee-sus loves you! Jesus loves you, Mary!" Joyously, he flung a morsel of grace into the snowy sky. It descended, gently, and touched a child of God named Mary, whose backward-looking gaze was caught by the all-seeing eye of Reverend Price, a divine 'gotcha' moment at his corner tabernacle on Euclid Avenue at Ontario Street.

"Mary, give your life to Jeeeez-sus," striking His name with a vocal thunderbolt. Mary was transfixed, her eyes on God's messenger. She received Reverend Price's nod as a beatitude, then smiled and turned to catch the crowd hurrying across Ontario Street in the headlong rush to prepare for Christmas, 1969.

The Reverend Price, animated apostle of the abbreviated epistle, clapped his thick, worn Bible and elevated it as a sacrament. Spirit shook his body, his eyes widened with joy as he called out to another soul, passionately dispensing deliverance to the procession of shoppers, whose only interest was in waiting for the traffic light to change, so they could worship at the altar of the god Xmas.

Snow flurried as my bride Helen and I hurried past the Bible-thumping Reverend Price and coursed with the crowd into Higbee's department store. Later, just moments after we exited with bags of gifts, a power failure hit downtown, and Christmas disappeared.

Helen looked at me, surprised and frowned, "What's that?"

"The city's lights seem to be going out, a lot," I observed.

"Maybe it's the weather," she offered.

"I don't know, Helen. We've been having blackouts no matter the weather," I said.

When the lights go out, what can you do? You wait for them to come on. That's life in the big city, except I had just been elected to the Cleveland City Council, and I had every intention of showing that things were going to be different.

I went to a pay phone to call the city's light system, and, after several attempts, got through.

"Division of Light and Power," a harried voice answered.

"This is Dennis Kucinich. I'm the new Councilman from Ward Seven. Could you please tell me why the lights are out? It's four days before Christmas and…"

"Hold on, hold on, hold on," the man growled. "You're the kid who beat Bilinski."

Yes, that was me, at age twenty-three, often mistaken for a paperboy in his early teens when I campaigned door to door. I defeated the Ukrainian Robin Hood, John Taras Bilinski, on my second time around with the help of the Cleveland Police, Paul DeGrandis, the Deputy Director of the Cuyahoga County Board of Elections, and 6'6", 320 lb. Scott Sikorski. Scott was a campaign worker and high school classmate who, after several failed attempts by election supervisors to get those inside a polling place in Ward Seven to open the door, tore it clean off its hinges.

It was there an hour earlier, in the basement of St. Augustine Church, Bilinski's ward machine, which officiated inside the polling station, ejected our designated witness, barricaded the windows and doors, then silently, desperately proceeded to count the paper ballots creatively, until they could come up with enough votes for Bilinski to win. Once Scott opened the door, the police and county election officials rushed inside like it was an Eliot Ness raid of a bootleg joint. The ballots were impounded and taken by police car to a secure place at the Cuyahoga County Board of Elections.

The official tally would take place at the Elections Board, where I won by sixteen votes in a recount. So, that's how I became the Councilman of the neighborhood where I went to high school, where church spires and pipe-organ smokestacks reached to a smudged sky. A neighborhood populated by a steely league of nations who spoke Polish, Greek, Slovak, Ukrainian, Russian, Arabic, Spanish, and occasionally English. It was a neighborhood of narrow streets lined with old men wearing white shirts and suspenders, and old ladies wearing babushkas and carrying shopping bags that dangled just above their socks, parading up and down the small commercial district on Professor Avenue.

It was on that very street in August of 1960, the St. John Cantius

Jayhawks varsity football squad gathered on the school steps for team pictures.

As a thirteen-year-old, 4'9", 98 lb., third-string varsity quarterback, I was being prepared for a career in Cleveland politics with every blind-side tackle, sack, forearm in the face, bell-ringer, dirt-eating episode known as "the game." As the last boy on the team, I practiced a gritty resilience against physical odds, a trait which would ultimately serve me well in the smash-mouth ward politics of the Tremont area.

I made the St. John Cantius varsity team as a freshman despite the misgivings of the coaches who, understanding the notion of contributory manslaughter, were alarmed at my lack of size. They humored my desire to enter into a single scrimmage, certain I would be easily dismissed given my first assignment, which was to take out the biggest person on the squad with a cross-body block. Once I executed the play perfectly, I made the team.

And play I did, lettering in my first year, for three reasons. One, the first-string quarterback was injured. Two, the second-string quarterback was injured. And three, I was the only other person on the team who knew all the plays, so I took to the field when the regular quarterbacks were sidelined.

My biggest challenge? I couldn't see over my center's rear end, but the other side couldn't see me either. I never recognized or even respected physical boundaries and odds, which was also good training for a career in politics. Once the ball was snapped, I was on my own and I loved the contest, a quality I inherited from the home life of my youth.

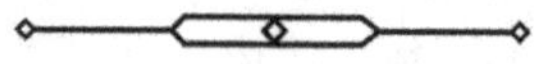

"Don't try throwing any weight around here you don't have yet, kid. You're not a Councilman for a couple of weeks. I keep track of those things." His phones rang continuously in the background. "Now you've got it straight. There is a power failure. All over the city. Number Six boiler's out. We're working on it. No steam for the turbine generator.

Here's somethin' for you. We don't have an emergency backup, no interconnect, so the whole system's down. CEI (the Cleveland Electric Illuminating Co.) is shafting us. They won't give us a back-up. We're stuck with outages. I gotta go."

"Wait. When will the lights go back on?"

"Look kid, I'm a boiler operator, not a fortune teller. People are gonna have to wait. Bye!" He hung up the phone. Little did I know how this exchange with a frantic boiler operator would impact the course of my life.

I turned to Helen and said, "How hard can it be to keep a light system going? Muny Light is always breaking down. People pay their electric bills. They have a right to expect the lights will come on when they flip the switch," I said.

"Once you get on the Council, things will be different, right?" Helen said in reassurance.

"Uh, yes," I said. After all, I knew about utilities from the time I was a child, because my parents had trouble paying utility bills. I had an eleven-year-old's memory of a three-room, upstairs apartment on St. Clair Avenue, where seven of us lived. Our suite had a cracked bathroom mirror, rusting tub, newspapers covering the windows and a red, paint-blistered bedroom floor which held a stained, torn mattress on which my two brothers, Frank and Gary and I slept.

Under a dim yellow light my parents counted pennies on a chipped, white metal table, trying to set aside enough money to pay the electric bill. CLICK, CLICK, CLICK. The pennies dropped, one by one. CLICK, CLICK, CLICK. From our cramped bedroom, I could hear the pennies dropping. CLICK, CLICK, CLICK. I could hear the pennies dropping in my sleep. CLICK, CLICK, CLICK as they hit the metal table.

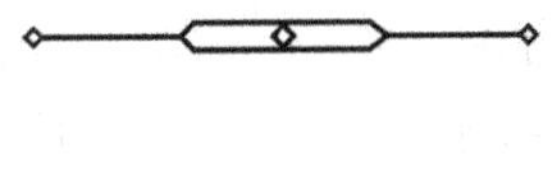

The blackout continued through the night and holiday merriment was churned into anxiety in the darkened neighborhoods served by Muny Light.

The next morning at City Hall, Council President James V. Stanton reminded the media that CEI had long refused to cooperate in establishing an interconnection from Muny Light to CEI's plant, to provide a backup in the event of a power failure.

Physically, an interconnection is like an extension cord connecting Muny Light to CEI and a web of transmission and generation systems across America, known as the national grid. This allows utilities to both trade power and share in the economic savings of interconnection.

There was a 1.6 mile line in place that temporarily tied the city's system with CEI, but it was seldom activated. Lacking an interconnect, Muny Light was isolated and vulnerable to blackouts which occurred when power demand exceeded generating capacity. A range of technical faults and equipment failures also caused blackouts at Muny. Even before taking office I'd heard that CEI had used its influence to block legislation to repair Muny's generators.

"Scrooge! CEI's like Scrooge!" Stanton seized the moment, invoking Dickens' miserly shopkeeper as he defended Muny Light's sixty-thousand customers. "CEI won't give us a tie-in, won't sell us emergency power," he said, deriding the private utility behemoth.

CEI was expanding rapidly and planning to construct two expensive nuclear power plants. Their system covered an area of seventeen-hundred square miles in northeastern Ohio, had twenty-two times the power production capacity of Muny Light, twenty times the annual revenue ($500 million to $25 million) and more than three times as many customers in the City of Cleveland, where it competed door-to-door with Muny in one-third of Cleveland's geographical area.

This head-to-head competition between overlapping service providers was unusual and stemmed from a seventy-five-year battle by CEI to block the development of Muny and to contain its service area. It had also resulted in a duplicate electric utility infrastructure and a tangle of Muny Light and CEI poles and lines in several Cleveland neighborhoods.

"Mayor Stokes must demand the Federal Power Commission [FPC] force CEI to provide Muny Light with a tie-in," Stanton told the media gathered in his second-floor office. Tall, handsome, with a stentorian Kennedy-esque speaking style, he commanded attention. The power failure was cast by the news media as a fight between him and CEI, with the administration of Mayor Carl B. Stokes on the sidelines.

In 1967, Stokes became the first African American elected a big-city Mayor. He was an intellectual, a formidable speaker and a charismatic leader who measured his words carefully.

Cajoled by Stanton and embarrassed by the power outages, Mayor Stokes pledged to keep the lights on and sought a Federal Power Commission order to force CEI to establish a permanent interconnection with Muny Light. When Stokes was elected Mayor, he had intended to sell Muny Light to CEI, and, although the power outages advanced the case for the sale, they also damaged Stokes' image as an administrator.

Outages occurred at the most inopportune times for Muny Light, weakening its competitive position while battle lines were forming between public and private interests. The City Council was being ripped by Muny Light customers angry over the blackouts. As I received increasing complaints from customers of the city's system, I sought to learn everything I could about public power in Cleveland.

CHAPTER 2

The Racket

My City Council career began amidst the conflict between Muny Light and CEI. Bristling with the energy of victory and the vulnerability of naivete, I entered the Cleveland Council offices to the consternation of elderly elected men and women.

"How did you get here? Who put you here, kid?" The question came from a grandfatherly colleague.

"Hey," a man, more my father's age, sidled up, asking confidentially, "Where'd you get your money to get elected?"

"I didn't have money. I campaigned door-to-door for two years," I said.

"Sure kid, sure."

Another Councilman joined in with a laugh, "You beat Bilinski's machine by knocking on doors? I don't think so." It was outrageous to my new colleagues that shoe leather counted for more than cash in defeating an entrenched ward machine. Ah, there was the smell of the con about this kid they figured, because they saw the world in their own image.

"Door-to door campaigning? Hah! Nice try," a portly veteran interjected as the clutch began to dissolve, amid amused smiles and exchanges of knowing glances.

"You'll fit right in," one Councilman said, slapping my back. These pros knew that every one of the thirty-three Cleveland City Council seats were won with campaign contributions from banks who held city deposits, money from phone, gas, and electric interests, or downtown real estate developers who never lost an election because they always bet on both sides.

One middle-aged Councilman, an attorney from a neighboring ward, let's call him Richard, befriended me, confiding, "Dennis, there are a lot of legitimate ways you can make money in politics. Nothing dishonest, mind you. Opportunities come to people who hold office," he said.

"Opportunities?"

"You know, you do favors for people. They do favors for you."

"Favors?" I didn't understand.

"Attorneys elected to Council get law business thrown their way. Insurance salesmen get policies. Travel agents book trips for people they help. Real estate guys get commissions from property deals called to their attention," he shared. "It's all legit."

"I'm still in college, I pay for my own books. I don't need anything," I declared, "I'll get $12,500 a year, just for being a Councilman." That was a lot of money, paying more than any job I'd ever held. I was a janitor's assistant and a stock boy in grade school, working to pay my siblings' and my own way through Catholic school. I also paid my way through Catholic high school with money I'd earned as a caddy and a part-time sportswriter.

After graduating from high school, I worked two full-time jobs, toiling at least eighty hours a week, mornings as an orderly and then a surgical technician at St. Alexis Hospital and afternoons and evenings as a copyboy at the *Plain Dealer.* This, while enrolled at Cleveland

State University, full time. At CSU, I fell in love with English romantic poetry and the theater and had even adapted a book for the stage. I loved translating ideas into form, offering audiences an alternate view of the world. I was torn between devotion to the dramatic arts and a commitment to politics.

Joseph Garry, the university's theatre director and my academic advisor, allayed my quandary "Politics and the theatre? They're the same thing." Joe's partner, actor David Frazier would later add, "In theatre the lines are better written." Comforted with such sterling insight, I transited from structuring plays to mapping campaigns and was hungry for the knowledge and the poetry of action. I didn't just burn the candle at both ends. Ambition cut the candle in half and I burned all four ends.

Earning $12,500 a year, I'd have to work only one job while going to school full time. Paychecks would come regularly. Paying bills wouldn't be a problem. At twenty-three, I had a measure of financial independence. Still, my new colleagues preached a psychology of acquisitiveness.

"You'll need something," my new Council counsel said. He was showing me the ropes, and a ladder invisible to the uninitiated.

"Something will come up, it's the nature of life. Everyone needs help at one time or another. You, your family, your friends. We help people, people help us. All you gotta do is play ball."

"Play ball?"

"Yeah, everyone here plays ball."

"I don't understand."

"You gotta vote right. You vote right, you do OK. It's the system."

"Vote right? What do you mean? I came to change the system not join it."

"Sure. We all want to change the system, but you're not on the outside anymore. You are on the inside."

"I didn't run for Council to help myself," I reflexively dismissed the 'insider' status. I'd come to Council to shake things up.

He studied me, nodding, "Of course you ran to help people," his tone had an unsettling, patronizing inflection.

"Right!" I was emphatic, because after all, I was an heir to the philosophy of President John F. Kennedy who in his Inaugural Address summoned a new generation to "Ask not what your country can do for you, ask what you can do for your country." I came of age in 1968, during a period of joyous rebellion, with a sense that all things were possible. I wasn't going to cheapen my idealism by asking what I could do for myself.

"Then help the people, and help yourself a little too," he said, gently. "Be smart," The word 'smart' rattled in his throat. Then he patted me on the shoulder and walked away.

This wasn't Mrs. Malone's seventh grade civics class of a decade earlier at St. Colman's, with its standardized charts of the legislative, executive and judicial branches. There was nothing theoretical in the boodle hunt here in the Cleveland City Council, where opportunities were picked as they arose.

As I entered the Council chambers for my first official meeting, I saw Councilman Jack Russell, former Council President, known for his ten-gallon hats and his campaign literature in different shades for different colors of voters. Russell had survived over a dozen elections in a district part-Hungarian and part African American. He looked up briefly from his newspaper, pointed to my nearby seat. Through teeth clenching a cigar he said imperiously, "Sit down and don't say nothin'," and went back to reading his newspaper, held high so no one could see him.

After the Council meeting, I returned to the Council offices, where I continued to be greeted felicitously. "Bide your time," said Mike Zone, a fatherly man from Ward Three, an Italian area on the West Side. He put his arm around my shoulder and took me over to the "Wall of Fame" where class pictures hung of former Council Members whose fixed smiles created the effect of a menagerie of antique Cheshire cats. He nodded to those who graduated to higher office. "You'll get your chance to move up, maybe to county recorder or another big office. Here you go along to get along." He then set his hands squarely on both of my shoulders. "Listen, son, don't be in such a hurry."

As I checked my official mail, I encountered Charles V. Carr, an elderly Black Councilman whose name I first heard when I was an inner-city child. He owned Quincy Savings and Loan and lived on a farm in Ashtabula County, ninety miles from his ward. I marveled at the simplicity with which he handled his mail. The waste basket was his filing system. He threw all of his correspondence, unopened, directly into it.

"You sure you're old enough to be here?" Carr's tired, watery eyes were kind. His voice though, was harsh, "Don't rock the boat. We got no use for people around here who rock the boat." Then, he smiled broadly. "You're young. You could become a big man in this town."

I campaigned for two straight years to be elected and after going door-to-door in Ward Seven, understood the election was about the People, not me. I came to City Hall with images of people with hands outstretched, people who lived in humble, clapboard houses with tar-paper roofs, pleading, "When you get in there, don't forget us little people."

'Don't rock the boat?' I came to rock the boat, but as a matter of courtesy, first wanted to meet the deck hands.

Rotund, cigar-chomping and irascible, Councilman James H. Bell, at a Monday night dinner before a Council meeting complained to me Council leadership had excluded him from unspecified financial opportunities. "I voted right. I don't ask for much," he said, his tongue loosened by a few glasses of port wine at Pat Joyce's Tavern, near City Hall. "All I want is a little ice cream," his face brightened with the wide-eyed anticipation of a political confection. He opened his mouth, lolled his tongue, and with child-like abandon licked an imaginary cone, his diamond pinky ring sparkling in the bar lights. "Just a little ice cream. I'm not a pig," he repeated. "I want what's mine. Some ice cream." His tongue again licked the air, gleefully anticipating his just desserts.

Cleveland City Hall was at that time a land of unbounded opportunity for a member of Council. If the assumed privileges and material benefits of membership eluded you, yet came easily to others, it sparked the pique voiced by Mr. Bell. There was a general claim to emoluments members could access at the right place, the right time, or by cutting the right deal with the right person.

In the hustling Council Offices, I was made aware of those also on a hunt for money and privilege, but on an exponentially larger scale. They were not members of the City Council, although they frequented the Council offices much more than elected officials.

"Who are those fellows wearing the expensive suits?" I asked Don Spears, one of the Council clerks. He was ever-alert, a thin dark man with tufts of gray hair sitting atop his head like a light soufflé. He was always in a hurry, a stack of important papers under his arm, but he focused to entertain a question from this fledgling representative.

"Do they work for the city?" I asked.

"Hardly," Spears chuckled. He motioned to one angular, crew-cut man. "He represents East Ohio Gas and takes Councilmen on fancy outings." Spears nodded toward a white-haired man sitting in the back of the committee room. "Phone company, Ohio Bell." He motioned subtly toward a cubicle. "He owns the Yellow Cab company, gives Cleveland Browns football tickets to Councilmen. Season tickets! I hear they are the best seats in the Stadium."

By now he was talking closely, confidentially, attempting not to be too obvious in disclosure. "The tall elderly man talking to Councilman Carr? He used to be Cleveland's Law Director, now he is CEI's man at City Hall. CEI gives away Cleveland Indians baseball tickets and also electric appliances to council members."

"I see these guys here all the time. Why?" I naively asked Spears.

"It's their job. Each one of their companies needs a special license to operate, called a franchise, which is awarded by the city. Council votes on the franchises. Franchises are worth millions of dollars. These guys want to be everyone's friend," Spears said quietly. "Council has a life and death power over their businesses. They stay close."

"Can anyone get a franchise agreement?" I asked.

"No sir. Not here. These company guys are good at what they do. They have it all locked up. Their business gets a franchise, sometimes for ninety-nine years. It's a monopoly. No competition. Everyone has to buy their service and there's no choice, you pay what they charge. A franchise is a cash cow. CEI has a franchise but they have to compete with Muny Light in parts of the city and don't like it. They have to watch what they charge for electricity in neighborhoods where people have a choice," Spears explained.

Utility lobbyists were among the best friends a lonely Councilman could have. Constant dinner companions, they threw expensive parties, organized trips, provided prime seats for theatre and sports events and campaign funds on demand and even helped get jobs for Council members' relatives.

All they wanted in return was a vote and they burrowed deep into City Hall. The very existence of private, investor-owned utilities depended upon politics and the political system. In the process of dispensing and seeking favors, utilities achieved control over local government officials.

I was not comfortable with fawning influence-peddlers who tried to capitalize on social exchanges or tokens of friendship which would be paid for handsomely by my constituents, so kept my distance and spared myself compromising entanglements. I grew up under conditions where I never relied on material things for comfort. Material things did not interest me, and no one could influence me by giving me anything. I lived in a world of ideas and my most treasured possessions were books.

CEI's man at City Hall tapped me on the arm after one Council meeting, soliciting camaraderie, "Councilman Kucinich, did your wife get the apron we sent from Mexico? It was tied to a bag of chili peppers."

"She already has an apron," I snapped. "Wait," I asked this utility welcome wagon wanna-be, "I want to give back those items." I went to retrieve the apron and the chili peppers, but they had disappeared from the secure Council cloakroom.

CHAPTER 3

Sell Muny Light

"We're the energy makers, your neighbors and friends. We're the energy makers, our job never ends," CEI's commercial jingle jammed the airwaves. I skipped from one radio station to another while driving Helen's serviceable gray Volkswagen downtown to City Hall.

CEI endeavored to establish a public profile as a friendly, community-spirited organization through radio, television and newspaper ads. At the same time, I witnessed their lobbyists stealthily block an interconnection for Muny, try to force rate increases and stymie improvements, while undermining the city system's competitive position and its reliability, all with the unmistakable intention of forcing the sale of Muny Light.

"Councilman Kucinich, may I speak to you?" Lee Howley, the former city Law Director, who plied Council for CEI, approached me in the Council offices.

"Yes, sure," I responded, asking, "Why won't CEI provide Muny Light with an interconnect, so it can be part of the national grid?"

"We are trying to help Muny Light," Howley said with well-practiced sincerity. Middle aged, taut physique, upright posture, brush haircut, he had the aura of a military officer, precise, direct, and regimented in his expression.

"Why won't you provide a tie-in?" I demanded, picking up on Stanton's criticism that CEI was blocking the interconnect for no legitimate reason.

"We've offered to interconnect," Howley said. "Our company wants to work with the city."

"CEI is trying to force Muny Light to raise its rates first," I challenged. Muny Light was able to offer electricity at rates about 20% cheaper than CEI because it didn't advertise, pay dividends to shareholders or pay high salaries to executives, including lawyer-lobbyists like Howley.

"If you raised your rates to our level, your system would be more reliable. You wouldn't have blackouts," he said, but I knew, with CEI blocking Muny improvements in Council, we would still be prone to blackouts and it was the blackouts, especially during holidays, which were undermining public support for Muny.

The interconnect had to be unconditional. Once Muny's system was tied into the national grid any power reductions at Muny would be immediately corrected by throwing a switch to get temporary power through CEI, a back-up source. The interconnect hardly required a great engineering feat, but was simply three wires linking the two utilities, enabling Muny to access the grid. There were over two thousand municipally-owned utilities in America and very few suffered the isolated condition of Muny Light.

"We can help with a temporary interconnect. You still have problems with your generators," Howley said. This was my first encounter with treachery attempting to pass for earnest discourse. I kept my guard because each exchange with Howley would serve as a measure of how well I was prepared to enter the larger debate over Muny Light.

"Provide us with an interconnect and we'd be reliable," I responded, careful not to reveal my assessment that I was in the presence of a man skilled in the art of prevarication.

"Imagine what it would mean for the people in your ward if the city had an extra forty to fifty million to spend for more police, for more recreation. You can do it, if the city sells Muny Light."

There it was, CEI's golden carrot, dangled in front of the lurching, aging horse of a city. Howley knew the city's financial condition well as he had been Law Director. He proffered a deal too good to be true: Fast cash, no consequences.

"Muny's power is cheaper. It's making money, why sell?" I countered.

"Sell Muny Light," Howley continued. "The sale is the solution to Cleveland's problems. We'll buy it and run it like a business."

Howley's certainty was unsettling. There was a national trend of larger, private electric systems taking over smaller, municipal electric systems, and, in Ohio, dozens of smaller utilities had succumbed to takeover efforts.

"Read this booklet," he said, handing me material in the manner of a Jehovah's Witness distributing an issue of The Watchtower. "It's about the company."

The Company. Before I came to City Council, I believed CEI was a pretty good outfit. After I lost my first Council race, I went to their headquarters to apply for a position of copywriter, a job that came with security, good pay and benefits. At my interview in their office tower, I was led through a warren of sterile cubicles which had the emotional depth of a bureaucratic gulag. I sat inside one of the chilled cubes until a man entered, sat across from me, briefly glanced at my application and promptly dismissed me as not having enough experience.

Now an elected member of Cleveland City Council, I found myself at cross purposes with CEI. I came to understand that the abrupt rejection I received from CEI was one of those hidden turning points when life had something else in store.

CHAPTER 4

Memorial Day Blackout

Memorial Day, 1970

In the Cleveland suburb of Brooklyn, a solemn semi-circle of Russian Orthodox priests in ornate robes hovered over well-tended graves in St. Theodosius Cemetery. Praying in their mother tongue, humming triple blessings, their swinging silver censers glinted in the rising sun, offering smoky wisps of myrrh that mingled with the sweet souls of the long departed. It was time for me, the Councilman representing St. Theodosius Parish, and St. Olga and St. Tikhon Streets, to speak a few words in Russian, transliterated with the help of a Russian-born precinct committeeman. I had borrowed heavily from Pericles' speech to the Peloponnesian warriors, and afterwards received sincere compliments for my pronunciation. I felt as Russian as the Volga Boat March.

Helen was with me, waiting patiently through the long ceremony because I'd promised that when we returned home, we'd change clothes and hurry to the wide-open country, thirty miles east of Cleveland.

On the ride back from the service, as we entered the city, traffic lights were out. When we arrived home, all three phones were ringing.

"Let them go," Helen said, since we had planned a getaway.

"Rinnnnng!"

"Helen, I should answer the phones. What if something is wrong?"

"There is always something wrong," she said laconically. "Now let's leave." The picnic basket she had packed was sitting on the table.

"Rinnnnng!" I looked at my beautiful bride for a long moment as her blue-green eyes turned to ice, and felt torn between the call of the wild and the wildly ringing phones.

"RRRRRIIIINNNGGG!"

"Dennis, you promised," she said, unwilling to sacrifice any more time to a public oblivious to the personal happiness and enjoyment of public servants and their families. Bending to my sense of duty, I picked up the phone.

"Hello, this is Councilman Kucinich, may I help you?"

"Kucinich, you son of a bitch!" The jarring invective poured into my ear. "I've got a refrigerator here full of food. It's spoiling because goddamned Muny Light is out again. I have a mind to dump my spoiled food on your front step."

"Hold on, please," I covered the mouthpiece and directed a perplexed glance toward my wife. "Those traffic lights? It's Muny Light. The lights are out everywhere." Our lights were on. We had CEI.

She stared at me, blankly, then objected, "Every time we make plans..."

I ended the call, and faced Helen who looked at her watch, unsympathetically.

"Muny Light is out," I said.

"I know," she said, very irritated.

I couldn't help it. Once in Council, I faced everything with a sense of urgency. People were counting on me and I had to be there to help, even at the risk of disappointing my wife. Muny Light was out and people were sweltering in their homes, staring at dead refrigerators, televisions, stoves, radios, stereos, and audio tape players. They were furious and called our home in droves.

There is one rule for a Councilman. When the city government breaks down, it's your fault. The people, in a medley from Councilmanic hell, let me have it.

"Can't you guys run an electric system?"

"What's with all the outages?"

"I've had it with Muny Light!"

"I'm going to call CEI."

"Sir, I'll get right back to you," I said to one caller, "I'll call Muny Light."

I got through to a worker at the Division of Light and Power.

"The whole system is down, the whole damn thing," he sputtered.

"Not possible," I said. Muny Light, according to City Hall, had in place a temporary interconnection, a tie-in with CEI, guaranteeing the city system's reliability.

"This isn't supposed to happen," I said, remembering CEI's assurances.

"You are not going to believe this. Some @&%#$ disconnected the tie-in!" he stammered.

"You're kidding," I said.

"Nope. No interconnect. Sixty thousand customers, no electricity."

"Oh, God," I sighed and ended the call.

Helen stood with her arms crossed. She was beautiful in jeans, her long, blond hair falling softly over a sweatshirt. An outdoors girl, she exuded earth energy. "Helen, the Muny Light system is down," I said, anxiously.

"So," she shrugged her shoulders. "Like you are going to fix it?"

I was a Councilman. I fixed broken things, or at least tried. People were calling for help, wanted answers and I had to get those answers. The interconnect was down, there was no backup, we were stuck with an extended power outage, and it was the Memorial Day weekend.

"Dennis, is anyone else going to wait for phone calls on a holiday?"

She had me. I relished public service. It was the fulfillment of a dream and I worked at it eighteen hours a day, raising hell to the delight of a bored press corps and to the dismay of the City Hall establishment.

Helen and I never settled comfortably into our second-story apartment, high above the industrial Flats, next to the carrier pigeon coop of my Polish landlord, Jan Krzmien. I was perpetually late coming home from Council and neighborhood meetings and when I did get home, went right to the phone to indulge in the lamentations of constituents and the mysteries of politics in Cleveland.

Now, with a power outage on a holiday, I trapped myself in a closed loop of hubris and responsibility. The plight of my constituents was my chief concern. I wanted to take hold and resolve matters on my own while remaining painfully aware that my control was limited.

My wife was done marking time and headed for the door, picnic basket in hand. Stopping briefly, she turned to me and said, "Dennis, maybe you want to stay here all day answering the phones. Look," she opened the door, "It's a beautiful day. I'm going out."

My eyes lingered at the note we had clipped to our refrigerator, "The family that plays together, stays together." We left the house, with the phones still yammering.

"Dennis," she said, beaming, as we arrived in the country, "What a wonderful day. How I love spring. See, the roses are coming out. Can you smell the air? It's so fresh and fragrant. Dennis? Dennis! Helloooo? Earth to Dennis."

"Oh, uh, sure honey." I was thinking about the Muny Light blackout.

She shook her head. I had married a child of springtime, to whom the natural world was the simple truth. If I'd harnessed my inner poet instead of my inner politician, I would have compared my bright, blonde wife to the hope of love which springs eternal, instead of pondering artificial city lights.

On behalf of the people of Ward Seven, as one supper after another cooled on our kitchen table, I demanded light, improved public safety, housing, recreation, transportation and pollution control.

I was the people's Councilman, their voice, their watchdog, salivating to each ring of the phone that brought new challenges, making sure the garbage was picked up, the police responded quickly, the streets repaired, the lights on, tending to each emergency and to a myriad of crises, caring for everything. Everything but our marriage.

Helen and I were married in July of 1969. As the honeymoon airplane lifted toward the stars, en route to New Orleans, I passed a hand-written note from one of my favorite songs, to assure her of my abiding love:

"Today while the blossoms still cling to the vine,
I'll taste your strawberries and drink your sweet wine.
A million tomorrows shall all pass away.
'Ere I'll forget all the joy, that is mine, today."

I was forgetting.

CHAPTER 5

Sabotage

Sabotage!" In tremulous cadence and with a piercing nasal tone, the florid-faced Larry Duggan, chair of City Council's utilities committee, called a meeting to order and propelled the controversial Memorial Day blackout into a political uproar. Speculating that CEI had covertly interrupted the city's power, he channeled the anger of his irate, powerless constituents, most of whom were Muny Light customers. It hadn't occurred to me that the blackout was less mechanical than contrived. The idea that CEI could create blackouts on the Muny system seemed a stretch.

Duggan had aged gracefully through two decades of public service. His well-fitting suits, clear glasses and pate of white hair gave the appearance of a banking official more than a populist Councilman. He peered into the packed City Council committee room and leveled his accusation of sabotage directly at the CEI lobbyists who stood in a supervisory pose underneath the floodlights at the back of the room.

The context of the blackout mattered to Duggan. CEI had been building public pressure for the sale of Muny Light and had a sympathetic Mayor, a cooperative news media and an uncanny knack for capitalizing on Muny Light blackouts, which occurred at the most inopportune times, usually during holidays.

"This is another one of their dirty tricks," Chairman Duggan said of the Memorial Day outage. In his youth, Duggan was a star pitcher in semi-pro baseball, but now "Lefty," as he was known, was throwing directly at CEI.

"I'm sure CEI is at the bottom of this blackout," he said, redirecting his fire at Utilities Director, Ben Stefanski, Jr., who was the picture of restrained congeniality at the hearing table. The most sensible members of a Mayor's cabinet did not attempt to win testifying at Council meetings; their task was to survive a mugging.

Immediately after the blackout, Stefanski had obtained a written agreement from CEI to provide for transfers of power to the Muny system, using a temporary interconnect, which was in place, in theory, but, in practice not always connected. Duggan was not to be placated by the piece of paper Stefanski waved, knowing that CEI could feign cooperation and ultimately do nothing.

In the history of the relationship between Muny and CEI, there were lengthy talks, numerous memoranda going back and forth, offers, counteroffers, agreements, and then untimely reversals by CEI. It was a paperwork pantomime.

Chairman Duggan pressed for the Federal Bureau of Investigation to look into the blackout.

"There is something fishy here," Duggan said, again alluding to direct interference in the operations of Muny Light.

There was no unanimity in the committee room and one Council member voiced the concerns of wards not serviced by Muny Light and switched the onus from CEI onto Muny.

"Muny Light doesn't work as well as CEI," he said. "It's time we start saving Clevelanders money and headaches. We ought to sell Muny Light."

CEI's lobbyists, poised like vultures at the rear of the committee room nodded in agreement. Duggan scowled contempt at his colleague's blind fealty to CEI and then adjourned the meeting.

Afterwards, I approached Duggan to tell him of my encounter with CEI's Lee Howley.

"Mr. Chairman, Mr. Howley says they want to help the city..." Duggan cut in, "Listen young man, Howley is not to be trusted. The interconnect is temporary. It may be up. It may be down. CEI controls when and if we receive help. If there is no interconnection, we are on our own, except we can ask for a routine load transfer, a transfer of power from CEI to Muny Light customers. Here is what I think happened, CEI created the outage with the way they handled the load transfer! It wasn't a mistake. They sabotaged us. I know their game."

"I don't understand. How?"

"Let me make it simple. Let's say a substation has two sets of plugs for electricity, one for Muny Light, the other for CEI. If Muny needs power, we let CEI know we need to plug into their system. But they make us unplug Muny before they will let us plug into CEI and again when we want to reconnect to our customers. They create the blackouts," he explained.

Duggan also related that after the blackout, CEI sent salesmen door-to-door in his ward.

"They were trying to get people to switch from Muny Light to CEI, pressuring them saying 'You keep having a lot of blackouts. Why don't you go with CEI?' And then they put contracts in front of Muny Light customers' noses, promising things like free wiring and electric appliances if they agreed to sign."

"Free wiring? For switching to CEI?" I was incredulous.

"Yes. They'll rewire homes if people switch."

"How can CEI afford it?" I asked.

"Wiring is a one-time expense. If they get more customers, they make more money. Rewiring costs CEI half what a Muny Light customer would pay to CEI for electricity in a single year. In the long run, CEI profits, heavily."

There was another thing the city could do to fight back. Duggan reminded me that the same provisions of the Ohio Constitution which gave cities the right to grant utility franchises, also gave cities the right to revoke CEI's franchise and use eminent domain to condemn their generation, transmission and distribution system and take them over, making the whole of Cleveland the province of public power. The city could pay for the acquisition of CEI through issuing bonds, secured by the annual revenues of the expanded Muny Light, and pay off the debt in thirty years, saving millions on electric bills, lowering taxes, controlling utility rates and attracting businesses.

I discovered a city report which showed Muny customers had saved over $50 million from its inception in 1919 to 1940. If Muny Light had taken over CEI in 1937, the city would have saved an additional $30 million in four years. Excess revenues could retire the expanded system's indebtedness and lower taxes. Cheaper electricity and lower taxes, using the Ohio Constitution. It was irresistible.

After reading the report, I sought out Chairman Duggan in Council to find out why the city did not take over CEI.

"CEI lobbied heavily. The takeover lost by a single vote in Council," he said with sadness.

"The people of Cleveland would have saved a lot of money," I said, wondering why such an obvious benefit could be blocked, even by a lobbying effort.

"That's the answer, Councilman," he said, "The people would have benefited. People would pay less for electricity, have more money for their families, and have lower taxes. CEI is trying to put us out of business. Muny's a threat to their profits."

Elsewhere around the state of Ohio, CEI was aggressively taking over smaller, publicly owned utilities, often without a fight. I could only imagine the skulduggery that occurred as community after community succumbed to the private utility's takeover strategy.

Prior to election to City Council, I never gave much thought to the system creating the power and summoning the light. Like most people, whenever I needed light, I'd turn a switch from "off" to "on." But turn the switch, and then no lights? That can get you thinking. I needed to know the mechanics of the electric system. The person to ask was the Commissioner of Muny Light, Warren Hinchee.

Early one morning, I entered the empty Council committee room for a private tutoring session with Hinchee. The space had the feel of a sanctuary, with the morning sun kissing the long, white sheer curtains, creating a gauzy, halo effect.

Hinchee was lanky, and professorial, with a ring of curly hair resting upon his head like a small wreath. His eyebrows arched as he unfurled a drawing of the Muny Light system, superimposed upon a map of the City of Cleveland.

"Here's Muny's system and the areas we serve."

He pointed to the northeast, to Larry Duggan's neighborhood. Then his finger traced the system's contours west across the city, to the near west and southwest wards of Cleveland, in a visual depiction of where Muny competed, house by house, with CEI, in an area covering one third of the city.

He pulled an artist's sketch pad from a long, thin case and began to illustrate the components of an electric system. He drew a series of boxes, labeling them "fuel," "boilers," "steam," "turbines," "generators," and "electricity." He connected the boxes with arrows and explained.

"Muny Light generates electricity using coal, sometimes gas. Coal fires the boilers, which heat water to create steam. The steam moves the turbines and the turbines spin the generators which create electricity."

Then he drew another series of boxes, illustrating how electricity is transmitted and distributed. The electricity moved from the generating plant at very high voltage along major trunk lines to transmission towers, then to substations. The voltage was continually lowered, or "stepped down" after which the electricity was distributed to homes, businesses and industry.

"Why so many blackouts?" I asked.

"Repairs are overdue. As you know, CEI is doing everything it can to persuade city council not to make repairs. If a couple of boilers are down, that reduces our power. If the turbines don't work, that reduces our ability to generate. If the generators don't work, everything goes dark. Problems along the line anywhere can create problems everywhere, including blackouts," Hinchee said. "Then there are the games which CEI plays with the interconnect and the load transfer which result in blackouts. And, of course, with the blackouts we lose customers, then we lose money."

Hinchee told me that whenever Muny Light suffered a blackout, it had to buy emergency power from CEI, at a price high above Muny's retail rates, causing further revenue loss.

Hinchee said Mayor Stokes, who had advocated the sale of Muny Light, became suspicious when after the 1969 Christmas blackout, the company accelerated efforts to acquire Muny. Mayor Stokes appealed to the Federal Power Commission for help. CEI had a legal obligation to connect Muny Light to the national grid. It was federal law. Almost every electric utility in America was connected to the grid, for reliability and efficiency. Utilities were not permitted to refuse each other emergency power to back up their system.

As Mayor Stokes pursued relief from the FPC, top executives of CEI who played a key role in Stokes' election, became unhappy with the Mayor and began to criticize him in business, political and media circles.

"Their plan," Hinchee said, "is to raise Muny Light's rates to CEI's level, causing our customers to drop off, then goodbye Muny. They want us to agree to fix prices, which is illegal. Competitors can't have any agreements on prices," Hinchee said. "CEI is sinister. It tells Muny, 'you don't want an interconnect, because if you had one, you could end up with unwanted blackouts, if there was a fault on CEI's system,' a fault, which they could create, on purpose. Every blackout increases the pressure on Muny Light to make repairs. Then CEI gets certain City Councilmen to prevent the repairs, and we end up with more blackouts," he said.

CEI was denying Muny Light an interconnect, while touting its own reliability-enhancing back-ups, building yet another new interconnect with Ohio Edison, a private utility.

Muny tried to break its reliance on CEI's high-priced emergency power, seeking arrangements with the public power systems of the cities of Painesville and Orville. But Muny still needed to go through CEI's territory to connect with this public power. CEI declined permission, while keeping the city's aspirations for a permanent interconnect suspended in endless rounds of negotiations.

At Hinchee's initiative, the city and CEI met and shared diagrams of their generating plants. CEI promised an engineering study for the interconnection, yet never delivered one. After a long delay, the Mayor's office formally requested the study.

"CEI told us the study did not exist. It was as if none of our meetings had ever happened," Hinchee said.

"Did not exist?" My head was spinning. This type of deception was beyond my experience. My election to City Council had opened a window to a new world. I came from the neighborhoods of the city, places where you took things at face value. On the street you recognize the hustlers, the practiced deceivers. One day in my youth, uptown on St. Clair Avenue, a guy on the corner rolled up his sleeve and showed me shiny watches all the way up his arm. Even though I didn't have the few bucks to buy one, I wouldn't, because I knew the watches were fake.

"I don't mean to be disrespectful Commissioner, did it ever occur to you they were lying?" I asked.

"Yes. But you can't do business with people thinking they are lying to you all the time," he said, annoyed. He was a technocrat, not a politician.

It wasn't only CEI's lies which bothered me. I have a deep sense of fairness, an innate objection to dirty tricks and a willingness to fight back. I went into politics not knowing the ways of business competition. I was learning that anything goes in the pursuit of money and power.

Next, Hinchee explained, Cleveland looked outside CEI's service area and attempted to acquire cheap power over lines from utilities in other states. CEI thwarted Muny's efforts to obtain an allotment from the Power Authority of the State of New York and also stopped Muny from accessing power from an Ohio cooperative, Buckeye Power.

A new organization, American Municipal Power of Ohio emerged to assist Muny Light but needed permission from the utilities which owned the transmissions lines, to bring in cheap power over CEI's lines. CEI and other privately-owned utilities would not cooperate.

CEI had formed an organization of private utilities, the Central Area Power Coordinating Organization, (CAPCO) which included Toledo Edison, Ohio Edison, the Duquesne Light Co., and the Pennsylvania Power Company.

All member 'investor-owned' utilities could coordinate their assets, sharing generation resources and saving each other money. The CAPCO utilities refused to let Muny Light join their group, and without transmission access, Muny Light was locked into CEI, which made power available only at a premium, undermining Muny's profitability.

Hinchee looked at his watch. The sun was full up now, glaring into a room which in an hour would be bustling with a committee hearing. Hinchee had another meeting, packed up his charts and diagrams while I took the drawings and thanked him for the education.

On the way out of the Council offices, I asked him, "Muny Light has been around for seventy years. Yet CEI is desperate to knock out Muny Light now. Why now?"

"CEI has been measuring us for years, keeping close track of city finances, coming up with one scheme after another to try to falsely link city finances to a supposed windfall from the sale of Muny Light. Now it has an urgent reason to force the sale of Muny. It has incurred massive construction loans to complete two nuclear power plants. CEI must expand its revenue sources to cover its increased costs and debt service, which means utility rate increases for existing customers. A CEI takeover of Muny Light would add in excess of 50,000 customers. CEI's revenues would grow by automatically charging Muny customers CEI rates. They would increase the cost of street lighting to the city. Once Muny is out of the way, they can virtually name their price for electricity in the city and get it. The more financial pressure CEI feels, the more desperate CEI will be to grab Muny," Hinchee added, "They have to get the nukes in operation and on-line to pay their bills and are having difficulty doing that."

Hinchee was not a fan of nuclear power. "Personally, I think nuclear is an expensive way to boil water. But the industry sees nuclear power as its 'savior,' because of the rising cost of coal," he said.

The education I received from Hinchee underscored the gravity of delving deeply into all matters Muny Light. When attending grade school at Holy Name Elementary, the nuns drilled into students the importance of doing homework, of preparation for tomorrow. It was a valuable lesson because, now in charge of my own education, I knew I had to become an expert on utilities in order to defend the economic and political interests of those who elected me. I had to do my homework before every meeting, if I was to be able to see through the lies presented as business-as-usual in the theater of governance.

Once I knew the mechanics of a light system and had a better understanding of the way CEI operated, I could keep a close watch on the company's dealings at City Hall. I also felt empowered to speak out. My unrestrained enthusiasm for change earned scathing criticism from the status-quo media. I had to admit that seeing my name cast negatively bothered me.

Warren Hinchee had described a duplicitous world far removed from the humble concerns of the six inhabitants of a small apartment on St. Clair Avenue where my parents counted pennies to pay the electric bill. The memory of that childhood experience was a constant tug on my awareness. People continued to count pennies to pay rising electric bills while underhanded, behind-the-scenes players were conspiring to force them to pay more and more. I took it upon myself to even the score.

CHAPTER 6

Grisanti, The Pride of Notre Dame

One afternoon I was walking briskly through Cleveland's Arcade, a three-tiered indoor architectural marvel of colorful small shops built in the 1920's.

Deep in thought, perhaps looking glum, I was met by a man charging forward with a bulging, frayed leather briefcase tucked under his right arm. He bristled with energy. A slightly slicked, otherwise untamed mane of silver and black hair gave the appearance of a brilliant, eccentric scientist.

"Hey, you're the new Councilman, Kucinich, right?" he said, with unexpected enthusiasm.

"Yes sir."

He understood I was preoccupied. Was it obvious? "Kid, don't let them get you down. I tell you every knock is a boost." Rapid fire, he jumped the conversation, without taking a breath. "Hey, you got a minute? Do I have a story for you!" Before I could respond, he extended an invitation. "I have an office nearby." He reached into his briefcase bundle and handed me a reprint of a Reader's Digest article that exposed

Cleveland's urban renewal program gone awry.

"Could you come with me for a minute?" he implored. He was seized with an idea and his enthusiasm broke my funk. I was compelled by the energy of this encounter to follow him to his office.

When he turned on the lights, stacks of paper suddenly materialized. He removed a pile of correspondence from his chair, sat down and gestured for me to sit across from him.

"My boy, I am going to give you an education and it won't cost you a dime." He patted a large pile of papers on his desk. "I've got it all here, the biggest scandal to ever hit this city and no one else will speak out." He put up his hands defensively, "Believe me, you'll be glad you came to see Al Grisanti."

Grisanti ran a hand through his unruly shock of hair. "By the way, this picture," he smiled at a sturdy, no-nonsense young man clad in the football togs of yesteryear. "That's me when I played for Knute Rockne at Notre Dame. Rockne, now there was a man. Did you ever hear of 'The Four Horsemen? Miller, Layden, Crowley and Strudehler? They were legendary."

Shifting from his reverie he continued, "Of course today," he lifted his chin for effect, "I'm not in as good shape. But, I can still keep up with those guys at City Hall." This was Attorney Al Grisanti, captain of his own legal offense, grappling with six-foot stacks along the wall, files which encroached on his desk approaching from weathered cabinets, gathering as the Four Horsemen of a paperwork Apocalypse in a tightening huddle, waiting for Grisanti to call the play.

He spoke hurriedly, as if he was accustomed to visitors searching for the exit. I wasn't planning to leave. I was drawn in by his intensity, riveted by his earnestness and unable to get a word in edgewise. I sat respectfully, silently, hoping for useful information.

Grisanti went into detail telling me that ten years previous, the city's afternoon newspaper, the *Cleveland Press*, pressured City Hall to commit to what proved to be the largest urban renewal program in America.

City Hall used eminent domain to move three thousand families, mostly blacks, out of their inner-city homes without any relocation assistance or alternative housing. People ended up in overcrowded tenement houses and apartment buildings in the Hough neighborhood. When space couldn't be found in Hough, people began to move to another neighborhood, Glenville, where my Mom and Dad rented out apartments. A decade later, the overcrowded and decrepit conditions gave rise to the Hough riots.

"Urban renewal wrecked thousands of families and a half-dozen neighborhoods. It destroyed downtown and cleared out good businesses. They even took a place owned by my mother. Euclid Avenue used to be the biggest retail center, but urban renewal shifted business activity away. It was the beginning of the end of downtown," Grisanti said.

"That's just your opinion, isn't it, Mr. Grisanti," I said, having trouble grappling with Grisanti's claim downtown was ruined and city neighborhoods were wrecked by a single program run amok.

He was stricken at my off-handed comment and paused, his face reddened, then he continued. "My boy, may I remind you I was the City Councilman for the downtown area."

Oh.

This was former Councilman Alfred Grisanti, of the downtown district. I had heard his name at City Hall. He had taken on the political establishment, and the media over urban renewal. He was a man of hard experience, beaten, but unbowed. Possessed of an evangelical fervor, he was relentless in his efforts to expose wrongdoing and provided an insider's primer on urban renewal.

"Uh, please excuse me, Councilman Grisanti," I said sheepishly, grateful he ignored my ignorance.

"Call me Al," he replied. His eyes were smiling, forgiving. "Now, as your unofficial, unsalaried and unpaid advisor," he continued, "Let me tell you what we have as a result of urban renewal - $30 million in unused and untaxed land and buildings, and seventy-five acres of prime downtown land which was picked up by real estate speculators."

"How did it happen?" I asked, rapt.

"First, the city used its power of eminent domain to acquire the land. The Federal government put up two-thirds of the acquisition costs, encouraging the clearance of the land. Then the land was resold to private developers," he said.

"Private developers?" I asked, puzzled.

"Yeah, can you believe it? The city took away private property from one group of people and used federal dollars to help another group get it."

"I heard urban renewal was a good thing," I said.

"I understand. This program was billed in the media as the biggest and best thing ever to happen in Cleveland. It covered over six thousand acres of land and was going to put Cleveland on the map. Instead, it took a large part of Cleveland off the map. The program was a mess. The Feds eventually put a freeze on it," Grisanti said.

"How come this has not been exposed in the newspaper, Mr. Grisanti?"

"Come on," he made a face, elongating his words, the irritation causing his head to jerk to his left, as though he had been slapped. "Wise up! This was the *Cleveland Press*' program, get it? The *Press* drummed up the publicity so the politicians would support it. The television stations paid attention to what was in the *Press*. 'Urban Renewal' became a catchword for Cleveland's civic boosters. The real story has been ignored for years."

OK, I was a freshman Councilman, vulnerable to the persuasions of old salts. This was a cautionary tale. However, urban renewal was history. I expressed regret to Mr. Grisanti for his family's misfortune.

"What does this have to do with my ward?" I asked, which is the first question a new Councilman should ask.

"Ah, I was coming to that," Grisanti said. "Your ward is in the newest urban renewal-type program."

I moved to the edge of my chair. "What?"

"It's called the Neighborhood Development Program, the NDP. City Hall will tell you it will mean a lot of money for your ward but don't believe it. I happen to know an attorney investigating the NDP. His name is Milt Schulman."

"Milt Schulman?" I restrained a jeer. Everyone at City Hall knew Milt Schulman. He visited committee hearings, taunted Councilmen, often leaving the room in an uproar. He told judges where to get off, and they would threaten to put him in jail. He filed lawsuits against the city like they were flying off a copy machine and most at City Hall considered him a crackpot.

"Ah, Miltie is a shrewd one," Grisanti said, with affection. "City Hall is pulling fast ones all the time. Milt is onto them. Ahh, I could go on and on," he grinned broadly.

"My boy, you are in for a hell of an education."

I was to learn this was a stunning understatement. I developed an increased respect for going with the flow of a casual encounter and how it can change one's life.

CHAPTER 7

The Meanest Son of a Bitch in the Valley

I followed Al Grisanti to Milt Schulman's office in the Standard Building, one block from the county courthouse. He looked in and called, "Hey Milt, I have a new Councilman here who wants to meet you."

The office was small, lavish and gold filigree shone from the corners of Schulman's desk. He motioned for me to sit on a plush French provincial couch and I noticed a sign on the wall near his desk depicted a grizzled, knuckle-dragging character who carried a cudgel, slung low. The inscription, a profane version of the 23rd Psalm:

'Yea though I walk through
The Valley of Shadows
I shall fear no evil.
For I am the meanest
Son of a bitch in the valley.'

"Go ahead, sit there," Schulman beckoned. "It's comfortable. I ought to know, I made it." Schulman left the furniture business, earned a law degree, and became one of the foremost real estate attorneys in Cleveland. He was the embodiment of Cleveland fashion, with a gray, wide-lapel suit, a crisp white shirt, black bow tie and suspenders. He strolled into government offices wearing a gray velvet bowler which added an air of nonchalance to his spiffy appearance, while providing cover for his balding head.

Physically imposing, he had considerable weight to throw from his six-foot frame. He was combative not by nature, but by neighborhood. Growing up in the Glenville area, he frequently encountered antisemitism, so he fought back physically. His talent turned to boxing and he became a prize fighter, under the name of Mickey O'Schul.

He was driven, redefining middle age as a time of new beginnings, having finished Cleveland State Law School when he was past his fiftieth birthday. He put his two sons, Jack and Howard, through Harvard Law. Schulman was a tireless civic rabble-rouser and a keen businessman.

His wife, Agnes, who managed the small law office was as sweet as an allegro played by the Cleveland Orchestra. Milt, much less.

"You met Grisanti. He did a hell of a job on the Council. But the downtown interests broke him." He shifted the conversation. "Now what can I do for you, young man?"

"Mr. Grisanti said there was an urban renewal plan for my ward," I said.

"Yes, and you have to kill it," he said emphatically, as I noticed a .38 revolver tucked into the ample waist that slumped over his belt line.

"It could mean a lot of federal funds," I said.

"You think that's good?" he challenged, his dark eyes hardening through thick, black-framed glasses. "The Federal government has wasted billions of tax dollars with urban renewal!"

"It's free money," I said.

"Free money? Young man, nothing is free. Did you know your

neighborhood must be declared 'slum and blighted' before it can receive funds?" Schulman asked.

I was not aware that, once the city declares a neighborhood 'slum and blighted,' it undergoes 'concentrated code enforcement.' Schulman went on to detail the workings of that program. The city sends in teams of housing inspectors to issue citations. Property owners must complete repairs, or face fines. Most of the homeowners in Ward Seven were elderly, with pension income too high to qualify for federal low-interest loans. In order to finance required repairs, they would have to borrow at high interest rates. This worked for the banks but could jeopardize the personal finances of those subject to the program. Those homeowners who qualified for low interest loans still would not be able to borrow enough to fix up their places and had no sure way of repaying, risking default and foreclosure.

Schulman's tone softened. "Once those housing inspectors start swarming, there will be headaches. In the end, people will have to sell, and property values will go down. They are going to tell you they'll also build new apartments in your area, if you approve the program, but you can get apartments built without chasing away homeowners. Have you read the plan for your ward?"

"No." I hadn't heard of the "NDP" until Grisanti brought it up.

Schulman handed a thick binder to me. "You have to read this. You'll want to take your ward out."

I thanked him and took the three-hundred-fifty-page document home with me and read it straight through. As Schulman said, the Tremont community was slated for a concentrated code enforcement, which would have forced over two thousand homeowners to fix up their properties, whether they had the money or not. As part of the program, over four-hundred apartment units would be built on a seven acre site.

Based on Schulman's advice, I proposed an amendment in Council committee to delete Tremont from the plan. It was accepted. The Stokes administration, which supported the NDP, objected while numerous city administration officials appealed to me to reconsider, telling me if I didn't take millions of federal dollars, someone else would.

Word reached my ward and there was an uproar. People could not abide losing 'millions,' especially while living in homes where the thinking was in terms of five and ten dollar bills. I had to give detailed justification for my decision, knowing it might not be enough to placate constituents disaffected because I turned down the money.

I went to the site where the units of housing were to be located. It was an isolated tract of land in the northeast quadrant of my ward, in sight of the downtown Cleveland skyline. While I had campaigned for more than two years to get elected to Council and personally covered every street and back alley, I was not familiar with this particular location. I walked the land, as an inspector might. Something was wrong. I called Schulman.

"Mr. Schulman, the area off Brevier Avenue, where the city wants to put in housing?"

"Yes. I presume you went there?"

"Yes. It looks like a dump."

I met Schulman the following morning at the County Recorder's office, where titles and deeds of property are kept. Then we proceeded to the County Auditor's office to review property records and property maps. Once we determined the ownership, we would have a clue to the land use. We poured over records and maps. It turned out the land had been owned by a chemical manufacturing company.

"Now let's go look at the land," Schulman said.

We drove to the site and walked a few hundred feet to the edge of a large excavation pit where the soil changed from solid, dark earth to a crumbling, ghostly gray.

"Get some of that gray soil. We have to get it analyzed," Schulman said, pointing to the ashen earth. I went back to my car and took out the morning newspaper, rolled it into a cone and scooped up some soil.

There was a lab located a few blocks away where I presented the sample to a chemist who took a look and said, "There's not much I have to do. It's limestone."

I reported the chemist's observation to Schulman.

"Now call the city engineer and ask him to go over the sewer maps with you. Ask him if the limestone would be able to take the kind of construction the Mayor's office is supporting."

"Jesus," a city engineer said, with a look of alarm, his eyes widening as I showed him my discovery, which I carried in a small Mason jar. "Look kid, I don't want to get involved in this thing. Do me a favor, don't tell anyone you came to see me," he said nervously claiming his God-given right as a bureaucrat, to anonymity. "Let me get the information and I'll meet you somewhere in the Flats."

The city engineer and I met in an abandoned bridge house in Cleveland's industrial Flats, above the Cuyahoga River. He was armed with several maps. "I have the information. Listen, don't get me involved in this," he said as he indicated the site on the map. "I went there this morning. No way they can build on a limestone pit, not unless they want to sink pilings a hundred feet below the limestone. The cost would be prohibitive," he said.

He showed me another map, and its parallel lines. "These are the sewers which are not on limestone. You can't build anything on them. They would be crushed by the new construction. You have to build new sewers. That would cost a lot of money."

"New sewer construction is not in the plans," I said.

"I ain't saying nothing," the engineer replied. "I told you nothing. You don't even know my name." He emphatically instructed non-disclosure of his identity, rolled up his maps and left.

Because I acted upon the advice of two independent thinkers, Al Grisanti and Milt Schulman, who were unafraid to challenge City

Hall, my refusal to accept so-called 'free money' saved my community millions and stopped an abuse of taxpayers' dollars. One jar of randomly collected soil from the site illustrated the unsuitability of the land for construction. Together we had saved the city millions of dollars in design, architectural, engineering, and site preparation costs for a plan which should never have been written. The city administration had looked at a topographical map and decided to build without understanding the territory.

Larry Duggan, Warren Hinchee, Al Grisanti and Milt Schulman helped me become a student of forensics, a political archaeologist and a better public servant, imbued with the spirit of a detective, a quality I'd never have developed if I'd pursued a path of aligning myself with the most popular and politically powerful people. Milt Schulman and Al Grisanti were ridiculed by interest groups at City Hall, their opinions pushed hard to the periphery as politically unacceptable.

Yet truth lined the margins along which they operated.

CHAPTER 8

Weissman the Wizard

Even allowing for the rigged inner workings of the city's political system, it was never easy to predict who would win the mayor's office. In the autumn of 1971, Republican Ralph J. Perk, a skilled ethnic politician of Czech descent and a man of prodigious appetites, was viewed by the political pros as a long shot against Mayor Carl Stokes' hand-picked successor, Arnold Pinkney.

Mayor Stokes executed a stunning political maneuver in the 1971 primary election. He backed businessman Jim Carney, Sr., in the Democratic Primary against the Democratic machine candidate, City Council President Anthony Garofoli. Carney won. Stokes then directed his supporters to switch their support in the General Election from Carney to Pinkney, an independent candidate, who was poised to become Cleveland's second Black Mayor.

Using what was then a new technology, a recorded telephone message which was automatically dialed, Mayor Stokes announced to his legion of supporters in the Black community, "In the primary I asked you to vote for Jim Carney, and you did. Now I am asking you to vote for Arnold Pinkney to continue the progress we have achieved." Many voters believed that they had received a personal call from "Carl."

Bob Weissman, the President of UAW Local 122, had carefully guided my own electoral success with an exacting and acute sense of timing. He saw an opening in the politics of the city which no one else had discerned.

Weissman was mathematical and spoke with precision, never wasting words. An incisive thinker, he had a compelling certitude.

"I think Perk will win. Look at the numbers." Weissman said, spreading before me sheets with voter registration numbers and precinct turnouts, together with his projections.

At this point in the mayor's contest no one, except Weissman, considered Ralph Perk as a serious candidate, let alone a future mayor. Perk was a stranded Republican bobbing in a sea of Cleveland Democrats, a no-hope candidate. Weissman believed, based on his statistical analysis, that Perk would win.

He knew he was right. Weissman was a man of commanding intellect, who chose a career as a labor leader because he saw the potential of the union movement to bring social and economic change. Weissman's personal manner was mechanical. He had a well-practiced economy of words and gestures with only a slight tinge of emotion. He was without artifice, dressed plainly, with an open shirt and a sport coat, and was unremarkable in appearance, except for thinning black hair. Black glasses framed the bright searchlights of his eyes, which instantly assessed, calculated, and summed up the worldview of the person he was meeting and its relevance to the moment. Most of Bob's conversations were short and he wasted no time with people to whom the world of ideas was foreign.

His intellectual skills were such that he was perceived as arrogant. He could win by mental intimidation, without bluster, and had an uncanny ability to assess and distill the potential outcome of onrushing events into varying degrees of probability. When he calculated an outcome, he was unshakable in his forecast, calling elections within a tenth of a percentage point. Bob had the hard edge of a labor bargaining team member, the innate courage of a student protester and was brutally honest.

"How can Perk win?" I was unconvinced.

"The general election vote is going to be split. Democrats are upset at the way Garofoli was defeated and how Carl Stokes manipulated the primary vote. Perk can pick up most of Garofoli's vote, and some of Carney's, and he'll win."

"What do we know about Perk?" I asked, not an unimportant question since Weissman was considering helping him become the Mayor.

"He's a Republican. He's fairly independent. He's the County Auditor. He is not close to the downtown business community. Look, someone has to win every election and it might as well be Perk. He'll win, if we help him." Weissman said.

This was a stretch. Perk was a Republican and I was a Democrat, though not a party man. Perk's outsider status was attractive and this was a chance for Bob and me to influence events inside City Hall, through helping elect a mayor.

Weissman and I scheduled breakfast at a downtown hotel where we were met by a well-dressed Ralph Perk who carried himself with the congenial assurance of a man who knew his place, and never overreached. His life was a celebration of calibration, the well-practiced caution of the plodder. He lived within his means and as with others whose avocation was politics, his means kept expanding as he moved up, his tastes more refined.

Perk ordered breakfast, then turned to me.

"You think I can win?" he asked with a deep, sonorous, sleep-inducing voice, the kind of political chops appropriate only for short speeches, small audiences, and fast departures.

"Bob has gone over the numbers. He believes you can win." I nodded toward Weissman.

"I am not so sure," Perk shook his head in disagreement. "Stokes put

Pinkney way out front and I don't think anyone can beat him." It was apparent he was considering dropping out of the race.

"How much money would this take?" He asked in a worried tone, given the task of defeating Mayor Stokes' personal choice.

"Very little," Weissman responded with unnerving confidence. Perk pushed back from the table in disbelief, ready to leave. He had dealt with ambitious people before and he was not going to be misled into a humiliating defeat. Ralph Perk wanted more than the approval most politicians crave. He wanted a guarantee. His perplexity made it likely he would run, not for the Mayor's office, but away from it.

Weissman, sensing the moment nearly lost, methodically demonstrated winning numbers with such irresistible certainty that Perk edged back toward the table. For a moment he sat silently, exploring the trajectory of his life, his career, his ambitions. Weissman was guaranteeing the outcome. What if he was right?

Once Perk embraced a degree of certainty, he accepted our offer of support and in this moment Cleveland history revolved, spun by the mathematical mastery of Weissman. With Weissman, things had to add up first, then everything else was possible. Bob's additional polling convinced me Perk would win, and, once the outcome could be envisioned, probability necessitated deeper discussions. What would happen after the election?

I wanted two commitments from Perk. One, protect Muny Light and two, create a new consumer protection agency. Perk said yes to both. His Muny Light pledge was easy, because he had been a defender of the people's electric system from the earliest moments in his political career. Uncommon as it was to the transactional nature of political commerce, I didn't ask for anything for myself.

In order to construct a bridge for other Democrats to cross over to support a Republican candidate, I formed "Democrats for Perk" and campaigned at Perk's side, firing up crowds before he spoke. I set up a campaign office, on the corner of West 11th Street and College Avenue, across from Lincoln Park, to greet potential volunteers. It was there that I encountered a sinister dimension of politics.

As we opened Perk Democratic headquarters, I glanced out the broad windows of the Tremont storefront looking out on Lincoln Park to see a tall, thin-as-a rail, ebony man step from a long, dark Cadillac. He was immaculately clad in a pale green suit, white shirt and a white tie. A diamond stick pin glinted from his lapel. He approached the door, opened it, lowered his head in a respectful manner, and inquired, "Mr. Q-sin?" His neatly trimmed mustache accented a close smile.

"Yes sir." He was a man of such impeccability, I considered it inappropriate to correct his mispronunciation of my name.

"I'm Bill Seawright. I'm here for 'Raff'," he said, pronouncing candidate Perk's first name as though he was describing a buoyant, floating platform. "You running Raff's campaign?"

"Yes, I'm organizing Democrats for Perk. May I help you?"

"No," he said smartly. "There's nothing you can do for me. There is something I can do for you, I mean 'Raff'. Hold on, Mr. Q-Sin, I'll be right back."

As I watched, he returned to his Cadillac, opened the trunk and tugged at a large, battered suitcase which, with additional effort, he dislodged, trundling it into our office.

"I have important information here," he said, patting the suitcase, "'Raff's' going to need this, Mr. Q-sin," he said, slapping the suitcase for emphasis. He glanced back to the door. The coast was clear. He motioned subtly with his chin toward a rear office partitioned from street view, where research papers were piled high on a lunch table. I was crafting the Perk platform here, on an Olympia typewriter. I cleared a space.

Thud! Seawright set down the suitcase. Its exterior was well traveled, its frame sturdy. He clicked open the locks, and swiveled its contents for my full view, proudly announcing, "This is for 'Raff.'"

My jaw dropped. The suitcase was jammed with thousands of dollars, hand-weathered tens and twenties stashed in large bundles. Legend had it such suitcases fueled political campaigns, tilted political decisions, and, upon discovery, occasionally sent someone to prison. The apocryphal became reality before my startled eyes.

I sensed danger. Seawright's smile was sickly, less congenial and more like a greeting by the proprietor of a funeral home who was welcoming the only visitor of the day to a one-car political funeral, in this suitcase - - mine. I instantly had the creeps.

"Don't worry, it's real," Seawright said, as if counterfeiting was my concern. My God, I knew what money looked like! It's just I had never seen so much cash, so close, offered for my control. "It's all for the campaign, Mr. Q-Sin. Understand, I don't want anyone to know about this," he said with the emphasis of a man of well-practiced discretion.

What had I gotten into by offering to help run a Mayor's campaign? Oh, Jesus. There were laws against this. I could become complicit in an under-the-table political transaction. My eyes lingered at the contents of the suitcase. My thoughts raced.

Momentarily, Seawright and I were joined in the room by the spirit of Sister Leona, my sixth grade teacher and the principal of St. Aloysius Catholic Elementary School in Cleveland in 1958. She came to my awareness, in full black and white habit, scribing onto the blackboard a short poem, "The Minute," which admonished her unruly pupils to regard carefully the spiritual consequences of right or wrong that were present in every moment:

"The Minute"
I have only just a minute,
Only sixty seconds in it.
Forced upon me,
Can't refuse it,

Didn't seek it,
Didn't choose it,
But it's up to me to use it;
Give account if I abuse it,
Heaven help me if I lose it.
Just one tiny little minute,
But eternity is in it.

The lesson was of the essence of conscience and appealed to moral sensibilities in the education of this young Catholic. Sister ordered the class to write the poem fifty times, at home, and the repetitive mechanical aspect of a painstakingly handwritten paper was received as severe punishment. As I wrote page after page of "The Minute" I wasn't just scribbling on paper but was inscribing a spiritual lesson on my soul: Each moment has a moral calculus. Do the right thing, no matter the consequences, whether or not anyone is looking. It would prove a great teaching, with Sister Leona a constant spiritual guide.

Sister Leona's essence left the room, leaving me alone again with Mr. Seawright. Upright and elegant, he looked at me expectantly as a master considers a squire. I took a deep breath, surveyed the cash, looked him directly in the eyes, lowered my head, gently folded the suitcase, locked it and pushed it back across that divide of time and space in which swirl black holes which swallow souls - - toward the puzzled Mr. Seawright.

"Uh, this is not my department," I said.

I referred Mr. Seawright to Republican headquarters, which handled contributions for the Perk campaign.

"I see." He straightened up. His eyes narrowed. "Yes, of course, Mr. Q-Sin, I'll take this money downtown." He gave me an imperious, dead stare as he removed the suitcase from the table.

"What kind of a campaign is this?" he asked, incredulous, shaking his head as he lugged the suitcase back to his car.

My thought, exactly.

Mr. Seawright "used to" run the "numbers," a lucrative underground lottery involving a network of neighborhood stores and taverns which paid off daily to those lucky gamblers who had correctly guessed a number based on the last three digits of each category of advances, declines and unchanged in the Dow-Jones daily stock market report.

On the streets of Cleveland, where I grew up, people bought dream books to try to discern the winning numbers in their sleep. Invoking the science of the subconscious, for ten cents a player could decode the wisdom buried deep within their dreams and dutifully play an esoteric number, in hopes of climbing out of debt, paying the rent, buying clothes or having a night out on the town. While there was always the possibility of winning free money, the biggest winner was always the person who ran the game.

Numbers were illegal, part of Cleveland's tempestuous underworld of gambling, payoffs to politicians, police raids of numbers houses, and street violence for anyone who crossed onto the turf of the numbers kingpin, who raked in large sums of cash, each month totaling in the millions.

Street cash in suitcases moving secretly into a mayor's race could tip the balance in a close election, with "walking around" money given to politicians to help get out the vote. I hoped Perk didn't operate this way. If he won, I'd see for myself. I didn't want to consider that corrupt interests had latched onto my candidate, or vice-versa, so I continued to concentrate on constructing the Perk platform and organizing the campaign.

CHAPTER 9

The Kishka Caper

Much like his spiritual predecessor, Cleveland Mayor Frank J. Lausche, (Cleveland Mayor 1942-1944) of whom it was said could cry in any language, Ralph J. Perk could eat in any language. He plunged from one campaign event to another with a hungry eye and the sunny abandon of someone who enjoyed himself thoroughly, while having only the slightest anticipation of winning.

The campaign for Mayor of Cleveland in the fall of 1971 was an unending polka of brass bands playing the 'oop-pie shoo-pie' music of Polka King Frankie Yankovic at ethnic picnics festooned with the multi-colors of the motherland, crammed with brigades of bright babushka-wearing, gray-haired ladies and heavy-set men with white shirts, downing pierogis, pigs in the blanket, and czarnina as beer-sloshed crowds merrily whirled to accordion music and the driving beat and dancing frenzy, invoking the esoteric question of a purloined Polish sausage set to song:

"Someone stole the kishka,
Someone stole the kishka,
Someone stole the kishka, from the butcher shop!

Hey!
Who stole the kishka?
Who stole the kishka?
Who stole the kishka?
Someone call the cops!"

And everywhere there was Ralph J. Perk laughing in Italian, eating in Hungarian, singing in a deep baritone Niepewnosc, which asks "Is this Friendship or is this Love," promising a new day at City Hall, a new chance for Cleveland's eastern European ethnics who were eager to regain political power lost during the reign of Mayor Stokes.

Perk was elected Mayor on November 9, 1971, just as Weissman had predicted. I was at Perk's side and even as the final returns showed him with a sizable victory margin, he was beset by worry.

Helen and I prayed with the new Mayor at a Mass of Thanksgiving at his neighborhood parish, a Czech Catholic church, Our Lady of Lourdes, then we stood at his side when he was sworn in. After the swearing in, we were at his home when he received a special delivery letter from Cleveland City Councilman Francis Gaul, warning that Bob Weissman was a dangerous radical, arrested in his youth for distributing leaflets against the Korean War.

Perk, ever the vehement anti-communist and champion of freedom, the revered founder of the Captive Nations movement, frowned as he read the letter and then declared, "Gaul? Why he was for Carney!" and threw the poison missive into an antique, square wooden wastebasket.

As a result of the central role I played in helping to elect Mayor Perk, the *New York Times* declared I was Cleveland's most prominent Democrat, praise which did nothing to win me the affection of the local Democratic Party, because I had helped to elect Cleveland's first Republican mayor in forty years.

Partisan labels were confining to me. I was on a mission and in electing Perk, I had helped to save Muny Light. Further, for the first time in Cleveland's history, a department of consumer affairs would be established, to protect people in the marketplace.

Even though my goal had been accomplished, I was in motion and wanted to advance to Congress, as Jim Stanton did. In Congress I could be of even greater service to those people with whom I grew up, those who were struggling to make ends meet, and people like them across the country.

I had an understanding at an early age that my life did not belong to me alone. It belonged to others, through public service. Weissman encouraged me to plan a race for the U.S. House of Representatives, from Ohio's 23rd Congressional district, a primarily suburban constituency.

I was on fire with ambition and every moment scintillated with urgency. I carried a sense of dread from my early childhood that life was short, and never expected to make it to the first grade, let alone graduate from high school. I was hungry for experience, in a time famine of my own making, where sleep was my enemy. There was much to do and the relentless arc of the second hand on the clock alerted me that I was almost out of time.

After all, I was already twenty-five years old.

CHAPTER 10

The Memo

"Good afternoon, Cleveland! This is the Electric News Magazine, with your host, Steve Clark. The Cleveland Electric Illuminating Company is reported to have spent over $7 million for promotions and advertising, or about $11 per customer. The *Plain Dealer* pointed out that, during that same period, CEI spent about one-fourteenth of that figure on research. What do these figures mean to you?"

This was noteworthy. The top radio news commentator in Cleveland was attacking CEI. Steve Clark of WERE radio had a clear, powerful voice which commanded attention. I stayed with him on my car radio as I drove from City Hall.

"Another interesting fact of the article was the information that CEI realized a net profit of $40 million last year, or more than sixteen cents for each dollar of operating revenue. Still the utility has announced CEI will seek a 20% rate increase from the Ohio Public Utilities Commission, the state agency that regulates utility rates. This rate hike would generate an additional $54 million annually for the company, which was granted a 6.5% rate hike in 1970."

"We, the body politic, grant monopoly status to these public utilities in order to avoid costly duplication of effort and equipment, hoping to keep rates within reason. We empower an agency of our government to look out for our interest in the regulation of such monopoly companies. It appears that we must find a way to dramatize to these agencies and then insist that they remember just who they are working for. This is Steve Clark."

Clark had a reputation as a no-nonsense interviewer. I accepted an invitation to be on his show to discuss the new administration at City Hall and spent a few hours preparing for the encounter. I arrived at the radio station and was greeted by a large man of the stature of the legendary lumberjack, Paul Bunyan, with a full beard and red and black checkered shirt. It was Steve Clark. His laugh reverberated. Everything about him was expansive and when I asked him about that particular show, he guffawed "Oh THAT! Did I get into the soup! My boss is still steaming."

"Why? The report was solid," I said.

"Someone from CEI called my boss after the broadcast. You know how those things go." Actually, I didn't know how those things went. I did not understand the relationship between advertisers and broadcasters.

Clark did not appear overly concerned. He changed the subject and we proceeded with the interview. I was invited to return and called him a few days later to work out a date. A different-sounding Steve Clark answered the phone.

"Hi. Listen. Your appearance on my show? Hold off." His voice was halting. It wasn't only my invitation being placed on reserve.

"Is everything OK?" I asked.

"No, it is not," Clark sounded stressed. "I really shouldn't discuss it."

I understood from his pause I had to extend the shelter of confidence. "Look, anything you discuss with me is private."

"OK. Remember I told you my boss got a call from CEI ?"

"Yes."

"Well, CEI was very angry. My boss called me into his office and said I was hurting his reputation in the business community. He reminded me who I am working for. He told me not to discuss anything on the air embarrassing to advertisers. The station gets at least $70,000 a year from CEI. I think he is making a play for more advertising dollars," Clark laughed nervously, then pivoted to what was uppermost in his mind.

CEI told his boss to send over tapes of that show and any show where the utility was mentioned. Clark may have determined the content, but the station belonged to his boss, whose primary concern was the comfort of advertisers. Until I spoke with Al Grisanti and Steve Clark, the implications of behind-the-scenes influence of advertisers on the news had escaped me. I accepted at face value most of what I heard on radio and television or read in the newspapers.

"I might lose my job over this," Clark said. "CEI has a new advertising campaign. It is filing for another rate increase at the PUCO and wants to minimize objections. I stepped into the frying pan. CEI is off limits, way off limits."

A few days later, a sealed, plain brown letter-sized envelope was placed in my Council mailbox. "Councilman Kucinich" was printed neatly in the center, but it had not been posted and there was no return address.

When I opened the envelope, the word M E M O R A N D U M was centered, in capital letters spaced under the letterhead of the Cleveland Electric Illuminating Company. It was a photocopy of a thirty-six-page memo, dated October 9, 1970, to Lee C. Howley from R.H. Bridges, another CEI executive.

Someone had given me a copy of a CEI inner-office memo.

Why?

I looked around the Council offices. It was early in the morning. I asked Margaret, a clerk, if she knew who put the memo in my box. She did not. Only official visitors, such as Councilmen, staffers and lobbyists had access to the area. I tucked away the memo.

At home, I studied the CEI internal communication. It was a secret document detailing a highly structured, clandestine program to take over Muny Light. Item two in the plan was already in process: "Curtailment of further development and expansion of MELP requires positive action."

"Positive" in this sense meant negative action against Muny Light, working to undermine Muny Light's reliability and blocking necessary repairs through influencing City Council. "The longer MELP continues the more difficult and costly will be the solution to us."

"Solution" was a euphemism for wiping out Muny Light.

Item five of the memo would prove to be prophetic. "Continuation of our present policy of keeping up to date files of information on the Muny operation and municipal finances generally." Even though Muny Light was a separate 'enterprise' fund, apart from the General Fund of the city, CEI's linkage of the two was ominous. It hinted at the company's intent to undermine not only Muny Light's finances, but those of the entire city government, with the help of CEI's finance and legal departments.

The memo outlined a program of "continuous education" of politicians and newspapers in the community to the economic unsoundness of the MELP [Muny Light] operation. Translated, political contributions to the politicians and advertising revenue to the media.

The plan was to use CEI's advertising dollars to subvert the media and undermine public support for Muny Light. Near-term and long-term corporate objectives were described in the covert plan.

The memo bragged of CEI's influence over radio and television broadcast decisions and "the favorable service editorial time devoted by WKYC-TV to the company's efforts to reduce pollution, stories about the Municipal Light plant and by WEWS-TV to the nuclear power general controversy." CEI calculated that it had received a thousand minutes of free news and public service time from radio and television stations, in a single year.

The Bridges Memorandum made clear that even more important to CEI than the free coverage, was what the local media did not cover as a result of CEI's editorial influence. As public concern arose over the Davis-Besse nuclear power project, inquiries into its efficacy, cost, environmental impact and safety were thwarted.

"Open communication [with the media] was expanded with press-radio-TV which has resulted in less intense reporting," read the memo.

CEI's success in concocting a case for the sale of Muny Light was a study in subversion of news managers. News articles, editorials, unsigned and undated letters to the editor relating to Muny Light, were prepared by CEI for submission to editors who would publish them, verbatim.

The Bridges Memorandum revealed that the information process in a major metropolitan area was a concoction of anti-Muny Light, pro-CEI propaganda, perpetrated by the private utility whose very existence depended upon public permission. The Cleveland media had become CEI's paid mouthpiece at a time when CEI was plotting the destruction of an electric system owned by the people of Cleveland. I had the proof in my hands.

How did CEI develop such a superlative talent for getting the media to write or broadcast whatever they wanted? The Bridges Memo proved that it was the calculated use of advertising dollars, which enabled CEI to push a rising tide of news and editorials determined to take over Muny Light.

Under a torrent of negative press, how could the media-consuming public conclude anything other than that Muny Light should be sold? What's more, CEI customers paid for the ads, since the cost of advertising was included in the determination of utility rates. CEI also used its advertising dollars to pump up support for nuclear power.

CEI coordinated both overt and covert actions to delay a permanent interconnect, to block Muny Light's repairs, to stop Muny's development and expansion, to eliminate Muny Light's rate advantage and to weaken Muny's financial condition. These, together with the media strategy set forth in the memorandum, were part of a campaign, in the words of the Bridges Memo, "to reduce and ultimately eliminate Muny Light."

Those words, "reduce and ultimately eliminate" had the feel of an organized crime hit, or the bureaucratic equivalent of a special military operation.

An independent journalist, Roldo Bartimole, in his publication, *Point of View,* unearthed a decades-old memo by former CEI President, Ralph Besse, revealing that Besse espoused a military strategy in the operations of CEI, "a military organization, with military lines drawn, military procedures enforced, military discipline imposed ..." Bartimole described Besse as an adherent of the leadership style of German General Erwin Rommel, the 'Desert Fox'. Under Besse, CEI's company divisions became private power Panzer units aimed at obliterating competing public power systems. CEI honored Besse by co-naming its first nuclear power plant, Davis-Besse.

Another major player in the development of CEI's strategy against Muny Light was John Lansdale, Jr., a powerful strategic thinker, the top player on CEI's legal defense at Squire Sanders and Dempsey, Cleveland's largest law firm. He added gravitas to Squire Sanders' presence in Washington, D.C.

Lansdale, Jr., a graduate of Virginia Military Institute and Harvard Law, was the army intelligence and security officer for the Manhattan Project, which developed the atomic bomb. He gained fame for his role in Operation Harborage, a daring raid deep inside enemy lines, which resulted in the capture of a large supply of uranium, and significantly, a half dozen of Germany's top nuclear physicists. He was hailed as the man who captured the secrets of Germany's atomic bomb program for the United States.

Colonel Lansdale was exceptionally skilled at his craft of interdiction, disruption and dissecting congeries of abstractions and would one day be named to the Military Intelligence Officers' Hall of Fame.

World War II had not ended for the gifted men who guided the investor-owned utility. The new battleground was in every city and town which had a municipally-owned power system. The power of the people, symbolized by Muny Light, was the new enemy which must be defeated, at all costs.

It was not hard to imagine CEI management and attorneys holding meetings in a war room, simulating the movement of assets, getting reports from the field, and determining the resources which were needed to clear a path to the destruction of Cleveland's light system.

And what was CEI's motive to capture and kill off Muny Light? In a single word from the Bridges Memorandum: "Profits."

That a private business would go out of its way to develop and execute a plan to seriously damage the city was stunning to me. This was the type of dirty trickery foretold by City Council Utilities Chair Duggan. Once I read the Bridges memo I knew that CEI could never be trusted and that I would confront them, even if most in Council were reluctant. Someone had to stand up for the people of the city.

Sleuthing was only part of my job as a Councilman. I answered anywhere from a hundred to two-hundred-fifty calls a day, (when it snowed). My first responsibility was to help to make city government responsive to people's requests. It was this service-intensive approach which gave me license to go deeper into city affairs, to ask questions from which others would shy away.

After reading the Bridges Memo, I excitedly called Steve Clark.

"I've got something huge, Steve."

"Excuse me Dennis," he cut me off. "I can't talk. I've been fired."

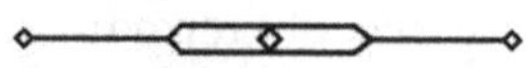

I took to the floor of City Council and read a transcript of Steve Clark's broadcast about rapidly rising utility rates and charged CEI with engineering his firing to quell criticism of their advertising practices and to intimidate newsmen, invoking an Orwellian scenario, the "Spectre of

1984" and what Steve's firing meant in terms of the free press.

"Today, it is Steve Clark," I looked at the reporters who maintained a permanent station to the right of the Council President's rostrum. "It happened to him. Tomorrow it could happen to you." As I spoke, the members of the Council were suffocated by boredom. Some gave me a lemon-sucking look, as if to say, "Hey kid, you just figured this out?" There is nothing so obnoxious to those in public life as a declaration of the obvious from a political neophyte.

News reporters covering the Council meeting were a sketch of supine immobility, a confession of the futility of expression without independence. If CEI worked to influence editors, the editors in turn would place limitations on their reporters. I could not expect any help from the "free press."

CHAPTER 11

Another Christmas Blackout

After receiving the results of the decennial census of Cleveland, the City Council redistricted its thirty-three wards to equalize ward populations. In an attempt to oust me from City Council, the Council leaders cut my ward into three pieces, so I chose to run in a newly-drawn ward five miles west of the former Ward Seven. I campaigned door-to-door and based on the prominence I received through helping elect Mayor Perk, I won.

Helen and I obtained a 7.5% interest rate on a mortgage of $22,500 and purchased a two-story, wooden-frame colonial on Milan Avenue. The two-year old house had a gas lamp in front and two large ferns framing the front picture window. A big apple tree stretched above a grassy backyard.

There was a time in my life when I could not have imagined living in a house, with wall-to-wall carpeting, central heating, a kitchen with wooden cabinets, three bedrooms upstairs and a finished basement below. Growing up in Cleveland and moving constantly, desperate to find a rental where we could all live, our family had to settle for substandard conditions with rats, roaches, broken windows, holes in the wall, leaky pipes, and wildly fluctuating apartment temperatures.

Our arrival on Milan Avenue in December of 1971 marked a moment of wonder. This was our first Christmas in our new home. A blaze of holiday lights warmed our sacred enclosure, despite another city-wide Muny Light holiday blackout.

We were CEI customers. Muny Light wasn't available in our new neighborhood, something I intended to change.

The Cleveland City Planning Commission issued a new study which showed a path toward economic prosperity for the city, saving its businesses and industries and its residential utility customers a combined $28 million a year, using eminent domain to take over CEI's generation, transmission and distribution system within the City of Cleveland.

Muny Light's cheap electricity could become a magnet to attract business and industry to Cleveland, the Planning Commission showed. This would provide a clear example of the benefits of public ownership. Under Muny Light, commercial, industrial and residential customers could save up to 45% on their electricity, providing Cleveland with one of the lowest electric rates in America.

In order to accomplish the acquisition, the City Council would first have to revoke CEI's franchise in Cleveland, a monopoly status granted by legislation. CEI would be paid, by law, fair-market value for its facilities in Cleveland. The purchase price, estimated at $289 million, would be paid with mortgage revenue bonds, secured by the newly expanded Muny system's property and a projected $90 million in annual revenue. CEI's massive market outside the city limits would not be affected.

Muny Light, according to the City Planning Commission report, had the wherewithal to buy out CEI, even as the company was lobbying Council members to sell.

Muny Light provided low-cost electricity to seventy-six city facilities and lit most of the city's streets. If CEI took over Muny, the result would have been automatically raised rates for Muny Light customers and necessitated a multi-million-dollar tax increase for all Clevelanders, to pay the higher street lighting bill.

The conundrum Cleveland faced was how to extend the benefits of municipal ownership, lower utility rates and lower taxes, while corrupt interests were exerting control. The effect of CEI's predatory conduct and its inflated cost of electricity would be felt by everyone in Cleveland. Privatization was solely for private profit.

The City Planning report was never acted on, and instead of a forecast expansion, Muny Light faced a nightmare of stunted growth. Ordinances to repair generators, to improve street lighting, and to strengthen Muny's financial position froze in Council committee amid continual blackouts.

CEI continued to feign cooperation in routine paperwork exchanges, proposing an alternative temporary interconnect of limited capacity which could be constructed expeditiously, as opposed to a permanent interconnect with the capacity needed to assure Muny Light's reliability. When, on July 7, 1972, the FPC ordered CEI to install a permanent 138kV synchronous interconnect, the company moved covertly to fund a taxpayers' suit to block it.

The competitive dynamic in Cleveland had turned toxic, with CEI using every means possible to frustrate Muny Light's ability to provide low-cost electricity, while continuing to force its own captive customers to pay higher and higher electric bills, profiting both CEI's shareholders and the banks which held the electric company's debt.

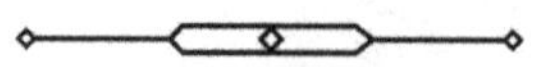

Utilities Chair Francis "Frank" Gaul, entered the committee room to take center stage at a meeting he had called to advance CEI's plan to acquire Muny Light. Gaul had a well-preserved physique from his days as an All-American tackle at Notre Dame. He was drafted into the ranks of pro football by the New York Bulldogs in the 20th round of the 1949 draft and had played one season. Short, square and trim, his very presence intimated strength and speed, fast enough to block or tackle anyone within his reach. Hard-nosed and impatient, he had the air of a man on a mission to take down Muny Light. Moments before Councilman Gaul's review began, he huddled closely with CEI executives who stood with him behind the committee table.

I secured a seat at the table and witnessed CEI's men passing several sheets of paper to Gaul. As they emphasized different areas in the documents they'd given him, Gaul frowned, perplexed. He was, at last, an outstanding athlete who ran the plays he was told, but this was a new playbook. He clearly did not understand the direction he was supposed to take. His eyes narrowed, his chin bunched as he furtively looked up and down the committee table, distracted, while increasingly animated utility executives tried to overcome his inattention, with gentle nudges, then agitatedly redirected his gaze to the papers they had placed in his hands.

Gaul finally called the meeting to order. Lights! TV cameras! His coaches from CEI had prepared him well. Despite appearances, I had never seen Frank Gaul more capable, nor more informed, as he read from the statement which CEI's lobbyists had given him. He was possessed with detailed knowledge of Muny Light operations and spoke in technical terms of net income, costs per kilowatt hour and megawatts.

"How can the plant be in such a condition that it can't consistently put 100 megawatts on the line, out of a capacity of 238 megawatts?" He spoke with the tinny ring of corporate authority concluding, "Thus, in the last four years, the benefits traditionally provided to all residents have virtually disappeared and all residents have increasingly been saddled with the increased costs of operating Muny."

He had made CEI's case and his performance was greeted approvingly by his CEI mentors who had moved to the private utility's customary post, overseeing events from the back of the committee room.

The media left the room to rush Councilman Gaul's ominous assessment of Muny Light to public notice.

It was my turn to speak but the room had thinned. I declared that CEI was using the media to pursue a deceitful plan to achieve a monopoly, but unfortunately all of the news media had left the room.

Commissioner Hinchee was next to testify and staunchly defended Muny Light, refuting Gaul's charges, while producing volumes of economic analysis, financial documentation and an historical narrative of Muny Light's success. Hinchee explained the urgency of proceeding with capital improvements to the Division of Light and Power, since the lack of repairs made Muny Light vulnerable to blackouts. Council members were unmoved and it was common knowledge that CEI lobbied to block Muny's repairs.

CEI continued to dawdle over an interconnect, placing upon the public system extreme operational pressures. As power emergencies increased in frequency, the city was forced to turn to CEI, who in turn, charged Muny Light nearly triple the going rate for emergency purchased power.

The cost of electricity rose sharply in the Cleveland area, with CEI's ever-escalating rates given a green light by the Public Utilities Commission of Ohio.

I went to Washington, D.C. to testify before the Federal Price Commission on the economic importance of stopping the rise in utility rates. After my testimony, I visited the office of U.S. Senator Lee Metcalfe of Montana, who had cataloged the sharp practices of utility monopolies and detailed unfair utility rates in a work entitled "*Overcharge.*" I met the Senator's co-author and administrative assistant, and handed him a letter asking for a further Justice Department investigation of CEI.

Vic Reinemer had closely studied the company and shared his insight. "CEI is proud they never miss a dividend. They are very aggressive.

You've got an unusual situation in Cleveland," he said. "Your Muny competes with CEI, street-by-street. That doesn't happen in too many places. It's either all public, or all private in most cities," he said.

I related Muny Light's perilous operational and financial position to Reinemer, as well as its vulnerability to blackouts. Then I handed him a copy of the Bridges Memo, which he perused.

"CEI could end up with an antitrust case on their hands," responded Reinemer. "Most Americans don't pay enough attention to utilities, except when rates go up. People are getting gouged. Public power is important. It gives people a choice to have control over their rates, to have cheaper power and accountability."

"CEI is trying to take away our choice," I said.

"People have a right to own an electric system. Remind Clevelanders of that principle. There are nearly two thousand publicly-owned systems in America. It is important to all of them that Cleveland stays owned by the city." He handed me a signed copy of "*Overcharge,*" promising to keep an eye on CEI from Washington.

"Muny Light is worth fighting for," he said as the meeting ended. "It empowers people. It enables economic freedom."

Council Majority Leader George Forbes, from Cleveland's Glenville neighborhood, emerged as a vocal proponent of the sale of Muny Light. He had been one of Mayor Stokes' top lieutenants. A former housing inspector, Forbes was an attorney, a self-made man who put himself through law school while studying the neighborhood political process. He was known as a cunning infighter. Tall and thin, with a razor tongue, Forbes was a feared political combatant.

Forbes and I may have been destined to be opposites. In my first appearance, in 1967, before city council's Legislative committee, Councilman Forbes cut me short as I advocated reducing the size of council.

"You are testifying on legislation which could put me out of a job," he said.

"I don't believe Council should be an employment agency," I retorted.

"You're not here yet," he shot back.

"I will be," I promised.

Skillfully exploiting Cleveland's primarily White business establishment by his personal experience of the economic and social effects of racism, Forbes provided corporate leaders with the comforting illusion that he was the one man of power and color with whom they could make deals. He would help the business community attempt to mollify the Black community, through doing political business - - with him as the bargaining agent. He became corporate Cleveland's go-to guy at City Hall.

Enigmatic, Forbes was a man of a thousand hidden agendas, no one ever knew what he really wanted. Everything he did, he always did for a reason, but no one ever knew the reason, because he was the master of misdirection and was never in anyone's camp, save his own.

"Sell it?" he responded to a question from the media regarding Muny Light. "Sell it. Now. Yes. Double 'yes'. I'm opposed to keeping it. It is unprofitable."

The incumbent Cleveland City Council President, Edmund Turk, had been appointed to the Public Utilities Commission of Ohio by Republican Governor James Rhodes. Turk enjoyed close relationships with all the city's private utilities and was a good fit for a commission whose policies leaned heavily toward corporate needs.

Forbes became the consensus choice of the business and political community for Council President. He was the first black person to ascend to that office, no small accomplishment in a community where the majority of the electorate and the Council was white. Other than Gaul and Forbes as proponents of the sale, and myself and Larry Duggan as opponents, most Council members chose not to be too involved with the Muny Light debate.

I spoke to Steve Clark about this, asking, "Why is it that most Councilmen are afraid to weigh in on Muny Light, especially when their constituents could have lower utility rates?" I asked.

"They are terrified, because CEI can put money into campaigns against them, or help to field opposition. CEI can do to the politicians what the company did to me, shut me up. It is a much more comfortable existence for a politician to say nothing and do nothing, rather than to risk the wrath of a powerful corporation like CEI, " he said. "This is what 'to get along, go along' means."

Politicians are risk-averse, and will not fight corporate interests, unless they have support among their constituents or a competing structure of equal power. Always vulnerable to the influence of interest groups, politicians were willing to tap the largesse of Cleveland's corporate community, which paid for campaign advertisements. I on the other hand, campaigned door-to-door, relentlessly and built a personal following which was a healthy substitute for corporate contributions.

Elected through a grass roots effort, I was able to steer clear of the compromises, the favors from special interests and the money which incapacitated many of my colleagues. Because my commitment was to my constituents, I was able to speak and act freely, but learned quickly that in public life, you must protect your freedom to act.

CHAPTER 12

"The Great White Father"

I was never much for cocktail parties, small talk or drinking, so when the Greater Cleveland Growth Association, our 'Chamber of Commerce' held its annual reception for members of Council at a private dining room in downtown Cleveland, I didn't plan to attend. I had successfully resisted what I saw as political meat markets, where politicians are on display for interest groups who ply them with food and drink. Besides, I had helped to end the Growth Association's pet project, a new jetport, built in Lake Erie, that would have required the issuance of $3 billion dollars in bonds, a sum approximating the total value of all land in the county.

Squire Sanders and Dempsey had written the law creating the new jetport authority, helped pick a majority of authority members, and was in a prime position to make tens of millions of dollars on the bond work.

Overlooked by political and business leaders cheering for the project were the financial liabilities, environmental effects, and inflated job numbers, concerns I brought to public attention through convening special hearings, called 'The People's Hearings on the Jetport.'

In the hearings, expert testimony from economists and

environmentalists concluded that the number of jobs created by the project were wildly exaggerated, the cost was grossly underestimated and environmental effects had not been considered. The dredging of the lake for construction of the jetport would release toxic quantities of cadmium, nickel and lead from the lakebed, poisoning aquatic life, and ruining the sole source of drinking water for millions. The building of a massive structure in the lake would increase soil deposits on the west shore and create erosion to the east, wiping out a section of Euclid, Ohio, one of Cleveland's largest suburbs.

In the hearings I was able to activate the innate power of community, which is often ignored by institutional economic power, the media and the political establishment enthralled with seldom-challenged powerful interest groups.

A woman testifying before a Council committee hearing summed up the plight of many people: "We're not the 'silent majority.' You are not listening to us."

In such circumstances, matters relating to necessity, economics, environment and safety were easily swept aside, creating no openings for a public response, which, otherwise, if organized, could change the outcome.

The jetport hearings were an opportunity to create public space for a discussion, empowering people through rallying civil society. Was this an act of defiance? Yes, entrenched power begs to be challenged and when I stepped forward on the jetport issue, the process of rallying large groups of people at the grass roots became emblematic of all my efforts. I began to insert myself into the daily life of the city and discovered the potency of standing up, speaking out and organizing for improved public transit, to save public parks, libraries and fire stations; for clear packaging of meat, for dating and labeling of perishable food, and against waste, fraud and abuse of taxpayer's money, leading the way against unnecessary taxes and excessive electric, gas and telephone utility rate increases.

The job of a Councilman was to vote and to answer phone calls from constituents and to act upon their requests. In my efforts on behalf of the community, I was called a 'rebel' and worse. I was rebelling - against a smug, rigged system. I held a public office and was required to step forward, proactively, instead of letting events pass by.

If I came across as a rabble-rouser, it's because I had this romantic notion of relentlessly challenging power, undaunted by defeat, untroubled by the paradox of detaching myself from the system while within the system, priding myself on independence of spirit, not exactly a path to success in a partisan political setting buttressed by powerful financial interests, seen and unseen. As with any politician, I wanted people to like me, but when given the choice between being liked and actually standing for something, I chose to risk popularity.

The energies that I brought to each cause stirred political activism in the community and people signed petitions to get involved. I wrote issue-oriented leaflets with Weissman's help and distributed thousands of missives everywhere, to excite participation. I made phone calls, announced meetings and developed neighborhood organizations.

My time on the City Council was an opportunity to redefine and redirect power through using my position inside the government to empower and rally people outside, creating a new political reality by helping people and their causes become visible, viable and consequential.

In the case of the jetport in Lake Erie, I was in direct opposition to the Greater Cleveland Growth Association and a major law firm. Mrs. Mercedes Cotner, the Clerk of Council, suggested I attend a GCGA reception, notwithstanding my position on the jetport. She said it would be a good opportunity to build bridges.

"They can't be mad at you forever. They were for the jetport. That's their job, to support business. It won't hurt for you to be seen by them," she said, sharing the wisdom of a veteran, practical politician.

I considered her entreaty. Yes, the Growth Association tried to perpetrate a fraud on the community. They did their job, and I did mine. We stopped the jetport.

"OK, Mrs. Cotner, I'll go."

At the reception, as I hopped from one beer-and-whiskey-drenched discursion to another, a stout, bespectacled man in his sixties intercepted me.

"Mr. Kucinich, I'm James Davis," a deep voice, smooth as whiskey, announced. I did a double-take. This was *the* James C. Davis, the most politically powerful attorney in Cleveland and managing partner at Squire Sanders, a law firm with 175 attorneys in six states and three countries, with annual billings of $43 million. Squire Sanders was not only bond counsel to the City of Cleveland, it represented virtually every governmental authority in northern Ohio on financial matters. I was surprised he sought me out. I was only a Councilman.

James C. Davis was the man Council President Forbes called the "Great White Father."

Since this exalted man introduced himself to me, I respectfully listened to what he had to say. "Well, well, Mr. Kucinich, I've been waiting to meet you. I've been watching your career," he said, as he swirled a maraschino cherry in his drinking glass. "You do get your name in the news quite a bit."

A surmising smile spread under his carefully trained mustache. "I've seen you standing up there and talking about 'the people' all the time. Always going against those 'big companies.'" His mouth opened a bit and he tossed back a chuckle, the word 'big' a little elbow of camaraderie before a knee-slapping joke. He winked, and sensing my discomfort, touched my arm as if to reassure me. "I want you to know I like you. Yes, I like you, Councilman. And let me tell you why I like you. Because when you talk about the people-this and the people-that, you don't believe a goddamned word you are saying. It's quite a show."

He looked into his glass, sloshed his drink, spinning his ice cubes and through his thick eyebrows and glasses, winced as his shoulders heaved slightly. He smirked and before I had a chance to respond, he walked away shaking with laughter.

It was a valuable lesson to bear witness to the contempt felt by members of the Cleveland establishment toward anyone who dared challenge them. I wasn't dissuaded by such treatment, but understood that the price of popularity with corporate Cleveland required that I agree to the transfer of millions of taxpayers' dollars to their private interests. I couldn't do it. It was fundamentally unfair and wrong to take taxpayers' money and give it away to powerful interest groups just because they demanded it.

My objections reverberated in Mr. Davis' ears and those of his colleagues and set me on a collision course with utilities, banks, real estate interests and their law firms.

The longer I was in City Council, the more I understood what I did not know. Milt Schulman helped propel my early Council career by providing me with documents on land frauds, corrupt federal programs and capital improvement boondoggles. He invited me to come to his office to school me on the arcane aspects of city finances, in this case the issuance of bonds.

"This stuff looks complex, but it's not," he said, setting me at ease. "They want to keep everyone dumb, especially Councilmen, so you won't ask any questions. Let's begin. The city finances the building of bridges, roads, that cockamamie Justice Center and police stations, by selling bonds and paying the investors an interest rate."

"Yes, like those thirty-year bonds they sold on the 1st District Police Station." I reflected.

"Right. The city pays off the bond issue with property tax dollars in two ways. Sometimes people vote on the bond issue in what is known as voted debt. Sometimes the city issues bonds without a vote of the people, called unvoted debt. I don't like it, but it happens. People should always have a vote on anything that raises their taxes."

Milt explained the difference between notes and bonds. Notes are short-term loans, for one year. They can be renewed by the city for up to five years, during which time the city waits for long-term interest rates to become favorable. The yearly renewal is called a rollover and is done all the time. Within five years however, the city has to convert the notes into bonds. Bonds are long-term financing.

"Look, all this is academic," Milt said. "Here's what you need to know. Bond financing has become a racket for law firms, underwriters, investment bankers and Wall Street. You get a group of architects, engineers and bankers who dream up something to sell to the public and it doesn't matter if it's needed or not. The bond guys go for the big projects. The bigger, the better for them. They build things to make money off the public. It's what makes the world go 'round, young man. Law firms, banks, investment brokers, rating services, Wall Street, they are all in on it. They run the financial system and they are all a bunch of crooks."

According to Milt, the government was run by a "bunch of crooks" who he was going to "get" at one time or another. Like a Jewish Robin Hood with a quiver full of taxpayer suits, he would launch one arrow after another at the evil Nottingham empire on behalf of middle-class taxpayers. I knew there was corruption, but surely not everyone at City Hall was in on it.

"Milt, how can you say they are all crooks!"

"Because I say it." He was imperious, angry at my insolence.

"Look at the Justice Center. We didn't need it. First, they said it was going to cost the taxpayers $62 million, next thing you know it was up to $120 million. By the time it is over it will cost close to $200 million. They could have fixed up the old Central Police station but no, they had to take a big chunk of prime property in downtown, removing tax-paying businesses. They call it a Justice Center but it's about anything but justice. It's about law firms, bond counsels, underwriters, investors, rating services and Wall Street."

When Milt Schulman talked, you could feel the physical power of his words spin off his ample physique. He was intimidating and when he showed up at Council committee meetings, members looked for the exits, rather than be subjected to his withering onslaught. He was an uncompromising ass-kicker of politicians, bureaucrats, judges, news editors, investment bankers, bond counsels and anyone else who he believed was sending his country, America, the greatest country in the world, to perdition.

"How does this relate to Muny Light and CEI?" I asked.

Milt explained that Squire Sanders is the bond counsel for the City of Cleveland and had the municipal bond business locked up in Ohio. Squire Sanders bond work necessitated close contact with underwriters and bond ratings services. Once underwriters and ratings agencies got on board, cities sold their bonds. The more bonds the city sold, the more fees Squire Sanders made, the more money the rating services and underwriters made, and the more money taxpayers owed, a system that encourages expensive projects.

"And that's just Squire Sanders municipal bond business," Milt said. "Do you know Squire Sanders' biggest corporate account?" His vest shifted as he grabbed his lapel, revealing, opposite a gold watch fob, his fancy .38 caliber rent collector. He was obviously preparing to deliver a punch line, since I had no idea of the law firm's corporate clients.

"No." I answered.

"The Cleveland Electric Illuminating Company! Squire Sanders is advising CEI and the city at the same time. You think the City of Cleveland is getting a fair shake when Squire Sanders makes most of its income from CEI? Mark my words, Squire Sanders is causing the city to be over-committed with bonds for projects which aren't needed. You think Muny Light is safe with CEI's attorneys inside of City Hall?"

I was trying to absorb the world of politics and finance which Milt

Schulman was unveiling.

"Young man! Open your eyes! Wake up! This is the way the city is run. They are all double-dealers. They are all a bunch of crooks."

"I'll talk to the Mayor," I responded.

"Perk?! He's in with them! I'm going to get that guy yet. The worst thing you ever did was to help him get elected," Milt said in a harsh, accusatory manner. "You think Perk's election helped the city? It hurt the city. You think it helped you? It hurt you."

"Milt, you can't say that."

"I'll say it and I did say it," his voice began to boom. His wife, Agnes, nervously approached his office. "Name one thing Perk has done since you got him in there," Milt needled.

"He's for Muny Light." I offered. I could feel the ridicule of this seer.

"Well you watch, young man. If he gets the chance, Muny Light will be gone. And you, young man, you got him elected," he shook his head to shame me, twisting the verbal knife he placed between my ribs.

Then his composure became amiable. He understood I was at the beginning of my journey, navigating a very corrupt system. I was young and not fully schooled in the ways in which private interests were ransacking the city treasury. Milt was determined to provide for my education. "You'll make up for it. You're still a mensch and Milt Schulman is going to help you beat these crooks."

CHAPTER 13

Campaigning to End the War

We find our fortune at the most unusual times and places. The midway at the Oktoberfest was a crush of sun-burned revellers, some men dressed in lederhosen, ladies in dirndls, all seeking music, beer, lining up at makeshift stands selling der weinerschnitzel, sauerbraten, and sausage.

I saw an opening and entered the main tent where clouds of cigarette smoke billowed to the inside peaks. A thousand people chattered in many languages against the din of a German polka band's brisk foot-stomping tunes. Polka music has a natural rhythm which syncopates with the shaking of hands from table to table.

A frail, white-haired lady with a grip of steel cornered me, grabbed my hands, and led me toward the center of the dance floor, pumping my arms up and down, as we twirled around. I tried to avoid the dancing, because it slowed me down in circulating the room, but never avoided hand shaking. Hand shaking is the great fun of campaigning and it's an art. The close, personal contact with people, the touching, grabbing, laughing, sharing, is an accelerated emotional experience which energizes the campaigner and the voter. After my polka, I plunged into the crowd. "Hello, my name is Dennis Kucinich and I'm running for Congress."

I won a hotly contested race for the Democratic nomination in Ohio's 23rd District, on the strength of a door-to-door campaign against the war in Vietnam. "Kucinich Says End the War," read the mimeographed missive I distributed door-to-door in the most conservative areas of the district.

"President Nixon now admits his policy of de-escalation in Vietnam has failed. The choice is to re-escalate or get out, the President has stated."

My campaign focused on the human and the economic costs of the war "Let's stop wasting American lives, American resources and the American taxpayer's dollars. Every American family has been paying over $500 a year for the direct military costs of our participation in Vietnam. We can't afford this drain on our economy. We can't afford the continuing loss of priceless American lives. We must not accept the increased costs of the insane gamble of widening this war." I asked the people of the district to send me to Congress to vote to end the war.

I faced veteran U.S. Representative William Minshall, an eight-term Republican, in the 1972 General Election and continued a relentless campaign schedule. Wherever people gathered within twenty miles of my district they could expect to see me at large crowd events. As I campaigned, if people said something favorable, I didn't let it go to my head. If they said something negative, I never took it to heart, but kept moving, shaking hands.

Our message challenging the war was resonating in blue collar areas thought to be sympathetic to the war. Their children were being called upon to put their lives on the line and opposition to the war was much deeper than had been assumed by politicians and the media.

I remembered when, as a copyboy at the *Plain Dealer*, I was assigned to "art runs," driving a company car to pick up photos of soldiers killed in combat in the early stages of the war. Most houses I arrived at were weather-beaten and badly in need of paint, with rickety steps which groaned even under my slight frame, screen doors in need of repair, flapping slightly in the wind. A blue star in the corner of the front window was a sign of a service family, with a loved one at risk.

With each assignment, I knocked on the door and was greeted by a person whose eyes were brimming with tears. I would introduce myself and offer my condolences and say I was there to pick up a picture. I was welcomed in and there was always something familiar. Things hanging by a thread, worn carpets, frayed furniture, a portrait of Jesus on the wall next to one of President Kennedy. Atop the television, a framed photo of a young man in military dress. Again and again, I witnessed the sad, slow-motion walk to the treasured photo, a clutching of it close, then the presentation of the photo for printing in the next day's newspaper. What was striking was who was paying the price for involvement in the war. The casualty lists expanded from city to suburb to rural areas.

I also was mindful every moment of the danger to our own family. My younger brother, Frank, signed up for the Marines and saw fierce combat in Vietnam. We corresponded frequently and I fretted for Frank during his combat tour. He returned, suffering from severe post-traumatic stress disorder. Several close friends I played baseball with went off to war and were killed.

This was personal. I could not enlist because of a heart murmur. Otherwise, I would have followed a path of military service, a family tradition. My Dad served in the Marines and sustained bullet wounds to his knee which affected his mobility for the rest of his life. He had raised all of us to be Marines, loyal to our country, faithful to the corps, standing up for America.

I had another type of battle to carry on. I was on a mission to help end an unwise, immoral war and gratefully, my father agreed with my position. He had seen war and death up close. The war in Vietnam made no sense to him and now his namesake was at risk in combat.

While campaigning at the Oktoberfest, I felt a tug at my sleeve. A painted lady, whose cheeks dripped with orange, red, and brown make up and whose chestnut eyes half slept beneath a sea of green eye shadow, spoke. She had a large yellow and red headdress, fastened at the center by a small, star-shaped pin. She wore a long blue gown, with a jeweled trim.

"Do you want to know your future," she said in a husky voice. Her eyes widened as she studied my face. She handed me her card. "Zehta. Fortunes Told."

I hadn't seen any new polls. The only thing I wanted to know was whether I would win the congressional race.

"Uh…sure. Why not?" I said.

She took up my right hand, studying it for a moment. "This is your lifeline. It is very long. It branches here." Her finger traced a crease in my palm.

Longevity is fine. I survived a grueling childhood and made it to age twenty-five. There were personal matters I could have explored with the fortune teller but already knew those answers. Yes, I occasionally had blood in my urine from kidney stones. Yes, I was dealing with the devastating on-going symptoms of Crohn's disease, which had already cost me half of my colon and small intestines. And yes, my peripatetic life as a Councilman put enormous stress on my marriage to Helen, primarily because I wasn't present, but living at the threshold of a relentless effort to save the world. I was a public man, not a private one and was piling everything on the altar of ambition. I wanted to know one thing and one thing only. Will I win this election?

I pressed her. "Tell me, please, am I going to win this election?"

She placed her right hand on top of my palm and held my hand, as she met my expectant smile with a solemn pronouncement.

"No. I'm afraid this is not to be. You will not win. I see in your future you will be a mayor."

I think people consult fortune tellers the same way politicians counsel with pollsters, to hear what you want to hear. When you get information which is contrary, you reject it. Mayor? I didn't think so.

I built a campaign team and a constituency as a direct result of my door-to-door campaign and appearances at hundreds of community events. I'd appear at public transportation hubs in the early morning, schedule group meetings through the noon hour, and then begin knocking on doors after lunch, seeking out individual voter's support, until darkness fell. Whenever I found an enthusiastic supporter, I'd ask them to join me as I campaigned.

My campaign literature consisted of a simple mimeographed message, produced with the help of Bob Weissman who also set up an apartment to receive returns from our issue-oriented fund-raising mail solicitations. We purchased a bus, renamed it the "Voteswagon" and set it up outside of high schools. As a result, we gained hundreds of young volunteers who would help us place orange and black bumper stickers on thousands of cars at shopping centers. As the campaign grew, our efforts produced thousands of yard sign locations which provided for a striking visibility, generating momentum. Wherever people turned, they could see evidence that a major effort was being made to win their vote.

The incumbent Congressman, William Minshall, refused to make joint appearances or participate in debates, so I began to stage my own debates, with a ventriloquist dummy. This added an element of circus to a campaign which was volunteer-driven, a low-budget, high-energy effort that caught the imagination of district voters.

The Republican party understood that Minshall was in trouble. A week before the election, President Richard Nixon came to the district to try to rescue Minshall. As the Presidential motorcade wound through Cleveland's western suburbs, it stopped, and Minshall nervously clambered onto the limousine carrying Nixon, who, upon seeing the Congressman, exclaimed "He's the best man for the job."

Although I was outspent twenty to one, I lost the election by less than two points, as the Democratic Presidential nominee, George McGovern, whom I strongly supported, was defeated in the district by a landslide.

Election night, I was crestfallen but Steve Clark, who with Bob Weissman helped to guide the campaign, encouraged me to push past defeat.

"Sometimes people are comfortable with myths, like 'bigger is better', or that American history is the story of a righteous people at war with the forces of evil," Steve said. He continued, "When someone comes along to tell the people what is really going on, they have trouble believing it, because it conflicts with what they think they already know. There is nothing harder in the world than trying to wake people up. You do things not because people will vote for you, but because those things are right. People can get mad at you today and then change their minds tomorrow to agree with what you said yesterday, so stand up for what you believe."

Steve also did what he felt was right. Thanks to Weissman's tireless work on his behalf, an arbitrator awarded him a $25,000 cash settlement, concluding he had been unjustly fired by WERE for his on-air criticisms of CEI. Despite his vindication, there were no long-term opportunities for Steve Clark in Cleveland and he soon headed west to seek a new life, while I turned my full attention to Cleveland City Hall.

With Weissman's help, I refocused keenly on a wide range of economic issues affecting the people of the Cleveland area. Once Weissman taught me how to analyze the city budget, I was equipped to delve into taxes, spending levels and personnel. With his encouragement and with the assistance of a former chair of Ohio's Public Utilities Commission, Henry Eckhart, I learned how utility rates were structured and I understood more deeply how utilities cheated people. I launched a series of public campaigns to challenge the rate-making practices of CEI, East Ohio Gas, and Ohio Bell, as well as scrutinizing local water and sewer rates.

While Mayor Perk had established the Department of Consumer Affairs at my request, it was still necessary to push back against Council efforts to suffocate consumer rights. With Weissman's help, I pursued the dating and labeling of perishable foods, as well as the clear packaging of meat.

Political resistance was always overcome when we took the issue directly to the people, in the form of petition drives or leaflet-driven civic action. One effort which fell short was an attempt to establish free transit in Cleveland, backed by a half percent increase in the income tax. Opponents expressed concern that, if transit was free, everyone would ride the bus. My point exactly.

There was another economic issue, government corruption, which claimed more and more of my time and drew me into learning City Hall's deepest secrets.

CHAPTER 14

City Hall and the Mob

It shakes you when you are inside city government and you realize that your city is run by a criminal element. Crime was flourishing in Cleveland. City fathers hypocritically went on crusades against some types of crime, while enabling vice to profit. Vice was inevitably connected to organized crime.

The Perk administration had 34% fewer vice arrests for prostitution, gambling and liquor violations than the Stokes administration and the police were involved in the corruption. A tavern owner charged he had paid police over $3,000 dollars so he could sell liquor after hours. Cops became robbers, chauffeuring machine-gun toting burglars, fresh from the scene of the crime, in their squad cars, splitting the loot, and absentmindedly leaving $900 in soggy cash from one robbery under the seat of the police car.

Police were running a payoff racket, protecting after-hours drinkers at night and fixing traffic tickets during the day. If someone had actually been arrested, convicted and sentenced, not to worry, it was said some cases disappeared at the courthouse, while the few who were actually incarcerated were caught breaking back into jail after spending nights out on the town.

Prostitution flourished openly in downtown Cleveland, including at the Sterling Hotel, notorious for its organized crime connections. An honest vice cop cracking down on the Sterling was transferred and according to the *Plain Dealer*, it was Mayor Perk's labor advisor, Mickey Rini, who effected the transfer, at the request of the owner of the Sterling Hotel, with Rini telling the Mayor, "We've got to get the bum out of there."

Rini denied the charge, saying "If someone would drop a bomb on City Hall, you'd say Rini did it."

In a mob gathering place above a restaurant in "Little Italy," a colorful Italian neighborhood on Cleveland's East Side, people lined up to pay homage to an aged man who blessed their endeavors. If someone had a problem at City Hall, the god-fatherly elder would bid them to "go see my man, Mickey Rini."

I raised questions whenever law enforcement was arbitrary and political when top city officials befriended criminal elements. I believed honesty was absolutely essential to governance. I may have appeared idealistic and holier-than-thou to those who saw City Hall as their private fiefdom and city resources as their private loot. I questioned the role of Mr. Rini, who I referred to as the "vice-mayor." Rini was a short, stocky man with a deep tan, who parted his graying slicked-back hair in the middle. A sharp dresser, his trademark was a crooked stogie, a Culebra, which hung loosely from his mouth, like fruit drooping from a banana tree.

A former Teamster official, he had the complete confidence of Mayor Perk and functioned on behalf of the Mayor. His portfolio was labor, but his activities went beyond the call of duty to workers. He intervened in police exam policies and the awarding of contracts. Coincidentally, a director in the Perk administration was the target of an assassination attempt over the awarding of contracts.

A police department vice officer was accused of receiving $3,500 from the Sterling Hotel to protect the prostitution and high stakes gambling blocked by the cop ousted by Rini's orders.

A compassionate policeman who was assigned to vice in the area of the Sterling Hotel was said to be paying a prostitute's rent.

People engaging in actual vice in Cleveland were in less trouble than people who were showing pictures of those engaging in vice. The city moved to shut down places showing pornographic movies.

With the orgy of vice and police corruption overtaking the city, and reaching inside City Hall, Mayor Perk brought the Cleveland media together to announce his solution. "I think we have had too much concentration on material things in this world and not enough on spiritual values and spiritual leaders available to us," he piously intoned. He then appointed a group of clergymen to investigate police corruption. The clergymen corruption-hunters, dubbed "the God Squad," received $100,000 in federal funds to launch their probe of crime and the rackets, while City Council was considering legislation to legalize church bingo for charitable purposes.

I had proposed legislation to deal with police corruption, an "Ethics and Corruption Control Commission." The Mayor had not properly constituted the existing Ethics Board, had nominated two individuals, but never submitted the names to City Council, rendering the board useless.

I continued to question Mickey Rini's influence on the police department.

The phone rang at my home. It was a close friend from the Tremont area, Florence Gioitta, whose husband, Chuck, worked a produce stand at the Central market.

"This is a friendly call," she said cryptically.

I laughed at her conspiratorial tone, which was so Florence. I spent many holidays at the Gioitta's home, where, surrounded by images of Jesus and eastern mystics, I would indulge in feasts of spaghetti, sausage and pizzelles while she regaled us with information from the street.

"I am calling as your friend," she said, emphasizing the word friend. "Now don't get mad at me. I'm delivering a message. 'Lay off Mickey Rini or you're going to get hurt.'"

"What?" I was incredulous. "Is this a threat?" I could not be intimidated. I had an informed fearlessness from my youth, encountering gangs and getting beat up; weathering violence at home, suppressing physical infirmities, and rejecting the imperatives of size in sports. My childhood reading of English romantic poets informed courage of heart and soul. Television brought to my awareness the exploits of Robin Hood, Wyatt Earp, the Lone Ranger, Superman, all of whom were dedicated to fight for the right.

"Of course not. I care about you. Rini has a lot of friends. Be careful going after him. I'm just relaying a message."

"From whom?"

"Never mind. This is serious."

"Why? What's he going to do?"

"I called to pass along a friendly warning. Rini is not someone you mess with," she said. End of conversation.

Rini was quoted in the *Plain Dealer* speculating I could use a couple of bodyguards, because I "might get roughed up." I encountered him in the shadows of the City Hall Rotunda. He gave me a long, cruel stare, the kind intended to instill fear. I stared back. He clenched the Culebra in his teeth. The back of his hand moved under his chin, he then flicked an Italian curse at me from his smoky, raspy throat, "Va fungool!" I turned away, without responding. But, in case I didn't understand Italian, he called after me forcefully, "Fuck you! You punk."

I returned his curse with a smile.

I considered Rini's invective forensically. When someone is unsuccessful in making you afraid, it becomes their problem, unless of course, they really do want to kill you.

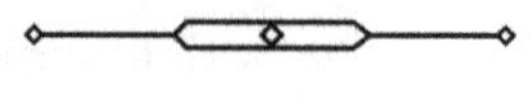

Mayor Perk's second term had the feeling of a top going wildly out of kilter, with the swirling psychedelic colors of administrative breakdown bleeding into what had passed for the stable machinations of legitimate governance.

Bob Weissman and I labored to deconstruct the city budget, a fundamental task preliminary to any discussion of municipal priorities. Once I understood how Perk's budgeting worked, I was able to discuss it in public forums. Weissman and I discovered that city budget crises were being manufactured to create a pretext for a tax increase. City income was deliberately underestimated, expenses exaggerated and there was no projection of growth rates. Finagling led to breakdowns in labor negotiations, and to a city truck driver's strike, affecting garbage collections.

As irate citizens protested growing mounds of uncollected waste outside the doors of their homes, Mayor Perk, in an attempt to take the pressure off City Hall, called upon citizens to dump their garbage in public parks.

On April 28th, 1974, garbage began to pile up in city parks at a rate of three million pounds per day. The fetid mountains were doused with disinfectants, baited with poisons to keep out rats and sprayed with insect repellent. It was all ineffective. Maggots instead of ground balls churned in the infield at the old League Park. The hallowed outfield, where Babe Ruth once played, was filled not with fly balls, but with balls of swarming flies and when it rained, sandlots across the city bubbled with a toxic stew of new disease vectors.

Police and Councilmen guarded the parks from excessive dumping. A lawsuit was filed but the judge, repelled, refused to inspect the sites. By the time the strike ended, fifty million pounds of garbage had accumulated, most of it in the city's parks.

The financial game-playing hurt recreation. Class "A" night baseball in Cleveland, a hundred-year-old tradition showcasing the city's best amateur players, was temporarily canceled because the lighting systems at the baseball park had not been maintained.

The Mayor announced layoffs of some city employees in order to pay for wage increases for middle management Republican political appointees.

Although I had helped him win the mayor's office, I recognized that Mayor Perk was not in charge of his administration. I could not abide the corruption, the waste of taxpayers' dollars and the almost comic mismanagement, so I challenged it and organized opposition to the administration's policies.

The cemeteries division was closed, burials were postponed and bodies piled up at the county morgue while in the midst of the demented circus known as City Hall, civic boosters unveiled a happy, new slogan.

"Cleveland: The Best Things in Life are Here."

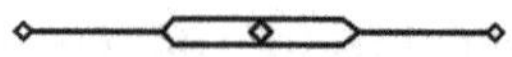

Blackouts continued at Muny Light, costing the public system hundreds of customers and lost revenue. The rate gap between CEI and Muny became smaller. Each and every blackout caused Muny Light customers to switch.

A renewed push for the sale of Muny Light began in the media, led by WERE, the radio station which fired Steve Clark for criticizing CEI. I asked the Federal Communication Commission to investigate WERE's conduct. WERE had every right to take an editorial position, but, given the station's history, its strenuous effort to promote the sale of Muny Light seemed like a payoff for CEI's advertising and future patronage.

The Federal Power Commission finally ordered CEI to proceed with the interconnect. Strangely, the use of the interconnect was subject to termination in an emergency, when it was most needed. CEI stalled implementation of the tie-in while warning its customers a switch to Muny Light would make them vulnerable to blackouts, especially when the new interconnect was disconnected for "maintenance."

As the company pursued its nuclear ambitions, it experienced legal and financial pressure to cooperate on an interconnect.

CEI's application for licenses to build nuclear power plants was subject to a mandatory antitrust review by the Nuclear Regulatory Commission. Previously confidential company files would be made public; any and all of CEI's business tactics and strategies regarding Muny would surface. Any finding of anti-competitive conduct by CEI could impede nuclear licensing and invite the US Department of Justice to enter the case.

With its range of legal options to thwart Muny Light diminishing, and with federal investigators hot on its trail, CEI attorneys created a paper trail to make it appear that the company was cooperating with Muny not only on the interconnect, but in access to nuclear power, and transmission of cheap power from outside the area which, of course, it wasn't. CEI's duplicity paralleled its political manipulation of City Hall, where it blocked $9.8 million in bond financing to repair Muny's generators.

Councilman Gaul, who had received gifts and other benefits from his friendship with CEI executives, attempted to force public disclosure of the objectives of the negotiating strategy Muny was using versus CEI. He tried to get the city administration to retract its previously declared interest in nuclear power, which would undermine a city legal claim against CEI that the company tried to block Muny's access to such power.

Muny Light confronted additional jeopardy. Under the misguidance of the city's financial advisors, the sale or lease of city assets had become public policy, with proceeds of sales sustaining the administration's bulging middle management payroll.

As a result of these policies, control of municipal services passed from elected local officials to regional authorities appointed and staffed by political insiders partial to corporate interests. This led to higher utility rates, higher fees and higher taxes.

City Hall's privatization policies were a major part of Cleveland's big business agenda and were a deliberate effort to deconstruct the city government, to reduce it to a status as a collector of tax revenues and a distributor of revenue and resources to corporations which lined their pockets with tax dollars, in the name of improving the city's image.

While the Perk Administration was liquidating city assets, the downtown business community was the recipient of tens of millions of dollars in the form of subsidies for bankrupt hotels, speculative developments and additional giveaways of hundreds of millions using tax abatement law.

While the property tax-dependent Cleveland schools were at the brink of bankruptcy, tax abatements totaling $15 million were given to National City Bank, the most profitable bank in Ohio, to build a headquarters which it had already decided to construct. There was no need to offer any kind of tax incentives after the fact. This was an example of banking interests corrupting city government.

Business leaders whose companies were hunting property tax reductions voiced their concern about the plight of Cleveland's schools, even taking positions on civic committees to bewail the declining quality of public education, while their own tax-avoidance schemes further depleted the school's financial resources. A favorite tactic, of which the public was generally unaware, was for a corporation to hire an attorney who would file a case at the County Board of (tax) Revision, seeking a dramatic cut in valuation on prime downtown land.

If the Board of Education did not fight it, a single corporation could reduce its long-term obligation by millions of dollars, thus shifting the burden of property taxation to support education, away from corporations and onto area homeowners. Corporations showed an interest in school board elections solely to elect persons who would not resist their continual efforts to avoid paying a fair share of property taxes, as Cleveland's school system, starved for revenues, would be forced to consider tax increases.

Standard Oil, one of the wealthiest companies in the world, was offered a tax abatement by Perk's City Hall. The largest newspaper in Ohio, the *Plain Dealer*, had a city street blocked off, vacated and given for its exclusive use. Major new public construction focused only on downtown. A project known as "Gateway" was to be financed by $6 million in bond anticipation notes for a marina which had no feasibility study, no marketing survey, and no tenants.

Milt Schulman had already pointed out to me that a new City-County Justice Center was planned at a cost of $62 million and mushroomed into a $200 million bond-financed boondoggle.

Hundreds of millions of Clevelanders' tax dollars were being squandered, while city officials and business executives affected a façade of "cooperation" and "progress," which became the central proposition of governance in Cleveland, a "public-private partnership," where the public subsidized private profit, a partnership which can be likened to a vampire forming a compact with a host for the purpose of extracting a red viscous fluid.

As I battled the waste and misapplication of taxpayers' dollars, I made a second run for Congress.

With the fervor of a grassroots campaign again challenging the Vietnam War, and attacking high utility rate increases, I set out to accomplish something which few individuals have been able to do: Achieve election to the U.S. House of Representatives from Ohio, as an Independent, attempting to defeat two powerful political machines embodied in the Democrat and Republican parties. My grassroots activism had gained attention throughout the west side district. New suburban supporters, not tied to either political party, joined our ranks. We had a door-to-door campaign, similar to my first congressional race, with thousands of our campaign signs and bumper stickers flooding the district.

I learned I did not need the permission of a political party to run for office. The campaign was a declaration of political independence which brought to my side those who understood the failings of the two-party system - - the self-serving brokerages which gained power and privilege because they had not been challenged. I found a surprising willingness to eliminate the middleman party bosses and their group-think, overturn both major political parties, and insist on direct representation. When presented with a real choice supported by a broad campaign based on things people care about, jobs, wages, education, health care, housing, retirement security and peace, voters were ready for political independence.

An independent candidate requires an independent organization ready to engage in direct voter contact. This we did. In a close three-way race, only a few thousand votes separated the candidates. I ran third, but through the effort, built a following which increased pressure on the political bosses. I returned to my duties in City Council with a renewed zeal, refreshed by the air of political freedom.

CHAPTER 15

Blood

"A bombshell is going to be dropped at Council's utilities meeting today," a clear voice informed me in a six a.m. call on February 25th, 1975, rousting me from a deep sleep. Fortunately, Helen had not been awakened.

"Hello, who is this?"

"This is Norm Mlachak from the *Press*. Did I wake you?" A conversation opener at 6:00 a.m.

"No Norm, I had to get up to answer the phone." No apology from this sleep-wrecking typewriter jockey. His was the grimy business of manufacturing the news no matter what the hour.

Mlachak continued, "I heard attorneys for the U.S. Justice Department are in town, investigating CEI for possible antitrust violations against Muny Light. We got calls last night about a CEI bombshell."

"A bombshell?" The *Press* and the *Plain Dealer* played a significant role in determining the television coverage on any given day. Their top stories became the top stories of the television stations. Newspapers, at the time, set the agenda and had a high impact. CEI knew this, so when the *Press*' first edition hit City Hall, the rest of the news media would follow in herd.

It didn't take much to figure out the hearing had been called for CEI's convenience and necessity. The "bombshell" was aimed at blowing up the budding federal investigation of the private utility. I did not voice any suspicions to Mlachak but knew I had to attend the hearing.

Mlachak provided me with a scoop. I arrived at the committee room early, parked my papers in a prominent place at the table, and conducted a stakeout, waiting for CEI to show up. My patience was rewarded.

Lee Howley strode into the room, briefly glanced in my direction, took a seat, and waited to be called to drop his "bombshell." At the microphone, Howley swept the committee table slowly with his gaze to own the space, encircling all the members of Council and the TV cameras, then recited his carefully rehearsed lines.

"Here and now, we have no designs on the Municipal Light Plant. We don't think there is anything to buy. We have our hands full with our own problems. All we are trying to do by coming here is to be good citizens. We do not think Muny Light is viable. We think it is costly to the general fund," said CEI's man, speaking with practiced gravity, in hope that attorneys for the U.S. Justice Department would notice his performance and exonerate CEI.

Such was CEI's confidence in the local media that the mere act of turning a committee meeting into a press conference was certain to have its desired effect. Television cameramen kept angling around the table for a better view of Howley, so when he arrived at the top of the Six O'Clock News, he would very much appear the part of the skilled, trusted, professional communicator reaching hundreds of thousands of homes with CEI's get-out-of-jail-free cue card, "We don't want Muny Light."

Howley's was a great gambit, well-timed, and convincing. The more attention paid to his presentation, the hotter the lights in the room, the less heat CEI would feel.

I finally got my say. "Mr. Howley, it is unfortunate CEI is using this forum in an attempt to absolve itself of an antitrust investigation. It is general knowledge CEI is conducting a systematic campaign to drive Muny Light out of business." I related that CEI had called the media to promote its "bombshell." My Council colleagues evoked a disinterested boredom, unaware and uncaring supernumeraries in Reddy Killowatt's grand opera of denial.

After the committee meeting, I went directly to the office of Council President Forbes to inquire why the committee had been turned into CEI's theater of the absurd. Forbes had not been present at the hearing but listened to the proceedings from a speaker in an office he shared with the Clerk of Council, Mrs. Cotner.

Once Forbes became Council President, Cotner remodeled the leadership offices and strategically located her desk in the same room as Forbes. Mrs. Cotner was Forbes' close confidant and sounding board, an astute politician, former Councilwoman and mayoral candidate who was alternately a lovely, white-haired grandmother or an effective political hatchet-woman, as the situation necessitated. Forbes and Cotner were an imposing duo, an effective, experienced political team with strong emotional ties. Forbes had said he was as close to Cotner as he was to his own mother.

"Why are you always causing trouble?" Mrs. Cotner inquired. "Lee Howley is a good man. You know the light system isn't working."

"Because of CEI's interference," I rejoined.

She acted as though she did not hear me and began to distract herself with paperwork, casually relating, without looking at me. "I used to be for it, too. Now I think it should be sold. Why do you always have to be so difficult, Dennis?"

"Let him go," Forbes called loudly across the room. "He's a rebel, isn't that right?"

Then Forbes addressed me from his desk, his wiry frame insinuating contempt. "You're a rebel and you just have to be opposed to things, Dennis. You are always arguing against stuff. Why are you always making things hard on yourself?" Forbes expressed a mixture of puzzlement and disdain.

"It is wrong to sell the light system. And it's wrong for CEI to steal it," I replied.

"You think it's wrong to sell the light system?" His voice climbed. "But you aren't telling us where we are going to get the goddamn money to save it, are you? Muny Light is losing money. Where are we going to get the money to save it?" Forbes glowered. Each time he said the word 'money' it was with renewed emphasis, stretching, punching, pulling and beating the word into shape, like he was preparing to make bread.

"People pay their utility bills, that's where the money comes from," I replied.

"It's not enough," Forbes said emphatically. "I'm telling you, it's not enough. This system is going down."

He suddenly became sympathetic. "I don't want to see it go either. But it's going down." Forbes had this uncanny ability to do an emotional pirouette. Kind at once, then mean, ecstatic then morose, victim then aggressor. He would put on one mask, replace it, try on another, sometimes for effect. It was easy and dangerous to be drawn in by Forbes, who masterfully melded theatrics and politics. He was psychologically disarming, grabbing thoughts from the periphery of a discussion, making them central and conjuring one scenario after another with dizzying speed and mystifying impact. A discussion with Forbes required full concentration and emotional distance.

A flash of anger leaped out of the frying pan he had prepared for me to step into. "Now why don't you just forget about the goddamn light system," he said, forcefully. Then the pirouette, "You can't do anything about it," he counseled softly.

This was the crucial moment when entrenched power, represented by the Council President, asserted its unassailability, posing the age-old political question, "What are you going to do about it?"

Boss Tweed posed the same question to those who criticized his actions at Tammany Hall more than a century ago. The response is acquiescence or capitulation, which is why things don't change, because those asked "What are you going to do about it" lose their nerve. I estimated Forbes' intent was to protect something or someone else and I pushed back, hard. "I'm going to fight you on this, George," I responded curtly.

Forbes frowned, his lower lip curled downward. "Heh, heh, heh," the smoky laughter, glowing embers of menace, smoldering in the cauldron of his belly were moving close to the surface. He cocked his head in a manner to size up prey, widening his eyes. He looked at Mrs. Cotner, who tossed me a sharp glance of disapproval, a shake of her head, an urgent pursing of her lips. It was too late.

Forbes erupted. His voice climbed several octaves, nearing falsetto. He called to Mrs. Cotner, his head pitching in my direction. "This motherfucker," he said, pronouncing each syllable slowly, with growing emphasis, "This motherfucker is going to fight me?! Do you hear him? He's going to fight me! " He breathed his fire in my face, "Why are you going to fight me?"

I did not respond.

"OK then, fight me! I'll play your gutter politics, I'm your kind. Remember, what goes around comes around."

Mrs. Cotner was alarmed. "I think you better go," she said, motioning to the door. Forbes was still in a state of fury when I left, bellowing to Mrs. Cotner, "Did you hear that? He's going to fight me. Fight me! Moth-er-fucker."

As Mrs. Cotner shut the door, I could still hear Forbes' voice.

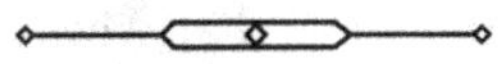

CEI coveted Muny Light, while declaring the opposite to the media. After Howley's staged performance, the *Plain Dealer* took notice of CEI's newly expressed antipathy with an editorial bemoaning Muny's situation as hopeless. "Even CEI is not interested." CEI had a special way of demonstrating disinterest. It intensified its media advertising and its political expenditures, accelerating to an all-out attack.

At the City Council utilities committee, on April 2, 1975, Utilities Director Raymond Kudukis woefully related the city's inability to sell Muny's capital improvement bonds. He reported that Muny Light lost $3.9 million in 1973. Kudukis predicted higher Muny Light deficits, unless the 85MW generator was repaired, at a increased cost of $13.3 million.

Kudukis was a professional engineer, well qualified to be Utilities Director. He and his wife, Grace, were two nationally-known activists from Cleveland's politically influential Lithuanian community, which had a bloc of votes in the northeast side of Cleveland heavily serviced by Muny Light. Kudukis dressed like a diplomat, with broad, blue pin-stripes and tailored shirts. He had the capacity to repel members of council who tried to trap him to serve their own purposes. Fact-oriented, and not on a political mission, he was soft-spoken in his presentation to the committee as he drove home a Muny Light truism, "We have to generate our own power to make money."

Absent access to cheap outside power, the deteriorated condition of the generators was placing Muny Light in financial peril, he told the committee. However, he did not mention that CEI had successfully thwarted all efforts to repair Muny Light's power-producing capability.

Kudukis and I communicated easily. We had worked closely together to elect Perk in 1971 and were friends, even though I was not on good terms anymore with the Mayor.

After the committee meeting, where he bemoaned Muny's condition, he further acknowledged to me that Muny's greatest peril was the blackouts, and CEI was lobbying against the repairs.

"I wish you had said that to the committee, Ray," I said.

He opened his hands in a gesture of futility. He was, after all, a stalwart in the Republican Party and a strong supporter of the corporate community, which believed the city had no business operating its own electric system. Kudukis had to pretend, for political reasons, that Muny's problems were purely internal. Privately, he was forthcoming.

"CEI has cut us off from raising money," he said. "Our bond sales have been undermined by Gaul's amendments. We received bad representation from our bond attorneys at Squire Sanders. They haven't been honest with us. I'll tell you one thing, though, CEI is in for a surprise," Kudukis said, hinting at turning the tables.

"Really? What?"

"I'm working quietly with Law Director Davis to stop CEI in its tracks," he said. If someone else at City Hall said they were 'quietly working' on a major matter, I would translate it into, 'I'm doing nothing.' I trusted Kudukis. I felt a flicker of hope.

"How?" I asked.

He smiled, "I can't say more."

Stop CEI in its tracks? As I waited for the unfolding of the city law department's strategy, the FPC dug in and finally ordered CEI to provide Muny Light with the long-sought permanent tie-in which CEI had successfully forestalled for three years. Muny's reliability was further degraded during that period.

Frank Gaul, now the appointed treasurer of Cuyahoga County, surfaced again to oppose repairs to Muny's generators. "A professional money lender looks at that operation and he can't professionally lend it five cents. If the Utilities Department thinks it is going to get $13 million of tax money to put down a rat hole, they are crazy," Gaul declared, threatening a taxpayer's suit to block repairs. As word of Gaul's newest attack on Muny circulated at City Hall, I called Kudukis.

"He is at it again, Ray," I said.

Kudukis fretted, because a lawsuit by Gaul would postpone repairs, lock Muny into CEI's tripled rates and drive up operating costs. Without repairs, blackouts would continue, more customers would be lost and additional money would be spent on a court fight. Further, Gaul had the vocal support of the *Plain Dealer*'s editorial board, which reiterated its support for the sale, but repeated CEI's latest position that it did want Muny.

On May 21, 1975, the FPC also ordered CEI to provide Muny Light with access to cheap hydroelectric power. CEI sought yet another rate increase, even though CEI customers were already paying the sixth highest electric rates in America. The FPC order and CEI's request for a rate hike gave Muny a chance to improve its competitive position.

Kudukis' surprise arrived on July 1, 1975, when James B. Davis, the Law Director of the City of Cleveland, (no relation to James C. Davis of Squire Sanders) filed a $330 million antitrust damage suit against CEI and four other utilities, charging the utilities with monopolizing the wholesale and retail electric power business through refusing to grant a permanent interconnection, refusing to transmit power from other energy sources and price fixing, refusing to interconnect unless Muny Light agreed to charge its customers the same price for electricity as CEI charged.

CEI was gravely jeopardized, because the antitrust lawsuit and the NRC's antitrust probe were based upon the same facts. The required production of internal CEI documents would soon prove that CEI had repeatedly broken the law in its conduct of business with Muny Light.

It was the Fourth of July holiday weekend, but instead of attending fireworks, I was a patient in University Hospital. I was much more excited that Muny was to get relief from CEI's conduct than I was concerned to get relief from the pain of a kidney stone which lacerated my right kidney, necessitating removal of the upper lobe. I had ignored blood in my urine until the acute pain re-focused my attention.

After surgery, the wound looked like a shark bite. It hurt. But who needed painkillers? I was euphoric. CEI finally had to account for its conduct that had hurt Muny Light.

I reached for the phone in my hospital room and called Kudukis. "How did this happen, Ray?" I asked, as I shifted in my hospital bed, careful to avoid any sounds of physical distress.

"Law Director Davis has been all over this. We have been in conversation for nearly a year to counter CEI."

"And this isn't a negotiating ploy?" I asked, to smother any lingering doubt. A nurse entered the room to take my temperature and asked me to place a thermometer under my tongue. I signaled for her to wait.

"No. Davis is very serious. He won't back down," Kudukis said.

"And the Mayor signed off?" I was checking the boxes to determine if the lawsuit against CEI would go forward.

"Oh yes. He approved it. We couldn't proceed without him."

The nurse asked me to set down the phone for a moment. I said goodbye to Kudukis. My temperature had soared to 104 degrees. The nurse notified the doctor and blood was drawn, revealing that I had a massive post-surgery infection.

I was in serious condition. I entrusted my life to the doctors and nurses, because I couldn't trust it to myself, with the long hours, no sleep, and a driving ambition which denied pain, ignored blood, and overlooked dangerous physical symptoms. I had a horrible diet with only myself to blame. Cheeseburgers, fried chicken and caffeine-laced colas were staples. I was seldom home for dinner, missing out on the one meal a day certain to be nourishing. I had frequent stomach cramps, which caused me to double up, writhing on the bathroom floor until I could get back to work. Mind over matter was both a path of survival and a postponement of a day of reckoning.

Health and love were sacrificed. I was seeking to give and receive love not from one person, but from the masses, with a relentless quest to challenge wrongdoing in government. Seven days a week, from sun-up to midnight, I ran a marathon of meetings and phone calls, gripped by ward matters, city issues, elections, and Cleveland's unique brand of bare-knuckle politics.

I created distance from Helen and never invited her in, never shared what I had learned during those long meetings. From the moment I was elected to City Council, though we appeared coupled, we were not. I loved her dearly and knew she deserved someone genuinely present. This was my loss.

Helen had a healthy skepticism about politics, a sense of proportion, a reserved and common sense perspective, while for me public events achieved out-sized importance in our lives. A computer programmer by training, she studied the arrangement of data, looked for patterns, to make sense of things. She was an ideal partner, intelligent, funny, charitable, well-organized, and all she wanted was for me to be there, in measure, to celebrate our marriage. She was a good wife.

I badly needed to create a good life with that good wife. I chose instead the solitary path of the priesthood of public service. I was a bystander in our relationship. As it began to slip away, I did not know how to save it, and once it was lost, I did not know how I could live without her.

My priorities were public. The same single-minded intensity, the political drive which crowded out a personal life, rescued me from abject depression over its destruction. Politics was my vocation, my amusement, my distraction, constantly calling forth visions of upcoming elections. I placed my name on the ballot for the city-wide office of Clerk of the Cleveland Municipal Court, the second highest elective office in the city.

Yet, here I was, in a hospital bed, thinking about parades, picnics and parks and the crowds gathering before dark when fireworks light up the city sky. I was seized with the fear that my election hung in the balance on this particular weekend, and everything depended on my physical appearance on the campaign. Instead, I was tethered to IVs and a catheter.

I called Weissman. He had prompted me to run for Clerk of Courts, because he saw it as a direct path to the mayor's office. With a voice weakened by illness, tinged with fear of losing, I confessed "Bob, I'm in the hospital. I may not be able to campaign for a while."

"You don't have to campaign," he said tersely. "Focus on your recovery."

"What do you mean? You always have to campaign."

"You don't have to do anything to win this race. There is no way you can lose. Take a break. Just show up to be sworn in at the beginning of next year," he said.

His certitude quelled my anxiety. My recovery took four months, most of it in seclusion at my home on Milan Ave. I had three meals a day delivered by Frank Zappone, the brother of Tony Zappone, the owner of Tony's Diner. Otherwise I was not taking visitors because I felt vulnerable, both physically and emotionally.

A knock at the door.

I struggled to rise from the sofa bed situated in the front room. I moved back the front curtain to see who it was. I had to open the door for this person.

"Hey, Dennis, I wanted to stop by for just a moment to see how you are doing. If there is anything you need, let me know. Everyone in City Council is asking about you. They want to see you back at work. Be well." Then he left.

It was George Forbes.

CHAPTER 16

The Golden City

During the term of Mayor Ralph Locher (1962-67), his top aide, Bronis Klementowicz, was said to have a drawer in his desk where he could reach in and magically find money needed for a specific project. Mind you, Klem's cash was city money, off the books.

Klem was long gone by 1975, when Cleveland was either flush with cash, or broke, depending who was talking. Two months after Perk took office in 1971, the city's debt was $323.7 million. Four years later, it was $369 million. In that time, City Council had approved $86 million in new borrowing, all of it without a vote of the people. The city was within $28.7 million of its legal debt limit.

As the city's debt obligations soared, and as options for further borrowing narrowed, the city began a process of leasing or liquidating valuable assets. The Perk Administration sold the city's sewer system for $36.6 million to a regional authority; leased the stadium to a private corporation for $150,000 a year; sold the city's transit system to a regional authority for $8,875,000; and sold millions of dollars in city property. Under consideration was the sale or lease of the Public Auditorium, the sale of land on which the city workhouse (jail) was located, the sale of a city golf course which served the city's east side and the sale of a major city park on the west side.

As one-time windfalls from the sale of city assets vanished, the administration ignored the increasing debt. Its budget director, Vince Campanella, assured everyone that more money would be available for improvements the following year, because the debt would decrease. Then, the city announced a General Fund shortfall and commenced to lay off five hundred workers, including bridge tenders whose absence isolated the city's industrial Flats, stranding dozens of businesses and provoking the observation that in Cleveland, bridges fell up, not down.

City personnel records were a mess. Layoffs included employees who had previously resigned, retired, transferred or died. City workers were demoralized. Labor leaders were irate, because a series of contract negotiations for wage increases was stalled.

Three thousand workers, over a quarter of everyone who worked for the city, went on strike. It became clear, once again, that the labor negotiations had been designed to fail, in order to manufacture a crisis. City workers were conscripted to push for a tax increase, less to help themselves, more to secure the city payroll supporting a politically-appointed class with no discernible responsibilities for work.

As the city foundered financially, Mayor Perk committed $3 million to buy three cruise ships, redesigned as floating hotels, with plans to anchor them in shallow, tempestuous Lake Erie, in a bid to attract the 1976 Republican Presidential nominating convention.

Despite all of this, budget naysayers were ignored. The city's long-term financial health was set aside, as financial experts pronounced the City of Cleveland financially sound. Claude M. Blair, President and CEO of National City Bank, Chairman of the Growth Association and head of a tax committee which scrutinized the city's finances, credited the work of his committee with helping the city's notes receive the highest rating possible from the Wall Street ratings agency, Moody's Investors Service, Inc.

Campbell Elliott, the President of the Greater Cleveland Growth Association said, "Cleveland is not in the same category with New York and other cities." New York City had secured a $396 million state loan to avoid default. Cleveland had no such imperative, according to the people who worked with money every day, Cleveland's leading bankers and its Chamber of Commerce, the Growth Association.

The *Plain Dealer* confirmed the good news on July 12, 1975:

"GROWTH ASSOCIATION COMMITTEE FINDS CITY IS FINANCIALLY SOUND"

When a Brookings Institution study raised doubts, showing Cleveland's central city to be one of the most troubled in America in terms of income, housing, jobs and other economic factors, Wall Street placed an exclamation mark of investor confidence supporting Cleveland's financial credibility.

Standard and Poors investor rating service joined Moody's in its positive assessment of Cleveland's finances. The president of S&P, Brenton Harries, dismissed adverse assessments of Cleveland's financial standing, noting Cleveland, like nine other impoverished cities in the nation, still paid its bills and deserved an "A" rating.

Wall Street rating agencies provided access to credit markets by legitimizing the continued sale of Cleveland bonds. This meant continued fees for the same rating agencies.

In a matter of a few days the *Plain Dealer* produced diametrically opposed news accounts of city finances. "Experts say city near fiscal crisis" was set against the "Experts rates city fiscally sound."

A debate was ignited with the publication of a five-hundred-page study by two Cleveland State University economics professors, John Burke and Edric Weld. Their findings were disturbing. "The city's financial system appears to be so complex, that there may be no one who knows all of its components. City finances are like a magician's coat with 40,000 pockets, and no one pocket knows what is in the other."

"The city's accounting system predates Medici banking," said Burke. He and Weld predicted that "…the city's financial problems will become particularly acute in 1978 and 1979, when the notes first issued in 1972 and 1973, must be turned into bonds."

City finances are not supposed to be a guessing game. Either the city finances were solid or they were not. Which was it? Could two Cleveland college professors and two out-of-town think tanks be right? Was it possible that the Wall Street ratings agencies, the city's bond attorneys and financial advisors at Squire Sanders, and, most of all, the city's banks were not aware?

The contradictions in Cleveland's fiscal health were worrying. I knew taxpayers' money was wasted. But I assumed the banks were paying attention when they renewed loans to the city and purchased city debt. My experience was that one couldn't get so much as a car loan from a bank without proving an ability to repay.

Was Council President Forbes posturing, when, earlier in the year, he pronounced the city "nearly bankrupt?" Forbes implied a concealment of the actual state of the city's finances. "When Perk leaves office, I pity his successor. Our indebtedness is so high we may never pay it off."

As Weissman had predicted, I was elected Clerk of the Cleveland Municipal Court, a local office with patronage powers. Another Kucinich, my younger brother Gary, a Marine veteran, won the seat I had held in Cleveland City Council.

As my public career advanced, my personal life hit bottom. Helen and I divorced. Living alone, I poured myself into the world of events.

I was specially prepared, from the earliest age, to be Cleveland's Clerk of Courts. My childhood was a total immersion in eviction notices, garnishments, and liens. By the time I was age ten, court bailiffs were my instructors at the door. Our family's world was unpredictable and precarious, riddled with illness, financial insecurity, drinking problems, arguments, and fights. My psyche journeyed through the emotional labyrinth of the socially dysfunctional, wherein the simplest daily tasks became overwhelming, and, if you survived, you were damaged goods with keen childhood memories imprinting hap and horror.

I had witnessed my parents trying in vain to contend with evictions, crooked used car salesmen, unscrupulous television repairmen, and the con men who plied inner-city neighborhoods selling things like insurance policies for children, because parents, at the least, owed their children a decent funeral. All nine of us were covered by death insurance, but there were no similar guarantees on everyday life.

As a result of witnessing affluent people who had tried to cheat my parents, I had trouble associating with people of means and money, and had much more in common with the tens of thousands of people who found themselves in the maw of the local justice system at the Cleveland Municipal Court. Ironically, my formal name was now the harbinger of bad news, as every garnishment, attachment, and enforcement order from the Cleveland Municipal Court was sent from the Clerk's Office with 'Dennis J. Kucinich, Clerk of Courts' emblazoned on envelopes and official documents.

The Clerk's office administered paperwork for the civil and criminal divisions of the Municipal Court. I could, by my own action, release from jail defendants who were awaiting trial on misdemeanors. My word was their bond. Several of my uncles would have fantasized such succor.

Rita Cestaric was one of my appointees who worked a PBX switchboard in the clerk's office. A line lit up on the board, the operator plugged in a cable, answered the phone, "Clerk of Courts' office, may I help you?" The call was switched to its intended recipient. The operator released her connection, over and over, hundreds of times a day. Rita's reticent demeanor and her 1950's style of dress evoked a red-haired

Harriet Nelson, of Ozzie and Harriet TV fame, rather than the prim housewife who built an influential political organization in suburban North Olmsted.

One afternoon, she approached my desk hesitantly, quietly confessing, "Dennis, I have been listening into people's phone conversations from the PBX."

"You know you shouldn't do that, Rita. Stop it. Ok?" I wondered how she had time. It was awkward to lay down the law to a kindly lady old enough to be my mother.

"I was listening. Joe (not his real name) is planning to remove case files from the criminal division," she said. Rita then gave me details as to time and place.

My staff determined an unusual number of misdemeanor cases had no file available when the case was called before a municipal court judge. If court files could not be presented when the judge called the case, it would be dismissed. A notation was made on the docket, "NP" meaning no papers. The local justice system may have been subverted for years and, if what Rita said was right, it was about to occur on my watch.

Shortly before a certain midnight, I took a camera and lay in wait behind case file cabinets in the clerk's office at Central Police Station. The eerie green glow of cabinets, the dull fluorescent lighting, and the whir of the HVAC system lent to a creepy-crawly feeling similar to the morgue I worked in while an orderly at St. Alexis Hospital a decade earlier. Promptly at midnight, as Rita had discerned, the locked office door opened and in came "the angel of justice," the clerk who would make petty criminal travails vanish into the cardboard netherworld he was carrying. He went to a file cabinet and, with great diligence, systematically began removing cases, disappearing them into his box.

I waited a minute, then I popped up with a cheery greeting. "Hi Joe, I have something for you to sign."

Yes, he was quite shocked to see me. I presented him with a carefully prepared letter of resignation. He read his departure letter and signed it without saying a word. I placed the criminal case folders back into the cabinet. Nothing stolen, nothing lost and it put a stop to the practice right then and there.

My focus remained on the administration of my new office, on maintaining the semblance of normalcy in the court, not the criminal prosecution of errant employees who could easily be separated from public responsibilities. We had inherited a 14,000 case backlog and our full energies were needed to resolve it.

A few weeks later, Rita Cestaric again approached my desk, sheepishly. I could tell it was trouble again.

"I know, I know, I know," she said, shaking her head, exhibiting disgust with herself, not even waiting to confess she had been eavesdropping, again. "I shouldn't listen in."

"Rita, Rita," I said. "We can't do those kinds of things. You must stop."

Then, before I could further reproach her conduct, or set an appropriate path of discipline, she stepped closer, her tone changed to confidential, and she whispered of a man who regularly called one of our clerks and asked him to dispose of outstanding traffic tickets.

"You mean parking tickets?" I asked.

"No, tickets for speeding, reckless driving, DUI's, things like that. They're fixing the tickets." Stanley, another of our employees, was taking the tickets, pulling the originals and the copies from the files. Case dismissed, disappeared.

"Oh brother!" I said, shaking my head, grateful for our erstwhile, repentant snoop.

I spoke to my senior staff. We worked out a plan. If Stanley's accomplice, named Harry, called at a time when Stanley was not in the office, Rita would direct the call to my desk and I would pretend to be Stanley, impersonating his voice.

I did not have to wait long. The following day she notified me she was rerouting a call.

The caller told me "This is Harry, I've got the stuff. Meet me in the Flats."

Jim Barrett, my Chief Deputy Clerk and the former assistant city safety director joined me as a witness. We arrived at the appointed place and time, in Cleveland's Flats, on the east bank of the Cuyahoga River. A new Cadillac was parked at the rendezvous. A man I presumed to be Harry was there, with a half-dozen people, members of his family, crammed into the car. I approached. Harry recognized me, in what he assumed to be a random encounter which pivoted with whiplash speed.

"Hey, Harry, I'm here to pick up the papers," I said, imitating Stanley's voice to effect. Harry's friendly smile melted to a sickly grimace. He began to speak, I shook my head and waved my hand for him to stop.

"Look, I know what you are doing. Do not ever do this again. Do you understand? Pay the tickets and stay away from my employees!"

"I'll never do it again," he stammered. "Never. Never again." That was my introduction to the 'King of the Gypsies.' His arrangement was over, as was Stanley's service in our office.

I drove back to the Justice Center from my encounter in the Flats, to review the plans for a new Clerk's office, which would necessitate a move from the City Hall building to the new Justice Center. I witnessed another Clerk's office employee standing at the back of a car, with the trunk open. Was he changing a tire? I braked momentarily to offer help when my eyes averted to the contents of the trunk. There was an array of heavy weaponry, including several Yugoslav machine guns which I easily recognized, an ethnic thing. When I returned to my office, I invited the clerk/gun dealer to meet.

"What's with the guns?" I asked.

"Just getting rid of some guns," he replied, in a way that was unnervingly casual. Perhaps it was common for him to display a weapons cache in the basement of the Justice Center, home to the police, the courts, the jail, and soon our new offices.

"You mean you are selling the guns!?"

"Yes," he admitted, "I'm trying to make a few extra bucks."

"You know what this means," I said.

"Yes. I'm gone."

"That's right." He was my responsibility and yes, he, too, could have been prosecuted, but I felt it was enough to end his public employment. These were good-paying jobs with great benefits, so losing his job was punishment enough. With no fanfare, I was cleaning up a dirty office, saving my outrage for grave offenses against the public trust, which I could not singularly dispatch. I was on the trail of much bigger crooks, the kind Milt Schulman described, and I was not going to be distracted.

My childhood was not sheltered. When our family rented a few rooms above Martha's Delicatessen on St. Clair Avenue, police sirens were the music of the night, sometimes punctuated by gunshots. But the noise inside our apartment was louder than the street. We were never sure where we were going to live or where any of us would go to school. Evenings in the apartment, I attached an alligator clip to a radiator to activate my rocket-shaped crystal radio, purchased with money I earned carrying groceries, to listen to crime reports of street attacks, robberies, muggings, knifings and occasional shootings. Then there was the bloody, sheet-covered body removed by police from the apartment building behind ours.

I didn't fear the street. On the sidewalks of St. Clair Avenue, no one paid any attention to me. I was small for eleven years old, carried a St. Jude medal for protection, wore a devotional scapular, and went to mass every day at St. Aloysius Church, where I prayed for timely intercession from my guardian angel. You can't be safer than that.

On those occasions when we had a functioning TV in our apartment, I became steeped in the lore of Eliot Ness, one-time Cleveland Safety Director, the 1930's gang-buster immortalized in the TV series "The

Untouchables." Cleveland was dotted with the relics of speakeasies from that era. Gangland wars were fascinating, the subject of tales short and tall. I knew little of Cleveland's underbelly, never saw much evidence of "organized crime." It was the spontaneous street crime, not organized crime, that had to be carefully regarded.

When I worked at the *Plain Dealer* as a copyboy, occupying a large phone console during late nights in the City Room, calls poured in with tales of political graft, corruption and various reports of wrongdoing. I would transfer those calls to the Police Beat, located in the Central Police Station, where a reporter would take the information and decide whether to investigate the seamy side. Perhaps as a result of my father's devotion to *True Crime* magazines, I acquired a knack for figuring out who-dunnits, discerning the missing puzzle pieces in a crime. I didn't have what Herman Melville called a "vision of evil." I was imbued with a romantic notion of natural goodness and human perfectibility, with a dash of street smarts.

Early in my first term in Cleveland City Council, a business leader, whose development projects I opposed, introduced himself, "You ought to get to know someone before you start attacking him," he said, extending his hand, which I accepted and shook firmly, maintaining eye contact. This was not a man who was wounded by criticism. He was intent on extending his influence. He came back to me minutes later, and presented me with a handwritten note in black ink from a small personal notepad:

"The shedding of innocence is the beginning of wisdom."

I took this as an educational offer from a professor of realism to a student of idealism, from the man, who by reputation never lost an election because he bet heavily on both sides. Here was a handwritten invitation to commerce's political inner circle, to learn how things work, to get wise to the ways of the world as it was, not as I wanted it to be. It was a provocative notion, setting innocence at odds with wisdom, especially when wisdom was presented as a path to take when it benefited one's self at the expense of one's constituents.

City Hall reeked of mendacity, of checking one's spiritual beliefs at the door like a beat-up coat and entering into circumstances where unseen forces were dictating decisions, demanding consensus, and meting out punishment to those who denied the deal-making. This was, after all, politics, the dominion of amorality, where personal advancement relied on pragmatism operating in shuttered light, without the imposition of conscience.

Inside City Hall, I had surveyed gun running, case fixing, and ticket fixing in the Clerk of Court's office, police wrongdoing, people connected to City Hall shot, or killed, and heard dark whispers that the 'black hand' of organized crime reached inside the mayor's office. The dirty tricks played by CEI and Squire Sanders was simply business, which, in Cleveland, didn't count as crime.

Outside City Hall, violent crime echoed, as rival organized crime rings vied for control of rackets. A bomb damaged the offices of Bill Seawright, the quiet financial backer of Mayor Perk, who had offered me a suitcase full of thousands of dollars for Perk's first mayoral election campaign. Another bombing took the life of Larry D. Steele, a thin, fashion-plate, raconteur who wore a Paladin-style black hat with a geometric silver band during frequent visits to City Hall. Steele worked in a drug rehabilitation program.

Robert Doggett was one of Mayor Perk's top officials. He ran the "Model Cities" federal anti-poverty program, which dispensed millions in housing grants, much of which was misspent or went unaccounted for. Doggett, who had earned a reputation as an honest man, barely survived an assassin's bullet. All suspects were tied to organized crime which had put its hooks into front companies seeking Model Cities contracts. A former employee of a spurned contractor, one of several persons under investigation for the Doggett shooting, was found dead, floating face-down in the Ohio River, the personal telephone number of a top city official the only scrap of paper in his waterlogged pockets.

Criminal elements had infiltrated the banking community. In May of 1975, *Cleveland Magazine* reported the demise of Cleveland-based Northern Ohio Bank, because, ". . .examiners were continually uncovering bad loans, totaling in the millions, to persons with organized crime ties."

An all-out war for control of the Cleveland rackets was waged with thirty mob-related bombings and occasional assassinations. A car bomb killed a local crime figure, Alex "Shondor" Birns, right across from St. Malachi's Church on West 25th and Detroit Avenue, a mile from City Hall. Another person active in the rackets, Danny Greene, had his house blown up. He survived that blast, only to be killed in another.

Cleveland's mob factions were blowing each other up with such elan, city streets and parking lots were a bloody street version of the finale of Tchaikovsky's symphony, the War of 1812.

Cleveland became known as "America's Bombing Capitol." A *Plain Dealer* editorial denounced the bombings as bad for Cleveland's image. Since looking good was more important than being good, civic boosters took out positive ads in *Forbes Magazine*, to spread the Cleveland gospel. Mayor Perk, ever sensitive to the image of the city, if not to associates in his office, declared that there was no organized crime in Cleveland.

CHAPTER 17

Law Firm Double Deals City

Wall Street stock manipulations were beyond my education, although four of my siblings went to Harvard. Harvard Elementary School that is, and we once lived close to the stock yards, also not exactly Wall Street-type experience. You wouldn't want a seat at that exchange. You couldn't walk past the place because of the smell and the god-awful sounds. And lawyers? Our family had an attorney named Phil Lustig. He was right up there with the President and the Pope. He kept trouble away from our door. It was the other guy's attorneys you had to beware.

Wall Street bond rating agencies had confidence in Cleveland, because they had confidence in the law firm of Squire Sanders, one of America's most highly regarded bond counsels. An overwhelming presence in municipal bond finance, Squire Sanders, as it was commonly known, had been described as "virtually a shadow government" with the power "to stop a legitimate bond sale."

The city trusted Squire Sanders so completely that it didn't keep its own files on bonds and notes, the firm had them. While Squire Sanders advised the city, the Perk administration mismanaged city accounts, padded city payrolls, wasted millions on harebrained schemes, and incurred hazardous levels of debt.

Except for Milt Schulman alerting me as to the conflict of Squire Sanders simultaneously representing CEI and Muny Light, I can't say I paid much attention to the firm, at first. I knew Squire Sanders supported the jetport proposal. I also recalled Squire Sanders sent couriers to the Council offices, where I witnessed fully-prepared legislation removed from large envelopes which had Squire Sanders' mailing label affixed. Otherwise, the city law department drafted legislation. Squire Sanders, in its special relationship, was an extension of City Hall.

Milt Schulman called "Dennis, I have to see you," he said.

"I'm at City Hall, Milt. I'm working."

"This is about City Hall. Something big has happened. It involves the Law Director and Squire Sanders. We need to talk - - now." There was no denying Milt. I left City Hall and walked over to his office two blocks away. As I entered, he dispensed with niceties.

"Remember I told you Squire Sanders represented both the City and CEI?" His eyebrows raised in surmise, waiting for my acknowledgment.

"Yes."

"Law Director Davis, who is leading the antitrust lawsuit against CEI, is trying to knock Squire Sanders out of the case at the NRC."

Davis' action could adversely affect CEI on several fronts. As the Justice Department conducted an antitrust review, the Nuclear Regulatory Commission (a successor of the Atomic Energy Commission) and its Atomic Safety and Licensing Board were gathering materials relating to CEI's business conduct with Muny Light. Given its primacy in all matters relating to CEI, in a sense Squire Sanders was CEI. How do you separate a shadow from its body?

"How can Davis get Squire Sanders removed from representing CEI?" I asked.

"Squire Sanders had a conflict of interest because they told CEI about confidential financial advice they gave the city on the bond issue to fix

Muny's generator. Davis presented those facts to the NRC and Squire Sanders has been knocked out of the case." Milt held up the January 20, 1976 early edition of the *Cleveland Press*. "Look at this headline," he exclaimed with excitement.

"LICENSING BOARD SUSPENDS SQUIRE SANDERS"

I tried to grasp the implications of CEI not having access to the firm which guided the company's legal fortunes since its inception, near the turn of the 20th century.

"What does this mean, Milt?" I knew he would guide me into the deeper meaning of Davis' action.

"War!" he said sharply. "Davis has declared war against two of the biggest players in town, CEI and Squire Sanders. He filed the antitrust lawsuit against CEI. He knocked Squire Sanders out of the NRC's antitrust review. He's trying to remove the firm as CEI's counsel in the city's antitrust case. He has dismissed Squire Sanders as the city's bond counsel. He's on fire. He's cutting all ties with them. He intends to win the antitrust case."

This was an act of courage, a sweeping rejection of powerful City Hall insiders. "Maybe the Mayor is finally standing up for Muny Light? He is Davis' boss."

"Perk? Don't kid yourself," Milt said with disdain. "Davis is calling the legal strategy, until Perk gets rid of him. Davis can't be pushed around. I know. I've had to deal with him. Mark my words, he's finished."

Milt was unshakable in his conviction that City Hall was controlled by Perk's financial advisers at Squire Sanders. He laid it out this way: Squire Sanders took money from CEI for corporate work. They also took money from the city for financial advice and bond work. If Squire Sanders puts Muny Light out of business, they'll make more money from CEI. If the city sells Muny Light, the sale proceeds can go to retire bonds. Then the city can issue new bonds. Squire Sanders will get paid for doing more bond work. City Hall was Squire Sanders' cash machine.

"That is how they do it," Milt said. "Squire Sanders controls city finances. It has Perk overspending. What will Squire Sanders say to Perk?"

"Sell Muny Light?" I said.

"Who do these bastards think they are fooling?" He roared.

Early the next morning, I returned to Milt's office with a copy of the morning newspaper, headlined:

"SQUIRE SANDERS ACCUSED OF CONFLICT IN CEI CASE"

The article noted Squire Sanders' sabotage of the Muny Light bond issue, to the competitive benefit of its client, CEI. "Law Director Davis discovered that Squire Sanders, while representing the city, reported to CEI the advice they gave to the city on the bond issue to fix Muny's generators, and the bonds never got sold."

"Forget the *Plain Dealer*, Dennis," Milt said, as I tried to read aloud salient paragraphs. "I have the NRC case transcripts and other documents here," Milt said, passing to me a stack of papers containing unpublished sworn testimony before the NRC.

"We are going to read," he said, motioning to me to sit in what had become my chair in his office. "Let's get started."

I began to review Law Director Davis's account to the Atomic Safety and Licensing Board of the NRC. On the other side of the desk, Milt glowered, occasionally looking up to offer a pointed narrative.

"That bond issue to repair the generators…" he began.

"Yes. CEI was in the committee room, coaching Councilman Gaul."

"Forget Gaul, this is about Squire Sanders. They knew Muny's finances, kept all the records and knew how to hurt Muny financially. Squire Sanders made it impossible for Muny to sell its bonds to get the money to repair the generators. They wrote legal restrictions into the legislation. They deliberately gave the city bad advice." Milt's teeth clenched.

"Listen to this. See how they operate!" He quoted aloud from Davis' testimony:

"...Because they had access to the finances of the MELP [Muny Light] they knew how certain actions could damage the city how certain restrictions placed on the 1972 bond issue, first selling it on the outside market, would destroy the bond issue and deny the city the use of capital funds that were needed. That is what happened. Those bonds that Mr. Brueckel [of Squire, Sanders & Dempsey] prepared, never sold. The city was never given the use of the $9.8 million. Yes, we are suspicious they were sabotaged."

"Squire Sanders should have disclosed to us that they were writing opinions to CEI that were justifying such things as the refusal to give us an interconnection, the refusal to permit us into CAPCO...their insistence of raising our rates which served to damage the city's position."

Milt was in a rage. "They sabotaged the bond issue. These dirty bastards helped put Muny Light in a hole and set a trap for the city," Milt dropped his right hand on his desk for emphasis, like a judge striking his gavel. "See what is going on here? Squire Sanders got Perk to borrow more than he could pay back. They weakened the city, to force the sale of Muny Light to CEI."

I now clearly understood the Muny vs. CEI contest was about corporate conspiracy, espionage and sabotage, to undermine and then steal a public power system, to gain a monopoly to raise utility rates to the sky. This was the betrayal of the City, abetted by trusted public officials and news editors who were not impartial arbiters, but men whose opinions were dictated by their advertisers.

This crowd was capable of anything. Was it even possible to stop them?

"Squire Sanders took money from both CEI and the City. They had a conflict of interest. This is why people hate lawyers. I hate the crooks in our profession. It gives us all a bad name," Milt said, while passing me another sheaf of NRC transcripts and documents. "Read these. You have to know what is going on at City Hall, if you are going to make a difference. Young man, you have your work cut out for you."

I re-calibrated my understanding of the world with each revelation of City Hall's power relationships. In this element, I did not take anything at face value. I asked more questions. When things at City Hall didn't make sense, it was sure to be bad news for my constituents. Those who said government did not work were wrong. It has been working, in this case, for CEI and against the people of Cleveland.

I left Milt's office and headed to City Hall, eager to share my new awareness with my former Council colleagues. I attempted to engage several members but was greeted with blank stares. They had little understanding and even less interest in Squire Sanders' subversion.

At the threshold of Forbes' office, I pondered for an instant whether to share my discovery. Why bother? He knew. The Council President was committed to the sale, recently telling reporters, "Taxpayers don't have an endless amount of money to finance improvements."

Law Director Davis formally dismissed Squire Sanders as the city's bond counsel, hiring a New York firm, and calling the switch "the beginning of the end" of Squire Sanders' bond monopoly in the state.

The decision by the Licensing Board on Squire Sanders, adjudging the law firm to be in a conflict of interest, triggered another review by a special NRC panel, presented with the same facts.

A strange reversal occurred. Only a few days after the Licensing Board found Squire Sanders in conflict, the special panel found "no unethical conduct" and reinstated the firm to represent CEI, saying the city should have known about Squire Sanders' manipulation. The January 26, 1976, *Plain Dealer* headline read:

"U.S. CLEARS CEI LAW FIRM"

I was shocked. The city had presented documentary evidence of Squire Sanders' duplicity. I called Schulman after reading the depressing news.

"No unethical conduct? The city should have known Squire Sanders advised the city against its own interests?! What is going on?"

"What is going on," Milt explained, "Is that Squire Sanders has a lot of friends in Washington, and that place is more crooked than City Hall."

Then, Mayor Perk met privately, or so he believed, with Federal Judge Robert Krupansky, who was presiding over the antitrust case. Perk's contact with the court raised eyebrows in the legal community, as he went over the head of Law Director Davis. It was a sign Perk had decided to sell Muny Light.

Law Director Davis had created forward momentum for the city on the antitrust lawsuit. He had challenged CEI's application to operate a nuclear power plant, and he started an appeal of the special board's decision which reinstated CEI. For his efforts, as Schulman predicted, he was forced out by the Mayor, placing at risk all city legal initiatives to protect Muny. It wasn't long before the *Cleveland Press* captured Perk's intentions on Page One.

"TALKS MAY BRING SALE OF MUNY LIGHT TO CEI"

The physical damage to Muny Light, the boilers and turbines whose repair had been blocked by CEI and Squire Sanders, the outages, the mounting debts, and the triple cost of power purchased from CEI was ruinous. Muny was spoken of in the past tense.

The *Press* wrote "Who Killed Muny Light?" while Frank Gaul, ever ready to be Muny Light's pallbearer, pronounced Muny Light "dead as we know it, kaput."

In keeping with the public burial of Muny Light, postmortem plans proliferated. CEI was ready to finally execute on its post-acquisition strategies which included an immediate rate increase for Muny Light customers. The sale of Muny's functioning generating units to CEI was contemplated, subject to an internal review of whether the generators, whose repairs CEI subverted, could be repaired and operated economically within the CEI system. Once firmly in control of Muny, CEI, with the city's help, would be able to secure inexpensive public power from the Power Authority of the State of New York (PASNY), which CEI had blocked Muny from accessing.

CEI was making record profits, and using ratepayers' money to expand their advertising campaigns to soften public resistance to additional rate increases.

The growing multi-million debt for purchased power, which the city owed to CEI, curiously was not a topic of discussion, even though in 1974 the Federal Power Commission ordered Muny to pay the bill.

The unpaid light bill was another trap. The resolution of the city's mounting debts, which included settlement of the light bill to CEI and the stabilization of city finances, was now being tied to the proceeds of the sale of the light system.

CHAPTER 18

Stealing Muny Light

When government goes behind closed doors with a utility monopoly, taxpayers and ratepayers had better hold onto their wallets. Federal Judge Robert B. Krupansky ordered the parties to try to settle the disputes represented in their litigation. The City went into negotiations with CEI on the antitrust lawsuit with the stated intention of restoring Muny Light, and helping it recover from CEI's and Squire Sanders' treachery.

On March 14, 1976, after a lengthy meeting in the office of Squire Sanders the City emerged from behind closed doors with a tentative agreement to sell Muny Light to CEI.

It was a total capitulation. Muny Light would be sold, the antitrust case would be dismissed and the conflict of interest charges against Squire Sanders would be dropped. The city would withdraw its complaint against CEI at the NRC and terminate its complaint at the Justice Department. CEI would get its license to operate nuclear power plants.

CEI, which had been under legal scrutiny for blocking the city's access to PASNY's low cost hydroelectric power, had planned to use the city's authority to obtain cheap public power for itself. Muny would exist on paper only, reduced to a distribution-only function in a limited zone.

The *Plain Dealer* blared that Muny Light was about to be extinguished:

"TENTATIVE OK REACHED IN SUIT TRANSFER OF MUNY LIGHT TO CEI NEAR"

The *Cleveland Press* printed the death notice, 'Who Killed Muny Light?' with Frank Gaul delivering a curt eulogy, "The plant is dead ... a veritable scrap heap."

A key element of CEI's strategy, which Gaul tirelessly advanced, was to deliberately characterize Muny's underfunded and subverted lake front generating plant as being synonymous with the entire municipal power system, which included not only generating, but also transmission and distribution services to its industrial, commercial, and residential customers. A confused public wondered why so much attention was directed toward a single building.

Council President George Forbes pronounced Muny defunct. "Now all CEI has to do, at the rate things are going, is to wait a couple of months and just come and take it," he said.

The sale of Muny Light was a done deal.

Weeks later, for no apparent reason, Forbes reversed field. He threatened to resurrect the antitrust lawsuit, cancel CEI's operating franchise in the City of Cleveland and invoke eminent domain against CEI, which meant the condemnation and purchase of all of CEI's electric utility assets in Cleveland. This was the option detailed in the City Planning Commission report.

Forbes, who had vociferously called for Muny Light to be sold to CEI, now wanted Muny Light to absorb CEI's operations within the City of Cleveland, at a cost of $300 million. The city could realize a net profit of $165 million in thirty years, according to City Planning.

"The Ohio Constitution gives us the right to take over all of CEI's operations which serve Cleveland, providing we give them a fair price.

It's an unbelievable thing. It's too good to pass up," Forbes said with elation, announcing he would present to the voters a charter amendment to create a new city power authority.

Was Forbes schizophrenic? No. He was a master manipulator who knew what CEI wanted, gave it to them, then took it away and threatened the private utility with losing everything. CEI was the mouse to his cat. He had an agenda and the audacity to purposefully play CEI openly. He hired the law firm of Kohrman and Jackson to evaluate the sale and the antitrust lawsuit. He also attacked CEI's newest rate increase, a 26% hike, and called for public hearings.

As Forbes pressed CEI, an unnamed official of the beleaguered private utility made calls to the media, charging that the Council President hired the Korhman and Jackson law firm at city expense because it had represented him in an attempt to purchase a Cleveland radio station, WERE. The implication was clear and risked inciting the Council President's volatile nature.

In a moment of self-reflection during a timely *Plain Dealer* interview, Forbes described his political philosophy "You scratch my back, I'll scratch yours. You shoot me in the back, I'll cut your throat." In retaliation for CEI's misstep, his knife's edge was set at the company's throat. He ordered full-page newspaper ads ripping CEI.

Mayor Perk, taking a cue from Forbes, pledged to hire two new attorneys to prosecute the antitrust case, which he had previously ordered to be canceled. CEI was once again vulnerable on legal, financial, and political fronts.

The ensuing months resembled a prize fight, with Muny Light gaining strength from an allocation of hydroelectric power, at one-fourth the rate CEI had been charging. CEI struck back, again blocking the city's access to this cheap power, arguing CEI's competitive position would suffer from such a concession.

Judge Krupansky formally denied the city's effort to disqualify Squire Sanders as CEI's counsel in the city's antitrust case. Then came the moment CEI had dreaded. The U.S. Justice Department filed its brief with the Nuclear Regulatory Commission, charging CEI and other utilities with a "conspiracy to monopolize." The NRC determined that "proof concerning the accomplishment of the objectives of a conspiracy may be persuasive evidence of the existence of the conspiracy itself."

According to the Justice Department, CEI, joined by the other private utilities, had achieved the goal of nearly destroying Muny Light, not with a 'superior product' or 'business acumen,' but through anti-competitive actions.

As a result of the NRC filing, CEI's misconduct became public, just as Muny Light was gaining access to cheaper, market-priced power. The city's antitrust lawsuit against CEI, covering the identical issues being litigated before the NRC, threatened the utility.

An upcoming decision by the Atomic Safety and Licensing Board of the NRC could also place CEI's nuclear power plant licenses in jeopardy.

The Justice Department had given a ringing endorsement of the value of competition, writing that competition helps regulation, it spurs efficiency and innovation, it enhances, even surpasses the purpose of regulatory agencies. Little Muny Light was entitled to survive, though surrounded by giant utilities and pursued relentlessly by CEI. With Forbes' new campaign against CEI and a mighty assist from the U.S. Justice Department, it looked as though Muny Light would make it.

Then, on September 8th, 1976, Forbes revolved again.

"Muny is like a small grocery store compared to a gigantic supermarket chain," he said. "Muny Light is not an asset, it is a liability," Forbes continued. "Muny Light is much too small an operation to be profitable in today's society. If we kept it much longer it wouldn't be worth anything."

Within a span of a few months, Forbes had gone from favoring the sale of Muny Light to championing the takeover of CEI by Muny. His game. His rules. He was leading the way one more time, to sell Muny Light to CEI.

Squire Sanders crafted a sale agreement which Mayor Perk and Karl Rudolph, the President of CEI, promptly signed. A key provision of the agreement required the city to drop all legal action against CEI, including the $330 million antitrust suit.

The afternoon Press of September 8, 1976 screamed the end of Muny Light:

"PERK, CEI OK MUNY LIGHT DEAL"

The next morning's *Plain Dealer* echoed Muny's demise:

"$158 MILLION SALE OF MUNY LIGHT TO CEI TENTATIVELY APPROVED"

I knew this "sale" occurred because Cleveland politics and media were in the service of CEI. Easy arithmetic showed that the city was selling the light system to pay an excessive bill, approaching $10 million for power, for which CEI had overcharged.

The deal was a classic swindle. The remaining proceeds would go toward paying CEI for future light service to city facilities and for future costs of street lighting, which had previously been provided by Muny Light, at a discount to the city.

The *Cleveland Press* wrote "Its sale will add nothing to the city's General Fund. It will disappear merely to settle debts... The old plant stands as a monument to municipal bungling - - run into the ground so that at the time of its passing it did not benefit the city and its people one bit."

The *Plain Dealer* "commended" Forbes and Perk for, "striking an exceptional bargain."

CEI's attorneys then sent a letter to the Atomic Safety and Licensing Board of the NRC, arguing that the sale would make antitrust violations "academic."

"If the city chooses to sell its electric plant to the Illuminating Company, or anyone else, that again, is its own business."

The Justice Department's response was a testament to the diminishing hopes of Muny Light to survive. CEI and the other defendant-utilities, had "finally driven Cleveland to the wall," they lamented.

Throughout the past few years I had been tracking the most subtle movements affecting Muny Light in the Council lobby, the committee rooms, the Council chambers, in editorial suites, and in news coverage, stepping forward at a moment's notice to stand for the right of Clevelanders to own an electric system. Whenever behind-the-scenes negotiations surfaced, I was prepared.

As the drama of Muny Light seemed to reach a climax, it became clear to me that the goal of Forbes and company was to keep the public off balance in order to preempt any organized opposition. It worked. Muny Light's status was confusing, at best. Muny was past tense, whether the reason was cutthroat competition, political corruption, or mechanical failure, the light system was gone, and everyone in Cleveland was called upon to accept it, in the mournful manner of accepting the untimely death of a loved one. CEI had finally put Muny out of business. It was considered a disrespect of reality to assert otherwise and unless I was prepared to put my reputation and every ounce of personal energy I had on the line, higher utility rates and higher taxes would follow.

I would not accept that the political system had failed the people of Cleveland and let the matter rest. I witnessed the betrayals. If I did not challenge them, I was complicit. I had to try to save Muny Light. It matters that people have a choice. It matters how much people pay for electricity. It mattered for that family, years ago, which counted its pennies in a St. Clair Avenue apartment. I could hear those pennies dropping, again, on that old, chipped, white metal table. CLICK, CLICK, CLICK.

As Clerk of Courts, my office sent court notices to people who had failed to pay their electric bills. That's as close as I was connected, legally, to Muny Light. What I lacked in statutory standing, I made up for in political involvement, claiming jurisdiction as the number two administrative official elected city-wide.

Legislation authorizing the sale was introduced in the City Council. I sought advice from Bob Weissman. If anyone knew how to throw oneself into the middle of a battle, it was him. I was startled at his assessment.

"Dennis, look, it is over. The sale is done. There is nothing you can do to change it. I don't want to see you wasting your time," he said emphatically. Bob wanted to assure that I was on course to run for mayor. He did not want me to get side-tracked.

"Bob, I can't just stand by. This is wrong."

"It is wrong," he acknowledged. "There are a lot of things wrong with City Hall, which you will fix when you are mayor. You are not mayor yet. Don't pick a battle that is over," he said impatiently.

Through thousands of conversations, over a period of eight years, it was one of the few times Bob and I found ourselves in sharp disagreement. He brought cool logic to our partnership, an irrefutable assessment of the observable world. I was intuitive. Our different ways of looking at the world balanced, like a simultaneous audit of a checking account.

Not now. He knew any involvement in Muny Light at this point was a waste of time. I knew I had to reverse the sale, whether or not it was of political benefit. This disagreement with Bob represented a personal crisis. He was my mentor.

"Bob, I've got to try to stop the sale," I said.

"Suit yourself," he said brusquely.

I was on my own. I had to come up with a plan to change the outcome and I did not have much time.

Late one night, at my home on Milan Avenue, I was unable to sleep, kept awake by simmering anger over the sale, the twists and turns, the legislative reversals, the feints, all to kill off Muny. The manipulation was blatant, and CEI's advertising revenue induced amnesia in Cleveland's media editors. The assault on the public interest had succeeded. No other elected official had stepped forward.

I got up from my bed. Searching for inspiration, I retrieved from my library a popular history of the city, "*Cleveland: The Best Kept Secret*" by local author and *Plain Dealer* columnist George Condon. I learned that seventy-five years earlier, CEI used political and legal maneuvers to block the creation of Muny to preserve its monopoly in Cleveland. Aided by Squire Sanders, CEI plotted to thwart Cleveland Mayor Tom Johnson's plan to give Clevelanders low-cost electricity by blocking a special bond issue election in 1903. Johnson then attempted to annex a suburb, South Brooklyn and its light plant. CEI again moved to block.

As Condon described it, Mayor Johnson's campaign to annex the town was fiercely resisted, so much so that the mayor openly charged fifteen Republican members of the City Council with misfeasance and two democratic councilmen with bribery. Johnson eventually annexed South Brooklyn and Muny Light was born. The addition of the Village of Collinwood and its light plant enabled the city to provide electricity at a savings of 20% as compared to CEI.

Mayor Johnson, in his autobiography, "*My Story*," envisioned public power as epitomizing the basic right of people to determine their own fate in a democracy:

> *"I believe in public ownership of all public service monopolies for the same reason that I believe in the municipal ownership of waterworks, of parks, of schools. I believe in the municipal ownership of these monopolies because if you do not own them, they will in time own you. They will corrupt your politics, rule your institutions and finally destroy your liberties."* [1]

Condon made Cleveland's history vivid. As I read of Mayor Johnson's struggle, I could sense his spirit, hear his voice calling across the time and space of three-quarters of a century, with a plea, "Do not let them sell the light system."

1 - From his autobiography, "My Story" by Tom L. Johnson. Published by B.W. Huebsch, New York, 1911 • Page 194

This was not communicating with the dead. Mayor Johnson's ideals were alive. It was up to me to give them expression, to take a stand. Muny Light was being stolen. I knew it. I had to act. Everything I ever learned: how to create an issue, how news is made, how to challenge government decisions, how to rally the public, and how to change the outcome, would be brought to bear.

In my home on Milan Avenue, I have a glass globe with a cityscape of Cleveland. When the globe is shaken, artificial snow which has settled at the bottom begins to stir. The more the globe is shaken, the more the "snow" expands, until a virtual blizzard is created. Events are often created in the same way. Stirred and shaken by external forces, they confront, confound, become irresistible, demanding attention and resolution.

Restless, I took a yellow note pad in hand, and, sitting at the top of the upstairs steps under a stark white light, I began to sketch a plan to save Muny Light. Once the plan was set in motion, Cleveland's city scape would begin to experience unusual political weather:

THE PLAN TO SAVE MUNY LIGHT

- Attack the sale price as a giveaway.
- Demand an appraisal of Muny Light.
- Demand a competitive bid, to slow down the sale.
- Seek another bidder, to make CEI's bid an issue.
- Show Muny customers how their rates would go up.
- Show CEI customers how their rates would go up.
- Analyze Muny Light's finances.
- Demonstrate that Muny Light is making a profit.
- Search all legal avenues to challenge the sale.
- Develop a grassroots campaign to save Muny Light.
- Create a campaign for a referendum to tie up the sale.

The plan was ready. So was I.

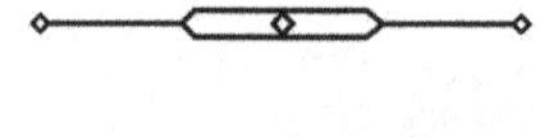

Could I reverse a consummated sale? The execution of the plan to save Muny Light had to be precise, engage the working press, and exploit each and every opening. Every thought, word and deed had to be aimed at stopping the sale. I could not do this alone. I called Warren Hinchee, now the former Muny Light Commissioner, who lived in Louisiana. It was Hinchee who, years earlier, instructed me on the workings of the light system and its financial position.

A few days later, Hinchee and I met at my home. There, he helped fill in my plan, beginning with dissecting the sales price.

"There are three dimensions to the price," Hinchee said. "One, what is Muny Light's actual worth as a going business? Two, we have to analyze the agreement, which set the sale price at $158 million. Three, what is the impact of the sale on city taxpayers, Muny Light customers, and CEI customers?"

I knew if we could make the price an issue, we could slow down the sale.

"There is a rule of thumb most people use in calculating the value of a municipal utility," Hinchee said. "The value of a system is ten times the annual sales. Muny Light sells $24 million - $25 million a year in electricity."

"It could be worth $250 million?!" I exclaimed.

"It is worth more," Hinchee replied. "When you look at the terms of the agreement the city signed, CEI will pay Cleveland only $38.5 million of the $158 million up front. The remaining $120 million, will be repaid over a period of thirty years, at $4 million a year, interest free."

"Interest free?" I had not considered that the city would not receive interest on the unpaid balance.

"Yes," Hinchee replied, "the present-day value of $120 million, repaid interest-free at $4 million a year, over thirty years, is $49.6 million. The actual sale price is $88.1 million, not the $158 million the public has been told. So, the city is being cheated out of at least $161.9 million. It is loaning CEI money to buy themselves a monopoly," said Hinchee. "Plus, Muny's lakefront land is worth at least $10 million."

"So the city is being cheated out of $172 million on this deal?" I asked.

"It's worse," Hinchee declared. "The city buys its electricity from Muny Light. Once CEI takes over, the city will pay $2.6 million more each year to service seventy-six city facilities and pay another $400,000 annually for higher street lighting charges. Building in expected rate increases and allowing for inflation, conservatively the city will pay at least $150 million extra for electricity over the next thirty years. Now, where do you suppose the city will get that money?"

"Higher taxes," I responded.

"Exactly. Public power enables the city to pay less for power. It keeps taxes low," Hinchee said.

"Won't both Muny Light and CEI customers pay more for electricity?"

"Yes. Muny Light customers' rates will instantly rise to those of CEI's, once the sale is final. They will pay at least an extra $5 million a year. Over a thirty-year period, former Muny customers will pay at least $150 million more for electricity, not including rate increases," Hinchee added. CEI customers' rates could also go up to pay for the acquisition.

Here was the crux of the campaign to stop the sale. Over a period of thirty years, CEI will make a $172 million profit on the sale of Muny, plus another $150 million from increased charges to the City for electricity, plus at least another $150 million from increased electricity costs from Muny's former customers.

The estimate of close to a half a billion dollars in undervalued assets and increased rates was explosive. I was convinced we could overturn the sale, if the information could get to the public. Hinchee said CEI customers could become our allies. Then, there was the $330 million antitrust damage suit.

"It is a viable lawsuit and potentially has great value. If the city won, it could even pay for the takeover of CEI in Cleveland. But don't count the money yet," Hinchee cautioned.

With Hinchee's help, I was able to move from an outline of a plan to a detailed analysis of the sale for presentation to the Cleveland City Council and to the Cleveland media. Hinchee returned to Louisiana, ready to offer further assistance.

I gathered the facts and went to City Hall. "This is potentially one of the biggest swindles in history," I declared at a news conference. "The people promoting it could end up in jail." I handed out my analysis of the deal.

The calculations of concern to Cleveland media managers did not involve stolen municipal assets or sharply increased utility rates, but rather, the advertising revenue CEI spent, enhancing profitability, while extending CEI's influence on editorial and news policy. The media could not be relied upon to protect the public.

A *Cleveland Press* editorial belittled my claims, demanding, once again, the sale of Muny Light "The plant has outlived its usefulness and the city should just get the best deal it can." Above the editorial was the newspaper's logo, a beaming lighthouse emblazoned with this motto:

"GIVE LIGHT AND THE PEOPLE WILL FIND THEIR OWN WAY"

CHAPTER 19

The Plan is Set in Motion

CEI named the largely discounted price it would pay for Muny Light, without an appraisal. Councilman Theodore E. "Ted" Sliwa, was Chair of the Real Properties Committee, which dealt with the disposition of all city property.

"Ted," I said, reaching him at his home office on Cleveland's West Side, "the administration is advancing the sale without an appraisal. I spoke to former Commissioner Hinchee. He said the system could be worth as much as $250 million. But, based on the present value of the sale, CEI is paying only $88 million."

"No appraisal?" He snapped, with a slightly nasal tone. "Is that right?" He was surprised.

"Ted, we need you to raise the issue."

He grasped the urgency. Sliwa's committee had broad jurisdiction over elements of the sale, consisting of the lakefront generating plant, the transmission and distribution system, the land, rolling stock and other assets. He was a strong-willed Pole, independent-minded, a World War II veteran who fought under General Patton. He won five battle stars and a silver star. At Council meetings Sliwa cradled under his right arm, as a bible, a dog-eared copy of a biography of five-star U.S. General Douglas MacArthur. And like his idol, Sliwa had the urgent air of a man who was ever prepared for combat. He religiously produced a May 30th Veterans' Day commemoration each year at his parish church of St. Barbara's. Some Councilmen cynically viewed Sliwa's fervent devotion to God and country as anachronistic. I saw it as the mark of a man who had integrity, someone who could be counted on, no matter the odds.

"Where in the Sam Hill did they get that figure?" Sliwa barked in his Council committee meeting, demanding an explanation of the discounted sales price. "A true value has never come out. We're taking somebody's word for it. We need hearings. As Chairman, I am not going to be bulldozed." I had slowed down the sale by raising questions. An appraisal could take at least a month.

Sliwa prepared legislation requiring an independent appraisal, setting off a bitter debate. One Councilman wanted an appraisal *after* the city sold the system. Another Councilman objected to any appraisal, claiming it would show CEI paid too much.

Meanwhile, Hinchee continued talks with a non-profit, American Municipal Power of Ohio, which coordinated the sale of inexpensive power to city-owned utilities. I invited both Hinchee and the executive secretary of AMP-Ohio to my home.

When AMP-Ohio's leader walked through the door, he had the appearance of a latter-day Einstein, a shock of white hair, an alert expression, and the fixed, widened eyes of someone who minutes earlier may have experimentally stuck his finger into a live electric socket. This was the man who had the intention, the know-how, and the means to scuttle the direct sale of Muny Light to CEI. He also had a fabled name in the electric industry, Powers Luse.

"The deal has been made to sell Muny to CEI. It is a direct sale," I said to Mr. Luse. "There was no competitive bidding. There was no request for proposals, no effort made to get anyone else to bid."

"You've a great friend here in Warren Hinchee," began Luse, as I nodded. “It’s clear your Council has no idea of Muny Light’s value,” he smiled. “Some in Council do not want to know. We are going to help change the situation. We are prepared to make a bid for Muny Light.”

“Where will you get the money?” I asked.

“We have the ability to issue mortgage revenue bonds to finance the sale. Muny Light has 46,000 paying customers to help retire the debt. No question, we could make a profit. There would be no problem raising the money,” Luse said.

“Muny Light is making a profit, even with everything CEI has done to hurt it financially,” added Hinchee. “Once AMP-Ohio indicates it is ready to bid, if the city nevertheless gives Muny Light to CEI without a competitive bid, we can sue and tie up the sale.”

“How ironic,” I said. “The city won’t borrow money to fix up Muny Light. The newspapers are saying it is not worth anything. Yet, AMP-Ohio can finance the purchase and operation of it.”

“Yes,” Luse said enthusiastically, “we’ll maintain it as a public enterprise. We’ll keep it out of CEI’s hands and structure the deal to return it to the city.”

I worked with Hinchee and Luse to craft a letter to Mayor Perk and Council President Forbes asking for that the sale to CEI “be held in abeyance, so AMP-Ohio may also enter into purchase negotiations and make a competitive offer for purchase.” I personally delivered a copy of the communication to Councilman James Bell, Chair of the Public Utilities Committee.

“They’ve been puttin’ a lot of pressure on me,” said Bell outside the committee room. “I don’t like the way this thing is comin’ down. It ain’t right. And I ain’t goin’ along with it no matter who is for it.”

“Jimmy, you can help here,” I said, hoping to enlist the second key committee Chairman in an effort to block the sale. “Would you release the letter? Once people know there is a second bidder, the question is going to be ‘Why a direct sale to CEI?’”

“George ain’t goin’ to like this,” Bell said. “I don’t give a damn. He ain't done nothin' for me," he said, striking the word "nothing" bitterly. Chairman Bell circulated the letter to the media, prompting stories of a second bidder.

As AMP-Ohio's offer circulated at City Hall, a third bidder appeared. Cuyahoga Disposal Inc. had offered the same price as CEI and the same payment terms, with one major modification - - they offered to install a garbage recycling plant, near Muny Light's lakefront operation, to power Muny's boilers. This bidder was traced back to the mayor's labor adviser, Mickey Rini, who "vouched" for the firm.

Utilities Director Kudukis broke ranks with the Perk Administration, scrutinizing Cuyahoga Recycling's financing, which included a form letter from a Wall Street firm that assumed the city would back any bonds the firm issued with the city's "full faith and credit," meaning that if the firm could not pay off the bonds to finance the purchase of Muny Light, the city would be stuck with paying off the bonds, another giveaway. Cuyahoga Recycling's offer also contained a trash disposal contract which would cost the city one-third more than it was currently paying for garbage disposal.

The *Press*, in a copyrighted story, charged that Cuyahoga Disposal submitted bid documents in a 1973 bid, and again in its 1976 Muny Light bid, misrepresenting its experience, qualifications, and backing, including falsely claiming financing from the Teamsters Pension Fund, falsely claiming incorporation in Nevada, and touting industry experience with a sister company, which turned out to be a cocktail lounge.

When questioned, individuals named as principals in the bid denied knowing anything of its details, or even agreeing to participate. The only story which checked out asserted that Cuyahoga Recycling was close to Mickey Rini. Cuyahoga Recycling's bid was certain to fall apart under public scrutiny, encouraged by CEI's well-placed friends in the media.

Warren Hinchee revised estimates of Muny Light's revenue stream and determined that it had a $300,000 profit in the third quarter of 1976, and would make a profit of $2.5 million in 1977, enough to finance $50 million in revenue bonds for capital improvements.

CEI, now under close federal scrutiny, slightly lowered the rate it charged for power sold to Muny, improving Muny's financial profile. Although the Council would not budge on authorizing $15 million for Muny repairs, Hinchee said Muny's financial position would improve even further, once the NRC ordered CEI to provide it access to cheaper, market-priced power. Hinchee met with Council members to share his findings.

He and I demonstrated to reporters and editors alike that the light system was worth upwards of $250 million. Nevertheless, *Plain Dealer* management continued to back the sale to CEI "... in no way should City Council be detoured from the main objective of getting rid of the Muny Light plant."

Thanks to Sliwa, Bell, Luse, and Hinchee the pace of implementing the sale slowed. Council President Forbes blamed me. CEI increased its pressure and Mayor Perk threatened to shut down Muny or lay off a thousand city workers, unless the light system was sold.

There was a procedural barrier to the sale. City Council could not act on a sale of Muny Light until a charter-required hearing was held by the City Planning Commission, an appointed board. If the planning commission disapproved, City Council would be required to muster twenty-two of thirty-three votes, instead of a simple majority of seventeen votes, to proceed with the sale. Based on discussions I had with individual Council members, I believed we could get at least eleven firm votes, particularly from Councilmen representing Muny Light customers. Planning Commission disapproval would, therefore, put us within reach of defeating the sale outright.

When the sale of Muny Light was placed on the agenda, I was in attendance. One member of the board, Monsignor Francis Carney of the Cleveland Catholic Diocese, wearing a black suit with a Roman collar, asked the Chairman of the commission, Wallace Teare, to cast his vote for him. Then, he left. I objected loudly from the audience, upsetting the decorum of the otherwise staid committee.

Chairman Teare called the roll and voted against the sale. Teare then cast Monsignor Carney's phantom vote in favor of the sale, resulting in a 3-3 tie. Not counting the absentee Monsignor's vote, the proposed sale was disapproved 3-2.

"The vote was three to two," I called to the chair, again disturbing the library-like silence. "The vote was three to two!" I protested loudly.

An uproar ensued. The planning commission members retired to a back office. When planning commission members emerged, a re-vote occurred. Teare and City Councilman Gerald McFaul, both of whom had voted against the sale legislation, had switched their positions during the recess. The sale of Muny Light to CEI was approved by a vote of four to one. I declared that I would sue over the phantom first vote, as a further means of blocking the effort to get rid of Muny.

The sale was totally tainted. The questionable price, no appraisal, no public evaluation of Muny's worth, no competitive bid, no public inspection of Muny's finances, and a phantom vote cast at a topsy-turvy meeting of the Planning Commission. Any of the objections we raised should have been enough to stop the sale.

My brother, Councilman Gary Kucinich, and fellow Councilmen Benny Bonanno, and Ted Sliwa, and I formed the "Save Muny Light Committee," rented the ballroom of Cleveland's Lakeside Holiday Inn, and asked for volunteers to come forward and circulate petitions to place a charter amendment on the ballot requiring a vote by the people of Cleveland on the sale. I knew if we were able to rally people and build an organization, we had a chance to prevail. The first crucial test would be the response to our plea for help.

The afternoon of the meeting, hundreds of Cleveland residents from nearly every neighborhood, responded with a unified determination to protect Muny Light and to rebuke City Hall.

They streamed into the Holiday Inn ballroom, most dressed in green or blue work clothes, ready to circulate petitions that had been prepared by Milt Schulman's son, Jack, a new attorney.

Councilman Sliwa, wearing his veteran's blue garrison cap, led us in the Pledge of Allegiance. Each elected official spoke, exhorting those in attendance to remember this moment in the history of our community was a chance for citizens to strike back at the questionable conduct of their government.

Before the distribution of petitions, the program concluded with a solemn pledge. Each person in the room raised a right hand and in unison recited a vow to save Muny Light: "I will circulate petitions to save Muny Light for the people of Cleveland. I will do all I can to stop the sale of Muny Light, and to work for a viable Muny Light system, to keep utility rates down. Muny Light belongs to the people, not to a giant utility monopoly."

As they recited the pledge, I could feel the power of unity surging from Clevelanders and for a moment, the Cleveland of 1976 was in a rendezvous with the Cleveland of 1903, led by Mayor Johnson, Muny Light's founder.

As citizens filed out of the Holiday Inn ballroom with petitions and ward maps in hand, each also took up a fluorescent-lime bumper sticker, which, with its electric flash graphics, would become the banner of one of the most consequential citizens' campaigns ever to sweep Cleveland:

"POWER TO THE PEOPLE
MUNY LIGHT"

CHAPTER 20

Ethics? I Thought You Meant Ethnics!

City Council readied "tax abatement" legislation, which granted tens of millions of dollars in property tax giveaways, to a few of the most profitable businesses in America, which happened to be located in Cleveland. It was beyond outrage for a financially stressed city, with underfunded schools, to give taxpayer dollars desperately needed to highly-profitable, large corporations.

City government was subsidizing businesses, picking winners and losers based on political connections for projects which would have been built anyway. This smacked of moral hazard and political payoffs. Under "tax abatements" buildings constructed on prime downtown real estate would be tax-free for fifteen years. The burden of taxation in the Cleveland area was increasingly shifted to residential homeowners.

When it came to protecting low utility rates, the Mayor and the Council President said Muny Light had to be sold because Cleveland was going broke.

Cleveland's public schools depended upon the property tax as it was their main source of revenue. The schools were on the verge of insolvency, unable to obtain bank loans, and had no vote on the giveaway by City Hall.

The tax abatement law, was brought before the finance committee of City Council for review on Monday afternoon, December 13, 1976. As the finance committee meeting ended, Council President Forbes said he had asked for $2,000 from the "Growth Association" to enable Council to sponsor Christmas parties for children of the poor. Forbes apparently wanted to deliver a good Christmas to both business and underprivileged children. His charitable instincts raised questions, since the solicitation and giving occurred in the context of pending legislation.

"Is this an ethical problem?" asked Councilman Gary Kucinich. Gary had no hesitation in asking the kind of questions many on Council would not. We were brothers in every significant way. The Council President did not immediately respond regarding the ethics of his request for $2,000 from the Growth Association for a Christmas party for poor children, while it had legislative interests before Council.

Gary brought the matter up again at the meeting of the full Council. Rather than raise the question of Forbes admitting to asking money from a beneficiary of pending Council action, Gary Kucinich gave the Council President the benefit of the doubt. He instead put the onus on the Greater Cleveland Growth Association, proposing they had offered Forbes $2,000 "for a Christmas party for inner-city children."

Gary Kucinich inquired of the city Law Director, Malcolm Douglas, who served as the parliamentarian at Council meetings "Mr. Douglas, the Growth Association is one of the chief proponents of this piece of legislation. The Council President has admitted the Growth Association has offered him a few thousand dollars to throw a party for the kids in various Council members wards. My question is one of ethics."

Council President Forbes interrupted from the chair. "Just one moment. Just one moment."

Gary continued, "Mr. Chairman, I would like to ask the Law Director whether it is appropriate for this legislation to be before this body when such an offer was made to the Council President. Mr. Chairman, I think the question is in order and I would ask the Law Director be allowed to respond."

"Are you inferring I was bribed?" Forbes demanded.

"Mr. Chairman I am not making any charges of pay off," Gary stated firmly.

"Just one moment. You did your thing. You have done your thing. You made a very serious accusation. Just one moment," Forbes said, directing his comments to Gary, who continued to stand by the microphone at his desk.

"I'm asking whether it is proper…"

The Law Director edged toward the microphone to respond. "Just one moment Mr. Douglas," said Forbes.

"Perhaps if we had an ethics law…" Gary said.

"Just one moment. I think everybody heard you. This is a very - I take it to be a very serious accusation," said Forbes.

"It's not a question of payoff," Gary countered. "It's a question whether it's proper or not."

"Just one moment, Mr. Kucinich. Just one moment. Please. Mr. Kucinich stated the Growth Association was the chief proponent of this legislation. That was the first statement that was made. Mr. Kucinich then stated that the Growth Association had offered me two thousand dollars. This is not the usual Council rhetoric. Mr. Kucinich inferred that I have been offered two thousand dollars."

"Mr. Chairman, you have been offered two thousand dollars."

"Just one moment," Forbes repeated. "Mr. Kucinich has inferred that I was offered two thousand dollars by the Growth Association for passage of this legislation."

Gary countered "Not for passage of this legislation, Mr. Chairman.

You were offered two thousand dollars… by the chief proponent of this legislation." Kucinich said.

"Just one moment," Forbes said.

Gary continued to speak "Not for passage. No accusation of payoff on this legislation."

"My integrity, I insist, I insist, I'm not going to leave here with the people in this audience, my colleagues, the media broadcasting this, that somehow I have taken two thousand dollars." Forbes said.

Gary answered, "I said you were offered, Mr. Chairman, which is exactly correct. There were members of this Council who were present when you stated you were offered two thousand dollars from the Growth Association for a Christmas Party for kids in the wards. And I am asking whether or not it's appropriate at the time when this legislation is before this body. I asked the Law Director a valid question. No charge of payoff was made and if there is any inference of a payoff charge, I would respectfully submit that is not the point, Mr. Chairman. The point is that we now have before the Council legislation which affects the Growth Association. And the point, Mr. Chairman, is that the Growth Association did offer you two thousand dollars for a party in the downtown area so that Councilmen could bring the kids down there."

Forbes charged back "I'm going to ask you point blank, are you inferring that I took two thousand dollars to pass this legislation?"

"No, Mr. Chairman, not at all. That is not my intent. My intent…" Forbes cut him off.

"Just a moment. Sit down. You're out of order." Forbes had Gary's microphone turned off. Gary took his seat. Forbes did not explain his ruling. The tax abatement legislation was called forward and passed.

Forbes then returned to the subject of the Growth Association and the $2,000, stating he had solicited, not merely been offered, $2,000 from the Growth Association for a Christmas Party for underprivileged children. Since Forbes had declared, twice, that he had solicited money from the Growth Association, he accepted the very ethical, if not a legal, burden from which Gary sought to absolve him.

Debate ensued. One Councilman after another rose to attack Gary's character, one even asserting he was "on the take." Gary left the floor of the Council and called me as the debate was underway.

I was meeting at my house on Milan Avenue with Hinchee, Powers Luse, and Alex Radin of the American Public Power Association. I excused myself, to speak with Gary.

Gary's tone was urgent. "They want to kick me out of Council," he said.

"Gary, there's a commotion in the background on your end and I don't think I heard you correctly," I replied. He was calling from the media room, off the Council chambers. "They want to kick me out of Council."

"You're kidding, aren't you? "

He wasn't. I begged off the meeting in my living room.

"I raised a question whether it was proper for Council to vote on the Growth Association's tax abatement legislation at the same time the Growth Association was donating $2,000 for a Council sponsored Christmas party for children."

"And?"

"Forbes said I impugned his integrity."

As a VietNam era Marine veteran, a sergeant, an instructor in physical education, a boxing and weight-lifting champion, my brother Gary carried himself with a cheerful assurance. He was politically adept at maneuvering the rocky territory Forbes had tried to lead him into, even to declare he was not charging Forbes had been bribed, but to no avail.

Gary was suspended from Council for two weeks, not for his remarks, but for Forbes' characterization of his remarks.

Gary was a key Council member opposing the sale of Muny Light and his single vote was critical. He was also my point of contact for organizing opposition within the Council.

The day after Gary's suspension, Forbes brought before four Council committees the legislation to sell the light system to CEI.

CHAPTER 21

Love and Death

I was in love again. One of my top appointees in the clerk's office, Joe Tegreene, noticed that I returned to the Clerk's office with a big smile after a lunch meeting.

"Uh oh, something's going on, I can tell," he surmised, smiling broadly.

"What?" I deflected his prying. "I went to lunch."

"Who did you have lunch with?" he pressed in a lyrical manner.

"Sandy McCarthy, a schoolteacher from Berea."

"Oooh, I understand now." Tegreene said. Educated at Kenyon College and as top organizer in my congressional campaigns, he had a natural aptitude for management. Clear, concise, efficient, he understood the outlines of the world, even if he did not have the life experience to read between those lines. He was funny, and loyal, but had a glumness which attended him on occasion, the seriousness of someone who quietly wrestled with deep questions and was attuned to the suffering of others. He saw how much I was affected by the divorce from Helen and while no one could tell outwardly from my public appearances, in the past year I had personally turned inward after separating from Helen and kept a solemn demeanor.

I knew I had spurned love in exchange for the fleeting favors of the public, and destroyed a marriage which, with the smallest effort could have worked. It was a self-created tragedy. Any change in my mood, even a smile, would be noticed by anyone in close proximity and Tegreene noticed.

Yes, in fact, I was in a blossoming relationship that began with a speaking appearance at Berea High School, in February of 1976, where Sandy McCarthy taught English.

"When's the wedding?" Tegreene asked, jumping the narrative.

"Slow down, Joe," I said.

"Yeah, right," he responded, knowingly.

As Sandy and I spent more time together, I was entranced by her intuitive nature, her colorful personality, and her love of literature. Much of my own life's philosophy was derived from reading the English romantic poets, so of course I had fallen in love with an English teacher.

While visiting her classroom, I witnessed her manner with the young people in her class and was impressed. Sandy was intelligent in a casual way, had a natural flair for drama, an outgoing personality, large, dark-brown eyes and long, natural platinum, curly hair. She was well-known locally, having sung on a television variety show for several years. Her voice was beautiful. She brought music, poetry, and a sunniness into my life, and I accepted her gifts with deep gratitude and love. A wedding date was set, January 15th, 1977.

Ten days before the ceremony, on the evening of January 5th, Sandy and I were at Milan Avenue, making last minute arrangements for our wedding. We talked excitedly as Sandy wrapped gifts in the dining room for the wedding attendants. I turned on the TV so that we could watch the "Scottsboro Boys," a cautionary true story about racism, a rush to judgment and a miscarriage of justice. I sat on an ottoman near a window, when I was swept with desire to be at Sandy's side, so I moved to cross the room. Suddenly, the wooden house shook, as if slapped by a giant hand.

Sandy and I exchanged glances.

"What was that?" she asked.

I looked outside. The weather was calm. We ignored the intrusion and went to sleep.

Early the next morning, I arose before dawn. Sandy had already left for work. What was the shock to the house, the burst of sound? I noticed what appeared to be a spider on the wall behind the ottoman, where I had been sitting. Upon closer inspection, I saw it was a hole. I was perplexed. A hole in the wall? I took a flashlight and went outside the house, where and saw a similar hole, level to the one inside.

I called the police. Two plainclothes detectives arrived and began their assessment.

"Someone took a shot at you," one detective said, after glimpsing at the holes.

"It is right by the chair I was sitting in," I described the scene when the house shook. The detectives looked at each other when I told them I had just left my seat. They found no bullet in the living room, only a hole. They traced the bullet's trajectory from outside the house, through the inner wall of the living room, then through the dining room. There was another hole in the dining room's interior wall.

The police asked for a ladder and went to the backyard to examine the outside wall of the house. Seven feet above the ground, in line with the hole in the interior wall, a blue wooden slat had been shattered and the facing of the outside gutter had been split. A detective took a ladder and examined the facing of the gutter. He took his pocketknife and dug a fragment of metal from the wood.

"This is what we were looking for," he said. "This is a round from a high-powered rifle. If you hadn't moved from that chair when this bullet entered your house, you wouldn't be here." Then, a few moments later, they found a second bullet hole. My desire to be at Sandy's side had saved my life.

I was questioned at length as to who I may have made angry. I was the Clerk of Courts, a relatively conflict-free job. The only major public issue I was involved in was Muny Light. Was I risking my life for a public light system?

Sandy arrived from school as the police were leaving. She sought assurance. "What are you going to do about this?" she demanded of the detectives.

"We will give the house special attention and assign someone to further investigate the incident," said one of the detectives, closing his notebook.

"I don't want publicity. It only encourages these kinds of things," I said.

"You know we have to file a report," one of the detectives replied. "It's a public record."

"We can't control that, sir, sorry," said the other detective. And then they left.

Sandy looked at me, incredulous, her eyes brimming with tears. "Is this what I can expect, being married to you?"

I was silent.

"Becoming a young widow is not in my plans," she said.

"Sandy, the police will try to find out who did this," I said confidently, concealing my concern. I was alarmed. Sandy could have been struck by a bullet. I quietly wondered if it was safe for her to live on Milan Avenue. No bride should have to accept such risks. Sandy vocalized my concerns.

"I don't like it. Dennis, I'm scared," she said. I tried to console her but was unconvincing. This was a bad way to begin a new life.

Word got out and the media swarmed the house, but we avoided comment. The news eventually moved on to other things, but the shots fired at me brought a better-informed sense of caution, and a serious concern for the safety of my new wife.

CHAPTER 22

CEI Deliberately Caused Blackouts

Thursday, January 6, 1977

Blackout! It was the middle of the night, one day after the attempt on my life. Temperatures were below freezing. Muny Light had another massive outage, affecting every one of its 46,000 customers and shutting off city streetlights and traffic lights.

The Perk administration blamed the weather, claiming icing on porcelain insulators on the CEI/Muny Light tie-in caused the blackout. Suspicions abounded however, that CEI helped effect the blackout, to further undermine support for Muny Light. The city owed CEI nine million dollars for purchased power. Behind the scenes, CEI's patience on collecting was seen as strategic: Induce the sale of Muny Light to pay the ever-increasing electricity bill.

Later that same day, in Washington, D.C., the Atomic Safety and Licensing Board of the Nuclear Regulatory Commission charged CEI with deliberately causing blackouts on the Muny system, imposing severe operating problems, transferring power in arbitrary ways, and intentionally causing brownouts, blackouts, or voltage reductions. Cleveland City Council Utilities Chairman Larry Duggan, had been right. CEI had sabotaged Muny Light. A federal investigation had confirmed it.

As an expert witness would testify, "Power was provided [by CEI] at the load transfer points by means of a dead load transfer, which meant that an outage occurred each time MELP/MUNY took power from CEI and each time that service was returned to MELP customers."

CEI then prolonged the blackouts it had manufactured, through administrative delays in providing emergency power. The blackouts helped CEI advance its public claim that CEI's system was simply more reliable. The frequent power outages caused Muny to lose customers.

It was revealed that in December 1972, Muny suffered a major outage and needed emergency power. CEI refused to provide it unless the city signed a contract to purchase power from CEI for street lighting. The city did so, but under duress. CEI's attempts at price-fixing were ruled "per se" violations of antitrust law.

Donald Hauser was CEI's corporate attorney. He was not an engineer, but required routine operational decisions such as transfers of power, normally the province of engineers, to go through him. He invented justifications for disrupting or shutting off power to Muny and personally ordered delays in transfers of power, causing Muny Light to experience blackouts, brownouts and voltage reductions.

Hauser claimed his involvement in engineering decisions and processes was to facilitate the FPC order for CEI to interconnect with Muny Light. In fact, he was subverting the FPC order, searching for ways to justify delaying, interrupting, or terminating service to Muny.

The NRC termed CEI's interference with Muny Light's expansion as "destructive competition" and scored the private utility for denying Muny benefits of coordinated operation, pointing out that CEI took five years to come to an agreement with the city over a permanent interconnection.

The ASLB/NRC initial antitrust decision imposed specific licensing conditions attaching to CEI and associated utilities, licenses for Davis-Besse and Perry nuclear power plants. Both CEI and its private partners had to refrain from requiring Cleveland to drop legal action. They were further ordered to provide interconnections, wheel power, provide membership in CAPCO, sell Muny maintenance power, emergency power, and economy power, share reserves upon request, and provide access to nuclear power.

The January 6, 1977, NRC ruling was a total victory for Muny Light and set the stage for the resurgence of public power in Cleveland. It exposed in great detail CEI's illegal attempt to put Muny Light out of business. What's more, the CEI internal office memos, which were in the NRC record, would be of great use in the antitrust case. The previously hidden documents confirmed charges the city had made in its $330 million lawsuit against the private utilities.

CEI deliberately caused blackouts to undermine Muny Light as a viable business. The company, in its cancerous greed, threatened the health and safety of the people of Cleveland every time the lights went out. Further, it overcharged the city for power, presenting a fake crisis, providing Mayor Perk a flimsy pretext for selling Muny Light to pay a light bill.

What could be the appropriate sanction or punishment for the betrayal of a community? Cancellation of their corporate franchise in Cleveland? Condemnation of their facilities and a takeover by Muny Light? State action to rescind their corporate charter in Ohio?

All eyes turned toward City Hall to reverse years of CEI's duplicity. Mayor Ralph Perk summoned the media to the ceremonial Red Room for a pronouncement, presumably of a new dawn. Enter Mayor Perk:

"Now CEI will have to buy Muny Light," he declared to a bewildered press corps. "We believe the NRC decision will prevent CEI from withdrawing from the original agreement . . . [to sell]."

The "Law of Contradiction" states that something cannot be true and untrue at the same time. It was true CEI had committed grievous offenses against Muny Light and the Cleveland community. Yet, it was Muny Light which stood to be punished.

When the laws of logic are totally debased, one need not search for an explanation in an alternative universe. No, Mayor Perk's capitulation at the moment of victory was a clear sign the political process in Cleveland had been totally corrupted by CEI and its supporters and I was more determined than ever to fight back.

Local media reports ignored the gravity of the findings, focusing instead on Muny Light gaining access to nuclear power. The *Cleveland Press*, without providing much detail, said the ruling could "breathe new life" into Muny Light.

Only one individual out of the entire City Hall press corps of perhaps two dozen reporters, Jim Cox, a veteran newsman for television station WJW, approached me at City Hall to discuss the NRC ruling. He had called it to the attention of his news director, who approved a series based on the agency's landmark decision.

Cox was respected by City Hall politicians and reporters alike as a dogged interviewer. Tough, fair-minded and thorough, over a period of several weeks he read thousands of pages of documents which exposed CEI's misconduct.

Curious, I asked to see his research, but he promptly ended the discussion. "Look for yourself. Go read the files."

While Cox was developing his series, there was a change in WJW's management and his exclusive expose was killed. Cox was stunned.

When Roldo Bartimole, independent journalist, discovered that Cox's series had been canceled, he wrote a scathing piece in his publication, *Point of View*. The station's new management obviously did not have the stomach for a confrontation with CEI, so it took Cox off the City Hall beat. They imposed changes to his schedule, and he encountered, for the first time, complaints about the quality of his reporting. He was replaced by reporter Bob Franken, who would ultimately have his own confrontation with station management.

Prior to his planned probe into CEI, Cox's fact-based journalism was widely acclaimed. He was a respected, even feared, truth-seeker. But the collision with station management over the CEI series meant the end of his TV news career.

I knew it was unlikely that any other media outlet would mine the NRC files. Cox's advice to me to "read the files" became an imperative.

I arrived at a public library thirty-five miles east of Cleveland, where documents from the NRC and the City of Cleveland's antitrust case were available. A librarian escorted me to large stacks of paper sitting on gray, metal shelves. I looked at the collection warily.

Through several sittings, I sat riveted, paging through the secret history of CEI's attack on Muny and set aside hundreds of pages for copying. I gathered boxes of information and went straight to the man who could help me decipher the documents, Milt Schulman.

There is a certain type of excitement experienced when one is on the verge of discovery. When I entered Milt Schulman's office, struggling with a cache of records, his eyes widened and he laughed, "What do you have there?"

Perhaps I hadn't told him the size of the collection to be reviewed. Nevertheless, he had cleared his schedule and his desk to help me study the CEI case file, as he had previously helped me decode documents to understand Squire Sanders' conflict of interest.

"Milt, I have the information Cox couldn't get on the air, " I began.

"Let me tell you something, young man. The newspapers, the radio and TV stations want CEI's ad money. They don't give a damn about the city. Those bastards at CEI are trying to steal the light system and their advertising money is helping," his voice boomed across the office.

His wife Agnes, looked up from her desk to see if Milt was all right. "Milt?" she called.

Upon Agnes' notice, Milt's voice dropped in volume. He maintained his commanding tone, and in an expansive gesture of encouragement, imparted his fire. "And you, my boy, YOU are going to stop them."

"I have a plan, Milt. I'm ready."

"Remember, CEI is in financial trouble. They built nuclear power plants they didn't need. Now they want Muny Light to help pay their bills." Milt circled behind his desk. "You have something for me to read?"

We began sifting through the boxes of hearing transcripts.

I pulled a document from the box, "Proposed Findings of Fact and Conclusions of Law and Brief in Support Thereof of the City of Cleveland," and began a rapid read.

It was a brilliant compendium of CEI's offenses against the city, including engaging in cutthroat and destructive competition, price fixing, creating blackouts, refusing to provide emergency power, and subverting the FPC interconnect order. It referenced the investigative products of the Department of Justice, the NRC, and the city. It charged CEI and the other utilities with a 'conspiracy to deny small electric utilities access to the benefits of coordinated operations and development of economies of scale and access to nuclear generation.' It presented a formidable obstacle to CEI's receiving a nuclear license.

The city's Washington antitrust counsel filed the "Proposed Findings of Fact" with the NRC on September 8, 1976, the same day Forbes did his instant pivot on to sell Muny Light, the same day Mayor Perk signed the sale agreement, which required dismissing both the city case at the NRC and the antitrust lawsuit.

The city was caught in a contradiction of having simultaneously advanced a case against CEI in Washington, D.C., while capitulating in Cleveland, moves which would cover-up major corporate crimes, to no discernible benefit for the people of Cleveland.

"The timing is incredible," I said to Milt.

"Yes it is," he agreed. "The city pushed CEI to the edge of a cliff. Then the city jumped."

The 'Proposed Findings of Fact' document was the product of

testimony and evidence developed by the city over a period of eighteen months and presented at a series of NRC hearings. It included citations from thousands of pages of transcripts of sworn testimony, evidence gathered by the Department of Justice, supported by extensive antitrust case law.

In order to understand the gravity of Mayor Perk's decision to call for the sale of Muny Light in response to the city's victory at the NRC, it is critical to know that as a result of information gathered pursuant to the city's antitrust lawsuit filed on July 1, 1975, the city had presented reams of evidence to the NRC regarding CEI's dirty tricks. This was before the draft document of the 'Proposed Findings of Fact' was reviewed by the city's lawyers on August 23, 1976; before the September 8, 1976 filing of the 'Proposed Findings,' and before the January 6, 1977 NRC decision.

Milt and I became engrossed in the files. I broke the silence, waving a document at Milt which provided background on the event which first drew me into the Muny Light saga - the 1969 Christmas-season blackout.

A month before the blackout, CEI decided that if there was ever a catastrophic failure on the Muny system, it would *not* provide the city with an interconnection.

It had publicly promised a tie-in, but privately, CEI's management was communicating to key personnel that, "A permanent underground tie is to be avoided like the plague." It had no intention of providing the city with any type of tie-in, underground or overhead, temporary or permanent. Its officials repeatedly lied to a trusting public about CEI's intentions

Following the 1969 Christmas-season blackout, CEI told the media it wanted to help Muny Light, then started to ply Council to sell Muny to CEI.

"They said one thing publicly, and did the opposite privately," I said, noting the contrasts.

"It's called duplicity," Milt said, jaded.

We spent hours studying documents and making notes. The totality of CEI's efforts had the feel of a military strategy produced in a corporate war room. I kept thinking how CEI management had adopted General Rommel's blitzkrieg tactics and employed the superior military intelligence skills of the utility's leaders. The company executed a plan which, but for the NRC investigation and the antitrust suit, would have remained secret. Now it was exposed. The long list of anti-Muny actions involved much planning, and uncommon risk-taking.

Early in the evening, Milt and I compared our findings from the NRC's files. CEI's quasi-military strategy was apparent:

- CEI created blackouts on the Muny system.
- After the blackouts, CEI culled Muny's customers.
- CEI blocked a permanent interconnect for five years.
- CEI attempted to fix Muny's rates and street lighting charges.
- CEI publicly said "yes" to interconnect, privately, "NO!"
- CEI attempted price fixing.
- CEI engaged in "destructive competition" against Muny.
- CEI would sell emergency power "at a (very high) price."
- CEI interfered with Muny operations and maintenance.
- CEI refused to wheel power, isolating Muny.
- CEI: Drop anti-trust and all probes to get nuclear access.
- NRC: CEI'S conduct an "outrageous affront" to antitrust law.

The company blocked repairs to Muny's generators so Muny Light would have to buy power from them. Then, they sold Muny limited amounts of power at a high price to blow a hole in Muny's budget, while calculating that Muny's allegedly wretched generators could later be put back into service and add value to their own system.

CEI's actions had caused serious monetary harm to Muny Light and inhibited its past and future growth. This was the key argument of the antitrust case. Unless it engineered a takeover of Muny, CEI would be exposed to a huge liability in damages for the economic consequences of its refusal to interconnect, refusal to wheel, and Muny's subsequent loss of customers.

On the other hand, by acquiring Muny, CEI projected that its earnings per share would increase by $2.723, providing greater than 10% growth. It called the takeover of Muny "inevitable."

"OK Milt, I get it," I said, setting down the papers. I took a deep breath and shared a short-hand version of my read of the files.

"CEI subverts the political system, prevents repairs and improvements at Muny, blocks the interconnect, sells a small amount of power to Muny at a high price, wipes out Muny Light's rate advantage, weakens the finances of the system, and with this deal, takes over Muny, gets a monopoly, escapes accountability, profits from its misdeeds, and pays down its nuclear debt," I said.

"Congratulations, son. You figured it out," Schulman said, pleased he had taught me to better understand both the light system and the political system of the city.

Milt and I continued to review documents. "Milt, here's a memo showing CEI plotting the takeover of Muny Light, get this, 'in the best interests of the Company.' They write of 'a consciousness of good timing, when to move in and how far, when to drop back, when to act, and when to wait.' They were predators, stalking Muny Light."

"Cutthroats," Milt interjected.

"Here, they're trying to 'keep a jump ahead of the sheriff.' They knew they were on the wrong side of the law," I said. I was agitated.

"Most people are honest, and have trouble comprehending how crooks operate. You have to know how they work, so you can fight them - and win," Milt said.

"They are even going after Painesville's public power system, thirty miles from Cleveland," I noted. Painesville was a small town, only 3% of the population of Cleveland.

"It is not the size of the town, it is how many millions CEI can make with a monopoly," Milt said. "This is about power and money."

The documents showed that CEI had carefully studied the acquisition practices of other private utilities and their campaigns to defeat attempts to create municipal systems. CEI's private utility partners had aggressive municipal acquisition programs. Since 1965, Ohio Edison had acquired Lowellville, Norwalk, Hiram and East Palestine. Toledo Edison was made up of 190 companies, gained through merger and acquisition. It targeted the publicly-owned electric systems of Pioneer, Waterville, Liberty Center, and Napoleon.

"They have taken over a ton of municipals, and they are still looking for more," I said to Milt.

"I know one they are not going to get," he said.

Milt took a blue pencil and underlined something. His mood clouded as he shook his head in sharp disapproval. The corners of his mouth receded. "They're killers," he said, handing the papers to me. "Absolute killers. Read this."

I studied the scored lines from the CEI internal document. "There is no precedent for the acquisition of a municipal system as large as Cleveland. Because of this, a victory for the company might well be a real contribution to continued private ownership of the electric power business and therefore be worth an extreme effort and sacrifice." Milt studied me as I read, watching for my reaction.

"'Extreme effort!' 'Sacrifice'! Are they crazy? Why in the world would they put it in writing?" I asked.

Milt countered CEI's belligerence. "Because they think they cannot be touched. They will do anything to get Muny Light," Milt said. "You had better watch yourself. They'll go after anyone who stands in their way. You don't have to be afraid of them, because they are a bunch of no good, lying bastards and the people will be on your side," Schulman said, brightening for the battle ahead. "And Milt Schulman is on your side."

There was only one Milt Schulman, but I knew this one brilliant, cantankerous iconoclast would help me take on CEI, their supporters in Council, the media and the business community.

The problem was, the public didn't understand the issue.

"The people don't get it yet, Milt. CEI still has a pretty good image in the community. The media keeps pushing the sale, ignoring the deeper story."

"You tell the people their electric rates are going to go up once CEI gets a monopoly, and they'll start paying attention. And the media? Keep raising hell, they'll cover you, even if CEI objects. There is a limit to how much control CEI has. Maybe this gang has been able to take over electric systems everywhere else, but you will stop them." Milt lent encouragement.

I knew the dimensions of the fight I faced, the size, the resources and tactics of my opponent. I was somber, but Milt would have none of it. "Son, let me tell you why you will stop them." He drew his six-foot, 270 lb. frame from his leather chair, removed his glasses, and held forth as if presenting a closing argument to a court.

"Because they are in business, they think they are real Americans, protecting free enterprise at all costs. Real Americans are fair and honest. Real Americans are for competition. Real Americans don't try to steal from their city. You are going to beat them, son, because you tell the truth, because you are not afraid, and because the people will back you. You'll stop them because you're a pretty tough little mensch."

He sat down, smiling.

CHAPTER 23

Dupli-City

City Hall was one happy celebration of a "public-private" partnership, pushing the sale of Muny Light. Forbes' legislation to finalize the sale had been prepared in the law offices of Squire Sanders, with representatives of CEI and the Perk administration in attendance.

The *Plain Dealer* boiled the pot for the sale, conjuring layoffs, service cutbacks, negative credit issues, and injury to bondholders, all because of Muny Light. Mayor Perk claimed the city's credit would be ruined unless the city could find at least $9.5 million to pay the CEI light bill.

In a speech to the prestigious City Club, given the NRC decision, I signaled an escalation of the fight to save public power, and drew editorial fire.

As details of the NRC ruling became widely known in political circles, Forbes, in violation of an Ohio law requiring public business to be conducted openly, held a private meeting of City Council members in his office to discuss Muny Light. When Forbes emerged from behind a closed door, he was confronted by the working press, who challenged the meeting as a violation of the state "Sunshine Law" which required open meetings on legislative matters. Forbes instantly pronounced the private gathering a luncheon, not a meeting.

"Do you expect the public to swallow that?" came one reporter's inquiry.

"The public can swallow what they want to swallow," said Forbes, brushing aside the impertinence of such irksome fourth-estate representatives.

Seven hours after the "luncheon" meeting in his office, Forbes called four committees of City Council into session, ostensibly to approve the sale and to move it to the full Council.

Unexpectedly, the committees, at Forbes' instruction, rejected the sale of Muny Light. Speculation over his motives was brief, because Council then convened and voted against selling Muny Light, by a 19-2 vote, with twelve members absent.

"Prior to the NRC ruling," Forbes explained, "we would have sold Muny Light." Forbes said the city should now pursue the $330 million antitrust damage suit.

What was going on? Was Forbes stringing along CEI? Was there something that Forbes wanted he had not yet gotten? Was he simply demonstrating his domination of the Mayor?

CEI was fearful that the antitrust lawsuit would hold up the licensing of the Davis-Besse Nuclear Power Plant, scheduled to open in April. The agreement to sell Muny Light, however, required the city to drop all of its litigation against CEI. So, before Forbes' about-face, Perk had already fired the attorneys who had prepared the NRC case to block CEI's nuclear license.

At Forbes' insistence, Perk had hired a second set of attorneys, who were instructed to reverse course, to proceed with the sale of Muny Light, to kill the antitrust case, and to withdraw legal action against CEI at the NRC. Forbes' newest change of direction caused Perk to be afflicted by an almost comedic whiplash. The Mayor once again made prosecution of the antitrust case official City Hall policy.

The Chairman of CEI, under renewed legal pressure, called Council's vote against the sale "unfortunate." He said that if the city was not going to sell Muny Light to pay the long neglected light bill, it would have to find another way to ante up, quickly, since CEI's "patience" was at an end.

CEI went to court, demanding the $9.5 million already owed for purchased power, plus an additional $8 million for recent power purchases. CEI also sought a court order requiring Muny to surrender all operating revenue to pay the bill, and if necessary, seize city assets. CEI again tried to force Muny Light as well as the water department into rate increases.

Mayor Perk and Council President Forbes, in their newest alignment to "save Muny Light," vowed that, if CEI persisted in its aggressive collection tactics, they would make sure everyone was informed of the NRC ruling. They threatened to damage CEI's image by placing ads in the *New York Times* and the *Wall Street Journal* to inform potential investors of the company's legal vulnerability in the city's antitrust action.

Forbes and Perk again spoke of a city takeover of CEI through eminent domain and condemnation of CEI's facilities in Cleveland, this time backed up by a bond issue and a million-dollar advertising campaign to thwart CEI in Cleveland.

"CEI is not fighting another private corporation. They are fighting the people of the City of Cleveland," exclaimed Mayor Perk.

"This is no longer a battle between little Muny Light and the powerful CEI. Gentlemen, this time the scales are balanced. The U.S. Department of Justice has joined Muny Light. It is a battle between them and the power mongers," said Councilman Richard Harmody, whose ward was saturated with Muny Light customers.

So stirring was the Forbes-Perk counter-attack on CEI, that it could have been set to the martial music of John Philip Souza, with each threat of exposure of CEI's perfidy worthy of the clashing of cymbals. This was brass. Who knew Mayor Perk still had it in him to beat the drums for

Muny Light with such fervor?

Even the moribund Cleveland media stirred from its slumber, with the *Press* enumerating CEI's misdeeds, albeit three weeks after the NRC had announced its decision:

"U.S. CHARGES CEI CAUSED MUNY OUTAGES"

"A federal regulatory agency has charged that the Illuminating Company deliberately rigged its interconnection policies to cause Muny Light power failures," the *Press* wrote. The news story cited key provisions from the NRC report. "When Cleveland needed power from CEI, the load transfer was operated in such a way as to cause an outage on MELP's system. MELP is the Municipal Electric Light Plant - an archaic media acronym for Muny Light.

"The resultant loss of power proved damaging to MELP's relationship with its customers. CEI was aware that MELP outages resulted in the conversion of customers from Cleveland to CEI and solicited the affected MELP customers after these outages. CEI's load transfer procedures were arbitrary, cumbersome, and not in keeping with modern prudent engineering practices. The switching operation could have been accomplished with only a three to five-second service interruption, without jeopardy to either system.

"Administrative delays. Connection at 69 kilovolts required CEI executive clearance and would at times take up to twelve hours advance notice before CEI would take any action on MELP's request. MELP's system would experience brownouts, blackouts or voltage reductions while awaiting CEI approval of a request for power."

A few days later, in a sidebar to a larger story entitled: "Who Turned Off Muny Light?" the *Plain Dealer* skimmed the NRC decision, but conceded: "CEI provided power to Muny Light in such a way that it increased the city's financial burden and caused brownouts and blackouts."

The NRC 's findings were now widely published, especially that CEI had caused blackouts and brownouts on the Muny Light system. City Council, led by Forbes, rejected the sale of Muny Light. CEI, not to be denied, or cowed, gave the city until March 15, 1977 to sell to them Muny Light to them, or else.

At the peak of his renewed campaign to rescue Muny Light from the clutches of CEI, to expose CEI to investors and customers alike, and to prosecute the case at the NRC, Forbes welcomed all into his City Council magic box where causality was confetti, time was a mirrored illusion, and words were blue smoke.

Forbes, it seems, had an epiphany in the middle of a blizzard and once the snow stopped swirling, the light he grasped belonged not to Muny Light, but to CEI.

Changing his position for a fourth time, he instantly marshaled the votes to sell Muny Light.

He had held CEI in check until an unspecified accommodation was reached. He was again moving forward with the sale, as would his hapless dance partner, Mayor Perk, who had at one time vowed to protect Muny Light "with his dying breath." The Mayor apparently discovered another source of oxygen. He celebrated the off-again, on-again sale of Muny Light as a demonstration of Forbes' exquisite display of legerdemain: "Forbes is the greatest Council President in Cleveland's history." Mayor Perk was right. Never had any Council President been possessed of such uncommon mastery of the art of political theater.

Last year, George Forbes wanted CEI to buy Muny Light.

Then, he determined Muny Light should buy CEI.

Next, he advocated CEI buy Muny Light.

Then, he brandished eminent domain promoting a city takeover of CEI.

Now, after two and a half circles, he was offering CEI one more opportunity to buy Muny Light.

What did he want? And from whom? Even Forbes' attorneys knew CEI's original offer cheated the city. What was the game of this grandmaster of multi-dimensional political chess, who could convincingly argue mutually contradictory propositions simultaneously with such sincerity, while playing most of the City Hall media like an electronic xylophone?

He could make up anything, and who would know? For a reporter staring at a blank page, and thinking of a mortgage to be paid, who cared? "Council President Forbes said it. We'll print it."

Forbes' media spinning wheel could exceed the velocity of a Lake Erie tempest. He could change direction with dizzying speed. No one could grasp his movement, let alone catch him. Better to fact-check the wind. Forbes wasn't just good copy, he was *great* copy, a reputable news source, summoning from his cornucopia of chaos the morning headlines, the afternoon news, the bulletins, and the blazing afternoon headlines in the five-star final. He was a walking, talking, relief program for voracious reporters.

Were Forbes' gyrations on Muny Light part of a Machiavellian posture to get millions more from CEI for the people of Cleveland? Was the city about to receive a windfall of cash? One Council member was convinced Forbes would get another $30 million out of CEI.

Can any additional insight be gained as to Forbes' motive? He had proudly told a reporter a story about a shipping company he said he had established, "not knowing the difference between an ore boat and a rowboat," by obtaining a verbal sale agreement for some ships. According to Forbes, when White shippers heard a Black person was about to enter the business, there was an immediate cancellation of the sale agreement, resulting in Forbes' new entity getting a $30,000 settlement, causing Forbes gleefully to boast, "I ripped off the big boys up town." Had Forbes once again ripped off the "big boys" over Muny Light? Whatever, it was all speculation, like concluding winter had come to Cleveland because the leaves were gone from the trees, and it was freezing outside.

What happened? Forbes' consistent intention was to present himself as the sole political power at City Hall. He was training CEI and their attorneys to come to him, first. If any deal did not originate with him, the approval of the Mayor alone meant nothing. If CEI went to Forbes first, he could cause Mayor Perk to acquiesce. Forbes asserted his authority constantly, proving he ran City Hall. It was all in the open.

The Mayor directed Muny Light to mothball its generating unit by April 1. This was, coincidentally, the same date the Davis-Besse nuclear power plant was scheduled to go on line.

Mayor Perk, a brilliant street politician with a PhD in Pierogis from the Polish Women's Hall, and a minor in Wienerschnitzel from Karlin Hall on Fleet Avenue, perhaps received a Pentecostal visitation of a tongue of fire, reminiscent of the extraordinary moment at the opening of the Chemical Convention in Cleveland, when his hair went alight. A spark jumped from a metal ribbon he was cutting with a blowtorch and danced onto his thinning pompadour. Whatever, Mayor Perk suddenly became miraculously gifted with fluency in the intricacies of the Wall Street bond market and proffered that unless the city acted to sell the light system, and soon, Muny Light bondholders could place the system in receivership and auction it for, say, $20 million.

Then, still another blackout hit the Muny Light system, leaving thirty-five thousand customers without power.

Cleveland's leading corporations placed the sale of Muny Light at the center of the municipal agenda. Although a snowstorm struck downtown Cleveland, Council President Forbes convened an emergency meeting of business leaders, at Cleveland City Council chambers, ostensibly to review city finances. Actually, it was staged to give visibility to key participants in the cheering section for the sale of Muny Light to CEI. Once again committed to the sale of Muny Light, Forbes, like Mayor Perk, raised the specter of foreclosure by bondholders, even though the system had made all of its principal and interest payments and was not in default.

Presidents and officers of international corporations, bankers and utility lobbyists slogged through the snow into the overheated City Hall building. As a former member of Council, I would normally have had the privilege of sitting inside the Council rail. But every Council seat had been taken by the corporate community. I sat where the general public gathered.

Forbes addressed the assembled leaders from the platform of the Council President, elevated five feet above the audience. "I'm telling you," he said leaning forward for effect, "we've got a problem here. Some people want to save Muny Light, but they don't want the city to go broke. They can't have it both ways. Unless the Muny Light issue is resolved, the city, as we know it, will cease to exist." Then Forbes, coordinating his inaugural public meeting of the corporate government, called upon the assembled business leaders to share their unique insights.

Tall, thin, with hard, dark eyes and slicked black hair, Richard B. Tullis, Board Chairman of the Harris Corporation, announced that the city itself was guilty of unfair competition against CEI. Tullis, who was also a member of the CEI Board of Directors, apologized, saying he could not stay for the balance of the meeting. He had to catch a private flight to Florida, where he had moved the Harris Corporation from Cleveland.

Since a CEI Board member had taken the opportunity to speak in the Council chambers, as a former Councilman, I stood and raised my hand, to assert the same right.

Forbes, expressionless, looked in my direction, as though he would call upon me, and then, without refocusing his gaze, recognized the city's Wall Street bond counsel, who was seated on the other side of the Council chambers.

"If Muny Light goes into default, it will be a long time before Cleveland ever sells another bond," said the bondsman, Peter Kinney of Wilkie, Farr & Gallagher.

Earlier in the day, at a meeting of the Utilities Committee, the Perk administration's Finance Director, Warren Riebe, said of Muny Light, "the only real option is to sell it." The Finance Director, however, refused to answer Utilities Committee Chairman James Bell's probing questions. It emerged that $2 million in uncollected delinquent accounts were owed to Muny. Prospective income was not being collected, creating a false deficit. Bell proved that Muny Light was actually operating at a profit. Forbes tried to intervene at the committee table to block the questioning of Riebe.

"You don't overrule me," Bell said, shutting down Forbes. From a parliamentary standpoint, Bell was correct. But Forbes generally ran Council under the boxing rules of the Marquis of Queensbury, not Roberts' Rules of Order. It was a dramatic moment to witness a committee chair shut down Forbes, who backed off.

At the corporate Council meeting, another CEI board member, Herbert Strawbridge, who was also president of the Growth Association, pledged in a soft, gentlemanly manner, to help create advisory groups to "make more efficient use of city assets."

A Councilman who opposed the sale, David Strand, stood close by me as he also attempted, unsuccessfully, to gain Forbes' attention.

A Perk administration legal advisor on the antitrust lawsuit, Arthur Galligan, echoed Forbes' funereal tone. The proceeds of the sale "might just pay for the burial expenses of what remains of Cleveland." He also mentioned, parenthetically, that he thought the city had a pretty good antitrust case.

This corporate Marching Band and Chowder Society for the Sale of Muny Light to CEI was too much to stomach. I did not want to be disruptive, believing that in most circumstances, manners count. I again raised my hand to speak, calling out loudly. Everyone in the chambers could hear me, "Mr. President!" Councilman Strand joined the commotion.

Council President Forbes summarily adjourned the meeting.

City Council Utilities Chairman James Bell, who earlier tangled with Forbes in committee, stood near an exit throughout the proceedings, as if to bait the Council President. As I left the chamber, Bell approached me. "You know who made up the invite list for this meeting? The Growth Association! It's a don't-mean-nothin' joke. I want George to know I'm eyeballin' him. He don't scare me," Bell said with contempt.

A *Plain Dealer* editor wrote of the City Hall corporate gathering, "With few exceptions, the feeling was the city should sell." The meeting was "...the sort of gathering the city could use more often." It was an editorial worthy of CEI's creative authorship.

Have you ever heard of someone selling their house to pay an electric bill? The city had no plan to pay CEI the $9.8 million light bill, other than selling Muny Light.

"Let's get on with it," wrote the editors at the *Press*, self-styled guardians of the public trust, except when CEI ghost-wrote their editorials.

The city did not know how much money Muny had, was owed, or was worth, since the Perk administration had been illegally destroying Muny Light records.

"How could you tell if any money is missing, if you don't keep a good set of books and controls?" Donald Lesiak, the State Auditor's financial resident examiner logically stated. The stocky, white-haired auditor was every bit the nerdy accountant, with thick, dark-rimmed glasses. A Lesiak visit had a high "yikes" quotient among city bookkeepers. His appearance at City Hall offices would cause eyebrows to be raised, eyeballs to roll, and every manner of furtive dive-under-the desk grimace as rivulets of sweat rolled down from the temples of those city officials of whom he simply inquired: "Can I see your books?"

"How do we perform an efficient and accurate audit with poorly organized records, not fully reconciled according to generally-accepted accounting principles," he complained to a City Hall reporter. Lesiak cast aspersions upon the city's financial establishment through challenging the veracity of the city's financial disclosures to the Securities and Exchange Commission with regard to bond and note financing.

CHAPTER 24

Something Wicker This Way Comes

It was the spring of 1977. As it waited for opposition to the sale of Muny Light to dissipate, the Perk administration was in search of innovative ways to increase city revenue. It settled on a sports gambling enterprise, known as jai alai.

A mixture of handball and lacrosse, its contestants used a scoop-like apparatus to launch small spheres off a walled space. Characterized by the Basque government as "the fastest sport in the world because of the balls," jai alai also had the capacity to rapidly separate bettors from their money.

City fathers envisioned a revenue stream faster than taxes, more money than horse racing, a cash windfall into the bare public till. Whatever ailed Cleveland would be cured in the unerring counting room of a jai alai sports palace, Perk's parimutuel pride, the frostiest fronton in the world, where the only thing faster than the balls coming out of the wicker are the winds whipping off Lake Erie.

Only in Cleveland could ice fishermen and bocce players line up, side by side, to place their bets and take their chances, on jai alai. As for its shady reputation of gamblers who worked to fix jai alai matches, when it came to such types, this city had dealt with pros. The Ohio Legislature, generally unconcerned regarding that which comes out of northern Ohio, caught the scent of new money and was anxious for the state's cut. The political juices flowed in the state capital, Columbus, to bring jai alai to Cleveland.

As Muny Light and jai alai consumed passions at City Hall, Federal Judge John M. Manos overturned Gary's suspension, ruling that the Councilman's free speech rights had been violated when he was suspended from City Council for questioning the Greater Cleveland Growth Association's financing of neighborhood Christmas parties, while the business group had tax abatement legislation in front of the City Council.

Our Save Muny Light Committee brought a boisterous uproar to the city's neighborhoods, drawing support from many community groups. Our referendum campaign was at the ready. We were waiting only for the Council to approve the sale, then we would go to the streets with referendum petitions.

Forbes, fearing a referendum, came up with a strategy to derail it. He devised a "special election," where voters would be asked to increase property taxes to save Muny Light, then accept the predictable failure of that proposition as proof of public approval for the sale.

"If the public wants the city to keep Muny Light, they are going to have to give us additional revenue," Forbes said. City Council approved his proposal by a 26-7 margin and scheduled a vote. Muny's debt to CEI was now $15 million, but the ballot initiative called for raising $15 million each year for five years, for a total of $75 million. The disposition of the extra $60 million was anyone's guess.

Forbes' property tax gambit was ingenious. Muny's service area covered only one-third of the city. Homeowners in the other two-thirds were being asked to increase their property taxes to pay off the debt. Yet they had no access to the direct benefit of lower electric rates, principally because of an informal, years-long allocation of markets between city officials and CEI. It was a levy designed to fail.

Editors at the *Press* celebrated Forbes' ploy with an "ends-justifies-the-means" editorial: "The strategy is for the issue to go down and for that defeat to be a signal to Council that the people do not want Muny Light. This is transparent and cynical, but if it is the only way to get this millstone from around the city's neck, so be it."

The United Auto Workers and I led opposition to the property tax scheme, opposed by both sides of the Muny Light issue. Mayor Perk added to the muddle, sending a request to City Council for a 20% increase in Muny's rates.

Judge Robert Krupansky, the federal judge supervising the antitrust case would not wait for the tax levy election to resolve the debt. CEI obtained still another judgment against the city, this time for an additional $547,155 for emergency power from 1970 to 1972.

Mayor Perk ordered the shut down of Muny Light's six boilers. The city would now be forced to obtain all of its power from arch-rival CEI, and, as a result, run up an even larger light bill.

Muny Light was now attracting national notice. The *New York Times* reported on Muny's "almost certain exit from the public power business," and noted the agreement with CEI "to settle its electric bill by selling Muny Light."

Forbes' property-tax levy failed by a three-to-one margin, no surprise. The Cleveland media interpreted the results with headlines consistent with their tainted editorial policy, typified by the *Press*' headlined story:

VOTERS PULL PLUG ON MUNY

"Cleveland's sixty-year venture into the municipal power business appeared near an end today after voters slaughtered a property tax levy allegedly designed to save the city's light system."

George Forbes, who, with a straight face, promised he would be guided by the results, concluded, "The people said, 'We're not going to fix it.'"

I answered Forbes, "The people weren't tricked into voting for an unfair tax."

Muny Light, nevertheless, appeared to be nearing its end, while, on the very same day, CEI made a new beginning. The NRC approved the operating license for the Davis-Besse Nuclear Power plant. CEI began fueling the 906,000 KW facility it owned jointly with Toledo Edison.

George Forbes had delivered Muny Light to CEI's grasp. He could not resist engaging in a form of political sadism with esoteric torture of his friends. He proclaimed, "As of now the deal to sell Muny Light is off," adding "CEI must increase its offer, and Council will negotiate a new agreement."

The timing of Forbes' hold-up of the sale placed ever-more pressure on CEI. The company was laboring under a financial burden to pay construction loans on its nuclear plant that were due September 1, 1977. It raised cash by selling 2.4 million shares of its common stock, at $33.125 a share.

A month passed as CEI's difficulties mounted, as it faced questions over the necessity of its expansion plans. An electrical engineer, who had worked for CEI for thirty-five years, charged that his former employer had jacked up its revenues by increasing voltage along its distribution system, secretly forcing unwitting customers to use more electricity. The creation of a new statewide agency to represent consumers on utility rate increases made it ever more imperative for CEI to eliminate Muny Light as a competitive yardstick, since lower rates anywhere in CEI's service area were a threat to CEI everywhere.

CEI apparently discovered a way to overcome the Council President's professed objections. Forbes called the City Council into session for a long debate that revolved around the Muny Light debt to CEI, the city's credit rating, the threat of receivership, and a court takeover of the light plant. Pressure to sell increased with strong newspaper editorial support disparaging Muny Light.

As the meeting dragged into its eighth hour, Forbes sent aides out of City Hall and across the city to bring in Council members whose votes were crucial. As the full Council slowly assembled, Forbes said, in the intervening period, that, as an enticement for the sale, he had negotiated a new concession from CEI - the private utility agreed to build a new fishing pier near its lakefront plant.

Forbes, from his platform high above the Council, studied the chamber. All members were, at last, in their seats as CEI's General Counsel, Donald Hauser, looked on from the gallery. The moment had arrived.

"All right, we've discussed this long enough," Forbes snapped, directing attention to Mercedes Cotner, the Council Clerk. She stood below the president's rostrum, pencil in hand, poised to tally, as Forbes ordered up the vote on the sale of Muny Light.

"Madam Clerk, call the roll."

Minutes later, after checking and rechecking her tally, Clerk Cotner announced "Eighteen yeas, fifteen nays."

"Muny Light is sold!" Forbes banged his gavel with finality and adjourned the meeting, his labyrinthine journey to deliver Muny Light to CEI at an end. The terms Council approved were identical to those which four Council committees had rejected earlier in the year, including cessation of the antitrust suit.

The following day, May 24, 1977, the *Cleveland Press* assessed the city's gain in a news report under this banner headline:

"COUNCIL SELLS MUNY LIGHT
AND GETS A FISHING PIER"

Though Forbes switched his positions on Muny Light back and forth a total of seven times, each pose with great drama and effect, the news article noted that "...the only concession the Illuminating Company yielded in the negotiations was a $250,000 fishing pier on Lake Erie," located not too far from Perk's planned jai alai palace.

There is no such thing as a private moment when you hold public office. My doorbell rang early. A tall, elderly White man wearing a powder-blue garrison cap with gold lettering stood at attention on the front step. I opened the screen door and welcomed him. He said he couldn't stay. He had something for me, a plain white envelope. I opened it to see four fifty-dollar bills.

"We want to thank you for getting us the carnival permit," he said. In the summer before I took office as Clerk of Courts, as Ward Seven Councilman, I had signed a permit for his organization's carnival to take place on a vacant lot on West 117th St.

Standing right behind him at the door was the spirit of Sister Leona. This was another minute fraught with spiritual implications.

"No, no, no." I shook my head and gave the envelope with the money back to him. "I get a salary from the city. I can't accept this."

"Sir, it's only a small token of our appreciation for your help." He called it a 'small token.' Rule Number One: When you hold public office, a gift is not a gift, it's a bribe. No need to insult this veteran by lecturing him on the law. I had only to say "no."

"You are welcome and I'm glad to help, but I cannot take your money. I get a paycheck for doing my job," I said gently, and he left, disappointed.

Our encounter was brief, I've spent more time holding the door open to fetch the morning newspaper, but I understood the visit. Members of

City Council had a life-and-death power over permits for carnivals. If a Councilman objected, it stopped the permitting process in its tracks. So, carnival operators were eager to ingratiate themselves with Councilmen, either through contributions to ward clubs, favorite charities, or cash in plain envelopes.

Once a Council representative, in his or her discretion, determined the carnival to be a worthy community enterprise, the carnival would proceed to a building department inspection of the rides. The permit is granted, pending final safety certification. Inspections are vital. Safety is the big issue with carnival rides, and compliance with the city code a must; otherwise a building inspector can shut down a ride or close a carnival.

Occasionally, Council members intervened with the building department on behalf of carnival operators and attempted to short-cut the inspection process. This can bring risk to the public. Carnival rides provide thrills for children and adults. The rides are also big, heavy, and sometimes dangerous pieces of machinery. Amusement can turn to horror when a carnival ride fails due to mechanical malfunction - or political interference in the inspection process.

When permits are cleared, it's carnival time and empty city lots are transformed into fantasies of swirling, flashing, multi-colored neon, lighting the night with mesmerizing pulsations. Along the midway, there are games to play, and tests of skill and the lure of good luck induces the sucker's trance. The carnival's fluttering lights alternate between light and dark, a large rainbow of colors arcing toward the mirage of a tiny pot of gold, or at least a golden trinket. It's yours, if you are good enough. If you accept the dare, the goad of the carny, you try your luck in the kingdom of the swindle, where the genuine test of skill is the exemplary practice of larceny.

"Come on!" A carny offers you a basketball. You shoot. You do not score. The rim is small. The ball is large. The basket elevation is too high. Try pitching a softball into the milk can. You can't see the steel concave plate welded into the neck of the can. You can't understand why your perfect arc keeps bouncing out. You move on to once again test your skill, tour the midway, hear the siren call and see the fun-house-mirror distorted face of the barkers.

"C'mon ring toss, ring toss, win a big prize." You see the watch fixed to the post, you see the ten and twenty bills waiting to be covered with your ring, with an easy touch. You are the easy touch. The blocks are shaped so the rings never will fit over them.

"Over heah, hey over heah, knock down the fat cats! Win a prize!" You wind up, you pitch. A small board, unseen, props up most cats. They stand, sentinels to your gullibility.

"Hey, you! Tip the milk bottles, tip the milk bottles. It's simple. Everyone's a winner." The bottles are weighted against falling. You're a loser.

The woman who proudly parades past you on the midway with her hero, hugging the largest stuffed animal in the world, is a shill, a hired employee of the carnival. Everything at the carnival is fixed. Everyone is in on the scam, except the easy mark, er, visitor from the neighborhood.

Welcome to scammers paradise in the off-kilter Kingdom of the Bilkers, where nothing is what it seems, except losing that's for real in this multi-billion-dollar yearly American enterprise.

Carnivals are vacuum cleaners with the business end inserted into the pockets of the players, the bettors, the gamblers. Once you get pulled into the din, you can hear the roar of the machine as it extracts money set aside for rent, for food, for utility bills.

The biggest stiffs drift off the midway, crowding around craps or card tables, holding fists full of money.

Lady Luck's smile is demented. The big payout is a promise denied to all but the house/carnival operator.

In the Spring of 1977, a man visiting a carnival on the Southeast side lost $160 on one game and filed a complaint with the Cleveland police. Cleveland Police Vice Sergeant, John Joyce, led a raid on that carnival because that person had the nerve to complain they were cheated by professionals. Sgt. Joyce arrested employees of Sebring Amusement Company for operating illegal gambling.

Cleveland Police Detective, William Riedthaler, who participated in the enforcement action, was approached by Officer Curtis Watkins, an off-duty Cleveland policeman, who moonlighted as the director of security for the carnival company.

"I want a receipt for everything you take," Watkins, the off-duty officer, advised the on-duty arresting officer. "Don't break any of that. Because if anything is wrong, you're going to have to pay for it," Watkins said, adding, "You are going to regret this at some future date."

This portent was not to be taken lightly, because Officer Curtis Watkins was also the personal bodyguard of City Council President George Forbes, whom he protected at least seventy hours a week. The arrests went from routine to remarkable in minutes as Watkins asked Sgt. Joyce to walk to a nearby pay phone to take a call. Watkins handed Joyce the phone.

"Get the hell out of there, let this thing slide," shouted a familiar voice into Sgt. Joyce's ear. It was Council President Forbes. "Go make some raids on Catholic bingo games," Forbes taunted. "I'll call the Mayor and you'll be ordered out of there. Even if you make the arrests, they'll never go to court."

"I have made the arrests," Sgt. Joyce responded to Forbes. "I have to do what I feel is right."

"Then I am going to have to do what I have to do," Forbes threatened reprisal. "I'll chop your head off."

According to the *Plain Dealer*, Forbes replaced Bill Seawright as Sebring's "go-to" guy at City Hall. Forbes' relationship with Sebring was checkered. In 1974 he discussed legislation which could have blocked Sebring from operating in Cleveland, yet would come to represent the carnival company The arrests proceeded and Forbes' law firm represented the arrested carnival workers.

Mayor Perk summoned the Chief of Police, Lloyd Garey, to his office and chastised him for the carnival raid.

"Let's talk about Sgt. Joyce's harassment of Council President Forbes," Mayor Perk said curtly to Chief Garey, who served at the Mayor's pleasure.

"Sgt. Joyce was doing his job," Chief Garey replied.

"He was acting improperly," the Mayor countered.

"He's a damn good man, doing his duty," the Chief said defending his vice cop.

A week later, Chief Garey, a thirty-three-year member of the police department, was told by a reporter that he had been dismissed. George Forbes celebrated the firing of Chief Garey, declaring Perk "Mayor for Life."

CEI wasted no time executing its acquisition of Muny Light. Once Council approved the sale of the city's electric system, CEI dispatched its top officers to Muny to examine the books, correspondence, diagrams, charts and operations, to begin the integration of the two systems.

I objected since such conduct invited a continuation of CEI's illegal activities. Besides, we had one last chance to change the outcome.

I called a news conference to announce the beginning of the referendum campaign. Petitions were ready. We needed to collect over 18,500 signatures to repeal the ordinance.

We began our campaign on June 2, 1977. We had only forty days to gather sufficient signatures and file them, or else the legislation would go into effect and Muny Light would be gone.

The *Cleveland Press*, doing the bidding of CEI, continued to use its editorial pages to try to disband our growing movement "Kucinich can't seem to comprehend that Cleveland voters spoke on the issue last month. He should channel his energies into other pursuits. Why prolong the inevitable? No one should let Kucinich's political smokescreen obscure that fact."

This was not a good season for customers of private utilities. CEI's rates had gone up 23% in the past year. People were angry over winter utility bills, some higher than rent or mortgage payments. I reminded Clevelanders what a private utility did to an elderly man who couldn't pay his electric bill. Ohio Edison cut off his power on one of the coldest days of the year. Eugene Kuhn, a retired factory worker from Mansfield, Ohio, sixty miles south of Cleveland, froze to death in his bedroom, because he couldn't pay an electric bill of eighteen dollars and thirty-eight cents.

Sewer bills had tripled when Cleveland sold its sewer system to a regional authority. High utility bills cut sharply into family budgets. People were fed up. People sat in apartments and homes and made choices every day about which bills to pay. When there was not enough money, first went health care, then utilities, then cuts in the food budget.

People had long believed they could not fight the private utilities and their ever-increasing rates. Our Muny Light referendum campaign was their chance to try. It evolved into a classic battle of public interest versus private interest.

We gathered signatures from supermarkets, barbershops, churches, and sports events, from bus passengers and from senior citizen's clubs, and we went house-to-house in Muny Light neighborhoods as well as those served by CEI.

Bill Casstevens, Regional Director of the United Auto Workers, together with Assistant Regional Director Warren Davis, had UAW members circulate Muny petitions on the shop floors of the Ford and Chevy plants, helping us gain momentum. People in the city were eager to sign the petition to save Muny Light. The message our volunteers brought back: "Tell CEI and all those politicians downtown to go to hell."

Councilman David Strand and I discovered that Muny Light had $4 million in unanticipated revenue. This built Muny's 1977 profit margin.

The administration claimed the failure to pay the light bill to CEI was ruining the city's credit. Yet, Cleveland marketed a $25.58 million bond issue at 5.94%, a full percentage point better than a previous city bond sale. Riebe speciously claimed, under questioning by Councilman Gary Kucinich, that the bond issue received favorable treatment because the city was preparing to sell Muny Light. This while Wall Street supposedly was placing more stringent requirements on municipalities and a crackdown on the misuse of bond funds, namely the use of capital funds for general operating purposes.

"Markets recognize the city is in sound financial status," said city Finance Director Riebe, contradicting his own testimony to council amidst the increasingly desperate effort of Mayor Perk. His Honor now asserted that the referendum itself would damage the city's credit and undermine future bond sales, causing Cleveland to forfeit both its light system and its water system.

On July 1, 1977, the day before the sale of Muny Light was to become final, as a result of the stirring grassroots petition drive involving hundreds of volunteers, I placed 30,000 signatures on the Clerk of Council's counter. The ordinance providing for the sale was immediately blocked, until Council either repealed the sale legislation or scheduled a referendum.

The tens of thousands of signatures broke the media myth that I was the only one who cared for Muny Light. It also forced the media to cover Muny Light as an ongoing news event with an outcome yet to be determined, instead of it being yesterday's story.

I met with local television news crews and repeated what I had heard while gathering signatures "People are fed up with high utility rates. They do not want to be ruled by a utility monopoly." The *Plain Dealer*, however, minimized the petition drive, writing that anyone with organizational ability could secure 30,000 signatures for anything.

Our petition drive blocking the sale had another benefit. It kept alive a federal appeals court ruling requiring the Federal Power Commission to examine a long-standing city claim that Cleveland was overcharged $500,000 by CEI for electricity from 1970 to 1972.

I followed up with a new request asking the FPC to block CEI's acquisition of Muny Light.

Mayor Perk, sensing complications for his re-election, pushed back, claiming the referendum would mean receivership and the liquidation of Muny Light. Councilmen could even go to jail for contempt of court, he asserted if the CEI debt was not paid by July 29th, 1977. Meanwhile, Perk and CEI quietly agreed to extend the deadline for that payment.

Perk said the referendum was unnecessary, because Clevelanders had already voted against Muny Light by rejecting the property tax increase, and that Muny Light had been neglected for thirty years.

"The city ought to be strengthening Muny Light and protecting the antitrust suit," I countered. At this point, I understood Perk was in a politically weakened state, given to having garbage collectors distribute questionnaires door-to-door to assess public attitudes about his war on pornography. I had to respond to his increasingly erratic statements by pointing the way to a viable alternative: Save Muny Light, keep utility rates low, repair the light system, prosecute the antitrust case, and stop the sale of other valuable city assets.

The Muny Light referendum campaign awakened the city. As I went door to door, I could feel support growing for Muny Light. I was gathering a constituency, to save Muny Light, and to press for broader changes at City Hall. Those circulating petitions had come back with another message "People want you to run for mayor."

I had a premonition at age sixteen that I would be mayor of Cleveland by the time I was thirty. I had turned down a "draft" effort in 1971 because it was too early in my career and I was unprepared. Now, after a decade of involvement in city issues, I moved forward with a purpose higher than the attainment of an office. I would run for mayor to save

Muny Light and to protect the people's right to have an electric utility, and a city government they could call their own.

CHAPTER 25

I Run For Mayor

July 7, 1977

The excitement in the ballroom of the Sheraton-Cleveland Hotel was building as the hour neared for the announcement of my candidacy for Mayor of Cleveland. A week earlier, we filed petitions to save Muny Light. This week another set of petitions would go into circulation, to place my name on the ballot in the non-partisan primary election.

I outlined my platform: Save Muny Light, protect the antitrust suit, end tax abatements, and improve city services with no new taxes.

After my statement, well-wishers passed by Sandy and me, as if congratulating a wedding party. A slight scuffle at the entrance of the ballroom drew scant notice. Police pulled a suspicious-looking man from the reception line. Under questioning, he explained to police that he was merely passing through Cleveland from Pittsburgh. The visitor saw the crowd, was curious, and wanted a closer look. He was searched. Police found a long knife hidden inside his boot. The man was an overnight guest at the Sterling Hotel, the notorious hangout for politically-connected local crime figures.

Clerk of Council, Mercedes Cotner formally notified our Save Muny Light Committee that sufficient signatures had been filed for the Muny Light question to be brought before the Council. According to the Cleveland City Charter, Council had to first consider legislative repeal of the ordinance. If the Council voted to repeal the sale, we won. If it voted against repeal, the issue would go to the voters at the next election.

After feasting on pork dumplings and roast duck in a backyard picnic at Perk's home, Forbes returned to City Hall and refused to permit a Council vote on repeal of the Muny Light sale. Instead, he directed the Council to send the issue directly to the ballot. It did, by a vote of 26-4. I threatened legal action since the Charter required Council first to consider repeal of the ordinance authorizing the sale.

Then, Forbes sent a legal opinion drafted by his private law firm to the Elections Board, seeking to bar the Muny Light issue from the ballot on the grounds that the petition language mentioned the antitrust suit. The language in the referendum petition referring to the lawsuit came from the original sale ordinance, written by Squire Sanders and approved by George Forbes.

Our attorney, Jack M. Schulman, told the Elections Board that under the City Charter, referendum petitions are required to reflect the language of the ordinance they are seeking to repeal, the wording was factual, and it would be a misrepresentation if references to the antitrust case had been omitted.

City Council's attorney said we had created a climate of deception and unconscionable partisanship. The Board of Elections, made up of partisan political appointees, ruled 3-1 against placing the issue on the ballot.

Three county political appointees denied thirty thousand Clevelanders a vote on Muny Light.

In an editorial entitled "Enough of Muny Light," *Cleveland Press* editors once again called for the sale, while conceding, "It's possible the city could win a lawsuit somewhere in the neighborhood of $300 million against CEI if Cleveland had chosen to press its case forward."

This blithe dismissal of the harm inflicted on the city by CEI's illegal conduct and the callous rejection of economic justice for the people was a grim illustration of the media's total abandonment of the public interest. Such was the climate in the Cleveland metropolitan area.

In the previous nine months, despite verifiable evidence of CEI's perfidy against Muny Light and the city, area newspapers were fully enlisted by CEI in the effort to gin up public opinion for the sale.

It was easy to visualize the heavy traffic back and forth between CEI's headquarters and editor's offices of Cleveland's newspapers, with CEI executives delivering editorials and news copy to favored editors and getting material published verbatim.

A brief listing of the cavalcade of news and editorial product was telling:

"We think the light plant should be sold."

"... sale of the light plant would be in the city's best interests."

"The Perk administration should not be censured for its decision to sell the Muny Light Plant."

"Anyone want to buy a turkey?"

"Maybe some politicians think they are making points with Clevelanders by talking about preserving the plant. But in opposing the sale they are whipping a dead horse."

"Murky Outlook for Muny Light."

"Push Light Plant Sale."

"Muny's future still dim."

"The only real offer to buy the light plant has come from CEI."

"This newspaper has said several times that the debt-ridden Muny Light plant ought to be sold....A child could understand the basic facts about Muny Light."

"Anybody wanna buy a light plant?"

"Muny Light sale a mess."

"Muny on Council's back."

"Muny Dark."

"Muny, except for its brightest and newest years, has been a born loser. Nobody, with the possible exception of some unthinking Councilmen, loves a loser."

"Muny Light a loser. The loser should be sold."

"Sell Muny Light... ...and we are convinced that through the years CEI has contributed to the Muny Light Plant's harm."

"All the evidence points to the practicability of selling the plant."

"It is too late to wring one's hands anymore at what has happened to Muny Light."

"...City Council should proceed with hearings aimed at the eventual sale of that utility to the Cleveland Electric Illuminating Co..."

"Sell the smudge pot."

"Don't just sit there, sell."

"Quit stalling on Muny Light. Shed a tear, if you like, because Muny Light was a great idea that went wrong."

"The municipal utility system is in a condition of wreck and ruin, it is beyond saving."

"Muny Light is gone. No one should let Kucinich's smoke screen obscure that fact."

"Muny Light Sale. All candles half off," (Cartoon).

"There was no other way out of the Muny Light mess then, there is no other way out of it now, but to close the sale."

"Enough of Muny Light. Frankly, we are getting tired of the Muny Light issue, and believe most Clevelanders feel the same way. Let's hear about some of the other, more important issues, Dennis."

Enough indeed.

I hold both Bachelor of Arts and Master of Arts degrees in Speech and Communications from Case Western Reserve University. I have studied the effects of mass media closely. There was nothing academic at work here, only the desire of Cleveland media for CEI's advertising dollars.

The concerted effort to disparage and degrade Muny Light was having an effect, creating a sense of the inevitability of the sale. Facts mattered less than constant promotion of the fear of approaching disaster, if Muny Light were retained.

In order to prevail we would have to have our own structured series of messages built around the economics of Muny Light and the economic dangers of utility monopolies and be able to deliver those messages in leaflets door-to-door across the city.

I knew well the risk of taking on the media. I became a target, subject to transference of the enmity they had directed at Muny Light. I dispensed a long time ago with the idea that my political advancement depended upon currying the favor of newspapers, or by agreeing with their editorial or news policy, which wasn't really theirs, but that of interest groups they were fronting. Our best hope to bring to the public an alternative message was the organization I built during the Muny Light petition drive and the Mayoral campaign.

All it took to challenge the institutional power structure of Cleveland was a dedicated group of citizens who were prepared to canvass the neighborhoods, fan out across the city to meet people wherever they gathered and present them with literature informing them of their stake in protecting Muny Light.

It was our ability to deliver an alternative message in person, in print, to affix bumper stickers to thousands of cars, and to place lawn signs announcing personal support for Muny Light which made our efforts visible and catalyzed public involvement.

A leader should show others how to lead, in their own neighborhoods, at work and at play. We brought forth thousands of new leaders, independent thinkers who began, for the first time, to understand the workings of power in Cleveland, and, in doing so, empowered themselves.

The sale hovered despite our referendum campaign. I promised to take the ballot issue through the state courts, to further delay the execution of the sale.

Whether the Cleveland Electric Illuminating Company, the Cleveland media, the Cleveland Mayor, or the Cleveland Council President liked it or not, Muny Light became the central issue of the 1977 Cleveland Mayor's race, with the help of our determined campaign of volunteers from every Cleveland neighborhood.

"CEI will never own Muny Light," I declared, with complete confidence.

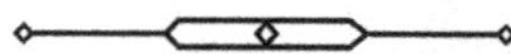

At the beginning of my campaign for Mayor, I arrived at Cleveland Trust's office tower on East 9th and Euclid Avenue with great expectations. I was to meet the head of the bank, established in our city in 1895. Three decades later, it had become the sixth largest bank in America. I wanted to introduce myself to Ohio's premier banker, M. "Brock" Weir, to let him know that if I was elected Mayor, I was ready to work with him, in the interests of Cleveland.

The elevator opened to a top floor covered with plush, money-green, wall-to-wall carpeting, intimating piles of cash, wall-to-wall money. This was the executive suite of Ohio's number one bank, the 33rd largest in America with nearly $4 billion in deposits, approximately $250 of it mine.

I can't say I understood money. All I knew, growing up in Cleveland was that it was scarce. When it appeared, it materialized from nowhere, or from the racetrack. My Aunt Betty, an expert handicapper, would take me with her to Thistledown Racetrack or to Northfield Park and split her winnings, so I could buy school clothes. Aside from Aunt Betty, I didn't know anyone who had money, or those in my family who did, kept quiet, or went to jail for taking money which did not belong to them. I once took an occupational aptitude test as a freshman at St. John

Cantius High School, and the results said I was best suited for banking. The results did not include any information on how to get money, or on how to keep it once you had it.

I did not understand money and I did not understand people with money. They were, well, different. They dressed differently, talked differently, acted differently, and sure lived differently than we did growing up. Then, I went to work as a caddy at Beechmont Country Club, a Jewish country club where successful businessmen and women, doctors and lawyers and others of means gathered. Golfers paid caddies $3.50 a bag to carry clubs for eighteen holes, sharing along the lush fairways Yiddish exclamations such as "Oy Gevalt!" and "Oy vey iz mir" as they slowly advanced toward the green.

For some of the members, a round of golf became an opportunity to do a mitzvot, a good deed. Caddies would benefit, and not only from the fees they received. If a member took a personal interest, it could change a young caddy's life. It was my good and great fortune to meet Mrs. Violet Ludwig Mendes, a tall, thin, platinum-haired lady with a beautiful smile, pretty eyes and a solid golf game. Whenever she saw me waiting for work at the caddy shack, she would ask the caddy master, Vic Popa, to call me forward.

One morning, as Mrs. Mendes and I progressed through the front nine, she noticed I was glum. "Are you all right, Dennis?" she asked.

"No," I answered. "I found out that I won't be able to play football anymore, because I have a heart murmur."

In my freshman year, I joined the varsity football team for the St. John Cantius Jayhawks. I made the team, among other reasons, because I could take a hit and get back up again, and probably because the coach let anyone play who came out for the team. I even earned a letter. I loved football. I did not want to give it up for any reason, even a heart murmur.

"Oh dear. Who told you could not play?"

"The team doctor, after I took a physical." I began to tear up. I looked away.

She put her hand on my shoulder. "I have a friend who is one of the best heart doctors in town. I'll call him and set up an appointment for you. I'll make sure you are ok," she smiled warmly.

"I'm afraid I can't pay for a doctor," I explained.

"Don't worry, it will be taken care of. Let me make the call for you."

Dr. Samuel Hantmann, cardiologist, was Mrs. Mendes' friend. He practiced in the University Circle area. Upon examining me, he confirmed the heart murmur. He also determined I'd had a passing attack of rheumatic fever which scarred my heart's mitral valve. Dr. Hantmann put me on Penicillin G Potassium. I took it every day for several years, to protect against further infections. If Mrs. Mendes hadn't cared enough to provide me with the best medical attention, my health would have been permanently compromised.

Years later, as I was making my way in the world as a struggling student, copyboy, orderly, she would call me occasionally, asking me to meet her to give her an update on my progress. As every meeting ended, she would go into her purse and pull out an envelope with "Dennis" written on it. "Here, please take this, it will make things a little easier for you," she'd say. Mrs. Mendes' generosity proved that there were people who have money who do care for those who don't. It was a valuable lesson, and it helped me move from stereotyping people of means.

As I stepped off the elevator and entered the spacious office, Cleveland Trust's Chairman and CEO, Brock Weir, did not get up from his desk. He was writing on a pad. He looked up briefly, barely taking notice I had entered the room. He returned to his writing. Large glass windows were behind him, affording a panoramic view of the city. I stood at a distance, to avoid familiarity.

"So you're that cowboy from the West Side," he said gruffly, still looking down. Cowboy? I was running for Mayor of Cleveland. I did not understand the instant contempt. I didn't come for an argument. I respectfully waited for him to continue.

"You don't really believe what you say about Muny Light, do you?" He didn't wait for my answer. "I don't think the city should be in the electric business," he said with strong emphasis on the 'I'. "It shouldn't be competing with private enterprise. The city should sell the light system." His tone was less declarative than imperative, more an order than a statement. I could have gotten into an argument. However, Brock Weir impressed me as someone who would remember how he was treated, not how he treated someone else.

Maintaining the space between us, I replied, "The city could operate a light system, if CEI stopped interfering."

"That's the trouble with you politicians," he responded, with irritation. "You'll say anything to get votes."

This was not going well. He was clearly annoyed.

"Politicians!" Harrumph! "You're running for Mayor?" he shrugged his shoulders and shook his head and continued talking into his desk. "It doesn't matter who gets elected Mayor. What happens at City Hall doesn't affect us. You politicians come and go. We'll still be here. Politicians like you just get in the way."

"Mr. Weir, I am running for Mayor," I said, attempting to remain upbeat, "and I simply wanted a few moments of your time to let you know that if I am elected, I will work with you." That was how I had intended to begin the conversation with Brock Weir, not end it.

I could not understand his air of dismissal. His bank had purchased millions of dollars of city notes under Mayor Perk, yet here, there was no discussion of city finances, Cleveland Trust's role in the city, or reciprocal relations. Weir had mastered the art of condescension, not even looking at me. A man not prepared to notice your presence is someone you should never want to ask for money. I thanked him for "seeing" me and then left.

I wondered why he consented to meet, if he didn't want to have an actual meeting. How would I deal with Brock Weir should I get elected? What was this foreboding which gripped me as I exited the building?

Was it Weir? The Cleveland Trust tower? Or was it the land on which the Cleveland Trust tower was built? Legend had it that the bank was built on an Indian burial ground.

CHAPTER 26

Sandy Saves the Election

Because I'd spent much of my childhood living in the Black community, every visit was a homecoming. A shared cultural experience can be comforting, grounding, and enriching. It was imperative, given Council President Forbes' advocacy of the sale of Muny Light, that I return to beloved people with whom I shared a wealth of experience, growing up in the inner-city. Each Sunday morning, Sandy and I made the rounds of Black churches within a sympathetic ministerial alliance, where, if given the opportunity, I would address the congregation and make a brief presentation of my candidacy, with appropriate scriptural references.

The Black church is a religious, social, and political hub, the source of cohesion, strength, and political movements. While I was raised Catholic and found much solace in the Mystical Body and tried to live the principles I was taught in catechism, the Black church, particularly the Baptists, spoke to a place inside me where the word of God is set to music, where my soul dances and shouts "Amen!"

After services in one church, the faithful gathered in the basement for cookies, tea, and a discussion of matters vital to the neighborhood, flooding problems, sewer repairs, general municipal housekeeping. The matter of greatest concern to the churchgoers, indeed, the entire Black community, was the police department, its arbitrary law enforcement practices and its unresponsiveness to confronting street crime in Black neighborhoods. I planned to appoint a Black safety director. I could not announce it, lest it be seen as pandering. I was very clear that my expectations of law enforcement would be color blind, responsive, and respectful. I knew, if elected Mayor, the protection of the civil rights of all Clevelanders, and my success, would depend upon fair and impartial law enforcement.

As the questions proceeded in a friendly manner, a voice called from the back of the crowd "What are you doing in OUR neighborhood?!" The challenging tone, the emphasis on "our" meant a nasty storm was brewing. The gathering separated. A thin,familiar-looking man emerged, injecting racial and sexual toxins into the amiable gathering. "How dare you come into our community when you used a Black girl from the Clerk's office, a member of this church, for sexual favors?"

His tone was menacing and instantly a distraught young woman, who was in fact, a clerk in my office, was brought to the man's side. She was in tears, emotionally a shambles. What was this? I had not auditioned for a part in this play.

"What did you do to her?!" The accuser was relentless in demanding an answer. The young woman's mother came to her side, hugged her daughter, wiped away her tears, and then cradled her like a baby. "What did you do?! Answer me!" the man shouted. "How dare you come to our community when you took liberties with one of our Black women?"

I was alarmed at the ferociousness of the attack. I fumbled for words, as a hush fell over the room. It was not silent for long. Sandy, who stood by my side, comprehended what was transpiring. The charge of sexual harassment was a set-up, contrived to create an incident in the Black community, to turn Black voters against me.

"How dare YOU?" Sandy confronted the thin man. "Who are you?

Bringing garbage into the basement of a church? You are the one who should be ashamed of yourself! I know Dennis. He didn't do what you said. You know it, too. You are a liar, a liar. Get out of here with your lies." In full fury she stepped toward the thin man. "The people won't have to put up with your garbage after this election."

And with that, the thin man, one William Seawright, who I had met six years earlier when he presented me with a suitcase full of cash for Perk's mayoral campaign, beat a hasty retreat. In business, Seawright had a reputation of never backing down. Sandy's fury cowed him.

Seawright had a long reach, from the open streets of the city to the pulpits of dozens of churches, and even to heavily protected government offices where security breaches are uncommon. A County Prosecutor's office held secret indictment papers relating to Seawright. The office had been broken into and ransacked. Cash seized as evidence in an investigation of Seawright had been stolen from the second-floor office of the vice squad at a district police station as Seawright was under indictment for running an illegal numbers clearinghouse.

Vice was a sensitive matter in the Perk administration, given organized crime's ties to City Hall. Mayor Perk had confidence in Seawright's knowledge of the street, even inviting him to screen candidates for Police Chief. Who better to protect the status quo? Local government was Seawright's province, City Hall his business. He held several city contracts for supplying equipment, notably snowplows.

In the basement of the church where Seawright hawked his incendiary charges and then skulked away, Sandy was steaming mad to the point of tears. "The nerve of him. I couldn't stand there and let him say that about you, about us. I'm sorry if I flew off the handle," she said.

"You were terrific," I said. "If you weren't here, he would have smeared me, and made the smear a campaign issue. You saved the day."

The crowd, slightly shocked when witnessing the tense exchange, gathered closer as I said, "Won't she make a fine first lady of Cleveland?" Sandy was given resounding applause.

With less than two months until the election, I was entirely focused on campaigning to both win the Mayor's race and to save Muny Light, despite continued blackouts which roiled my political base. A personal appearance by a candidate can motivate voters and I moved frenetically from one stop to another, convinced that victory depended on my effort alone

After one stop, I received a call about my brother Perry, who had long suffered from mental illness. Perry had jumped through a large second story window at St. Alexis Hospital after being admitted to the emergency room with a drug overdose. His injuries were serious and arteries in his arms and legs had been cut when he plunged through the plate glass. I rushed to his side.

You can run for office, but you can't run from your family. It is where you come from. We may not be defined by our siblings, but we shared common experiences and were all affected, though not in the same way.

Perry was a gifted artist, who struggled with schizophrenia. I was the fortunate one, because people would appear in my life, like angels lifting me up when I could have fallen through life's cracks. Perry was a very sensitive soul, severely impacted by our family's social disorganization. I escaped home physically to avoid the fighting, the yelling and screaming and it had taken me two full years of living alone to adjust to the quiet. Perry, nine years younger than me, stayed, but checked out both mentally and emotionally. I spent long, silent hours at St. Alexis Hospital at Perry's side, aware of the importance of protecting his privacy.

I was cautioned by advisors not to mention Perry's mental illness, because it would reflect on every member of my family, myself included. Politicians and their families have to live their lives like everyone else, without fear of disclosure or ridicule. Not everything can be political and I was not going to deny that my brother, or others in my family had emotional difficulties. You don't grow up the way we did, moving constantly, living in twenty-one different places by the time I was seventeen, including a couple of cars; exposed to constant conflict inside and outside the home and emerge entirely unscathed. You meet life's difficulties and soldier on.

When Perry broke from his self-imposed solitude in his hospital room, he was a lucid guide to a journey through his tormented psyche, his metaphysics, his alternative universe. My political concerns by contrast, were small and my brother was in danger. I have an index of thousands of mental images inside our home where reality collided with his tender soul, any one of those moments could have driven a healthy person to permanent distraction. I did not know how to spare Perry the pain of his dissociation, his nomadic, trance-like walk through life. Instead of judgment, he required love and understanding, art supplies, four packs of cigarettes and several quarts of coffee a day to wash down his meds and two pounds of sugar a week to sweeten the coffee.

CHAPTER 27

A Mayor is Born

I love Cleveland. It is easy to fall in love with this city. I love the Croatian Tamburitzan festivals, where a single phrase, 'Ja sum ponasen da sum Hrvat' (I am proud to be a Croatian) can electrify the crowd. I love the Blaskapelle at the Danauschwaben Oktoberfest strolling to the music, I shook hands with thousands of revelers. I love the ineluctable softness of the Italian brass band of Our Lady of Mount Carmel, the members dressed in black pants, white shirts, and black ties, sitting on an elevated platform lit by the stars and a string of incandescent lights, playing so sweetly you could see the tears of the old-timers glisten in the moonlight.

Those inspiring Poles of Warszawa, little Warsaw, wearing small red and white flag pins crossing the staff of Old Glory, rose proudly in banquet halls, chests forward, canes resting on the back of wooden folding chairs, singing Jeszcze Polska nie Zgniela, they lift praise to Matki Boskij Czestochowskiej and the village of Jasna Gora, home of beloved Cardinal Woytyla who came to St. Stanislaus Church to visit before he became Pope John Paul II.

Cleveland is the polka capital of dancers whirling in sawdust to frenzied drummers and accordion players, until the floor becomes a human top decorated with the blur of faces spinning to the up tempo tunes. I love the calliope-like music of the Czech and Slovak instrumental groups at Ceska Sin Sokol hall, mixing with the draught and the high humidity, causing people to nod off to a sitting sleep at the picnic tables. The excitement of the Hallelujah Chorus of the storefront churches in Cleveland's Black neighborhoods, the converted temples where hymns of paradise are channeled through blue and golden rhythms of the choirs who call forth Jesus Christ. The country western Jamboree star working up an e lek' trik git' tar storm, while men in flashy rhinestone-studded shirts and pretty li'l women with big, puffy hairdos clap their hands in jubilee from flatbed trucks parked in city parking lots.

Cleveland is America come together, dreams held fast in celebration and reverie. When you are with the people, when you take the time to be with them, to speak with them, eat with them, to laugh with them, to mourn with them, to confide in them and let them confide in you, to argue, to agree, to pray, to sing, you learn politics must be more than the wink, the gliding hand, the greased palm, candidates' floating heads, disembodied voices and vanishing media images. Politics is connecting with those voices and spirits singing in every language to hearts and souls. It is reaching out to bring people together to build neighborhoods, a city and a nation.

Constituencies are gathered when you show up. Cleveland is honeycombed with community, ethnic, religious, fraternal, veterans, senior and neighborhood organizations. I reached out and I showed up. I knew the neighborhoods and promised tangible things, a traffic light here, an improved street there, sewers, improved recreation facilities, to deliver specific physical improvements. It showed people I was paying attention to their concerns, and they, in turn, paid attention to mine, a desire for their votes. Slow police response was a major issue. It heightened public safety concerns and, of course, there was Muny Light. It was now a powerful election issue, because it was directly connected to higher electric rates.

State Representative Edward Feighan, the Democratic mayoral candidate, Mayor Ralph Perk, and I made joint appearances, heightening interest in the election. Feighan, though slightly younger, with thinning hair, appeared older and more mature. A former seminarian, he was intelligent and measured in his approach. As we debated across the city, it became clear that his low-key, logical manner was not a match for the passion our campaign exuded, the clear-cut positions and the commitments I was ready to make.

I wanted to be Mayor and I was ready to govern. Feighan was the candidate of the Democratic party machine and, while certainly very capable, he seemed to be running out of a sense of obligation, more than desire. Feighan's campaign was deliberate and paced, ours electric. I bolted from one ethnic event to another, from East Side to West Side. Anywhere people were gathered, I showed up. Feighan relied on the Democratic city organization. I relied on a swelling tide of dissatisfaction, engaging people who had been at the margins of city politics.

Mayor Perk was counting on the power of incumbency to guide him through the primary. Everyone, except Weissman, thought he would survive.

Bob came to me a month before the non-partisan primary election with a poll he had taken indicating we were leading. Perk was in danger of being forced out, and we were headed into a contest with Feighan. His prediction proved true, for on the evening of the primary, Mayor Perk was defeated. The city was stunned. The man whom Forbes had declared "Mayor for Life" ran third, leaving Feighan and me in a closely contested General Election.

A surprise endorsement came from the *Plain Dealer*, which continued to insist upon the sale of Muny Light, and the resolution of the mounting $18.3 million debt to CEI.

The decisive factor in gaining the *Plain Dealer's* support was my interview with editor and publisher Tom Vail in which I convinced him of my willingness to close off organized crime's access to City Hall and to stop its infiltration of law enforcement. Vail was horrified at the Mob's presence and its reach into every area of local affairs, from padded city contracts, to appointments, to open mob warfare.

Three weeks before Mayor Perk's term came to a close, he dispensed, without competitive bidding, unnecessary contracts for computer services, waste collection and professional services which would cost the city millions of dollars and cut-rate leases of prime city land to political insiders. Then, to cap his going out of business rally, his financial advisors "discovered" a $4.5 million "surplus" in the city's debt service fund. Would the money be used to pay the storied interest-gathering debt-bomb utility bill to CEI? No. It was used to cut everyone's property taxes by 10%, a grand going-away gesture from Mayor Perk to the cash depleted city government he was leaving behind. In a year that $4.5 million giveaway from a debt service fund would leave the city wide open to an attack by Cleveland Trust Bank.

The General Election was uncertain until, in the closing weeks, Alva T. "Ted" Bonda, President of the Cleveland Indians baseball club, and partner in the Airport Parking Company of America loaned our campaign a large sum for television ads. His financial assistance helped us win.

On the evening of the General Election, November 8, 1977, Cleveland's Lakeside Holiday Inn, rocked with shouts and cheers of victory as Sandy and I entered the ballroom. I began joyously shaking hands, which came at us from every direction. Calloused hands, wrinkled hands, hands with fingers missing, hands with dirt caked under the fingernails, White hands, Black hands, Brown hands, hands not wanting to let go, hands reaching out. Blue streamers soared through the air and multi-color confetti broke in showers while TV lights focused their heat, center stage.

Sandy and I reached the platform and waved into the searching, cross-cutting beams. Eloise Bryant, a campaign worker, raised up a star-spangled red and black hand-lettered cardboard sign, passed it to me, and I held it in triumph:

"A MAYOR IS BORN"

I was Mayor of Cleveland. At age 31, the youngest Mayor in Cleveland's history. The youngest person ever elected Mayor of a major American city. I didn't want to be the youngest Mayor. I wanted to be the best.

"We want Dennis, we want Dennis," the chant at our victory celebration mixed with cheers. "Looks like I'll get to throw out the first pitch at the Indians' opener," I said laughingly to Sandy. This job would be fun.

There was another meaning to this moment, as I opened my heart to my city. "I remember many years ago, as a very young person, I prayed to God that someday I would have a chance to do something important. Sometimes life in the urban ghetto has a way of obscuring the future. But with the help of so many people, like those here this evening, I have had a chance to share in a part of the American Dream."

Mom and Dad stood beside me. Mom was thin, her once ivory-freckled skin taut, a bit jaundiced. She struggled to catch her breath. Her green eyes spoke defiance of her shaky health. She had arrived fresh and pretty from her neighborhood beauty shop.

The bosses at Werner Transportation gave Dad the day off from truck driving. He rarely took time off. He had spent the day at the polls in his only suit, which hung loosely around his shoulders. Dad leaned toward me, gripped my arm solidly with his work-scarred hands, and said "I'm proud of you, kid. I always knew you would do it. You did good." Mom pulled close for a kiss. My brothers, Frank, Gary, Perry, and Larry, and my sisters, Terrie and Beth Ann, were at my side, as was Aunt Betty.

My God, it had been a journey for us! Living in all those places, always renters, never owners, living through sickness and poverty, daily on the edge of disintegration and insanity, living, but most of all, persevering. What every member of my family understood in that moment is in America, anything is possible, and in Cleveland, the impossible happened. We had traveled from living in a car on the edge of the industrial valley to becoming the First Family of the city.

After the victory reception, Sandy and I headed to the *Plain Dealer* to thank its editor, Tom Vail, for his paper's general election endorsement.

I met Vail in the lobby of the *Plain Dealer* at 1801 Superior Avenue, N.E. He was immaculately dressed in a three-piece pin-striped suit with an understated four-in-hand. His hair was graying at the temples. He was more the image of a senior statesman, a U.S. Senator, or a high-ranking diplomat, than the news boss of a city.

I caught a whiff of the news, as the smell of fresh newsprint from the mail room permeated the lobby. I knew well the full press-run scent of ink and paper, the newsroom aroma of cigarette smoke and stale coffee, and the oily, acrid composing room one floor above.

I had worked in the same City News Room a decade earlier, along with other copyboys with names like Juniewicz, Pasela, Kopinski, Jacobs, Lauridsen, Hatch, Kryll, Weinberg, Fleshin, and Brown, stuffing news stories and headlines into a Plexiglas pouch to send up the pneumatic tube to the composing room, where Linotype machine operators would pound hot lead into words, while the ashen, smoking scrap of the castings smoldered in buckets on the floor.

Five nights a week, I waited for marked-up news copy, while standing behind a battered 20th Century dictionary, amidst editors who dreamed of writing great novels, sailing the Atlantic in an eleven-foot boat, or winning a Pulitzer Prize. Many saw their dreams realized. Now, though a former copyboy, it was my turn. I strode to the pneumatic tube with Editor Vail, to send to the composing room a story which would be on the front pages of newspapers across the country:

"Dennis J. Kucinich defeated Edward F. Feighan in a close race last night to become Cleveland's 52nd Mayor and the youngest chief executive of a major American city."

After leaving the grand moment at the Plain Dealer, I received a phone call from Jack Schulman. "Don't rest too easy," he said. "We have a meeting to go to in the morning."

"What are you talking about? I'm going to take a break, I've been up since 5:00 a.m."

"You'll be up for this one. I just received a call from Perk's former law director, Jim Davis. He was tipped off that tomorrow morning the Board of Control, (which awards city contracts) will put the sale of Muny Light on its agenda, based on the legislation Perk and Forbes negotiated," Jack said. "They're going to sell Muny Light before you take office."

"Can they do that? I asked Schulman, who was my law director-designate.

"They can argue that since the repeal election has not occurred, they have the legal authority based on council approval of the sale last May," he said. "You can kill the sale once you take office, but that's five days after the Board of Control meets. So, yes, they can do it," he said.

I wondered why, after an election which centered on stopping the sale of Muny Light, the Perk Administration would demonstrate such open contempt for the voters they would go ahead and sell Muny Light anyway. Jack and I decided that the next morning, the day after the election, we would quietly appear at the beginning of the Board of Control meeting, ready to disrupt the meeting.

We entered the meeting place of the Board of Control, the so-called Red Room, known for its deep-red wall coverings and other regal appointments. Soon Ralph J. Perk's portrait would join other former mayors in a place of honor in this storied room.

Members of the outgoing administration were surprised by my presence, which suggested a breach of protocol. Jack and I were seated. We witnessed top officials exchanging nervous glances, hushed asides, heads nodding in disagreement. The meeting began. One item after another was brought forward, and passed, but no mention of Muny

Light. We left the meeting without a word. I was unsure if we were sent on a wild goose chase.

Afterwards, Jack received another call from former law director Davis.

"Well, you did it. They were floored when Kucinich walked in. They pulled Muny Light from the agenda. They did not have the stomach for an open fight," Davis told Schulman.

Did we save Muny Light just by showing up? If former law director, Davis, who championed Muny Light in court, was to be believed, yes. If so, it was a new experience for me in the exercise of political power. Sometimes you just have to show up to make a difference.

Six days after the election, on November 14th, 1977, at Cleveland's Music Hall, I took office as Mayor. Flanked by former mayors, congressmen, editors, businessmen and thousands of supporters from Cleveland's neighborhoods, Sandy and I put our hands on our family Bible and I pledged "To faithfully execute in all respects, and in the public interest, all the duties and powers of the office of Mayor of the City of Cleveland," as Ohio Supreme Court Justice and former Cleveland Mayor, Ralph S. Locher, (who during his term had resisted CEI's repeated overtures to sell Muny Light) administered the oath.

It was later noted in news accounts that I added the words 'in the public interest' to the traditional oath. I completed my speech by asking everyone in the Music Hall to join hands in an expression of unity.

Elected independent of both the Democratic and the Republican political machines, I intended to go beyond the partisanship which characterized so much of politics and to call my fellow citizens to a higher purpose. I addressed those in attendance with this challenge: "What an important moment to express the power of our humanity, to participate in that ongoing act of creation which man alone is capable of - fusing the imagination with the barren earth, using human hopes and desires as implements to rebuild a city."

What is a city? A city is not simply the buildings, the granite skyline, a dateline written in an out-of-town news report. Nor is a city an elite group which dictates events within certain geographical boundaries. A city is a spiritual being, a composite of genius and stupidity, sanity and absurdity, sanctity and depravity. It is the collective will of a people, or impassiveness, apathy and inertia of inchoate masses. A city is a statement of ideas and ideals, or lack thereof, motion, with or without reason.

I had a vision of what Cleveland could become. I was impatient to match that vision with action.

The hour I waited a lifetime for had arrived. After the swearing in, I walked across Lakeside Avenue to City Hall as Mayor, skipped up the broad steps, and moved briskly through the tall bronze doors, excited, climbing the white marble stairs two steps at a time, to the second floor, passing under the three-dimensional wooden letters, 'Mayor's Office'.

Six-foot-high, gold-framed portraits of Cleveland's legendary industrial giants paneled the mayor's outer office. A reminder of who was in charge? The adjacent kitchen was equipped with a microwave oven, Corning top stove, dishwasher, washer and dryer, butler sink, and cupboards stocked with linen napkins, crystal, fine china and silverware to supply a private dining room, where Mayor Perk held receptions.

At the threshold of the inner office, I marveled at the tapestried inner sanctum with its hand-carved thirteen-starred flag, crowned by a symbol of unlimited bounty, four cornucopiae; the rococo plaster menagerie of cattle, griffon and Pegasus; the winged warriors carved in stone along the ten-foot-high fireplace with its twin brass lions guarding the huge, gas-jetted logs.

Potted palms lounged wearily over a harlequin patterned, grey and blue-green French provincial couch, banked by two brilliant copper spittoons.

A large brown mahogany desk top, no drawers, was softly accented by caramel-colored velvety drapes which hung nearly twenty of the twenty-five-foot-high room, framing two ten-foot-high windows which opened onto a balcony. A richly crafted blood-red, royal blue and off-white Persian carpet lay luxuriously, nearly wall-to-wall.

None of my constituents lived this way.

It would be easy to pretend to royalty here. Easy to let one's aspirations fold into each gilded layer, to let fantasies shimmer in the light of the enormous chandeliers in the middle of this grand private office, to see one's own light shine from the pearl-textured globes which open to the ceiling. This office could cause its inhabitant to think differently, to become enamored of materiality, so ensnared in the trappings of office to defend its perquisites, rather than stand to express democratic principles. Better to think of the surroundings as expressing the grandeur of government of the people, rather than the exultation of a single person.

Except, I was a child of the city, a wanderer, as my family moved from place to place, looking to accommodate our growing numbers, given increasingly severe financial constraints.

I learned not to rely on material comfort, did not seek it, and, when it presented its lure, I was unmoved. The only concession I made upon election as Mayor was to buy a couple of new suits, which was, for me, a landmark event.

I received a call from Maurice "Maury" Saltzman, an internationally known entrepreneur, philanthropist and the founder and Chairman of Bobbie Brooks International clothing company. Maury played a key role in organizing financial support for my election. He had a compelling life story as an orphan who became a self-made man. He was an expansive thinker, a compassionate philosopher, an important advisor, and a friend.

"Dennis, now that you are Mayor, I want to introduce you to my tailor. He's going to measure you for a couple of new suits."

"I can't pay for them just yet, Maury. I haven't received my first check."

"Don't worry about that. You can pay for them later. I want to make sure you look your best. You are the Mayor now!"

So, Maury and I went to Harry Jacobs' clothier, where I was measured for the two best suits of my life.

As the tailor assessed the fit, I looked into the mirror and saw the same person who appeared before me every morning, but I had to admit there was something about this moment. It wasn't just that I had suddenly become Mayor, it was that I was looking at a newer image of myself.

I didn't feel more important, but in that moment I sensed a new experience of abundance. It felt good. No more shopping for bargains in May Company's basement, searching for boy's size 20. The days of borrowing coats from my diminutive Uncle Lenny or of possessing only one pair of pants for a couple years were over. I was stepping into a new realm, with the help of Maury, who made his own climb, yet ever mindful of the words of George Bernard Shaw in his play St. Joan: "Dressing up don't fill empty noodle."

I always remembered where I came from. New clothes would not change that. It was that memory of my inner-city Cleveland experience which would inform my every decision as Mayor. It would guide my major appointments, as well. Since many of the neighborhoods we lived in were in the Black community, I felt comfortable working with Carl and Louis Stokes to assure that half on my top appointments came from the wealth of talent available in the Black community. If anyone would want insight into my heart, let alone my politics, they need only understand where and how I grew up, and who were my neighbors.

In homage to the pulsation of the street, I placed on my desk a small cartoon, given to me by artist Tom Wilson, his Everyman character, the helpless, hapless "Ziggy."

This little Ziggy, dwarfed by the intimidating opulence and power symbols of the Mayor's Office, appealed knowingly, expectantly: "Good Luck, Dennis. Don't forget us little guys."

CHAPTER 28

City Hell

The sale of Cleveland's municipal electric system, Muny Light, was effectively canceled the moment I took office, although there was an issue that arose about missing documents pertaining to the antitrust suit. At last, I could turn my attention to running the city. I made an unannounced tour of City Hall, winding my way from the basement to the attic. I found city workers asleep at their desks, while their phones rang and rang. Others were reading paperback novels at desks strewn with half-eaten donuts and crumpled coffee cups. One employee was filing her nails while the public waited impatiently at a service counter.

The smell of rock-concert-scented smoke came from underneath the door of one unlit room. Concerned there might be a fire, I opened the door.

In the wispy, pitch-dark room, pinpoints of glowing orange embers suspended in the air. When I turned on the light, two employees of the housing department were toking in the dark. Eyes widened, red-faced, they coughed and coughed until I turned off the light.

As I made my way from floor to floor, through dimly lit corridors and staircases to the roof of City Hall, I could hear faint strains of trumpet music. I followed the sound up a metal staircase through the eaves where a shaft of skylight shone upon a partition, enveloping it, illuminating a solitary man atop a stool, playing solo as sweet as any I've heard on Bourbon Street in New Orleans.

He was good and obviously well-practiced. I complimented him on his artistry, wished him well in his city planning job and returned to my office.

An administration changed, but City Hall had not. This place was in for a shock.

I gathered my staff members in our new meeting room, former Mayor Perk's exclusive dining suite. There was an air of boisterous excitement, an anticipation of great things. There were experienced hands present, like Weissman who, at age 40, functioned as a taciturn Chief of Staff. Jim Barrett, 38, Safety Director, served as an assistant safety director under Mayor Stokes. Isabelle Hendricks, 39, was a neighborhood activist who became Director of Economic Development and our Human Resource Director was Dr. Bancroft Henderson, 42, whom I met when he taught a prescient college course on The Democratic Policeman.

Pete Pucher, 41, was the new Properties Director, whose jurisdiction included Parks and Recreation. Pete had coached me at St. John Cantius High School and taught me one of the most important lessons in life: Keep your promises. Earl Williams, Community Development Director was 44. Law Director Jack Schulman was 35. The city's chief counsel, Jack's brother, Howard was 32. Press Secretary Andy Juniewicz, 31. Health Director David Strand, 33. Morris Pettus, Service Director, was 33. Consumer Affairs Director, Herman Kammerman, 43. Utilities Director Louis Corsi was 42. My Executive Secretary, Blanche Nofel, was 42. Personnel Director Don Bean was in his early 40's.

Each was seasoned, mature and brought a wealth of professional and personal experience to their positions. Exceptionally gifted young people were in that first meeting as well. Betty Grdina, 22, became Community Development Director. Joseph G. Tegreene, 24, was the new Finance

Director Rich Barton, 24, was at Muny Light. Tonia Grdina, Betty's sister, became an assistant Safety Director, at age 21. Each was known for scholarship, activism, and integrity.

As a result of my own relative youth, despite the mature age of most of my top appointments, local wags termed our administration "Kiddie Hall." Our endeavor was not juvenile. We were aiming at cleaning up a corrupt, lazy, indifferent, unresponsive government, to turn it from a mob-connected racket into an instrument of public service.

I shared with the staff the results of my impromptu tour of City Hall and asked them to make their own inspections. When their reports came back to my office, I understood in grim detail the task facing our administration.

A numbers gambling operation was flourishing in the service department. In the city's water department, a daily craps game rattled in the yards, as new fire hydrants, worth close to $200,000 were carried off. New tires were missing from the tire repair shop, gasoline was stolen from city pumps, copper wire pilfered from the utilities department. The city received rebuilt engines that came from stolen trucks. There were irregularities in the accounting of six-figure concession contracts at Public Hall.

Milt Schulman called as we were conducting our inventory. "Remember, I told you to get an audit." He was right. It became apparent, things not nailed to the floor or screwed to the wall had disappeared.

I met with Safety Director Jim Barrett, a police department veteran. "Jim, we need to get a handle on what's going on in the police department. I want a thorough report."

Days later, Barrett revealed that parking ticket money was not being properly accounted. Police were re-selling confiscated guns, taking parts from impounded vehicles, overlooking drugs sold on East 86th and Hough, ignoring a big gambling operation on East 105th near Euclid Avenue. Officers were taking city cars on personal trips out of town. A lieutenant was drinking at his girlfriend's house while on duty.

A captain drew his service revolver and blasted a clock off the lunchroom wall in a police district station.

"Hey!??!" A fellow officer cried out in fear and objection, "What the hell are you doing?!"

"Killing time," he retorted.

More reports: Building and housing inspectors were taking payoffs, city firemen bought their way to promotions by paying senior officers to retire. A community development worker was tending bar, on city time. He said he was on his break.

A gun club was operating out of the water department lab at the five-mile crib water intake on Lake Erie. An adjacent boathouse was used as a rifle range by gun-toting city employees.

Service department employees, whose job it was to collect residential garbage, were privately paid for picking up waste from commercial establishments, using city trucks.

Water department employees were surreptitiously selling developers the right to water connections for new suburban residential areas.

A review of existing city contracts was undertaken by the law department, with Weissman's help.

The review disclosed that elements of Cleveland's organized crime were involved in the city's garbage hauling contract. The city had a garbage hauling contract with a landfill that provided for a reasonable charge per ton dumped. But it guaranteed 900 tons a day of garbage, far in excess of the amount the city actually dumped. The phantom garbage cost the city $250,000 a year, an exorbitant expense. Corruption in contracting was a hidden tax. It enabled organized crime to operate inside City Hall, to appear legitimate, while taxpayers were being ripped off. It inevitably resulted in kickbacks, political contributions and other means of defeating the public interest. The systematic review of millions of dollars in city contracts brought with it the consideration that many of them were either unnecessary or fraudulent.

Jack Schulman informed me that a local businessman had congratulated him on becoming Law Director and that the position "should be worth at least an extra fifty grand a year."

A computer company which had not performed on its first contract was recommended by a city purchasing official, for a second contract. It was no surprise. The official was getting payments from the computer company, as a consultant, while simultaneously allowing another contractor to overcharge the city $90,000 for copy machines.

New Mayor, old City Hall, driven by larceny, penny-ante rackets, and serious criminal activities. The old Mayor? Among the "gifts" Mayor Perk left was a specially-equipped fleet of brand new Fords, one for each cabinet member, a costly extravagance and a clear indication of the former Mayor's vain expectation of victory.

As I gathered the nightmarish reports of institutionalized government breakdown, I looked out a window of my office, across the street, to the Public Auditorium. Silver, furs, books, linen, file cabinets, jade trees, china, glass and even crutches were being taken out of the building by the carload.

What was this?

It was a charity event, the annual "White Elephant Sale," the biggest honest rummage sale in town.

The padded city payroll was imposing a substantial financial burden on our budget. I took immediate action to lay off two hundred bureaucrats, who for years were consigned to a Hades where reports had to be made of reports of reports. The layoffs would have saved taxpayers $5 million dollars a year. However, a judge ruled against them. I had rattled the Gates of City Hell and the Beast issued an ear-splitting roar of defiance, reminding our administration, as were the passengers of the storm-tossed ship in Shakespeare's Tempest similarly warned, 'Hell is empty, and all the devils are here.'

CHAPTER 29

Lien on Me

The most aggravating creditors are those who demand payment from you for bills you did not incur. When the City of Cleveland's budget for 1977 was first drafted in 1976, the Perk administration omitted the $15.8 million owed to CEI.

When we blocked the sale earlier in the year, Forbes and CEI quietly worked out a deal. CEI would get a court order to pay the entire light bill immediately, empowering CEI to virtually shut down the city to collect its money. The city's tills could be raided and nearly 70% of the city workforce laid off by the end of the year, for lack of operating revenue.

I was Mayor less than two weeks when CEI launched its first attack against the city to collect $13.5 million for the light bill. I had correspondence and records I hadn't even unpacked. Jack entered my office to give me an update.

"They filed the lien to put pressure on us before we can develop a plan to counter them. You stopped them from grabbing Muny Light and these guys are not going to give you a pass. CEI could foreclose on Muny Light to satisfy the bill," he warned.

"They wouldn't dare," I responded.

"Theoretically they could, Dennis. Most likely, CEI will put tags on city property, claiming specific assets to sell at auction to pay the debt."

"What does this mean for our finances?

"Let's get Tegreene in here. He has been meeting with the banks," Schulman said.

Joseph G. "Joe" Tegreene had a good, analytical mind for numbers and a sharp eye for detail. I was criticized for appointing him, given his youth. He looked at least ten years older, was uncommonly mature and had an officious manner suited to his essential position of Finance Director. I trusted him. His service as a Chief Deputy Clerk of the Cleveland Municipal Court was exemplary. Schulman, Weissman, Tegreene and I were jointly involved in weighty financial decisions.

Joe entered the office with a sheaf of papers.

"CEI filed a lien against us," I said to him.

"I know," Tegreene replied. "I've been meeting with bankers to discuss rollover of the city's one-year notes. Wall Street is nervous because of the Cleveland schools' financial situation and the Muny Light debt. If we decided to issue bonds, we could end up paying a higher interest rate."

"We are not going to the bond market," I said.

"Not right now," Tegreene agreed. "By the way," he changed from a serious tone to a lighter discussion, "It would be helpful if you made nice with business leaders. They can make things easier for us." Joe was a conciliator. He believed in reaching out to try to build relationships. Of course, most of the people we had to build a bridge toward tried to defeat us, tried to take Muny Light, and were very unhappy with our opposition to tax abatement.

We won the election. We could afford to be magnanimous.

"OK, I'll meet with the business leaders. But on my turf, not a downtown hotel," I said. "Tony's Diner?"

Tegreene and Schulman both laughed.

I ate breakfast every morning at Tony's Diner on West 117th St. and

Lorain Avenue, the crossroads of the West Side. Tony's Diner never advertised. Its owner and proprietor, Anthony Zappone, believed the best ad was the food on the plate, at an affordable price. He opened Tony's in 1946, then threw away the key, establishing one of Cleveland's few twenty-four-hour neighborhood restaurants.

Tony's Diner was the great equalizer. I wanted to send the clearest signal that a shift of power had occurred, to the neighborhoods of the city. There was no better way to drive home the message than to meet at a local diner. The participants would have to travel through the city to get to the diner, to see where city people lived, to get a feel of the grit from whence I came. I was at home at Tony's Diner.

Here, I could deliver, with the bacon and eggs, a pledge to work with business, as well as a promise to contest their untoward demands. As one very well-dressed business titan after another filed into Tony's early on a cold, December morning in 1977, it was easy to sense their discomfort at the plebeian setting. Tony's customers, mostly blue collar workers, looked up briefly from their coffee. Sideways looks, shoulder taps and elbows were exchanged along the counter, in the manner of "get a load of fancy pants." Once I was spotted, Tony's regulars correctly assumed I had a method to a dress-up breakfast. And what a sight it was, Cleveland's top executives crammed into a booth at Tony's. If they were uncomfortably seated, wait until they saw the menu and learned how much they had been overpaying for restaurant food.

At Tony's, food was wholesome, home-cooked, and affordable. Waitresses' aprons were stained from trundling back and forth from the bustling kitchen, where numbers were barked out from a couple of cooks coordinating orders across a hot grill. Here in the diner, I was the host. I could make nice. I could also deliver a message to CEI through their peers, in an informal setting.

We exchanged pleasantries and then, before breakfast was served, I offered something not on the menu. "Gentlemen, I think we can work past our differences. I want to work with you. On the matter of CEI, I want you to know we intend to pay the city's bills. I also want you to take a message back to CEI: "Don't push too hard. I'll fight back."

The eggs, sausage, bacon, cereal with fruit, toast, and orange juice arrived, and the topic promptly changed to matters less fraught with tension. I picked up the check and fed six people for under $25.

I did visit one Cleveland business leader on his home turf. Art Modell, owner of the Cleveland Browns, had supported my opponents in the primary and the general election. He greeted me warmly in his office at the Cleveland Municipal Stadium. Perhaps the only thing Modell and I agreed upon was our love for football and the Cleveland Browns.

"Dennis, I want to be very clear, I did not support you, I supported another candidate. You were not my man in the election, but you won, so you're my man now. I have no hard feelings," he said jovially. "Just to prove it, I'm going to let you run back the opening kickoff at our next home game, against Houston."

No thanks. I was a quarterback, not a kickoff return specialist.

I received an invitation to join another elite Cleveland organization, the Mob. Jimmy Trusso, the head of the garbage collector's union, an Ambassador from the Street, entered my office. Head down, eyes squinting, looking furtively left and right, "We gotta talk," he said in a low whisper.

"Hi Jimmy, what can I do for you?" I greeted him as a friend, and a member of the Teamster family, like my Dad.

"Da boys on da Hill are worried dat you gonna crack down on dem."

The hill Trusso was speaking of was Murray Hill, an Italian neighborhood on Cleveland's East Side, rich in family and religious tradition, jammed with neat, wooden-framed and brick houses with American and Italian flags. Some of Ohio's finest restaurants and bakeries were on the main street, Mayfield Road. Murray Hill was also a well-known hangout for a generation of wise guys, who long controlled rackets in the city, prostitution, drugs and gambling from an area where there was solid attendance at Daily Mass. While Cleveland's

Italian community promoted the cultural, commercial, academic and legal success of its members, the Mob's presence brought unwelcome stereotypes which fraternal groups sought to overcome. Still, the Mob was a reality.

"Wait, Jimmy." I put up my index finger to signal a suspension of the conversation.

I was elected to a two-year term and had no interest in a term of say, 10-20 years. The one thing I learned from Mayor Perk was where to have this kind of discussion. As part of a million-dollar renovation, Ralph Perk had a shower installed in the Mayor's office. It was a place where he could freshen up, debonair he was.

It was also a protected space where he held confidential conversations with the shower running full blast, creating such clatter as to make a face-to-face discussion barely discernible. What with the city for sale, contracts and concessions up for grabs, the mob inside his office, and fights with police who could bug his office, Perk was cautious about where his conversations were held. I ushered Trusso into the necessary room, turned on the water, and shut the door, providing a liquid sound screen to drown out any recording device.

"OK Jimmy, now tell me."

He got right to the point. "Da boys are bein' boddered by da cops. Da heat's on," his expression was pained. "Ya know, da boys have a little card game on da 'Hill,' a little gambling here n' dare, it's nuttin. Nuttin' at all. Dey're not bodderin' no buddy n' dey doan wanna be boddered by no buddy."

Cops, vice, broken syntax, broken legs, the language of the street, when it rolled off Trusso's tongue, it came as an order, not an explanation. He wasn't asking me. He was telling me.

It called for a straight-forward response "Jimmy, you can't ask me not to enforce the law," I said emphatically.

The scrunch on his face tightened. It was a menacing look reminiscent of someone standing in front of you, pounding the business end of a baseball bat in his hand, inviting cooperation. He was unhappy. I stood motionless, waiting for him to speak. The cascading water sounded torrential in the silence. A puzzled look, extended hands, palms up, the nonverbal 'c'mon,' Jimmy struggled. "Dey're not askin' for no speshul favuhs. Unnerstand? Dey wanna be left alone. Who dey bodderin? Huh? C'Mon," hands extended, again palms up, "Who dey bodderin? Dey're not bodderin no buddy! Yuh heah me?" his chin flinched back, "C'mon!"

Well, there was this matter of a gangland war in Cleveland for control of the rackets, including gambling. The unexpectedly dead had piled up in recent years. I didn't want to hurt Jimmy. I couldn't do anything to help him.

I was being tested. This wasn't about one card game. This was about one mayor, one police department, one standard of law enforcement in Cleveland. I was receiving my first invitation to become one of "da boys," to keep the game going from the Hill back to the Hall. We were moving forward, away from pernicious influence, and I was determined not to go back.

"I understand, Jimmy," I said, more than I could let on. "I don't have plans for a crusade against your friends. But, tell them no one is going to get any special favors. I won't tell the police not to enforce the law. If your guys get busted in a raid, they are on their own, Jimmy. "

He stood there glaring, his lips twisted, jaw tightened, eyes blinking. He had to account to The Boys on the Hill to whom, I guessed, he made a promise he thought he could deliver but just learned he could not. He had a lot of thinking to do on his way back to The Hill. This was an awkward, painful meeting, with potential for danger. But, Jimmy and I had a bond transcending politics and The Hill. His daughter had been very ill in a local hospital two years earlier. I visited her often and called Jimmy frequently to inquire about her health. It was a grim period for Jimmy while the life of his beloved daughter was in the balance.

He never forgot I reached out to comfort his daughter and to console him. I couldn't help my friend on this one. I had to break this kind of influence.

I turned off the water and walked out of the Mayor's office with Jimmy in a gesture of friendship.

"Ya gotta see what ya can do," he narrowed his eyes again, recognizing he knew what I had to say to him, and I knew what he had to say to me. He needed something to bring back to the Boys on The Hill, anything.

I understood, but could give him nothing.

The Bible says it is easier for a camel to get through the eye of a needle than for a rich man to get to Heaven. True, except in Cleveland, where the wealthiest corporations had found Heaven at City Hall, in the form of huge tax abatements. Woe betide the person who would raise moral questions about taking from the poor and giving to the rich.

National City Bank had received a total of $14 million in tax abatements in 1976. The Chairman of National City Bank, Claude Blair, directed fire at Cleveland's Episcopal Bishop, John H. Burt, who noted the tax abatement on the National City building cost the ailing Cleveland schools $10 million and the city $4 million, when both institutions were experiencing financial difficulties. Blair promptly quit the church.

When I became Mayor, I tried to cancel the giveaways. Blair was as unhappy with me as he was with Bishop Burt. Law Director Schulman advised me that the National City abatement, as well as another one granted to Sohio, formerly Standard Oil of Ohio, were granted legally and impossible to overturn in court.

Bishop Burt discovered what I had already known, that the wealthiest of downtown interests had a sense of entitlement to public resources and were deeply offended when challenged. What Bishop Burt said was true. National City, one of the state's most profitable banks, was taking tax dollars away from a bankrupt, inner-city school district. While I could not stop the National City or the Sohio tax abatements, both granted by the previous Mayor, I ordered the end of the tax abatement program, creating a jarring collision with local developers and their Council allies, who vehemently objected to my vetoes of four tax abatements, and a veto of an additional multi-million dollar tax giveaway to Sohio. I was accused of chasing industry out of Cleveland, although it had a good head start out of town, long before I became Mayor.

Tax abatements were opportunities for corruption on a grand scale. Millions of dollars in tax revenues, instead of going toward city services were instead given away to certain business interests, who gave political contributions and God knows what else to their elected benefactors. This was a moral hazard. What about the businesses not getting tax breaks because they lacked influence at City Hall? The tax abatement system was a cancer on the body politic, and the sooner it was excised, the healthier the city would become.

Although seventeen labor and community organizations supported my position on tax abatement, the Council overrode my vetoes by a 28-3 margin, then proceeded directly to an "override" holiday party with food and drinks, thrown by the ever-generous Greater Cleveland Growth Association.

Cleveland's school system was not at the party. It was facing a $50 million dollar deficit, unable to meet payroll for its 11,000 employees, planning school closings, the layoffs of hundreds of teachers and cuts in extracurricular activities exacerbated by the City Council giveaway of school property tax revenues. Furthermore, over $15 million in loans from National City Bank and Cleveland Trust were due to be repaid, by the schools to the banks, by the end of the year. This was an example of the immorality of the tax abatement system.

CHAPTER 30

Baby Face

A parade of out-of-town business and development interests came to town to inquire how we might subsidize their pet projects. Blanche Nofel, my executive assistant, frequently greeted them.

Setting a stately and elegant tone for the Mayor's office, she would extend a well-manicured hand and diamonds would sparkle from several rings. Her dark red hair beautifully coiffed, perfect posture, a broad smile, Blanche welcomed visitors with great grace. Mother of three boys, she was the President of Cleveland's largest PTA, at West Tech High School. Wife of an auto worker, her sensitivities were keen on matters of wages and benefits and worker's rights. She had been appointed to the Civil Service Commission by Mayor Perk, where she closely guarded the concerns of workers. Behind the pretty exterior was the heart of a lioness, a fierce protectiveness of her family, and of me. She was the alert guard at the door.

In those early days, Blanche would usher visitors from out of town into the Mayor's office. As I would arise from my desk to welcome them, puzzled looks and questions hung in the air "Mayor? Where's, oh, you are the… Mayor? "

"Gentlemen," she would say, in a tone both forgiving and official, "This is the Mayor."

Yes, the rumors were true. Cleveland had elected a very young Mayor. I admit I did not look the part. I was now 31, and by media consensus, looked to be in my teens. This sparked a great deal of interest among young people who wanted to know how one of their own became a big-city Mayor. It also inspired among elderly politicians fear of the onrushing future.

Why did I appear so young? Genetics, an optimistic outlook on life? I did not drink, smoke or do drugs, didn't spend much time in the sun, and I had boundless energy. I was short and carried a sense of levity about my stature, appearance, and office. The cartoonists had a field day, depicting me in a playpen with blocks or in a crib with local services as mobiles.

When I was introduced by Ohio Governor James Rhodes to Bob Hope at an event in Cincinnati, America's famous humorist looked at me from the balcony of his hotel suite and said "Mayor of Cleveland? Are you sure you aren't the Mayor of Boys Town?"

Premiere entertainer Bette Midler, brought her act to Cleveland, announcing "Cleveland's got a new Mayor, a baby Mayor!" Then in the middle of the stage she got on her back, shook an imaginary rattle and bawled like a baby. The audience loved it when I walked on stage, to her surprise, to give her a hug.

National news, celebrity jests, pictures, television news clips all centered on my youth, so I became known as the "Boy Mayor." Cognitive dissonance occurred when interest groups expected to have their way with "the kid" who ran City Hall.

When it came to business negotiations at City Hall, with Jack Schulman and Bob Weissman in the room, there was no frivolity. Favor seekers discovered a new way of doing business. They did not have to pay. They had only to be honest and not cheat the taxpayers.

One man, whose convention center contract was canceled due to a short count on revenues owed to the city, appealed to Weissman, who dispatched him with this pronouncement "Here's the problem. You are a crook. You know you are a crook. We know you are a crook. Everyone knows you are a crook. We can't do business with crooks." Bob's job was to put the crook on the crooks, so the crooks could not put their hooks into City Hall.

Law Director Jack Schulman, was a study in unflappability. His demeanor was of a man who carried with him a secret joke, a good cheer which lit up his countenance. Those who interpreted Jack's nonchalant brilliance for a lack of seriousness were set at an immediate disadvantage. Jack had accepted the Law Director's position, despite an aversion to politics. He had an instinctive contempt for politicians, no doubt inherited from his father. He had a law degree from Harvard and was trained for business. He was the top appointed city official and was pleased to leave the politics to Weissman and me. Once inside City Hall, he discovered everything was political. Jack's legal acumen, and that of his younger brother Howard, our Chief Counsel and the number two city lawyer, was such that they could successfully challenge teams of attorneys from any of Cleveland's top corporate law firms.

Outside the courtroom Jack was amiable, self-effacing. Inside the courtroom he was feared for his instantly accessible legal skills. His lightning-logic cut opponents to the quick. I had confidence that Weissman and the Schulmans would handle a range of city matters in my name, as I worked to reach out to the business community.

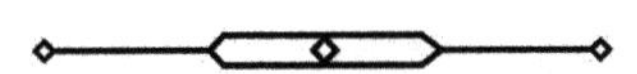

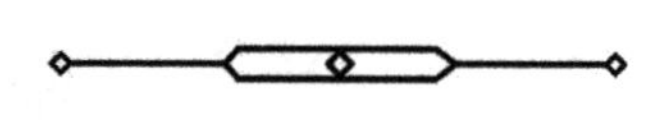

PHOTOGRAPHS

Kucinich Family home at 8110 Finney Avenue in Cleveland, 1957; one of 21 moves the family made over a period of 17 years.

The 1960 St. John Cantius Jayhawks, third string quarterback Dennis Kucinich, #26, (front row center).

Recount of the 1969 Council election, with Scott Sikorski, who weeks earlier had torn down a polling place door so police and election officials could stop the election from being stolen. © The Plain Dealer

Cleveland City Council, 1971, Councilman Kucinich speaks.
Councilmen George Forbes (L) and Ted Sliwa (R).
Photo by Frank Libal, United Photo Company

Carl B. Stokes, Mayor of Cleveland.

Cleveland Mayor Ralph Perk (1971-1977)

Lawrence W. Duggan, Cleveland City Council, Utilities Committee Chairman (1969-1971)

George L. Forbes, Cleveland City Council President.

Election night victory declared, 1977.
© The Plain Dealer - Photo by James A. Hatch

Mayor-Elect Kucinich and Mrs. Sandy Kucinich revisit his days as a copyboy at The Plain Dealer by sending the story of his election to the composing room.
Photo by William A. Wynne - © The Plain Dealer

"Ziggy" - from famed cartoonist
Tom Wilson to the new Mayor, 1977.

(L to R) - Law Director, Jack Schulman, Mayor Kucinich,
(Row 2) Service Director, Morris Pettus and Finance Director, Joseph Tegreene,
(Row 3) Properties Director Pete Pucher.

Mercedes Cotner, Clerk of Council.

James H. Bell, Cleveland City Council,
Utilities Committee Chairman (1975-1979)

Mayor Kucinich and Bob Weissman.
Photo by Tibor Gasparik, City of Cleveland

Mayor Kucinich with Andy Juniewicz.
Photo by Tibor Gasparik, City of Cleveland

Mayor Kucinich with Police Chief Jeff Fox.
Photo by Tibor Gasparik, City of Cleveland

Young members of the Kucinich Administration (Standing, L to R) Joe Tegreene, Finance Director; Richard Barton, Muny Light Commissioner; Morris Pettus, Service Director and Mayor Kucinich.
(Seated L to R) Bill Smuckler, Asst. Properties Director; Eloise Bryant, Mayor's Office; and Tonia Grdina, Asst. Safety Director.
© The Cleveland Press - Photo by Tony Tomsic

Dennis at the Mayor's desk.
Photo by Tibor Gasparik

Blanche Nofel and Dennis. UPI Photo by Ron Kuntz

Photo by Tibor Gasparik, City of Cleveland

Dennis and Sandy Kucinich with President Jimmy Carter.
Official White House photograph

Cleaning out City Hall.

Dennis, wearing a bullet proof vest, throws the first pitch at the 1978 Cleveland Indians' opening game.
UPI Photo by Ron Kuntz

Photo by Diane McNees,
© The Plain Dealer

Mayor Kucinich explaining local government to visiting school children.
Photo by Tibor Gasparik, City of Cleveland

Dennis at Tony's Diner in Cleveland.
Photo by Tony Tomsic
Cleveland Press Collection at Cleveland State University Library

Dennis and Sandy Kucinich meet with City Council President Forbes and his wife Mary at Tony's Diner.
Photo by Tony Tomsic
Cleveland Press Collection at Cleveland State University Library

THE PLAIN DEALER

OHIO'S LARGEST NEWSPAPER — CLEVELAND, FRIDAY, DECEMBER 15, 1978 — 15¢

Cleveland Trust: Pay up

Bank would relent if Muny Light were sold, Forbes believes

By Joseph L. Wagner and Frederick E. Freeman

Cleveland's hopes for avoiding default were dealt a serious blow last night as Cleveland Trust Co., the city's largest bank, insisted on prompt payment today of $5 million in loans.

The five banks holding the remaining $9 million in notes due at the close of business today will be closely watching City Council — which is meeting this morning — but are apparently leaning toward going along with the city's refinancing plan.

If council and the mayor cannot agree on a package, the other banks would be likely to refuse to refinance the notes.

Council President George L. Forbes, D-20, who met with bank executives yesterday, said he believes Cleveland Trust "could change its mind if Muny Light were sold." Mayor Dennis J. Kucinich has said repeatedly he will never sell Muny Light.

Saying "I want to save the city from default," Forbes called an emergency council meeting for 9 a.m. today at which time council leaders would push for passage of:

• Enabling legislation for the 50% income tax hike and a $30 million bond issue with specific language that these issues would become effective only after Kucinich sells Muny Light.

• A resolution asking the Ohio Legislature and Gov. James A. Rhodes to establish a multimember board of fiscal control to supervise city financial administration. Kucinich has opposed a board, but has agreed to establishment by the state of a single fiscal agent.

Last night, Forbes ruled out any referendum on Muny Light.

In a letter to Finance Director Joseph G. Tegreene, William J. Clutterbuck, Cleveland Trust vice president for public investment, said the city's bailout plan was deficient. He appeared to leave the door open for new proposals that might affect the loans.

"While we commend the administration's recognition of the need for additional revenue, we still feel that the plan is too reliant on speculative contingencies which are beyond control of the administration.

"If, prior to maturity, you have any other proposal that will deal with alternatives that have more materiality, we will be happy to review them."

Forbes said this was a reference to Muny Light.

"I spoke to the chairman of Cleveland Trust and he indicated he could go with the sale of the Muny Light Plant," Forbes said.

The chairman is M. Brock Weir.

Clutterbuck's message on the notes was officially terse.

"This will advise you of our intention to present our notes for payment at the office of the city treasurer of Cleveland on Decem-

Continued on Page 10-A

• Ohio legislators discuss a bill that would permit Cleveland to hike the municipal income tax. Page 7-A

• City consultant reports that the Municipal Light Plant will make a profit of nearly $1 million in 1978. Page 10-A

• Andrew M. Juniewicz, the mayor's news secretary, says local news reporters have sometimes been irresponsible or inaccurate. Page 11-A

Newsmen waited in vain through the day for reports on the city's financial situation.

$4,000 payment owed Leftwich halted by board

By Christopher Jensen

The Cleveland Board of Education voted last night to stop payment on almost $4,000 that Dr. Charles W. Leftwich is owed in severance pay until questions concerning about $95,000 in unpaid bills are answered.

The board also voted to begin paying Supt. Peter P. Carlin $50,000 a year to run the 105,000-pupil district. Before being appointed superintendent, Carlin had been receiving about $35,000 a year as assistant superintendent for special projects. Carlin's new salary, effective today, is about $2,000 less than his predecessor, Paul W. Briggs.

The Leftwich bills include charges for lodging, meals and, in some cases, liquor. They were run up by consultants as well as Leftwich, who was, at the time, deputy superintendent of desegregation implimentation, and his staff.

Before the vote, board member George Dobrea said he was appalled at some of the bills and described billing liquor to the board as brazen.

"The lifestyle of our former superintendent in charge of desegregation was not too good," Dobrea said. Later, he told board members, "I think we have a fraud being perpetrated on this board."

The $95,000 in bills are part of the $193,000 package owed vendors including the Bond Court and Hollenden House hotels. About $38,000 of those expenses may be payable, said the board's clerk-treasurer, Michael J. Hoffmann, but the remainder is questionable.

In a report Hoffmann made to the board, he noted "excessive restaurant charges and liquor charges." He also told board members the standard reimbursement for employes is $3 for breakfast, $4 for lunch and $7.50 for dinner. He said the normal procedure is for employes to pay, then be reimbursed.

The board decided to hold the payment until its lawyers can determine what recourse the school system may have and decide when Leftwich's relocation costs ended, and his personal living expenses began.

An order from U.S. District Judge Frank J. Battisti said Leftwich's relocation expenses should be paid, but it did not specify when they should end.

Carlin's salary makes him one of the better paid superintendents in the country, according to a 1977-78 survey by the Educational Research Service in Arlington, Va. That survey indicated the top paid superintendent in the United States got $62,797 for managing Los Angeles' 653,000 pupils.

Continued on Page 11-A

Suburbs shun 'save-the-city' session

By W.C. Miller

Dozens of reporters and businessmen flocked to University Heights yesterday, expecting to see an equal number of suburban mayors discussing Cleveland's money problems.

The television cameras whirred at Temple Emanu El. The businessmen listened. But most of the mayors weren't there.

The meeting was scheduled for University Heights City Hall, but was moved to accommodate an expected large turnout.

But only nine of Cuyahoga County's 61 suburban mayors and city managers showed up to hear an ambitious save-Cleveland plan presented by University Heights Law Director Guerin L. Avery.

"I have seldom seen so much media attention to a suburban meeting," one mayor exclaimed later. "Everyone was there. The only thing was — our people didn't show."

Avery's pitch called upon the suburbs to unite and guarantee Cleveland's outstanding debt. The suburbs would actually contribute money only if Cleveland were to default.

The mayors gave the proposal mixed reviews. Garfield Heights Mayor Raymond A. Stachewicz suggested Cleveland look in the mirror and solve its own problems.

Even Avery admitted the legality of his plan is questionable.

He asked the suburban Council of Governments to review and develop his proposal and to offer

Continued on Page 10-A

$2 lettuce is possible if superbug wins out

LOS ANGELES (AP) — A "monster bug" has attacked the nation's lettuce crop and may destroy half of the big California winter planting, sending lettuce prices as high as $2 a head, farm experts say.

The bug — a budworm — has a ravenous appetite and an apparent immunity to convential pesticides. Mike Wallman, director of the Imperial County Farm Bureau, estimated that unless a new poison proves effective, surviving heads of lettuce could cost consumers up to four times the current price of about 50 cents.

"This is a superbug, a monster that's becoming resistant to almost every pesticide we've got," Wallman said.

But there may be hope. Last week, some farmers seemed to be gaining some control over the budworm in fields sprayed with a largely untested new family of pesticides, poisons called pyrethroids and marketed as "Ambush"

Continued on Page 10-A

Tongue-tied

Thought of discussing sex with children leaves parents with lump in their throats

Cleveland parents, despite the much-touted sexual revolution, are still shy about talking to their children about sexuality.

Even so, parents believe they are their children's primary source of information, but the decidedly un-shy television set, they say, is the second.

The difference between parents and the television set, when it comes to talking about sex, is that it is up to children in most cases to start a conversation with their parents on the topic. The television set has no such reticence but parents do not have a high opinion of what it says.

Younger children ask questions more readily and get easier answers, according to a survey conducted here in the past two years. Parents, however, are aware there are topics about which older children should be informed but which find them tongue-tied unless children take the initiative and ask.

On the other hand, interviewers found that parents in many cases expressed acceptance of more liberal, less traditional attitudes than those they actually practiced.

Researchers suggested that parents' awareness that values and attitudes are changing may account for some of their reticence about talking to their children about their beliefs.

The Harvard-based Project on Human Sexual Development is to report today at a luncheon at the Hollenden House on its survey of 1,400 parents in this area, aged 16 to 60.

They were questioned about their own attitudes and about what and how they tell their children about sexual facts and issues. All of their children were between 3 and 11. About 30 of the parents took part in follow-up interviews after the first 90-minute session.

Researchers define sexuality as all behavior, including life-style, that is affected by an individual's gender and by others' expectations if they are based on gender.

Continued on Page 16-A

Brad Norris, lead attorney in the city's antitrust case vs. CEI.

Kucinich prepares to address Council as the clock moves toward midnight on the evening of default, Councilman White speaking (R)

The 1978 Polish Constitution Day parade.
(L to R) Councilman Joseph Kowalski, Dennis, Joe Tegreene,
Councilman Benny Bonanno, and Sandy Kucinich.

Photo by Tibor Gasparik, City of Cleveland

Dennis explains the connections between
Cleveland Trust, CEI and other corporations.
UPI Photo by Ron Kuntz

Mayor Kucinich with Ralph Nader; photo courtesy of Ralph Nader

Dennis takes his case about corporate corruption to Capitol Hill.

Dennis and committee staffer as Mayor Kucinich prepares to testify at the Congressional hearing on default.

Testifying before Congress at the investigation into default. From left, Julian McCall, National City Bank; Dennis Kucinich; Joe Tegreene, John Gelbach of Central National Bank; and Brock Weir, Cleveland Trust.

Dennis and his parents, Frank and Virginia Kucinich, with Bob Hope at the 1979 Eagles Grand Aerie in Kansas City, MO. Hope presented Kucinich the award for "The Outstanding Public Official in America."
Photo courtesy of the Fraternal Order of Eagles

America's first African American Mayor, Carl B. Stokes of Cleveland endorses Mayor Kucinich based upon a powerful record of appointing African Americans to top positions in city government.
Photo by Tibor Gasparik, City of Cleveland

Cleveland Mayor Tom Johnson (1901-1909)
Photo by Bakody-Berger

Cleveland Municipal Court

JUSTICE CENTER · 1200 ONTARIO STREET

MAILING ADDRESS · P.O. BOX 94894 · CLEVELAND, OHIO 44101-4894

CARL B. STOKES, JUDGE

(216) 664-499

April 12, 1993

Honorable Dennis Kucinich
c/o WJW TV-8
5800 S. Marginal Road
Cleveland, Ohio 44103

Dear Dennis:

Sometimes it is better for someone else, other than the person involved, to write an explanation for that person as to why he did or did not do something.

But there is no one, alive or dead, who could have better written the Plain Dealer column on "Default" than you did in today's edition.

It was written simply. The facts cited were clear. The conclusions reached were patent from the facts.

Truth jumped out at the reader of the column. Emotion did also. There are few who read this article who won't react to the manifest injustice done you as you did what was best for our city and its people.

You have overwhelmingly and fully explained the true history of a villainous political act done by a bank, solely in the interest of self-profit, at the expense of the reputation and well-being of this city.

I was Mayor of our city before you were. Every reference that you offer in your article as being fact, I attest to its accuracy. I am glad that I never had to weigh my entire political career on a single decision -- as you did. I worry whether I would have had the same selfless courage that you demonstrated.

Thank you, Dennis.

Sincerely,

Carl

Carl B. Stokes
Judge

CBS:kb:

Original drawing above by Artist Bill Dotson.

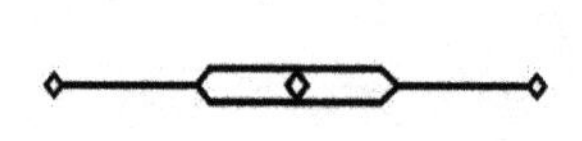

PART TWO

THE MAYOR WHO SAID "NO!"

CHAPTER 31

Still Another Christmas Blackout

Blackout! Muny Light went dark and Christmas disappeared, exactly as it had eight years earlier, almost to the day Muny Light entered into my life.

As Mayor, I had experienced the joy of throwing a light switch and watching Public Square be reborn in a swath of electric Christmas colors, attended by neon angels and fluorescent stars brightening as darkness fell. Days later, the Muny Light system was down and all homes, businesses, and streetlights were dark at the peak of Friday's holiday rush hour.

Lights were restored inside City Hall when Richard Barton, one of my young staffers, ingeniously jumped City Hall's emergency generator with a floor scrubber.

As I had earlier in my career, I called Muny Light operations. "This is the Mayor, what is going on?!" I asked the supervisor who answered the phone.

"The voltage metering transformer, which sends power from CEI to Muny, went down," he said.

"Why? When will the power be back?" I asked.

"We're working on it. We'll be down four, five hours," he predicted.

"Can you get the gas turbines up?" I asked, anxious to limit damage from the blackout.

"Yes, we're saving that power for downtown," he said, reciting the policy of the last administration.

"No, you are not." I replied.

"What? That's what we always do," he said plaintively.

"I want that power sent to the neighborhoods. Get it into Collinwood, right away." I expressed a silent note of gratitude to Chairman Larry Duggan, who years ago schooled me on the politics of Muny Light, the dirty tricks of CEI and the priority on city resources given to corporate Cleveland.

The business community was upset that a city neighborhood, not downtown, had power restored first. They had every right to be upset. They had just launched a new $500,000 PR campaign called, "Cleveland, a New Generation." Cleveland's business leadership was solidly behind CEI's efforts to take Muny Light.

No question in my mind, CEI had precipitated this holiday-season blackout to punish my constituents for electing me. The private power company knew that if I was blamed for a blackout, it would weaken me politically.

CEI continued to promote the acquisition of Muny Light and made it clear that it would "take its gloves off," starting with the filing of a lien against the city as my term began.

My first week in office, I asked Muny Light officials to obtain a second interconnection, so that the city would have a back-up, if the main tie-line with CEI failed. A second interconnect would have prevented a blackout. CEI's Rudolph responded defensively, stating that the request had arrived only a day before the blackout.

It was a familiar lie. CEI had delayed a permanent interconnect for years, as it tried to acquire Muny Light. The fact Muny Light had to rely on CEI for most of its power made the system always vulnerable to CEI's manipulations. CEI did not accept the results of the election and was going to do everything it could to destabilize city government in the manner of oligarchs using their financial clout to rule banana republics. I was onto their game and was pushing back with the help of Jack Schulman and the law department.

The NRC had already documented blackouts caused by CEI on the Muny System. We pressed to access power from outside the CEI system. This was not unusual, since 75% of municipal power systems in the U.S. operated on purchased power. We would need CEI's permission to "wheel" or interconnect to other sources of power. They refused, even in the face of the NRC's order and Justice Department's action on behalf of the city. Another agency, the Federal Energy Regulatory Commission determined that CEI charged the city double interest on the outstanding debt, a $1.5 million overcharge.

The Christmas blackout lasted four hours. It was a warning of what we could expect from CEI. They had become accustomed to running City Hall on their own behalf and they were having difficulty adjusting. In their obsession to take Muny Light, they lost sight of their responsibilities to their own business, which was at risk due to the ever-escalating costs of construction of nuclear power plants.

Sandy and I were preparing to welcome in the 1978 New Year, when I checked the late afternoon edition of the *Cleveland Press*, a feature column by its editor, Herb Kamm:

"KUCINICH RECALL? FORGET IT!"

"Reports keep circulating that a recall election is being sought against Dennis Kucinich – by a group of non-admirers said to be unhappy over the Mayor's seeming stance against downtown business, as evidenced by his recent flurry of tax abatement vetoes."

Yes, I did veto several tax abatements for downtown developers, and, with the support of neighborhood groups and labor, I issued more vetoes in a few days than other mayors had in an entire term. Council overrode the vetoes, but could not, however, require me to grant a tax abatement.

A recall? Excuse me, I just got here. In Cleveland, anyone can attempt to call a special election to recall a mayor, for any reason, or no reasons; the only requirement is to have the requisite signatures on recall petitions. I won the Mayor's office by a margin of one percent of the votes cast.

Kamm's column was a message from downtown corporations. They rejected the election results. Preparations were underway to cut short my term.

CEI and their supporters wrongly assumed that given the choice, I would be more interested in being Mayor than continuing to resist the predatory conduct of a utility monopoly.

Although we failed to disqualify Squire Sanders from representing CEI on the antitrust case, we kept the lawsuit alive and brought back the legal team that Mayor Perk had fired. We intended to win the lawsuit.

"We've got a winner. CEI is going to pay. I'll be as merciful with them as they've been with the city," I promised. I instructed our attorneys to seek a level of money damages sufficient to put CEI out of business. If CEI's executives thought I'd knuckle under to their high-handed tactics, they would soon be disabused of the notion.

We demanded the NRC shut down CEI's nuclear operations until the company agreed to transmit cheaper hydroelectric power from New York, per the NRC ruling of January 6, 1977. CEI was vulnerable to NRC action because of its nuclear power construction loans. If their nuclear power plants were shut down, the company would hemorrhage cash.

CEI and other Ohio private utilities, amidst a million-dollar-a-year image-building media campaign, paid for by ratepayers, also clipped their customers in 1976 for almost $60 million in federal income taxes that they did not forward to the federal government. Anticipating record profits, with a three-for-two stock split underway, CEI continued its potentially deadly policy of turning off power in freezing temperatures for customers delinquent in payments. Only Wall Street could understand a stock split occurring while CEI was in trouble with its payment on its nuclear debts. Main Street understood turning off the electricity and plunging disadvantaged customers into freezing darkness. This harsh debt collection practice was hidden behind the manicured image of the private utilities.

CEI again struck at Muny Light, using a federal court order to interfere with operations. Court directive and clipboards in hand, U.S. Marshals, accompanied by CEI attorneys from Squire Sanders, moved through Muny Light's main plant and then to its yards, methodically tagging generators, boilers, acetylene torches, clamps, valves, copper tubing, two-way radio equipment, typewriters, and office furniture. At other utility department facilities, cars, trucks and vans were similarly attached. Government agents cleaned out the cash registers at the water department, seizing $1,400 dollars for CEI. Such openly mendacious conduct of a corporation against a city government has seldom been observed.

"You can't put a red-tag on a city," I protested to a hastily called City Hall news conference.

CEI's Chief Executive Officer, Karl Rudolph, stated his company's terms through the media, "To terminate this action, and remove the tags, all the city has to do is to pay what the federal district court ordered them to pay.... the court has jurisdiction to eventually sell the tagged assets at auction and apply the proceeds against the debt."

I reiterated that we would pay off the light bill without selling the light system. We developed plans to sell $20 million in "judgment bond," specifically to retire the court-ordered payment to CEI. We were also deeply curbing the spending levels of the previous administration, without reducing services.

As our battle with CEI escalated, I received a call at home late one evening from Maury Saltzman.

"Mayor, this conflict with CEI is bad for the city. You have got to find a way to put an end to it."

"You aren't talking about selling Muny Light, are you, Maury?"

"No. The city and CEI need to stop the fighting. I want you to meet with Karl Rudolph, the man who runs CEI. Have you ever met him?"

"No. I know who he is. Haven't met Rudolph and, frankly I don't care to meet him," I said. I didn't want to offend Maury. I trusted him. It was hard to say "no" to Maury, even if he was asking me to meet with CEI's leader.

"You two should talk," he said.

I had to be direct "What's the point? He wants Muny Light, and he can't have it," I replied bluntly.

"You're making sure CEI doesn't get Muny Light. The lawyers can sort out the other matters. Sit down with him. See if you can establish a relationship. This climate of bitterness is awful for the city," he repeated.

The no-longer-secret record of the company's predatory conduct was enough to justify reluctance to meet and CEI showed no sign of relenting in its attacks. Yet, there was something irresistible in meeting with Karl Rudolph.

Leadership requires meeting with opponents. How else can things change, except through personal diplomacy? Given the history between CEI and the city, if there was even the slightest chance that I could get CEI to back off, it was worth a try.

It was late in the evening. There was no time to consult Jack Schulman or other key staffers. "OK, Maury, I'll do it. It has to be private. Don't expect anything to come of it," I added, feeling a need to temper my friend's enthusiasm.

The next morning, Maury led me into the small boardroom at Bobbie Brooks. Light was streaming through a bank of windows facing the street. A stocky, older man was standing, looking out the window. He was not much taller than me. As he turned to face us, I recognized him. It was Karl Rudolph.

The three of us sat down. Maury opened the meeting. "I know both of you gentlemen, and I am sure you want what is best for the city. I wanted you to meet, to see each other as human beings, and try to find a way to get along, even if you disagree," he said.

I politely nodded. Karl Rudolph sat rigidly, lips clenched, his head down slightly, his elbows extended outwards, his clasped hands resting on the desk in front of him, the same way my uncles used to sit at a long table, when Aunt Betty and I would bring tasty chicken dinners with French fries to the visitors' room of the state prison, where they were inmates.

"Maury called me last night, Mr. Rudolph," I redirected the conversation. "I agreed with him. It would be good to meet."

Rudolph nodded and then spoke gruffly. "Look, we are tired of fighting you. All we want is the money the city owes us."

"You do know we are seeking legislative permission to issue bonds to pay off the debt entirely?" I said.

"That's not a guarantee," he responded. It occurred to me that a word from him to Forbes could move along the bond issue. "This thing has dragged on long enough," Rudolph continued. "No sensible business would let such a large debt remain outstanding for such a length of time."

Yes, I thought. CEI's interference stopped Muny Light from generating its own electricity and blocked the city from buying power at below-market prices. CEI overcharged Muny, let the bill run up, then pushed for the sale to satisfy the bill. The implicit was better left unspoken. If, in the moment, I delved into CEI's categorical misconduct, it would mean the end of the meeting. I demurred. I was searching for a resolution, not a confrontation. But Rudolph's uptight, non-communicative manner lacked the expansiveness essential to create a breakthrough.

"We want to pay our bills, and we will, " I assured him.

"This talk about taking us over doesn't help either," Rudolph said. Surely Rudolph was not mistaking me for Forbes' lieutenant, Council

Majority Leader, Basil Russo, for whom talk of a takeover was a ploy.

I wanted to say to Rudolph, "Yeah, it's OK for you to put Muny out of business and destroy the city financially." Instead, I said drolly, "I'm all for live and let live. That should work for both of us. We do have outstanding legal matters to contend with."

He became stony at the slightest reference to the city's lawsuit. The meeting came to an abrupt end. Maury interjected, with understated haste, "This a good place to stop. We made progress. I got you two fellows in the same room and you've talked to each other! Now you have to find a way to keep talking, for the good of the city."

We shook hands and left the boardroom.

Back at City Hall, I met with Law Director Jack Schulman and told him of the brief, private meeting with Rudolph.

"What? That's not good," Schulman said. Clearly irritated, he shook his head in disapproval. "You met Rudolph. What did he say?"

"Not much. He wants his money. He said they're was tired of fighting us. I didn't tell him I was tired of the fight, because I'm not."

"His attorneys would skewer him if they knew he met with you," Jack said. "Meetings between principals are always viewed as a signal of an intention to capitulate."

"We didn't discuss anything legal. It was simply a "get-acquainted" meeting.

"Get acquainted? Aren't we already acquainted? Don't tell anyone else. I don't want anyone to think you are softening. It would encourage new attacks," Schulman cautioned.

Then his tone changed. "I have something important. Brad Norris, the outside counsel we hired to work with us on the antitrust case, came up with a draft of an action plan for Muny Light. It calls for negotiating a second interconnection, rehabbing the turbines, paying the debt, and gaining access to cheap power. I'm working with him." Jack handed me an outline of the plan.

"CEI hasn't answered us on a second interconnection, have they?" I asked, as I perused Norris' road map to stabilize Muny. "No," Schulman answered.

"They are deliberately exposing our customers to equipment breakdowns," I said.

Yes, I met with Karl Rudolph. I explored a path to peace. Rudolph had no similar intention. While we met in Bobbie Brooks' boardroom, CEI continued to damage the city's interests, and not merely with respect to the sabotage of Muny Light politically and operationally. CEI threatened our budget, our credit, our tax rates, our utility rates, and our ability to run city government. The Cleveland business establishment, of which CEI was a key member, viewed City Hall and taxpayers' dollars, as corporate assets. The economic power they wielded brought political power, used to enhance the wealth of their shareholders. They were in it for their next earnings report. I was in it for the next generation of Clevelanders, to assure a City government they could call their own. While I was interested in resolution, I was also prepared to press forward with Brad Norris' plan.

"Let's push this plan and the lawsuit," I told Jack. We redoubled our efforts to resist CEI's takeover. It was unlikely Mr. Rudolph would want to meet again.

One of Muny Light's most formidable opponents in Council, Majority Leader Basil Russo, reprised the Forbes negotiating strategy of simultaneously selling Muny Light to CEI, while proposing legislation to take over CEI's assets in the City through eminent domain. In a surprise attack on CEI, Russo claimed CEI's assets in the city were worth a billion dollars, and the private utility paid property taxes on only $170 million in assessed value, while racking up a profit of $111 million in 1976, with $25 million coming from the people of the City. Well noted.

CHAPTER 32

The 100 Mile Per Hour Blizzard

A monster snowstorm approached Cleveland. It was our first week in office. This would be an early test of our administration, and our chance to show city government could work.

I called my Service Director, Morris Pettus, who I had appointed a Chief Deputy when I was the city's Clerk of Courts. Morris was steady, reliable, hardworking and well-organized, traits needed in the man responsible for thousands of city employees who repaired and cleaned the streets and cleared the snow. He was lanky, built solidly, and sported a medium Afro. His years of work as an activist in the Black community inspired the confidence of the service department team, which had substantial membership from the Black community.

"Morris, nothing is more important than making sure the snow is removed, ASAP. Get the salt trucks and the snowplows ready. Let's get ahead of this storm."

"OK Mayor. I'm on my way to the service garage. I'll call you after we dispatch the crews to salt the main roads and prepare the plows." This would be challenging, but we could meet the test. We would not run out of salt because Cleveland sits atop a huge salt mine. We had to get the vehicles on the road to hum the City Hall snow mantra: Salt and plow. Salt and plow.

"Thanks Morris, I'm headed to the front of City Hall to discuss our preparations with the media. I'll let people know we talked. Please get back to me right away," I said urgently.

Whirling snow dervishes danced upon the steps of City Hall, taunting me as I took a wide shovel in hand and scraped off a layer of the rapidly falling white stuff, personally assuring Clevelanders my administration was going to be removing the snow from the streets as fast as it accumulated. I had returned to my office to confer with safety and emergency management officials when Service Director Pettus called back.

"Mayor, I have some bad news," he said. "What?"

"I don't know how to tell you this..." Morris had great personal strength yet spoke in a surprisingly halting manner.

"What?! Morris, tell me. I don't have a lot of time."

"We don't have the plows we need," he said, sounding upset.

"We don't have the plows?" I asked plaintively. "What do you mean?"

"We are supposed to have seventy-five plows," Pettus explained. "Only seventeen of those seventy-five snowplows are ready. The rest were put into repairs by Mayor Perk a few weeks before he left. It'll take months to fix them. And some of them can't be fixed at all."

Was this a set up? No, the Perk administration had no competency for such tricks.

"Oh no," I was suddenly filled with anxiety. "Seventeen snowplows for the whole city. We're going to get blitzed."

Pettus continued with the sad litany. "We have suppliers who have not been paid for months. We can't get new suppliers on short notice. One of the suppliers Mayor Perk was working with is represented by Mr. Seawright. The city wrote the specs so that Seawright's client could get the contract. They got the bid. The city paid for the trucks, but Seawright's client did not deliver them."

Seawright again? "Morris, can we, at least, clear the main streets?" I asked, in exasperation.

"No. We need at least another twenty trucks, for the mains. We need fifty new trucks for the whole city. We don't have the plows to do the job."

We don't have the plows. I was beginning to process what it would mean for Cleveland, and for public confidence in our administration.

"I'm sorry, Mayor," Morris said.

He's sorry? I looked outside my windows to see snow swirling furiously. A shape-shifting white beast was stalking the city and would enter our gates without resistance. As it advanced, temperatures would drop, the way they do in a Stephen King novel as evil enters the room. The wind, like a giant ghostly gray wolf, would howl mournfully. The snow would accumulate, blowing vertically, with winds approaching 100 mph, six-foot snow drifts covering Cleveland like a massive funeral pall, a complete whiteout. He's sorry? No, Morris, I will soon be the sorriest man in town.

As an exercise in tension reduction, I raced over to the service department garage on the lakefront, where vehicles were housed. I thanked the few drivers who would venture into the storm.

The wind-whipped snow subsided briefly. I looked out the door of the department shanty onto a soft fluorescent snow sculpture. Hundreds of autos were already stalled in the snowbound traffic on Cleveland's Shoreway. Dim silhouettes behind the steamed car windows intimated people were inside the snow-capped vehicles, some trapped, their cars running out of gas. The frieze disappeared in a blinding cascade of spectral snow, on the wings of a minus-50-degree wind-chill. Legions of icy angels of death streamed in from Lake Erie, 100 yards north.

I felt fear, but I could not indulge it. I had to act. I called the command center we had set up.

"Have the police help those people out of their vehicles. Tow those cars! Hire private contractors." Then, the lights went out at City Hall.

I received word the airport had shut down. Visibility was zero. Thousands of travelers were stranded inside the terminal. The city was paralyzed at seven degrees above zero, the coldest recorded temperature for that date since 1871.

Dawn revealed Cleveland as a frozen tundra. Thousands of calls came to my office. People could not get out of the side-streets to go to work. Those who made it to the main streets were caught in traffic snarls for hours.

Airport management had plows. Then a prankster deity intervened. While the storm raged, the crews became lost on the airfield, unable to determine their location or direction. As a result, snow mistakenly was plowed perpendicular to the main runway, creating a series of snow barriers, making takeoffs and landings impossible.

We didn't have the plows.

If it had not stormed a second time, bringing the accumulation to over twenty inches, what a great improvement we would have made upon our first dismal effort. Nature had overwhelmed the city's limited capacity to handle the snow.

I asked the National Guard to help rescue our snowbound city and Governor Rhodes ordered a hundred and fifty Guardsmen to Cleveland. We set up a temporary emergency shelter inside of City Hall with cots, food and water for stranded travelers including a bus load of snowbound passengers from Buffalo. At the airport, more than 1,000 people were unable to travel.

We didn't have the plows. Poorly maintained salt spreaders pressed into service broke down on the streets, creating roadblocks. The sixty new trucks Council had approved would not be available until next winter.

If it had not snowed a third time, a blinding blizzard, with 100 mph winds creating whiteouts, and wind chill factors of seventy below zero, we could have regained public support.

It did snow. The snow accumulation for the first third of winter was at a record, over 100 inches. When the full fury of the third storm hit, Sandy and I were in Washington, D.C. for meetings at the White House and the U.S. Senate. Joe Tegreene ably commanded the city's response, but no one ever had to deal with anything like this storm. I had to get back.

Sandy and I were finally able charter a plane to fly into Cleveland's Burke Lakefront Airport. As the plane landed we were welcomed by snow piled ten feet high on the sides of the runway. Everything was a splendid white desolation. We could have landed in Siberia and not known the difference.

I used to love Cleveland winters, the crispness of the air, the quiet beauty, the luminescent houses and trees, the shrubbery in magnificent frozen stillness stark against a blue sky, families sledding along the Edgewater Lakefront Park. I cringed as I viewed the storm damage from a National Guard helicopter. I saw thousands of cars stuck on hundreds of streets, commerce garroted by ice, a winter blunderland. Where were the snowplows and salt spreaders?

Only two months ago, it was Perk's snow. Now it was mine. The Old Testament cautions, "Pray that your plight not be in the winter." God, I'll take my chances with spring rains and flooded basements and even power failures on hot summer nights. But snow? Impassable, and as cold as the hearts of those angry callers who claimed I was personally responsible for the strokes, the heart attacks, the man freezing to death in his car on a vacant lot, the auto accidents, the frozen water pipes, the closed schools, the closed airport. I was facing my first crisis in confidence.

Then, a major water main broke and put a neighborhood under icy water. I was living inside a disaster movie and someone else was writing the script. I arrived just as hell broke loose.

If I'd had more life experience, I could have better appreciated the wisdom of Buffalo Mayor Jimmy Griffin, who, knowing a devastating storm was slouching across the lake toward his city, simply told his constituents to "Stay at home and open up a six-pack."

The snow would remain on many streets until warmer weather melted it. On the positive side, Cleveland could look forward to a white Easter.

Cleveland's snowstorm was uppermost in my mind, even as Sandy and I were in Washington to meet the President. The novelty of being American's youngest Mayor caught the attention of the White House, who contacted U.S. Senator Howard Metzenbaum, a Democrat from Ohio, to set up the appointment with President Carter in the Oval Office.

As Sandy and I prepared for the visit, my thoughts went back to the neighborhoods my family lived in, when the White House was an abstraction. I had seen President Kennedy up close when he was a candidate appearing at a Labor Day event in 1960, at Euclid Beach Park. I saw him again, from a distance, when our St. John Cantius senior class visited Washington, D.C. in 1963, a little more than a week before his assassination. I later rubbed shoulders with President Lyndon Johnson during a Cleveland rally. Meeting the President in the Oval Office was a fantasy.

This was an opportunity to advance the needs of Cleveland and other cities. I prepared for the trip by drafting a proposal to rebuild America's infrastructure, to place it directly in the President's hands.

When the day arrived, we were escorted by Senator Metzenbaum into the Oval Office. I wondered at the pale-yellow colors of the room, the curved doors, the President's desk, trying to take it all in. Sandy and I were positioned next to the President. Senator Metzenbaum made the introduction to President Carter. A throng of photographers appeared, captured the moment, and then vanished.

I presented my infrastructure proposal to the President, who handed it to his aide. President Carter mentioned he had heard from people in the Transportation Department that I had refused $41 million in federal money for an elevated rail transit system known as a "People Mover," a driver-less rail vehicle to circulate through downtown. I had studied the People Mover and realized that it was a solution for a problem Cleveland didn't have. Cleveland needed improved public transit in the form of wider distribution of bus service, increased frequency and lower fares. I felt the People Mover was a waste of federal taxpayers' dollars. The federal money was there for the taking, but I refused it. Money was less available for practical things.

"No one turns down federal money. The Department of Transportation doesn't know what to do. They say no one has turned down their money before," President Carter smiled. He then said a few words to his assistant, who nodded.

There was a question I had been waiting to ask this President, or for that matter, any President, and it was, "What is it like to be President?"

His answer reflected humility and the experience of a year in office. "It's like this. Everyone thinks since you are President, you have all this power. Well, in some matters, you do. But sometimes I give an order, and the bureaucracy is so big, I never know if it gets carried out. That's what it is like." Humility is an important character trait in public officials. President Carter possessed it in abundance; when you are in constant battles, it is a hard practice.

CHAPTER 33

The Chief

Sometimes your best is none too good. I hired a new Police Chief, Richard Hongisto, the Sheriff of San Francisco County, to help reform the Cleveland Police Department, deal with police corruption and brutality and improve police response time. Weissman had recommended Hongisto. Bob and I agreed that ingrown police department corruption needed someone from outside the city for a clean-up. Hongisto had demonstrated courage when, as Sheriff, he refused to evict tenants of a San Francisco apartment building, even under threat of court action. He came to Cleveland for a lengthy interview in the Red Room with me and a few cabinet members. I invited Sandy to sit in.

I began the meeting with a question to learn his philosophy of government.

"What do you believe in?"

"Nothing," he said. His response surprised everyone in the room. Was he a philosophical anarchist, a nihilist, a Zen sheriff? In the give-and-take, he expressed a willingness to take on the challenge of reforming a generally unresponsive police department. A light-hearted banter settled in, then the meeting broke up, with most appearing satisfied we had the right man.

Sandy remained silent during the meeting. She took me outside the Red Room, closed the access door, looked me in the eye, held up an index finger and warned, "Watch him! He is not what you think he is. He doesn't believe in anything, except his own interests. I see trouble."

"Trouble? Sandy, we have an out-of-control police department. I can't go inside the department for a Chief. Weissman said Hongisto is one of the best prospects he's seen."

"Watch him," she repeated, in a sharp tone. Sandy and I had been married a year and I had come to respect her intuitive capacities. She wasn't new to politics. Her father, Dan McCarthy, had been President of the local Bricklayers Union and was now a state official of the U.S. Department of Labor. Sandy inherited her sense of informed caution from him. I considered her negative reaction to Hongisto, but I did not see what she saw. I offered Hongisto the job. He accepted.

The only question he asked me was if he could have city business cards printed, post-haste. "We'll take care of it," I said, asking safety officials to place the customary order through the city print shop.

I never get bored, and I've been known to enliven the work environment with elaborate practical jokes, like when I made a fake radio broadcast to convince Weissman his political activities as a student in the 1950s were under scrutiny. Then, there was my good friend in Council, who on April 1st, had to suffer a private gasp over a fake arrest warrant for non- payment of a rather substantial collection of delinquent parking tickets.

As a practical joke to demonstrate working with me would be fun, I had an aide present Chief Hongisto with a sample of a "new" business card, with my name, not his, front and center in large type, and his name in small type in the corner of the card. Such a card to a top level official, as a matter of City business, would have never in reality been printed. It was a joke.

I detected a hint of vanity when I met Hongisto. A good-natured ribbing could spark an upbeat, high-spirited interaction with others in our administration where a bit of humor helped balance the seriousness of our tasks. When the Chief came to back me with a question about his business card, I would let him in on the game, we would have a great laugh, and bond.

If only I had known the Chief did not have a sense of humor.

The media gathered in my office where I introduced Richard Hongisto, of San Francisco, as "The Best Police Chief in the United States."

A few days later, Jack Schulman said during a snow storm he had been offered a ride home from the airport by the Chief. Throughout the ride Hongisto kept asking Jack what various people thought of him. "He reminds me of some criminals I defended. They were constantly scheming, and that is the way he thinks. He is paranoid. He may be your Police Chief, but I won't be in a room with him without a witness present," Jack said.

"Come on, Jack, give him a chance," I appealed.

Jack shook his head. "Watch yourself with this guy. He thinks like a criminal."

What did Jack and Sandy see that I could not?

Undeterred, I introduced "The Best Police Chief," a reformer, to meetings with editors, neighborhood groups, and district police.

His sympathies with San Francisco's legendary liberalness spawned rumors regarding his sexual orientation. Detractors inside the police department protested that I had hired a "homosexual Police Chief." The bigotry of the times was strongly against any person rumored to be gay. It was especially an issue with my conservative Catholic constituency. I was not to be dissuaded by popular prejudice.

It made no difference whatsoever to me whether or not Hongisto was gay. A person's sexual orientation is a matter of personal privacy, not grist for the City Hall gossip machine. The gay rights movement at that time was stirring in San Francisco through the power of Harvey Milk's moral suasion; to observe the movement had not arrived in Cleveland is to greatly understate the moment.

Members of Cleveland City Council, learning of Hongisto's advocacy of the rights of gays, objected with the language of homophobic bigotry, as did the leader of the Cleveland Police Patrolmen's Association.

A wavy-haired, well-manicured television commentator uncrossed his legs, stood and sidling up to the new Chief, whispered into a live microphone in confidential tones, "Tell us, once and for all, Chief, are you a homosexual?"

"No," the Chief replied to the live television audience. It didn't matter, the rumor was proof enough. The news media coverage heightened the question. As a sexually-charged controversy roiled, callers to my office were outraged at his appointment.

"How could you, a Catholic, hire him?"

"I'm through supporting you. If you hired a homosexual, you must be one, too."

"Why can't you get someone from inside the police force?"

"Can we trust him around our younger policemen?" a top police union official rasped. A councilman called for an investigation to see if, "what they say is true."

My parents brought us up to be inclusive. I understood from an early age not to judge people by the color of their skin, their ethnicity, their religion, their gender, or their sexual orientation. The twenty-one different places in which we lived as renters were very diverse and we were taught to honor, not criticize differences and to stand up to prejudice. In some neighborhoods, we were the minority and experienced stereotyped characterizations because we were White.

As my career advanced, at each stage I faced ridicule of my youth or my height, another lazy way to dismiss a person. Once you develop a personal resistance to ridicule or discrimination, it is easier to stand up for others who face it.

The media and the political establishment were latching onto controversial innuendo surrounding the Chief, in order to lure the public into a political blind alley where imaginations ran wild with titillation. I never had much interest in who was partnered with whom. I was concerned with those apparently upstanding, church-going politicians who were in bed with special interests and the mob. Opposition to Hongisto was less related to sexuality than police department insularity and resistance to reform.

Police union contract talks had not been resolved under Mayor Perk. The Perk Administration had promised a windfall from the sale of Muny Light. Several unions deferred job actions, hoping the Muny sale proceeds would help pay for their wage demands.

Cleveland's patrolmen had been working without an agreement since June of 1977. The Cleveland Police Patrolmen's Association obtained sole bargaining authority, replacing the Fraternal Order of Police. We began negotiations with the CPPA as soon as we took office. Here, Weissman's experience as a top labor official was invaluable. We wanted city workers to be well paid, but the CPPA expressed a militancy aimed less at increasing wages and more at dictating law enforcement policy. It's crucial to have advice from those on the front line of law enforcement, but the city charter places ultimate responsibility for public safety with the Mayor.

As Hongisto arrived, an epidemic of "blue flu" infected one shift after another. Police weren't showing up for work. The police department was, in effect, on strike. The timing of "blue flu" with the appointment of a new Chief was unmistakable. I knew I had to assert the charter authority of the mayor on matters of law enforcement. I was prepared to use the CPPA's sudden and illegal job action to replace the recalcitrant workers with new hires, if necessary. I believe police must be well paid, and well controlled by civilian authority.

Council President Forbes entered the fray, and without any legal standing, offered wage and benefits increases to the CPPA. Council intervention in criminal law enforcement matters and contract talks invited further corruption of the police department.

I objected strongly, stating, "If Councilmen can play games with rezoning and liquor licenses, think of what they can do by manipulating labor negotiations."

I asked Chief Hongisto to sign necessary warning letters to striking policemen, requiring them to return to duty. Surprisingly, he balked. "I don't know enough about the circumstances of the strike," was his only response.

"Chief, it's like this," I said. "They didn't threaten Perk with a strike. He had a year and didn't come up with a wage deal. They are testing us, because I brought you in from out of town. You are the circumstances, Chief. I need you to sign the letters, now!"

After much negotiation, the new Chief agreed to sign a toned-down version of the letter to police. Police, facing discharge, returned to work. Talks with the CPPA resumed. Relations with the Chief, however, became a serialized nightmare.

CHAPTER 34

Paper Cash, Paper Bags

On January 12, 1978, the *Plain Dealer*, in a copyrighted story, ran this extraordinary headline:

"FORBES ADMITS TAKING MONEY FROM CARNIVAL GAMBLING FIRM, USED FUNDS TO HELP WARD CLUB CHARITIES, HE SAYS"

"For more than three years, City Council President George L. Forbes, has quietly assisted and accepted cash from a Cleveland carnival company which runs illegal gambling and raises funds for Democratic ward clubs, the *Plain Dealer* has learned."

According to the *Plain Dealer*, the Council President promoted Sebring Exhibit and Supply Company to the other councilmen. He helped secure carnival permits from the building department. He provided legal defense for Sebring employees accused of illegal gambling. His driver, a Cleveland police officer, became Sebring's Security Chief.

The *Plain Dealer* also reported that Forbes accepted paper bags full of cash, thousands of dollars, from Sebring. He asserted that he gave the money to carnival sponsors, charities, or Democratic ward clubs, but political organizations were not recognized as tax exempt charities and, therefore, could not legally receive proceeds from carnival gambling operations.

Most of the illegal Las Vegas-style gambling at carnivals took place in the Black community on Cleveland's east side. One former Sebring employee, speaking of carnival-goers in the Black community, told the *Plain Dealer*, "You can rob 'em blind and they'll come right back."

The County Prosecutor John T. Corrigan, subpoenaed Forbes' records and those of eight present and former Members of Council, requiring them to deliver the files to Cleveland Police to determine what had happened with the carnival proceeds.

The investigation began in May of 1977, six months before I became Mayor, when Cleveland Police Sgt. Joyce filed his report of his personal encounter with Officer Watkins and his telephone encounter with Forbes. The carnival probe was now in full swing, with the Cleveland Police, the FBI, and the County Prosecutor's office working in concert. Since the investigation was already progressing, and since it involved a large number of Councilmen, including my political arch foe, Council President Forbes, I recused myself from it and instructed city safety appointees and law appointees to keep a distance from the probe, hand's off and let it take its course. I had no desire nor any intention to smear Forbes.

Our administration was gearing up an attack on organized crime with a new unit focused on illegal gambling, arson, narcotics, loan-sharking, and white collar offenses. Jack Schulman was challenging the mob-tainted vending machine business. It had extensively infiltrated the tavern industry through millions of dollars in loans. Financial assistance had been given to bar owners in exchange for the placement of pinball, jukebox, and other lucrative vending machines in their establishments. We announced legislation to ban such loans, because, through them, the mob was building the financial base of a criminal syndicate.

When we began to crack down on the vending machine racket, Jack Schulman's life and his family's personal safety were threatened. Mob elements saw Schulman's efforts as cutting into the profits of local crime bosses, at least one of whom was on trial for the murder of Danny Greene, a colorful local figure who ran rackets from the Cleveland Port.

Hongisto and I met to discuss Schulman's security situation. The Chief changed the subject and asked what we were going to do with the carnival kickback case.

"It's already under investigation. There is no need for us to do anything," I said to Hongisto. This was the only carnival-related conversation I ever had with him.

Ten days later, after a newspaper account reviewed the progress of the carnival investigation, Hongisto, inexplicably, charged that he had been blocked from expanding the carnival probe. This had to be news to the Cleveland Police Intelligence unit, who, along with the FBI and county prosecutors had already expanded the probe to eleven present and former Councilmen, including Forbes.

The briefest review of the public record would have demonstrated that no one could block a matter under investigation by multiple government agencies. Since the newly arrived Hongisto falsely claimed that he was stymied in a high-profile investigation, the *Cleveland Press* ran screaming front-page headlines, on Hongisto's allegations of 'unethical conduct':

WHAT HONGISTO CHARGES:
PRESSURED TO CURTAIL AN INVESTIGATION
PROMOTE A POLITICAL FRIEND
IGNORE AN ENEMY

I had been told Hongisto was spending late evenings at a watering hole for local reporters. I assumed it was an effort to ingratiate himself with the media. I wondered if perhaps after a few drinks he spewed out frustrations distorted at the bottom of his glass.

After reading the published charges, I summoned Hongisto to my office. Schulman, Weissman, and Juniewicz sat in. I asked the Chief to provide proof of his sensational charges of unethical conduct. Two of the Chief's assertions involved personnel matters. The third charge, curtailing the carnival investigation, bordered on the insane.

My reputation was on the line. It was critical to call him to account for the charges published in his name. He walked into my office, with a small clutch of papers under his arm. He looked harried. He sat down.

"What is all this?" I asked, indignantly, holding up the newspaper headline.

For a few moments, he appeared to be gathering his thoughts. Then, without a word, he suddenly got up and ran out of the room. I followed him to the elevator; by now a group of reporters and TV cameramen made the elevator a merry mix. I asked the Chief to return with me to the Red Room.

Transparency in government is always to be desired, but, as I learned, personnel matters are better resolved privately, just as hindsight is better than foresight.

As the media watched, I demanded the Chief produce proof of the allegations. "If you do it, if you reveal it all, if any wrong has been done, I'll bring those individuals to justice. But if you can't do it right now, I really think you ought to resign." No proof was offered. I placed the Chief under suspension until he came up with proof. I took no exception to news reports which described the session as bizarre.

It was Good Friday, 1978. I had been in the Mayor's office only four months. City Hall was closed, except for dozens of reporters in the Red Room, a two-story ceremonial office paneled with the portraits of former Cleveland mayors. The room was bisected by a thirty-foot-long mahogany dinner table, purchased from the bishop of the Cleveland Catholic Diocese.

I walked into the Red Room, and, through the courtesy of live television, into the living rooms of a city atoning for its sins, dyeing Easter eggs, stuffing baskets with multi-colored sugar candy and chocolates, smoothing out Sunday-best for services celebrating the Resurrection of Jesus Christ, Alleluia! Across the city, worshipful penitents crowded churches, revering the crucifix, His suffering! There was spiritual calm, broken by the irrelevant conflicts of politicians.

I went live on the Six O'Clock News, and based on the Chief not backing up his charges, fired "the Best Police Chief in America." I had let public life become as a self-contained vignette in a glass ball, and I was shaking up my own landscape, energizing the tempest Hongisto had conjured.

I forgot the world outside City Hall. I was more intent on affirming the power of the Mayor's office and disciplining an insubordinate Police Chief. I don't believe the Chief was corrupted or bought off. He was letting off steam. His remarks reached print. He was in trouble, had to save face, and upped the ante, creating a full-blown municipal crisis in an already volatile political environment.

The man I brought in to help with the clean-up had instead unloaded a garbage truck full of political debris on the front steps of City Hall. My commitment to honesty and integrity were unchanged. I felt like the kid who wore a white suit to a mud-wrestling contest. I can't deny though, that two of my most trusted advisors, Sandy and Jack, had seen this trouble coming.

Livid at the outrageousness of the charges, I dismissed the Chief I had recently hired.

Fire the Police Chief? I couldn't hear the people screaming at their television screens, as they were eating their dinner, "Dennis! Who cares? It's Easter time, for God's sake. Shut up!" By Monday morning, callers to my City Hall office were ready to fire me.

Hongisto had accused my administration of trying to *hinder* the carnival investigation. At the same time, George Forbes said Hongisto told him I was *promoting* the carnival investigation - trying to put him in jail.

These contradictory statements were precisely the reason I avoided politicizing the investigation of Forbes and the rest of Council. This was a criminal investigation with allegations of payoffs, charges of theft in office, and alleged criminal misuse of public authority to provide assistance to crooked carnival operators who would also short-cut safety rules on their rides. It was the biggest scandal to hit Cleveland City Hall in years. If the investigation resulted in removal from office and jailing of several city legislators, so be it. The law is the law.

Hongisto's charge brought me to center stage, attacked simultaneously for blocking and for prosecuting the investigation. The contradiction summed up the convoluted state of City Hall snake-pit politics.

Forbes' charge that I was behind the investigation were repeated at dozens of meetings throughout the Black community, where his allies in Council insisted that I had instigated the carnival probe. Racial passions were stirred with images of a White Mayor trying to put Black Councilmen in jail.

The allegations of racially motivated prosecution were a political maneuver to damage me in the Black community, and to help Forbes regain the control of City Hall he lost when Perk was defeated. Forbes understood better than anyone the sensitivities of the Black community when it came to racial injustice, and he stirred the pot to political effect.

Insight into the color of Forbes' political palette may be discerned from his candid public explanation of pretend-feuds he occasionally had with Mayor Perk when they were top City Hall officials.

"A lot of you may have thought that Ralph Perk and I were enemies. We're really friends. We helped start a phony fight, so that I would be all right with Black folks and he would be all right with White folks, so both of us could get re-elected. But in Ralph's case, it failed," Forbes recounted with a touch of hilarity.

One prominently published fictitious report in the *Press* claimed I had announced at a cabinet meeting I was going to "put the screws" to the County Prosecutor's office, over which I had no authority, statutory, political or otherwise, to pursue indictments of Forbes and the Council.

After I announced the Chief's dismissal, many councilmen involved in the carnival kickback case, who Hongisto supposedly was prevented from investigating, enthusiastically announced their support for him. One councilman claimed at least twenty of thirty-three members supported Hongisto

"It'll be bad for the city if he leaves. He's done a good job. The Chief is well-liked by the people in the city, as well as the men in the department. He's been responsive and hard-working," said safety committee Chairman, Caesar Moss.

Hongisto's firing set off ringing declarations of support from the most unlikely quarters. This demonstrated the overwhelming desire of my political opponents to pile on, no matter who or what was in the heap. Accolades for the Chief came from lawmakers under investigation and from police officials who discovered, to my consternation, that the outsider, Hongisto, presented no threat to police insiders. Hongisto, once fired, gained popularity in the city's political class, because he could be played to accommodate any narrative, no matter how outrageous, to destabilize our administration.

I was getting rocked by a political tornado that I had helped to spawn. I thought back to the danger presenting itself guilelessly at my doorstep three years earlier. A carnival sponsor had attempted to give me an envelope containing a cash gratuity, simply for signing a permit. I had declined the envelope. If I had accepted it, I too would have been imperiled and in the dock, right alongside George Forbes.

CHAPTER 35

Easter "Shotgun" Sunday

I am the Resurrection and the Light," a priest said, reading from the scriptures at the Easter Sunday Mass Sandy and I attended. It was the perfect day for us to embrace renewal with a visit to the tropical environment of Cleveland's horticultural wonderland, the Rockefeller Park Greenhouse. There, underneath an expansive skylight, thousands of colorful plants brought to Cleveland from all over the world were a reminder that nature exists beautifully outside the unnatural realm of politics, and of the importance of seeking beauty, appreciating it, embracing it, and holding it in your heart.

Accompanying Sandy and me were Richard Ben-Veniste, a Watergate prosecutor, and his friend, folk singer Mary Travers, of Peter, Paul and Mary fame, who was performing in town. I was proud of Cleveland and the City Greenhouse. I wanted to share the beauty of our city with our illustrious visitors. Afterwards, we dropped off our guests at their hotel and headed home.

As we pulled into the driveway, I waved at the policeman guarding our house. He sat alone, in an unmarked police car. Our dog, Daisy, part German shepherd, part Husky, was barking loudly, perhaps to welcome us?

"Sandy, I'm going upstairs to bed," I said, exiting the car, opening the door of the house, and climbing the stairs to our second floor bedroom, with Sandy close behind.

Suddenly, loud noises and shouts came from the side of the house. Moments later, our police guard pounded at the door. I answered it. He looked disheveled. He was hyperventilating.

"Mayor, … just chased … away from … side window." Breathing deeply, he bent over, his hands on his knees. "He had … a shotgun! Tried to tackle … threw awning at me … got over … fence. Lost him."

Sandy and I exchanged fearful glances, and invited the stricken policeman to step inside the house to catch his breath and to calm down.

"Sorry he got away." He was very upset. He was stationed at the house specifically to prevent any attempt at violence.

"It's OK, we're fine," I reassured him, as I stepped away from the windows.

"How do you want me to handle this, Mayor? Want me to call for backups?"

"No need to. He's gone. You saw a shotgun?"

"Yeah, yeah, he had one. I missed grabbing him. He threw an awning at me that was sitting at the side of the house and then jumped over the fence, by the trees. I couldn't shoot. He escaped through bushes. I couldn't see where he went."

"You did the right thing," I patted his shoulder, imagining what would have happened if he had been shot or had shot someone.

"This could cost me my job," he said, still in a panic.

"It's all right, let's not make a big deal here." I explained that whatever security problems we might have now, once an incident is broadcast, we would have even more worries. It puts ideas in people's heads. "Let's forget it, OK?."

"Ah, Mr. Mayor," he reminded me, "I still have to file a report." Word would get out.

"Of course. Well, I am glad you are OK. Be careful," I said, as he returned to his post.

Sandy and I sat down, shaken. We held fast to each other. "Daisy was barking. You went upstairs so fast. If you had stayed downstairs…" she said, tearfully, as her voice trailed.

"We can't keep thinking about this," I said as my eyes moved to the spot in the interior wall where a rifle shot had missed my head. Who was this shotgun-wielding assailant? Was he acting on his own? Who sent him? At this point, all I could do was guess. I knew I could not dwell on it. There are risks for taking on the status quo. It was part of my job.

It is one thing for an office holder to expose himself or herself to danger, but one's spouse? Sandy's safety was my paramount concern, my responsibility as her husband. I immediately ordered increased security for her, assigning her a policewoman bodyguard. I would not be able to function fearing for her safety.

I was concerned that my unceasing challenge to corrupt interests had increased our vulnerability and upended our home life. I had already sacrificed one marriage to politics, and I was determined not to let it happen again. We both needed a private, home life to balance our public lives. I could not back off on Muny Light or any other position based on threats. My loved ones should not have to be vulnerable because of my decisions. I refused to live as though under siege. This was our home, and I was not going to be chased from it. I did not intend to get into the habit of seeing bogeymen everywhere in the shadows. Caution was an appropriate companion, paranoia not.

Juniewicz called an hour later. The report had become public.

"Reporters are asking for comments," he said.

"Andy, no way. The less said, the better."

The Anchor of the Six O'Clock News on TV 8: "We are receiving reports of a man in the area of the Mayor's house with a shotgun. Police kept the house under surveillance all day today and into this evening. Kucinich himself had no comment on the gunman story, and police officials would neither confirm nor deny that any threat had existed. News Center 8 has learned, however, that the reported gunman fled officers, escaping from them at one point by hurling a section of awning at the cops."

CHAPTER 36

Baseball is Life

A boy's baseball dream dies hard. Monday morning, public fury over the firing of the Police Chief was at its peak. Recall petitions had been prepared. The political mercury rose fast, impacting the Opening Day plans of the Cleveland Indians' baseball club, whose General Manager Gabe Paul came to my office with a plea.

"Mayor, no offense, I don't think you should throw out the first pitch," he said softly.

It was a prime ceremonial duty of the Mayor of Cleveland to attend the Opening Day and to throw out the first pitch of the game. I was offended by the suggestion that I should be the first Mayor denied the honor because of a political balk.

I love baseball. Years earlier, as a high school senior, I was runner-up in the Cleveland Indians' bat boy essay contest. The winner got to wear the team uniform and be at all home games, on the field, handing the bats to the Major Leaguers ready to go to the plate. My consolation prize was two general admission season passes. I went to many Cleveland Indians' home games in the summer of 1964, accompanied by St. John Cantius classmates.

When I was elected Mayor, I was determined the office would not change me. I declined to live in a fifteen- room mansion, preferring to remain on Milan Avenue, in our 1208 sq ft. home. I rid the Mayor's office of catered dinners in the Mayor's private dining room and passed up being chauffeured in a black Lincoln limousine, preferring a nondescript car with a police radio. I declined the "Mayor's box seats" at the Opening Night of the Opera, giving the tickets for Rigoletto to my barber, Tony Scibilia. But I was not going to give up a perquisite prized by anyone who grew up in the neighborhoods of Cleveland cheering for our beloved major league baseball team

"Mr. Paul, every Mayor throws out the first pitch," I said.

"Not every Mayor is in the trouble you are in," Paul said. "Besides, I don't think you will be safe walking onto the field. I'm sure you are aware that there are a lot of upset people out there. We can't protect you. We certainly would not want something to happen to you. It's not good for you, and it's not good for baseball," he said.

Gabe Paul was kind, in a grandfatherly way. He knew baseball. He was the General Manager of the New York Yankees before coming to Cleveland. He knew politics, too. He came to appeal to me not to be visible at the Opener. He offered a compromise.

"You could toss the ball onto the field from behind the first base dugout. We would not announce it, there would be no crowd reaction, and it could still be said you threw out the first pitch."

"People will say I was afraid to walk out on the field," I said.

"Mr. Mayor, with all due respect, this is not about you, it's about the game," he said.

The Game. It was much bigger than me. I could not argue. I seized upon the canard of "tradition."

"If anytime a Mayor does something unpopular, and can't go onto the field to throw the first pitch, sooner or later no Mayor will be there on Opening Day. People were waiting in the weeds ready to pounce on any mistake I made, and sometimes I helped them.

I really wanted to throw out that first pitch. I was faced with a choice: The death of a childhood dream or the danger of real death by assassination. I preferred "Take Me Out to the Ballgame" to "take me out at the ballgame."

Dreams die hard. I decided to take the risk, go to the mound, and make my pitch.

"Mayor, it is not a good idea. We won't stop you. Know what you're getting yourself into," he said. "You could have 60,000 people yelling… but at you," his eyes smiled pleadingly.

Major league teams seek tropical climates for spring training, to prepare for the season opener. I had no such luxury to prepare to throw out the first pitch, although I did have a few potted palms in my office to simulate Florida. When I walked to the mound at Cleveland Municipal Stadium, I would wear an unusual uniform: A blue, waist-length kapok jacket which covered a bullet-proof vest.

I had to get used to throwing a ball from inside that cocoon. I practiced wind-up and pitch motions in my office, using a plastic sphere. I did not ask anyone on my staff to help. It would only start rumors that I had lost my mind trying to find my pitch. I didn't think anyone would understand why this was so important.

I was never a good athlete, although I went out for every sport in school. My distinction? I was the smallest person on the team. Spirited and wiry, I could take a hit and get back up. Another two feet of height and an extra hundred and fifty pounds and I could have been a contender.

When I wasn't playing sports, I was writing sports for the school newspaper, the yearbook, and later the *Plain Dealer,* as part of my weekend sports rewrite duties. I had finished first in sports-writing in a journalism competition at the Northeastern Ohio Scholastic Press Association. I was born a fan. I'd even had a 1948 Cleveland Indians World Series Championship pennant over my crib as a baby. You need more?

Opening Day, 1978. Exuberant crowds filed into Cleveland Municipal Stadium, as a dozen people waved clipboards outside, encouraging fans to sign the recall petitions. The recall crew mingled cheerfully among vendors hawking scorecards and baseball souvenirs. American League pennants ringed the roof of the upper deck of the Stadium - no, wait, those were police sharpshooters. Temperatures were in the low forties, feeling chillier with the wind from the Lake.

Then Baseball's Voice of God, the stadium announcer, called fans to attention. "Now, please join us in welcoming the Mayor of the City of Cleveland, Dennis J. Kucinich, who will throw out the first pitch." Upon the mention of my name, tens of thousands of fans rose as one, producing a hearty, standing BOO!! It rocketed around the Stadium, a home run cheer-in-reverse. Chairs rattled like the grim thunder of townsfolk barricaded at the walls of the city, pounding makeshift cudgels on the ground, demanding entrance. I knew who the vociferous fans were addressing when I heard "Kill the Bum," because the umpires had not taken the field. Amid the cacophony of jeers, I strode briskly to the mound, wearing a Cleveland Indian's baseball cap, the blue snowmobile jacket, and my trusty bulletproof vest, well prepared to throw out the first pitch.

On the pitcher's mound, I swatted away the thunderous boos, I ignored the shouted invective, and forgot the recallers outside the stadium. Then, a moment of doubt. Maybe Gabe Paul was right. Maybe this was a bad idea.

No! Focus! I had practiced. I was ready. I was standing on the mound. I had to throw the ball. For a brief moment I apprehended the grave political consequences of a wild pitch, the perceived preternatural awkwardness, worse, the unforgiving metaphor, if, when I launch this small white sphere toward its target sixty feet, six inches away, it instead fell short, spinning crazily in the dirt.

Focus. I was on a mission. The Indian's catcher, Ron Pruitt, went into a crouch.

Focus. The deafening noise dissolved. The agitated crowd disappeared. It was me and Pruitt. One pitch. I tugged my cap as a Major League pitcher might, I concentrated on the dark center of the catcher's leather glove. I wound up and flung the ball into the void, its trajectory an arc of hope carried over the center of the plate, true to Pruitt's mitt, for a strike.

The crowd suddenly returned to my awareness. The storm of boos broke like a vanishing Lake Erie tempest, jeers turned to cheers. The catcher hustled toward me, to give me the ball, the good seed from which would spring the Indian's 1978 season.

"I'm glad to meet you Mr. Mayor, because I've been waiting to talk to you about the condition of your streets," catcher Pruitt said with playful banter.

The bright sunshine of a smattering of applause lit my return path from the mound to the dugout. I waved broadly to the crowd. People waved back. It augured well. The Indians won the game, 8-5.

I had to take my chances, go to the mound, throw out the first pitch. I'm not a spectator.

Mayor Locher once said there was nothing wrong with Cleveland that a baseball championship couldn't take care of. Baseball is life. This town loves a winner, if only for a day.

CHAPTER 37

Recall Madness

The word "recall" used to mean "to remember," but that was before I became Mayor. Now it meant people could vote me out of office well before the end of my two-year term. All that was needed to start a recall was a major blunder to acquire signatures, and I provided it.

The recall became Cleveland's prime sporting event. Whatever happened in the city, a wildcat police strike, a pending garbage collection strike, problems with Muny Light, insinuations of a giant, hidden financial deficit, the weather, all hastened the gathering of signatures on the recall petitions, because, since I was the Mayor, it was my responsibility, and my fault.

Politics was lumbago. The recall was the cure. I had visited chaos, illogic, and waltzed at the precipice early in life, so I can't say I felt personally threatened by each cycle of insanity. You want "normal?" It's a place in Kentucky. I was born in Cleveland, Ohio, where in my childhood "recall" only related to a song about Rudolph, the most famous reindeer of all.

My frenzied childhood prepared me for this moment. It was 1956.

We had moved in with Uncle Pete and Aunt Marge after spending a few days driving around the East Side in a 1948 Dodge, searching without success for a rental to call home. My cousins Maryann and Junior did not know sleep, nor did we at their wayside inn, because Pete and Marge's marriage was a brawl. They fought over how much money he made from the scrap he stole from railroad cars. They fought over the last beer in a daily twenty-four bottle case. They fought over Marge's beautiful blue and white parakeet, Pretty Boy. It fluttered freely around the house, angering Pete.

One afternoon, as my cousins and I were watching American Bandstand on a grainy black and white TV screen, Pete, unshaven, suspenders tight over a tobacco-stained t-shirt, chased Marge around the house with a claw hammer because she had yelled at him for flushing Pretty Boy down the toilet after the bird had escaped its cage.

I've seen life on the edge, and from the other side of the edge, where reality is vertiginous. So too, with the recall. No legal or ethical violations were charged, none were cited. I was charged with bad publicity and bad form for being Mayor of a corrupt, corporate-run city.

The recall was spurred on by the signatures of dead people, of ghosts from vacant lots, of people from other states and other countries whose signatures were affixed, some multiple times, to the petitions.

It was Daschbach's Law at work. When I was a copyboy at The Plain Dealer, a senior reporter named J.C. Daschbach, was a rumpled, ink-stained sociologist, a refugee from Ben Hecht's days of Front Page journalism. Daschbach once boasted that he could easily circulate in downtown a petition demanding the hanging in Public Square of the Cleveland Mayor. He professed it would be simple to obtain sufficient signatures. "People will sign anything!" he said confidently.

Daschbach's Law. The recall signature tally rose, promoted by the media coverage. It was a toxic political version of the United Appeal. 'We have 5,000 15,000 30,000 signatures, ...47,547 signatures! Even with half the signatures invalid, the requisite numbers were obtained.

The petitions were presented to the Clerk of Council. She certified them with alacrity.

Reporters, sound men, and cameramen followed Clerk of Council Mercedes Cotner from her office. They clambered across the second floor of City Hall to Juniewicz's space, where the clerk handed him an envelope.

"This is for the Mayor," she said, ceremoniously. Juniewicz turned to deliver the message. The cameramen who missed the hand-over of the letter wanted her to do it again, so they could focus on the writ of ouster, and the old hand passing the poisoned letter to the young hand, signaling the commencement of an unhappy political new year.

"Wait!" the Clerk stammered. "Can I have that envelope back?"

"Can't we do it again, Andy?" a cameraman pleaded, "C'mon, Andy, give us a break."

Juniewicz, a model of stoicism, with the patience to watch oil paint dry, responded only with a smile. An early riser, Juniewicz was the first person in the office in the morning and the first person to light up a cigarette. He made it a point to be on top of the news as it was reported overnight. Athletic and youthful, he was up to the rigors of what would prove to be a sixteen hour-a-day job, at the least. He was my "distant early warning system," my flak catcher. I hired him from the *Plain Dealer*, where, as a City Hall reporter, he had a reputation for accuracy and fairness. He also possessed an appreciation for irony, a spontaneous sense of humor and grace under pressure. He was steady under all circumstances. He headed toward my office with the message.

"This is from the Clerk." He handed me the sealed letter. "I think you should read it," he said without affect.

I opened it.

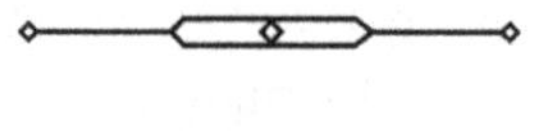

City of Cleveland

MERCEDES COTNER
CITY CLERK
CLERK OF COUNCIL

June 23, 1978

Dear Mayor Kucinich:

You are hereby notified that a sufficient recall petition and amended recall petition, demanding your removal, has been filed with me and this date submitted to the Council with my certificate to that effect.

Pursuant to Section 18 of the Charter of the City of Cleveland, you have five (5) days to resign from office.

Sincerely yours,
Mercedes Cotner
City Clerk
Clerk of Council

MC:o

"Five days to resign. Generous, especially since we've been here seven months," I said. Andy and I laughed and went back to work, knowing we were caught up in the politics of destabilization, where any ordinary occurrence could achieve out-sized importance and add fuel to the recall fire.

The city was at the brink of a financial crisis, compounded by the federal court order to pay CEI an accumulated $18 million by year's end. Just as it was our snow, it was our budget, our debt, our financial crisis. We inherited fourteen labor contracts. Projected increases in expenses drew, from council leadership, predictions of layoffs, tax increases and more demands to sell Muny Light.

The recall was depicted to be homey, operating from a rundown storefront on the West Side which was once a funeral home. It was a Potemkin village. The recall was funded from corporate office towers, where dozens of officers and directors of Cleveland Trust, CEI, National City Bank, Central National Bank and Society National Bank and their law firms were quietly raising large sums of money to retake control of City Hall.

Undeterred, our administration moved ahead with plans to protect Muny Light, to develop Cleveland's economy without tax abatement, and to improve city services, all while cutting government spending.

One major misstep had opened the possibility of my becoming the youngest Mayor with the briefest term, for taking an action that was a tradition in Cleveland - - firing the police chief. The city had hired nine police chiefs in the past fifteen years. Perk had fired his police chief, and Forbes celebrated: "Perk just got himself re-elected."

While editorialists declared the recall "premature" and although the Chief produced no evidence for his accusations, the recall bandwagon accelerated, as wacky as a Mad Hatter's Tea Party. Neither the announcement of the construction of a new $50 million office building, without tax abatement, nor a heart-tugging, handwritten, letter-to-the-editor from my own dear mother, could break the momentum. Every meeting of the recallers, every rally to attack the administration brought major news coverage, though attended by the same people, saying the same things, from the same storefront office. Neighborhood groups supporting our administration were ignored as the recall scaled heights of hysteria.

Bob Weissman spoke at the Union Club, where waiters were Blacks only and women were not permitted through the front door. The Union Club was the House of Have, the clubhouse of the financiers of the city and the financial backers of the recall.

Facing the gathering of hostile business leaders, Weissman impoliticly observed "mayors can govern without getting along with council" and "big business ought to pay its taxes and not meddle in the affairs of city government," which sounded reasonable to me. No reporter was present at the meeting. However, a man whose company was under scrutiny by the city for excessive noise at his metal forge provided his insider's version of the Weissman speech the next day, sparking headlines:

"COUNCIL, BUSINESSMEN, TARGETS IN BLISTERING WEISSMAN ATTACK"

Weissman's speech brought demands for his resignation. His assignment at City Hall was to help me get rid of the corruption, cut expenses, save taxpayers' money. At Weissman's direction, the city payroll, 11,600 persons when I took office, was reduced by 150 positions a month. Sharp budget reductions were initiated, overtime was cut, unnecessary contracts canceled and efficiencies introduced to improve city service.

Weissman helped run the city as a business on behalf of its owners, the taxpayers. He was a hard-nosed pragmatist who did not allow emotions or sympathies to affect his decisions, sometimes creating politically-awkward moments.

He chased the Little Sisters of the Poor out of City Hall as they went from office to office, seeking donations. He fired the City's 86 year-old Coordinator of Patriotic Affairs. He laid off a man with two blind parents. The 'Good Humor Man' he was not, more like Dr. Spock as deputy Mayor. The city had not seen a more honest, more capable administrator committed to making government work, through the sheer villainy of trying to get people to actually do their tax-funded jobs. But honest government was not universally in demand. We were under attack at every turn for every effort to stop the waste and the theft, of taxpayer dollars.

In an effort to precipitate Weissman's resignation or dismissal, grossly exaggerated accounts of his clashes with City Hall bureaucrats appeared regularly in the *Cleveland Press*.

Weissman came to my office as criticism reached a crescendo.

"Dennis, I'm a target. I don't want to hurt you. I'm ready to resign if you think it would help." This was an extraordinary moment with the man who was almost singularly responsible for my political career.

"Not a chance, I'm not going to give in to this crowd. If they can push you out, they'll think it will be easier to get me, and the attacks will become even crazier."

Ted Bonda, who had provided funds to help us win the 1977 election, came to my office and demanded Weissman be let go.

"He's hurting you and undermining your efforts. You have to get rid of him," Bonda said forcefully. "He's going to take you down." Bonda had been speaking out against the recall, and, I believe, had my best interests in mind.

"Ted, I'm taking full responsibility for him. He's staying."

"You are making a big mistake," he said, angrily. Then, Ted Bonda, who raised campaign funds assuring our narrow victory, stormed out of my office.

There was no way I was going to let go of Weissman. His integrity and dedication were unmatched. I could not be intimidated into firing him and refused to accept his resignation.

My misery required the most competent company.

By late June, the Chief of Police, was forgotten, as were his incendiary, unsubstantiated charges. Once the political fires were raging, who cared who started the recall, or why? Attention shifted from one topic to another and eventually to the ultimate question: Would I survive? Political death watches intimate interment.

As the recall reached the ballot, I knew every political decision would impact it, but I had to move the city forward. I could not stop governing. There were dozens of decisions to be made every day. I had to act as if there was not a recall, while being aware the recall existed and could end my mayoralty abruptly.

The burden was less administrative then emotional. It meant preparing for an election where my opponent was myself, or rather a distorted image communicated through media promoting the recall. The political pressure increased and the stigma of being subjected to a recall was, in and of itself damaging.

The recall ballot language was devious, crafted by George Forbes to create consternation. If someone wanted to vote for me, they would have to vote against the recall. Anyone who wanted to vote against me, would have to vote for the recall. If total confusion reigned, I'd have an even chance.

CHAPTER 38

A-Bomb

You hire people to tell you the truth. Bob Weissman, Jack Schulman and Joe Tegreene grimly walked into my office.

"Touche Ross, the accounting firm we hired to audit the bond funds, has determined that the Perk administration was balancing the city budget by illegally using bond funds for general operating purposes," Weissman said gravely. "Money meant for capital improvements, like street repaving, sewer construction, and rebuilding bridges, recreation centers and fire stations was spent illegally on payroll."

"Perk engineered a constant infusion of new bond and note money into the treasury to cover the fact that the old money had already been spent for the general fund," added Tegreene.

In his first term, over my advice, Mayor Perk sought authority to tap bond funds for payroll. He was denied by Council, but did it anyway. Squire Sanders helped Perk issue $178.6 million of bonds and notes during the period 1972 to 1977, purportedly for capital improvements, creating a slush fund.

We had commissioned the audit to determine exactly how much expended and unexpended cash existed in the bond accounts. The head of the Growth Association said it was the first full audit in the city's history.

"How much bond fund money is missing?" I asked, with dread.

"At least $17 million," Tegreene continued, "There was no system to separate the bond funds from the general operating funds. Bond and note money was instead commingled in the General Fund account, along with income tax and property tax proceeds," Tegreene elaborated. "It took seven months to sort this out." Ultimately, Touche Ross determined that from January 1, 1972 to June 30, 1978, the city used over $50 million in bond funds to cover cash shortfalls. This bled into programmed spending at the beginning of our administration.

Previous to our election, whenever anyone came to City Hall to inspect financial records, they concluded that the books were not auditable, that is, to the extent the books could be located. Perk's finance officers had the political cover to misspend bond and note funds for general operating purposes.

The deception enabled Perk to maintain an inflated payroll, employ an army of consultants, pad contracts, spend lavishly on City Hall decorators and parties, and sharply increase spending for outside legal counsel, all with the approval of both city council and the business community. Meanwhile, Perk was intentionally failing to pay CEI's light bill.

"This is another reason why Perk wanted to sell Muny Light. The proceeds from the sale would have gone into the general fund and covered the deficit, " Jack observed.

A year ago, Perk predicted that Muny Light was a "fiscal atomic bomb." His administration built the bomb, with CEI's help. Russo and Forbes long maintained that unless we sold Muny Light and paid the CEI debt, the city would become insolvent.

Jack's analysis was spot-on. The practice of using bond funds for general operating purposes would have been concealed, had Muny Light been sold and Perk re-elected. Proceeds from the sale of Muny

Light could have been placed in the general fund account, and no one would be the wiser.

"We've got to find a way to resolve this. It could sink us," I said, knowing the field day the media and Council would have with this news.

"Joe, anything from our financial advisors?"

"I'm meeting with First Boston, and several investment banking firms, including Salomon Brothers. This report will not help our ability to refinance the city's short-term debt," Tegreene said, an understatement. He was methodical in his approach. He had been meeting with accountants, bond counsel, and other finance officials to develop a refinancing program, to convert the city's outstanding one-year notes into long term bonds.

"They'll use this newly-discovered deficit to come after us on Muny Light," predicted Schulman.

"Of course, Jack. This is what it is about anyway, isn't it? Sell Muny Light, cover the deficit. Sell Muny Light, cover up illegal spending. Sell Muny Light, save the city's finances," I said. "What a mess."

"Look," Weissman cut in, "We can't panic. If we do, it will affect the recall election. We can still balance the budget. We have to let the people of Cleveland know we are not exceeding our expenditures."

True.

We did not have the cash the books showed we had. Now, even reduced levels of expenditures were depleting the city's cash reserves. We had gone down a financial rabbit hole and awoke to find giant numbers marching upon us, menacing us with destruction, like the minions of the Queen of Hearts, poised to make heads roll. Here we were, $17 million in bond funds missing and under a court order to pay CEI $14.5 million, including interest, while facing a recall election where city finances were at issue as a means of forcing the sale of Muny Light.

The corporate interests who contrived to lead Perk and the City of Cleveland into a fiscal swamp would become the very individuals who purposely blocked our efforts to restructure the city's debt. We were paying penance for Perk's profligacy. In the very act of cleaning up a mess, we became responsible for it. This dynamic encourages politicians to go with a false flow, maintain the status quo, and leave office before anyone knows.

As the meeting broke up, Tegreene added, as if in apology, "Mayor, we do not know exactly how much money is missing. It could be a lot more." Tegreene, gifted of intelligence leavened with naivete, could increase the anxiety level in any meeting.

The bond fund deficits were revealed and as we expected, recall advocates screamed that we were leading Cleveland into bankruptcy. George Forbes, who used the adverse fiscal report to further his plan to force the sale of Muny Light made a stunning admission: "We have to wear the jacket for Perk's policy of using bond money for general fund obligations. Council could have forced the issue and told Perk, 'You don't do it.' We could have brought the city to a halt then instead of today."

CEI added pressure for collection of the debt. According to the newspapers, radio, television stations, the Growth Association, and the Democratic Party, the solution to the city's rough financial straits was to successfully execute the recall, or sell Muny Light, or both.

CHAPTER 39

Bank Shot

Brock Weir, Chairman and Chief Executive Officer of Cleveland Trust bank, was in a singular position to help the city refinance nearly eight million dollars in notes, which were coming due on July 7, 1978. We needed Cleveland Trust's cooperation to organize a bond or note sale for the national market. As Tegreene and I sat before Weir, I hoped for results better than I'd had as a candidate for Mayor when I made my first visit to the green and chrome tower.

Weir sat before us, ramrod straight. He seemed to have a problem with the vision in one eye and leaned forward as I spoke.

"Mr. Weir, the city will need to refinance the notes coming due and held by your bank. We would appreciate your help."

He shook his head slowly, and barely audibly uttered, "No. I can't do that. You have serious financial problems. If we loan you money, it won't help solve your difficulties. You've got to find another way to solve the city's financial problems."

"How can we do that without you extending the term of the existing debt?" I asked.

"I think I covered that," he responded. His body language suggested that this meeting was at a conclusion.

"Mr. Weir, you wouldn't want the city to go into default, would you?" I asked.

He sat back in his chair, relaxed, for he had all the time, and money, in the world. He looked at me directly for the first time.

"Default might not be so bad for the city. It might help you get your financial house in order," he said.

Two years ago, Brock Weir's bank loaned Mayor Perk's administration $7.8 million. Did he know then whether the city would have the ability to repay it in 1978?

People who borrowed money for a new car were asked more questions regarding their ability to repay than the banks apparently asked the city in 1975, when they loaned Cleveland $125 million, ostensibly for capital improvements.

I was not applying for a car loan, nor was I asking for *more* money. I requested only that the Chairman of Cleveland Trust refinance a debt the previous administration had incurred under this banker's watch.

Weir exuded a perverse, sadistic pleasure as he spoke of the possibility of default. "Default, not so bad?" The city treasury could be rushed by creditors. Money for payroll, depleted. Severe cutbacks in service could ensue. Court battles with creditors. Inability to attract investors. Federal funds forfeited. A court-appointed receiver to run the City of Cleveland. The city's name and reputation damaged.

Bill collectors do not faze me. When I was growing up in a tenement district on the east side of Cleveland, within sight of this office tower, bill collectors visited our apartment with such frequency that I assumed they were relatives. Our mailbox was always overflowing with legal confetti. We had to scramble every day to come up with money. Mom clipped coupons from newspapers and entered every kind of contest for money prizes, Irish sweepstakes, church raffle tickets, punch cards, in hopes of winning twenty-five cents to a dollar.

I had my responsibilities, scrubbed floors at the school, searched garbage cans on pick-up days for glass deposit bottles, sold magazine subscriptions, carried groceries home from the A & P, went to local meat markets to get free bones "for my dog," shined shoes, distributed political and real estate leaflets, swept the floor at Martha's Delicatessen, stacked bottles in exchange for bottle caps redeemable for hockey tickets, which I either gave to friends, or sold. I even fished for coins deep under commercial district sidewalk grates with a wad of gum attached to a string. There is money all over the streets, you just have to know where to look. The cash went to Mom. I always helped my family find a way to produce a few extra dollars to brush off the "money stealers" who danced around us like milkweed pods. Today it was my responsibility to find a way to come up with millions for my extended family, the people of the City of Cleveland.

Weir wouldn't budge.

As Tegreene and I left, I could hear tapes playing in my head. People with lots of money screwing people without money. Tegreene was stunned by the brevity of the meeting and Weir's dismissal of the city's plight.

"What a bastard," he said, shaking his head.

Cleveland Trust was preparing to push Cleveland over a financial cliff. According to a congressional investigation, Weir moved decisions regarding the city's debt, "from the commercial bank level to an executive committee at the holding company level" indicating the management of Cleveland's $5 million debt was a very high corporate (political) priority of the $4 billion financial institution.

Tegreene checked to see if there were water department bond funds available to invest in the $17.8 million in city notes coming due in July, 1978. The water department had its own segregated bond fund accounts, which could be legally invested until proceeds were needed to pay for water system improvements. I directed the water bond fund to buy the $17.8 million in notes, avoiding default.

Mayor Perk and Forbes blasted the transaction, and once again called for the sale of Muny Light. The duo claimed the city treasury would be unable to redeem the notes, the city would lose ownership of the water system to the suburbs, and water rates would go up. Lawyers for the suburbs raced into court, demanding a regional takeover of the water system. They echoed the Forbes-Perk claims. If the city forfeited the water system, a trustee was waiting in the wings to run it, CEI's Lee Howley.

In September, 1978, $3.3 million of the $17.8 million of notes now owned by the water system came due. If we failed to refinance, it would trigger the default Forbes, Perk and the suburban mayors forecast. Tegreene found another fund that could invest in the $3.3 million.

The city's credit rating was downgraded by the Wall Street ratings agency, because the impoverished school system, stripped of resources through tax abatement, had undermined the "long term attractiveness" of the City of Cleveland. Under Ohio law at the time, the school system's finances were governed by an elected school board and were separate from the city's.

I had no jurisdiction over the schools, although I did try to protect their revenue base by stopping tax abatement. Nor did I have any responsibility for a Cleveland school board member who was arrested as he stuck his bare rear end out a car window, in full view of a traffic cop. I received blame for that as well, as the media was finally getting to the bottom of things.

The credit downgrade meant the city would have difficulty attracting investors. We would be required to pay a higher interest rate, if we could borrow money at all. The city's investment potential further deteriorated amid the continual public warnings by Council that bankruptcy was imminent unless Muny Light was sold. It didn't matter that we had unearthed the misspending and put in motion a plan to replace the bond funds. No one was interested in the city's financial history.

I could feel our support slipping. The *Cleveland Press* editorialized, "To be subject to a recall, all an official must do is act so the tide of public opinion runs strongly against him. And that Dennis Kucinich has done."

The word "Recall" was stamped across my picture on TV news stories, an electronic pro-recall campaign poster. The opposition of the Cleveland media, the banks, CEI, both political parties, developers, and elements of organized labor appeared insurmountable.

Dozens of the people in my new administration had dropped their own careers to join my effort. I knew each one of their stories. We were family. I brought some of them into politics at a very early age, inspiring the highest expectations, the highest possibilities to create positive change through dedication, perseverance and honesty. These individuals were charged with making government work, carrying out necessary change in every city department, fearlessly. The satisfaction of making a difference was their only reward.

I gathered this team together in the mayor's dining room to inform them of the perilous path ahead. Our experiment in democratic municipal governance could soon be over. Their lives, their commitment, their service and their futures weighed heavily on my heart. They were under the harshest attacks, yet focused and maintained city services, uninterrupted.

"We are going to have to get ready for this recall election," I said looking around the room. "It will be the toughest election any of us has ever faced. We could lose. But I am asking you to believe we will win, and we must work to win. Remember our commitment to the people of this city. Remember what happens when you challenge entrenched power. Do not falter. I ask you to join with me, one more time, to protect the right of Clevelanders to have a government they can call their own."

Their youthful faces showed trepidation, but they were also ready to fight back.

"Save the city, sell Muny," was a civic chorus, no matter the good news Muny Light received from the NRC, which issued a notice of violation against CEI for blocking the city's access to cheap power.

Ted Bonda asked for another meeting. At our previous meeting, he told me to fire Weissman.

When he entered my office again, he was direct, no-nonsense, to the point. He spoke in imperatives. "You didn't listen to me about Weissman. I'm here about Muny Light. You made your best effort. Now you have to sell it. Otherwise, it's going to cost you your job," he said sternly. He sincerely believed it was best for me and the city, to sell Muny Light. I sincerely believed he was wrong.

"Ted, there is no reason to sell Muny Light. CEI and Council have worked to undermine it. I'm not going to give it up, even to protect my own career."

"Suit yourself. You may lose the recall because of it. Then, they'll sell it anyway," he warned. The meeting was brief and unfortunately, unfriendly.

Meanwhile, our effort to issue $20 million in judgment bonds to pay CEI was blocked by the Ohio Supreme Court. We had to devise yet another plan to pay the bill and to hold onto our public power system.

Every day, I received briefings in my office on the status of private utility activities in the state of Ohio. I read annual utility reports voraciously, utility industry analyses, and Public Utility Commission of Ohio rulings. Those most affected by high utility rates did not understand the system that was exploiting them. Our city government was one of the few raising the issue of utility rates. The inevitability of death, taxes, and utility rates is ingrained into civic acceptance. I never lost sight of why we were persevering - to stop the economic exploitation of the people of Cleveland.

Each time a utility rate increase occurred, for many families it meant less money for food, clothing, and shelter. There was an aspect of involuntary enslavement here to an insular, private system of extraction. I found this condition repugnant, and I was always prepared to resist and try to change it. People were carefully counting their pennies, as did my parents, while the owners of investor-owned utilities' were counting their millions, with the active assistance of government, which rigged the game.

Nationally, investor-owned utilities had municipal electric systems in a price squeeze, charging cities more for purchased power than they charged their commercial accounts, effectively creating a cross-subsidy. Ohio's privately-owned utilities had jacked up the price of power, buying and selling electricity among themselves, increasing prices as much as 72%, according to the *Youngstown Vindicator.* CEI had resold that power at a 34% markup.

Led by CEI, private utilities were on a rampage against Ohio consumers, gouging customers coming and going. Competition mattered more than ever.

A switch from coal to fuel oil during a miners' strike enabled utilities to automatically pass through to consumers tens of millions of dollars in costs each month, through a fuel adjustment clause, while at the same time telling customers to conserve energy. CEI used the increased costs to ask for another 12% increase in electric rates. Then, while its use of oil declined, it increased its rates by an extra 3% in March, following a 10% increase in February. Utility rate regulation in Ohio was non-existent. CEI had the state regulatory agency, known as the Public Utilities Commission of Ohio, (PUCO) in its pocket.

At its annual meeting, CEI's Karl Rudolph bragged to shareholders that dividends on common stock had increased every year for twenty-five straight years, while nine senior citizens brought 16,636 pennies to CEI's headquarters to pay their light bills.

Ohio's Consumers Counsel wanted the PUCO to order CEI to refund $50 million to electric consumers. This paralleled a Federal Energy Regulatory Commission investigation of CEI overcharges. CEI purchased an excess of power during a coal strike and then marked it up 32%. Court-approved air pollution control standards aimed at controlling sulfur dioxide emissions in Ohio were met with a predictable response from CEI: If people wanted clean air, the company said callously, they were going to have to pay higher electric rates.

Whenever comparing itself to Muny Light, CEI touted its status as a taxpaying corporate citizen, criticizing city-owned utilities for not paying taxes. However, *Plain Dealer* reporter Amos Kermisch determined that while CEI customers were charged $72 million to pay CEI's federal taxes, the company remitted only $3 million to the federal government. A former CEI employee claimed the company had increased its sales for years by transmitting more voltage than customers needed .

CEI's attempts to keep its new Davis-Besse nuclear power plant on line faltered, with a 30% shutdown rate. CEI's customers were billed for the higher-cost replacement electricity, due to the unreliability of the nuclear power plant. Davis-Besse's companion Perry Nuclear plant, situated upon Ohio's northeastern shore, had been built on an geologic fault line and was cited by the NRC for faulty design. The NRC assessed a stiff fine, and shut down work at Perry for sixty-six days.

CEI and other state utilities used their advertising budget to dominate state-wide media. The PUCO ruled private utilities could charge their customers for unlimited ad expenses. When a vacancy arose at the PUCO, Ohio Governor Rhodes offered it to Council President George Forbes, who declined.

Finances reigned as the recall reason. Cleveland City Council, six years too late, passed an ordinance to prohibit the city from using bond funds for general operating purposes. Since bond and general funds were, at the moment, inextricably commingled, Council's intent was to fuel the recall drive by freezing the city's ability to issue paychecks.

We estimated a balanced general fund by year's end. Council opposition showed a deficit at the six-month mark.

The Wall Street rating services denied the city access to bond markets, until the Muny Light debt was resolved.

We devised still another plan to pay CEI. It involved the sale of valuable, though unneeded, city-owned land, plus advancing income tax and Muny Light revenues. A *Plain Dealer* "analysis," however, said both the land and Muny Light should be sold, to straighten out city finances.

The state auditor issued another finding: The city's books were not auditable for each of two fiscal years ending on June 30 in 1977 and 1978. The fine print in the news article said, "This condition was inherited by Mayor Dennis J. Kucinich's administration..."

Never was an inheritance so thoroughly unwanted, yet wholly owned by its recipient.

CHAPTER 40

Recall Madness II

Opportunities for extortion abounded in the toxic political climate. A few weeks before the recall election, Republic Steel, the city's largest employer, hinted at the closing of its mill and the loss of 9,300 steel worker jobs, unless it was given a 25-year lease on prime space in the Port of Cleveland, for construction of an ore unloading facility.

When Republic Steel representatives first unrolled the ore dock plans on my desk, I wanted to help. After all, the company provided thousands of jobs. As steel companies were a focal point of our efforts to curtail air pollution, they constantly threatened to leave town, unless the city relaxed air quality standards. That, I would not do.

I understood from growing up at the edge of the industrial valley that the people got the pollution, a decreased quality of life and adverse health effects, while the industry took the profits. Each time I saw a plume of rust-colored smoke rise over the city, I knew the steel company did not give a damn. When I became Mayor, I was determined to enforce emission standards to protect the air and water quality. United Steelworkers' officials supported our efforts, because it was the workers who bore the first burden of damaged health from the pollution coming from the mills.

Steel company officials grumbled, but I knew they would not move, because Cleveland is a great place to make steel. The area has a trained labor force, easy access to interstate highways, and superior river, lake, rail, and air transit of benefit to industry. I looked for ways I might be supportive and, learning of the ore dock project, asked top administration officials to consider it favorably.

Republic officials, early on, maintained that the ore-unloading facility could be located either in Cleveland, or, alternatively, in Lorain, Ohio, 25 miles west of Cleveland. The ore could be transported from Lorain to the Cleveland steelworks, at equal expense. But locating the ore dock in Cleveland would mean jobs and would serve as visible proof of Cleveland's industrial strength, since people would see the 1,000 ft. ore carriers docked at the Cleveland port. I asked Law Director, Jack Schulman to analyze the proposal.

When Schulman presented his conclusions, my enthusiasm for the ore dock waned. Republic was forecasting record-breaking income and profits. Schulman determined the ore dock deal provided the corporation with a $153.5 million subsidy, a multi-million dollar annual giveaway through low royalties paid to the city for tonnage unloaded.

Taxpayers would also have to pay an estimated $18 million for dredging a channel for the larger ore carriers. The project would remove $6.4 million in land from the city's tax roll. City, county and Cleveland school taxing districts would thus lose $16 million in revenue over the 40-year term of the lease.

The publicly-funded Port Authority would have to borrow $7 million to buy the necessary land, Republic would repay only $3.5 million and gain exclusive use of the dock.

In exchange for the multi-million dollar handout, the Port Authority would receive nothing. Schulman determined the ore-dock facility would mean only ten new jobs, and cost a hundred longshoremen jobs, as the new construction would replace at least 25% of the existing dockage used for general cargo.

Three years earlier, the Port Authority had commissioned a study recommending Whiskey Island, a site west of the mouth of the Cuyahoga River, as the ideal location to receive the 1,000 foot ore carriers. This site was the terminus of Conrail's railroad tracks, which transported the ore to the steel mills. The Army Corps of Engineers consented. But, when Republic Steel and the Port Authority came to an agreement to build the ore dock east of the river, Conrail, unable to compete with a taxpayer-subsidized ore dock, dropped its plans to move ore.

Republic would have the only ore dock in town accommodating the 1,000 foot boats, leaving competitors J & L Steel and U.S. Steel, to either pay Republic's price or be unable to bring in iron ore pellets via the larger, more economical vessels. With this single agreement the city would be picking a winner and two losers in steel-making competition, something I could not permit.

We asked Republic Steel executives to come to City Hall to discuss Schulman's findings. Corporate leaders who once smiled at the 'wonderful cooperation' received from City Hall became resentful.

George Forbes had once served as President and Chairman of a short lived shipping concern, Marine Transit, Inc. That firm's former executive vice president was now in charge of planning the ore dock for Republic Steel. Council President Forbes said I had thirty days to approve the original terms. I refused. Forbes then brought the Council together to approve the ore dock lease.

I rose to object, pointing out that Council refused to act on a new computer contract, which would save the city $8 million annually, yet acted with dispatch to give away $153 million to Republic Steel.

"You are out of order. Stick to the subject," Forbes interrupted.

"I'm the Mayor, not you. You can't censor me." I replied, hotly.

"I'm the Council President and I run these meetings." Forbes said, ordering a Council employee to electronically shut off my microphone.

"I will not be silenced, Mr. Chairman. This is a corrupt deal!" I shouted.

Our administration exited the Council chambers, in objection to Council's attempt to ram through the agreement.

Prior to adjourning the meeting, Forbes slipped through legislation legalizing various carnival gambling machines, to the benefit of Sebring Exhibits. Forbes said he passed the carnival legislation on behalf of the Catholic Church, to help it make more money. The 'Penny Fall' game was one in particular Forbes wanted to shield. In it, quarters are moved onto a vibrating plate toward a chute where players expectantly await a mass of coins to cascade into a tray, delivering a Vegas-like metallic windfall. The game originated in Great Britain, where it was played with pennies. Players had about as much of a chance at winning at Penny Fall as Cleveland taxpayers had at benefitting from the ore dock.

Cleveland area steelworkers, naturally attuned to Republic's statements hinting at closing the mill, watched with great apprehension as nearby Youngstown Sheet and Tube shut down.

Steelworkers were told by their union leaders that the only way to save their own jobs was to get rid of me. This was devastating since the steelworkers, under United Steelworkers District Director Joseph Kender, was one of the first unions to support my political career when I was the city councilman of the Tremont area.

I was in the Public Auditorium to address thousands of delegates to the state convention of the largest labor organization in Ohio, the AFL-CIO. On cue from a local union leader, as I began to speak, more than one hundred steelworkers walked out. They coursed across the street to the steps of City Hall. They marched as Republic Steel, the media, and City Council called forth awful images of grass growing in factory parking lots, mortgages foreclosed, and families hungry, sick, and disintegrating, when the mills shut down.

Frank Valenta, the District Director of the United Steelworkers, issued a statement, "The only way to save Cleveland and our jobs is to vote for recall on August 13."

Rough-hewn men in plaid shirts and safety helmets appeared in recall television commercials asking fellow Clevelanders to save their jobs by voting for the recall.

This was a nightmare, manipulated by corporate interests who were trying to shake down the city government for millions.

How do you tell your strongest supporters they are wrong, when they believe their jobs are on the line?

The best labor leaders know when they are being played, when the political or financial establishment tries to appropriate their support in one moment and then wields economic power against them in the next, driving down wages and benefits, and, in the end, making jobs less secure. I had been elected to defend the economic rights of the people, but this was no time for philosophical reflections or working class economics. My political base was cracking.

A dynamic tension was building in the community between supporting an independent government or capitulating to dependence upon the corporations who were exploiting it.

Sohio then announced that it would not build a $70 million dollar office tower in Cleveland, even though the city had offered a $7.5 million federal grant to repair adjacent roads. The oil company's reversal was viewed as still another reason for the recall.

As the recall moved forward, I could not shirk my responsibilities, no matter the political risks. In my visits to primarily Black public housing communities during my election campaign for Mayor, I had learned from shattered families of twenty-three murder victims in 1977, of hundreds of break-ins, of the theft of household goods and frequent rapes, muggings, and robberies. So, in July of 1978, I issued an order for Safety Director Barrett to assign fifty Cleveland policemen to individual foot patrols in Cleveland's public housing estates.

The leader of the police patrolmen's union burst into my office, unannounced, to object to the new assignments. He stood in front of my desk shouting, "Ya dunnit dis time, an I ain't goin' alone into da jungle wit doze animals."

I took strong exception to his racist characterizations and asked him, "If armed police would not walk the housing projects alone during the day, what about the paper boys, mailmen, and those who live in the projects who were victims?"

"Well, dat's it! You do whut you gotta do 'n I'll do whut I gotta do!" He stormed out of my office.

On the way out he angrily threatened horticultural violence to Sandy, who volunteered on special projects in the office, "Ya know dose flowers ya planted today in Willard Park? Well, by tomorrow, we're gonna pull doze flowers up by da roots!" He was bitter as he threatened Cleveland's First Lady, who was shocked by the officer's sudden entrance and exit.

Thirteen policemen were fired for refusing to patrol public housing estates, in individual patrols during the day and in pairs at night. I modified the order to try to avert a strike but upheld the public safety director's action against those who had refused the new assignments.

Nineteen hundred policemen, most of the department, walked off the job.

Public housing residents appreciated my intervention. The rest of the city was in an uproar over lack of police protection.

We obtained a midnight court order to require the police to return to duty. It was left to me to get the word out. The only way to do it was to travel immediately to the six police district stations to broadcast the order to the striking policemen over my car's public address system.

Assistant Safety Director Tonia Grdina, *Cleveland Press* reporter Peter Phipps, Sandy, and I were driven by a member of my personal security staff, Detective John Zajac. We were not prepared for the uproar at the Second District police station.

A riot of drunk and disorderly policemen were discharging firearms, hurling threats, "Don't go home tonight!" I tried to read the court order over the car's microphone. Curses, obscenities, middle-finger gestures followed. Beer cans sailed through the air. Police sirens and car horns drowned out my words. Our car was surrounded, and rocked violently, as faces distorted by rage crowded the windows.

One protester in blue bellied up to Detective Zajac and said, "I hope you aren't a cop, because I'll remember your face."

Everyone in the car was afraid. Things were totally out of sync as we left in a hail of beer cans. The police department was in open rebellion and its members were fully armed.

In the wake of the riot by police, I called the White House and asked for federal troops to patrol the streets of Cleveland. I was referred to Ohio's Governor, James A. Rhodes, to ask for the National Guard. Governor Rhodes declined.

The police returned to work the next day, under threat of heavy court fines to individual officers and union members. I agreed to arbitrate the dismissal of the patrolmen. The absence of police from the streets for nearly a full day gave the recall more ammunition.

Fear joined the recall. The people weren't interested in who was at fault. Policemen, both on duty and off duty, now pushed the recall. Bumper stickers supporting the recall appeared on police cars. Increased complaints of ever slower police response poured into my office.

Provocative TV news reports followed, "Telephone police and tell them you've been raped, robbed, or shot and you can expect help - - thirteen minutes later!"

"There are not enough police. There were 2,500 in the Stokes' administration now there are only 1,950."

A few days later Safety Director James Barrett toured a public housing estate and found two policemen asleep in their car.

I was glad someone was getting rest.

CHAPTER 41

We Could Lose

The media intensified its editorial barrage on behalf of the recall. Usually, I paid little attention to media coverage. I left that to Andy Juniewicz and his assistant, Joe Stewart, who would share key news reports with me. Otherwise, I instructed them to file the reports and someday, perhaps many years later, I would review them.

When you are in public life, as it is for athletes, writers, artists, or any type of performer, you have to be inner-directed to be successful. If you look to each report or review to find out who you are, it is a distraction sapping vital mental and physical energy.

That approach worked fine until the recall election.

I had to pay careful attention, with trip-wire sensitivity to all news reports. I picked my way through a fusillade of recall editorials which were being repeated, almost hourly, in the media.

WKYC-TV 3, the NBC affiliate, was terse: "Dennis Kucinich should not continue as Mayor of this city. He also inherited a monumental mess from a procession of political leaders who have done a thoroughly rotten job of managing this city. But he knew about that when he asked for the job. As much as we opposed recall, and we did and do, it's now a fact and the time has come for someone else to put the pieces back together."

WGAR Radio: "Dennis will continue to fight for what he believes in while Cleveland goes down the drain. For that reason alone, radio station WGAR supports the recall…"

WHK Radio: "He sees Muny Light and now the water system in a state of financial and structural collapse… Financial mismanagement has us careening toward municipal bankruptcy. …Cleveland does not need Dennis Kucinich as Mayor and Cleveland must say so this Sunday, August 13th."

The *Cleveland Press* wrote: "Our support for the recall is based solely on our fear that the mood and the atmosphere in City Hall today frustrates those who want to help Cleveland move forward and we see little hope for change. "

The newspaper of Cleveland's Black community, the *Call and Post*, compared a vote for the recall with the end of slavery. "Blacks more than any other racial group, trapped as they are in the inner-city, for their own best interest must vote for the recall. Let's all of us make Sunday, August 13, Emancipation Day in Cleveland."

The recall was not about logic, or the community, or the city's interests. It was a crude, high-level power play to regain control of city government. The Cleveland media, as an extension of Cleveland's corporate community, was in no position to make an independent evaluation of events, because they too, were caught up in the recall fever. Their role was to prophesy doom unless I was recalled.

Seventy-five years previous, in the golden age of journalism, with publications like *McClure's Magazine* bringing forth the best journalists in America to focus on social and economic injustice in American cities, the spirit of reform swept across the nation and fostered a new breed of journalistic "muckrakers," who exposed wrongdoing and thereby created shifts in American politics. The muckrakers' spiritual heirs in Cleveland had lost their jobs, leaving the public clueless as to corporate crimes and social injustices.

As the recall election drew near, various players presented their summation as an indictment. Removal from office for refusing to sell Muny Light, refusing to approve the Republic Steel ore dock deal, and for financial mismanagement. The Chief of Police, in whose name the recall commenced, was now a muddled memory of distorted recollection. The recall was duck soup du jour.

Dick Feagler, a *Cleveland Press* columnist, was the only person in the establishment Cleveland media who challenged the hysteria. "…Dennis had not caused these horrible problems, who else was there to recall, if not Dennis? … They couldn't say Dennis got in through a rigged election. Couldn't say he failed to keep his campaign promises. Couldn't say he had committed any crimes. About all that was left was to say that Dennis just doesn't fit."

As I counted down the days to my political reckoning, I woke up tired every morning. The clock radio alarm played newly-programmed editorials demanding my recall. My stomach was wrenched in knots. I told no one that I was passing blood. If I went to the hospital, the recallers would claim I had a mental breakdown.

I was in trouble.

I knew it.

I found solace in reports coming back from the field. Our razor-thin margin of support, somehow, appeared to be holding. The constituency I had gathered through the struggle to save Muny Light, through the victory in the mayoral primary and general elections, was steadfast. People stood up for me, because I stood up for them.

When our campaign visited Clevelanders at their homes, we learned that many quietly resented the constant attack by interests exploiting the city. "Man on the Street" TV commercials drove home that theme. In one, an elderly Italian man angrily proclaimed in broken English, "They don't wanna honest man in there." Another ad, featured an African American man, opining the reason for the recall was "Probably 'cause he's stepping on some pretty big toes."

Our campaign mailers sharply drew comparisons between the type of city government people had under our administration and what people could expect if we were ousted.

A terse mailer, on pink paper, was a "utility shut-off notice," sent to Muny Light customers, reminding them that, if I lost the election, their Muny Light service would, truly be discontinued.

A few days before the election, another nightmare. Forbes precipitated a garbage strike. He refused to authorize raises for city mechanics, falsely maintaining the city did not have the money, in order to promote the public perception city finances had been drained by Muny Light. The city mechanics struck, stopping garbage trucks from making their rounds.

As bags of rotting garbage began to pile up on tree lawns on humid August afternoons, the citizenry did not want to know whether or not it was an illegal strike, nor were they aware the city had the money to pay retroactive raises to avoid the strike. They just wanted the garbage picked up.

Sandy and I had arrived home late from a night of campaigning against the recall. We went upstairs, I took off my tie and began to stare vacantly across the room.

"What are you thinking?" she asked, anxiously.

"I don't have any idea how this is going to turn out. The television commercials, the editorials, the distorted news stories, the political reality of the city has been twisted. Everywhere I go, people ask, 'How can you stand it?' What they mean is they can't stand it. We could lose."

Her eyes widened. "You've never said that before."

"You know me, I am always the optimist. I always try to win. Now, with Muny Light, the shaky finances, the police strike, the garbage strike, Republic Steel threatening to leave, Sohio threatening to pull their project, the Sunday election, the paper ballots. Victory may be beyond our reach." I was melancholy. "Remember we won this office by less than one percent."

Sandy was taken aback. "Do you think people are so stupid that they believe all that stuff?" she said angrily.

"How can you expect people not to believe what they see on TV and read every day in the newspapers? The media is promoting the corporate consensus. This is Cleveland's establishment reshaping the city in their image. How else do people get information about the government, except through corporate media? People could easily believe everything in Cleveland was OK, until I got elected."

"Why should you even bother?" Sandy said in disgust. "The city was corrupt before you came in. It will be corrupt after you leave. They don't want anyone honest. And, why aren't people speaking out to defend you?"

"Our supporters are intimidated. We are getting indications at the door that our support is holding, even if it is quiet. Hopefully, people will speak for us through their votes," I said.

I took a deep breath, changed into my pajamas and moved near to Sandy in bed. "Hey hon?" I whispered to her. Her eyes fluttered open. "Thanks for staying close through all this. I'm sorry it's been so tough."

"Shhh…" she said, and turned out the lights. We fell asleep in each other's arms.

CHAPTER 42

Prophets of Poison

It was a beautiful morning. The birds nestling in the tree outside our bedroom window were chirping merrily to the baby blue sky, while the scent of pine wafted to our side window. I peeked through the blinds to see rays of sunshine splitting golden clouds on the eastern horizon. A new day. It was good to be alive. I sensed something good was going to happen.

"Dennis? Are you up? Come on down, we've got to get started." Sandy was preparing breakfast. "Wait 'til you see the *Plain Dealer*!" she said in a disquieting tone.

At the kitchen table, I saw the banner headline placed in front of eggs and toast:

"SELL MUNY LIGHT OR RISK TAKEOVER CLEVELAND FINANCIAL ADVISOR SAYS"

I read the story. Its source was George Forbes, not a "Cleveland Financial Advisor."

Another headline read:

"CITY TO RUN OUT OF CASH FOR PAYROLL"

This was not true, but couldn't be disproved in only a day.

A third front-page story discussed a poll showing 22% of the people believed services in Cleveland were better since I became Mayor, 26% believed services were worse and 52% didn't see any change. The headline:

"SERVICE WORSE UNDER MAYOR, POLLS SHOW"

The recall was fait accompli. The Democratic Party Chairman unveiled a new Mayor:

"HAGAN'S CHOICE: MAYOR FEIGHAN"

Tim Hagan, Democratic Party Chairman, was Edward Feighan's campaign manager nine months ago, when I was still a young man. My successor had been anointed with printer's ink, and I was not yet dead. I looked at the *Plain Dealer*'s recall propaganda edition a second time. I had to laugh.

Media use their power to confirm their predictions. In this case, the *Plain Dealer* had abandoned any pretense of honest journalism. If America ever descended to a state-run press, I saw a preview worthy of the USSR's Pravda.

The *Cleveland Press* sent a signal to my supporters: "Don't bother voting, the election is already over. You lost." On the day before the recall, a *Cleveland Press* columnist conjured, "Kucinich will lose as backers stay home."

The editorial page sent me a message on behalf of their corporate advertisers, "Message to Kucinich, there is no conspiracy." Why would I have thought that?

I could not win with the corporate media. I had to win the recall with the support of the people in the neighborhoods. So, in the closing hours, I was back on the streets, where my campaign first began, where my career began, where my life's work was informed. I was on the streets, reaching out to people, asking for help, asking for a chance to continue to serve. I knew, if I had any chance at all, it was here.

Life, as with politics, is being in the right place at the right time. The Feast of the Assumption was one of Cleveland's most colorful pageants. A procession of devout marchers moved solemnly through the Murray Hill neighborhood festooned with Italian and American flags for the celebration of the Assumption of the Blessed Virgin Mary. The recall election was less than twenty-four hours away.

Sandy and I knelt before a makeshift shrine next to Holy Rosary Church. Hundreds of dollars of hopes were pinned to the green and white money diadem of a statue of Mary, above a crescent of flickering votive lights.

We blessed ourselves and returned to the street with our pug-faced guide, Jimmy Trusso, the Cleveland labor leader who knew "The Hill." His "goombah's" were here. He had passed the word on my behalf.

I had disappointed him when I would not promise to overlook gambling. Today he said, "Look, we know ya ain't gonna be out dere for someone else. We'll live wit dat."

Trusso was crucial on this day. Murray Hill was Councilman Basil Russo's neighborhood, and Russo strongly supported the recall. Jimmy Trusso knew the most influential people on The Hill.

A posse of reporters from state and national media followed us as we bounced from stand to stand, sampling pizza, sausage, lemonade, watermelon, and pastry, while gently resisting a few fortune-tellers eager to let me know if I had a future. The cameras focused tightly as I pressed into the crowd, my eyes searching for a friendly face.

"Buongiorno," I exclaimed.

I received a smile and hoped the media trailing me would witness at least one positive response. I looked up Mayfield Road, toward a small, animated circle of men shaking their wrists and shooting dice against the corners of a green felt table stacked with piles of money, while an off-duty policeman, in uniform, stood watch nearby. My eyes met the operator, who lowered his head. The circle at his table drew tighter and the policeman stepped back into the shadows.

Without a word, I changed direction, darting across the street to steer the media away from the crap game. I looked down an alley where slot machines were set up. Back across the street, a modified roulette wheel. Illegal gambling, protected by politicians and police, was a continuing issue. I didn't permit it. I told police officials to enforce the law. The day before we came to The Hill, vice detectives closed down a Vegas-style craps game and removed slot machines.

The carnival kickback scandal was fresh. At least a third of the City Council was under investigation for allegedly taking payments from carnival operators who sponsored illegal gambling.

Two years ago, John Nardi reportedly sought a cut of The Hill's gambling take, run by James T. Licavoli, the Godfather of the Cleveland Mob. Nardi was killed by a car bomb. Licavoli later went on trial for the murder of Danny Greene, another Cleveland crime figure.

"Hey, Mayor," a man, eyeing the cameras, met me in front of a lemonade stand. "Come on in the back. The boys want to meet you. We got some slot machines back here." My eyes widened. Then, he burst out laughing. "Hey, I'm just busting your balls," he laughed and slapped my back. "Don't worry, you'll be alright. Jimmy Trusso put out the word. We gotcha covered."

Sandy and I, hungry and exhausted, chased back and forth across Mayfield Road, as crowds numbering in the tens of thousands coursed along. The media was close behind.

We reached a restaurant. I turned from its entrance, and entreated the media, "Look, we are going to get something to eat. We'll meet you here in an hour. Thanks."

We transited from blinding sun to pitch-black darkness. The lights were out in the restaurant. Escorted by Trusso, we walked a narrow aisle to a secluded patio behind the kitchen, where a few rays of light filtered through closely fitted slats of a black wooden fence.

"Ya gotta try dis food. It's da greatest on da Hill," said Trusso. "Try da veal parmigiana. Hey!" He hailed a solitary diner who sat hunched in a corner, "Jack, hey Jack, howyadoin'. Evuh meet da Mayuh? Here's da Mayuh, Jack," Jimmy said jauntily as he corralled me by the shoulders and marched me toward Jack's table.

"Mayuh, say hello to Jack."

I nodded, extending my hand. Jack, sitting down, accepted it. He was a well-built man in his late sixties. He waved, grandly, for us to join him.

"Try the veal," he said as he fixed the spaghetti bib covering his white shirt. We dined on veal, spaghetti, and Italian salad with oil and vinegar. Jack motioned toward me with his head and twirled a forkful of spaghetti as he spoke to Jimmy.

"I've heard a lot about this kid," he said. Trusso squinted, pensively. "Always wanted to meet him." He took a mouthful of spaghetti and then his knife cut sharply into a large slab of meat. Tilting his head slightly, as if to size me up once more, his faced loomed as large as a moon. Jack had presence, a sense of command.

"I hear you got big balls, kid. Bigger than an elephant's," he said. "I like that." We laughed. Sandy gave me a sideways glance. A compliment is a compliment, and the recall election was tomorrow.

"Thanks, Jack," I said.

"I like a guy who has balls," he continued. "Most politicians are weak. Got no use for them. They disgust me," he said the word 'disgust' with extra feeling.

We ate and talked about the wonders of Murray Hill, Italian food, and City Hall. He knew politics, and he knew Cleveland. The meal was excellent. Even if it was hard to see the food, it set well with me. If tomorrow was to be my last day as Mayor, it was appropriate that my favorite food, spaghetti, be my last meal.

It was time to go back to the street. Jack had been gracious, unassuming, a warm grandfather. As we left the dinner table, we shook hands, Jimmy said goodbye, and then added, "Passa la parola," Italian for "pass the word."

"Va bene," Jack answered, his hands moved, as in a subtle blessing.

We wended our way to where the media was waiting on the other side of the restaurant door. I shielded my eyes as we moved from the darkness to daylight. As we were about to step into the news scrum, Jimmy turned to me and cupped my head with his hands to whisper into my face.

"Boy am I glad none of dose newspaper guys came in. Da ball game wudda been ovah." He made a face as if he had sucked on a lemon.

"What are you talking about, Jimmy?"

"Jack's not really bad as dey say," Jimmy said, distracted, furtive, rummaging through fragments of thought. I did not understand what he was trying to say.

"Come on, Jimmy, we've got to get back to the campaign," I said anxiously, as camera crews hovered and microphones began to appear.

He continued, sotto voce, whispering into my ear. "He's a businessman, ya know?" He spun the pronunciation of the word "businessman," stressing the first two syllables, elongating them. "He's a businessman, ya know whad I mean?"

"So who is he? What does he do?" I was impatient. There were votes to get. Time was running out.

Jimmy gave me a look of wild surmise. "You don't know Jack? Jack, he's da boss. Da BIG boss. 'Il Capo.'" Jimmy's face scrunched tightly, as if the sunlight was bothering his eyes.

A shiver went through me. I saw the election lost. My career a cold meatball. What would happen if the people of Cleveland found out that, the day before the recall, Sandy and I had lunch on Murray Hill with "Jack" White, AKA the notorious crime boss, James T. Licavoli, the Godfather, who not quite three months earlier was found innocent of involvement in the bombing murder of well-known organized crime figure, Danny Greene.

Would I survive this onslaught?

There is another city, one apart from the synthetic creation of special interests. The real city takes shape in conversations across backyard fences, at the shop, in area taverns, on the sidewalks in front of churches, inside beauty parlors, in diners, on buses, at card parties, and in hundreds of other places where people came to discuss the recall and the city of Cleveland as they felt it, as they lived it, apart from the events conjured in editors' offices, or the dancing electrons of theatrical distortions coursing through the circuitry of television sets into homes.

People in positions of power and influence have trouble understanding life at the street level, where the led do the leading while their practical aspirations are seldom addressed by politicians.

People at the street level wonder how they can make ends meet. They worry for their jobs, their wages. They wonder why they pay so much in taxes and get so little in return. They see politicians supposedly representing poor people become millionaires while supporting the interests of large corporations. They wonder why they never hear editorials protesting high food prices, high interest rates, high utility rates, utility monopolies, or criticism of a daily advertiser. They wonder, as they look to retirement, after a lifetime of work, why they still face the same uncertainties of their younger years. They do not see answers in the popular culture and are suspicious of popular prejudice. They turn the TV dial to see if their experience is shared by others. But they seldom find evidence it is.

On the street, there was a growing understanding that I was fighting for the economic interests of ordinary people and a wariness of the powerful forces constantly battering our administration.

Both Democratic and Republican political parties were working for my ouster. Party officers and their ward political machines were in charge of the polling stations, they appointed the people who conducted the election and counted the ballots in the precinct. At least twenty-four of thirty-three ward machines were campaigning for the recall.

When paper ballots were ordered for the election, I remembered the attempt to overturn my first election victory, proving the saying "It ain't how the ballots go in that counts, it's how they come out." I held classes for my staff and volunteers to urge them to beware of mis-marking, strike-overs, ballot defacement, smears and smudges invalidating paper ballots cast against the recall. We were concerned the election would be stolen, dead persons voting, votes recorded for individuals not present for the election, people double voting in absentia and in person, people voting from vacant lots and abandoned buildings, pre-marked ballots for the recall substituted for ballots actually marked against the recall. A slow vote count could mean ballots were being altered. I learned my lessons well from the Bilinski machine in Tremont, where I won my first election by sixteen votes in a recount of impounded paper ballots. I knew from experience that, despite all our efforts to win the election, in the face of bi-partisan opposition, we had to protect the election on Election Day. We certified volunteers to be "challengers," who would verify voting eligibility inside the polling places or be present as witnesses to the counting of the ballots by precinct officials.

When Sandy and I awoke, early on Recall Sunday, church bells were summoning the elect and the electorate. A camera crew slept in a car outside our home. It seemed inappropriate for the recall election to be held on such a beautiful, clear day.

We voted early. I was the 13th voter in my precinct on this, the thirteenth day of August. The Sunday election had been arranged by Forbes. He assumed that tens of thousands of Black voters in churches whose pastors allied with him, upon receiving spiritual guidance, would proceed to the voting booths to dispatch me to perdition's lowest circle.

Sandy and I set out across the city for a final round of campaigning, stopping to make last-minute appeals at churches in the Black community, hoping to say something to turn a vote. I knew the election would be close.

Before the vote totals came in, a network television crew asked me: How many votes will you win by?"

My answer: "One."

It was the evening of the recall. The polls were closed. Our campaign workers, who had been distributing literature and asking for votes at polling places throughout the day in key wards, returned to the Plaza Hotel to await the results.

Sandy and I stopped briefly at Tony's Diner, greeted supporters, ate, and then went home. The recall campaign at an end, I could feel a wellspring of emotions. The recall had been an ordeal, a journey through a hall of distorted mirrors, screams, bright lights, threats, portents, and lunacy. I went up to my study to begin to write down my thoughts. I wrote two speeches, one for victory, the other a concession. I was ready for either outcome.

Downstairs, Sandy played "As Time Goes By," softly on the piano. She was the only other person who knew what kind of hell we had been through in the past months. We drew near, bolstering each other's confidence and courage, despite being opposed by nearly every interest group in the city. Each day we looked ahead, never sure of the outcome, knowing only one thing: Not to quit. A practiced perseverance and our love steadied us.

Time suspended as we waited to hear from Weissman, who was analyzing precinct results at the Board of Elections. Bob would know from early returns whether we would remain in office.

The phone rang.

Eternity expressed itself.

It was Weissman.

"You won!"

I grabbed Sandy and held her close for a long time, while we both shed tears of relief.

Weissman reported that the large turnout recallers were hoping for did not materialize. Eight of ten Black voters walked out of church and headed home, without voting. Black voters saw the recall as a White person's thing. They knew our administration represented the community, equally and fearlessly, and despite the near unanimity of Black leadership for the recall, Black voters disengaged. Forbes' strategy for a successful recall depended upon stirring up enough hostility in the Black community to spark a turnout against me. It did not work.

Sandy, *Cleveland Press* Columnist Dick Feagler and I got into a detective car and headed for our election night reception at the Plaza Hotel in downtown Cleveland, where I would reclaim my mayoralty.

The band played the theme from "Rocky" as I jumped to the platform with the echoing cheers of hundreds of campaign workers. Our margin of victory was two hundred and seventy six votes, 0.2 of one percentage point. I knew to be gracious in victory and, remembering Lincoln's Second Inaugural, spoke of binding up our city's wounds. I was prepared to forgive and forget the political attacks.

CHAPTER 43

They Will Kill You

The next morning, the recall leaders, in a gesture of futility, argued that I should resign. They wanted me to hand them the victory denied to them by the voters.

Back at City Hall, Jack Schulman entered my office to offer congratulations.

"Well, you did it."

"No problem." I laughed for a moment and then grew serious. "Jack this was unbelievable. I'm glad to get it behind us."

"You think what you just went through was bad?" Schulman said. "Let me tell you something. You won the battle, not the war. Your enemies came close to getting rid of you. They smell eventual victory. They will now go out and get a bigger gun. CEI, Forbes, and the banks will break the city if they have to, in order to get you," he said with the same certainty, the same timbre his father, Milt, had used to make his point.

I claimed a victory and was not going to let it evaporate, based on the seismic sensitivities of my Law Director. "Jack, the war is over."

"You'll see," he continued. "They'll refuse to roll over the notes that come due on December 15th. They'll put the city into default. They figure it will finish you."

"Jack, no way will the banks put us into default. Bankers live here, too. Forbes and CEI want me to sell Muny Light. They won't ruin the city to get at Muny."

Jack was not to be placated. "Wrong. They will break the city to get rid of you. There will be another recall, a financial one," he predicted.

"Jack, we won, enough of the crepe-handing," I thought.

"They will try to kill you. They already tried once."

"Twice," I said. I was paying attention.

After the recall election, I called Council President Forbes and invited him to meet at Tony's Diner to discuss governing, over grits. Diners were quite aware of the rivalry, so when we sat down for breakfast, it created a stir.

George appreciated the fanciful nature of a post-recall parley. We sat across from each other, and for a moment, silently looked each other in the eyes. Then we both burst out laughing, Forbes' way of acknowledging the ferocity of the recall campaign and congratulating me for still standing, and my way of telling him that I won despite everything he threw at us.

My supporters celebrated a tremendous victory, which they believed strengthened my hand at City Hall. My detractors were ready to start another recall, when the statutory time-period tolled. Call it a hangover.

There was no need to rehash anything with Forbes. Little had changed. I remained the Mayor He was still the Council President. I did have objectives in calling the meeting. First, I wanted to signal to the city that such a meeting could occur. Second, I wanted Forbes to know that we should make an effort to reset our relationship, because I was going to be around at least until November of 1979.

We did not get into details at Tony's. I was not looking for political security from Forbes, only an opportunity to speak one on one. There were many serious matters to attend to. We had to communicate first.

A few days later, at my request, Forbes called a meeting of the City Council's finance committee to bring forward our latest plan, land sales to repay the CEI debt. Council approval was needed to clear the way for us to pay the CEI debt and relieve other financial, banking and credit pressures.

This would be the first test of whether the Council President was prepared to take Muny matters in a new direction, or whether he was unalterably committed to CEI and would not permit any legislation to pass, short of the sale of the city's electric system.

Forbes made his position clear in an interview with the *Cleveland Press,* published in the morning edition. "This Mayor is such a bad Mayor that he doesn't care about what happens to this city," Forbes said, ending our brief truce, renewing his pledge to deliver Muny Light to CEI. He took a committee vote on our proposal, and it was promptly defeated. Perhaps his only reason to meet me at Tony's was to sample the grits.

The *Press*' final edition correctly predicted, based on Forbes' comments:

**"COUNCIL SET TO DEFEAT
SAVING OF MUNY LIGHT"**

It was no surprise that the only way we would get approval of any financially-significant legislation, according to Forbes, was if I sold Muny Light. The *Plain Dealer* reported on Page One:

**"COUNCIL REFUSES TO OK LAND DEAL
FORBES DEMANDS SALE OF MUNY LIGHT"**

Forbes reverted to political theater. It was an act I had seen before. He would appear conciliatory, until we approached a solution for retaining Muny Light. He would not cooperate with our administration until we made clear that we would sell Muny Light. Each refusal brought a new tirade from Forbes The city was going broke, because of Muny Light. Nothing would change until I changed my 'attitude,' meaning, until I agreed to sell the light system.

I tried to reach out to the Council President to remind him I would not bend on Muny Light. One phone conversation from my office to his was telling.

"George, we have to work something out to protect the city's finances. Time is short."

"Now, Dennis, why are you calling me?" he said with a patronizing touch of amusement. "You know what you have to do."

"That's a non-starter, George. It's a big city. Aren't there other things you are interested in?"

"I'm telling you, I'm not moving anything until we deal with the light system."

I had offered Forbes a compromise on the ore dock in exchange for an agreement to secure our finances and protect Muny Light. He may have viewed my offer as weakness, because he turned it down, calling for both approval of the ore dock and the sale of Muny Light. Then, he threatened to hold up the police and fire payrolls, unless I yielded on Muny Light.

During one committee meeting, Forbes and I sat in close proximity. He raised his chin a bit and peered down his nose at me and laughed and said, "I'm telling you, no way you are going to stop me from selling the light plant."

I paused, looked at him, and said, emphatically, "I'll go to hell first, George."

I was not going to permit Muny to be held hostage, no matter my desire to strike a deal.

While in my office, I received a call from a local minister whom I had known from events in the Black community. "Mayor, I need to see you." I was pressed for time, but I remained generally available to religious leaders, as they represented large groups of people from the neighborhoods. His church was not far away from City Hall. Over the lunch hour, I had Detective Plank drive me to meet in the sanctuary, off Cedar Avenue.

The pastor met me at the door and gave me his card, "For yet a little while, and He that shall come, will come and will not tarry," - - Hebrews. As I was contemplating the spiritual guidance of the pastor's card, he excused himself.

Across the empty church, a slight figure emerged from the shadows, walking slowly, steadily toward me, as an apparition. It was Bill Seawright! *This* was the minister's emergency?

"Mr. Mayor…" he began softly, head bowed in a gesture of humility.

"Whoa, whoa, whoa, whoa," I stammered. "Where are we going with this?" I had a keen memory of my last encounter with Seawright in a church. I measured my steps to the exit.

"It's all right. I don't mean you no harm," he said. "You know Ralph Perk was a friend of mine. I stand by my friends."

"Why did you arrange for me to be here?" I asked, mindful that anything could happen when Seawright was present, set-ups, suitcases full of money, or police raids.

"I wanted you to know, I don't mean you no harm. I won't do anything to hurt you. I don't want nothing from you. I support a lot of people, and don't ask for anything in return," he said. Translated: 'Don't do anything to hurt me.'

He was asking me not to judge him. He did not live for money, as much as he did for respect. Money was the means to appreciation and honor. Those he supported included dozens of ministers and their churches, including this one, I assumed.

How Seawright gained money was another matter. As I considered my difficulties with Cleveland's 'legitimate' financial community, I was reminded of Bertolt Brecht's observation in The Three Penny Opera, "What is robbing a bank compared with founding a bank?"

Seawright reminded me that we had met more than ten years ago through Gerrie Williams and Rosetta Gregory, who worked on Carl Stokes' campaigns. He had direct contact with Mayors Stokes and Perk. This was an effort to do the same, with me. That's the way he did business. This was also a sign he accepted the results of the recall election.

I wondered, since Forbes was solidly behind the Sunday recall, and Seawright and Forbes were implacable foes, based on their conflicting business interests, did Seawright use his influence with the pastors on his payroll to tamp down recall enthusiasm as a means of thwarting Forbes? Had I gained favor with elements of organized crime in the Black and the Italian communities simply because I was not in anyone's pocket?

Our minister friend did not return. Then, "He that shall come," Bill Seawright, left gently, and I returned to City Hall, mindful not to take yesterday's opponents for granted. They may have personal reasons to support you today.

CHAPTER 44

Not Banking on Cleveland

Cleveland's banks were not banking on Cleveland. We tried to get $14.5 million of Mayor Perk's one-year notes re-financed, by asking each major Cleveland bank to buy a share of new city notes to replace the maturing notes they were holding. They refused.

The city was fully capable of repaying new notes, as long as the Council President authorized repaying them.

We were not asking the banks for more money, only a rollover of the loans they gave the previous administration. In fact, we were correcting the financial aberrations created by Perk and the banks.

Dan Marschall, an economic development research specialist, sent me a report showing that the banks holding the city's debt had combined assets of more than $14 billion. They had $2 billion invested in municipal bonds outside of Cleveland. Their profits in 1977 were over $122 million, even after reserving millions of dollars in losses for bad loans all over the world.

There was no reason for the city to be considered a "bad loan." Cleveland had all the assets needed to meet its obligations. Nevertheless, the groundwork was being laid to use the city's tenuous credit standing as the fulcrum to privatize Muny Light.

Marschall's report showed the banks made their money in Cleveland, then moved the money, abandoning the city's neighborhoods, to invest everywhere else.

I called in Juniewicz to get the information released.

"Andy, this report reveals Cleveland Trust, National City and Central National have the biggest consumer deposits in the city, while they continue to decrease the amounts they loan into the city. Millions come from the people in the neighborhoods of Cleveland, as well as millions in deposits from City Hall. At the same time, the banks invested comparatively little in Cleveland homes and businesses."

"Call them out on their loan practices. They spend a lot of money on burnishing their images," Juniewicz said. "People should know they are red-lining city neighborhoods and moving capital out of Cleveland. Challenge them."

I chose a live radio show to deliver this message:

"Cleveland's largest banks seem committed to destroying the city. They won't buy Cleveland's bond offerings and they continue their systematic looting of Cleveland's financial resources in pursuit of profits elsewhere in this country and overseas. Unless the banks respond, there will be a citizens' uprising against them. These banks must be brought under control, and this administration will be at the forefront of the movement to severely hamper the operations of these banks."

The *Plain Dealer* responded "...Banks have nothing to do with the financial chaos of the City of Cleveland." The *Cleveland Press* linked the banks' reluctance to purchase the rollover notes to the financial condition of Muny Light.

The Chairman of the local Democratic Party accused me of attacking the free enterprise system, of pitting rich against poor, the haves against the have-not's and barred me from participating in major party events. When a political party is dependent upon corporate interests, it cannot serve the public interest.

Our conflict with the banks had drawn national attention. An "angel" called my office. It was Edward DeBartolo, a shopping center magnate from nearby Youngstown, Ohio.

"Mr. Mayor, I hear you have a problem. I'd like to help. We would be glad to buy a few million in notes to help ease the city's financial condition." He asked me to keep the call confidential until the transaction was cleared. I expressed great appreciation and called Schulman, who predicted the banks would object to DeBartolo's participation.

The debt crisis had empowered the banks, giving them extraordinary leverage over the city. The irony was that banks were created through the sovereign power of the people, as expressed by the state. The granting of a bank charter by the state was a political act, a confirmation of social power to create, hold, and loan money. Though creatures of the state, banks could wield enormous influence, and use credit to usurp the government. The financial game in Cleveland was rigged by the banks, against the city. As Schulman had predicted, the banks refused to consider DeBartolo's offer.

The banks had created the crisis in Cleveland by loaning the Perk administration money without evaluating the city's ability to repay. Bank officers formally certified the city's financial stability, helping Cleveland achieve an A-1 credit rating, while Mayor Perk tripled the city's long-term and short-term debt and inflated the city payroll.

The city's banks could have easily rolled over the outstanding one-year notes. Instead, they were threatening to call the loans, manufacturing a crisis. Demand for immediate repayment would squeeze the city, creating cash shortfalls across city accounts, imperiling vital city services.

Liberal bank lending under Perk had placed Cleveland at the mercy of banks, enabling the financial institutions to use credit as a political weapon. The city's vulnerability to the banks holding its short-term debt occurred while the city deposited tens of millions of dollars in taxpayers' funds, every year, into the same recalcitrant banks.

I spoke to our Commissioner of Economic Development, Jack Nicholl, and asked him to find a way out of the trap. He came back with a plan for the city to establish its own economic development bank to rebuild the city's infrastructure, and to help stabilize city finances. Such a bank was already in operation in North Dakota.

One immediate justification for such a dramatic move: A *Plain Dealer* report on Northeast Ohio Areawide Coordinating Agency (NOACA) study, showed that Cleveland financial institutions made nearly 91% of mortgage and home improvement loans outside the city. Norman Krumholz, City Planning Director told the Cleveland Press that 94% of deposits in local lending institutions come from within the county, but 53% of deposits returned in the form of loans for residential purposes.

The Cuyahoga Plan, a fair housing agency, named race as a factor in lending patterns, where the city's financial institutions were less likely to lend to Black areas than White.

When word of our plan to establish our own bank became public, Cleveland's bankers were irate. This single proposal, for the city to establish a bank, had the potential to change the power equation in Cleveland. Financial independence was the key to local self-governance and to an equitable distribution of financial resources throughout the community.

There was a time in America when banks did not have the final word on government matters. It was prior to the creation of the Federal Reserve Bank in 1913. At the founding of our nation, Congress had the power to coin or create money. It was given away in the Federal Reserve Act. That legislation, passed in 1913, set the stage for a debt-based monetary system. It put the banks above the government. It forced governments to borrow money from banks to meet the needs of the people. Maybe in a small way, Cleveland could expose this condition, or even better, begin to reverse the tide.

The banks, CEI and Forbes put me in a box. Creative thinking by an intellectually gifted staff helped me step out of it.

CHAPTER 45

Death Rides the Ferris Wheel

Three days before her tenth birthday, Cheryl Winiarz and her eleven-year-old sister climbed onto the Ferris wheel at the parish carnival at St. John Cantius Church, on the city's southwest side. At its sixty-three foot height, the "Rampage" provided the girls with a thrilling view of the Tremont neighborhood surrounding the small Polish parish.

Both Cheryl and Elizabeth were secured in their seats by a safety bar, but as the Ferris wheel was cycling, it bumped another ride, the "Zipper," incautiously stationed too close. The safety bar on the Ferris wheel flew open, and Cheryl was pitched head-first onto the asphalt pavement while Elizabeth held on, grabbing the side of the car.

Cheryl's injuries left her in critical condition, and an investigation revealed Sebring Exhibit and Supply Company had been operating the Ferris wheel without the required city inspection. It was the second major accident in three years at a Sebring-operated carnival in the Cleveland area. Fifteen people had been hurt earlier when a Sebring ride collapsed at a Cleveland festival in 1975. That ride however, had been inspected twice and approved by the city.

The same day as the Ferris wheel accident, the Cuyahoga Grand Jury met to hear continuing testimony on the carnival kickback case from George Forbes, Bill Seawright, former Police Chief Lloyd Garey and Mayor Perk, who claimed no knowledge of Forbes' role. While the Grand Jury was underway, a Molotov cocktail, a beer bottle containing a flammable liquid, landed a few feet short of my house, where it exploded without creating any damage.

Cheryl Winiarz' mother and father kept a bedside vigil for their young daughter but tragically, Cheryl died of her injuries. I was grief-stricken. I had known the Winiarz family since my days as a student at St. John Cantius. The parish community was devastated. The corrosive carnival system of payoffs, political favors, cheating the public and unsafe rides had converged to claim the life of a little girl.

CHAPTER 46

Bloody Hell

Forbes was out for blood. He sharply escalated the political conflict, describing a speech I had given at the National Press Club as "a mixture of communism, McCarthyism, and racism." He told the City Council's Democratic Caucus that I was the person most responsible for prosecuting the carnival investigation, repeating a theme he used during the recall election.

Forbes directed his remarks to me, "Absolutely nothing is going to move until you change your attitude. If you think you can run this city by yourself, you better start trying," Forbes said, adding that I understood "only the force of the two-by-four."

I needed expert advice on how to deal with the Council President, who was demonstrably more agitated than ever. I called Carl Stokes, the former Mayor, now a news broadcaster in New York City. Forbes had been one of Stokes' lieutenants during Stokes' mayoralty, 1967-1971. Stokes flew to Cleveland to meet me. We planned a late breakfast together at Tony's Diner. After our meeting, I was to be the Grand Marshal of a parade in Cleveland's Black community, sponsored by the *Call and Post.*

It was Saturday, October 14, 1978, just before 10:00 a.m. I paced the house awaiting Stokes' arrival. A talk with him was essential to expand my perspective on dealing with Forbes.

He was late so I walked into my back yard where the leaves on the apple tree were fading from dark green to lime yellow. The cranberry-colored barberry bushes alongside the stockade fence glistened in the early morning sunshine. The air was cool and clean. I felt refreshed, returned to the inside of the house and walked upstairs to my study, overlooking the backyard and watched from an upstairs window, amused as two blue jays cavorted in the spruce tree.

I turned away from the happy sight.

Suddenly, everything went black.

I slumped into the rocking chair.

When I came to, Sandy was holding my hand. She was terrified. Blood was everywhere.

I had trouble speaking. "Wha… what happened?!"

I tried to get up. I was too weak. I fumbled to comprehend.

"The ambulance is on its way. I called Dr. Pensiero. He will meet us at Hillcrest Hospital."

"What happened? Why all this blood?" I was woozy.

"Sandy, uh," I tried to get up. I pitched back.

The doorbell rang.

"Hold on," she called out. Sandy hurried to the top of the stairs. "Come upstairs, quickly, please," she shouted.

"Sandy, is everything all right?" I heard Carl Stokes' voice.

"No, Carl, it is not. Please come up here."

He came upstairs and entered the study.

"Sandy, he's white as a ghost," Stokes said with alarm. A well-built, strong man, he eased me up and carried me to the bedroom, removing my bloody suit. I vomited blood. I hemorrhaged blood from below. Dark gobs of blood were gathering on my lower torso, sliding down my legs. He helped me slip off my clothes. I was not in pain. I was fading in and out.

"Jesus," I heard Stokes say, softly.

The Emergency Medical Service arrived. Stokes and Sandy accompanied me inside the ambulance, as the siren hit loud and long.

"Where are we going?" the driver asked.

"Hillcrest, Hillcrest Hospital. His doctor is waiting there for him now," Sandy said with urgency.

One medic was already checking my blood pressure and phoned the results into the hospital. Suddenly, I had clarity. I had been swallowing all of the pain I had felt from the stress of one battle after another. While I may have outwardly appeared calm, I had internalized the conflict. I ignored taking care of myself, and my body was registering the consequences. My system exploded in a blood-drenched fury. I could feel my life ebbing. My thoughts raced. Who was going to run the city? There was so much work to be done.

"Carl, could you please call W. O. Walker," who was the publisher of the *Call Post* newspaper, "and tell him I can't make the parade?" This was awful. I was to be the Grand Marshal in the parade, a major event in the Black community.

"Sandy, please contact Andy Juniewicz, Weissman, Schulman, and Blanche Nofel. Tell them to keep track of Muny Light and the financial situation and be ready to give me updates. I want a report on the federal grant we're trying to get for snowplows." Stokes put his hand on my head to try to calm me.

Sandy pressed my hand tightly. I caught her passing a look of futility to Stokes, who clasped my other hand as we sped along the freeway toward the hospital.

Stokes shook his head. "Dennis, this job is not worth the kinds of things you have to go through."

When the ambulance arrived, I was rushed into Hillcrest Hospital's emergency suite, as Sandy and Carl stood watch. They were soon joined in the waiting room by Andy. A jackhammer ripped into concrete in an adjacent room that was under construction as Dr. Mario Kamionkowski, Chief of Gastroenterology, moved a tube down my esophagus into my stomach.

"His blood pressure is dropping," said a nurse. I could hear whispers. Dr. Donald Pensiero, my personal physician, entered the room.

Dr. Kamionkowski spoke. "He's got an acute bleeding ulcer opening on an artery. He's lost several units of blood."

"Send for more blood," said a voice.

"I want him infused with Vitamin K right now," said Dr. Pensiero, tersely. "His prothrombin time is much too slow. We've got to get it controlled."

I passed out and when I woke, the clock had jumped ahead an hour and a half. Dr. Pensiero went to the waiting room to meet with Sandy, Carl and Andy.

"Is he going to be all right?" Juniewicz asked.

"To be honest," Dr. Pensiero said solemnly, "we could lose him."

As the shock of the prognosis settled in, Dr. Pensiero assured the trio that everything was being done to save my life. As Andy later related to me, they stood in stunned silence, each one contemplating how things could suddenly change, for my beloved wife, my closest aide, my dear friend, and my city, unalterably.

Dr. Pensiero returned to the Emergency suite as I slipped in and out of consciousness.

"Dennis, we may have to remove part of your stomach to stop the bleeding," Dr. Kamionkowski said gently, as I rolled over. I couldn't reply because of the tube in my throat.

"We will wait a few minutes to make the decision," he said.

As a former surgical technician, I knew if I went to surgery, I was in more trouble. With a clotting mechanism deficiency, there was a risk. I was in shock. The bleeding was uncontrolled. The team attending me came back with another tube, this one with a camera, enabling doctors to image the bleeding artery inside my stomach. More time passed.

"The bleeding is slowing," Dr. Kamionkowski said with a hint of optimism. "Look," he motioned to Dr. Pensiero to look at the camera images.

"Let's wait a few more minutes," Dr. Pensiero said, instructing the surgical nursing team to stand by.

I fell asleep, woke up, fell asleep. Minutes became hours. The bleeding stopped, neither doctor was sure why. I was moved to recovery and then to a private room.

I had been blessed. When I collapsed at home, Sandy contacted Dr. Pensiero as he was preparing to leave for a Florida vacation with his family. He knew my medical history and had everything ready for me when I arrived at Hillcrest. At another hospital, without prior knowledge of my medical situation, they could have cut me open and, complicated by a severe loss of blood, I could have had trouble surviving the surgery. In all, I was transfused six units.

Sandy had taken charge at the moment of extreme peril and made necessary contacts. I was aware of Sandy's comforting, constant presence as I was guided into the emergency room. I did not know how close I had been to death, but would learn the details later from Sandy, Carl and Andy.

The word of the bleeding episode swept through the city. Juniewicz established a series of medical bulletins, broadcast outside the hospital, to advise the media of my condition. Had I been conscious, I probably would have objected to going public with the details. I was very private as to health or security concerns. Once a public figure begins to advertise frailties, opponents seize an advantage. Tears of sympathy are a fast-drying fluid, especially among crocodiles.

The TV news monitor in my room informed me how I was doing "This is the 5:30 Evening News. We have a special report from our staff Doctor, Leigh Thompson, concerning the Mayor," began anchor person Mona Scott.

"Well, as you know, in the stomach you have a lot of acid, and this breaks down food stuffs, but, at the same time, its an interesting question as to why it doesn't break down the stomach, and there are a variety of reasons for that," Dr. Thompson began, with a diagram of the stomach as a visual aid for his viewers:

"There's a barrier right on the edge of the stomach, and all the acid that's leaked into the stomach is usually carried away by the bloodstream. But if you have too much acid from stress, one would turn off the acid production by taking out a lot of the stomach, that red part here, that produces the acid… "

What is this? That's MY stomach he's dissecting. He's taking out my stomach on the TV screen.

"… or you might actually take out this blue part of the stomach, and by cutting this out, and reconnecting the intestine, you solve all the problems."

When people complain to City Hall that there's a chuckhole deepening for weeks, or a water leak flowing for years, they make the ultimate, desperate threat: "If you don't take care of this, I'm going to call the television stations." It was the darndest thing. They would call, the TV news crews would dutifully come out with their cameras and show it on TV, and the chuckholes would get filled and the water leaks plugged. You can get things more things done with a TV camera that you wouldn't otherwise accomplish with asphalt mix, shovels, tampers, steamrollers and a road crew. It never fails.

While my actual doctors spared me from having my stomach removed, the TV doctor had taken my stomach out, full color, in view of hundreds of thousands of witnesses. Cut out the red part, took out the blue part and reconnected my intestine in two minutes. I didn't feel any pain. I didn't even get an insurance form from Blue Cross. In two minutes flat, TV-me was ready to return to work, except that the real me was pinioned to a hospital bed, with IVs carrying blood and other fluids back into my body.

There was twisted consolation as an outpouring of "concern" came from Council members. They demanded release of my medical records, expressing regret that I might have terminal cancer, or had suffered a mental breakdown.

This was true blood sport, and a new opportunity to take over political decision-making at City Hall.

CHAPTER 47

The Murder Plot

I stepped away from my "danse macabre," after my first week at Hillcrest Hospital, and summoned enough energy to speak with the city's Personnel Director, Jeff Fox. It had been considering him to be the next Chief of Police. A trusted administrator, Fox had a depth of experience in handling difficult assignments for Mayor Stokes. He was a chief deputy clerk when I was Clerk of Courts, chief negotiator in police department contract talks and was in charge of security for school desegregation, which was to be fully implemented by September, 1979. As personnel director he oversaw policies which affected 10,000 city employees. Fox accepted the appointment as Chief of Police. Safety Director Barrett swore him in two days later.

One of Chief Fox's first orders to the police department was to increase security at my hospital room. There were already two policemen outside my room and one inside my room. I noticed several Cleveland police cars in the hospital's parking lot. I was embarrassed, not impressed, by the level of security. Worse, it was a waste of taxpayers' money. I complained to my personal bodyguard, Detective Plank.

"Chief's orders, boss," he said with characteristic brevity.

"Tell these officers to go back to their assignments in the city."

"Mayor. They are there on the orders of the Chief," Detective Plank said. He was loyal to the chain of command.

He was forgetting something.

"Dusty, I give the Chief orders."

"Then you better call him, Mayor," he replied.

It was a perplexing moment, as gray as the sky outside my fourth-floor room. I couldn't get information from my own bodyguard.

Why all these police?

"Dusty, get me the Chief." Detective Plank dialed the number and handed me the phone.

"Jeff, what is going on? What's with this heavy security?"

"I can't tell you over the phone. Believe me, the security is necessary. Lieutenant Kovacic and Detective Vanyo of the Intelligence Unit are handling this matter. Jack Schulman will be over with Andy Juniewicz. You need to see them. I'll be there soon," Fox said.

When Schulman and Juniewicz entered the room, I was sitting up in bed, agitated.

"Listen," Jack began, "You have to get better and get out of here. But don't go getting yourself worked up. Everything is under control."

Schulman came to give me the news that, together with our financial advisors at First Boston, we had been able to persuade the Ohio Legislature to change Ohio's bond laws to allow us to gain access to the credit markets. As a result, Salomon Brothers, the Wall Street investment firm, was prepared to underwrite a $50 million bond issue to convert $40 million in Perk's notes, all of our short-term note indebtedness, to long-term bond debt. This included the $14.5 million of notes maturing in December. This would surely demonstrate the city's financial viability.

If this plan was permitted to work, we could save Muny Light and avoid default. All we needed was for the Council to approve the deal. But no one could predict Forbes. When he appeared to be ready to deal, he was off to another game. He was single-minded in his efforts to transact the sale of Muny Light. I was single-minded in my efforts to save Muny Light. Was there room for compromise?

The physical trauma of the bleeding episode had left me weak. I needed rest. Otherwise, as Dr. Pensiero warned, I could risk a recurrence of the bleeding. I was still healing inside.

Chief Fox was due to arrive in my hospital room. I did not have to worry with Fox in control of the department. He was a fair man, a no-nonsense administrator. He entered the room and assessed that I was ready to receive a startling report.

"There is a plot to murder you. The deed was going to be done at the *Call and Post* parade," the Chief said. "Instead of being in the parade, you ended up here, in the hospital, so the attempt was postponed."

I was shocked. "You mean if I had been in the parade..." The Chief did not respond to my speculation.

"Mayor, we have been in contact with law enforcement officials in Maryland. They have a man working undercover who provided this information. They are in touch with Detective Kovacic. It comes down to this: The local mob has hired someone to kill you, and the hit man was prepared to execute you at the parade."

I felt a chill. I drew the covers closer. The bleeding ulcer, which had almost taken my life, had, in fact, saved it. Is this what Thomas Hardy described as "crass casualty...dicing Time," things happening randomly, or was there a larger plan? The synchronicity in the timing of the two events was not to be easily dismissed, or understood. Either way, blood would be shed.

Throughout my life, I had been delivered from hazardous circumstances. This was of another magnitude. If I had not believed in miracles before being placed at death's door in a hospital, I certainly believed when I learned of the planned assassination attempt, had I been in the parade.

I contemplated deeply my mortality, my loves, my purpose in life, the reason I got into public life, and what would happen if I suddenly departed. Like a Dickens' character awakening from a bad dream, I was poised to rededicate my life, if given more of it - - but I had questions first.

"Who's behind this?" I asked the Chief.

"It's a business decision," he said coldly. "Someone wants you out of City Hall. If the only way is to kill you, well, they are ready to pay money. I can't tell you not to worry," Chief Fox continued. "We'll do everything we can to provide you with protection. When are you leaving the hospital?"

"Dr. Pensiero told me to take a couple weeks convalescing before I return to City Hall, " I said, unhappily.

"That's a good idea - for a number of reasons. Don't tell anyone where you are going."

"Jeff, is Sandy in any danger?" Great anxiety returned when I thought her life was in jeopardy.

"Only insofar as she is with you," he said. "I'll notify her. We don't think anything will be directed toward her. They want you, not her."

CHAPTER 48

You've Got Your Problems, We've Got Ours

It's easy to disrupt a government: Don't pay the workers.

Forbes used Chief Fox's appointment to attempt to trigger another police strike, by defeating a routine transfer of funds into the safety department to cover the police payroll. This was the same destabilizing tactic Forbes used on the eve of the recall, causing a garbage collection strike, through his refusal to pass legislation for contractually-obligated pay increases for the city mechanics who serviced the trucks.

Echoing Forbes' ire over the choice of Chief Fox, Council Majority Leader Basil Russo called it "...the gravest threat to democracy yet posed by this administration."

The tempest over the new Chief receded, when a dramatic development occurred in the carnival kickback investigation. On October 28, 1978, after several months of testimony from over 130 witnesses, the Cuyahoga County grand jury indicted eighteen people on

498 counts of bribery, theft in office, and engaging in organized crime. It was the largest number of indictment counts, delivered from one investigation, in the history of Ohio. Council President George Forbes, was indicted along with five present and two former councilpersons.

The indictments set off a political firestorm. The Black community rallied behind Forbes. A defense fund was established. I wasn't available for comment. I was recovering from the bleeding ulcer.

I did not associate myself with the investigation, the indictments, or the results. Nonetheless, Councilman Terrence Copeland charged that I had instigated the investigation, that the indictments were racially motivated, and that I was trying to put Black leaders in jail.

Forbes pleaded innocent to the charges. Then, Forbes promptly approved the police payroll, ending the threat of a strike.

One of his co-defendants, the former building commissioner, Carlton Rush, also pled innocent to three counts of engaging in organized crime and four counts of theft in office. Rush was implicated because, once Council approval had been obtained for a carnival, the building department had the responsibility to inspect the carnival rides and to green-light carnival permits.

The Council President expanded his political manipulation of the police payroll to the manipulation of all city workers, railing against Muny Light as a threat to everyone's paycheck. This was not lost on Teamster's officials who, even though they knew Forbes was playing a game, threatened a strike by snowplow drivers, if their December paychecks were withheld.

"Look Mayor, you've got your problems, we've got ours," one union leader told me. "If he screws with our paychecks, we have to strike."

The newest theme became that, if Muny Light was not sold, the city would go bankrupt. The *Cleveland Press*, in its centennial souvenir edition, which it printed in the type-face of a bygone era, parroted Forbes' "payless paydays" theme, legitimizing the budget crisis he was attempting to manufacture. This was a routine day in the *Cleveland Press*' tireless campaign to force the sale of Muny Light:

"CRISIS SEEN
PAY-LESS PAYDAYS
DEBT DEFAULTS
LOOM IN CITY

PREDICTION

SALE OF MUNY LIGHT
IS CALLED WAY OUT

OFFICIALS ARE SHAKEN

RUSSO AND WHITE ASSAIL TEGREENE
SAY HE IS A BOLD FACED LIAR"

"The city of Cleveland faces the very real possibility of pay-less paydays and default on its debts unless the Muny Light Plant is sold," the *Cleveland Press*' news story asserted. Forbes, ever the great director, deserved a byline, since he was the person manufacturing the payroll crisis, boiling the pot for the sale, and auguring default. Forbes also filed a lawsuit to try to sell Muny Light directly to CEI, under terms of the agreement he reached with Mayor Perk in 1976.

CEI's legal counsel, Squire Sanders, revealed a previously hidden humanitarian side when it came to Forbes' defense in the carnival kickback case, with a pledge of "pro bono publico" representation. "Pro bono publico" is a Latin term meaning "for the public good." Forbes would now be represented by one of the state's top legal minds, Squire Sanders' partner Charles Clarke, for free. CEI also hired Carlton Rush, the former city building commissioner.

Dr. Pensiero informed me that I would need at least three more weeks of rest before returning to work, lest I begin to bleed again. I did not take it well.

"Look, I have to be on the job. People are taking advantage of my absence. I'm ready to go back."

Sandy was alarmed. Dr. Pensiero spoke curtly, "You may be the Mayor. I'm your doctor. I'm putting my foot down. You are not physically ready to go back to work. You need rest. If you start to bleed again, you will put your life at risk."

I was too weak to argue. We accepted Dr. and Mrs. Pensiero's generous offer to travel to Florida, where they provided the seclusion of their personal condominium for our use. I would rest and be sheltered from the hounds of organized crime, who were now looking for an opportunity to kill me physically, and the press hounds who were trying to kill me politically.

Guidance of city matters was under control of the team of Weissman, Schulman, Tegreene and Juniewicz. I had to let go. I had no choice.

The phone rang. Only Blanche Nofel had my Florida number. No one else was permitted to call me, per Sandy's instructions, and no one knew my location. "Dennis, I have Andy Juniewicz here, he needs to speak with you," Blanche said.

I opened the blinds and sunlight poured into the room, a degree of illumination uncommon in Cleveland, especially in late Autumn and Winter. My city is constantly besieged by cloudy days, perfect for inducing melancholy.

"Hi Andy, what's up?" I asked cheerfully.

"How are you?"

"I'm feeling better, getting stronger."

"You'll be glad to know you are missed. The Cleveland media is looking for you and the *Press* is offering fifty bucks to anyone who can get a picture. Rumor is you were spotted on a beach in Florida."

Spotted in Florida? I did not have any security staff with me and anonymity was my new best friend. I was recovering from a near-death medical experience and hiding from the mob.

"TV stations have sent out camera crews to search for you," Andy warned. The media had no idea the risk their political scavenger hunt would bring. If cameras and TV crews suddenly appeared, could the mob be far behind?

"That's not why I called," Andy continued. "I need to bring you up to date on an urgent matter," Andy said. He went on to report that our team had a solution to the city's financial difficulties.

As a result of the efforts of John Carhuff, the city's Wall Street financial advisor from First Boston, Salomon Brothers had finalized the plan to purchase $50 million in newly-issued City of Cleveland bonds, then go into the market and resell the bonds at a profit. The bond financing was to be anchored by a $2.4 million annual increase in property tax revenue, produced by restoring the last-minute property tax cut Perk had enacted. This initiative required only approval by Council.

At Forbes' direction, Council held three votes. Each was against issuing the bonds. While bitterly criticizing the city's lack of access to credit markets, Forbes rejected a Wall Street-approved refinancing plan. He continued to demand the sale of Muny Light, while promoting the fiction of an approaching financial catastrophe.

"They think they can blackmail us into selling Muny Light?" I said heatedly. "This is plain wrong. There isn't a financial problem. There is a political problem. This is a pretend crisis. What is wrong with Forbes? I wish I was back there right now."

Sandy, who was standing near, shook her head in disapproval as I became more animated.

"Take your time," Juniewicz said wryly, "It will all be here when you get back." Law Director Schulman was filling in with gusto as acting Mayor, charging Council with creating the financial crisis by concocting a $34 million deficit, in order to help CEI take over Muny Light. At every opportunity, Schulman explained to anyone who would listen that we had the money to meet payroll and have a balanced budget at the end of the year. The deficiencies were only in the bond accounts, money required by law to be used only for capital improvements.

"If you don't have the money to build things, you don't build them," Schulman, with typical simplicity, advised the Council. He also informed the Council that the misspent capital improvement bond funds had already been funded automatically, by legally-required adjustments in the millage of the property tax, which occurred when the bonds were issued. There was no deficit, and no crisis. At worst, the city might have to pay higher interest rates in the future, depending on the market.

"Andy, this is a fake crisis," I said.

"Yes, I know," he answered. "The media is swept up in a false narrative. We are seeing an increase in intensity to sell Muny. Reporters want a comment from you, not me, not Jack, or anyone else. I was reluctant to make this call. You must respond, right away," Juniewicz said.

"Tell them I said Muny Light will not be sold. Issue a statement calling yesterday's vote a last ditch effort on the part of CEI and their supporters in Council to steal Muny Light. I can't believe the Council will continue to conduct itself so irresponsibly as to deliberately force the city to default on a debt that can be so easily funded. Say that."

"Got it." Andy replied

I may have been convalescing a thousand miles away, but I was in a combative mood. The *Cleveland Press* rushed my statement into its headlines, but it wasn't what I said:

"I'LL RISK DEFAULT"
KUCINICH WARNS COUNCIL ON MUNY

The next day, things were Cleveland-normal. "On this epic day in the life of our newspaper," the *Press* wrote in its Centennial edition, "it is a pleasure to report that the business community has raised some 70% of the $4.3 million it will use to tell the world what a great city Cleveland is, and never mind some of the quaint events that have been happening of late."

CHAPTER 49

Cleveland Dream

The jukebox was playing Johnny Paycheck's "Take This Job and Shove It." A cigarette haze hung over the lunch counter at Tony's Diner, batting around in a breeze of chatter from customers in plaid hunting jackets and green and gray work clothes. A waitress set down a plate of sizzling chicken. I took up a drumstick and began to eat. Sandy, my brother Gary, and Gary's wife were with me in an orange vinyl-covered booth.

Instantly, I felt an explosion inside my head, heard a popping sound, and heard glass breaking. I pitched forward. I heard screams. I was bleeding profusely from my head. Blood was running down the back of my neck. The music was…fading. The diner…fading.

God, this is it.

I woke up in a profuse sweat. Wait!

It was a dream. I wasn't dead at Tony's Diner! I was alive, safe, in an air-conditioned hideaway on Florida's Gulf Coast. We were a thousand miles from danger. It was a dream. I had another chance. Waking up from that nightmare was transformational. I felt as though I had met death and surmounted it. There was nothing to fear.

The morning light bounced around the chrome furniture and the green and silver-plaited wallpaper. I clung to Sandy. She stirred. We fell back to sleep. I didn't want to bring a nightmare to our vacation bedroom. I kept the dream to myself.

As the plane broke through the clouds, I could see Lake Erie was stirring. Choppy waves peaked and lapped over the break-wall below. Cleveland's neighborhoods were easy to identify through the portal of the passenger jet.

"Sandy, there's the house, see?" I moved back so she could get a glimpse of our two-story frame house, visible on the approach to Cleveland Hopkins International Airport.

Our Florida respite was at an end. It was good to be home.

We were met at the gate by a special security detail, accompanied by Detective Plank. "The Chief wants to speak with you," Detective Plank said. "He's in the back parking lot." He turned to Sandy. "Mrs. Kucinich, would you please come with me, and we will meet them around back?"

I walked through a restricted parking area behind the terminal to a green detective car, where Chief Fox and Inspector Nagorski were in conversation. I sat in the front seat, next to the Chief. Sandy remained in a car with Detective Plank.

"I'll make this brief, Mayor," the Chief said in a bureaucratic tone. "We have received word of another planned attempt on your life. It could come at any time. Our sources have told us that the situation is a 'go,' as far as the hit-man is concerned. I have established a special security unit to tail your car, to determine if anyone is following you or checking your movements. The extra unit has been briefed regarding the possibility of an assassination attempt. These are men from the intelligence unit. They are well-trained. They can respond to any situation. I want to emphasize this could not be more serious. The attempt could come when you are leaving your home, entering or exiting City Hall, at a public meeting, across the street from the roof of Public Hall, inside City Hall, inside your office, anywhere."

He nodded toward Inspector Nagorski, seated in the back. A twenty-five year police veteran, who served as acting Chief until Fox's appointment, Nagorski was one of the senior officers whose advice I greatly valued.

Nagorski spoke "The Chief and I have talked this over. Here's what we are recommending: Limit your public appearances. Do not let anyone know your schedule. Stay away from your house. Do not observe any established routines. We have planned various routes in and out of City Hall for you. And, you should wear your bulletproof vest at all times."

I interrupted. "Is Tony's Diner safe?"

Nagorski shook his head. "You should definitely stay away from there. There are too many vantage points for snipers. Wait until this thing blows over."

"I think we should review the other facts we have been able to establish so far," continued Chief Fox. "On October 17th, Lieutenant Kovacic received a call through a contact from a national police intelligence agency who told us that a Cleveland-area crime figure had hired someone to kill you. Several calls have been made between our police intelligence and the contact. We have information the person setting this up is Tommy Sinito. The hit-man visited Cleveland during the week of October 9th to meet with Sinito, who offered him a large sum of money to kill you. Sinito is a member of La Cosa Nostra and is believed to have figured in a number of other murders."

"Why not arrest Sinito?" I asked.

"The problem is," Nagorski said, "the source is an undercover policeman who is right in the middle of this thing. He doesn't have it nailed down, yet. If his cover is blown, he's a dead man. This is an on-going investigation. We hope to be able to know every move the hit-man is making."

"Where did you get this information?" I asked, quietly.

"The Maryland State Police. It's their undercover man. Their undercover man met with Sinito in an Atlantic City casino, where a contract on your life was arranged. It is important that you do not mention this to anyone. We don't want to put the undercover man in jeopardy. We have received word there's a hit-man due, here, in Cleveland," Nagorski said. "That's why we came to meet you."

I looked to Chief Fox for good news. He was wearing his official mask, expressionless. I wanted more than a clinical assessment. I broke the formality.

"Jeff, what do you think the chances are, uh…" I fumbled to describe the prospects for my own demise.

"Let me put it this way - I wouldn't sell you life insurance." He didn't blink. He drew back, as if for effect, his lips tightly pursed on his solemn face. "Oh, by the way, boss, welcome home."

I spoke with Weissman, who had been briefed by the Chief. His view was pragmatic: "Just keep doing your job, don't let this distract you. Look at it this way, it's a compliment. What else do you do with a man who can't be bought?"

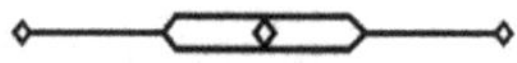

Someone wanted to kill me. But I wanted to go back to work.

In the Mayor's office, I had completed an hour of taking phone calls from the general public when Juniewicz entered the room.

"I hope you are feeling better, Mayor. Everyone here is glad you are back. I have a lot of interview requests," he said, reviewing a list on his clipboard.

"Let's start taking them in a few days. I need time to settle in."

"OK, most of these can wait," Andy agreed. "But I've got a videotape you'll want to see."

We went to Juniewicz's office, forward of the official reception area, where he turned on a television monitor. "This was the big news story last week on Channel 8," he said. He hit the play button, and a TV 8 anchor introduced the story

"Tonight, News Center Eight's Bob Franken has an exclusive report on behind-the-scenes discussions that make default look likely. Bob."

City Hall reporter Bob Franken picked up the lead-in from anchorman Judd Hambrick.

"Judd, if the banks holding $15 million in Cleveland debt refuse to refinance that debt when it comes due, December 15, the city will become the first to default since the Depression. National City Bank holds $4 million of that debt. News Center Eight has learned that National City's Board Chairman, Claude Blair, has been saying in private conversations that because of what he views as the Kucinich administration's antagonism toward the business community, he's considering not refinancing the notes held by his bank. This would probably mean the City would default. Sources quote Blair as expressing a willingness to accept the consequences for Cleveland as the price to pay to see Mayor Kucinich defeated in next year's election. My sources asked not to be identified."

The report showed file film of the construction of National City Bank's new downtown headquarters, as Franken continued. "This project is just one of the reasons Blair is reportedly saying he has had it with Dennis Kucinich. The Mayor has repeatedly attacked this project, which is going up with the help of tax abatement. But Blair is also characterized as disturbed by the administration's overall position on the business community."

"Blair was unavailable for comment today. News Center Eight has tried since Monday to interview him. However, today, in reaction to this story, the bank did issue a statement contending that no decision has been made on refinancing the debt."

"My sources go on to quote Blair as saying that default, with all its problems, might be the best thing that could happen to Cleveland, if it meant the defeat of Dennis Kucinich. What he proposes to do is to get all the banks to invest tremendous amounts to solve the financial problem. But only after a new Mayor takes office."

The videotape ran out. The monitor went blank. I turned to Juniewicz.

"How do we know it is true?"

"Oh, it is," he said. "Look at this."

Juniewicz put another tape into the video playback machine. Channel 8's News Director appeared. "Two nights ago, on News Center 8 at 6:00 p.m. and 11:00 p.m., we reported that National City Bank and its Chairman Mr. Claude Blair, had engaged in certain conduct and had made certain statements which would prove detrimental to the City of Cleveland. In making those statements we failed, in this instance, to check the accuracy of our sources of information. We now find that all of the statements we made were inaccurate and there was absolutely no basis for the report."

"Further investigation has led us to conclude that National City Bank and Mr. Blair are committed to the city's future well-being and financial stability. Therefore, we sincerely apologize for the derogatory statements we made and we deeply regret any embarrassment we may have caused National City Bank and Mr. Blair."

Juniewicz turned off the monitor.

"Well, what do we believe, Franken's news report or the retraction? I asked. "Franken does not have a reputation for making things up."

"No, he doesn't," Juniewicz took a long drag on a cigarette and blew a cloud of smoke up toward the ceiling. "I understand he had a dozen sources, all close to Blair. At least, that's the word going around Channel Eight's news room."

"I have to talk with Franken," I said. "We've got to answer this."

"You can talk with him. It may not do a whole lot of good," Juniewicz said.

"What do you mean?"

"Bob Franken resigned right after the station ran the retraction. After seeing the initial report, National City threatened to sue Channel 8. The station management broadcast the retraction, it said, in order to protect Franken's confidential sources from disclosure in a lawsuit. Word is that TV 8's General Manager, Bill Flynn, told Franken he didn't have to resign, but he was destroying Flynn's credibility in the business community, and the retraction was a business decision," Juniewicz said.

"What!?" I hit my fist into my palm. "Dammit!" A report by Channel 8's top City Hall reporter, a retraction, a resignation, an impending default. The same bank chairman gave Perk's handling of city finances high marks, while Perk doled out a $12 million tax abatement to his bank.

I opposed the expensive concession to National City Bank because it deprived the financially-stressed Cleveland schools of needed money, and it inflicted financial harm upon the city's general fund.

Bob Franken had exposed corporate Cleveland's behind-the-scenes maneuvers. He uncovered the bank's plan to use their financial power to bring the city to its knees. The corporate tax giveaways benefiting the banks and the largest corporations would then continue.

American corporations busied themselves with the overthrow of democratic governments in Central and South America. But in the U.S.? The banks could not run the city, so they were prepared to ruin the city, financially. Franken's report was a watershed event in Cleveland politics.

"Andy, please cue up the station's retraction again."

He put the tape in the machine. Watching the retraction of Franken's report was like watching a TV station chastise a weatherman for a tornado warning. It may have made the station feel better, but I was still watching the sky. This was not about only one station and one reporter. Franken was the second TV 8 reporter to leave his job after colliding with downtown business interests. Jim Cox had been fired a couple of years earlier by TV 8, after the station refused to run his story on the NRC investigation of CEI. And, there was Steve Clark, axed from his radio news commentary after CEI complained.

As a result of the TV-8 story, rumors about default abounded. Cleveland's corporate community had tipped its hand. Franken's initial story was evidence of their arrogance. The first report revealed their fear of public backlash. Franken's story exposed the collusion of media management, ordering a retraction, even though a veteran reporter had at least a dozen sources.

"There is speculation at the *Plain Dealer* that the City may go into default," Juniewicz said. "No one knows what that would mean," he said. "Do we?"

"We won't feed speculation. Tell them we are still expecting the City Council to approve our proposal to go to the national bond market with a $50 million dollar issue."

"Forbes made it clear he won't go for the bond issue unless Muny Light is sold," Juniewicz reminded me.

Open talk about default was a problem because it meant the city was being prepared for default. Franken's report said we would be the first city to go into default since the Depression. Me and Herbert Hoover, great! We aren't talking about the national economy here, or even the local economy for that matter. We were talking about rolling over fourteen and a half million of existing debt, money Perk had borrowed with the encouragement of the very same Cleveland banks now threatening the city.

"Andy, there's no reason for us to go into default. We are not looking for new money, we need an extension of existing credit. Franken's story is about weaponizing credit. I don't want to create a self-fulfilling prophecy by encouraging talk of default."

"Talk of default is going on, whether we encourage it or not," Juniewicz said dryly.

CHAPTER 50

Murder at City Hall

Chief Fox called, urgently "Mayor Moscone of San Francisco and City Supervisor Harvey Milk were just shot and killed at San Francisco City Hall."

"No, no, no!" I said, in disbelief. I had met Mayor Moscone at a national conference in San Francisco early in my term and had spent an evening with Harvey Milk at the California Democratic Council's state convention in San Diego in January. We were on the dais together with Congressman Allard Lowenstein and Governor Jerry Brown.

"Moscone's a decent guy. Milk's an amazing person, very committed. Courageous."

"They're dead, and because of that, you are even more at risk. I'm going to order additional security measures at City Hall. If we do it now, it will be seen as a precaution related to San Francisco. I want a metal detector installed outside your office. The problem now is the random person, the copycat, who gets an idea from the news out of San Francisco," said Chief Fox.

Threats loomed large. Mayor Moscone was killed inside his own office. Why? What drives people to believe you can change things by killing public officials?

I wanted to look out my window to view the expanse of Lake Erie, to reflect upon the lives of Mayor Moscone and Supervisor Milk, but I had to keep the drapes closed.

Why was I being targeted? Lieutenant Kovacic of the Cleveland Police Intelligence Unit had been coordinating the gathering of information critical to my security. A twenty-year veteran crime-fighter, with deep insight into the workings of organized crime, he had to know the reason for the plot. I asked him to come to my office.

He was a man of contradictions, gregarious but closed-mouthed, physically imposing yet not assertive, daring, as he challenged corrupt interests, though cautious in his manner and in his words. He had a desk job, but preferred to be on the streets. As he sat across from me, I acknowledged his dedication and that of his unit.

"It's our job. I'm not going to lose a Mayor on my watch," he said, "We are watching over you. The rest is up to God."

"Lieutenant, I appreciate you making sure word does not get out."

"We don't give information in the Intel Unit, we gather it. We don't discuss it outside of our unit. I know I can rely on our people. They are working on this around the clock. Also, there are people working undercover we have to protect."

I took a deep breath and asked the question for which perhaps Lt. Kovacic, alone among investigators, had an answer

"Why?"

"Mayor, you know I'm not involved in politics, so I can't say anything one way or another about your decisions. Based on everything we know, this is about Muny Light. You're getting in the way of some people making a lot of money."

CHAPTER 51

We Don't Want Your Money

No plan to save Muny Light was so good that it couldn't be rejected. As the murky financial tide continued to rise, we tried one idea after another to avoid default and to pay off the debt to CEI. We had already paid CEI $6.4 million since the beginning of the year, using unneeded money from an airport account. CEI, however, claimed that we owed not $6.4 million, but $10.8 million, including compounded interest. The private utility cited a "moral responsibility" to its shareholders to collect the money and threatened, once again, to foreclose on city assets.

Then CEI asserted a new claim against the city, this one for $2.5 million dollars for electricity sold to Muny Light between 1972 and 1975. We faced a new round of attachments of city property, and a rising debt.

Serendipity entered when a top official of the Chessie System railroad called Jack Schulman and informed him of the expiration of a ninety-nine-year lease of a sixty-foot-wide railroad right-of-way, which Chessie held on city land in the industrial Flats. The railroad wanted to purchase the property. The city could sell the land to the railroad voluntarily or, the railroad had the power, under Ohio law, to appropriate it from the city, since it was an active right-of-way.

Schulman ordered an appraisal. It came in at $2 million dollars, enough to nearly pay off CEI and, consequently, balance the city's budget. We felt the figure was a fair price and the Chessie System accepted it.

Schulman informed the Council of the deal.

Several councilmen objected, saying the land should instead be used for bars and restaurants, even though the land was on the industrial side of the Flats and was an active railroad right-of-way. It was the main corridor for shipments of iron ore from Cleveland's port to the steel mills in Youngstown and Pittsburgh.

Forbes opposed the land transfer, then supported it, then opposed it again. Forbes and his Council supporters were desperate to keep the city from getting the money to pay CEI. He refused to call a vote and the proposal for the sale of land died, with members of Council saying I should sell Muny Light and not city land.

We turned to another option - delay payment of $2 million in pension liabilities. We pushed certain payroll obligations into the new year, to ease financial pressure.

Forbes sought to block us at every turn.

Then, with tax abatement legislation due to expire on December 31st, Forbes proclaimed that nothing was going to move at City Hall unless I approved "the single most important issue facing Council," a tax abatement for the Terminal Tower, the epicenter of Cleveland's business district.

Schulman and our lead antitrust attorney, Brad Norris, came into my office after a meeting with the federal judge presiding over the antitrust case.

"Judge Krupansky is threatening to dismiss the antitrust suit, unless we finish paying CEI by December 31st," Schulman said.

"Does he have the power?" I asked.

"It would be an abuse of discretion. We would fight it," said Norris.

Tall and patrician, Norris was immaculately dressed, with matinee-idol good looks and a stunning pair of blue eyes, all hinting at softness. Yet by courtroom reputation, he tore the opposition to shreds with the passion of a Calvinist minister pointing a smoking finger at the damned. He was ready for a fight. This was good news. He believed the debt was a trap CEI and Squire Sanders had laid years earlier to ensnare Muny Light. The antitrust suit was the history of their joint, illegal efforts to undermine and take over the city's light system. Brad Norris had the intellectual, legal, and moral capacity we needed to help us win the case.

The Nuclear Regulatory Commission's findings of CEI's anti-competitive conduct entitled the city to legal recourse. Norris had engaged expert witnesses who had calculated that CEI's anti-competitive actions against Muny Light had an adverse economic impact on Muny of over $100,000,000. One preliminary report stated "The MELP system, with customers lost to CEI's illegal conduct and absent the other illegal acts, would have been a different, larger, and more efficient system than it is now."

"I don't think Judge Krupansky will dismiss the case," said Norris. "He would be inviting the Justice Department to intervene to reverse his decision, since it would lead directly to the sale of Muny Light and to CEI gaining a monopoly. Krupansky has said we are 'ignoring available solutions' to the city's financial problems. He could be referring only to the sale of Muny Light. If he clearly states that, we will have him removed from the case," Norris said. "There is another issue here, although the court will not take note of it. The reason why Muny owes so much to CEI is that CEI purposely charged Muny higher electric rates than it did other large customers, in an effort to put Muny Light out of business."

"Can we still pay off CEI by December 31st and meet Judge

Krupansky's deadline?" I asked.

"Sure," Schulman said. "It's not a matter of our ability to pay. Council has to authorize any method of payment. Forbes has boxed us in. We are not permitted to borrow money and are not permitted to sell land."

Moody's was downgrading our credit rating again. They were predicting default, saying we had no plan. We've had many plans. Every one of them has been rejected by Forbes and the City Council. A false choice has been constructed and repeated in the media "Sell Muny Light or default." "Sell Muny Light or miss payrolls." "Sell Muny Light, or the city will be destroyed. "

Responding to the escalating tension, the public appealed directly to my office with a flood of urgent calls, all demanding the sale.

In an effort to achieve a semblance of civic normality, despite the fiscal constraints, we went ahead with plans to hold the annual Christmas lighting ceremony and a parade in downtown Cleveland. Sandy was in charge of the large civic event, at my request and spent months on the planning. Dozens of meetings with participating organizations were held to ensure that the event, sponsored in cooperation with the Greater Cleveland Growth Association, would be successful. Certainly, Christmas was the one thing we could all agree upon.

I walked into the office Sandy used when she was at City Hall, from where she coordinated a wide range of civic activities. She was in tears. I moved quickly to her side.

"What's wrong?" I asked, concerned, because Sandy was seldom flustered.

"The Christmas Parade," she said, shaking. "The Growth Association called. They are withdrawing their pledge of money to sponsor the parade. They are canceling it!"

"What?"

"They said that under the circumstances, they don't see how the city can go forward."

"Under what circumstances? That I won't sell Muny Light?! You did a lot of work on this, Sandy. I'm so sorry."

"I'm not concerned for myself," she said. "There are hundreds of people who worked to make the parade a success. We had all those meetings. A hundred thousand Clevelanders come to the parade. It's a tradition. It's awful to cancel it. It's so sad. Even Christmas is political," Sandy sighed.

"Do you know who the Growth Association's two largest contributors are?" I asked her.

"Cleveland Trust and CEI?" she guessed.

"Yes. CEI is turning off the lights at Christmas, again," I said, recalling the private utility's role in Christmas-time blackouts on the Muny system

As we were preparing to notify Clevelanders about the Christmas parade, news reports falsely attributed the cancellation to either Sandy bowing out, or to my having had an ulcer. It was not as though we did not have other things to think about, so we let it go.

CHAPTER 52

Foreign Owned City

I never knew Cleveland banks were so provincial. They had, after all, invested millions in other countries. Finance Director Tegreene contacted the local representative of a West German bank to explore its investing in the City notes coming due on December 15th.

Word leaked to the media, setting off a firestorm of patriotic debt-mongering. Speculation was rife that the heavily-ethnic City of Cleveland could end up becoming a "foreign-owned city," as opposed to being lorded over by benevolent local banks which red-lined, dis-invested city neighborhoods, and moved depositors' assets out of the country.

"Money could be Arab," blared one headline.

"I'm caught in an irreconcilable dilemma. We are used to an open policy in American public financing, as opposed to the European business concept of secret negotiations," said Forbes, as he attempted to complete the sale of Muny Light under secretly-negotiated terms.

Not all of Forbes' efforts to peddle Muny Light to CEI were behind the scenes. As the clock ticked toward a December 15th showdown, Forbes filed a lawsuit seeking a writ of mandamus from the Ohio Court of Appeals (8th District) requiring me to sell Muny Light to CEI on the terms of the May 1977 ordinance which passed city council by an 18-15 margin and then was signed by Mayor Perk. This was the ordinance I had blocked with a petition drive.

The referendum was in legal limbo. My election as Mayor was buoyed by the Muny Light campaign, changed the city's political dynamic, and took Muny Light out of CEI's clutches. The May, 1977, sale ordinance was an outlier.

The Perk Administration had planned to use the ordinance to effect the sale of the light system, by contract with CEI, in a last ditch effort at its final meeting of the Board of Control. They backed off when Jack Schulman and I showed up.

Forbes said he filed the action to avoid the city's default. The *Plain Dealer* applauded him and suggested that acceding to Forbes's action was a "fine way" for me to save face, "but the fight is over."

Wrong.

I was certain Jack would beat back this latest gambit to grab Muny Light.

Meanwhile, another Schulman had his own ideas about how to deal with recalcitrant members of City Council. Milt Schulman headed to Probate Court with papers seeking the removal of several of them, charging "misfeasance in office." Under Ohio law, a charge of misfeasance requires an immediate hearing, the introduction of evidence, and a decision from the bench as to the status of the elected official in question.

"They are colluding with CEI to force the sale of Muny Light," Milt said. "They are not going to get away with it. I'm going to get them and get them good."

"Have you talked to Jack?" I asked. Milt's son was in charge of our legal strategy.

"I don't need to talk to Jack, I know what I am doing," Milt said, dismissively.

"Milt, Forbes will claim I'm behind this. He's blaming me for the carnival investigation. This will create chaos with Council."

"There's already chaos, and you're losing," Milt replied. "You need help and Milt Schulman is going to help. If we remove most of the Council they can't touch Muny Light."

Milt Schulman was intent. I couldn't dissuade him. Jack couldn't stop him. He filed the misfeasance charges in Probate Court and went to the Council offices at City Hall to personally serve each named member with a copy of the complaint. As he approached with papers in hand, Councilmen backed off, littering their hasty retreat with profanities. One Councilman, twenty years younger than Milt, approached and, without warning, took a roundhouse swing, striking Milt in the face, knocking him down. A few days to go before the default showdown and we were already taking casualties.

Adding to the circus, a few floors above the room where Milt was decked, federal agents were combing through records in the housing department, looking for evidence of an arson-for-profit ring.

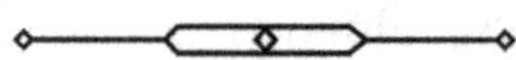

After much contemplation, we developed yet another plan to avoid default. Reluctantly, I agreed to ask Cleveland voters to increase the city income tax. The banks could then exchange their expiring notes for new notes, secured by the new city income tax revenue.

Rescued from default and strengthened by increased tax revenue, we would then market a $90 million bond issue in March of 1979, $40 million to redeem the city's outstanding short term debt, $40 million to replace misspent bond funds, and $10 million for essential equipment for snow removal, garbage collection, and street resurfacing.

Notwithstanding our increasingly sharp differences, I met with Cleveland bankers to inform them of this latest effort to safeguard the city's credit rating and to pay off the debt. At the meeting, I was asked to boost the tax request from 1/4 percent to 1/2 percent, yielding an extra $38 million.

I was opposed to tax increases in principle and campaigned against them. Generally, the more money the government has, the more it wastes. But the massive debt incurred by the previous Republican administration put the city in serious financial straits. A tax increase was the surest way out. I could roll back the tax after the city's credit was stabilized. I acceded to the banks' request.

It was Tuesday evening, December 12, 1978, three days before the deadline and thirteen months since I had taken office. I faced the people of Cleveland in a live TV broadcast, to speak of our dilemma and the necessity of a tax increase.

"Our city faces the danger of being in default to Cleveland banks... If this plan fails, we could find the City of Cleveland losing its water system, losing what's left of its sewer system, losing its Municipal Light System, losing a $325 million antitrust damage suit, and experiencing a drastic reduction in city services. The city will have no capacity for any kind of capital improvements whatsoever....If the plan succeeds, there will be no reduction of service and we'll be able to continue our capital improvement program."

Only the NBC affiliate, WKYC, broadcast my appeal. The two other network-affiliated stations, WEWS TV and WJW TV, refused. I protested to the Federal Communication Commission, since the Federal Communications Act of 1934 required broadcast licensees to operate in "the public interest, convenience and necessity."

Forbes and other Democratic leaders watched WKYC from a nearby holiday party. The Council President's response was, "wait and see."

Councilman Russo said Muny Light should be sold before any tax increase was recommended. Prominent Cleveland commentators supported the tax increase, yet continued to call for the sale of Muny Light.

Former Mayor Perk responded in his low monotone: "Dennis is a pathological liar. Every member of City Council, at least nearly every member, knows that. They've dealt with him before. They know that he can't possibly tell the truth, even if the truth is before him....He had so much money in the treasury. When those kids came into City Hall, they began a wild spending spree beyond anything the city has ever known."

Actually, we had cut city spending by 10%, without reducing services, and made payments on the CEI debt, without borrowing any money. We were probably the only city in America run on a cash basis.

Poor Ralph Perk. He knew only what his financial advisors told him: Don't pay the electric bill and then cut everyone's property taxes before leaving office. I wasn't upset with Ralph, because I always considered him, at heart, a decent human being. When he journeyed into the land of truth, with corporate Cleveland as his guide, he was in foreign territory.

Milt called, in high dudgeon as he mulled Perk's slander. "Milt Schulman knows exactly what's going on. The Republican guard wants to blame the young people in your administration for taking on their crooked friends. I always told you Perk was no good," he exclaimed. "You are the first Mayor who had the guts to take them all on. You beat them once, you'll beat them again. Ask the people for help."

I invited members of the City Council to lunch to present our plan to avoid default. Afterwards, we gathered around the large committee table in the City Council hearing room, jammed with onlookers, media, and utility lobbyists. I took an informal poll and the Council members present rejected the financial rescue plan, 14-13. Once again, Muny Light was cited as the reason for the dire financial straits. The failure of the straw vote gave rise to doom and gloom news reports.

Images of default flashed in the Cleveland media, with CEI sponsoring the news on Channel Five.

"This is Tappy Phillips, TV 5 News. If we don't come up with $15.5 million, we're going to be the first major American city to default since the Great Depression and this thought has caused a 'great depression' to settle over City Hall and its financial planners. There is also dread and anticipation in the minds of Cleveland's residents, who don't know what default will mean to them. It will mean one of two things. It would easily cost us all more money that the city will have to forfeit as a penalty for its now abysmal credit rating. And it will definitely mean fewer services."

Phillips put default in the perspective of a consumer loan. Her conclusion led back to Muny Light "The city's default is really the same thing as if you or I didn't pay back a loan. Eventually, the banks would want the money back. If the city doesn't pay back its loan, the banks can go to court and get a judgment against Cleveland. That means the banks can come and take city property of the same value as the debt, which is what CEI is doing by tagging city trucks to satisfy the Muny Light debt. There are several solutions to the problem. One is the ½ percent tax increase the Mayor offered us. Another is to sell what some are calling Cleveland's Alamo, the Muny Light plant."

"If Cleveland goes bankrupt, it will go from bad to worse," said TV-5's Dorothy Fuldheim, known respectfully as Cleveland's 'most distinguished news analyst.' "Those who oppose selling Muny Light argue that without competition, the cost of electricity will go up. Well, that's a lot of hogwash. Utilities cannot raise prices unless the Public Utilities Commission of Ohio allows it. The price we pay for electricity is determined by the Commission, based on what it costs to produce power. Even if there was some merit in the city's ownership of Muny, the fact is the city can't afford Muny. Besides, what does it prove to own Muny? The city doesn't own the gas company or the telephone company. These are utilities also. Muny is an oddball representing nothing. It cannot even produce electricity. It can only carry it. So what is it good for? "

"Dorothy, Dorothy, Dorothy," I called to the television. "Why are there two thousand city-owned light systems in America?"

CHAPTER 53

Propaganda or Truth?

Matt Quinn, ABC national news reporter, summarized the Council majority's position on Muny Light "The city councilmen would like to make the Mayor back down. They would like a little revenge. The issue, and the price for cooperation, is the sale of this municipally-owned light company. The Councilmen say that the sale would solve the city's problems. The Mayor refuses to sell, saying, "I'll never sell my soul to the devil. "

NBC's national anchorman, Tom Brokaw, came to the Mayor's office to interview me. He zeroed in on our youthful Finance Director, Tegreene.

"Mr. Mayor, your Finance Director is only twenty-four years old. Don't you think, under these circumstances, it might be wise to appoint someone with more experience?"

"I think there are people in their twenties in your business who have done very well," I responded.

Brokaw countered, "But I don't know how many of them could rescue the City of Cleveland, for instance, from its possible bankruptcy."

"I don't think age is the issue here," I responded. "The qualities in municipal government needed today are not simply having years and years of experience, if you want to call it that. But we're also talking about honesty, integrity, concern about people. These are qualities that are needed too," I said, pushing back against Brokaw's attempt to play on the 'Kiddie Hall' caricature. It was not idealistic, honest youth which got us into this mess in Cleveland, it was an old boys' network.

The default story percolated in the national and international press. Representatives of Cleveland's media, ever concerned as to how the city was perceived from afar, traveled to New York City to find out how people there viewed events in our much smaller city, 463 miles to the west.

A New York cab driver tooled through Midtown Manhattan while being interviewed by his fare, a clean-shaven, well-scrubbed Cleveland television reporter, acting for all the world like a bedazzled tourist in the Big Apple.

"What have you heard about Cleveland?" the reporter asked.

"Nothing, nothing at all," spoke the cabbie, eyes looking briefly into his rear view mirror. "What should I hear about Cleveland?"

"Well, we've got the same kind of financial problems there that you have here." The 'same kind? Yes, if you add several zeros to the amount and subtract a light system.

The reporter watched as the cabbie looked in the rear view mirror, to ask his own question.

"Is it propaganda, or is it the truth?"

""Well," the interviewer pressed on, "They tell us we're going to default."

"They tell you only what they want you to hear," the cabbie said without taking his eyes off the road.

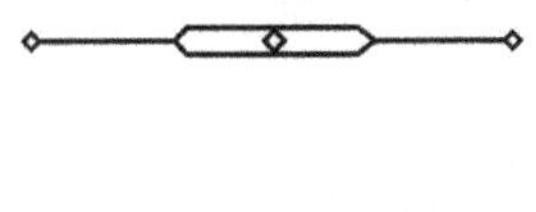

Thursday, December 14th

The Investment Plaza Building on East 9th St, and Chester Avenue.

We needed to postpone payment of Perk's debt to the banks to avoid default. We had the plan to refinance the debt and to pay it off. This situation was different from the many global clients of the Cleveland banks who had refused to repay loans totaling tens of millions. Banks charged off millions in bad foreign debt to operating expenses. We, the City of Cleveland, had every intention of paying the banks and we wanted, once more, to affirm our commitment, review the concessions I had made and close the deal with the banks.

Attending the meeting at the Investment Plaza, besides Tegreene, and myself were Council President Forbes, Clerk of Council, Mercedes Cotner, and the bankers involved in the December 15th note renewal.

Minutes before the meeting began, attorneys for CEI were once again affixing attachment liens on city vehicles, including water department trucks. A court order made it illegal to move any tagged vehicles, even to repair the dozens of water leaks flowing onto streets in the department's 545 square-mile service area.

I did not mention this in the meeting with the banks. I wanted to keep CEI and Muny Light out of this discussion.

"Council President Forbes, gentlemen, and the gentle lady, Clerk of Council Cotner, I went to the people on Tuesday with a request for an income tax increase to restore our credit. As you know, I asked for a specific amount, on the advice from the people in this room. I'm confident the people will pass the tax. Our debt to the banks will be secured with that income tax money. Once the tax passes, we will go to the national bond market with a $90 million issue, retire our short term debt, replace misspent bond funds and buy equipment needed for service improvements. I need your cooperation."

There was a long silence in the room, broken by Forbes. "Even if I agreed to it, there's no assurance from Mr. Clutterbuck," he said.

Clutterbuck was the Vice President of Public Investment for Cleveland Trust, which held $5 million of the maturing debt. The reference to Clutterbuck was odd since his boss, Brock Weir, was in the room.

"I just received this plan at 10:00 a.m.," Forbes groused, though the plan was announced the night before in a televised news conference, which Forbes commented upon as he watched with Members of Council and the media.

"I think it is appropriate for the individual bankers to state the position of their banks," I said, drawing the discussion away from Forbes, hoping to get one of the bankers to voice a favorable view, to end the threat of default.

Julian McCall, the President of National City Bank, spoke, "Our bank is in."

"We're in," said John Henniger of Euclid National Bank.

"So are we," said Michael Hricik of BancOhio Capital National Bank.

The dynamic of the meeting changed. The banks were ready to refinance the city's debt! Default would be avoided and the city's financial condition stabilized, once the tax increase passed.

The representative of Society National Bank nodded concurrence.

Four banks in, two to go. Central National Bank's president, Wilson Brown spoke. "There is one thing I would like to ask," he began. "I would like the city to offer something more than the income tax revenue as collateral, in case the tax fails. Would you be willing to put up property as collateral?" he asked.

"I have no problem with that," I said, without missing a beat. I had already pledged city property.

"OK, then our bank will participate," Brown pledged.

Five banks in, one to go.

Quiet descended upon the meeting, once again, as everyone in the room understood we were on the threshold of a dramatic breakthrough.

Tegreene broke in. "Well, that just leaves Cleveland Trust."

M. Brock Weir, Chairman and CEO of Cleveland Trust, had been standing to the side of the room, near an exit. He glared at his colleagues and said "I want you to know I resent this peer pressure. If Mr. Tegreene wants to know the answer, he should step outside in the hall, and I will tell him privately."

"Is Muny Light a condition?" Tegreene pressed.

I was not pleased. Joe was raising an issue I wanted to avoid as I saw it could box us in.

"No, Joe," I intervened, "I do not want that question raised. The city will withdraw the question."

We had, after all, the concurrence of five of six banks without Muny Light being mentioned. The light system was not part of these latest talks. I was not about to let it become negotiable.

"The question is withdrawn," I repeated.

"What about Muny Light?" Forbes, now animated, thrust the light system back to the center of the discussion. "We ought to find out about Muny Light, right now." His voice hit a high emotional frequency.

Bankers who had momentarily pledged cooperation began to fidget in their chairs. Weir slipped out of the room.

"What about Muny Light? What about Muny Light?" Forbes fumed after Weir's exit. The flow of the meeting had been broken, admitting confusion. The remaining bankers arose from their chairs and one by one, exited the room. Forbes, ever the skilled director of events, knew the value of chaos. With a calculated burst of anger, he had assisted Weir in blocking an agreement, keeping alive the threat of default unless Muny Light was sold.

As the City Hall building was closing for the day, Cleveland Trust's eponymous Mr. Clutterbuck delivered a letter to the city, refusing to rollover its $5 million of notes, adding, "If, prior to maturity, you have any other proposal that will deal with alternatives that have more materiality, we will be happy to review them." Cleveland Trust, precise as to matters of the city's debt, was imprecise on the matter of 'materiality,'" I tried to call Clutterbuck for an explanation. He was unavailable.

"Jack, what is this?" I said, waving the letter. "'More materiality'? We offered income tax collateral, property collateral, double collateral to meet the city's debt. That was not material?"

"You know what they want," Schulman said.

10:00 p.m. - The Mayor's Office.

I convened a meeting with Jack Schulman and his brother Howard, the city's Chief Counsel. Howard worked with Jack closely and was now one of my key advisers. Weissman also was present, along with John Carhuff of First Boston, our principal financial advisor, and Gene Crowley, partner at the Wall Street investment bank of Salomon Brothers, which was planning to underwrite our debt issue, and Dick Segal, Crowley's attorney.

There, in the tapestried inner sanctum of Cleveland City Hall, we began to calmly discuss Cleveland becoming the first municipality in America to be made 'bankrupt' since the Depression.

"The banks have their papers prepared. They have gone to court against delinquent creditors before, and they will do it again. CEI had attached city properties in the 1930's, during the Depression," Segal said.

"They would risk shutting down the city?" I asked. "Who is going to answer bank alarms when there are no police to respond? Who is going to answer fire calls? It's their risk, too. Municipal bankruptcy is a two-way street."

"Segal has an opinion on the effect of the bankruptcy law here," Howard Schulman said, deferring to Segal's expertise. "What provisions do you think would apply, Dick?"

Segal paged through a huge folder of papers and read, "The banks could petition the federal court to file against the city under Article IX of the Bankruptcy Act, Municipal Bankruptcy. The court would then appoint a trustee who would function as the Mayor, Council, and Board of Control which, by the way, awards city contracts. It would not be necessary to have any official action of elected city officials to go to court and begin disposing of assets." He shifted in his chair. His tone changed. He directed his next remarks to me. "Muny Light would be the first to go. Police, fire and garbage collection could be affected."

"How would they run the city without money?" I asked, deflecting the point.

"The court would have the power to impose property and income taxes on the people," Segal said.

"They would have a full scale revolt on their hands. This stuff sounds far-fetched. There is no way they will interrupt services in this city for $14.5 million, or for misspent bond funds in which the banks were complicit," I said.

"This situation is analogous to what has happened to the Cleveland schools," Howard Schulman added. A court-appointed trustee was running the school system and paying its debts, while the school's administration operated under his direction. Under this scenario, both major local governmental systems, City Hall and the school system, would be beyond the reach of the democratic process.

"So much for Home Rule and the government of the people. Well, we won't concede," I said firmly. "We still have one day."

All eyes turned my way. "Mayor, you have the power, but not the right, to put the city into default," said Segal in a subdued tone. "You are going to have to come to an accommodation. You must seek a compromise. Cleveland Trust has to be delivered."

"Accommodation." "Compromise." "Deliver." Those words attacked my sensibilities. I proposed a city income tax increase, backed up by city property. I was given a false choice. The consequences for the city were real. If I sold the city's electric system, we would avoid default. If I did not sell, the city would be placed in default. All circumstances would be merged in the psychology of a manufactured imperative. Public opinion had been hijacked in favor of the sale.

"Weir walked out of the meeting this afternoon, as we were nearing an agreement. No one in this room wants default," I responded obliquely. I knew exactly what my financial adviser was telling me. He was urging me to take a politically pragmatic approach, leading to little public resistance.

"Why can't we ask the other banks not to present their notes for payment?" Weissman asked a pivotal question, to try to limit the damage of default.

"The other banks will have to protect their legal interests. They'll present their notes if Cleveland Trust does," predicted Crowley. As a result of Cleveland Trust's studied recalcitrance, the five other banks were going to be dragged into default.

I sat deep in a plush red couch and looked around. This didn't look like a municipal poorhouse. Chairs costing hundreds of dollars, each, to re-upholster, fine Persian carpeting, wallpaper at $50 a yard, crystal goblets set for our guests, all purchased before I came into office. Here, in this office were intimations of affluence, declarations of resource.

Weissman pointed out that the banks were not obligated to present their notes for payment. "We could get advances of state and federal funds that will be owed to us. All banks could agree to wait two weeks before they press collection," he said.

"We can't do it," Carhuff said, "Without a program for new revenues, we'd be bankrupt."

"This guy," Segal motioned to me, "is too good to be sitting here not thinking if there is some better way."

The 'better way' was a very bad way. I was facing a horrible choice, keep Muny and default on loans, with all the financial consequences, or sell Muny and default on my conscience. I was not to be flattered by Mr. Segal. Instead, I spoke of consequences my financial advisors would dutifully repeat to the banks.

"If the banks grab our cash and we don't have the money for payroll, there will be no police protection. There will be massive layoffs on Monday," I said.

It was late and we were all tired. I dismissed the meeting saying, "I will be in the office early. Please stay in contact." As we prepared to leave, I told our Wall Street advisers, "I will try to reach an accommodation." The way forward was fraught, no matter what I decided. When you are the Mayor of a big city, could anything be more important than the credit of the city?

It was close to midnight when I arrived home to a ringing phone. It was my friend, Maury Saltzman. He called to express concern and offered to play a key, last-minute role to avoid default. He tried once before to temper the conflict between the city and CEI. I needed help. He was a trusted intermediary.

"Dennis, I want you to make one more effort to resolve this," he said. "I want you to come over to my office early in the morning for a meeting."

"With…?"

"Brock Weir and George Forbes. I think once you get together in the same room you can come to an agreement that will be good for Cleveland." Maury was a believer in personal diplomacy. I assumed he was not aware of the details of my on-going battles with Forbes, nor of Cleveland Trust's intransigence. He was motivated by a desire to help Cleveland. I felt compelled to share with my friend the reality I faced, so as not to expect too much at the eleventh hour.

"Cleveland Trust wants me to sell Muny Light to CEI, Maury. What's to be gained by another meeting?"

"You owe it to the city to keep trying. This may be your most important meeting." Saltzman said. Perhaps my friend was presenting the last best chance to avoid a financial calamity.

Events had reached a crescendo. Maury convinced me I had to explore every last possibility. His intention, as I understood it, was to get George Forbes, Brock Weir, and me in the same room, early in the morning, to work out a solution.

I decided to try, notwithstanding my misgivings. "OK, I'll be there, Maury, " I said. "Will they?"

"I spoke to them earlier. They are waiting for my call. They will be there." Was there a chance for a deal with Forbes and Weir, without the sale of Muny Light?

I woke up Sandy, who wisely had gone to sleep early in anticipation of the events of December 15th. "We have to leave first thing in the morning. I have a meeting with Brock Weir and George Forbes at Bobbie Brooks. Maury put it together. This could be big."

She opened her eyes, half-awake. "Be careful," she said, and went back to sleep.

CHAPTER 54

Judgment Day - "Pay Up !"

December 15, 1978 - 6:00 a.m.

The clock radio alarm proclaimed Cleveland's question of the century: "Will the City of Cleveland go into default or will Mayor Kucinich sell the city's electric system? That's the choice the Mayor has today, according to Council President George Forbes, who spoke with Cleveland Trust Chairman Brock Weir. Forbes quoted Weir as saying the bank would renew the city's loans, if the Mayor sold Muny Light. Kucinich has only…" I switched off the radio and turned to Sandy, who was awake.

"What a bunch of bull. Muny Light shouldn't be at issue here," I steamed.

"Calm down, Dennis," Sandy said and then kissed me. "Did you sleep well? Dr. Pensiero said you must have at least six hours of sleep. You don't want another ulcer."

I certainly did not want another ulcer. The nerve-wracking stress of being forced into an inexorable, though false choice, had taken an emotional toll on Sandy. She was paying a price which no spouse of any public figure should ever have to pay. Yet, she remained concerned about my welfare instead of her own.

"No, I didn't sleep much," I admitted.

Sandy went downstairs to get the morning newspaper and returned. "Look at the front page!" she said, as she handed me a broadsheet, black and white dun-letter, otherwise known as the *Plain Dealer.* The headline blared menacingly:

**"CLEVELAND TRUST PAY UP
BANK WOULD RELENT IF MUNY LIGHT WERE SOLD, FORBES BELIEVES"**

This day screamed of reckoning. The headlines demanded it. The banks demanded it. Cleveland Trust demanded it. George Forbes demanded it.

Sandy pointed to one paragraph. "It says here that Forbes talked with Weir. Cleveland Trust will give the city credit if Muny Light is sold." It was a neat editorial package, with one source, George Forbes.

"If Muny is sold, they will take the city out of financial jeopardy. They are establishing false terms, a lie agreed upon, appearing as truth," I said.

What if, based upon the extensive media reports of the dire consequences of default, most people sincerely believed the sale of Muny Light was in the best interests of the city? I had not only to choose between Muny Light and default, but the reality in which I participated.

Is this what politics is all about? Weighing the imperatives of one's commitments, beliefs and career against demands of interest groups deciding the price to be paid for personal success? And what of the implications for the city? Default was equated with the Depression, bankruptcy, and the poorhouse. People were buying in, assuming I could "save Cleveland," simply by selling Muny Light. Was I the only one concerned about the economic impact of infinitely higher utility rates, of higher taxes for increased street lighting charges? Didn't others know or care that Muny Light was undermined by CEI and Squire Sanders' dirty tricks to set the stage for an illegal takeover?

Corporate Cleveland cast the city into a contrived default hoping to annihilate me politically. I was the only official who had the power to say "NO!" and, as my financial advisor said, "I am thinking there must be a better way."

It takes a while to comprehend inverted reality. You check all your senses, your belief systems, your values, your ethics, and then, as you face the darkest deceit, you have to decide what you stand for. I had a sense that Cleveland's future and my own was on the line. If I sold Muny Light, I would protect Cleveland's financial future, as far as Cleveland Trust was concerned, and I would assure my own political career.

The conditions put to me were neither legal nor legitimate. Those conditions cast out Steve Clark, Jim Cox, and Bob Franken, truth tellers. In their cases someone picked up a phone and talked about truth as a threat to business interests. Perhaps truth is not absolute, but subject to an economic measure by a prevailing interests? I remember reading Ibsen's *Enemy of the People*, where the central character, Dr. Stockmann, discovered the town baths, the source of community income from tourism, were polluted. He disclosed the truth and was condemned for it. Was I to be condemned for disclosing the business community's corrupt exploitation of city government? Was this fight over an electric system worth putting my city's reputation and my name, and my life, on the line? At such a moment, one clings to the person closest, for support.

"Our love counts more than ever," I said to Sandy. Love was our rock.

"No matter what happens, I love you," Sandy said tenderly. We embraced, holding on tightly. We knew we had better protect love inside our home, because once we went outside on the street, there was no love, only the yammering of powerful bill collectors: 'Pay Up!' As the New York taxi driver advised his Cleveland visitor, "they only tell you what they want you to hear." Accordingly, the Cleveland media drew the masses into its Muny Light sale echo chamber, and people simply repeated the ubiquitous demands to sell.

"Maybe I can still work out some kind of compromise this morning," I said.

"Don't bet on it," Sandy replied.

"I have to try," I responded. I'm always open to changing the outcome. I carried a small card in my wallet, a quote from Miguel de Unamuno "Only he who attempts the absurd is capable of achieving the impossible." It was absurd to think I could change the minds of my chief antagonists on this day of destiny. Yet I could not let any effort go unexplored.

Sandy steered me into the kitchen. "Why don't you have breakfast now. You are going to have a long day, and I don't want you getting sick again."

My driver, Detective Plank, arrived in an unmarked police car, a silver-toned 1977 Ford. Sandy and I swiftly entered the vehicle, as a team of intelligence unit detectives prepared to follow us.

"Ready for the big day?" Detective Plank asked with an earnest smile.

"I'm ready. I don't know if the rest of the city is," I said.

Detective Plank worked through rush hour traffic, en route to a network television interview, prior to the big meeting. On the radio, talk show hosts were portentous, challenging, parroting the front page of the *Plain Dealer* "Will the Mayor sell Muny Light and save the city from default?"

"Please turn it off," Sandy requested.

Detective Plank detoured away from a traffic jam and guided us through the industrial Flats. Black, pink, purple, gray and white rings of smoke encircled the sun, splitting the sky over the valley, an Ansel Adams-type landscape. Black strip mills were tintypes, sharply outlined in the shadows. Southside bridges were rotting. Empty railroad sidings were decorated with Queen Anne's lace. Long, dark streaks of rubber were burned into pocked pavement showered with glittering fragments of white, green and brown broken glass. Everywhere there were signs of decay. Save the city, indeed. For whom?

"Dennis," Sandy asked, "What are you going to say in this interview?" She kept me focused. How could I explain, briefly, that $14.5 million was due tonight, on loans I hadn't taken out, and, when I wanted to repay those loans with income tax revenue, property taxes, or the sale of property, those efforts were refused because Muny Light was the only legal tender in Cleveland?

Who in TV-land understands notes and bonds? It's not a quantitative culture. People's eyes glaze over. Instead of relevant financial details, TV coverage centered on me, the drama of America's youngest Mayor in a showdown with the banks over an electric system, with default a possible outcome.

It was 7:20 am and my face felt frozen under the Kleig lights. The host from the ABC New York studio, David Hartman, was congenial, even sympathetic, as I explained my quest for a compromise. Their reporter, Matt Quinn, participated from the Cleveland studio. His question cut deeply.

"Mayor, if the price of a settlement, of a compromise, was your resignation, would you do that?" Quinn asked.

My face reddened. "I think that question is immaterial and irrelevant."

"But," his voice heavily tinged with judgment, "Your personality is not immaterial in this argument," he said.

"Personality" was shorthand for young, uncooperative, and obstreperous, regarding corporate Cleveland's interests. The dollar bill has a personality too. Money, not my conduct, was at issue and if I agreed to sell, I would be awarded a winning personality in the exchange.

I tried to stay on point, "I'm the one who has come up with a plan to keep the city out of default. If the city defaults, it won't matter who is Mayor or who is in Council, because they won't be running the city anymore."

Sandy was watching from a few feet off the set. She glared at the reporter as he ended the interview, confronting him, "You have a lot of nerve, asking Dennis to resign!"

"It's a fair question, Mrs. Kucinich."

"It is not," she answered angrily. "Do you even know what is happening in this town?" She challenged the reporter, who backed away. Media had journeyed to Cleveland from around the globe. It sought the answer to only one question: Will Cleveland become the first American city to default since the Great Depression?

It was left to me to explain Cleveland's crisis to reporters who had come to City Hall from Japan, West Germany, Switzerland, Sweden, Great Britain, Canada, Italy, France, Belgium and the Netherlands. A manufactured crisis is still a crisis. Its effects can change the history of a city and the lives of its people.

CHAPTER 55

A Minute in the Boardroom

8:00 a.m. - Bobbie Brooks, Inc., Corporate Headquarters

It could all come down to what happened here. I entered Bobbie Brooks' two-story yellow brick headquarters on East 38th and Perkins Avenue to meet with Weir, Forbes and "Maury" Saltzman. In our many discussions, Maury had never sought any favor from the government, nor did he try to influence any decision. He was a true friend, whom I could always rely upon for good advice. At this moment he was a crucial intermediary.

I walked down a long hall, past design rooms and racks of clothing catalogs to an elevator, to the second floor, and to a small, unpretentious boardroom, a rectangle nearly thirty-four feet by fifteen feet - the same place I had met Karl Rudolph of CEI. Numerous plaques lined the walls, testifying to Saltzman's humanitarian work for hospitals, foundations and the State of Israel. The dark oak meeting table was ten feet long by four feet wide, plenty of surface to negotiate.

The boardroom. The city's faith, goodwill, credit and image could be impacted by what happened this morning, in this room, at this table.

I entered to see Maury seated at the head of the table, in close conversation with Brock Weir. Saltzman's rise to the top of a clothing empire was legendary in the Cleveland business community. Yet for all his accomplishments, he was a humble man. He exuded warmth and precision. He rose to greet me and gave me a fatherly hug.

"Dennis, my boy. How are you this morning?"

"A little tired, Maury. I appreciate your efforts in helping to bring us together."

"Dennis, I want to help the city. I hope some good will come of this meeting."

We sat down, and Maury turned to Weir. "Brock, you know Dennis, of course." Weir gave a slightly perceptible nod and then stared down at the table as I took a seat across from him. His head was low between his shoulders. His hands rested on the table, palms crossed.

Forbes walked briskly into the room. He relaxed into the chair at my immediate left. Pleasantries were dispensed with, and Maury brought us to concentrate on the matter at hand.

"I've known Brock here for a long time. I've always had a good relationship with George. And, as you all know, I am one of Dennis' biggest supporters," Maury began. "I wanted you fellows to get together to see if we can do anything to stop default. The city is counting on you fellows. I hope you will do the right thing."

"Maury," I said, while my eyes acknowledged Forbes and Weir, "I don't want the city to go into default. I have offered alternatives. I'm ready to resolve this, here, now."

Weir, speaking in a low voice, addressed Saltzman, "Maury, remember the one business operation you had that was losing millions? You had to drop it, so the rest of your business could stay profitable."

"Yes, Brock," he replied.

I didn't like the parallel drawn between Maury's business activities and Muny Light. Maury faced me, squarely, and spoke. "Mayor, I had this operation that was losing $18 million. I had to sell it. When I did, my company rebounded. It was a tough business decision. It helped my company. It was the right decision."

"Once you did, things worked out," Weir chimed. "It was the best decision you made, Maury." Weir was somehow familiar with Bobbie Brooks' finances.

"Dennis," Maury crossed his arms over his chest and stated crisply, "I have always been against selling Muny Light. I even tried to get muny power here, at Bobbie Brooks. But, the city might go into default today, because of Muny Light, so I think you ought to sell it."

Maury was my best friend in the business community. Based on our underprivileged childhoods, I felt we had something in common. He helped me become Mayor. Why did he invite me here? Did he promise Weir and Forbes he'd convince me to sell? Maybe he had the best intentions for the city and for me. Yet when he spoke of his "business decision," it sounded too pat, especially given Weir's knowledge of Maury's company.

I had a business decision to make too. I was Cleveland's CEO, trying to protect a major city asset, Muny Light, from being taken over by its ruthless competitor.

When Maury made clear he favored the sale, the dynamic of the meeting shifted.

Forbes pounced on Maury's shift. "Dennis, Dennis," Forbes smiled slightly. "Even with all the problems we've had, I basically like you. But you won't listen to me, Dennis," Forbes gestured toward Maury. "Listen to this man. This man is your man. He pays your campaign bills. He respects you. He's telling you to sell it. If your good friend wants you to sell it, hey man, what does that tell you?"

Weir, sensing an opportunity, became solicitous, and, for the first time ever looked me in the eye. "You are faced with an inescapable conclusion. The city is on the brink of default and you will be subjecting the city to many problems, because you are holding onto a business that is losing money. We can help you, but you are going to have to show that you're ready for our help. You can't do it alone," Weir stated.

"You've got to learn to work with people," Forbes came back, his voice rising. "Dennis, I'm telling you. You can be anything you want to be in politics, anything. I've been telling you that for years," he said, "But first you've got to learn to work with people." Forbes leaned toward Weir. "Brock here is a good man, a decent man. I mean to tell you, he's never done anything for me and he isn't going to do anything for me. I don't do business with the man and never will, so I've got nothing to gain. Brock Weir wants to help the city." Weir's eyes, now trained on Forbes, softened at the Council President's generous characterization.

"Dennis," Forbes continued, "You are never going to get anywhere in politics, until you learn to work with people," jabbing his arms in my direction, for emphasis. Then his tone hardened. "I'm telling you that you got the wrong goddamn attitude. Brock here wants to help you, but you've got to make the first move. There's just one thing you've got to do."

"Maury," I struggled to maintain my position. "My plan will avoid default. I have a way to avoid default. There is no reason for Muny Light to be mentioned. It is making a profit."

"It is losing money, from everything I have heard," Maury responded curtly. "Brock and George think it should be sold. They tell me that it will continue to lose money. I think you should sell it. I wanted to say that in front of them."

"George, I've shown a willingness to compromise. I proposed an income tax increase. I never wanted to do that, but it was a way to resolve this situation. Yesterday, the other banks agreed. I have tried to be reasonable. I don't want the city to go into default." I said earnestly.

More specifically, I had proposed an income tax increase to pay off the last administration's debt. And Muny Light was hemorrhaging cash because CEI was slashing it with the razor blade of antitrust violations, blocking repairs, tripling the cost of power, and attacking its customer base.

"There's just one thing you've got to do," Forbes said, leaning slightly toward me.

Weir had been looking past his clasped hands, as if using his thumbs as a gun sight to line up a target. The boardroom lights were bothering his bad eye. He then looked up and made me an undisguised bribe. "If you sell Muny Light, we'll roll over the notes. I will get you $50 million worth of new bonds. We'll get the other banks to participate," he said. We could have credit (more debt) and no electric system or an electric system and no credit.

There was that headline again:

"CLEVELAND TRUST - PAY UP
BANK WOULD RELENT IF MUNY LIGHT WERE SOLD, FORBES BELIEVES"

"You know, he can make it very easy for you," Forbes nodded toward Weir. "Your problems would be solved."

My political future would be guaranteed, with the swipe of a pen. The endless calls to sell would end. The media trumpeting the so-called deficiencies of Muny Light would stop their barrage. The equation of the sale of Muny Light with the avoidance of default would end. If I sold the electric system under these intricately-contrived circumstances, the people of Cleveland would never know I did not have to sell. They would be offered a fictional tale of a happy outcome, agreed upon by the media, the business community, CEI, the banks, and the political establishment. It would be the fairy tale of a young Mayor who finally came to his senses and did the "right thing."

But I knew the truth.

The people would end up paying millions of dollars in higher taxes to the city for street lighting and other services. Without competition, CEI would continually raise rates. People in the city would pay millions more in higher electric bills. Yes, the city would have credit. It could borrow money and go deeper in debt. If I agreed to sell, no one in Cleveland would ever know what happened in this boardroom.

Today the world's attention was briefly on the impending default in a major American city. If I sold, tomorrow the big story would be 'The Escape from Default," the bookends of a complete political soap opera. Only I would know that Muny Light was stolen. I would have to conceal that knowledge, as I rocketed to political stardom with my newfound friends. I'd wave from a high platform at "the people." Unaware, they would think they were the ones who sent me to higher office.

I was thirty-two years old and Tom Snyder of the Tomorrow Show had begun a boomlet for me, for a presidential bid, even though I was far away from the minimum constitutional age of thirty-five to qualify. When he suggested I ought to be President, my office received thousands of letters of encouragement. Celebrated in some quarters as America's youngest big-city mayor, hailed as a rising political star, I could anticipate a bright future. If I entered into this single agreement to sell a light system, I would guarantee both political success and credit for my city.

But, if I turned down Weir's offer? The city would go into default. The people won't remember Brock Weir. All they will remember is that Dennis Kucinich was the young Mayor of Cleveland on that darkest day in Cleveland's history.

What a choice, sell the light system and protect my political career and betray the people of Cleveland or, save the light system, protect public power, guarantee lower electric rates, and end up an outcast. I did not become Mayor of Cleveland to be a martyr. Neither did I become Mayor to sell out.

Sister Leona's poem, 'The Minute,' came to mind, and breathed confirmation of the impermeability of my soul, and the brevity of a political career, versus the precipice of eternity.

I looked at Weir. "Isn't there some other way we can work this out?" I asked.

He was unmoved. He slowly shook his head from side to side, signaling 'no.' Maury, Weir and Forbes had come to the boardroom with the intention of convincing me that the sale of Muny Light was in the best interests of the city - - and my political career.

For a moment, the three men stared at me, hoping capitulation was at hand. My thoughts were not in the Board Room, but of an apartment, a couple of miles and years away, where my parents, trying to come up with enough money to pay the utility bill, counted pennies on a chipped white metal table.

'CLICK, CLICK, CLICK.' I could still hear those pennies dropping, I had not traveled far from that family and that apartment.

I looked at Weir and then at Forbes. "George," I spoke reflectively, "I know if I don't sell Muny Light, we will go into default and my political career will be eclipsed."

I knew it was not only me who would be affected. My mother and father, always in difficult financial straits due to poor health and social disorganization, relied on me for financial assistance, as did my brother Perry and my sister Beth. The young people who had moved to Cleveland to take part in my city administration had careers at risk, as did those administration officials who were not so young, who in mid-life took pay cuts and made sacrifices, forgoing other opportunities to unselfishly enter into municipal public service.

Forbes grew weary. "Well goddamn! If you know this thing is going to end your political career, why are you doing it? I'm telling you," he said, pleading, "You can be any goddamn thing you want to be in politics. If you know your career's going to be eclipsed, why ruin your political career? Sell the goddamn light system, get it out of the way!"

Forbes, the quintessential political wheeler-dealer, knew I loved politics, knew I ran for congress twice, and knew I wanted to advance. He dangled the bright, shining object of future attainment before the furnace of my ambition. If it was true that I could be anything I wanted to be, would it still be true no matter what I decided? Was my career, my name, and my life truly dependent upon making this one deal, or rejecting it? This was a moment of consequence.

The wind from Lake Erie was tapping on the windows of the boardroom. A chill came from Brock Weir's frozen face.

"Isn't there some other way we could work things out?" I asked one last time, as Weir's lower lip climbed upward. He peered into the dark table. I moved away and changed my tone.

"Thanks for your time, everyone. See you at the Council meeting, George."

I sat, while the leader of the largest bank in Ohio, with assets of more than $4 billion dollars, and the elected representative of one of the poorest neighborhoods in Cleveland walked out of the boardroom, together.

It was early in the day. I was exhausted.

I asked Maury for a drink of water. "Dennis, I don't know if this meeting did any good. I wanted to let you know how I felt. I think you are wrong on this. But whatever you decide, I'm still with you." He patted me on the back.

I stood up and exited the board room.

CHAPTER 56

City Light

How do you know where you are going if you forget where you came from? My roots in the city affected me deeply, because I knew from graphic experience what I wanted to change in my immediate environment, in my community and in my city. My early experiences growing up in Cleveland equipped me with a high tolerance for ambiguity, with a deep sense of compassion and an understanding of the dynamics of transformation. I needed the anchor of a different time, to reconnect with my roots, spiritually and emotionally, to remind myself of distance traveled into a future I had never imagined.

"Well," Detective Plank raised his reddish-brown eyebrows expectantly, as we moved forward, "Mayor, are you alright? You look a little pale around the gills."

"I'm OK."

I was not OK. I was contemplating the decline of my city and the unraveling of my political career. I could not hide it from a top detective. I asked Dusty to go back to City Hall by way of Perkins Avenue to East 30th Street, a few blocks from Bobbie Brooks' board room. We turned a corner, and I time-traveled back to 1957.

Dad spent days driving up and down side streets in the area, looking for rooms to rent. We had been living off St. Clair Avenue and East 101st Street, until Mom told the landlord she had named her fifth child after singer Perry Como, and the landlord told Mom we had to move, too many people in the small apartment. Dad packed all seven of us into the dirty gray 1948 Dodge with an ignition that ground like a bad sinus. We drove up and down the streets of the East Side. Every once in a while, Dad noticed a rental sign in the window. He'd stop the car and knock on the door.

After a brief conversation with a person on the porch, Dad came back with a sad look on his face. "Enh, nothing," he said, as he pushed his shoulders forward in a helpless way. The visor of his rumpled green hat was turned upward. His green work uniform was frayed at the back pockets.

Dad looked too thin for 5'7." Nevertheless, his arms were like Popeye-the-Sailor man pistons. He could flatten a guy twice his size, pick up any three of us kids at one time, or, on good days, steer 40-ft rigs through Cleveland's rush hour traffic. He was physically powerful. He could carry almost anything, except more troubles.

After another stop he announced, "They won't rent to kids," to his disappointed brood. We drove through the lower East Side, with our things jammed into cardboard boxes and paper bags stashed in the trunk. Mom, Dad, Frank Jr., Gary, Theresa, Perry, and me living and sleeping in a $95 dollar, four-door Dodge. In the evening, Dad went into the trunk and pulled out a couple of pea green blankets, WWII surplus. He threw one on the front seat and one into the back.

The interior of the Dodge was carpeted. Mom, Dad, and Perry slept in the front seat. Frank Jr., Gary and Theresa shared the back seat. I slept in the rear foot well.

As we were unsuccessful in securing a place to live, Dad drove south on East 30th Street. The car passed under a railroad bridge, and we parked at the edge of the industrial Flats, ready for sleep. I marveled at the starry expanse of twinkling lights. Many nights, I watched through the car windows to see a fiery fist shoot out from the steel sleeve of a long smokestack, opening its flaming fingers, thirty, forty, fifty feet, until the night around it dissolved into its outstretched orange palm. The fingers came together to form a torch. I could feel the light playing against the car, against my face.

Whenever we drove in the inner-city darkness, I looked for the emblazoned sky over the Cleveland Flats, for the torch which overcame the night. When I saw it, I was filled with awe and momentarily forgot we did not have a place to live. No matter how bad things appeared, the image of the light chasing away the darkness always gave me hope.

Now, as Mayor, I felt darkness enveloping my city. "Mayor, which way now? Hey where are you?" Dusty waved a hand in front of my face. He had stopped on East 30th St., awaiting directions.

I snapped from my reverie. "Let's go to City Hall."

Sandy and my brother, Gary, were in my office waiting for me. "I don't have anything good to report," I said. "Weir figures he has me where he wants me."

"What did Forbes say?" Gary asked. "He's keeping Council in the dark."

"Forbes kept telling me to sell Muny,"

"What about Maury?" Sandy asked.

"Maury told me to sell."

"He did?" Sandy said, her eyes widened in astonishment.

"Yes. I did not expect Maury to lead me there. I was hoping to stop default and to save Muny Light. They wanted the meeting to make one last effort to get me to agree to sell."

We moved to the inner office. I reviewed a stack of phone messages demanding "sell." In the chaos, Gary provided strength. "You've got to stand in there," he said, squinting his eyes for emphasis. People would occasionally mistake Gary for me. I don't know how. Gary was five years younger and weighed seventy pounds more. He spent four years in the Marines as an instructor in physical education. He won weight-lifting, wrestling, and boxing championships. His street experience shone in the steel of his gray eyes. One look and you knew he was a person to be reckoned with. The look he gave me spanned the time and space of our lives together, our aspirations, our struggles, our climb from the neighborhoods of the city to positions of leadership. We did not come this far to shrink from a crisis.

8:55 a.m. The Mayor's Press Office

I spoke with Juniewicz. A new report from consultants R.W. Beck, showed Muny Light made a profit of $1.2 million from June of 1977 to June of 1978. Muny would have a million-dollar surplus by the year's end.

"We have to get this information to the public, today," I said.

"No one will pay any attention to this, Mayor," Juniewicz said. "It's all about default."

9:00 a.m. Mayor's Office

"You better try all possible funding sources for the maturing notes, because we don't have much time," Weissman said. He stood at my side as I made the calls.

I first contacted Gertude Donahey, the Treasurer of the State of Ohio. "Sorry Mayor, I cannot legally invest in municipalities."

Next call went to Ohio Attorney General, William Brown, who sat on the board of the Public Employees Retirement System. "Sorry Mayor, pension funds are selfish. They would get a better return from the Sunbelt."

I placed a call to Jack Watson, President Carter's assistant for Intergovernmental Affairs, and asked for an advance on revenue sharing to cover the amount owed to the banks. "We sure hope you work out your problems. We don't want you to go into default," he said sympathetically.

A year earlier, I had asked the White House for permission to use a federal Community Development grant of $3 million to purchase snowplows. They were sympathetic then, too. The city was buried in snow, commerce was paralyzed. I couldn't get federal permission to purchase the snowplows. Instead, they promoted the city's acceptance of a $41 million grant for a system of individual monorail-type cars, which supposedly would substitute for walking in Cleveland's relatively small downtown. In a meeting at the White House, in the Oval Office, after I presented President Carter with a plan to rebuild America's infrastructure, I asked him to intervene to cancel the People Mover grant. He did. Weissman and Schulman visited the White House later in the year, attempting, without success, to get White House officials to intervene with the Cleveland banks.

"I can get money from Washington for programs we don't need and not get an advance to avoid default?" I questioned Watson. "We may go into default over a lousy $14.5 million!"

"We are sorry, Mayor, there isn't anything we can do. The feeling here is that it is a local problem," Watson said.

He was telling me it was a local problem?

Jack Schulman was waiting in my office. "Mayor, three banks presented their notes to the city treasurer for payment at nine this morning." The financial vise tightened. The other banks were pawns in Brock Weir's high stakes chess game. I faced what Weir called the "inescapable conclusion."

"We gave them receipts, but no money," said Schulman.

I walked over to the window behind my desk, quietly looking toward Lake Erie, the moody, shallow repository of fresh water legendary for its sudden storms imperiling Great Lakes freighters. The rapid cross-currents and powerful wave actions had the capacity to snap a thousand-foot ship in two and send it plunging to the bottom. There were physical, alchemical forces swirling here, too, in my office, with portents of destruction, if I did not sell the electric system. If I did not sell, the city would survive. My career in politics would not.

9:30 a.m. Mayor's Office

Several members of Council entered.

"I've never seen Forbes so upset. He really wants Muny Light," said Councilman James Rokakis of Ward 6.

"Forbes is not telling us what Council will do today," said Councilwoman Barbara Pringle of Ward 9. "We have a meeting in a few minutes, and no idea what will happen."

I knew that if I asked for passage of the income tax legislation in the morning, Council would not act on it. I decided to invoke my charter authority to call a special Council meeting in the evening, so the Council would feel the full pressure of the impending default, and, hopefully, seek another path to avoid it.

10:30 a.m. The Mayor's Press Office

Juniewicz handed me the first edition of the *Cleveland Press*. It looked like a tombstone:

"COUNCIL ULTIMATUM:
SELL MUNY LIGHT OR THE CITY DEFAULTS TODAY
CLEVELAND TRUST PUSHES SALE"

"Check out the lead," Juniewicz said.

"Mayor Kucinich apparently has but one option left to him today, sell the Municipal Light Plant or throw the city into default. A resolution before City Council which promises to send to the voters the Mayor's proposed tax increase, but ties it to the sale of Muny Light, was Council's apparent last word on Cleveland's financial crisis. Council's resolution was written last night after Council President, George Forbes learned that Cleveland Trust - which the city owes $5 million - had rejected the Kucinich proposals."

"There is something else here," Juniewicz said. "Bruce Akers, (Cleveland Trust's Vice President) says they will reconsider if you sell Muny Light and pass the tax increase."

The *Cleveland Press* article reported: "Bruce Akers, Cleveland Trust Vice President for public relations and one-time aide to Mayor Perk, explained that his bank would be willing to reconsider its position if Kucinich accepted something like Council's proposal to couple the tax increase with the sale of Muny Light. Otherwise, said Akers, Cleveland Trust will have to 'present our notes for payment at the office of the City Treasurer on December 15, 1978, in accordance with the terms of said notes.'"

Surprisingly, the newspaper carried a reference to the apparent split among leading bankers: "The *Press* learned that during private negotiations yesterday, Cleveland Trust was the only bank to push the Muny Light issue. The other five banks seemed to be fighting with Cleveland Trust over the Muny Light question and appeared to be willing to go along with the city's original plan for an income tax increase only, one source said."

"It appears, Andy, that Cleveland Trust now wants me to both sell Muny Light and to increase taxes," I noted the increased stakes. "All Weir asked me for was Muny Light. I could have gotten off cheaply," I laughed. A half-percent tax increase would raise $38 million. The city owed the banks $14.5 million.

The *Cleveland Press* also reported that Maury Saltzman went public with his support for the sale. He described the meeting in his boardroom. "Brock was nice, he said 'Look Dennis, get this out of the way. Sell the building, we'll roll over the notes and I will personally help with $50 million in bonds.'" If I didn't get the point of Weir's generosity in the meeting, Maury publicly repeated it to great effect.

In declining Weir's offer, I was seen as obstructing Cleveland Trust's efforts to "help" the city.

Blanche came into my office. "Dennis, you have to take this call, it is from your brother, Frank."

Frank? He never called me at City Hall. I asked for the call to be sent to my desk.

"Den," he began. "Now I know you don't want to hear this. I think you are wrong on Muny Light. I think you should sell it. It's bad news for the city."

Of all people, Frank's call was as disturbing as it was unexpected. We were close, had shared a turbulent childhood and when he joined the Marines and then left for Vietnam, we divided a dollar bill, each taking half and pledging to make it whole upon Frank's safe return. We wrote each other frequently, and when Frank returned home, emotionally battle scarred, I spent long hours with him as he related his anguish. He had a passionate love of country, expressed through military service to America. He paid a price for his Vietnam tour of duty, severe post-traumatic stress, seeing so many of his fellow soldiers killed or wounded in combat. He was haunted by images of death everywhere. Today he called, concerned about me and the city.

"You have to sell it, it's going to take the city down," he said. Then he paused. "I know I'm right," he said. Frank was apolitical, although once, when he returned home from leave, he helped in my first campaign. His views represented a more conservative segment of the population, which supported me, but believed I should sell Muny Light.

"Frank, I'm doing the best I can."

"You are my brother. I had to call to tell you this," he said before saying goodbye. I did not want to argue with him. I worried how this turmoil affected him and those loved ones who did not call.

CHAPTER 57

'The Bankers Will Run This Damn Country'

10:30 a.m. - City Council Chambers

The morning Council meeting was delayed as Forbes remained behind closed doors. I took the opportunity to announce the special Council Meeting, when Council would be required to consider an income tax increase not linked to the sale of Muny Light. It would be Cleveland's final chance to avoid default. I scheduled the meeting for eleven that night.

News media from around the world gathered to witness the countdown. A barricade of tripods was erected in an arc below the throne-like seat of the Council President. Councilmen and women drifted into the Council Chambers, moving slowly onto the red carpeting. They milled, shaking their heads, wagging their fingers, complaining Forbes had not said why he called the morning meeting. Members took their places at their oak desks, to read newspapers, and to stare at the immense space, filled with grand murals depicting the dignity of the people and the wealth of materials used to build the City of Cleveland.

I broke the torpor by personally serving each member with notice of the late meeting which they were required, by law, to attend.

Council clerks distributed Forbes' legislation. Jack Schulman and I read it together. The text paralleled Cleveland Trust's widely publicized demand for the sale of Muny Light. It asserted the banks would renew the notes, if I agreed to both the sale of Muny Light and an increase in the income tax. The bargain basement sale price was similar to what CEI previously negotiated with Mayor Perk. Muny would go to CEI for $40 million in cash and $4 million a year for thirty years, interest-free.

I warned Council members, that even if Muny Light was sold, the proceeds must first go to repay the system's bond holders. Once those obligations were met, the remaining proceeds from the sale would not be enough to replace the missing bond funds or repay the banks. The city would be worse off financially, not better off, if I sold.

"Forbes did not mention this legislation when I met with him a few hours ago," I remarked to Schulman.

"Doesn't matter," Jack replied. "It is illegal, because it has two subjects. It calls for the sale of Muny Light *and* an increase in the income tax. Under Ohio law, legislation can have only one subject. They can't schedule an election with this resolution. They can't sell Muny Light with it either," Jack said.

The light system could be sold only through a separate ordinance. It would then be subject to repeal by the voters and/or to antitrust action by the U.S. Justice Department.

Forbes made his entrance, climbed the rostrum, and announced to the confused Council, "I have just received a call from Cleveland Trust. I spoke to the Chairman. The bank approved this plan," he said, reprising his script from the morning headlines.

"We had better get ready," Schulman said to me. "He is going to try to pass something right now." I took a yellow pad in hand and began to write. Forbes used a parliamentary maneuver and placed his resolution on final passage. The floor debate was vitriolic.

Councilman Leonard Danilowicz bared his walrus-like teeth and rubbed his fist across his mustache, waving in the other hand a copy of Brock Weir's front-page demand. He lifted his voice in anger and tore into the Cleveland Trust-sponsored resolution. "If we allow the bankers to run this damn city, the bankers will run this damn country. If it comes right down to it, I'm voting against this damn thing, because it means a loss of freedom for me when I'm handed a damn ultimatum which I thought was gone when Hitler died. Someone tells me about the disastrous results of default? What are the disastrous results of loss of freedom?"

Danilowicz slammed down his microphone. He came from a Polish and Czech community whose residents resisted genuine dictators. His was a neighborhood of churches, bars, and steel mills, where people organized to fight for their rights to clean air, pure water, and neighborhoods free of crime. It was also an area with few Muny Light customers.

Michael White, Councilman from Ward 24 arose, defending the banks. "It is the Mayor who has backed us up against this wall. You talk about the banks? The banks have a legitimate right to question our fiscal policies."

12:05 p.m. - City Treasurer's Office

Two representatives of Cleveland Trust, wearing dark topcoats and carrying manila envelopes, presented their notes to the city for payment. City Treasurer Jack Cross III, reviewed the documents and gave them a receipt, but no money.

12:05 p.m. - City Council Chambers

The Council debate continued. Benny Bonanno of Ward 21 hit back forcefully at Cleveland Trust. "If Cleveland Trust wants to sink the City of Cleveland, the people of Cleveland will sink Cleveland Trust."

The Council Majority Leader, Basil Russo, a consummate political operator, asked to be recognized by the chair. As the leader of the Democratic caucus, Russo helped Forbes carry out Council policy. Slight of frame, from a distance he appeared unimposing. He was the son of State Representative Anthony Russo, a shrewd grassroots strategist, and had inherited many of his father's skills. When Russo spoke, councilmen listened, because he carried Forbes' instructions.

The two had not always been close. At one time Russo was an ardent advocate of keeping Muny Light and disagreed with Forbes on key political issues. Forbes had become so exasperated with the wily Russo that he once declared, "When that little ******* dies, they better screw him into the ground to make sure he doesn't come back." Today Russo was very much alive, as Forbes' trusted lieutenant. Thus are the vagaries of politics, a reminder that the person who may try to destroy you today could tomorrow be a valuable ally.

"The chair recognizes Mr. Russo."

"Mr. Chairman," Russo's voice was high-pitched, his manner fastidious and articulate. He spoke with restrained excitement. "Council has taken the initiative to draft a plan that would be satisfactory to the banks. The banks are ready to go with this. Obviously, the Mayor is not. It is up to Council to take appropriate action."

I turned to Finance Director Tegreene to learn of any late word from the banks. He checked with the city's financial advisor, John Carhuff, of First Boston Corporation, who served as a liaison to the banks. The best we could determine was that Cleveland Trust, and Cleveland Trust alone, was aware of Forbes' action.

I walked to the stand-up microphone positioned in front of my desk and queried Forbes on Russo's assertion. "Which banks, Mr. Forbes?" He did not look at me, nor did he respond. I asked again "Which banks, Mr. Chairman?"

I then addressed the Council, reading from notes.

"Members of Council, the Law Director has informed me that this legislation is illegal. Even if it is passed, it will not prevent default. Muny Light will not be sold. Therefore, the banks will not withhold action on default based on a resolution which requires the sale of Muny. This resolution means absolutely nothing. The question is: Will Council vote to let the people decide on the ½ percent tax?"

"As to the banks, five banks agreed to our plan. Only Cleveland Trust refused. The other five are still willing, if Cleveland Trust goes along. Let's put Cleveland Trust to the test. Put the ½ percent tax on the ballot. Then we will see if Cleveland Trust is ready to destroy the city in the interest of CEI."

Though the game appeared rigged, I felt I was swaying votes. "There are no apologies to be made after today. There is no way you can tell people you are sorry if you participated in the murder of their city. You cannot wash your hands of what you will do. The stain will always be there."

Forbes needed twenty-two votes to pass his resolution under suspension of the rules. The roll was called. Twenty Councilmen voted for it, thirteen against, enough to sustain a veto.

Forbes had suffered a rare legislative defeat. He would have to wait thirty days for the law to take effect, though its validity was in question. He adjourned the meeting in a rage, declaring he would ignore my call for a Special Meeting at 11:00 p.m.

A group of reporters encircled me. "What's the next move, Mayor?" I was asked.

"We have until midnight to come up with a solution," I said. I had four members' votes to change. As I worked on a breakthrough, I discovered Cleveland Trust's motive in aiding CEI's quest to obtain Muny Light.

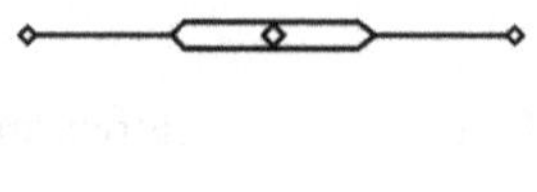

Jack Schulman sat impatiently on the red and white silk-covered chairs in the reception room, combing through documents.

"Dennis," he said, as I walked past, "We have to see you. Now. Brad has been investigating Cleveland Trust. You need to act on what he has discovered."

Norris and Schulman followed me into my office. "Mayor, we need to move fast in exposing the connections between Cleveland Trust and CEI," Norris began.

He was referring to research by Dan Marschall of the Economic Development Department and James L. Harkins, Jr., of the city's Law Department, exploring the relationship between the boards of CEI and Cleveland Trust. Marschall and Harkins had identified interlocking directorates between our two chief foes - - two persons serving on Cleveland Trust's board and CEI's board, at the same time. A third Cleveland Trust director was scheduled to join CEI in January.

Norris opened his briefcase and handed me several documents. "Cleveland Trust's conduct is aimed at coercing you to sell Muny Light, to the benefit of CEI. That's a violation of antitrust law. Since they are connected through their boards, we have the possibility of a conspiracy to violate the antitrust laws."

"They're working together to create a default?" I asked.

"It appears that way," Norris said, "based on what Marschall and Harkins have found, CEI and Cleveland Trust participate in the development of policies for both corporations, to each other's mutual benefit."

He elaborated "Cleveland Trust is one of the largest shareholders of CEI. Cleveland Trust's trust department holds over $27 million worth of CEI securities, including 782,798 shares of common stock. Cleveland Trust manages $70 million of CEI's $130 million pension funds."

Cleveland Trust and CEI were, in effect, branches of the same company, each laying claim to Muny Light, each using their resources to undermine the City of Cleveland to effect a monopoly takeover.

This collusion was beyond my experience, but not beyond our brilliant antitrust attorney's. Like a curator of Henri Magritte's paintings, Brad Norris working with the Harkins-Marschall findings, revealed a bay window in an otherwise impenetrable brick wall of corporate activity, and I looked upon a new political world: A conspiracy through interlocking directorates, a corrupt identity of interests among corporate fraternal twins.

This explained the disdain for Muny Light which Weir evidenced when I first entered his office as a candidate for Mayor.

"Read the letter Brad has drafted to the U.S. Justice Department," Schulman urged. "It will put CEI and Cleveland Trust to the wall."

Norris spread papers on a small black coffee table and handed me the proposed letter to the head of the Justice Department's Antitrust Division in Washington, D.C.

Dear Mr. Shenefield,

As Mayor of the City of Cleveland, I hereby request that you institute a formal investigation into the conduct of the Cleveland Electric Illuminating Company (CEI) and the Cleveland Trust Company, Ohio's largest bank.

You will note that I refer to last year's decision by the Atomic Safety and Licensing Board of the Nuclear Regulatory Commission, determining CEI had violated antitrust laws in its conduct with Muny Light, including creating a blackout on the Muny system.

We discussed the legal implications of the letter.

"CEI and Cleveland Trust's action is a continuation of their illegal antitrust activities. Remember, a federal panel took sworn testimony and concluded that CEI illegally attempted to put Muny Light out of business. CEI won't stop until they have accomplished that objective. CEI and Cleveland Trust are desperate to eliminate Muny Light, because as long as Muny Light is viable, so is the antitrust lawsuit. That suit threatens both companies' economic interests," Norris said.

"If Cleveland Trust forces the city to sell Muny Light, the antitrust suit is gone," Schulman said. "Dismissal will be made part of any deal to sell."

I took pen in hand. "Once you sign this, you are past the point of no return with Cleveland Trust," Norris said.

"It does read like a declaration of war," I said of the letter. "CEI has been fighting a covert war against the city for years." I said, putting my signature to the letter, adding "Let's not make this public right away, in case there is a chance we may reach an agreement with Cleveland Trust."

"Mayor, the antitrust case is still at risk. Judge Krupansky has informed me that unless the city comes up with its full payment of debt, he will dismiss it." Norris said. The federal judge was putting additional pressure on the city. We still owed CEI nearly $2.5 million for past power purchases.

"Brad, assure his Honor we have paid most of the debt and intend to pay all of it by the end of the year."

I called Juniewicz into my office and handed him a copy of the letter to the Justice Department. He moved his glasses up on the bridge of his nose as he read and nodded in approval, "Not bad, not bad," he said. "You know what? I heard this morning that some reporters at the *Plain Dealer* have been looking at the same interlocking directorates. They had a story ready to go last night about bank connections to CEI. The editors refused to run it."

"The *Plain Dealer* editors suppressed the story!?"

"Yes, and there is a battle going on in the City Room between the reporters and the editors over publication," Juniewicz said.

"Andy, can you imagine if Brock Weir awoke to headlines reading: Conspiracy? CEI-CleveTrust Tie Probed. Muny Sale in Doubt," I said, lamenting those days I spent as a *Plain Dealer* copyboy, when I believed the newspaper to be the conscience of the community, the repository of plain truth.

The *Plain Dealer* and the *Press* ran dozens of editorials and news articles calculated to make the sale of Muny Light a foregone conclusion. Antitrust transcripts revealed that they got their information from CEI. I was skeptical that a 'reporters' rebellion' would change anything.

"Dennis," Juniewicz expressed disagreement, "A lot of reporters at the *PD* care. There is a change in attitude in the city room. Reporters are opening up their eyes, because we are forcing the issue."

"It's late in the day, Andy," I said.

"Yes. *PD* management has an revolt on their hands over efforts to suppress this story," he said.

"Really?" I found it difficult to believe. Was Andy having reverie of his halcyon days at the *PD*? I found no comfort in his certitude. I knew what happened to reporters who challenged their bosses.

"Don't forget what happened to Steve Clark, Jim Cox, and Bob Franken at WJW. Honest reporters pay a price."

Andy cut in. "Okay. Okay." He had work to do. "There are a hundred hungry reporters in the Red Room. What should I tell them? They would like to go to lunch, if you don't have anything to say."

"Tell them I'll be right there."

CHAPTER 58

Putting 'the Crook' on the Deal

2:00 p.m. - The Red Room

I had a message to send to the people of Cleveland and to the broader public following events in our city. We were trying to resolve the crisis, but "It is immoral to inject political questions in an attempt to blackmail an administration to dispose of one of the most valuable assets this city has. And if it wasn't valuable, then why are such incredible efforts being made to try to get it away from the people of Cleveland?"

The TV lights were sizzling hot. I held the Cleveland Trust-sponsored legislation in my right hand and said, "There is no legitimate reason to include Muny Light in this 'deal' any more than there is a reason to sell City Hall, Public Square, Public Auditorium, or Burke Lakefront Airport. Why Muny Light? Why not any one of the hundreds of millions in assets the city has? I'll tell you why. It's a crooked deal. It's one of the most crooked deals in the annals of urban politics, because it involves hundreds of millions of dollars and potentially billions of dollars in future public assets."

As we came down to the wire, I wanted unambiguously to "put the crook" on this deal, because, as time moved away from this moment, any fair analysis of the circumstances would come to the same conclusion, no matter what the Cleveland media reported.

I concluded "I want the people to know we are not going to permit the municipal power system to be stolen. We are not going to permit this city to be sold out." I informed the media we had ten hours to see if the Council would act on the tax increase proposal, without requiring the sale of Muny Light.

A cacophony of questions arose, one a surprise.

"Mr. Mayor, some members of the CEI Board of Directors are also members of the Board of Directors of Cleveland Trust. Is this responsible for the behavior of the bank? Does it constitute a conflict of interest?" The question was disembodied. I could not see the reporter who asked it. He was jammed back in a queue of journalists jockeying for position. I heard him and wondered how this question, roiling the *Plain Dealer* city room, could have surfaced here? I looked at Juniewicz, who appeared surprised.

"I think any interlocking directorates ought to be studied," I said, without tipping our hand.

That afternoon, events accelerated.

2:00 p.m. - Cleveland Trust Board Room

Brock Weir told the executive committee of CleveTrust Holding, that if I agreed to sign the resolution Council passed earlier in the day, which called for the tax increase together with the sale of Muny Light, "the bank's position would be improved," and that would be sufficient for Cleveland Trust to agree to renew the city's notes. The board agreed. The two Cleveland Trust directors who also sat on the board of CEI abstained from voting.

2:00 p.m. - City Treasurer's Office, City Hall

The remaining banks presented their notes to the city and were given receipts, but no money.

2:00 p.m. - The Governor's Office, Columbus Ohio

Governor James Rhodes declared he would not allow the City of Cleveland to go bankrupt, but the state had no money to help Cleveland and the state would do nothing to help Cleveland, unless asked. Reporters walked away from the Governor's office scratching their heads.

2:15 p.m. - The Tapestry Room

Sunlight streamed through the white sheers covering the high windows. I shut the door to take a break. Searching for guidance, I picked up a desk-side copy of Mayor Tom Johnson's autobiography, *My Story*. I re-read the sections on his fight to establish Muny Light, his creation through a long, bitter battle with the City Council and CEI, early in the 20th century.

In 1903, the Cleveland City Council unanimously passed an ordinance authorizing a $200,000 bond issue providing for an "electric light and power plant." In *My Story*, Johnson wrote of CEI's role in defeating the ordinance which was intended to set up a municipal utility: "… The Cleveland Electric Illuminating Company … didn't want to be obliged to compete in the lighting business with its own best customer, the city. It went to Council. The Illuminating Company succeeded in winning over three Democratic members. These men, voting with the nine Republicans, defeated the ordinance when it was again introduced. Another example of what outside influence does to Councils."

There was still a way however, for Mayor Johnson to establish an electric system, through annexation of a small, neighboring village.

Johnson wrote: "South Brooklyn owned a small electric lighting plant and for this reason, corporate privilege was opposed to annexation. To have Cleveland acquire a municipal lighting plant in this way was as obnoxious to the Cleveland Electric Illuminating Company as the City's other plan had been, and its fight was now directed against annexation. I made the unfriendly Councilmen very angry by maintaining that the Cleveland Electric Illuminating Company seemed to have more power than forty thousand voters."

"Privilege" as Mayor Johnson put it, had to do with corporate power usurping government, seeking political and economic control of public facilities, privatizing them and selling the same service back to the public, at substantial profit.

Mayor Johnson spelled out the dangers to democratic governance emphatically when he wrote, "I believe in public ownership of all public service monopolies for the same reason that I believe in the municipal ownership of waterworks, of parks, of schools. I believe in the municipal ownership of these monopolies because if you do not own them, they will in time own you. They will corrupt your politics, rule your institutions and finally destroy your liberties."

I put down Mayor Johnson's book. My battle with CEI and Cleveland Trust had deep roots in Cleveland's political history. Mayor Johnson prophesized today's events. What was this destructive instinct infecting the Cleveland Electric Illuminating Company and its cohort, Cleveland Trust? Generation after generation, laws were broken, legislatures were corrupted, and now, the city itself was sent to the brink of fiscal destruction, to destroy public power and to replace it with rule by corporations.

"Mayor?" Intercoms were intrusive. I snapped to attention.

"Yes Blanche?"

A group of the city's financial advisors are outside, and they want to meet with you, now."

Financial advisors? What did I need them for now? People who come from Wall Street protect Wall Street. I needed to see a degree of independent expression from these men, not simply a regurgitation of the poisoned pablum that Cleveland bankers were feeding the financial community. Financial advisors? I needed a Reader and Advisor, a fortune teller, someone who could tell me what would happen to the city. Financial advisors speak with cold certainty, pinioned by questionable numbers. I was filled with uncertainty. I asked Blanche to arrange for us to gather at a nearby restaurant, Sorn's, although I did not expect much.

En route to lunch, seeking temporary refuge from bedlam, I made a stop at a nearby house of worship. I asked Detective Plank and the extended security detail to give me space, while I walked into the sunlit St. Peter's Church on East 17th and Superior Avenue.

I knelt down. I looked past rows and rows of empty pews to the altar and the large crucifix suspended over the sanctuary. St. Peter's was my first church. I attended first grade and made my first communion here and received, from the Good Sisters, formal instruction in the difference between right and wrong, a childhood introduction to spiritual questions one asks oneself, every day, in matters small and large.

Here, in faith, I could feel the presence of those gentle guiding hands of the distant past. I prayed for Cleveland. I prayed for the strength to make the right decision. I prayed and I listened.

I felt comfortable in St. Peter's Church. It was where I led candlelight processions, because I was the littlest altar boy. It was where I served my first mass, memorizing Latin passages now the signposts of my life. "Emitte lucem tuam et veritatem tuam,"... "send forth your light and your truth." Today, truth was less solid, more liquid, changing shapes depending upon the container holding it. Light? Its properties colored by desire. Here, at St. Peter's, I tried to access immutable light and truth. I believe there is such a thing as right and wrong. How could I sacrifice that belief to hard-edged political pragmatism without losing my soul?

I loved my city and its people. Was I serving them by taking a stand? Would I be betraying them if I did not sell Muny Light and the city was put into default? Or would I be betraying them if I sold Muny Light?

3:15 p.m. - Cleveland Police Headquarters

The Office of the Chief of Police. Maryland State Police called Cleveland Police Lieutenant Kovacic and informed him the hit-man had again been asked to visit Cleveland to receive new instructions on the murder contract. Kovacic advised Chief Fox.

3:15 p.m. - Outside St. Peter's Church

I returned to the car and received a phone call from Weissman, waiting at Sorn's restaurant.

"Where are you? We can't keep these guys waiting." He was annoyed at the delay. If Weissman had known the reason, he'd have a fit. He considered religion hocus-pocus.

"Do they have anything new?" I asked.

"You ought to find out," he said. "They are still working for us. They can be of use. They have an idea they want to discuss with you, a compromise to blow apart the phony argument that Muny Light should be sold because it is losing money."

"The report we released this morning does show Muny will have a million dollar surplus," I said. "No one is paying attention."

"It is being lost," Weissman agreed. "We may have a way to bring it to public attention, to show Weir is trying to coerce the city into selling a money-making city operation."

"What's the compromise?" I asked, eagerly.

"They'll tell you. Get over here. Forbes is reconvening the Council at 4:00 p.m. We don't have much time."

3:20 p.m. - Sorn's Restaurant

As our car pulled up to Sorn's Restaurant, an eatery located in the heart of Cleveland's Croatian and Slovenian community on the lower east side, a number of men wearing gray suits in various shades were standing in doorways awaiting my arrival. They were not financial advisers, but "security advisors," plainclothes detectives who had staked out the area to ensure my physical safety.

Inside Sorn's, three men in white shirts, pin-stripe suits, and dark ties sat at a large round table. Their faces had become familiar. I apologized for the delay. They were already chewing on fish, macaroni, steak sandwiches, weinerschnitzel - and pencils.

John Carhuff of First Boston spoke first. "Things are in a deadlock, and, unless a new development occurs, the city is going into default. You can offer a compromise to break the deadlock. At the 4:00 p.m. Council meeting, we suggest you present a plan to establish a Municipal Electric Control Board to oversee the operations of Muny Light. It would be independent of the Mayor and the Council. At the end of a year, if Muny Light is making money, the city keeps it. If it is losing money, the city sells it."

"Wait a minute," I stopped the discussion. "A controlling board for Muny? Who would run it? If I announce this, Weir will be saying, 'Hey, we're halfway home with this guy.' I can't expose the light system to the possibility of a sale. It would legitimize Cleveland Trust making Muny Light the issue."

"Mayor, whether you like it or not, legitimate or not, they have made Muny Light the issue," Carhuff responded. I didn't like it, but I had to concede he was right.

"You would be making a totally safe offer," a second advisor said. "The Beck Report demonstrates that Muny Light can make it during the test period. This would flush them out. You come forward with a compromise, you appear reasonable, statesman-like, in an effort to break the deadlock." It seemed safe, but the danger lay in that it could be misread as favoring the sale.

Weissman, sensing my hesitancy, interjected. "Remember, we are working on agreements to buy inexpensive power from out of state, reducing our dependence on CEI. CEI is under NRC orders to allow access to wholesale power and to provide wheeling rights, so we could bring in cheap, out-of-state power across the lines of other utilities. We could lower Muny's expenses. By next year Muny could be making $2 million to $3 million a year in annual profits. There is no great risk," Weissman said, "and it would protect the antitrust suit."

"Mayor, this compromise will actually make known Muny Light's profitability. If profitability is not the issue, then Cleveland Trust and Council may still refuse your proposal, but, in doing so, they would reveal their intentions are not honorable," a third advisor added.

"Oh, I've never had any doubt about whether their intentions were honorable," I said to laughs.

"There are few options at this late hour. Otherwise, events will run their course and the city will go into default tonight," Weissman said.

"Is this proposal legal?" I asked.

"We checked with Schulman. The Charter and the Ordinances of the City have nothing to prohibit it," Weissman explained.

Our financial advisors had devised a strategy to ultimately protect Muny Light. What they were proposing was difficult. I could be exposing Muny Light to the remote possibility of a sale. But I decided to take the calculated risk to break the deadlock. If this new development helped flush out Cleveland Trust, so much the better.

"I'll do it," I said. There was a discernible shift in the mood of the advisors. A new possibility emerged. The tension lifted. I had given them an alternative to take back to the financial community, and to Council, as well.

"Bob, ask the law department to get the legislation ready. I'll announce it at the 4:00 p.m. Council meeting. Maybe it will shake loose a few votes. Maybe we can get this and the tax proposal passed at 11:00 p.m. tonight!" I said.

Our financial advisory team had been in despair over an impending default. They could return to City Hall with hope.

"Wait a minute," I said gruffly, as the group prepared to leave. "Not so fast, gentlemen." They hesitated, nervously. "I have one more question." I grabbed a take-out menu. "Anyone want apple strudel to go?" They burst out laughing.

3:45 p.m. - Burke Lakefront Airport

Brock Weir left on a private jet, flying to a ski resort in Colorado.

CHAPTER 59

Any Time Now

3:55 p.m. - The Tapestry Room

"Mayor?" Blanche's voice came over the intercom.

"Yes?"

"Chief Fox is here to see you. He said it couldn't wait."

"Send him in."

The Chief of Police entered my office and shut the door. We sat facing each other, with Chief Fox wearing his now-characteristic look of unhappy concern. He spoke first, "Mayor, I have to inform you to take extreme caution today. An assassination attempt may be made soon."

"What do we know?" I asked.

"There has been movement by the prime suspect. We'll provide extra security at the Council meetings, extra men in both balconies, at all exits, and in the audience. We will have undercover police tail your car. I would advise you to wear the bullet-proof vest at the Council meetings and anywhere else you make a public appearance for the next few days, until we have this thing under control."

Raised Catholic, I appreciated the requirements of spiritual service. But I was not interested in martyrdom. I had a 1,400-page prayer book that contained the names of hundreds of martyrs. It was interesting to read about martyrs, rather than contemplating being one.

"Dennis, I've got a lot of good men working on this," Chief Fox said, "There are also out-of-state police working undercover, taking a lot of chances. We are going to provide you with back-up." He stood up, clutched his files closely. We shook hands. Then, he left.

I was reminded, once again, by Chief Fox to stay away from the windows in my office. The requirements of self-preservation can become a self-imposed cage, and I must be free. I walked to the tall, glass opening and looked down Lakeside Avenue to Sixth Street. It was a gray day. Cleveland may have more cloudy days than any city in America. The clouds' thick vapors marched toward Cleveland's lakefront slowly, nature's version of the Volga Boat March, perfect for somber reflection.

My public persona was being ruined. What had I created as a result of taking a simple stand years ago against the sale of the city's electric system? As one revelation after another presented, I began to access a deeper understanding of the nature of power, the consequences of unbridled greed, the role of the city in the life of its people. The light system was not mine to sell.

4:00 p.m. - City Council Chambers

Forbes called the meeting to order. He repeated his version of the morning's events, again averring that our plan was not acceptable to the banks - - well, one bank, Cleveland Trust. "I said earlier that I would not agree to meet at 11:00 o'clock. I have reconsidered. The Charter gives the Mayor the right to call a meeting, if he so chooses."

I stepped to the microphone. Forbes cracked the gavel. "This meeting stands adjourned." He had no intention of permitting me to address the Council.

"Mr. Chairman! Mr. Chairman!" I protested loudly. Forbes exited the chamber, leaving surprised Council members still in their seats. I stepped closer to their desks and, without benefit of a sound system, spoke above the din to the Council.

"I have a compromise," I waved a sheath of papers. "I have a compromise, which may make it possible for you to vote tonight to avoid default. If you are interested in helping this City, stay right where you are and listen to what I have to say." I described the proposal, with Muny's survival dependent on showing a profit. Reporters, cameramen, and other technicians moved forward to hear, drawing most of the Councilmen into the impromptu clutch.

The compromise was seen by many in Council and the media as a dramatic new development, an offer saving the day. The compromise is what Clevelanders would hear during afternoon rush-hour traffic. The compromise is the story television networks carried to a nation enthralled with our municipal drama. We had recreated the moment. Cleveland was set for a storybook finish.

4:15 p.m. - The Mayor's Office

"Dennis, Forbes is telling reporters that Weir is willing to keep his bank open until midnight," said Juniewicz. Indeed, the head of the Cleveland Federal Reserve Bank had called Tegreene and said he would keep the federal wires open until midnight, so that the banks could make and receive wires. I realized that Forbes agreed to the evening meeting, because he and Weir thought I would deal on Muny Light. I decided to add a little pressure of my own.

"Andy, how do you think downtown businessmen would feel, if default meant no police or fire protection for their establishments?" I asked. His response was a study in silent contemplation.

I did not want to have to reduce police, fire, and other essential services to any area of the city. I did not want to lay off any city workers. But, as the default approached, I had to consider that failure to pay our bills on time could result in a run on the city treasury by our creditors. We were particularly vulnerable to contractors who had agreements with the city for work to be paid out of the bond funds the Perk Administration had illegally spent for general operating purposes.

4:30 p.m. - The Tapestry Room

Years earlier, the Greater Cleveland Growth Association had been known as the Cleveland Chamber of Commerce. Its major players met at the Union Club. Then, as Cleveland began to lose industry, the Chamber of Commerce changed its name to the Greater Cleveland Growth Association. John Lathe, its president, was one of the few business leaders who understood that although I refused to sell Muny Light and opposed tax abatements, that did not mean I was anti-business. There were grants and infrastructure improvement for business development, which I supported, which did not adversely affect the city's underlying tax structure. Lathe had sought to work cooperatively with City Hall, despite the financial support provided to his organization by Cleveland Trust and CEI. I called Lathe, hoping he would communicate to his associates the possible impact of default."John, if they squeeze us on this, they'll break the city. The business community cannot escape the consequences."

"Mr. Mayor, I can assure you that the business community does not want the City of Cleveland to go into default. We are on record as favoring the sale of Muny Light. If you can pull this off without selling the light system, God bless you."

"John, if we go into default, by Monday there will be no policemen on the streets of downtown. Neighborhoods will have priority service for police and fire. Downtown will have to protect itself."

He paused. "We don't want that." He promised to call his associates.

Next, I contacted Herbert Strawbridge, president of Higbee

Company, one of Cleveland's largest department stores. He sat on both the boards of Cleveland Trust and CEI. He was one of the very first members of the business elite I visited when I began my campaign for Mayor.

"Mr. Strawbridge, the city will not be able to provide safety services for downtown." He listened in silence, unmoved, and then replied without expression

"Thank you for calling, Mayor," he said, putting down the phone.

4:45 p.m. - Federal Courthouse, Cleveland, Ohio

An agreement between Council President Forbes and CEI was filed with Judge Krupansky, releasing dozens of utility department vehicles needed by the water department. Cables and transformers, belonging to Muny Light, however, remained attached by the lien CEI filed against the city for failure to fully pay Perk's light bill.

4:45 p.m. - Juniewicz' office

Andy put down the phone as I entered his office. He sat back in his chair, leaning it against the wall. The corners of his mouth tightened, signaling bad news. "That was the *Associated Press.* Moody's Investor Service just announced it is dropping the City to the lowest bond rating, Caa, three notches below investor grade. That's the same place New York City was at a few years ago, near the bottom. It will make it tougher for the city to borrow money."

"This is a smear," I said. Perk's debts were overlooked. We've been running the city on a cash basis. We haven't borrowed a dime. What baloney! Moody's is discouraging investors in Cleveland." I was angry.

Andy sat quietly as I recounted the city's experience with the bond rating services and the role of Squire Sanders. Under the Perk Administration, that law firm had kept all of the city's financial records.

How could they have not known that millions were illegally diverted from the city's bond funds. Understanding their legendary legal, strategic and tactical skills, it was not beyond imagination that Squire Sanders, on behalf of CEI, laid a financial trap for the city, with the sale of Muny Light as the only escape. Two years ago, despite a "secret" massive deficit, and under financial conditions that were demonstrably worse, a committee of local bankers and lawyers declared the city financially sound, and City Hall received a high bond rating from Moody's.

5:00 p.m. - The Tapestry Room

Ohio Governor James Rhodes made a public pledge to help Cleveland. I called him.

"Mr. Mayor, I'm going to help. I won't let the city down."

"Governor, could you please assist us in getting a loan from the Public Employees Retirement Fund?"

He did not have direct oversight. But, if he put in a request, a loan could be arranged.

"Governor, will you help us get the loan?"

"Well, I can't do that."

"Couldn't you make a call?"

"I want to help. Why don't you call them, Mayor, see if they'll help?"

"I already called. They won't help. That's why I called you."

"Mayor, I said I will help. If you have any more problems, you give Jim Rhodes a call. I'll be in Florida."

5:30 p.m. - The Tapestry Room

"Do you want to go live with Channel 3 at six o'clock?" Juniewicz asked. "All you have to do is walk over to the studio. It's all set."

"I'm worn out, Andy. It's not a good time to go on the air."

"I think you should."

I was thinking of sinking into Perk's gauche couch in the inner reception room. I had little sleep in the past seventy-two hours. The plush red cushions bid me to rest up for the 11:00 p.m. meeting.

"What if I fall asleep on live TV?" I asked Andy.

"It would do a lot to tone down your image," Andy quipped. He motioned to the clock. "If you are going to do it, you have to leave now." I groaned and headed for Channel 3, one long block south of City Hall. Despite the objections of my security team, I walked, fast, to try to pump up my energy level, as three city detectives trotted alongside and a trail car kept watch.

CHAPTER 60

Live on the Six O'Clock News - Blackmail

6:00 p.m. - Action 3 News Studio

I had another chance to make my case to the people. I was seated next to news anchor Amanda Arnold, who nervously rehearsed her script. I was the one who needed a script. A production assistant counted down with hand signals and the red light on the studio camera beamed. We were live.

The show began with two of the station's reporters, Joe Mosbrook and Sheryl Brown along with co-anchor Doug Adair, waiting in the City Council chambers with a late-breaking development from Council Majority Leader, Basil Russo, Forbes' right-hand man.

Doug Adair: "Sheryl Brown has Basil Russo and some reaction to [the Mayor's plan."

Sheryl Brown: "That's right, Doug. Russo said this compromise a few moments ago was a joke. He said it was bunk and it was not going to work. He said he didn't buy it. He said the banks don't buy it. Basil is in Council Chambers right now, holding a live news conference. He is not going to be talking about this compromise. He has a major announcement concerning Cleveland Trust. Basil."

Majority Leader Basil Russo snappily picked up his cue and delivered one more ultimatum from Cleveland Trust, which was identical to the sum of the morning headline in the *Plain Dealer*, and to the offer I was made in Bobbie Brooks' boardroom, consisting of $50 million in 'help' if Muny Light was sold. It was essentially the same refinancing guarantee which Weir and the executive committee of CleveTrust holding voted to endorse four hours earlier, except this demand was live, on the Six O'Clock News:

"Thank you. If the Mayor will sign the resolution that was passed by Cleveland City Council this morning, the Chairman of the Cleveland Trust Bank has informed the Council that his bank will purchase $50 million worth of city bonds. In effect, what this means is that it will permanently end the city's financial crisis. It will save us millions of dollars in interest, and it will restore the city's credit rating. So, in effect, we now have a plan sitting on the Mayor's desk that will absolutely end the city's financial problems, if he will only put his signature on it," said Russo with certainty.

Sheryl Brown: "That is, if he will only agree to sell Muny Light."

Basil Russo: "That is correct. But in return for that, the bank is pledging a $50 million loan to the City of Cleveland, which is something no bank has been willing to do, until now."

Doug Adair: "Now we are going back, as I understand, to Mayor Kucinich who is in the studio right now with Amanda."

Amanda Arnold: "Doug, thank you very much," and turned to address me directly. "Mayor, as we just heard, the ball is squarely in your court. Mayor, if you will sign that resolution, we have Cleveland Trust saying that you can have $50 million in city bonds which will permanently end, according to Mr. Russo, the city's financial crisis. This is quite an offer from Cleveland Trust, considering the hour, considering the day."

"And especially considering the fact that everyone says that Muny Light is not worth anything," I retorted. "It is a significant offer, certainly. Strange they would cause the default of the City of Cleveland over a light system that is worth nothing. All I have to do is sign my name to this paper and we can have the whole city back together? Baloney!" I dripped sarcasm and continued, speaking directly to the viewers "Cleveland Trust cannot blackmail the people of this city. That is what they are doing. Sandy and I are going to be down at Cleveland Trust on Monday, taking our money out. I am urging everyone listening to do the same."

"When you get a bank that thinks it can run the community, that it can blackmail the Mayor, then you know that the bank has gotten too big for this city. I'm saying that I am not going to sell Muny Light, that it is not a legitimate issue. I have a plan right now, we can avoid default. Five of six banks agreed to a plan which did not involve the sale of Muny Light. That never even came up! This is being thrown in at the last minute, and the people of Cleveland do not want me to sell the soul of this city to this bank and to their buddies at CEI."

"I want to say one thing further. I want to let the people know that I have notified the United States Justice Department of what is going on here. I am going to ask Justice to investigate the action of Cleveland Trust and its connection to CEI. I have every belief that the investigation, should it be brought about, will reveal things to the general public which will bring shame upon CEI, Cleveland Trust, and everyone connected with it."

Amanda Arnold "You are turning down flat… "

"The city has hundreds of millions of assets," I replied. "We have Burke Lakefront Airport. We have the Public Auditorium. We have the Public Hall, itself. Now, why, with all those assets, would Cleveland Trust zero in on Muny Light, which everyone says is not worth anything? So, I think it is clear what we have here… "

Arnold interrupted. "Why would you hang onto it, when the City's financial future is at stake?"

This was an assertion that I was betraying the city I took an oath to protect. Does truth mean nothing? I tried to reclaim the narrative.

"Because this is blackmail. I believe, as Mayor, I have a responsibility to the public interest. And I can tell you right now, if Cleveland Trust determines that the only way we can avoid default is to sell Muny Light, they cannot blackmail the city, and I cannot permit them to do that."

Arnold was swept up in the moment, less anchor than broker. "You have turned down the offer that Mr. Russo outlined on behalf of Cleveland Trust. Doug is with Mr. Russo now to react to your response to the offer."

Doug Adair: "Basil has been listening to the Mayor and the Mayor has rejected it." Adair spoke to the camera and then turned to Russo with the microphone, "Obviously you have felt that you had something that he might agree to?"

"Yes, we did," Russo was emphatic, a tinge of excitement crept into his staid demeanor. "We obviously felt that we had the entire solution to the city's problems. I think we should point out that the bank obviously feels the same way that the Council does, that the Municipal Light Plant is at the root of all the city's financial problems, and until we get rid of that Light Plant, we cannot put our financial house in order. And, consequently, this isn't the time for us to be threatening one another and talking about blackmail and playing politics with the issue."

He lowered his tone, for effect. His rate of speaking slowed down. He assumed a paternalistic character, "We have to act responsibly. We've got to act mature. We only have a few hours left and we have got to resolve this issue in the interests of the City of Cleveland."

I responded on-air to Russo's characterization, which I had watched on a studio monitor.

"I want to let the people of Cleveland know that we are going to make every effort to work this out. I know that the people do not want me to submit to the blackmail of Cleveland Trust or City Council. This is fundamentally wrong. It's morally wrong to sell the Municipal Light System just because Cleveland Trust has decided that's the price. You have got to stand for something."

"Tell me now," Amanda Arnold pressed. "What's going to happen at midnight, if these banks do not accept your offer? You are not accepting their offer. What happens at midnight when this city goes into default?"

"That's a question that I will address directly to the people of Cleveland - - at midnight. I just want the people to know that we've offered an income tax that would solve the problem. We've offered a plan to stabilize the city's finances. I've offered a compromise so that the Council would have an opportunity to join the administration. All they are offering us is arm-twisting, blackmail, and it is unfortunate for the city. Because I know that it's a great city. But I know one thing. When the people put me in as Mayor, they didn't put me in there so that I would sell out the soul of their city."

"Well, we will be looking forward to hearing what you have to say at the midnight hour," Arnold said.

The interview ended. I stayed on the set. Weir did not have to submit to interviews.

Countless households watched as I turned down Cleveland Trust's $50 million offer, live on the Six O'Clock News. I looked far into the future, toward others who would judge this day. Would they understand, forty, fifty years from now, would anyone care about the one-term "boy" Mayor of Cleveland who drew the line, took a stand for the people, and told corrupt interests "No!"?

Or, would they wonder why I didn't take the deal?

Is it possible people can be blind to a major theft happening in plain sight? Lacking information, or suffering through misinformation and disinformation, the public can be misled.

Muny Light had belonged to the people of Cleveland for the last seventy-five years, and, if I had anything to do with it, it would belong to the people of Cleveland for another seventy-five years, and more.

I left the studio. My heart was breaking for my city.

6:30 p.m. - Juniewicz's Office

I returned to City Hall to join Juniewicz, to study videotapes of the news on Channels 5 and 8. On Channel 5, reporter Roger Morris interviewed Basil Russo in the City Council chambers. "Basil, exactly what fiscal controls must be implemented to assure that $50 million loan to Cleveland?"

"The bank [Cleveland Trust] said it was prepared to proceed with the loan, so long as the Mayor signed the ordinance that was passed by Council and that he agreed to keep the city's books in an orderly fashion," Russo said.

"In other words, sell Muny Light," Morris summed up Russo's argument.

"That is absolutely correct," Russo responded.

Morris then faced the camera to sign off from City Hall. "That is Council Majority Leader, Basil Russo, saying that the bank will give us the loan, if Muny Light is sold by the Mayor."

Andy then brought up Channel 8. It was Russo, again. "...If he [the Mayor] will just sign the resolution that Cleveland City Council passed this morning, the Chairman of Cleveland Trust has informed the Council that his bank will purchase $50 million worth of city bonds..."

"Okay, okay, okay, I've seen enough," I said.

Russo received saturation coverage on the evening news. No wonder the phones were ringing off the hook. All Clevelanders knew from the news tonight is that unless I sold Muny Light, as dictated by Cleveland Trust, the city would go into default. The compromise I had announced had been blown up. Now the story was "Will you accept the $50 million offer from Cleveland Trust?"

Andy handed me the final edition of the *Cleveland Press*:

"DEFAULT TIME ARRIVES AS THE NATION WATCHES"

Of course, I was concerned about how Clevelanders looked at the unfolding events. Now I had to worry about what the nation thought? The editors were trying to embarrass me into giving away Muny Light. You want embarrassment? I know embarrassment, wearing the same pair of dog-ripped, turquoise-blue pants to school for more than a year; my parents and siblings getting evicted from our small apartment, and passersby picking through our things set upon the sidewalk. Life experiences can move you to appreciate and sympathize with other people's hard luck circumstances. Cleveland was suffering not from hard luck, but hard corruption.

I looked again at the foreboding headline and read the first paragraph. "As the nation watched, Cleveland today was at the brink of becoming the first major American city since the Depression to default. With little apparent room for compromise, there were these developments: City Council met to consider a resolution that would give Mayor Kucinich but one alternative, sell the Municipal Light Plant or default."

7:00 p.m. - The Mayor's Office

Weir's early-morning ultimatum was recited in the board room. It was amplified in banner headlines in all the newspapers. It was put in the text of a Council resolution. It blared in radio news accounts and was recited by Council Majority Leader Basil Russo, live to all Cleveland media at 6:00 p.m.

Sell Muny Light. Sell Muny Light. Sell Muny Light!

Whatever Clevelanders read that day, whatever they listened to, whatever they watched, nothing else was discussed except Muny Light and default. It touched every discussion. People spoke of Muny Light in fearful tones, on buses, at work, in office towers, in their homes, in bars from one end of the city to another. Brock Weir's message was heard.

The foundation of City Hall felt like it was shaking with demands for the sale.

Appearance is everything in politics, wrote Machiavelli. It appeared a great calamity was to befall Cleveland. "The first American city to default since the Depression." The Great Depression. There it was, the images of bread lines, soup lines, long lines of people hungry, unemployed, broke, a broken city.

Based on the calls pouring into our office, Clevelanders thought I was taking the city down. The toughest part of politics is worrying what people think. They get mad at you today, then they change their minds tomorrow to agree with what you said yesterday. Slavering after public opinion is like dancing with clouds - your partner keeps changing shape as you try to defy gravity.

Weissman frequently told me that nothing is more important in life than to stand up and to fight for those things you know are true. What he didn't tell me was how I could do that *and* remain in elected office.

Detective John Zajac was guarding my office. He and Patrolmen Jim Benedict and Dan Mahon alternated security and bodyguard duties with Detective Plank. I played football at St. John Cantius with Zajac and Benedict. I remembered them as rough and tumble. That was why, after my election as Mayor, I requested their presence on my security detail.

"Mayor you look very tired," Zajac said.

"John, I need a break. I'm going into the next room to try to get a few hours rest. Make sure I am up by 9:45 p.m., okay?"

"What if anyone calls?"

"Tell them I will be at the Council meeting tonight."

I locked the door behind me, a habit. I took off my shoes, suit and shirt, pulled a light cotton blanket from behind the red couch and hugged the velour cushions. The light in the room was dimmed. Only the portraits of Thomas Jefferson and Cleveland Mayor Tom L. Johnson were visible. I studied Johnson's face. Could he have imagined the future battle his credo would ignite? His words echoed through time and reverberated tonight in the city:

"I believe in public ownership of all public service monopolies for the same reason that I believe in the municipal ownership of waterworks, of parks, of schools. I believe in the municipal ownership of these monopolies because if you do not own them, they will in time own you. They will corrupt your politics, rule your institutions and finally destroy your liberties.[1]"

At its core, the fight to save the Division of Light and Power was a fight for freedom. Freedom for people to control their politics, their communities, their own destiny.

This evening, I kept watch with Mayor Johnson. It was my turn to be a sentinel for something more important than my political career, more important than City Hall itself. It fell to me to keep faith, to keep alive a Cleveland tradition of true public power and to preserve the memory of the man who had the vision to establish it.

I drifted into a deep sleep, where for the first and only time I met in a dream someone I had long admired, who visited with me from the wellspring of my imagination or from that place where past, present, and future converge, where spirit and matter unite in consequence. He had come forward to thank me and to offer encouragement in the days ahead. It was Mayor Tom Johnson.

11:00 p.m. - City Council Chambers

Five hundred citizens jammed the Council chambers. Over one hundred news persons and a few bankers watched as Council President Forbes gaveled the meeting to attention at 11:00 p.m. Cameras zoomed to the City Council Attorney, John Climaco, who began a long series of legal objections to our proposal for a Municipal Electric Control Board. Council refused to put an income tax on the ballot. It refused to pass the

1 From his autobiography, "My Story" by Tom L. Johnson. Published by B.W. Huebsch, New York, 1911 • Page 194

secured note ordinance, which would authorize the city to refinance the notes due at midnight. A chronometer was displayed on one television station's screen, a countdown of minutes and seconds to default. As Climaco droned on, a few Council members visited at my desk, begging me to sign the Cleveland Trust resolution, selling Muny Light to CEI.

International and national media were present, drawn into the frenzy.

11:00 p.m. - The 11 O'Clock News, WEWS Television

A commercial introduced the show: "The 11 O'Clock News, is brought to you live by the Cleveland Electric Illuminating Company."

Ted Henry, Anchorman, "It's been one of the most suspenseful days in this city's history, as Cleveland has teetered on the virtual brink of financial disaster. The question the nation is waiting to hear tonight is 'Will Cleveland become the first city to default since the Great Depression?' Well, let's begin our coverage of a series of live reports from City Council chambers. Here now is Dave Patterson."

News reporter Dave Patterson, of WEWS TV, Channel 5, stood in the balcony of the Council chambers. His camera opened with a wide-angle view of the Council below. Patterson explained the latest developments to his viewers, "Well Ted, in many ways, this has been a disheartening and quite confusing day down here at Cleveland City Hall. The political polarization between the Mayor and City Council may well have paralyzed the city's efforts to avoid bankruptcy."

"We are literally less than an hour now before the deadline for the city to repay those $15 million in notes to Cleveland banks, and at this hour, Cleveland City Council has assembled for a special meeting requested by the Mayor."

"Council, as you know, continues to insist that Mayor Kucinich agree to sell the Municipal Light plant, something that he continues to say he will not do. They want it for the cash and to deal him a severe political defeat, something that he will not swallow at all. Today Kucinich did offer a sort of compromise. He agreed to set up a three-person financial oversight board…but that was not acceptable to Council and they're not going to approve that."

"I had a long talk tonight with two officials of Cleveland Trust, the bank that has been spotlighted as the most conservative of the banks. They are still insisting that they be paid. They did offer the olive branch, so to speak, saying that if there was some viable alternative, for example, if the Mayor would agree to sell Muny Light, and if there was some assurance of tighter financial controls in the city, Brock Weir personally said that he would lead an effort to sell $50 million in Cleveland city bonds," Patterson reported.

Ted Henry in the WEWS studio: "Well Dave, Cleveland Trust, if I'm not mistaken, is going to leave its front door unlocked there until about 12:00 midnight. So that gives the boys down at City Council and the Mayor just about forty minutes… to come up with some workable solution."

Patterson: "That's true. Cleveland Trust President Jerry Jerrold, and Vice President, Fred Cox, are both probably watching this newscast right now. They have no more idea than we do of what is going to happen. They told me they'll be watching television tonight to see what Council does."

11:00 p.m. - TV 8 Reporter Jeff Maynor with Susan Howard

Jeff Maynor: "…The bankers are here at City Hall tonight. Now Forbes has said the Mayor called this meeting for the purpose of voting on the income tax increase, and that's all that can be discussed here tonight. The people close to the Mayor told me tonight they can't get the votes they need for the tax increase in conjunction with keeping Muny Light under control of a board… Susan Howard was here all through the day today doing developments… Susan?"

Susan Howard: "…this has also been one of the most emotional and frustrating days. This morning, even though Mayor Kucinich had said selling Muny Light was like selling his soul to the devil, City Council introduced a resolution that unless Muny Light is sold, there will be no consideration of the Mayor's tax hike proposal. Debate over the issue is the most bitter I've heard...The Mayor attacked the bankers for requiring the sale of Muny Light and called for Clevelanders to attack the banks too."

11:30 p.m. - City Council Chambers

Reporters from local television stations, and cameras identifying every major American news network, ABC, CBS, NBC, plus the BBC, CBC, Japanese Television, and the Swiss network, were capturing the drama in City Council as Cleveland teetered.

CHAPTER 61

Not For Sale

Let me make a confession. I am ambitious. You don't get to be mayor of a major city by age thirty-one if you do not have large ambitions. I am not, by nature, a moralist. But, even non-moralists can, in their journey stumble across a moral dilemma.

As default approached, what appeared to be the easiest way out, to sell Muny Light, was not the path I would take. My city, members of my administration and my loved ones would suffer the consequences. It would mean for me, the destruction of a dream of public service, and the obliteration of a decade of striving.

I addressed the Council, inspired by one of my favorite Baptist congregations.

11:45 p.m. - WJW TV 8.

News Anchorman Tim Taylor: "Let's go back now to the City Council meeting for a live report from our City Cam reporter, Jeff Maynor."

Maynor: "The Mayor has just begun to speak to City Council."

At this moment I knew I was speaking to the future, because the decision to force Cleveland into a default had been made by Cleveland Trust and CEI and their supporters in Cleveland City Council. "Mr. Chairman, I began, " there has been no interest in compromise. The clock is ticking away, and what we got was filibuster..."

"There was an offer covered in the media that $50 million in assistance from Cleveland Trust would be extended, if the Council and the Administration will dispose of the Municipal Electric System. Is Cleveland Trust so corrupt that they're trying to buy off an entire city? Because the offer of $50 million, under these conditions, is an insult to the people of this city, and it's a totally dishonest device which reveals Cleveland Trust's underlying assumption that everyone has a price."

"Everyone has a price. Now that's the kind of psychology upon which people are sent into slavery. Everyone has a price. That's why legislatures and governments, entire governments, are bought and sold overnight, with the poor people paying the freight charges."

"Everyone has a price. Well, maybe that can carry them anywhere in the world, but it isn't going to carry them through the gates of City Hall, because not everyone in this city has a price. And if Cleveland is to go into default, at least we will not have sold our souls. They've offered to give us $50 million of help if we sell our electric system. Sell it at a discount. They'll give us $50 million if we sell Muny Light, but they won't extend our credit $5 million. I want it understood that I offered a compromise today with great reluctance."

"...it's unfortunate that the Chair dispensed with the prayer tonight, because maybe we need that more than anything in this city, with a story from the Book of Daniel, which tells of King Nebuchadenezzar, who made an image of gold... the King decreed whoever does not fall down and worship will, at the same moment, be thrown into the fiery furnace."

"Three administrators of Babylon, Chadrak, Meschach and Abednego didn't obey. The King summoned them, threatened them with death if they did not fall down and worship an image of gold. And they responded to the King, " 'Let it be known to you, O King, that your gods are not the ones we are serving, and the image of gold that you have set up we will not worship.'"

"Mr. Chairman and Members of Council, ultimately the history of Cleveland will reveal that Cleveland Trust and CEI and some members of this City Council brought shame to this city and besmirched its history. But it will also show that there were people who recognized wrong when they saw it and condemned it for what it was."

WJW TV-8 - Live at 11:55 p.m.

George Forbes' response was a colossus of convolution. "To set the record straight about $50 million and Cleveland Trust. I don't bank at Cleveland Trust, like you, Mr. Mayor. I've never had a penny there and I never will put one there. Cleveland Trust and the Chairman of the Board did not offer you $50 million to sell the light plant and you know it. The man [Brock Weir] stated that his bank held $5 million in notes. That the plan as proposed by the administration was not acceptable to his bank. He further stated that if he could give the money to you, he would, but he was a banker and could not. He further stated he was willing to go forth with and raise $50 million for this city to place itself on a sound financial basis, and he never mentioned one single solitary thing about Muny Light, and I will not have anyone believing Cleveland Trust and Brock Weir offered $50 million for the light plant."

Maynor whispered, "There are several microphones raised by Councilmen indicating that they too would like to speak. The discussion will continue for some time. We are now at about midnight, straight up, and past time when the notes were due. Apparently, the city is in default. We will be coming back to you, but we will return you to the studio now."

Anchorman Taylor in the TV 8 studio "I guess default is a foregone conclusion..."

Our income tax legislation was not acted upon. The electric-powered City Council chamber clock struck twelve.

Cleveland was in default.

One of the great ironies of the moment, was that Cleveland was put into default by the banks over loans taken out for the "City-County Justice Center" project, which according to Mayor Carl B. Stokes, Milt Schulman and others never should have been built in the first place. Supported by Mayor Perk, ground was broken on October 20, 1972, during his first term. The project, originally scheduled to cost $60 million, was completed in 1976, at a more than 100% cost overrun.

1:30 a.m. - December 16, 1978 - Milan Avenue

Sandy and I traveled from City Hall to our Milan Avenue sanctuary in silence. We wearily walked upstairs to the bedroom. I was filled with anger. We tried to leave the City outside, so that we could have each other, without the tension of city politics. Tonight, the City and Muny Light gripped both of us.

"We actually went into default. I can't believe it." I folded my suit. It smelled of smoke-filled rooms. I tossed my shirt and socks into a hamper.

"What a rotten mess."

"It isn't the whole town, Dennis. Just certain people," Sandy said, trying to smooth my feelings.

"Look at what happened today, Sandy. All day, radio, television, newspapers, Weir, Forbes, Russo, sell Muny Light, sell Muny Light; utter distortion, they put it out and people bought it. The future of Cleveland was put in the context of whether or not I sold the light system. No one was thinking of the long-term cost to the City, the higher utility rates, the increased taxes. Cleveland was fed a big lie."

Sandy was ready for bed. "Come on, Dennis, get some rest. You made the right decision. Now," she motioned to the pillow beside her. Emotionally, I was still at City Hall, on the Council floor, giving hell to

Cleveland Trust, to CEI, to Forbes. I stood in my jockey shorts, t-shirt and bare feet, declaiming to the only vote I was truly sure of, "People wonder what's wrong with our politics. It's the yes men, the politicians without any backbones."

"Dennis," Sandy motioned, "Bed!"

On December 15, 1978, everyone in Cleveland knew the choice I had been given: Sell Muny Light or the city would go into default. Most Clevelanders could not understand why I refused Cleveland Trust's offer of $50 million in loans in exchange for the sale of Muny Light to CEI. There was resentment toward me for passing up what was understood as the Cleveland Trust solution, to sell Muny Light and save Cleveland. I had been urged to hand over the keys to the city to a bank and a utility. When I did not, it was said I had shamelessly betrayed my city.

Saturday morning, the *Plain Dealer* finally published its story revealing the high-level connections between CEI and Cleveland Trust. The news analysis was so heavily edited, however, that the reporters who worked on it refused to put their names on the story. Nevertheless, the revelation of behind the scenes influence was beginning to see daylight, even if the story was buried inside the paper, a day late:

"CEI, BANK BOARDS OVERLAP
7 OF UTILITIES 11 DIRECTORS
ALSO SERVE CITY'S LENDERS"

Cleveland Trust's motive was exposed. CEI and Cleveland Trust had identical financial interests.

A few years ago, New York City technically defaulted on $3 billion of its debt and narrowly avoided precipitating a world-wide fiscal crisis. New York City gave up control of its finances to an un-elected controlling board. I received a letter of encouragement and a visit at my home from Paul O'Dwyer, who was President of New York City Council and on its Board of Estimates from 1974-1977, during its financial crisis.

"My dear Mayor: O'Dwyer wrote, " In 1976, the actions threatened by the bankers here would have driven us into bankruptcy. Our state and city officials turned handsprings and surrendered as a result. We have paid over $200,000,000 per year in exorbitant rates of interest and that will continue into the indefinite future."

"The rates of interest on bonds or notes in every town, city and county across the United States rose to unprecedented heights making a real windfall for the money lenders. Had we called the bankers bluff, as you did, we could not have been worse off."

"Bankers at the time told us our paper was not sellable on the open market, and that was true. They had created that condition by secretly unloading $2 billion dollars in New York City notes which they then held."

As New York Council President O'Dwyer lamented, the surrender to the banks cost New York dearly.

CHAPTER 62

$ Give Me it All - or Die

Monday, December 18, 1978

The banks and other creditors did not take action to collect their debts. They placed us in a technical default and held us there. No services were interrupted anywhere in Cleveland. Not a single city worker was laid off. Streetlights and traffic lights were operating. Policemen were at their posts. Garbage was picked up. Streets were repaired. We were in default, destabilized, yet still in business. It was ludicrous that a city with over $2 billion in assets was thrown into default over $5 million in notes which Cleveland Trust refused to renew.

It was reprehensible that a few weeks before leaving office Mayor Perk gave away $4.5 million in debt-service fund which could have been used to pay off our obligation to Cleveland Trust.

Sandy and I had a promise to keep. At noon, we left City Hall, and headed to Cleveland Trust's headquarters to withdraw $9,197.52, our life savings, in protest of the bank's action pitching us into default.

Detective Plank drove us through downtown Christmas traffic to Cleveland Trust's main office at East 9th and Euclid Avenue. The police radio crackled with a report "Bank alarm, East 57th and Broadway. Car on the way." How ironic an illegal withdrawal was underway as we were legally withdrawing our money.

Large crowds coursed through the sparsely-decorated retail district. Pickets six-deep lined the sidewalk, overflowing into the street, surrounding our car, chanting "You can't trust Cleveland Trust."

We had supporters.

A gaggle of reporters and cameramen followed us into the impressive rotunda of Cleveland Trust's headquarters. We were greeted by Christmas carolers, the famed Singing Angels, while media teams moved into position to capture the action at a teller's window.

"God Rest Ye Merry Gentlemen, Let Nothing You Dismay," came the sweet sounds of the Singing Angels.

We moved to a teller, presented our passbook, and withdrew our savings.

Moments earlier, across town, as reported by police radio, the bank alarm. A thin, blond-haired man wearing sunglasses and carrying a battered suitcase, had entered a Central National Bank branch on East 57th and Broadway Avenue and handed a bank teller a Christmas card, with a colorful cartoon of Santa Claus withdrawing toys from a toy bank. The teller smiled, opened the card. The handwritten note inside the card greeted:

$ Give Me It All - Or Die

The shocked bank employee, without a word, tripped an alarm and moved stacks of money over the counter, including one bundle designed to explode with a marking dye. The robbery suspect cleared the counter of the money, put it into his suitcase, and calmly walked out.

Sandy and I exited the lobby to the steps of Cleveland Trust bank, where I announced to the demonstration taking place, "I'm taking my money out, because I don't want clean money in a bank which is dirty." We invited other Clevelanders to do the same. Detective Plank approached me, as I was in mid-sentence. "Gotta go boss. They need you back at City Hall."

"What's up?" I asked. I did not want to leave.

"Don't know. They said to get you back, on the double."

As Sandy and I entered our car, I heard a fragmentary conversation on the police radio, "Bank robbery suspect in custody."

We hurried back to City Hall, to an ante-room of the Mayor's Office, where a morose Juniewicz stood with Blanche Nofel and Chief Fox, both of whose faces showed anguish.

What in the world?

"We've got problems, " Juniewicz said drolly.

"You brought me back here to tell me we've got problems? I'm trying to keep city services going without laying off thousands of workers. We have media from all around the world in the next room Andy, I know we have problems."

"I mean we've got BIG problems." Andy said.

"Big problems? What else could go wrong?"

Blanche, her face flush, her voice trembling, blurted out. "Your brother Perry just robbed a bank!"

Andy added a dagger thrust "Try... your brother Perry robbed a bank at the same time you were taking your money out of Cleveland Trust."

"Is this a joke? You've got to be kidding." I was horrified. "I have a press conference in a few minutes with the national media."

A grim Chief Fox explained, "Perry is in police custody. They are bringing him to the Justice Center. He'll be arraigned by a federal magistrate."

"We can't make this up," Juniewicz said. He gave me more details. I tuned out. I was reeling. A moment later, I regained my poise.

"You know Perry has been in and out of psychiatric hospitals? Gary and I have been trying to get him help. But..." I didn't know what else to say. I dreaded having to explain.

"Dennis," Andy wrestled to keep me at attention. He stepped close, braced me, and looked directly at me. "Here's the problem - - everyone, I mean everyone, wants to know about Perry. They aren't asking me about the default. They don't want to talk about Cleveland Trust. They don't want to talk about Muny Light. They don't care about you taking money out of a bank. They want to know about Perry taking money from a bank."

I looked toward the Red Room and the crease of bright white light at the bottom of the door. The room was floodlit for TV cameras. I stared back at Andy. He nodded slowly, sadly, in painful disgust. He motioned toward the door of the Red Room.

I had planned a low-key briefing on our efforts to maintain city services in the face of default. On the other side of the door, the story was Perry. I was faced with the terrifying task of discussing my brother's life difficulties, and our family's problems, with a roomful of strangers who would carry the story into the living rooms of tens of millions of people around the world.

Andy and I hastily drafted a statement appealing for compassion and understanding.

Every family has its story of heartache and tragedy. I could not tell them Perry had been institutionalized for many years, a paranoid schizophrenic, who shut himself inside a small room for days, weeks, months on end. He was a brilliant artist, a creator of thousands of small paintings, a philosopher, a visionary who dabbled in the black arts.

Perry carried a Jungian palette of emotional and psychological archetypes on physical display, emerging and acting out independently on any given day. Whom do you desire to appear? Nietsche? Nostradamus? Warhol? David Bowie? Marilyn Monroe? Or Gumby, the gentle, pop-culture cartoon character wrapped in asparagus-green rubber foam from head to toe? Gumby, a star of the Howdy Doody show, a triumphant, animated character who was certain to attract attention everywhere, because, well, because Gumby was all green and could have been a humanoid, a vegetable, or even your brother. Yes, Gumby, who after a call late one night from the Cleveland Police, I lovingly reclaimed from the psychiatric emergency room of St. Vincent Charity Hospital, as a half-asleep patient jumped up in a waiting room chair, pointed at me and Gumby/Perry as we walked past, alerting patients and staff alike, "Look, there's the Mayor with mutherfuckin' Gumby!" or maybe he said, "there's Gumby with the mutherfuckin' Mayor."

Politicians love being connected to celebrities, not upstaged by them. Gumby and I entered that emergency treatment bay where we discussed the next move.

"Dennis?"

"Yes Perry."

"Do I look like Gumby?"

"Yes Perry, you look a lot like Gumby. There's people here who think you are Gumby."

"Thanks Dennis. Why are you here?"

"Even Gumby needs rest, Perry. It's time to go home."

After a nurse checked Perry's vitals, I drove him back to his apartment and cautioned Gumby should not stay out late.

All of Perry's companions traveled with him in his perpetual Ziggy Stardust metaphysical road show, ready to materialize in wondrous detail, anytime, any place. I wondered who showed up at the bank and presented the teller with the Christmas card.

There was so much to say. My brilliant, troubled brother was infinitely more interesting than me. Juniewicz advised, "the less you say, the better."

I entered the Red Room and kept it short, calmly telling the media we would get Perry whatever help he needed. Pandemonium permeated the air. I had been catapulted inside a Salvadore Dali landscape, where the thin veil between what is real and what is not had been breached, where objects melted and all things had a woozy, blurry feeling. Reporters were jostling each other to ask questions. The din reached cacophony.

The Red Room was transformed into a fun house of characters

preening before distorted mirrors. Perry's emotionally train-wrecked psyche had collided head on with our financially train-wrecked city, and I was suddenly the focus of a Fellini-esque carnival of paid gawkers with cameras, pens and notepads. I read my prepared notes, left the room, shut the door, took a deep breath, closed my eyes, and slowly exhaled.

"Oh. My. God!"

Reporters and television cameras rushed to the Federal Court to see Perry, handcuffed, headed for his hearing before a magistrate. "Hi," he said breezily as he walked past a thicket of whirring cameras.

"Perry, Perry, do you have any comment?" Reporters shouted after him.

He stopped for a moment, looked briefly at reporters and replied, "I just did: 'Hi.'"

The federal magistrate, attempting to determine whether Perry had financial resources to defend himself, inquired of his assets.

"My cat," explained Perry.

Later that day, the national media recounted events in Cleveland. "A bizarre development in Cleveland today as the city entered default, the brother of Mayor Kucinich robbed a bank." It was a lead story on World News Tonight with Walter Cronkite.

The entrance to the city hospital psychiatric ward was decorated with holiday silver and green. I was led through a series of locked doors to visit Perry, who had been placed in a small, austere room. He sat upon a bed, still. I sat in the only chair available, a sturdy metal one.

"Perry, how do you feel?" I asked, gently.

"Fine, why do you ask?" he said in a heavily-medicated, mechanical cadence.

"Well, there are a lot of people wondering how you feel."

"Oh, I feel fine. Dennis," he replied. His eyes widened. He was suddenly present, as he offered why he robbed the bank. "I heard the city needed money, so I went to get you some. Did I help you, Dennis?"

"Sure, you did just great, kid," I said, putting my arm around my little brother. I sat with him for a time, thinking of his long struggle. Then I gave him a big hug, and, as I had many times before, moved past an attendant who kept Perry in a secure place. As the thick metal door shut, I remembered the travails of our family of seven children, the countless moves my parents made, living in cars, the topsy-turvy home environment that damaged Perry from an early age; his private struggles now achieved an out-sized public dimension. How difficult, yet essential, it was to try to protect him.

CHAPTER 63

The Division of Light and Power

December 20, 1978 - Mayor's Office

Reality inverted, as in a Kafka novel. History didn't repeat itself, it rewrote itself, as fiction. The City of Cleveland over the next few months became a pulverized landscape of odd, unfamiliar shapes, much like one of my brother Perry's paintings. Neither a psychotropic drug, nor an emetic had been invented to park or purge this affliction, which began as do many things in this story, with the Cleveland Electric Illuminating Company:

"CEI WITHDRAWS OFFER TO BUY MUNY LIGHT"

This single declarative headline in the *Plain Dealer* was meant to obliterate a seventy-five year span of CEI's corporate interference, scheming and sabotage. It was akin to the declaration of a fox, once inside the coop, denying its taste for chicken, but it brought the advocates for the sale forward; this time to mourn the opportunity lost by my unwillingness to let Muny Light be eaten by a utility monopoly.

"The reason [for the withdrawal of the offer] is that Mayor Kucinich, through delay and harassment, clearly killed the city's offer to sell when he repeatedly announced that he would never give up Muny Light. The political value of the facility has more importance to him than the money that might have prevented the city from defaulting," Rudolph told the *Plain Dealer.*

"The big lie technique is being exposed for what it is," Karl Rudolph, Chairman of CEI stated. This was not an act of contrition, since Mr. Rudolph's truth was not subject to criminal prosecution. This was the beginning of corporate Cleveland's gas-lighting of the city.

Cleveland Trust Vice President, Bruce Akers, told the *Cleveland Press* on December 15th that Cleveland Trust would reconsider, if I accepted their demand calling for the sale of Muny Light. Now, unnamed spokespersons said, "Cleveland Trust officials stated that the reporter asked Mr. Akers leading questions, that the remarks were taken out of context, and at no time did Mr. Akers suggest that a rollover of the notes [held by Cleveland Trust] was pre-conditioned on the sale of Muny Light."

On December 15th at 6:00 p.m., three Cleveland television stations had broadcast live Council Majority Leader, Basil Russo's, oft-repeated articulation of Brock Weir's position: Sell Muny Light to avoid default. Russo now declared he had "no conversation with Mr. Weir. Weir never said that. He never told me that. He never told Mr. Forbes that. He never told the Mayor that."

Forbes explained Russo's dilemma: "Russo misunderstood me and Russo may have been dazed by the glare of the television lights," he said with a smirk.

My good friend Maury Saltzman, who shortly after default told the media of Weir's offer linking Muny Light to the rollover, now maintained, "I will say right now that Weir did not link the rollover with Muny… At no time did Mr. Weir mention the sale of Muny as a precondition to rollover, or as a precondition to any other action." After his retraction, I received a staff memo that Cleveland Trust was listed as owning 26.9% of the common stock of Bobbie Brooks, my good friend Maury's company.

Council President, George Forbes had carried Weir's ultimatum through to the media.

Forbes' December 15th legislation to sell Muny Light embodied Weir's demand. It was "An emergency resolution to establish a fiscal policy for the stabilization of the City of Cleveland's finances which … requires the sale of both the Municipal Light Plant and an increase in the municipal income tax." It was followed by this passage: "Whereas, local banks have indicated a willingness to consider renewing outstanding notes…if both the above actions are accomplished."

Reclaiming his position as chief celebrant of Cleveland's tradition of double-speak, Forbes now proclaimed, "Weir never said anything about Muny Light." Forbes said I was lying when I said the bank linked its refinancing of city notes to the sale of Muny Light. He said Weir never offered to raise $50 million for the city, if the light plant were sold. "What Weir said was that he would personally help raise $50 million in credit for the city, if an acceptable financial plan were written."

Why the utter distortion of televised events witnessed by millions?

The letter Brad Norris had me send to the Justice Department was having an effect and the denial of Muny Light being the price of refinancing was now the official position of all those who made the sale of Muny Light the price of refinancing.

The Cleveland media dutifully broadcast the newly-minted claim that Muny Light had nothing to do with default, as they had broadcast, both prior to December 15 and on that day, the demand that Muny Light had everything to do with default. The denials became the "New Truth." The "old truth" was old news. Old news was no news. The New Truth was news.

The Irreducible Truth was that the City of Cleveland was in default. Why? According to Cleveland Trust, Weir, Akers, Forbes, Russo, and Saltzman, it had nothing to do with the sell-Muny Light-for-credit scam.

How could everyone have been so misled, on such a critical matter, at the zenith of a crisis?

December 19, 1978 Mayor's Office, Meeting with Chief Fox

"I'm authorizing additional security," the Chief told me in a one-minute meeting, "I met with Inspectors Nagorski and Gallagher and briefed them on the intelligence we have received regarding the plot. Lieutenant Vanyo will brief your security detail, so that everyone is on the alert. Be careful."

"Thanks Chief, I'll be careful."

What does 'careful' mean? Unless I hide in a box, I don't have any control over this. None.

December 19, 1978 Mayor's Office

It was the end of a long day. Sandy and I sat alone in the reception room. Perhaps, if the phones remained mute and no director rushed in with an emergency, we would have a chance to plan a holiday visit with our family. It was difficult to celebrate Christmas under these circumstances.

True, city services remained uninterrupted. Clevelanders moved about easily doing their holiday shopping as if nothing had happened. The phone calls to City Hall dropped off. As I moved about the city, I had to answer questions about why Cleveland Trust did or didn't offer $50 million if I sold Muny; why the sale of Muny Light was or wasn't ever a consideration of default; why I rejected CEI's offer to help the city avoid default. Except for a burst of mostly superficial national news stories, nothing much was said about the default. Our administration was still searching for the right combination of compromises to escape from its imposition.

The moments I shared with Sandy were precious, but our private space had been usurped. We were both wondering about the next steps for our city.

"Sandy, the banks may keep us in default," I said, certain Cleveland Trust would choose to ensnare us, without regard to the city's resources.

"Dennis, you have carried the weight of this long enough," she said.

"What do you mean?"

"I mean it's time for you to let the people help. If they want Muny Light, let them say so. Why should you keep sticking your neck out, if no one cares, and if everyone is damning you for standing up?"

"What are you suggesting?" I asked.

"Put the question of Muny Light on the ballot. Let the people decide. Ask them to back you up," she said.

"Sandy, the minute I put Muny Light on the ballot, Cleveland Trust, CEI, and their friends in the media will have a field day. I don't think we'd stand a chance."

"Don't you have confidence in the people?" she asked, challenging my own sensibilities.

"People can be manipulated by big money. Things can get pretty mixed up in an election campaign. Most victories go to whoever spends the most money."

"Dennis, let the people decide. It may be the only way out of this deadlock," Sandy implored. "You've got to let this go. This is killing us. Your political career is down the drain. You've escaped three assassination attempts. Your health has suffered. Let the people decide if they want Muny Light."

She was right. If I wanted to build public support, I'd have to engage the people of Cleveland and give them a choice at the ballot box. I tried two years earlier to accomplish a referendum on the sale. A public vote never occurred, because Forbes and the election board blocked it.

With Sandy's encouragement, I decided to seek a special election. It could be my kind of campaign, long odds, limited resources, a cause I dearly believed in, no one giving us a chance to win, and then, hopefully, victory. We would prepare for our fourth election in a year and a half, with another Mayoral primary and general election facing us a half year later.

"Maybe this could move Forbes. If he'll agree to put the income tax on the ballot, as a compromise, we could put forth a vote on Muny at the same time," I said.

When I presented the idea to Forbes, he agreed. Perhaps he saw it as his path to ultimate victory. The voters would be asked for a one-half percent tax increase to take us out of default. Simultaneously, the question of Muny Light would be put to a popular vote. Forbes agreed to hold the election on Tuesday, February 27, 1979.

Shortly after the special election was scheduled, Cleveland Trust purchased nearly 92,000 shares of CEI stock, anticipating CEI's takeover of Muny Light.

The stage was set for perhaps the most contentious, spirited, and deceptive issue campaign in the city's history. The fate of Muny Light hung in the balance.

December 28, 1978 Mayor's Office, Meeting with Chief Fox

"There is a new hit planned," the Chief said. "Our 'Intel' Unit has been in touch with the Maryland State police. An undercover agent has learned that an attempt on you will be made between Christmas and New Year's."

I listened, chastened once again by intimations of mortality, knowing my existence was dependent upon good police work and good luck.

Chief Fox continued, "The hit-man was set to meet with Tommy Sinito. Sinito has been seen talking with members of an organized crime family in Pittsburgh. At least one member of that family has allegedly been involved in a contract killing in the past. Remember, the hit-man met with Sinito in October. This is the second meeting we know of. The meeting took place yesterday at Port O'Call Lounge on Brookpark Rd.

We had surveillance on the place. The hit-man entered the bar, Sinito motioned to him. Then something funny happened, as if Sinito sensed he was being watched. He left."

"What now?" I asked.

"Nothing. We're watching, waiting. We don't have enough yet to make an arrest. I'm making sure everyone in the Intelligence Unit is on board."

On the advice of Chief Fox, I left a sealed envelope explaining possible participants and motives with U.S. Representative Louis Stokes, Chairman of the House Committee on Assassinations, which had retained jurisdiction of investigations of politically-motivated killings.

I knew there was a chance an attack could end my life. I could not dwell on it. I could not, would not go into hiding.

When I was five years old, standing in a whirlpool of family arguments, shouting, economic uncertainty, with no permanent home, I remember that I was gripped by worries that a particular day could be my last. I internalized the stress of our family's social and economic struggle, dealt with severe stuttering, and conquered it through speech therapy in the first and second grade with the help of nuns at St. John's College. Then came a debilitating case of Crohn's disease, literally twisting my insides in knots. Crohn's claimed half of my colon, six feet of small intestine and through complications, half a kidney by the age of 26. Pain was my constant companion as I knocked three times on death's door, in critical condition after massive surgery for Crohn's disease and facing a life-threatening post-surgical infection after the operation to remove part of my kidney. Then, as Mayor, the bleeding ulcer which almost took my life. This was my American version of Death on the Installment Plan.

An unyielding instinct for survival conquered my fears of life's brevity, so I pushed myself through a decathlon of physical threats, reaching beyond my limited self, to suppress inner pain, to attempt mastery of mind over matter, to align with purpose and to explore unlimited spirit intermingling with the energy of matter in perfect expression.

In this soul voyage, I found that deeper courage, perseverance, and compassion awaits when you step outside the narrow concerns of self. Faced with a grave threat to my life, I rejected the commonsense notions of retreat. The slightest courage creates new conditions, including the possibility of survival, even under extreme circumstances. I went from a focused battle over a light system to a peaceful search for my own inextinguishable inner light.

"Tis the best use of fate to teach a fatal courage," wrote Ralph Waldo Emerson. I read those lines when I was thirteen and, as the years unfolded, they have had greater meaning. Tragedy happens when fear causes one's potential and one's contribution to be unrealized. Equipped with such understanding, I could not be intimidated. Cleveland would survive, with or without me. And I would survive, with or without Cleveland.

After the meeting with Chief Fox, I huddled closely with Jack Schulman in the Tapestry Room and discussed succession, the possibility that as Law Director, he could suddenly become the next Mayor.

"Jack, I met with the Chief of Police and I have been informed that an assassination attempt could come at any time."

"No!" he said, not wishing to consider the implication. I explained my wishes to him as matter of fact, rather than indulge in drama.

"We have to be ready for anything. You know exactly what will need to be done. Don't change any policy or personnel. The only thing I want you to make sure of is that Sandy will be looked after. Will you promise me?"

He stared at me, clearly not wanting to accept what I had just shared. He responded simply, "Yes."

December 31, 1978, New Years Eve

Forbes continued his attack, with a new claim that our administration had caused a $100 million deficit. An extraordinary claim, since we borrowed no money in the market, had cut spending, paid off millions in debt, and came within a million dollars of balancing a city budget that had not been balanced in years. As to millions of dollars, misspent and long missing from bond and note accounts, the Council President knew it had happened under Perk, through Forbes' exercise of the legislative power of the purse. He permitted it then, but he denied our administration any relief unless we capitulated on Muny Light.

We complied with Judge Krupansky's order to pay the final installment of $1.8 million to CEI by year's end, thereby protecting the antitrust lawsuit. On the second to the last day of 1978, the tags CEI had put on city property were removed.

In 1978, we had run the city entirely on a cash basis, reduced city spending 10% without cutting service and, made payments of $15 million to CEI. Each accomplishment had the feeling of rolling a massive rock uphill. Gravity was not my friend. When rock bottom arrived, with the cheerful relentlessness of a Sisyphus, I accepted my fate and mustered the strength to push the rock back toward the top.

December 31, 1978, 8:00 a.m.

I opened the *Plain Dealer* to a newspaper ad, from Brock Weir: "We want to make it unmistakably clear, despite what you may have heard or read, that Cleveland Trust has not and will not make the sale of Muny Light a condition of our willingness to finance Cleveland's debt. We don't care who owns Muny Light."

If only that was his position on December 15, 1978.

December 31, 1978 8:00 p.m.

New Year's Eve: A small group of friends gathered with Sandy and me on Milan Avenue to celebrate.

I was never so glad to say goodbye to a year.

CHAPTER 64

Courageous Reporter Bob Holden Helps Turn the Tide

Muny Light's support declined precipitously, confirming Forbes' decision to allow a vote on the sale. The light system was blamed for the default and I was blamed for supporting the light system. In the first poll published after I decided to put Muny to a vote, WEWS-TV claimed 95% of the people would rather sell Muny Light than have city workers laid off. More than 60% were said to favor the sale, in a straight up or down vote. A telephone survey done for the Growth Association reported Cleveland voters favored the sale by a 70% to 30% margin.

The polls on Muny Light were published and broadcast, not so much to report on public opinion, as to shape it, to create a self-fulfilling prophecy, and roll the bandwagon for the sale. It worked. Momentum for the sale was building. The Muny Light election brought new waves of hysteria from Cleveland media questioning the city's finances, credit, image, and our administration's ability to govern. The Cleveland business community expressed concern the default and the Muny Light battle had ruined its own Harris poll on the city's image.

In order to stabilize the source of their strength at City Hall, the banks, CEI, and Cleveland's top law firms rallied around the indicted councilmen, raising large sums of money for their defense, as Forbes and the Council made a strenuous effort to disband the city's organized crime investigative unit.

On the eve of default, five of six banks had committed to refinancing the city's notes, without demanding the sale of Muny. Now Cleveland bankers and the rest of the business community were in solidarity, asserting that unless Muny Light were sold, the city would not be taken out of default, and worse, would face foreclosure. Forbes said an "unnamed banker" told him as much.

Cleveland returned to the fever pitch of sell-Muny mania, led by institutions whose existence derived from licenses and public franchises granted through the power of the people: Radio and television stations, banks, and CEI.

The "sell" campaign which depicted Muny Light as a broken-down clunker, had the support of the chair of the Democratic Party and most members of City Council.

We reached beyond Cleveland for political help. I went to Washington, DC to meet with famed consumer advocate Ralph Nader, whose work I admired greatly. His national stature could be pivotal in drawing the attention to events in Cleveland, the high stakes, and the national implications.

With Nader's help, we designed a broad, full-scale attack on CEI, employing political, governmental and media resources, to attack CEI's illicit effort to achieve a monopoly and to warn of the adverse financial impact the sale would have on all electricity customers. Nader helped create greater national awareness of the Muny Light issue. He wrote supportive newspaper columns. He recorded several TV commercials. He came to Cleveland and helped inspire more public involvement, including additional door-to-door volunteers who distributed reams of paper with a powerful anti-monopoly message. His involvement helped with fund-raising.

Jeff Moats, a member of our mayoral staff and an erstwhile Hollywood producer, had previously helped develop a key TV commercial against the recall, showing City Hall, in the form of a cake, cut up and devoured by corpulent men in pinstripe suits wearing diamond pinky rings.

Our newest campaign TV production hit CEI and its executives fiercely, with opening theme music from the 1950s TV police series, Dragnet.

William Hickey, the TV-Radio critic of the *Plain Dealer* captured perfectly the letter and the nuances of the commercial: "It is a rip-off of the Dragnet format of yesterday, complete with the dum-de-dum-dum musical score."

[Hickey describing the commercial] *"This is the city... Cleveland, Ohio... There are hundreds of stories in this city,"* a voice all serious and monotone says, while a backdrop of the Terminal Tower comes into view. Cut to a picture of the CEI office building and bring back the voice... *"The big story is behind the walls of this building, the Cleveland Electric Illuminating Company, (dum-de-de-dum) whose executives are wanted for price fixing, price gouging and price manipulation."* It should be noted that the background changes to a typical post office wanted poster and the sleeve of a four-stripe law enforcement officer appears. The voice continues, *"They are currently masterminding the rip-off of their careers. They are planning to steal the Muny Light system. The only way these thieves will have their day in court is by your vote against the sale of Muny Light."*

Two local television stations, Channels 5 and 8, refused to run it, setting off another controversy over CEI's influence upon the news. The *Plain Dealer's* TV critic and other news analysts swore that we had never really expected such a sharp-edged commercial to be broadcast and had calculated that a well-publicized rejection would be to our advantage. Once I announced the commercial was banned, calls flooded Channels 5 and 8, demanding to see it.

In Washington, D.C., Nader and I brought the Muny Light story to members of Congress who had oversight authority on banking matters. As the Muny Light issue heated up on Capitol Hill, pressure mounted on CEI. The embattled private utility overreached, interceding with *Plain Dealer* editors to squelch unfavorable reporting, precipitating a revolt in the morning newspaper's city newsroom.

"You are not going to believe what is going on at the *Plain Dealer*," Juniewicz said, breaking his restrained demeanor as he entered my office.

"Try me."

"You know Bob Holden?"

"Yes." He has covered utilities, very straight-forward in reporting facts."

"He was getting ready to write a three-part series for the upcoming Muny Light and tax election on the history of CEI's attempts to take over Muny Light. *Plain Dealer* management took him off the story," Andy related.

"Why?! I asked, well aware of Cleveland media managers' reputation for holding reporters hostage to corporate interests.

"Word from the City Room is that CEI now considers Holden their primary PR problem. CEI called the *Plain Dealer* to get him removed from the beat." When Juniewicz spoke of 'the word,' it meant he had received information directly from his life-long friends and colleagues who worked in the City Room.

"Holden was told by management he could not cover CEI any longer, because he 'would not be fair' to the utility. The whole City Room staff is in an uproar," Andy said. "Reporters are talking 'strike.' I've never seen anything like this."

"Strike?!" Cleveland had not experienced a newspaper strike in many years.

"Dave Hopcraft, the managing editor, went right over the head of Bob McGruder, the City Editor and took Holden off the utilities beat.

He assigned him to write book reviews. Book reviews!"

"No way."

"McGruder's been undermined, and he's ready to quit. I told you the reporting staff would never front for CEI," Andy said proudly of his former colleagues.

As a result of management's yielding to CEI pressure, *Plain Dealer* reporters voted to picket the newspaper's offices, an unprecedented uprising over news policy. The reporters issued a statement. "*Plain Dealer* management has acquiesced to cynical and self-serving external pressures that would control the news in their own best interests."

CEI's attempts to manipulate the media were now exposed from inside the *Plain Dealer*'s City Room.

The next day, Holden, with his wife clutching their infant daughter wrapped tightly in a blanket, protested in a freezing rain, waving a sign: "WHO RUNS THE PLAIN DEALER $." Other members of American Newspaper Guild Local Number 1, the reporters' local union, joined the Holdens on the sidewalk in front of the newspaper.

Make-shift signs challenged the *Plain Dealer*'s editors: "DOES THE PLAIN DEALER DEAL PLAIN?" "CEI-PD HOOK-UP UNVAILED," a play on the name of the *Plain Dealer*'s Publisher, Tom Vail.

In protest of Holden's removal from the CEI story, *Plain Dealer* reporters announced a "byline boycott" and removed their names from news stories for two days. This was a personal protest by Holden's fellow reporters since, in the trade, reporters generally seek credit for what they write.

Holden and the Newspaper Guild struggled to regain his full status as a reporter on the utilities beat. The Cleveland Newspaper Guild reached an agreement that provided for reinstating Holden, but management again censored his stories.

"We lost the battle - - the utilities are still off limits," Holden said. "Nothing is left for me to do, but resign."

Holden's resignation triggered yet a more powerful reaction from inside the City Room. *Plain Dealer* management was unable to suppress the story of an internal struggle between reporters and management over the coverage of the news. National publications were scrutinizing *Plain Dealer* management, questioning their integrity, drawing further attention to Muny Light, Cleveland Trust, and CEI. The paper's reputation had been damaged. Only a full-blown investigative disclosure of CEI's dirty tricks would suffice to redeem the *Plain Dealer* as an institution.

The narrative switched from skulduggery inside CEI's headquarters and collusion in the editorial suite to a new breed of muckraking inside The *Plain Dealer.* The City Room became charged with a spirit of rebellion and the electricity of discovery, as a backlash to CEI's attempt to suppress criticism. Suddenly, every *Plain Dealer* reporter became Bob Holden.

Under pressure from their own reporting staff, and under scrutiny by journalists around America, *Plain Dealer* management assigned two reporters, Daniel Biddle and David Abbott, to cover the upcoming Muny Light election. Now, instead of simply facing one dogged truth-seeking reporter, CEI had to contend with two unbridled reporters, who were fully supported by their enraged colleagues. *Plain Dealer* staff members were said to be circling Biddle and Abbott's desks as they crafted their report, with the air of expectant parents pacing outside a delivery room.

Biddle and Abbott, drawing on thousands of internal CEI memos from NRC and court documents, produced a comprehensive account of CEI's merciless attack on Muny Light in an "Election Special."

The tantalizing headline read:

"CEI OBJECTIVE: SNUFF OUT MUNY LIGHT"

"For nearly two decades, the Cleveland Electric Illuminating Company has campaigned publicly and privately, in the words of its own officers, 'to reduce and ultimately eliminate' Cleveland's Municipal

Light Plant, better known as Muny Light," the *Plain Dealer* wrote. This was exactly what was in the October 9, 1970 Bridges memo, secretly placed in my Council mailbox eight and a half years earlier, a document the media possessed, but had ignored.

Plain Dealer reporters enumerated a litany of CEI's secret activities in its private war against Muny Light. It was information Milt Schulman and I unearthed two years earlier, and repeatedly tried to bring to public attention. Once the list of assaults was exposed by a major daily newspaper, Muny Light achieved fresh, new importance. The story had a powerful public impact as it recited the litany of offenses by the Cleveland Electric Illuminating Company.

CEI had:

- caused Muny Light blackouts.
- publicly agreed to an interconnect, while privately delaying it for ten years.
- tried to force Muny Light into price-fixing, to set its rates at CEI's levels.
- imposed severe operational problems on Muny.
- blocked Muny Light repairs and expansion efforts.
- blocked Muny's access to cheap power.
- used an anti-competitive strategy which included distorting media coverage and corrupting public officials.
- a mutually-beneficial relationship with one-time Council Utilities Chair Francis E. Gaul, who was relentless in his efforts to close down Muny Light.

According to Muny Light officials interviewed by the *Plain Dealer*, if Muny had had access to PASNY power for the preceding five years, it could have saved on average, $266.58 per residential customer, an amount equivalent to fourteen months of free electricity.

For those seeking documentation of the charges, the reporters noted, "The Muny-CEI legal battle has produced more than two million pages of information." The internal memoranda and documents from the court and the Nuclear Regulatory Commission had been available for at least two years. Media disclosure had been suppressed by CEI's influence on editorial and news policy.

CEI's misconduct and corruption was communicated, at last, in detail to the people of Cleveland, through the front pages of The *Plain Dealer.* Bob Holden's courage, his sacrifice, and the persistence of his fellow Guild members had helped to achieve a turning point in the campaign to save Muny Light, illustrating the power of a free press, unshackled from the impositions of advertisers. CEI's dirty tricks were exposed, as we headed toward the final weeks of the special election.

The *Cleveland Press* was compelled by The *Plain Dealer*'s coverage, to run a similar investigative series. The revelations reinforced our campaign themes Save Muny Light to keep utility rates low through competition, stop CEI's monopoly, protect the antitrust suit, and end business domination of city government.

Thanks to the unflinching integrity of a single reporter, Bob Holden, the momentum for the sale had been broken. Things were finally moving in our direction.

CHAPTER 65

The Other 'City Hall'

I thought I knew Cleveland Trust.

Jim Harkins, of the city law department, working with research expert Dan Marschall, produced an extensive study of the bank's ties, a strong assist to our request for a congressional investigation of default. Jack Schulman gave me the completed report.

"Look at this. You'll know who and what you've been fighting," he said.

"As if I don't already know," I replied. "This concerns the connections between CEI and Cleveland Trust, right?" The initial finding of Harkins and Marschall were the basis for our appeal for a post-default Justice Department probe.

"This latest report is more comprehensive," Jack said. "Cleveland Trust, through their board members, is tied to every powerful corporation in the Cleveland area."

"I'm not picking a fight with all of them."

"That's what you think. Cleveland's corporate community has closed ranks to promote the sale of Muny Light. Weir is their leader. Don't forget you have thirty-three national corporate headquarters here, the only other cities in American who have more are New York and Chicago."

"Why would the other companies come after us?"

"Because this is war. They are on one side, you are on the other. Weir has said 'We're not talking about recovering $5 million. We're talking about recovering a city.' When he says 'we,' you have to understand that Cleveland Trust not only owns a big share of CEI, they own substantial portions of nearly every major business in Cleveland. Corporate Cleveland financed the recall. Cleveland Trust *is* Corporate Cleveland."

"I'm paying attention, Jack. The *Plain Dealer* says corporations are meeting to field a candidate for Mayor."

"Understand what you are up against. You are not taking on just a bank and a utility, you are taking on the entire system. It's the other City Hall. And it's not only corporate ties, it's relationships. They are friends who socialize and do business with each other. The personal relationships of corporate leaders are as significant as their financial relationships," Jack said.

"Come on, Jack," I repeated, "I didn't intend to pick a fight with all these people."

"It may not be how you started," he said. "But it is where you are. You have to read this report. It builds on the complaint letter that Brad Norris' drafted and you signed the day of default."

The Harkins-Marschall Cleveland Trust study provided me with a deeper understanding of the dimensions of the battle I had undertaken. Our researchers located an eleven-year-old congressional study of Cleveland Trust which concluded "...not only is Cleveland banking, from the point of commercial bank operations, dominated by the Cleveland Trust Co., but when the additional factor of trust investments combined with interlocking directorships is considered, the Cleveland Trust Company, along with the other banks surveyed in Cleveland, is probably the single most influential element in the entire economy of the area."

Harkins-Marschall's initial research discovered that on the day of default, two directors of CEI were also directors of the holding company of Cleveland Trust, the CleveTrust Corporation.

The ties between Cleveland Trust and CEI went beyond interlocking directorates:

Cleveland Trust was one of CEI's top stockholders and would have profited directly from the takeover of Muny Light. Cleveland Trust's action to attempt to force the sale of Muny Light would benefit CEI by adding 46,000 customers to CEI's accounts, wiping out the yardstick Muny Light provided on residential rates and forcing cancellation of the antitrust suit, a benefit to CEI's stockholders.

CEI maintained four demand deposit accounts at Cleveland Trust and had a $25.4 million approved line of credit at the bank. Cleveland Trust managed $70 million of the $130 million CEI pension fund.

CEI paid Cleveland Trust more than $100,000 a year for various financial services relating to the pension fund and the sale of stocks and bonds.

CEI's chief fuel was coal. Its prime source was the North American Coal Company. One of North American's directors was the Chairman of Cleveland Trust, until the Autumn of 1978.

Cleveland Trust's law firm, Jones Day, represented the Central Area Power Co-ordinating members, which, with CEI, had conspired to deny Muny Light access to power and which were named defendants in the city's $325 million antitrust lawsuit. CAPCO was a group of interconnected utility companies acting as a sub-grid, coordinating transactions and enabling the various utilities to depend upon each other to maintain reliability.

After reading the report, I called Schulman to discuss Cleveland Trust's investments in CEI.

"Utilities are cash cows for banks," he explained. "When people pay their utility bills, the banks get to use the utility's money. They make money off the float. They make money from loans to the utilities. And if a bank has a lot of control, as Cleveland Trust has over CEI, they promote CEI paying high dividends, causing the utility to rely even more on the bank. Banks love utilities," Jack said.

The Harkins-Marschall extended report described the financial behemoth I was fighting, a beast devouring the tax base, inevitably eating its own, since without sufficient tax revenue a city cannot provide basic services.

There is no better path to the control of city assets than through the acquisition and control of utilities. Mayor Tom Johnson understood this at the turn of the 20th century, when he predicted, of public service monopolies, "If you do not own them, they will in time own you." I understood this intuitively.

Now, seeing the corporate connections laid bare, and experiencing the demonstration of the raw money power of Cleveland Trust, I understood I was indeed taking on the whole system; a predatory financial machine for whom government was a mere subsidiary, an extension of its profit-making through the siphoning of tax dollars and the conversion of city assets to private, corporate benefit.

"The Other City Hall" needed the complicity of elected officials inside City Hall to pull it off.

We were on the threshold, not only of the special election, but soon I would have to declare that I was running, again, for Mayor. Led by Cleveland Trust, CEI, and Squire Sanders, corporate Cleveland sent out a casting call for a new mayor, looking for anyone willing to be wrapped in the garments of pretend 'municipal peace' and prepared to stand upon a stack of corporate campaign contributions so high he could not escape notice, to rescue the city from a manufactured crisis.

Leading bankers brought a Democratic campaign consultant from Boston to a hush-hush meeting at the Cleveland Plaza Hotel. Tape sealed the hotel listing of the morning's events from the eyes of inquisitive reporters. Guards were stationed outside the main ballroom. Inside the meeting room, the discussion focused on how to defeat Muny Light, pass the income tax and recruit a candidate for Mayor.

Brock Weir made the strongest pitch, according to one attendee. "If we don't put a stop to this mayor now, this thing will spread nationally," he said. "This thing" that Weir spoke of was a rising awareness of corporate exploitation of government. If our efforts in Cleveland caught on, a renewed civic consciousness had the power to transform the relationship between business and government and even put an end to dozens of private power company acquisitions of municipally-owned utilities.

A powerful challenge to the rationale for privatization of public assets was emerging. I was being contacted by citizens' groups and public officials and aspirants from across America who wanted to teach the Battle of Muny Light, how to resist corporate takeovers of municipally-owned services. Letters flowed into our office, urging me to consider running for President.

After the meeting of the bankers and their political consultant ended, NBC TV's local affiliate, Channel 3, caught Weir and other members of the Cleveland corporate community scurrying out a side door, dodging reporters, "almost like criminals being led away from an arraignment," according to TV-3 news reporter Joe Mosbrook.

The group expanded both its membership and its objectives. Its next meeting was held at the Union Club, ostensibly to raise $300,000 for the indicted councilmen.

While a political strategy was being crafted to try to topple our administration at the ballot box, Cleveland's banks were moving to gain control over city government by engineering a financial takeover bill through the state legislature in Columbus. A state controlling board would permit a court-appointed receiver to dispose of city assets, such as Muny Light, without the permission of the mayor, the council or even the voters of Cleveland. It amounted to the theft of a city. The "Other City Hall" was spoiling to reclaim its fiefdom.

U.S. Representative Benjamin Rosenthal, Democrat of New York, at Ralph Nader's request, contacted me to offer help. He wrote a letter to ask the Securities and Exchange Commission to review Cleveland Trust's and CEI's conduct.

"It would appear that the stockholders of Cleveland Electric Illuminating Co. may derive a substantial financial benefit from withdrawal of the city's antitrust suit if the Municipal Light system is sold to Cleveland Electric Illuminating Co.," he wrote.

"It would also appear that the bank's alleged refusal to extend credit to the city unless the Municipal Electric system is sold to the Cleveland Electric Illuminating Co., may have a material effect in contributing to the withdrawal of the antitrust suit," Congressman Rosenthal, the chairman of a banking oversight subcommittee asserted.

His efforts lent additional credibility to our plea to follow the monetary benefits which CEI and others would obtain through acquisition of Muny Light and the dissolution of the antitrust suit. There were individuals within the system willing to expose wrongdoing.

The special election drew near. The odds of saving Muny Light had improved, but the outcome was uncertain. The United Auto Workers came forward, under the leadership of Bill Casstevens and Warren Davis, who had long been a staunch supporter. Davis and Weissman worked closely on every major public issue. With the UAW's help, we mounted a slashing mass media attack on CEI. Ralph Nader appeared in our television commercials to inform Clevelanders of the plight of people in Fort Wayne, Indiana, who sold their public electric system and experienced a 40% increase in their electric rates over the next 18 months.

I received a call from *Plain Dealer* reporter Joe Wagner, who informed me of CEI's newest rate increase, a 25% hike for wholesale power. Wagner had doggedly covered the Muny Light story from business' perspective.

Since CEI was Muny's sole source for wholesale power, I knew CEI initiated this rate increase as a means of undermining Muny. By raising wholesale rates, on the eve of the election, CEI would show Muny's future rates could not be competitive with CEI.

"I'm not prepared to accept that scenario," I told Wagner. "CEI's latest rate hike underscores the need for competition and the need for Muny Light."

Wagner had unintentionally done us a big favor. He called my attention to CEI's wholesale rate increase, mid-afternoon, and inadvertently gave me an opportunity to get ahead of the story.

I hastily summoned local media to the Red Room and attacked CEI for the latest rate increase. I offered it as a prime example of the urgency of taming CEI's rapaciousness. The private utility's stratagem backfired. The CEI rate increase was criticized in the evening news. We made our point: Absent Muny Light, nothing would thwart CEI's predatory rate increase practices.

Our staff and volunteers canvassed Cleveland's neighborhoods, conveying the importance of competition, and the necessity to moderate rates, to protect the antitrust lawsuit. We alerted the people of the other City Hall's efforts to control our city government. As the private system ran Cleveland for its private benefit was exposed, Cleveland voters began to recoil at CEI's aggression against the city.

It took Larry Kramer of the *Washington Post*, a major newspaper located four-hundred miles east of Cleveland, to carefully document and illustrate the chains of interests which constituted our city's power structure and to expose to the nation the concerted effort, not only to force the sale of Muny Light, but to reassert corporate dominance of city government. The Cleveland story was summed up in this headline:

PEOPLE POWER VS. SHADOW GOVERNMENT

It was no fun being mayor when the advance people for my speeches were police snipers. They were stationed atop nearby downtown buildings as I traveled from City Hall to the City Club. Uniformed policemen directed automobile traffic. Suspicious-looking persons were denied entrance to the Cleveland Plaza Hotel. As I entered the ballroom of the televised City Club, armed plainclothesmen sat in the audience. Despite the assassination plot and other unrelated death threats, attending this platform was crucial to our campaign because this was an important public opportunity to make the case for keeping Muny Light.

The audience inside The Plaza were leading opinion-makers, most living in the suburbs, most opposed to Muny Light. The television audience included prospective voters. Detective Plank sat behind me, on stage, studying the pin-striped scoffers. I was wearing my bullet-proof vest underneath a tweed suit jacket.

Cigarette smoke drifted up to the podium, while forks merrily chipped away, creating a wind chime effect. I began my presentation with a recitation of CEI's attacks on Muny, listing the findings of the Nuclear Regulatory Commission, charges the *Plain Dealer* investigation brought more fully to public light, including that CEI deliberately caused Muny Light blackouts.

I traced a pointer over a chart which illustrated the web of connections between CEI and Cleveland Trust, the interlocking directorates, the coal company connections, the law firm connections, the utility coordinating connections, the significant financial investments which Cleveland Trust had in CEI stock, and its management of CEI's pension funds. I spoke of CEI's line of credit with Cleveland Trust. I told of how Cleveland Trust refused to finance home mortgages and home improvement loans, unless Muny customers switched to CEI.

The Plaza audience was unimpressed. They had heard such tedium before, and, watching their whispered exchanges, traded around the lunch tables, I could imagine the clipped characterizations of my remarks:

"CEI was in competition with Muny Light. If you can't compete, get out." "Interlocking directorates? So what! So Cleveland Trust and CEI do business together. That's smart. You don't understand business, do you, Mayor?"

"So what if Cleveland Trust was the major stockholder of CEI, holding 5% of the total stock. SO WHAT? They think it's a good investment. That's business."

"This stuff of denying home mortgages and home improvement loans if people don't switch to CEI from Muny? Have you seen those homes in Cleveland?"

This audience was underwhelmed.

I argued that the default occurred because Cleveland Trust made the sale of Muny Light a condition of rolling over the notes. In the lead-up to default, the media, the business community and the political community, led by Forbes, made it clear that the only way to avoid default was to sell Muny Light. Under threat of an investigation, however, all the public statements linking the rollover to the sale of Muny were reversed.

The audience was skeptical. The consistent post-default accounts in the news media had created instant revisionist history, i.e., the default had nothing to do with Muny Light. Except, I had a copy of a live TV broadcast the night of default. At my direction, the lights in the Plaza ballroom were turned off.

A video projector summoned the larger-than-life image of Council Majority Leader Basil Russo, live from the Council chambers at 6:00 p.m., on December 15, 1978, announcing that the Chairman of Cleveland Trust will avert default and purchase $50 million in city bonds, but only if I agreed to sell Muny Light.

The Russo videotape placed the onus for default on Cleveland Trust and its demand for the sale of Muny Light. The audience gasped at

Russo's earnest testimony. Where did that tape come from? Surely, that never happened! The audience was flummoxed into stunned silence, afflicted with cognitive dissonance. The Russo finale had impact. The audience, which included many of the Cleveland areas leading citizens, left the forum unsettled.

The Mayor is using the big lie technique, Karl Rudolph of CEI said in response. "The same old tired litany we've heard so many times before."

A circus maximus, declared the *Cleveland Press* "If you were looking for hard facts you were disappointed." Nothing new, reported Channel 8.

As the new narrative emerged proving the real reason for default, it posed a threat to the fabricated narrative. Until default, the political and economic life of Cleveland hinged on the sale of Muny Light. After default, the social and political reality of Cleveland was reconstructed by the Cleveland business and media establishment: Default did not concern Muny Light, but Muny Light still had to be sold. Then another reset; the sale of Muny Light was inevitable.

Then there was George Forbes. His Muny Light campaign strategy was simple, turn the Muny Light campaign into another recall election, attack me personally, which he did, in a fusillade of hyperbolics, employing stereotypes from across the political spectrum while demonstrating uncommon views of history and popular culture.

I had destroyed the city, he said, accusing me of government by intimidation, of running a Gestapo or a Stalin-like KGB, of operating a cult, like Jim Jones, who led his followers in Guyana into mass suicide. Forbes asserted we were checking the city income tax returns of politicians, businessmen, and journalists, and said I was leading a communist-type Khmer Rouge attack on the police department. Russo, at a meeting of Council, implied Bob Weissman was a communist.

Forbes' attacks were so ferocious that they became a point of discussion in a national TV interview. I was asked how I felt about being compared to Stalin and Jim Jones. "These individuals cover the political spectrum, from far right to far left. It shows how broad my appeal is."

I took Forbes seriously, but not his characterizations.

CHAPTER 66

Reds

Former Mayor Ralph Perk, wearing a red boutonniere, standing under a red exit sign in front of an image of a dancing Fraulein in a red dress painted on the wall of the HofbrauHaus Restaurant, while accompanied by live polka music, used the occasion of his 65th birthday celebration to speak in defense of his understanding of the free world:

"I've never seen anyone in high public office as Marxist and communist as Dennis Kucinich and Bob Weissman. Our people came from the old country and came to this country because they wanted to get away from this kind of Marxism that was developing in the old country. This class warfare, this attempt to pit one class against another. Our people came here because we have freedom and opportunity. Yet there's a man in high public office, two men, Dennis Kucinich and Bob Weissman, who preach the kind of Marxist theories that our people ran away from in the European countries that so many of you are from."

As I watched Perk on television, I felt sad that my friend was auditioning for leader of the bankrupt Freedonia in a remake of Duck Soup, blending Harpo, Chico, and Groucho Marx with Karl, confusing capitalism with theft.

I was not trying to take over the means of production. In fact, I was protecting competition. I was trying to stop monopolists from stealing Muny Light. Muny Light customers were investors, who had a right to expect that I would recognize my fiduciary responsibilities to protect their asset. Good governance, whether of private or public institutions, rests upon similar values of trust, frugality, and fidelity to the mission.

As he poured his last drop of birthday vitriol, Ralph Perk received a standing ovation, to the strains of his favorite song, "Melody of Love." Council President Forbes stepped forward. Laughing heartily, he grasped Perk's hand in a gesture of fellowship.

Calls poured into our office demanding to know if I was a communist or was ever a member of the communist party. "If you aren't a communist, you ought to go on television and say so," advised one nervous caller.

The *Columbia Journalism Review* quoted the managing editor of the *Plain Dealer*, David Hopcraft, as having raised the question with reporters in the *Plain Dealer* City Room "Well maybe we should look into that. Maybe he is a communist."

All this was right out of the CEI playbook, portraying the advocacy of public power as coming from adherents of foreign ideology. Forget there are 2,000 public power systems in America. This was Cleveland, where the rule of gold supplanted the golden rule and where no smear was so outrageous that it could not be put into the service of CEI's interests.

Given the intensity of the climate of loathing, a group of prominent citizens approached Forbes to start another recall drive, which would force me into a seventh election in two years. They were ready to gather signatures at the polls on the day of the Muny Light election.

Forbes said he would not do that, because "he wanted to be fair."

The city was still in default on the notes that had come due on December 15th. We crafted a new plan, with the help of our Wall Street advisors, to issue new notes to fund the defaulted notes. Tegreene said our new plan would resolve our financial problems while retaining local control; it provided for a balanced budget and limited financial supervision by the state auditor, whose review and certification of the city's budget would appease Wall Street and the credit markets.

Under our proposal, the state treasurer would purchase $50 million in city notes at 8% interest, enabling immediate payment of the defaulted notes and the replacement of missing bond funds.

We had reason to be confident. The *Wall Street Journal* reported a high demand for Cleveland bonds. Municipal bond speculators were placing purchase orders of $125,000 to $500,000 for Cleveland bonds, which were effectively paying 10% to 15% interest. Even notes, conceivably vulnerable to default, were in demand. Post-default investors understood default was a political event, not a financial one, and were prepared to take a nominal risk for a solid profit.

Even though there were many ways for the city to cure default, Cleveland Trust would have none of it. Weir was not agreeable to any of the alternatives we put forth. He openly fretted over his obligation to his stockholders, and said the city had to resolve default in order to restore its fiscal reputation among money lenders. We presented Cleveland Trust another new way, whereby the defaulted notes could be replaced by notes secured by both the income tax revenues and property of the City of Cleveland. Weir opposed it, saying we did not have the support of Council. Forbes opposed it, saying we did not have the support of Weir.

Weir entered the Muny Light election campaign. He told a downtown business luncheon, "Clevelanders should show bankers their desire for sound fiscal management by approving the sale of Muny Light."

This remark threw fear into his attorneys at Jones Day. According to one *Plain Dealer* columnist, Weir was told to keep his mouth shut. He had inadvertently exposed Cleveland Trust to liability by carelessly reprising his original lines from December 15, 1978, the day of default, when he linked the sale of Muny Light to refinancing the city's debt.

While denying the city any chance to repay, Weir expressed to his stockholders great confidence in the Cleveland-area economy, celebrating his bank's record deposits, loans and profits in 1978. "...the controversy has not been of any expense to your company's volume of business nor has it handicapped our ability to develop new business."

He went on to boast of Cleveland Trust's "seventh consecutive year of an increase in net income" and "the sixteenth consecutive year of increased dividend payments."

CEI, which announced a three-for-two stock split in December of 1977, cheered its 1978 revenue, $ 659.3 million, a record.

Squire Sanders drafted a bill for submission to the state legislature eliminating the Mayor's charter-derived executive authority, abolishing home rule and replacing both the city administration and the council with a nine-member controlling board. Weir endorsed the bill. Under Weir's preferred structure, the controlling board would have the power to sell city assets, settle all lawsuits and raise taxes without a vote of the people.

Led by Weir, the banks were using their self-serving interpretation of creditworthiness, or lack thereof, as a pretext to abolish local government.

Cleveland's charter provides for a "strong Mayor." Weir's proposal would have reduced the Mayor's office to a figurehead. "[If Kucinich] wants to go around the city handing out keys and cutting ribbons, I couldn't care less," one anonymous businessman was quoted as saying.

Weir's preferred board would have the power to award contracts, deposit city funds, and direct public services, determining the amount of money to be spent for police, fire, waste collection, street repair and snow removal.

"We aren't talking about recovering $5 million," Weir repeated a favorite line, "we're talking about recovering a city." A new mayor would be supported, "providing we have confidence in whom we are dealing with," Weir told *The Financier* magazine. In the same article Weir delivered a mind-boggling reprise of his December 15th offer of $50 million in credit for the sale of Muny Light (which he later denied.) Weir, as reported in *The Financier*: "I have said I would personally undertake a program, to develop an enthusiasm, for the banks to recognize the possibility, in the right circumstances, of putting together a consortium, that would provide up to $50 million [in bank loans]." The mash-up of subordinate sentence construction and subordinate financing could have come only from a banker who had strayed from his legal counsel. No wonder he changed the name of his bank.

Cleveland's financial entanglement with Cleveland Trust was compared to the difficulty New York had with its banks, but only as a pretense. The Cleveland banks invested a fraction of their money in the City of Cleveland. New York banks were heavily involved in that city's municipal finances.

Cleveland Trust's point man in the legislature, Rep. Harry Lehman, advanced the takeover bill, characterizing me as 'Hitler-like.' Representative Lehman's next job would be as an attorney in the Columbus office of Jones Day, Cleveland Trust's corporate attorneys.

The Growth Association said the city must have a controlling board, even if voters approved both the passage of the tax and the sale of Muny Light. Weir lamented "We and other members are responsible for not doing something a long time ago." Legislative action on the controlling board was delayed, however, pending the outcome of the tax vote.

It mattered not that we borrowed no money and ran the city on a cash basis with no reduction in services. If the tax passed, we could do the same in 1979. We were prepared to chart a course of frugality through the multiple hazards constructed by CEI, Cleveland Trust and Forbes.

In U.S. District Court, Judge Krupansky granted CEI and their co-defendants a request for a postponement of the trial of the antitrust case. The Judge, curiously, told attorneys for the city, who were ready to go to trial and who opposed any continuance, that they were actually *not* ready to go to trial, then granted CEI the delay it wanted.

CHAPTER 67

A Mayor and His People

A soft sunlight bathed the congregation at St. Paul's Baptist Church. I stepped to the podium for one of the last speeches of the Muny Light campaign. I looked toward the congregation of people from the inner-city, people I grew up with. I apologized for the distraction of media representatives sitting on the floor in the side aisles, who came to the service to report on the church, a mayor and his people.

I did not need a prepared speech. Here, I could speak from the heart.

"Some people can't understand why others are worried about paying utility bills. When you are cold in the winter and you can't pay that high bill, you know what the problem is all about. Our fight is for economic justice. Unless you have economic justice, you cannot be free. Because, if you can't survive economically, if you can't be free from high prices for food, for shelter, for clothing, if you can't be free of high interest rates, if you can't be free of mortgage and insurance red lining – if you can't be free from all those things, and someone tells you you've got political freedom, that's doesn't mean an awful lot."

"You probably have the game of Monopoly at home. One strategy that wins the game is to get all the utilities. They pay off double. The real world is the same. Monopoly is played every day. We're landing on their spaces and paying double every day."

The people in this church understood there was a lot more at stake than a light system. But, the *Plain Dealer*'s editors claimed that a vote to sell Muny Light was a vote to "Save Cleveland," but failed to say for whom.

Forbes and I engaged in a live, televised debate on the eve of the Muny Light election. He was unprepared, preferring to answer questions from a panel of reporters rather than engage in a previously agreed-to face-to-face debate format. I pounded away at CEI, Cleveland Trust, and the Council. The debate was described by the media as a draw. The *Plain Dealer* captured two unusual moments in their news summary: "Forbes also accused Kucinich of spreading rumors that he had been offered a $500,000 bribe if he pushed for the sale of Muny Light. Kucinich calmly denied the charge."

"Kucinich, who often quotes the Bible in speeches, quoted Jesus at one point after referring to the $50 million that he said the city was offered if Muny Light was sold. When Kucinich started to quote the Bible for a second time. Forbes objected, saying 'I hope you are not going to quote Jesus again.' Kucinich replied. 'No, I am not going to quote Jesus. I'm going to quote Moses.'"

As I debated and brought our closing arguments to the pulpits of Cleveland's churches, ABC news followed.

ABC News Anchor "...tomorrow is Cleveland's day of decision. Here's Matt Quinn:"

Quinn: "Tomorrow, the citizens of Cleveland vote on two proposals their leaders say will raise the money to save the city. There is no real organized opposition to the proposal to increase the wage tax. The second money-raising issue, the sale of a city-owned electric light plant, is a bitter emotional battle. Mayor Dennis Kucinich has made a career in politics by being against the sale of the city's electric plant to the huge, privately owned Cleveland Electric Illuminating Company, known as

CEI."

Kucinich: "When God said let there be light, He wasn't talking about CEI. Utility companies didn't exist in the time of Jesus."

Quinn: "On the last Sunday before the critical election, Kucinich carried his Muny Light campaign to the congregation of St. Paul's Missionary Baptist Church....Mayor Kucinich blames last December's default on bank loans, and, indeed, most of the city's financial woes, on what he calls a shadow government of Cleveland bankers and businessmen, who, he says, manipulate politicians for their own profit."

Kucinich: "And if money's your master, you're in trouble. There were three people, Shadrach, Meschach and Abednego, and they said, 'We don't care what you're going to do to us, we're not going to worship that idol.' Because they knew that a man can't have two masters."

Quinn: "The principal public spokesman to oppose Kucinich and to argue for the sale of the light plant is City Council President, George Forbes. Over the weekend, they staged a televised debate. Forbes argues the wage tax alone won't be enough to save the city."

Forbes: "And I'm stating to you and stating to the people out there, unless the tax is passed, and the light plant is sold, we will not be on the market, and we'll have the same problem on February 28 that we're having right now."

Quinn: "At Ferris' Steak House on Cleveland's west side, they watched the Kucinich-Forbes debate. Not many minds were changed."

Man: " He's a maverick Mayor."

Quinn: "And you like that?"

Man: "Very good."

Another man: "We've got a bubble-gum mayor, because we've got a kid in there."

Quinn: "Only about a fourth of Cleveland's voters will decide its financial fate. Matt Quinn ABC News, Cleveland."

I did everything I could do for the cause of public power. Now I had to rely on others. Tomorrow, I would find out whether the people would reaffirm the historic commitment Mayor Johnson made seventy years earlier. I would learn if the 'NO' I said in the corporate boardroom on the morning of December 15, 1978, was one voice against many or one out of many.

February 27, 1979. Election Night. The Bond Court Hotel.

Weissman feverishly calculated precinct returns from a hotel room above the ballroom. By the time all the leaflets were dropped at doors and all the commercials were run, with charges and counter-charges flying through the air like snowflakes in a Lake Erie blizzard, our precarious election endeavor, which began with an estimated 70% to 95% of the people in favor of the sale, had turned with a vengeance.

What we were witnessing seemed impossible. Neighborhood by neighborhood, we were sweeping Cleveland, both for the tax and for keeping Muny Light, by a two-to-one margin.

Sandy and I took to the ballroom's stage amid bright lights, bedlam, and an outpouring of great emotion from hundreds of campaign workers gathered for the returns. Quoting from scripture, I announced the results

"The light shines in the darkness and the darkness grasped it not." I was elated.

This was a turning point, and it would never had occurred except for Sandy urging me to take the Muny Light issue directly to the people, the principled resistance of Bob Holden and the *Plain Dealer* reporters' rebellion.

We had saved the Division of Light and Power! We could pay off the defaulted notes and get out of default. Financial recovery was in sight. We could cure all deficits and return to the bond market. We could prosecute the antitrust case. We could escape the quagmire dug by the Perk Administration, Squire Sanders, Cleveland Trust, and CEI.

The next morning, Jack Schulman and I met early at City Hall.

"Congratulations! You did it. You won. You beat the banks, CEI, the news media, and Forbes. You got the tax passed and you saved Muny Light. Unbelievable!"

"Jack, people responded to our message."

"It was a great victory. Too bad you weren't on the ballot, Dennis. You would have been re-elected in a landslide."

Suddenly, Jack's tone changed from light-hearted enthusiasm to another Cassandra-like warning. "Now you really have to be careful, Dennis."

"Jack, we saved Muny Light. Why hang crepe?"

"Yes, you saved Muny Light. Without you, it would have been gone, and the people would have been screwed. You get a nice pat on the back. But, the guys you just beat are not going to change course. They have never been defeated by any politician. And you have now beaten them three times in a row. It isn't about Muny Light anymore. They want YOU." His index finger was aimed, Uncle Sam-like, at me. I felt tired and ancient, as old as last night's victory.

I could take the personal and political attacks. Could the people of Cleveland withstand the relentless politics of corruption, default and destabilization? Would they understand the caterwauling issued from downtown was of an insatiable beast?

One would expect that things would change, after Cleveland's voters spoke resoundingly in favor of our administration, even to the point of taxing themselves. They didn't change. The day after passage of the tax, the banks reneged and refused to take us out of default, even though the city would have an additional $69 million income by the end of the following year. Nor would the banks extend credit to the city. Instead, they united to support the abolition of local government through advancing the imposition of a state controlling board.

The political nature of the default was ever more obvious. It never had anything to do with the creditworthiness of Cleveland.

Across America, a more accurate picture began to emerge. Jack came into my office with a copy of the *Washington Post.*

"You have to see this. The *Washington Post* says your victory has national implications. Listen." He read aloud. "In defeating a referendum to sell Cleveland's municipal power system on Tuesday, voters of that city have signaled what may be a new era of urban populism an era that could have a major impact on how, and by whom, our cities are governed."

"Wow. It should help us with a congressional investigation," I said.

"This proves to Cleveland corporations that there are bigger stakes. Weir keeps telling businessmen that 'we have to stop this here, before it goes national.' This shows everyone in his circle that you are a threat," Schulman once again added a strong dose of political reality.

Our victory had increased my national profile. Calls and letters continued to express hope that I would run for President. But victory also made me a bigger target. We were stuck on the assembly line of a crisis-manufacturing industry.

Amid the city's surfeit of cash, corporate Cleveland blocked our path to the national credit market. Audacious, new predictions of bankruptcy were circulated by Council and the business community. It was as if the approval of an income tax increase to pay off the defaulted notes never happened.

Members of Council, ignoring the will of the people, as expressed in the results of the special election, renewed their call for city government to give up control of Muny Light. This came as an administrative law judge of the Federal Energy Regulatory Commission, the successor agency to the Federal Power Commission, found CEI's conduct toward Muny had been "discriminatory."

Council balked at approving a routine block-grant application to the federal government, putting at risk $37 million in Community Development Block Grant funds.

Forbes put the city on the verge of another default on the water system notes which were held by the city treasury, placing us in jeopardy of losing the water system to a regional authority. His action threatened a tripling of city water bills, due to investors shifting the cost of new water and sewer infrastructure for new private developments onto the public.

Cleveland Trust and Forbes then constructed a legislative scheme whereby the banks would be treated as a preferred class of creditors. The banks wanted every single cent of the first $14 million of new income tax funds to go immediately to them, although they were only one class of creditors having a claim. The Cleveland Trust-Forbes plan would create a cash flow problem for the city, forcing the layoff of 1,200 city workers. I explained, in a letter to the City Council, that it would be unfair for the banks to receive all the money. "When you pay off a bank loan, you work out a payment schedule, you don't offer to give the bank your paycheck every month until the loan is paid off, because if you did, you couldn't put food on the table, gas in your car, or clothes on your back."

I chose to ignore the "bank preference" ordinance, and instead offered to begin repaying the banks at the rate of $1.25 million a month, a proposal subject to City Council approval.

The income tax had passed, but the scheming that had produced the default continued.

It was unbelievable that the people of Cleveland could vote by a 2-1 margin to rescue their city from a corporate-imposed, politically-motivated, fabricated crisis, yet what they got in return was the contempt of corporate Cleveland, which ignored the election results and used its financial and media power to project the image of a city government forever at the brink.

The *San Francisco Bay Guardian*, as part of their on-going investigation of Pacific Gas and Electric (PG&E) noted Brock Weir's role in forcing default over my refusal to sell Muny Light and illuminated how he may have ended up moving in 1973 from the presidency of the Bank of California (B of C) to his post at Cleveland Trust.

The *Bay Guardian* described the Bank of California as a major power behind PG&E, its largest stockholder in 1974 and speculated that Weir went to Cleveland to attempt "to pull off the kind of naked power play to kill off public power that B of C/PG&E and their power trust allies had pulled off by keeping Hetch Hetchy [inexpensive hydroelectric power] out of San Francisco for decades…"

Cleveland Trust and the other banks continually threatened foreclosure and bankruptcy, notwithstanding the new income tax revenue source. We had the money to cure the default. But no amount of money could cure the politics that created the default.

CHAPTER 68

CEI's Corruption Goes Nuclear

The turmoil at City Hall proved to be an advantage to CEI because it shifted attention away from a series of damning revelations about the company's haphazard management, falsification and cover-ups which set the stage for a potentially catastrophic nuclear mishap at Davis-Besse No. 1, and an extraordinary discovery at the site of the Perry Nuclear Power Plant 120 miles downwind.

I received a detailed study from the former Chair of the Ohio Public Utilities Commission, Henry W. Eckhart, "of every time the Davis-Besse Nuclear Unit No. 1 went out of service, was returned to service and the reason for the outage from the date it went on line, November 21, 1977 through January 13, 1979."

Eckhart, who was legal counsel to the City for utility matters, produced information that "the Davis-Besse Nuclear Unit No. 1 went out of service 38 times during that period" including being out of service May, June and most of July, 1978; 15 days in August, 22 days in October, 15 days in December with three outages in January 1979. He said Davis-Besse had the worst service record of all nuclear power plants in the United States, according to the NRC.

Among reasons for outages at the nuclear power plant: Control valve problems, low reactor pressure, containment vessel leak, reactor trip, steam leak, tube leak, broken control rod indicator, reactor cooling pump trouble, loss of radiation detectors and failure of the reactor coolant pump.

On March 6, 1979, an operator at Davis-Besse, located on Lake Erie in Port Clinton, Ohio, seventy-five miles upwind from Cleveland, improperly closed the wrong valves, disabling the reactor cooling system, creating a perilous condition which was duplicated just three weeks later and caused a partial meltdown at another major U.S. nuclear power plant.

On Wednesday, March 28, 1979, the Three Mile Island (TMI) Nuclear Generating Station, located on the Susquehanna River, about ten miles from Harrisburg, experienced a partial meltdown of its reactor and a subsequent radiation leak.

It has been described as the worst nuclear power accident in U.S. history. The government urged the evacuation of children and pregnant women within a five-mile radius, and an estimated 140,000 Pennsylvanians fled their homes. According to the *Plain Dealer*, the Three Mile Island nuclear reactor's troubled cooling system was designed by Babcock and Wilcox, the same system which vexed CEI's Davis-Besse.

CEI's falsification of safety inspection documents was brought to light. The *Plain Dealer* wrote: "During its construction, the NRC cited the Davis-Besse plant for numerous wiring problems that could have jeopardized reactor safety. Three former employees said they were ordered to falsify safety inspection documents."

An NRC inspector stated that he had sent memoranda to his superiors after CEI's operators at Davis-Besse, "responded improperly to confusing reactor pressure indications during two mishaps in the reactor" in late 1977. *UPI* reported that, "The same operator miscues in a similar situation have been singled out by the reactor maker, Babcock and Wilcox, as crucial actions that led to core damage and radiation releases at Three Mile Island last March."

Mindful of the deficiencies at Davis-Besse outlined by the Eckhart Report, as the danger of a total meltdown, wide-spread radioactive leaks and a potentially explosive hydrogen bubble at Three Mile Island escalated, I contacted him and we filed a complaint with the PUCO asking for a temporary restraining order to keep Davis-Besse shut until its safety was determined. Additionally, we argued that CEI and its nuclear partner Toledo Edison, should not be able to charge customers for a nuclear plant which was neither used nor useful.

The *Chronicle-Telegram* of Elyria, Ohio, one of the few newspapers to pay close attention to Davis-Besse's incident accounts filed with the Nuclear Regulatory Commission, reported on a near-meltdown which could have been more serious than Three Mile Island. Quoting from the NRC: "Between 2:00 p.m. on January 3 and 11:00 a.m. on January 5, two pumps critical to the Port Clinton plants emergency cooling system were 'considered to have been inoperable.'"

"Had the reactor, which was operating at full power...experienced a loss of primary coolant, the emergency safety cooling system most likely would not have worked, the [NRC] record suggested."

"The scenario could have led to the feared 'China Syndrome,' where the reactor, out of control without coolant, melts down and sinks into the ground spewing radioactivity over an immense area." The Chronicle-Telegram suggested that Davis-Besse came very close to a total meltdown with catastrophic implications.

The operation of a nuclear power plant required the utmost integrity. I tracked the construction of both the Davis-Besse and the Perry Nuclear Power plants, ever-alert for conditions which could jeopardize public safety.

The NRC made further determination of dangerous nuclear security lapses at Davis-Besse, including failure to have back-up diesel generators, essential to assuring the operation of nuclear safety systems.

Adding to questions about its ability to safely construct and operate a nuclear power plant, a former worker at the Perry Nuclear Power Plant came forward to accuse CEI of hiding crucial geological information about site preparation. A bulldozer operator revealed that at least one-hundred workers participating in excavation identified a geologic fault line. Workers were immediately ordered to keep quiet as the fissure was filled with thousands of tons of concrete and construction continued over the site.

The troubled Davis-Besse plant led CEI to seek approval for an additional $80 million rate increase, less than a month after receiving approval for a $60.4 million rate increase. It also announced it would seek approval from FERC for $3 million in wholesale rates it charged Muny Light. I anticipated CEI's newest threat to Muny Light, which could force a Muny rate increase. I had opened up negotiations with Buckeye Power Inc., to reduce our dependence on CEI and sharply cut our power costs, enabling our customers to save money and Muny to continue to show a profit.

The great irony is that the company's venture into the building of the Davis-Besse plant, with its nearly calamitous safety and extraordinary financial risks, may not have been necessary. In 1979, the staff of the Public Utilities Commission of Ohio, determined that even without the nuclear plant, CEI still had almost 15% excess capacity.

CHAPTER 69

Congress Investigates Default

Washington, D.C.

Ralph Nader visited the chairs of congressional committees with jurisdiction over banking and charged that Cleveland Trust tried to shake down our administration, conditioning its loans on political criteria, the sale of Muny Light. Members of the House Banking Committee gathered in a closed hearing room to weigh my request for a full congressional investigation of the default.

Straight-forward, intellectually-gifted, and incorruptible, Nader was beloved nationally for his constant vigilance of corporate conduct. He inspired a political movement of consumer's rights, product safety, and marketplace integrity. He stood apart as a lean, modest, singular figure in Washington, a restless crusader for the public interest, a determined man who inspired a new brand of citizen action. This national hero was at my side as I related the events of December 15th, 1978, and told of the extreme pressure brought by Brock Weir, CEI, and George Forbes.

Members listened intently as Nader described the back door dealings, details usually buried, except that in the case of Cleveland, "the Mayor said, 'No!'"

In Cleveland, I was attacked for misleading Nader and trying to hoodwink Congress into thinking Cleveland Trust made the sale of Muny Light the price of avoiding default. Weir and Forbes blasted Nader for interfering in Cleveland's business.

A major development occurred when Representative Fernand St. Germaine, Chairman of the House Subcommittee on Financial Institutions Supervision, Regulation and Insurance, promised to have his staff investigate and, if necessary, to hold hearings.

Representative Benjamin Rosenthal, Chairman of the Subcommittee on Commerce, Consumer and Monetary Affairs, directed the Federal Reserve Board to make a report on the default.

Prior to the release of the Fed report, the *Plain Dealer* bungled an attempt at acquittal-by-headline, rushing forward with a false report that CEI and Cleveland Trust were to be "cleared" of collusion:

FED TO CLEAR CEI, CLEVELAND TRUST
NO COLLUSION FOUND
BANKS CHIDED FOR LENIENCY TO CITY

The newspaper asserted that the banks were warned against further credit extensions to the city. The Federal Reserve, or "Fed", is an independent agency, not supported by taxpayers' monies and is funded by assessments on member banks. The Federal Reserve Bank of Cleveland was once chaired by a director of Cleveland Trust.

Rep. Rosenthal's staff termed the *Plain Dealer*'s account of the Fed Report "... totally false. The report didn't deal with, and therefore did not concern itself with collusion. The statement that the banks were lenient is absolutely false. There is nothing in the report warning the banks against further extensions of credit."

Rep. Rosenthal's summary of key provisions of the report concluded "The Federal Reserve staff memo fails to disprove and in many ways provides support for the allegations... The weight of evidence produced suggests that the sale of Muny Light played a prominent and perhaps a decisive role in Cleveland Trust's refusal to extend the city's loans."

The *Plain Dealer* carried Rep. Rosenthal's reply the next day, under this headline:

"REPORT ATTACKED, CLEARS CEI, CLEVETRUST"

Cleveland Trust and CEI were exonerated by the *Plain Dealer* and the *Cleveland Press.* Were they "cleared" by the Fed? The thrust of Rep. Rosenthal's rebuke rested on explosive passages in the Fed Report, mentioning Weir's $50 million offer, unreported by either daily newspaper: "Mr. Weir made a comment to the effect that if agreement between Council and the administration could be reached, he would volunteer to help raise up to $50 million for the City."

This was an abridged version of the conversation I had with Weir in the boardroom the morning of December 15th and corresponded to what Forbes, Russo, Akers and Saltzman unanimously asserted, then unanimously denied, despite voluminous reports in print, radio and television to the contrary.

The Fed Report had unearthed complete minutes of the meeting of the executive committee of the Cleveland Trust's parent committee, the CleveTrust Corporation, including this "smoking gun:"

"The minutes of this meeting state that the resolution adopted by the City Council on the morning of December 15, calling for an income tax increase and for the administration to sell Muny Light, if signed by the Mayor, would provide a basis for temporary renewal of the notes. In addition, the minutes state that the committee discussed management's plan to renew the notes for an interim period, in the event the Mayor signs the resolution. The committee concluded that CTC's position would be improved if the Mayor signs the resolution and advised management that it did not object to its plan."

Brock Weir told Congress that Cleveland Trust did not condition the temporary renewal of the notes on the sale of Muny Light. Yet the minutes of the board meeting of the Cleveland Trust corporation show otherwise. Not only was Weir reported as saying he would renew the notes if Muny was sold, his board approved that very position five days later!

July 10, 1979 Washington, DC
Congressional hearing on default

The gavel dropped with a sharp crack. "The committee will come to order," Chairman Fernand St. Germaine of Rhode Island began:

> *"This morning we open hearings on problems of the City of Cleveland, with particular emphasis on the role of the commercial banks... Few cities, large or small, have escaped the need to borrow funds and the crunch for many has been severe in the face of declining tax bases, increasing demand for services, and rising interest costs.... The credit powers, alone, can literally be life or death for business enterprises and individuals, and, as we have learned in New York and Cleveland, for large municipalities as well. When those credit functions are enhanced by trust investments, linked directorships and other ties, the potential for power and control is awesome."*
>
> *"We have just passed another Fourth of July, the 203rd anniversary of this nation's proud independence and its belief in the dignity of man. Without being overly repetitive of the Fourth of July speeches, we do not believe that the decisions of the people, whether we think them wise or unwise - - should be overruled by Government or corporations. Neither banks, nor corporations, nor government - - anymore than the King of England in 1776 - - have that divine right."*

He paused, looked at me, and then truth had its time "The Chair recognizes Mayor Kucinich." I was prepared.

I faced the committee, took a deep breath, and spoke empathetically, "I have accused the Cleveland Trust Company of attempting to extort the Municipal Light system from the people of Cleveland. The people's light system was the price Cleveland Trust demanded in exchange for an extension of credit." I eventually completed my lengthy statement.

It was Brock Weir's turn.

"The real issue is," he said, "shall political pressures be permitted to coerce one of the world's safest and most efficient banking systems into compromising universally recognized standards of prudent lending?"

Congressman John J. Cavanaugh of Nebraska questioned Weir.

"I have a news article ... from the *Daily Record* of May 3, 1979, in which it quotes you as saying 'We weren't asking the type of questions then (of the Perk administration) that we were asking this administration...The Perk administration was not as antagonistic toward the business community as to precipitate a showdown.' Is that an accurate quotation?'"

Weir, "It is."

Congressman Cavanaugh: "What disturbs me about that quotation is that I get a feeling that as long as you had a friendly administration in city government, that you were not disposed to engage in prudent lending practices. The problem with that is, if it is indeed a banking practice or standard, that it does impose a very serious threat to the relationship between public entities and financial institutions and lenders."

After Congressman Cavanaugh finished his questioning of Weir, Chairman St. Germain sent a message to the banks "I might observe that I think the lenders should remember one thing. They are not lending to Dennis Kucinich, the Mayor of the City of Cleveland, or rolling over notes to Dennis Kucinich, but rather dealing with the City of Cleveland... your decisions should be made on the financial picture of the city and its ability to repay, rather than on personalities."

One week after the subcommittee hearings, the *Washington Post* obtained a copy of the congressional staff report on default, and carried a front page story by Larry Kramer, headlined:

CLEVELAND DEFAULT LINKED
TO EFFORT TO UNSEAT MAYOR

"The Cleveland banking community apparently was making a deliberate effort to unseat maverick Mayor Dennis Kucinich when it forced that city into financial default by failing to refinance $14 million in municipal notes, according to a House Banking subcommittee staff report.

The report, by the staff of the Subcommittee on Financial Institutions Supervision, Regulation and Insurance, suggests that: "the deep animosities and political crosscurrents in which some bank officers became involved, rather than 'pure hard-nosed credit judgments' led to the decision to cut off the city's credit."

A copy of the report was obtained from subcommittee sources. It alleges that Cleveland Trust led the other five local banks involved in a game of 'chicken' with Kucinich to force him to sell the city's municipal power system to the local privately-owned utility before they would refinance the city's $14 million debt. If this was the case, obviously the Mayor did not swerve."

The staff report and news accounts which followed received scant attention in the Cleveland media.

The introduction to the "Staff Study on City of Cleveland Financing" noted that nearly one-half of municipal debt in the nation is held by commercial banks… "Therefore it is essential that publicly-chartered financial institutions utilize their vast money and credit powers in an even-handed manner and that their decisions to grant or withhold funds from a municipality be based on objective criteria undiminished by other factors or competing interests."

The *Washington Post*'s story established the validity of our charges, vindicated Clevelanders' support for Muny Light, and set the stage for my re-election campaign and the street fight between City Hall and its shadow.

As the Muny Light saga and its implications were exposed, the story captured ever more national attention. It was seen as an unprecedented frontal challenge to unbridled corporate power. The heat caused Cleveland Trust to announce a name change; effective in the fall of

1979, it became "AmeriTrust."

Our administration was gaining support from people across the America. The desperation of corporate Cleveland escalated.

I began my campaign for re-election on August 20th. Two days later I went before City Council to ask for a transfer ordinance to pay the banks on August 31st. We had the money, but the Council refused. Council would not approve legislation to facilitate the payment and then made an issue of the banks not being paid. The people of Cleveland had passed a tax to pay off the banks and now they couldn't understand why the banks did not get their money.

We needed Council permission for a rollover of $3.3 million of notes held by the water system's construction fund, which had enough cash to handle all current and foreseeable future needs. Council again refused.

As a result, on September 3, 1979, a city flush with cash went into default a second time, this time to itself, one month before the October 4th primary election. The media covered and criticized the chaos, never mentioning the political games.

Bob's polls showed we would run second to George Voinovich, the Republican Lieutenant Governor and candidate for Mayor, who had vote-getting strength among the same ethnic groups supporting me. A former County Auditor and state representative, Voinovich's political career was moved along with strong support from Cleveland's business community.

The primary campaign required personal appearances. I was careful not to attack any of half-dozen candidates who wanted my job, because the low-profile primary would be in sharp contrast to the high-energy, high-profile general election. In the primary, I focused on accomplishments.

My continued challenge was inside City Hall. Council's refusal to act on a simple request to rollover notes destroyed any chance Cleveland had of restoring the city's credit rating and regaining access to the national credit market. It also exposed the city to the possibility of loss of its highly profitable water system to a regional authority through court action

Council further balked at providing authorization for rolling over $14.1 million in notes coming due two days after the primary.

The first default was Cleveland Trust's retribution for my refusal to sell Muny Light.

The second default was fabricated to directly interfere in the mayoral election of 1979. The *Washington Post* said as much, pointing out Council would respond to a request for an approval of a roll over after the elections. The *Post* noted our Administration's singular position among American cities: "Because it is in default, the city cannot raise money through traditional means. It must operate on a cash basis in a way that no major U.S. city has had to for decades. …Through intense cost cutting, the city has stayed afloat and even begun to build up the coffers." A week later, Forbes decided to renew $14 million in notes held by the treasury.

Because of the contrived political turmoil, no one was listening when I brought forward a list of accomplishments in neighborhood after neighborhood.

Everything we had done, including making Muny Light profitable for the first time in ten years, reducing city payrolls by 17%, paying off the inherited $15 million debt to CEI, saving millions by eliminating outside contractors, improving police response time, tripling the size of the snow removal fleet, expanding recreation facilities, securing development without tax abatements, stopping the corruption, the kickbacks, the payroll padding, and the racketeering - - all of it was overshadowed by the malignantly engineered financial earthquakes and aftershocks.

The public had assumed, and I had hoped that all would be well and city finances would be stabilized as a result of the February 1979 special election. But, the Cleveland business establishment and their political partners would simply not permit stability. The manufactured crises left us politically vulnerable. I knew I would make it through the primary election. The General Election would require a tremendous effort. As with other battles I faced, I knew how to win, notwithstanding the odds.

CHAPTER 70

That's Politics

In the American system of justice, people are presumed to be innocent until proven guilty. It should always be so. Assistant County Prosecutor Donald Nugent, at the trial in the carnival kickback case, alleged that Council President Forbes accepted money from carnival operators in return for favors, while Forbes' attorney, Charles Clarke, of Squire Sanders, said there was no evidence supporting Nugent's charges.

Common Pleas Court Judge, James McGettrick, the judge to whom the case had been assigned, interjected himself repeatedly in the prosecutors' questioning of witnesses, over the strong objections of the prosecutors. The prosecution asked for a mistrial. McGettrick denied the motion, taunting prosecutors, "If they didn't like it, they could get another judge." County Prosecutor, John T. Corrigan, traveled to Columbus with a sworn affidavit of prejudice, resulting in the removal of McGettrick from the case.

A new judge was assigned, Common Pleas Court Judge, George Tyack, of Franklin County. Abruptly and without explanation, Tyack threw out the case without sending it to the jury, clearing Forbes and his co-defendants of all charges. Assistant County Prosecutor, Nugent called the acquittals "absolutely incredible." Chief Prosecutor John T. Corrigan would not comment publicly. He did tell TV reporter Tappy Phillips that he believed "something was terribly wrong with either the law or Judge Tyack…"

Andy notified me of the sweeping acquittals. "Almost five hundred charges. This visiting judge throws out everything?"

"This proves one thing, Andy," I said.

"What?"

"The system works."

Forbes appeared on a local television show to discuss his vindication.

"I had a phone conversation with Hongisto," Forbes told the TV audience, referring to the former Chief of Police. "I say Richard, while we got you on the phone, tell me, how did this carnival thing come about?" He said the Mayor took him to lunch and told him to get involved in it. He [Hongisto] said 'Look, the thing has been over with, I don't want to get involved in it.' Well, he told us on the phone that it came about because Kucinich insisted. I have no intention of forgetting it," Forbes said angrily.

Forbes had no intention of forgetting something which never happened. This account by Forbes was contrary to the account igniting the recall, wherein Hongisto claimed he was told *not to proceed* with an investigation which was being pursued by other authorities.

Weeks after the trial, Bob Weissman encountered the Council President in City Hall and brought up the carnival case, now a serious barrier between myself and Forbes, particularly since Forbes told the Black community I tried to put him in jail.

"George, you know full well we had nothing to do with that carnival case." Weissman said to the newly-exonerated Council President.

Forbes stifled laughter. His face lit up in mock surprise, as he let Weissman in on his merriment: "Hey man, that's politics."

October 8, 1979, my thirty-third birthday

As I had expected, I came through the low-key mayoral primary trailing my opponent, George Voinovich. His campaign, heavily funded by Cleveland's corporate community, spent over half a million dollars, three times more than any candidate for the office of Mayor of Cleveland had ever spent.

We had survived the recall. We turned around the Muny Light election. I believed we could also win in November.

As the general election campaign began, Sandy and I met Voinovich, his wife, and daughter Molly at a campaign event in Cleveland's Lithuanian community. Molly was such a darling little girl. At home in the evening, unwinding from a full day of campaigning, I remarked to Sandy, "Isn't Voinovich's daughter a beautiful child? It would sure be nice to have a child like her." I never lost sight that the other person in the race is a human being, with family and friends who love him.

The General Election race would be a knock-down. I would face continuous attacks over default, and I would respond by pairing Voinovich with those who capsized the city. I ran on a record of accomplishments, saving Muny Light, ending tax abatements while promoting growth, stopping the misspending of city bond funds, and cutting the city work rolls by 17% with no reduction in service. I knew the recitation would not be enough. I intended to challenge Voinovich's record as County Auditor, where he amassed political contributions from corporate interests for whom he facilitated significant real estate tax cuts or undervalued their prime downtown land, thereby reducing their property taxes. This revelation would put Voinovich on the defensive. It would be key to the election.

There were thirty days remaining until the General Election. Plenty of time to develop the dynamic needed to put us on the path to victory.

No one could have been prepared for what happened next.

Juniewicz and Mrs. Nofel came into the Tapestry room. They were both pale and shaken.

They gave me the awful news: George Voinovich's beautiful daughter, Molly, had been struck and killed crossing the street on the way to school. The shock I felt was deep and beyond words. In one heart-rending moment, everything stopped. Politics and elections became irrelevant. A deeply-moving personal tragedy had struck the Voinovich family. The city was engulfed in mourning and the emotional climate of the campaign became funereal. It took the death of a wonderful nine-year-old child to prove there are things in life much more important than elections.

When sudden death intervenes, people turn to matters of the heart and ultimate questions. In such a tragic environment, ambitions become petty and recede in the grim pageant of mortality. Strategies evaporate into nothingness. The death of a child is particularly devastating, as it is a cruel violation of the natural cycle of life. Sandy and I, who had hoped to have a child of our own, felt deep compassion for the Voinovich family.

As we sat in attendance at Molly Voinovich's funeral, an organist played, "Let there be peace on earth and let it begin with me." We watched the small casket roll by our pew, followed by the grieving Voinovich family. The emotional pain of the family was excruciating and struck everyone deeply.

We called a halt to our campaign, as an expression of solidarity in grief. We had tens of thousands of well-researched leaflets, scrutinizing Voinovich's public record, ready to be put in the hands of the voters. I ordered the distribution suspended. I could not and would not attack Voinovich while he was mourning the death of his daughter.

There was dissension in my own organization after the child's funeral, questioning why I continued to withhold all campaign activity. A warehouse full of campaign literature was placed on hold. TV commercials, on hold. I was on hold, shaken to the core by Molly's death. I rely on emotional energy in a campaign. It is what will arouse the public and has the capacity to change the outcome. I couldn't feel the election anymore. I was riveted to the Voinovich family's loss.

"You have got to get out there," Weissman demanded. "Otherwise you are handing him the election."

"Bob, he lost his little girl. I'm not going to attack him." I replied.

"Do you realize what is at stake? Cleveland Trust, CEI and company will take over the city. We didn't work day and night over the last eight years to let that happen. You have got to get back on the campaign trail. What is wrong with you?"

I simply did not have it in me to attack Voinovich, in any manner, at this grim hour.

Two weeks before the election, Voinovich resumed campaigning. So did we. We met him squarely on the issues, but the emotional climate needed to defend my mayoralty had evaporated. There was not enough time to contrast our public records.

We were outspent at least three-to-one. Still, we had prominent celebrities who stepped forward on our behalf. I was fortunate to receive substantial fund-raising help from singer Helen Reddy, who performed a brilliant concert in Cleveland. Heavyweight Boxing Champion Larry Holmes appealed to people in television ads "Hi, I'm Larry Holmes and I fight for the people. Dennis Kucinich is a Mayor who fights for the people. Let him stay in the ring so he can keep fighting for you."

A singularly important endorsement came from former Mayor Carl Stokes, who recounted that he had run for Mayor on a platform to sell Muny Light. He thanked me for saving it and also thanked me for sharing major political appointments with the Black community.

I returned to the streets of the city for the final week of the campaign, to get our record to the people, to try to climb out from one pseudo-crisis after another, to try to calm the atmosphere of hysteria carrying over from the recall to the default, to the Muny Light election, to the attempted state takeover, and to the extended default, which continued even though a tax had been passed to cure it.

I was taking another beating in the thunder of front-page headlines, the lightning of radio news flashes, the TV eye of the hurricane. Inside City Hall, the climate may have been mild. Outside, in the community, the images of City Hall were as electric flashes of forked lightning, provoking foreboding.

My God, it had been a long two years.

CHAPTER 71

Citizen Kucinich

Election Night, November 6, 1979.

I traveled to George Voinovich's headquarters. Sandy and I moved to the platform overlooking a large gathering of well-dressed, mostly older White people. Shouts, curses and boos rang through the air. As we stepped to the podium, I reminded Sandy, no matter what, keep smiling, always look like you are winning. It confuses the hell out of them. I conceded the election to Voinovich and asked for unity.

My term ended a few days later.

On my last night in office, I walked up the steps of City Hall, alone. I pushed through the revolving doors. It was nearly midnight. The cheers of a rapid progression of six election nights in twenty-six months were muffled in the eerie silence of the cavernous City Hall rotunda. I felt like a ballplayer walking into the gathering darkness of an empty stadium, watching ghosts hovering at every position, hearing the transparent roar of the crowd, then deafening silence as the lights dimmed. Tomorrow my successor would be sworn in.

I wanted a final moment, alone, here. I paced the Mayor's office width, measuring my steps and the steps of the thousands of others who visited, including policemen who regularly swept the office for bugs. I looked at the polished surface of the big desk that I had re-positioned so I would work facing the people of Cleveland. I sat down one last time in the Mayor's chair, gripping the sides, looking up at the tapestries. The time had come to leave behind my own tapestry of yesterday's battles.

We had a two-year war in Cleveland. I was lucky to get out alive.

Shadows danced as I dimmed the crystal ballroom lights. I turned and walked through the metal detectors, out of City Hall, and headed back toward Milan Avenue and into private life. A person can traverse a galaxy of interests which make up the time and space of a city and find his way back home again. For me, home is not a city, it is not a political office, it is not even a house. Home is the heart.

I was now Citizen Kucinich, driving alone on Lorain Avenue, past a moon-lit ghost town of square buildings alternating with empty lots. I looked for a moment toward the silhouette of St. Colman's at W. 65th Street, where I sat in Mrs. Malone's civics class and first began to learn about a government, "of the people, by the people and for the people."

I envisioned the "people" as the ones I grew up with, those who counted pennies to pay their bills, those teachers like Sister Leona who prepared me spiritually for public life. These are the people to whom I would now return, the people who gave me purpose, who moved my soul. I made a promise long ago, if I ever got anywhere in life, I wouldn't forget them, nor would I forget where I came from.

I kept my promise.

The new city administration, under Mayor Voinovich, changed the name of Muny Light to Cleveland Public Power. Due to the 2-1 results of the referendum vote on the sale of the former Muny Light, there was no political pressure to sell the light system.

Cleveland was repackaged by civic tub thumpers as the "Comeback City," with few aware that "comeback" actually meant Cleveland's leading corporations had returned in triumph to reclaim control of City

Hall. The Cleveland media heralded the city's return from the "dark days." My name, and mine alone, was synonymous with "default."

Sandy and I flew to Berkeley, California to take a break and to be with friends who understood the machinations of my Cleveland ordeal, Bob Scheer, author and national correspondent for the Los Angeles Times, and his wife Narda Zacchino, an editor at the Los Angeles Times. Scheer had written lengthy articles about my battles with corporate Cleveland, including conducting an interview which was published in *Playboy Magazine*. The Scheer-Zacchino household was bursting with continuous, upbeat energy. It had the feel of holiday, until Cleveland intruded.

Andy Juniewicz, functioning now as a voluntary press secretary, called.

"Hey, Channel 3 is running an investigative piece. A mob hit-man confessed that he was offered money to kill you," Andy said, "The station said a contract may still be out there. They would like a comment."

Didn't the Mob hear I lost the election? "No comment." A mob hit-man again!? It was just as well no one knew my location. Andy taped the news, called back and played the broadcast over the phone:

WKYC News Anchor Doug Adair: "Good afternoon, everyone. An astonishing story, an exclusive report tonight uncovered by our Probe 3 investigative unit. A story of organized crime and a plan to kill former Cleveland Mayor Dennis Kucinich. Probe 3 investigator Mel Martin says the plot may still be in effect."

The investigative report featured interviews with top police officials, Inspector Edwin Nagorski and Lt. Edward Kovacic, head of the intelligence unit, who confirmed the existence of the plot. In order to further substantiate intelligence provided by the police, TV 3 had arranged to interview the hit-man.

Reporter Mel Martin: "The man we came to talk to was brought in from another undisclosed location for our meeting. He knows about organized crime in Cleveland. He should, he's been part of it. A convicted hit-man for the Mob, he says he was offered the job of killing Mayor Kucinich, more than a year before the Cleveland police heard of the threat.

Hit-man: "I was supposed to do it. I guess the only reason I didn't get the job done was because I got picked up," he said in a gravelly voice, his image obscured in shadows by the camera.

Martin: "You say you were willing to do the job?"

Hit-man: "True. Everybody's got to make a living."

Martin: "What kind of money might have been offered for something like that?"

Hit-man: "If I was to do it, I would want at least $80,000. I know it sounds ridiculous and high, but you've got to go on what position the guy holds, what his head's worth."

Martin: "Why do you think these people would want to do the mayor in?"

Hit-man: "We can't buy Kucinich. That's what I was told. We can't buy Kucinich. He was cut from a different cloth, and they didn't know where he was coming from, what angle he was coming from, and so we had to go different ways with him. You can't get any more serious than that."

Reporter Mel Martin: "Our informant says he is willing to disclose the names of Mob people who offered him the job of killing Kucinich, but only to law enforcement officers… The Mayor's spokesman confirmed that Kucinich did know about the danger…"

TV 3 concluded its report with a comment from the hit-man saying, "that contract would still be on the streets."

"That's it," Juniewicz said.

After listening to the news report, the memory of potentially-deadly events played back in my head. The rifle shot through the house, as we were mounting the campaign to save Muny. The guest at a local mob hotel, a man with the long knife in his boot, waiting in line at the reception after my Mayoral announcement. The warnings when I went to the stadium to throw out the first pitch. The man with a shotgun outside our home, chased away on Easter Sunday, 1978, by a police guard. The murder to be carried out as I was the Grand Marshal of the *Call and Post* parade. Plans made to take a shot from the roof of Tony's Diner. The increased intensity of assassination planning reported by police intelligence in the run-up to December 15th.

This news report brought it all back and reminded me why I sought to downplay the danger and focus on my work, understanding that I was in a fight to survive personally, as well as politically.

Later, Cleveland's TV 8 delved deeper and secured an exclusive interview with Lt. Kovacic, who had since served as Chief of Police. Kovacic broke years of public silence over the information he gained as head of the Cleveland Police Intelligence Unit. He described the motive for the plot: "There is a light plant in Cleveland and if that plant can be sold, some people are going to make a lot of money, and Kucinich was stopping them from selling that plant," he said.

It was speculated that James Licavoli, aka "Jack White" the head of the Cleveland Mob, ordered a hit on me, the same "Jack White," who Sandy and I unknowingly shared a spaghetti dinner with on the eve of the recall.

CHAPTER 72

The Price of Saying "No"

After I left office, I had time to absorb what had happened to me in Cleveland, my ten-year climb to become Mayor, my collision with corrupt interests amidst the highest of hopes for the city. However hard I tried, I could not find a moral to the story. I was shattered, not so much from losing an election, as from the pillorying of the ethical signposts of my life: Right was wrong and wrong was right.

The inversion of reality was particularly shocking. The banks, the business and political establishment had now constructed, and the Cleveland media carried forth, a new fictitious narrative. The city on its way to recovery… from me.

Only the antitrust case still remained as a portal to journey back into CEI's sordid tale of the subversion of government and Cleveland Trust's corruption of city finances.

Sandy and I returned to Cleveland from California. I discovered anew the widening personal impact of my decision not to sell Muny Light. My loved ones, as well as those closest to me in the service of the city, were all suffering, financially and personally.

Part of my mayoral salary had gone to Mom and Dad, who were

struggling with ill health and living in deteriorated housing in a rough neighborhood. I no longer had money to be of help. My brothers, Perry and Larry, and my sister, Beth Ann, were hurting emotionally from the increasing deprivation and chaos at my parent's home and the wave of public criticism of their oldest brother. They too, depended upon me for financial assistance. I could no longer offer assistance, nor could my brother Gary, because he had lost re-election to the City Council. He was now looking for work, too.

The members of my administration now faced terrible personal and financial dilemmas, as well. Andy Juniewicz had sent out sixty resumes, resulting in a single interview, in which the prospective employer lured him in, only to berate him for working for me. His mail and his calls seeking work went unanswered as he pondered how he would be able to support his young family and pay his mortgage. He was forced to cash in his public pension.

Joe Tegreene, went to an employment agency, where the principal wanted the appointment only to gloat at the plight of the former city Finance Director, looking for work. Tegreene enrolled in law school, where one of his professors, in the middle of a lecture, made a caustic comment about me, adding, "I'm sure Mr. Tegreene is going to cry." After graduation from law school, Tegreene was interviewed by a major firm and questioned as to the soundness of his judgment, given his prominent role in our administration.

James Barrett, our safety director, also cashed in his pension. He found his years of experience in law enforcement, as a patrolman, a detective, and assistant safety director under Mayor Stokes, to no avail as he went from firm to firm, only to meet with rejection after rejection. He was hitting a financial wall, unable to meet his bills, with no source of income in sight. He shared with me, "It's because I worked for you. But I'm not working for anyone who thinks they can break my loyalty."

Morris Pettus, our service director, tried to return to City Hall as a worker in the same department he had led. He was blocked by a

Voinovich administration official. He next tried the telephone company, he had worked for previously. He was rejected because, he was told, they could not find his previous work records. Later he and Jim Barrett formed a construction company, but work was scarce.

During our term, Jack Schulman never complained about the impact of events on him and his family, the threats to his own life, and the intrusion by the media. He was, throughout, a rock of support, even though he paid a price professionally for defending Muny Light and protecting our administration from the Cleveland establishment's legions of corporate attorneys. Schulman, a graduate of Harvard Law, was now being turned down by prospective clients, because he had been our Law Director. He was rejected for the position of general counsel of the school board, for the same reason. He and his brother, Howard, ultimately began practicing law together, sharing space with their father, Milt.

Most of those who worked for me could not find jobs, blackballed by the Cleveland establishment. Several members of my team had to travel many miles out of town to find work. Most found themselves at a significant financial disadvantage. One, a brilliant city planner who had courageously challenged developers' schemes to extract millions from the taxpayers, committed suicide.

It was my decision and I paid a price, but regrettably, others also paid. The extraordinary thing is that no one, faced with what came to be the heavy burden of association with me, ever complained or bemoaned their fate. Still, pain abides in the consequences.

I received a notice from the Internal Revenue Service that my tax returns were to be audited for the years 1977, 1978, 1979, even though the only income I received for those years was from my salary as Clerk of Courts and later Mayor.

I showed the letter to Jack Schulman. "It's political, isn't it?" I asked.

"Of course," Jack responded. "Someone called them and claimed you were taking money under the table. They assume all politicians are crooks." I shook my head. The election may have been over. The Cleveland establishment and their allies were still on the attack.

"Dennis, you made only one mistake," Jack said. "You thought you were the Mayor."

I was later contacted by Treasury agents. I referred them to Jack Schulman, as well. Again under investigation, I had to produce every scrap of paper, every financial document supporting my income and my expenditures. This was actually very easy, because there wasn't much.

The Cleveland establishment, not satisfied with having destroyed me politically, tried to destroy me financially. No one wanted to be known as the person who gave me a job. Whenever and wherever I sought employment after leaving office, offers were extended, then withdrawn. A radio station wanted to hire me. A key advertiser told station management it had better not. A newspaper column was offered, then retracted. A television station official called, expressed interest in guest editorials, then nothing. A local company wanted to pay me $10,000 to do a commercial. The offer disappeared when one of their major customers, Republic Steel, objected. A Cleveland State University official who gave me a temporary, entry-level, part-time position as a course instructor was chastised by his superiors for not getting clearance from his Dean to hire me. I was blackballed in a city which I had served with integrity.

I graduated from Case Western Reserve University in Cleveland, with both bachelor's and master's degrees. I had nearly a straight A average in my graduate major, and I couldn't get a job in the city I had served faithfully as Councilman, Clerk of Courts, and Mayor.

Sandy tried to regain her job as a high school teacher, to no avail.

Bills were piling up.

"We can't live like this, not knowing where our next dollar is coming from," Sandy said, as we looked at a stack of payment demands one afternoon. The personal financial pressure had become intense. Sandy vocalized what I had been thinking but was afraid to admit. We were in trouble.

"All because of a damn light system," she added, bitterly.

"We saved Muny Light," I offered gamely.

"Nobody cares about Muny Light but you. People just care about themselves," she said, and began to cry.

"Sandy," I touched her shoulder, to comfort her.

"We'll find a way." She clasped my hand and we embraced. The uneasiness of the moment lingered as we lived with the harsh consequences of my stand. We had saved Muny Light from being stolen and in retribution, the Cleveland establishment was trying to steal my life.

Sandy and I had exhausted all of our financial resources and were on the verge of losing our home on Milan Avenue. The emotional pressure on our marriage was excruciating. I had spent a lifetime helping other people, yet found it difficult to ask for help for myself. I had pride in self-sufficiency and resourcefulness. It had been easier to find a job as a child, when I earned money scrubbing floors to pay my siblings' book bills at Catholic school, than it was to find work as the former mayor. Whatever personal strengths I had to meet adversity, all the doors were closed in Cleveland.

Then came an ironic and emotional blow, taking me back to the upstairs apartment above Martha's Delicatessen on St. Clair Avenue, where my parents counted pennies to pay the electric bill.

I received a notice that our own electric service on Milan Avenue was to be disconnected. Our account was past due. Muny Light was shutting off our electricity.

CHAPTER 73

What Goes Around…

Three Years After Default

After years of denying documented evidence that it tried to knock Muny Light out of business, CEI finally confessed in open court during the antitrust trial: "If intending to eliminate the only competitor is an attempt to achieve monopoly, this we admit," CEI's lead attorney, John Lansdale told the court… "The intent of CEI is not an issue. There can be no doubt, no question of our intent…"

The *Cleveland Press* reported the sensational confession:

CEI ADMITS TRYING TO FORCE MUNY LIGHT TO CLOSE DOWN

Seven weeks into the trial, Federal Judge Krupansky declared a mistrial due to a "deadlocked" jury. Five of the six jurors had determined to find CEI guilty. However, unanimity was required for a verdict. According to the jury forewoman, the holdout juror "never took notes on anything," and refused to participate in the deliberations. One significant development in the trial was the admission into evidence of the so-called "Miller Stipulations," that contrary to the company's testimony that it did nothing to interfere with construction of the FPC-ordered interconnect, CEI secretly sponsored a taxpayer's suit to block it.

In the second antitrust trial, Judge Krupansky refused to permit the Miller Stipulations to be introduced into evidence. Moreover, while the factual findings of the NRC were identical to the issues in the antitrust lawsuit, Judge Krupansky refused to permit the NRC's damning legal rulings to go to the jury. He also allowed CEI to retry issues decided adversely by the NRC.

Krupansky's rulings caused the city to lose the advantage of the legal implications of CEI's abuse of market power. Jurors were unaware of the Miller Stipulations and that CEI's refusal to interconnect contributed to Muny Light's going out of the generating business. Judge Krupansky also instructed the jury to "disregard evidence that CEI retained substantial market power through its power to control its prices." Denied by Judge Krupansky of the ability to introduce compelling evidence, the city lost the second case.

Robert M. Ginn, CEI's President and Chairman, while speaking of the utility's "Say Something Nice About Cleveland" marketing campaign, called for "the death" of Muny Light.

The city appealed and asked for a new trial based on the Trial Court's exclusion of the Miller Stipulations, and exclusion of the NRC's findings of fact. The city lost 2-1. The dissenting judge termed the exclusion of evidence as prejudicial error. The city failed to get the U.S. Supreme Court to review the case.

Were the legal battles all for naught? James B. Davis, the Cleveland law director who initiated the antitrust case in 1975, wrote to Brad Norris:

"When that case was started the overall objective was to save Muny Light as a long term asset for Cleveland....The antitrust case bought the time for the NRC proceedings to succeed, for CEI's stranglehold to be broken, for Muny's debts to be accommodated within the city, and the system righted....CEI's massive push to grab the system was defeated.

"You were not defeated on the facts, or the law, or the courtroom presentation," Mayor Perk's former law director wrote to Norris, "but by perversions of the judicial system which were the worst I have ever seen."

Five Years After Default, Washington, D.C., 25 January 1984,
Dirksen Senate Office Building, The Committee Room
Meeting of the Permanent Subcommittee on Investigations

Public discussion about personal security was a topic I avoided, downplayed and dismissed, for good reason. There had been three assassination attempts and an assassination plot, which was documented by Maryland state and Cleveland police intelligence. During my time in office, I never discussed the subject outside a small circle of trusted confidants. Sandy, Jack Schulman, Jeff Fox and Detective Plank, my bodyguard, were the only persons inside my administration who knew some of details I was provided by police intelligence. They kept my confidence, ensuring my security.

As a result of the plot, an increased police presence was noticeable. Political speculation said that I was obviously terrified of violent death, but I was not being haunted, I was being hunted. I fear neither life nor death, so I brushed off the threats and admonitions, and stayed focused on my job.

When I left the Mayor's office, TV3 News Cleveland, for the first time, unearthed the story which I had pushed aside. An exclusive interview with a convicted hit-man detailed a murder plot against me. The report brought derision from some quarters, and a few eye rolls. I refused interviews because I did not want to invite sympathy or skepticism.

Four years later, on January 25, 1984, the United States Senate Permanent Subcommittee on Investigations held hearings on a "Profile of Organized Crime: Great Lakes Region" in the United States Senate, the Dirksen Senate Office Building, SD 342. It was a detailed investigation into car bombings, mob executions, gambling, narcotics trafficking and political corruption in Michigan, Indiana, Illinois and New York and Ohio.

During the hearing, John F. Sopko, an assistant counsel to the Minority Subcommittee staff, gave sworn testimony about the breadth of criminal activity in Ohio. Prior to coming to Washington to work for the Senate, Sopko had been an attorney in the Justice Department's Organized Crime and Racketeering Strike Force in Cleveland, where he was credited, as a young federal prosecutor, with helping to put the leader of the Cleveland organized crime family. James T. "Jack White" Licavoli, and five other defendants in federal prison in 1982 for their part in the 1977 bombing murder of Danny Greene.

In his testimony, Sopko gave a gruesome account of the sociopathic and psychopathic killers involved in gambling and drugs and Cleveland's role as the bombing capital from 1975 to 1977. He discussed the Cleveland mob's infiltration, through bribery of a clerk at the local FBI offices, thereby gaining access to sensitive files. Sopko's testimony was a graphic depiction of the depth of the Cleveland mob's viciousness.

Sopko handled his task of testifying with a chilled, pedestrian air as he discussed the stakes in Cleveland: Huge profits from the sale of illegal narcotics, gambling, and "business" killings, to take profits or territory. Sopko then segued into the story that I had suppressed and ignored for the last four years, the mob's plan to kill me.

He addressed the Vice Chairman, Warren Rudman of New Hampshire, presiding, and Ranking Member Sam Nunn of Georgia: "During the scope of this investigation [into organized crime in the Great Lakes Region], the minority staff also received additional information concerning an alleged plot upon former Mayor Dennis

Kucinich. Sketchy reports of this plot were made public first in 1980, garnered from Mafia hit-man, Louis J. Aratari."

"Aratari's recollection is that there have been discussions among members of a Cleveland LCN [La Cosa Nostra] family about a contract to kill Kucinich. It has uncovered facts which showed that there was a plot attempted on the life of Mr. Kucinich. As a result of the minority staff investigation, we are able at this time to confirm that such a plot existed."

"Intelligence information gleaned by the Maryland State Police and Cleveland Police Department, confirmed that the murder contract was, in general terms, due to the fact that Kucinich had caused considerable problems for local dishonest businessmen, politicians and criminals. It was alleged that Kucinich had been impeding organized criminal activities and its ability to make money in the city. As a result, someone decided to do away with the mayor," Sopko testified.

I had something that I had to do away with: An attachment to the life-death narrative. I forgave everyone who was involved in any plot or effort to do me physical or political harm. I detached myself from playing out old conflicts, from being enmeshed in polarized thinking, without tether to any contestant, emotionally or spiritually, so that I could be light, empowered and ultimately, free.

Five and a Half Years After Default

It was the summer of 1984. Sandy and I, and baby daughter, Jacqueline, were in our new residence on Cleveland's southeast side, on Lansing Avenue. A year earlier I won an election to fill the unexpired term of Councilman Joseph Kowalski, who passed away suddenly. Although the City Council salary offered some degree of financial security, the trauma of the Mayoral term, and its aftermath, proved to be more than our marriage could bear.

One afternoon, a surprise guest appeared at the door. This was a meeting best held in the back yard, out of sight of curious neighbors.

The visitor got to the point. "It's like this has nothing to do with you, but it has everything to do with you," he began. "We want to go ahead with leasing Muny Light to CEI. CEI's ready to go. The Mayor's on board. Council is ready. A "Memorandum of Understanding" between the city and CEI has been prepared. Forest City (the development company) is waiting for the deal to bring 1,000 CEI workers to their new Tower City project. But Voinovich is afraid if he goes ahead with this, you will beat him up. He doesn't want to have to fight you over it," the visitor said.

My God! Voinovich ought to be afraid. He began his campaign for Mayor in 1979, standing in front of Muny Light, vowing to protect it. Five and a half years after default, CEI was back trying to take Muny Light, and I was once again inside City Hall, this time as a councilman.

"I appreciate you coming to me about this; it was thoughtful of you. It's called a lease, but we know it is actually a sale. Please take this message back to Mayor Voinovich: If he makes any move against Muny Light there will be hell to pay." I said, with a new key I had discovered in my emotional repertoire - - low.

And with that, appreciating the irony of the moment, my visitor, Council President George Forbes, gave me a knowing smile and with a barely suppressed chuckle, left my house to relay the message to Mayor Voinovich.

I avoided confronting Forbes in the moment, or mentioning that he and I would again be headed toward another battle. I don't think he relished that, nor did I. In my reflections I had come to see George

Forbes not as an enemy, but as one of my life's great teachers, someone to contest with, if necessary, but not to be judged. I had learned to step out of polarity. It was a challenging practice, but the most important lesson of my life. When I ran in the special election in 1983, Forbes very publicly promised my prospective constituents that they would be "screwed" - - cut out of city services, if they dared elect me. I did not engage him. I kept open the door for precisely the kind of communication he brought to me about still another attempt by CEI to take Muny.

Forbes conveyed my message about Muny Light to Mayor Voinovich. The *Plain Dealer* reported that Forbes thought "the mayor rejected the sale because the mayor feared Councilman Dennis Kucinich…would use the issue to politically damage Voinovich."

"I told George I disagreed with his decision," Forbes told reporters. When the deal became public, Voinovich claimed he had lost track of the negotiations and declared dead a deal which Clevelanders never knew was alive.

CEI expressed astonishment at Mayor Voinovich's reversal: "…his position…(not to sell Muny Light to CEI) seemed so completely to disregard what he charged to be reasonable negotiations between his representatives and ours that met all of his criteria," the *Plain Dealer* quoted a CEI executive.

While the behind-the-scenes negotiations to sell Muny Light were at their highest intensity, the city accepted a national award for its support of public power. When the story surfaced about his negotiations to sell Muny Light, Mayor Voinovich lashed out at CEI. "I honest to God believe that the folks at CEI - - I don't think they're straight dealers, I think they're sidewinders," he said.

The *Plain Dealer* described major elements of the proposed transaction: Sale of Muny Light at $40 million. CEI received a monopoly on electricity. City residents would get electricity 10% cheaper than suburban residents for 10 years.

Mayor Voinovich's deal with CEI was immeasurably worse than

anything negotiated by Mayor Ralph Perk years earlier, including the sale price. The promise of cheaper electricity? Muny customers were already saving 10% on their electric bills, as opposed to CEI's rates.

Fourteen Years After Default

I was at a friend's house on the West Coast. I received a call from a *Plain Dealer* reporter, Benjamin Marrison. "Hey, Mayor, did you hear the news?" he said in a cheerful voice.

"About...?" I asked.

"Muny Light. It's expanding. The largest expansion, ever."

"That's great," I said. "But it's been fourteen years since I left City Hall."

"People are saying there wouldn't be a Muny Light if you hadn't stood up and said 'no'," he said.

"I'm glad it is working out for Cleveland," I said warming to the tidings, "I hoped it would. I always knew I was right about Muny Light."

Much had changed since I had left the Mayor's office. Cleveland Trust was gone, swallowed by a bigger bank. CEI was folded into a larger power company. But, Muny Light, now Cleveland Public Power, had come back. Cleveland City Council voted to permit Muny Light to sell $146 million in bonds, enabling a major expansion.

Marrison reported "By approving that expansion, Council members lived up to the dream of former Mayors Tom L. Johnson and Dennis J. Kucinich, who wanted residents to be able to reap the benefits of competition between two electric companies through lower rates."

"Council President Jay Westbrook and his colleagues, talked of a young Mayor named Kucinich who put his political career on the line to save the struggling municipal electric company."

Fifteen Years After Default
December 15, 1993

On the fifteenth anniversary of default, WJW-TV ran a lengthy news analysis that demolished the established narrative. It said I had sacrificed my career to save Muny Light.

I lost the Mayor's office because I refused to sell Muny Light. But, in 1994, I rode the crest of a new wave of public appreciation, with a campaign slogan "Because he was Right," to become the only Democrat to defeat an incumbent Republican in a statewide election. Two years later, I defeated another Republican incumbent to be elected to the United States House of Representatives, on a campaign motto, "Light Up Congress."

Twenty Years After Default

Near the end of my first term in Congress I was asked to attend a meeting of the Cleveland City Council on December 14th, 1998, the eve of the twentieth anniversary of default.

Surrounded by members of Council, including Council President Westbrook, I was presented with a City Council resolution of recognition "...Today the City of Cleveland has one of the fastest-growing municipal electric systems in America. Currently, Cleveland Public Power is expanding to provide low-cost electricity to more and more people, providing power for city facilities and streetlights, thereby helping to keep taxes low and encouraging economic development. None of this would have been possible had Mayor Kucinich not refused to sell the City's electric system on December 15, 1978 now, therefore,"

"BE IT RESOLVED, that Cleveland City Council hereby extends its deep appreciation to Dennis J. Kucinich, for having the courage and foresight to refuse to sell the City's municipal electric system, which has saved the people of Cleveland over $300 million since that time."

I had surrendered two marriages, my health, and my career to stand for the people of Cleveland. Now, I stepped forward to receive the Council presentation in the same chamber where the city had plummeted into a contrived default over Muny Light twenty years earlier. Members of Council stood and applauded.

George Forbes was quoted in a special retrospective on Muny Light saying, "Dennis was right" not to sell the system.

He said the default never had to happen.

EPILOGUE

The process of writing this book has caused me to re-visit, re-assess, and re-evaluate everything I did as Mayor of Cleveland, as well as what has occurred since my term ended.

I began my career in politics as a naive optimist, excited about the wonderful things I planned to accomplish to improve the lives of the people who put me in office. What I soon learned, however, was that government, at least in 1970's Cleveland, did not function for the benefit of the governed. It functioned for the benefit of office-holders and for their co-opting patrons.

Politics is inherently transactional. It is a process of give-and-take, and compromise. The distinction between normal politics and corrupt politics can therefore, be difficult to recognize. The line is crossed when the reward is personal to the office-holder - - private sector jobs for friends or relatives, contracts for personal business interests, admission to a desirable network of associates, support for a favorite charity, and well-timed campaign contributions can be inducements that cause an elected official to favor a private interest over the public interest. Corruption is much more than cash slipped under the table. Its forms are endless.

This process is so endemic that it is actually accepted as "The System."

Every newly-elected office-holder, as I once was, must decide early on if he or she will participate in The System, or challenge it. Ignoring corruption or pretending it does not exist is not a real option, because, by acquiescing without trying to impede or stop it, you become complicit in facilitating it. Once elected, you must either join The System or fight it.

I engaged The System energetically, and it cost me dearly. What is worse is that many others, whose only sin was helping me, also suffered.

As I wrote this book, I constantly asked myself, "Should I have taken this stand? Was it worth it?" Having finished the book, I now know the answer; I really had no choice, if I wanted to live an authentic life with integrity.

The wizened Milt Schulman had a saying "You will never regret doing the right thing." Then a beginner, I did not fully comprehend what that meant.

I do now.

He was right.

I have no regrets.

GLOSSARY

Allocated service territory:

The Public Utilities Commission of Ohio (PUCO) has divided the state into territories allocated to investor-owned utilities.

AMP-Ohio: American Municipal Power of Ohio.

A state-wide organization of municipal electric systems, which has its own generating capacity.

APPA: The American Public Power Association:

A national trade organization of municipal systems.

Backup:

The ability to provide service, electricity, if the primary means of delivering that electricity fails.

Blackout:

Total loss of power affecting all electrical devices connected to a system.

Brownouts:

Characterized by intermittent power supplies, or lower voltage, which can cause lights to flicker and appliances to malfunction.

Buckeye Generation Cooperative:

An association of rural co-ops in the state of Ohio. Its generating facilities provide power to rural cooperatives.

CAPCO:

The Central Area Power Coordinating Organization. An organization of privately- owned utilities in Ohio, now defunct.

Cleveland Electric Illuminating Company:

An investor-owned utility operating in northeast Ohio, now a First Energy company.

Co-ordination:

Co-ordinated methods of operation between connected utilities.

Customers:

Those who subscribe to the service of a utility.

Delivery point:

In purchased power it is where the power is handed off between electric systems.

Distribution:

Facilities used to move power to neighborhood substations along poles and wires to customers homes and businesses.

Primary distribution lines:

The higher voltage lines that feed neighborhood stepped down transformers, providing electricity to residential and commercial districts.

Secondary distribution lines:

(lines under 600 volts) which connect with residential and commercial customers.

Economies of Scale:

The theory that it is more economic to generate from a larger unit than from a smaller unit.

First Energy:

An investor-owned utility operating in seven states, including Ohio.

Franchise:

An agreement between a municipality and an investor-owned utility permitting the operation of the investor-owned utility in the municipality, under certain terms, for a specified period in time.

Generation:

Producing electricity.

75MW boiler:

The size of a coal-fired boiler that produces steam turbines to spin the generators which produce electricity.

85MW steam turbine:

The generating unit which produces electricity for distribution to substations.

Isolated generation:

Not interconnected with any other utility.

Highest block rate:

First block in a declining block rate schedule. The more power a customer uses, the better rate they get. Generally used to recover fixed cost up front.

Interconnection:

An electrical connection between two utilities which allows power to flow in either direction, as needed.

Temporary interconnection:

Same as above, but not constructed as permanent.

69kV tie:

An interconnection between two systems at that voltage level.

69kV emergency open-switch synchronous interconnection:

The utilities are not interconnected, and power flows only when switches are closed. Power is available only under pre-arranged conditions.

138kV interim emergency synchronous interconnection:

An interconnection not permanently in place.

Investor-Owned Utility (IOU):

A publicly held company whose owners trade shares on various stock exchanges and who often pay dividends to their shareholders.

Isolated generation:

Not interconnected with any other utility.

Load:

The amount of electricity customers are using at any given time.

Base load:

The amount of electricity which customers use on an average basis. It is a consistent load regardless of seasonal variations or time of day.

Load transfer:

Shifting customers off the first electric system and onto a second electric system. This involves the disconnecting the first system from its primary voltage (which can create an outage) and then connecting with a second electric system.

Peak load:

The load which is required to serve customers at a time of greatest demand.

PASNY – The Power Authority of the State of New York:

Owns hydro-power generating facilities in Niagara and St Lawrence Seaway. It has its own transmission links and distribution on a grid; now called NYPA (New York Power Authority.)

Price squeeze:

Imposing an unacceptable level or actual loss on a competitor by narrowing or eliminating the difference between revenues derived from final product sales and costs. Also charging a competitive utility more for power than a utility charges its own customers.

Power:

Bulk Power:

Power that flows into a system from interconnected systems. Muny Light's 138kV transmission system is considered a bulk power system.

Emergency power:

Power required on an unplanned basis, not predictable, premium priced, must be delivered when an emergency situation arrives.

Firm Power:

Power delivered on a basis a customer can rely on, as opposed to power which can be curtailed at any time. Firm power is generally based on contractual agreements.

Maintenance Power:

Power purchased when generating facilities are down for maintenance. If a generator goes down, maintenance power would be purchased to cover the load it would otherwise provide.

Power pool:

A number of utilities coming together to fund or create a generating facility which serves their power needs.

Retail power:

Power sold to individual customers.

Short-term power:

Power purchased for a short amount of time; could be seasonal, or for several months.

Measurements of Power:

Watt:

A unit of power.

Volt:

An unit of electrical potential

Kilowatt:

(kW) 1,000 watts of electricity.

Kilowatt Hour:

(kWh)1,000 watts of electricity, over a one hour period.

Kilovolt:

(kV) 1000 volts, measure of the level of voltage.

Megawatt:

(MW) One million watts.

Municipal Electric System:

An electric system owned by a city or a municipal unit of government.

Outage:

A sudden power failure.

Public Utilities Commission of Ohio:

Also known as the PUCO. The state regulatory agency having jurisdiction over all investor-owned utilities, including rate-making authority.

Rate schedule:

Charges assigned to different components such as demand, kilowatt hours, etc. Rate schedules for IOU's are approved by the PUCO. Rate schedules for municipals are proposed by a city administration and approved by city council.

Reserve

Reserve Capacity:

A percentage of generation planned to keep available in case the customer demand unexpectedly increases.

Reserve Sharing:

Physical generating facilities are owned or financed by multiple entities be they municipalities or rural coops for the benefit of the ownership, but each municipality would have its own reserve unit.

Right-of-Way:

The path for physical transmission of power; rights that electric companies use to facilitate the delivery of the distribution of electricity. In some states, a power siting commission can grant a right-of-way.

Retail power:

Power sold to individual customers.

Rural cooperative:

An organization which serves unincorporated areas spanning multiple communities. Can be regional in nature.

Self-generation:

Power produced with one's own equipment as opposed to buying power from outside the territory.

Territory boundary agreements:

Enforced by the regulatory authority (the PUCO in Ohio.) These agreements treat investor-owned utility business conduct on the edges of service territories.

Territorial restrictions:

Imposed by the regulatory authority, in Ohio the PUCO, to prevent one investor-owned utility from raiding another utility's service territory.

Transfer points:

The physical facilities used to transfer loads of electricity from one system to another.

Transmission:

Distributing the highest voltage electricity through a system to another electric utility or to a substation.

Transmission Grid:

A system of all bulk-power transmission lines in a region or nation.

Wheeling:

Movement of power over transmission lines and through multiple jurisdictions or entities.

END NOTES

ABBREVIATIONS:

ASLB: The Atomic Safety and Licensing Board

CEI: Cleveland Electric Illuminating Company

FPC: The Federal Power Commission

MELP: Municipal Electric Light and Power (another name for Muny Light).

NRC: The Nuclear Regulatory Commission (formerly known as the Atomic Energy Commission).

PTX: Plaintiff's Exhibit from City of Cleveland v. Cleveland Electric Illuminating Company., No. C75-560 (N.D. Ohio, filed July 1, 1975).

PUCO: The Public Utilities Commission of Ohio, with jurisdiction over investor-owned utilities and their rates.

INTRODUCTION:

Documentation for this book is supported by federal court records, (the production of documents through the discovery process); the proceedings of the Atomic Safety and Licensing Board of the Nuclear Regulatory Commission; the report of the Federal Reserve Bank; Staff report of the United States House of Representatives, subcommittee on Financial Institutions Supervision, Regulation and Insurance of the Committee on Banking, Finance and Urban Affairs; "The Role of the Commercial Banks in the Financing of the Debt of the City of Cleveland," Committee on Banking, Publication, Serial 96-61; City of Cleveland records, personal files of the author; published newspaper accounts, and transcriptions of televised accounts.

The end notes include material from a selection of documents from the NRC Docket Nos 50-440A and 50-441A, in the matter of the Cleveland Electric Illuminating Company as well as the federal antitrust case, The City of Cleveland vs. The Cleveland Electric Illuminating Company, C75-560, representing only a small amount of the volume of evidence available from CEI's internal files, acquired by the City of Cleveland through the discovery process. The citations in the end notes detail CEI's dealings with the City of Cleveland on all matters relating to Muny Light, then also known as The Division of Light and Power.

For further information, an on-line version of the digest of the city's exhibits (PTX) in the federal court case, in numerical order, as well as the NRC's Initial Decision and the city's "Findings of Fact" presented to the NRC, are available here:

www.DLParchive.com

PART I: A CITY IN THE DARK

1. CHRISTMAS BLACKOUT

"The official tally"

Plain Dealer, 1 August 1967, Page One, "Protest With a Guitar? Not this candidate, 20," by James Naughton.

"CEI had long refused to cooperate"

City of Cleveland v. Cleveland Electric Illuminating Company, No. C75-560 (N.D. Ohio, filed 1 July 1975) hereinafter referred to as Cleveland v. CEI.

PTX 2615, CEI Memo, dated 9 June 1971, Sener to Hauser: "A chronology of meetings held between representatives of MELP and CEI concerning emergency standby service."

"They won't give us a back-up"

Nuclear Regulatory Commission, Before the Atomic Safety and Licensing Board, In the Matter of The Toledo Edison Company and The Cleveland Electric Illuminating Company (Davis-Besse Nuclear Power Station, Units 1,2, & 3) (NRC ASLB) Docket Nos 5-346-A, 50-500A, 50-501A.

The Cleveland Electric Illuminating Company, et al. (Perry Nuclear Power Plant, Units 1 & 2.

NRC Docket Nos. 50-440A, 50-441A ASLB NRC document, page 132, para. 5, re: S21 December 1969 outage.

PTX 1952, Muny Light outages, 1969. Proposed findings of fact and conclusions of law and brief in support thereof the City of Cleveland, 8 September 1976.

"known as the national grid"

Federal law required utilities be interconnected to assure the reliability of the national power grid. The city had a 1.6 mile line which temporarily connected the city system with CEI.

"There was a 1.6 mile line in place"

NRC ASLB Proposed Findings of Fact: 1.02: "a 138kV single circuit transmission line."

"Scrooge! CEI's like Scrooge"

Stanton referred to CEI as "Scrooge" for its refusal to provide a tie-in to Muny Light and for refusing to sell emergency power to Cleveland, thus prolonging a blackout.

PTX 2453, *Plain Dealer*, 25 December 1969.

PTX 2452, *Cleveland Press*, 26 December 1969, "Stanton-CEI feud Flares over Tie-In."

"Mayor Stokes pledged to keep the lights on"

PTX 2450, 22 December 1969, *Plain Dealer*, "No More Outages, Muny Light Pledges."

PTX 2451, 23 December 1969, *Cleveland Press*, "City May Ask Court to Order CEI to Tie-In line to Muny Light."

PTX 2455, 10 December 1970, *Cleveland Press*, "Stanton Says 25% Tie-In Not Enough."

"sought a Federal Power Commission (FPC) order"

PTX 2454, 27 December 1969, *Plain Dealer*, "Force CEI Tie-In, City to Ask FPC."

PTX 2456, 12 December 1970, *Cleveland Press*, "Permanent CEI Tie-In is Sought."

PTX 2426, 21 January 1970, *City Record*, "Resolution No. 119-70. Authorizing the Director of Law to make an application to the FPC for an Order directing a permanent interconnection between MELP and CEI."

2. THE RACKET

"Joseph Garry, the university's theatre director"

Plain Dealer, 12 May 1979, "Audience is Deeply Moved by CSU Student's Drama," by Elizabeth Jacobsen, page 3-B

3. SELL MUNY LIGHT

"I witnessed CEI's City Hall lobbyists"

PTX 2859, 12 January 1970, City Ordinance No. 115-70: "Emergency ordinance authorizing the Director of Public Utilities to enter into an agreement with CEI for temporary Muny Light switching and load transfer to CEI."

"We've offered to interconnect"

Plain Dealer, 27 December 1969, "Howley Supports Tie-In."

PTX 54, 29 December 1969, CEI Memo, "A permanent tie-in is to be avoided like the plague."

PTX 1509, 30 September 1970, Letter, Howley to Bergman: "Proposal re Phase III interconnection."

PTX 1509, 23 April 1971, "Summary of discussion of Phase III with attached sketches."

PTX 1507, 4 September 1970, Letter, Fitzgerald of CEI to Grant, FPC: "Update of summary of terms of agreement between Muny and CEI re: load transfer."

PTX 2429, 16 December 1969, "Chronology of MELP's request for a temporary load release during the time period in which precipitators were being installed."

PTX 1012, 17 July 1970, CEI Memo, Jankura to Davidson: "Ericksen of MELP requests a meeting to be set to discuss Phase III, a permanent tie between CEI and MELP."

"CEI is trying to force Muny Light to raise its rates"

PTX 329, CEI Memo 28 February 1968, Re: Revenue per kWh comparison between MELP [Municipal Electric Light and Power] and CEI. "The published rate schedules for the MELP tariffs which, for the same kWh usage, result in MELP charges roughly 15% lower than CEI."

PTX 332, CEI Memo 18 June 1968, Rate Comparison Study CEI vs. MELP Rates.

PTX 335, CEI Memo: 26 May 1969, "Cleveland pays MELP at least 25% less than CEI's rates for various mercury streetlights. Small residential customers now pay CEI about 6% more than they would pay MELP, general commercial customers pay about 7% more and CEI's large commercial rates about 7% - 8% more than MELP's."

PTX 336, CEI Memo 4 May 1967, "The history of Cleveland Muny is traced in precise detail, including capacity additions, rate revisions."

"You can do it, if the city sells Muny Light"

PTX 2095, CEI Press Release Draft, Re: purchase of MELP.

PTX 2640, 12 May 1960, CEI Memo, Kender to Rudolph: "Cost of efforts to compete with Muny."

PTX 560, CEI Memo, 7 January 1970, Re: "Advantage to the City of Cleveland if MELP were sold." Mentions city's outstanding debt of $25 million as another reason to sell.

"Muny's power is cheaper"

PTX 2161, 1969, Cleveland Financial Report: "Department of Public Utilities, Division of Utilities Fiscal Control, Light and Power Financial Report."

PTX 2512, 1969, Annual Report: "CEI Annual Report, 1969."

"The sale is the solution to Cleveland's problems"

PTX 692, CEI Memo, 19 September 1963, "...Sale of MELP plant would yield funds for the City's capital needs."

PTX 645, 6 August 1965, Letter CEI to Crawford: "...Sale of MELP to CEI would provide the City with money that can be used for capital improvement."

PTX 702, 10 January 1966, CEI Memo: "Sale of MELP Plant and advantages of sale to the City."

"larger, private electric systems taking over smaller, municipal electric systems"

PTX 639, 15 March 1965, Re: CEI position on purchase of MELP. "The trend in America for many years has been clearly away from municipal ownership of small, hence less efficient, utility systems...The trend is inevitable in view of the economy of scale made possible through the rapid technological advances taking place in generation and transmission."

PTX 640, 19 May 1965, *CEI Magazine* interview, Besse: "Throughout the country today the trend is toward interconnection and purchases of power by municipal plants..."

PTX 1763, 10 April 1967, CEI Planning, Marketing Group: "Planning project re elimination of isolated electric power generating facilities in eastern district."

PTX 541, CEI Memo, 23 June 1969, Re:... acquiring Muny Light. "We also should accumulate data as this acquisition is inevitable."

PTX 652, CEI Survey, January 1970, "Clevelander's Thinking on the Muny Issue," to reflect attitudes on MELP, interconnection with CEI, sale to CEI.

5. SABOTAGE

"CEI had been building public pressure for the sale of Muny Light"

PTX 1156, 16 November 1965, CEI Memo, Bridges to Howley: Wants to put pressure on the administration and Muny advocates to agree to sell Muny. Also wants to go to the public directly to get support for sale of Muny to CEI.

PTX 628, CEI Memo, 29 July 1960, "The sale of limited amounts of firm power may contribute to ultimate acquisition [of Muny Light]. There is no precedent for the acquisition of a municipal system as large as Cleveland... because of this a victory for the Company might well be a real contribution to continued private ownership of the electric power business and therefore worth an extreme effort and sacrifice."

"CEI could feign cooperation and do nothing"

PTX 1278, 20 January 1970, Letter, Howley to Stefanski: Confirms the understanding reached between the City and CEI. CEI will provide switching and load transfer service. Approved and signed by Stefanski.

PTX 1501, 18 June 1970, Letter Tomlinson, to Mayor Stokes: Response to City's 2 June 1970 letter re extensive outages at MELP, including information re FPC assistance; prior relevant communication included.

PTX 1041, 14 April 1970, CEI Memo, Bridges to Howley: (Suggests CEI was ghost writing public statements for Stefanski).

"CEI created the outage"

PTX 1951, 1968 Muny Light Report: Muny Light Outages.

PTX 1952, Muny Light Report: 1969 Muny Light Major Outages.

PTX 1953 Muny Light Report: 1970 Muny Light major outages.

"Mayor Stokes...became suspicious"

PTX 2982, 2 June 1970, Letter to Grant, FPC, from Mayor Stokes. "Summarizes three massive outages of MELP in past six months; caused serious problems not only to customers it serviced but to entire community. City requests FPC to assist in investigation or conduct own investigation."

PTX 2987, Response to Mayor Stokes by the Federal Bureau of Investigation, regarding his request for a probe: "...No investigation... warranted at this time."

"After the blackout, CEI sent salesmen door-to-door"

PTX 1790, 4 January 1964, CEI Commercial Sales Dept. Report: "Commercial Sales Department Planning project re: solicitation of Muny customers."

PTX 79, CEI Memo, 25 June 1969, "During the last year we continued to pursue our plan of selectively selling Muny conversions. In 1969 industrial and Muny conversions totaled $252,000, the largest in our company's history..."

PTX 112, 9 October 1969, "CEI had a net gain in all aspects of Muny competition of 381 customers and $469,305 EAR (Estimated Annual Revenue)."

PTX 141, 7 January 1971, CEI Memo: Muny to CEI Conversion Chart. "For the year 1970, CEI has net gain in Muny meter displacements...of 1,472 customers and $834,425 in annual revenues."

PTX 70, 15 June 1972, This document demonstrates CEI's execution of their 'conversion' strategy: CEI memo from Commercial Sales Department: Prompt and effective follow-up by salesmen on inquiries after recent Muny outages contributed to the above goal results, i.e. conversions exceeding goals.

PTX 1769, 15 February 1970, CEI Memo Hoehn to Zitsman: Report titled: "Why do Customers Convert to Muny?"

PTX 1747, 5 April 1973, City Memo Cristell to Hinchee: "Complaint re CEI sales reps' pressure tactics for switchover of service at Pentagon Plating Industries Inc, 7502 Carnegie Avenue."

PTX 2748, 1 May 1975, Letter, Pentagon Industries to Kudukis: "Report of tactics used by CEI to convert service."

"Free wiring? Just for switching to CEI?"

PTX 136, 14 March 1969, CEI Memo: "As the result of the extensive Muny outage Tuesday, March 11th, Commercial sales representatives converted 18 accounts for 306 KWD and $14,160 EAR..."

PTX 1770, 4 August 1970, CEI Memo, Farling to Gould: "Review of three conversions from Muny involving wiring allowances in excess of $1,000."

PTX 348, CEI Memo, 8 February 1971, "Estimate of EAR [Estimated Annual Revenue] per residential customer converted from MELP is $105."

PTX 123, CEI Memo: 25 March 1971, "We underwrite such wiring costs up to one-half of estimated annual revenues."

PTX 143, 6 January 1972, CEI saw the free wiring as being key to winning over Muny Light customers: "Muny to CEI Conversion Chart." CEI Memo, "The elimination (significant reduction) of CEI's Muny Displacement Wiring Modernization Program would have an adverse effect on displacement sales results."

PTX 260, CEI Memo, 1 August 1972, Chart: Expenditures for MELP Conversions 1969-1970-1971.

PTX 1772, 5 January 1973, CEI Memo, Greben to Gould: "Summary and chart illustrating Muny competition activities from '64 to '72."

PTX 165, 5 January 1973, CEI Conversion Chart, Muny to CEI Conversions, 1960–1964; 1965–1972.

PTX 261, 12 February 1973, Muny to CEI Conversions, Customers and Revenues; also Muny-CEI conversions. In 1971, largely as a result of blackouts, CEI gained 782 customers from Muny, and Muny gained 80 customers from CEI.

PTX 1748, 14 July 1974, Letter, Oppman to Cristell: "Complaint re instance of CEI's hard feelings because of switch to Muny." In 1972, CEI gained 1,097 customers from Muny, and Muny gained 95 customers from CEI. Muny Light lost almost a million dollars in customer revenue over the two year period.

"Ohio Constitution which gave cities the right to grant utility franchises"

The Ohio Constitution, Article XVIII, Section 4: "Any municipality may acquire, construct, own, lease and operate within or without its corporate limits, any public utility the products or service of which is or is to be supplied to the municipality or its inhabitants, and may contract with others for any such product or service. The acquisition of any such public utility may be by condemnation or otherwise, and a municipality may acquire thereby the use of, or full title to, the property and franchise of any company or person supplying to the municipality or its inhabitants the service or product of any such utility." The Ohio Constitution, Article XVIII, Section 12, states: "Any municipality which acquires, constructs or extends any public utility and desires to raise money for such purposes may issue mortgage bonds therefore beyond the general limit of bonded indebtedness prescribed by law; provided that such mortgage bonds issued beyond the general limit of bonded indebtedness... shall not impose any liability upon such municipality but shall be secured only upon the property and revenues of such public utility..."

"I discovered a city report"

The Proposed Acquisition of CEI by the City of Cleveland. 28 April 1943.

PTX 2863, MELP Graph: "Compares generating capacity of CEI and MELP, 1915 through 1942."

PTX 2728, 1931 article from issues of "Public Ownership," June-July, 1931: Titled: "Cleveland's Municipal Light Plant Still Pesters Power Trust," ibid. "That such large profits are possible is due largely to a reduction in the cost of capital."

PTX 3093, (Excerpt) Ohio Constitution: "Article XVII, Section 4, Acquisition of public utility; contract for service condemnation."

PTX 3093, (Excerpt) Ohio Constitution: "Article XVIII, Sect. 6, Municipal Corporations, Sale of Surplus."

"The takeover lost by a single vote"

Re: 1943 vote in City Council against acquiring CEI.

"Muny's a threat to their profits"

PTX 487, CEI Memo, 29 March 1957, The MELP's rates are too low for non-public customers [10% - 25% below CEI's].

PTX 489, CEI Memo, 9 April 1963, "MELP should raise its rates to private customers to the level of CEI's rates.

"CEI's efforts were spurred by its large advertising budget"

25 November 1970, *WKYC-TV3*, a sympathetic editorial, #128: "Sell Muny Light."

PTX 707, Bridges Report discusses placing company-written propaganda in local media.

"Here's Muny's system"

PTX 2064 Map: MELP (generating and substations and transmission line).

PTX 2077 Diagram: Illustrates generation, transmission and distribution.

PTX 2065 Map: MELP service area showing census tracts.

PTX 2066 Map: MELP service area and CEI service area.

PTX 2067 Bar graph: Illustrates magnitude of MELP kWh sales and number of MELP customers by class. [1960-1977]

"Problems along the line anywhere"

PTX 2162, 1970 "Department of Public Utilities, Division of Utilities Fiscal Control, Light and Power Financial Report."

PTX 2516, 1970 Annual Report: "CEI Annual Report for 1970."

And also PTX 2425, 18 November 1970, City Memo Bergman to Gaskill: "Report which covers the recent operations, finances and problems of the Division of Light and Power."

PTX 2070 Graph: Illustrates net number of

MELP customers lost or gained to or from CEI, 1960-1977.

PTX 2072 Graph: Illustrates percentage of MELP customers by certain classifications switching to CEI for stated reasons, 1960 – 1973.

"Mayor Stokes, who had advocated the sale of Muny Light"

PTX 334, 13 March 1969, CEI Memo, "...The present Mayor Stokes has taken the position that Muny Light should be sold..."

PTX 1023, 30 December 1969, CEI Memo, Briggs to Besse. "Attached letter to Mayor Stokes recommending sale of Muny to CEI."

"Their plan...is to raise Muny Light's rates to CEI's level"

PTX 487, 29 March 1957, "The MELP's rates are too low..."

PTX 494, 18 October 1963, CEI Memo: "MELP should save a $12,000,000 investment in a coal-fired generator by buying power from CEI instead. CEI would require a rate equalization."

PTX 628, 29 July 1960, "... report of the Muny acquisition practices of other companies based on comprehensive review of interviews with these companies. Usually the Muny's rates are higher than the rates of the acquiring company."

PTX 631, 12 April 1965, Speech, Howley to Turk [City Council Utilities] Committee:... "Muny people have been talking about and endorsing interconnections for years. The fact remains they continue to run an isolated plant....CEI's interconnections already tie us into 1,800 REA's and municipal systems – but not to Muny..... Sale of Muny would be in agreement with the national trend. Interconnection with CEI and rate equalization is another proposal that deserves consideration."

PTX 45, 25 July 1966, "CEI Will Not Agree... Unless Muny Rates are Raised."

PTX 171, 6 August 1973, CEI Memo: "Survey on why residential customers switch to Muny. Low cost is the main reason."

PTX 172, 22 October 1973, CEI Memo: "Why residential customers convert to Muny. Low cost is main reason."

"characterized the [permanent] interconnect as being 'in the public interest'"

PTX 2861, 13 July 1966, *Cleveland Press* Article, 13 July 1966: "Lindseth renews Proposal to Link CEI, Muny Light."

PTX 513, 14 July 1966, Letter, Besse to Mayor Locher: "Interconnection is in the public interest..."

PTX 531, 27 February 1968, CEI Memo Re: "Arguments that might be made in support of the 'philosophy against interconnection with MELP." (i) "As an independent system, MELP is protected against the cascading effect of faults on other systems."

PTX 50, 17 June 1969, "...we have been successful in finding a way to give MELP limited, temporary help without parallel operation."

PTX 754, 19 April 1971, CEI memo which summarizes the load transfer agreement between CEI and MELP. "Under no condition will the CEI system and the MELP system be paralleled at any voltage..."

"we end up with more blackouts"

PTX 1522, 7 September 1971, City [of Cleveland] Report: "Summary of system outage 7 September 1971."

PTX 1523, *Cleveland Press*, 8 September 1971, "Three of Six Boilers Out - - Muny Crisis Grows."

PTX 1524, *Cleveland Press,* 9 September 1971, "Damaged Boiler Expected Back in Service Monday."

PTX 2431, 10 November 71,Hinchee to Mayor's Task Force: "Special report for the Mayor's Task Force regarding the Division of Light and Power."

"denying Muny Light an interconnect, while touting its own reliability"

PTX 288, Letter CEI to Villa Angela Academy: "The most reliable electric system service available in the northeast Ohio area is furnished by the Illuminating Company. Reliability is assured by a modern, well-maintained electric system backed up by interconnection with adjacent state and interstate utilities..." "Your alternative choice is a public power system which has sustained increasingly more frequent power failures due to equipment and system breakdown in recent years."

PTX 291, 10 February 1972, CEI Memo: Muny Outage shut down the SIFCO plant for four hours. "Monday's MELP outages not only shut down their plant for 4 hours, but also prevented their boilers from operating. In near zero weather this could endanger their entire steam distribution system."

CEI Budget Planning Report for Year 1971, "...new transmission facilities to allow increased interchange of power between the systems...mutual aid in emergencies and storms, economical exchange of power, and improved scheduling of generating units." p. 12.

"Muny needed to go through CEI's lines"

PTX 693, 27 June 1963, Letter CEI to City of Cleveland. "The proposed interconnection Cleveland-Painesville-Orville is unsound economically and from an engineering viewpoint. The kind of interconnection that makes sense is one with CEI."

PTX 3109, 11 July [date missing], Letter Chaney, Black and Veach, to Murphy, Squire Sanders: "Response to request to evaluate and be prepared to testify re feasibility of MELP having initiated construction of transmission lines before August 1973 to interconnect with other utility systems outside of Cleveland. Concludes such was feasible and beneficial to MELP."

"It was as if none of our meetings ever happened"

PTX 2853, 25 May 1971, Letter from Hinchee to Department of Justice: "...CEI has pretended to prepare engineering study and proposal for interconnection with the city...at April 23, 1971 meeting CEI advised that no firm planning for interconnection had been made..."

PTX 2582, 27 July 1971, CEI Memo, Loshing to Miller, et al.: "Enclosing minutes of CEI meeting with Muny at City Hall."

PTX 1518, 2 August 1971, City Memo, Hinchee to Gaskill: "Summary of attempts made to discuss engineering plans for interconnection since 7/8/71 meeting."

PTX 2848, 23 August 1972, City Memo, Hinchee to Hollington: "Response to request that list of items to be negotiated with CEI be submitted as soon as possible. Following items to be negotiated with CEI: settlement of overcharges for service from Feb. 1970 to present; 69kV synchronous operation prior to completion of 138kV installation; renewal of duplicate service - - clean up and make clear cut respective service areas - - CEI or City; stop CEI - - special subsidy of Muny customers; negotiate for firm power at not more than 7.5 mills to be delivered through the 138kV; negotiate transmission charges for delivery of 30 MW of PASNY power or delivery of 50 MW of power from OP system."

"CEI thwarted Muny's efforts"

PTX 2853, 25 May 1971, Letter, Hinchee to Department of Justice: States that Muny has tried to obtain source of power from Niagara – hydro project - - since 1967, unsuccessfully.

PTX 38, 30 August 1973, "CEI not willing to wheel PASNY Power."

PTX 35, 5 December 1974, "Companies express objection to wheeling as a license condition."

"American Municipal Power of Ohio"

PTX 795, 18 August 1972, CEI Memo, Lester & Blank to Bingham: "Creation of AMP-Ohio opens potential new power supply for Muny Light,"... "estimating that the cost to MELP for power purchased from AMP-Ohio would range from 5.7 to 11.8 mills per kilowatt hour."

"CAPCO utilities refused to let Muny Light join"

Central Area Power Coordinating Organization.

PTX 1, 510, 11 May 1971, Complaint: "City of Cleveland v. CEI, filed before the FPC..." City [seeking] emergency power and also giving it access to a power pool created by five power companies, called CAPCO, the Central Area Power Coordinating Organization.

PTX 2853, 25 May 1971, Letter, Hinchee to Department of Justice: States that Muny has tried to obtain source of power from Niagara – hydro project - - since 1967, unsuccessfully. City has tried to obtain interconnection with CEI as first step toward participation in CAPCO power pool but has been subverted by CEI... "CAPCO members had long sought to constrain the purchase of electric power by the Buckeye Cooperative so its members could benefit from lower-cost, wholesale electricity."

PTX 969, 15 June 1973, Letter, Munsch to Duff: "No meetings were held between CEI and the City relative to the City's admission to CAPCO. Attached letters show that the city requested certain documents and CEI was unable to comply."

PTX 970, 7 August 1973, Letter, Munsch to Olds: Copy of letter from City to CEI requesting admission to membership in CAPCO… "City requested certain documents and CEI was unable to comply."

PTX 197, 4/30/74, Toledo Edison Common Stock Prospectus: In September 1967, CAPCO was formed "to create a power pool in the interests of reliability and economy, with future additional generating requirements of the members to be provided by sharing in the largest units feasible for pool purposes, mutual support of power requirements and provision of bulk power transmission required for such purposes. Certain definite agreements to put the arrangements into operation have been completed and others are in the process of preparation… CAPCO members have acted in concert to obtain lowest possible fuel prices. The City of Cleveland has requested that it be admitted to participation in the CAPCO group. The City has been advised that the participation of a municipality is not practical."

"CEI has been measuring us for years"

PTX 485, (1964), "This is a legal memo dealing with the disposition of funds obtained on the sale by a municipality of capital assets… discussing how the sale of MELP for $60 million could result in lower city property tax rates."

PTX 691, (undated), CEI Memo: "Cleveland is in a perennial financial crisis. There are alternatives to (a) city income tax…[the sale of MELP]."

PTX 2640, 12 May 1960, CEI Memo, Kender to Rudolph: "Cost of efforts to compete with Muny."

PTX 31, May 1960, [advocating non-growth of Painesville, Ohio municipal electric system in order to discourage municipal bond sales.]

PTX 505, 27 January 1966, "Solutions to city's financial plight…"

PTX 327, 27 January 1966, "City needs money…raise MELP rates…sell MELP…"

PTX 330, September 1967, CEI Memo, "Discussion re competition with Muny, blackouts and FPC compelling interconnection with Muny."

PTX 331, 8 April 1968, CEI Memo, mentions details of City Council Utilities Committee, Muny to install gas turbines, increase electric and street lighting rates; also mention of debt obligations.

PTX 252, October 1968, CEI '69 Planning Report – Industrial Sales Depts. Includes ten most important objectives, among which is preventing the installation of competitive total energy systems, isolated on site intensify efforts to convert existing competitive services.

PTX 1038, 21 May 1971, CEI Memo: "Information concerning Muny Light's debts to CEI."

PTX 2130, Table, Moore [CEI]: Net cash picture of MELP from 1960 through 1971. 1969 through 1971 is estimated.

PTX 1838, City Distribution List: [CEI] Lists of those to receive various Muny reports… Rudolph.

PTX 1805, 1 July 1975, Diagram: Illustrates relationship between CEI and MELP.

6. GRISANTI - THE PRIDE OF NOTRE DAME

"Urban renewal wrecked"

Cleveland Press, 9 March 1970, Page One, "Glamour Projects Hide Urban Housing Failure," by Paul Lilley

Cleveland Press, 10 March 1970, Page One, "Renewal is called a Sham," by Paul Lilley, [referencing quotes of Thomas Westropp, President of Women's Federal Savings and Loan.]

Cleveland Press, 11 March 1970, Page One, "East Woodland Mistake Typifies Urban Failures," by Paul Lilley.

7. THE MEANEST SON-OF-A-BITCH IN THE VALLEY

"frequently encountered antisemitism"

International Holocaust Remembrance Alliance, www.holocaustremembrance.com, [Excerpt] The unhyphenated spelling is favored by many scholars and institutions in order to dispel the idea that there is an entity 'Semitism' which 'anti-Semitism' opposes. Antisemitism should be read as a unified term so that the meaning of the generic term for modern Jew-hatred is clear. At a time of increased violence and rhetoric aimed toward Jews, it is urgent that there is clarity and no room for confusion or obfuscation when dealing with antisemitism.

8. WEISSMAN THE WIZARD

"The Minute," also known as God's Minute, is attributed to Dr. Benjamin Mays, the First Dean of the School of Religion at Howard University, January 1, 1934 – January 3, 1940; and the 6th President of Morehouse College, August 1, 1940 to July 1, 1967.

9. THE KISHKA CAPER

"Who Stole the Kishka?" Lyrics by Walter Solek, music by Walter Dana, popularized by polka artist Frankie Yankovic.

10. THE MEMO

"top radio news commentator ... attacking CEI"

Steve Clark Commentary, 28 October 1971, *WERE* Radio.

"Someone from CEI called my boss"

10 November 1971, Personal notes from author's conversation with Steve Clark.

Plain Dealer, 11 November 1971, "Fired for attack on CEI, says *WERE* man," by Brent Larkin.

"CEI has a new advertising campaign"

PTX 354, 12 July 1971, CEI Memo: "A rate increase by CEI will be viewed by the public 'as just another spiraling cost.' A program of 'the best bargain yet' type of advertising would be desirable."

"a...clandestine program to take over Muny Light"

PTX 707, 9 October 1970, CEI Memo, from RH Bridges to Lee Howley. "CEI Budget Planning Report for 1971."

PTX 3054, [predecessor document], 9 December 1959, CEI Memo, Fitzgerald and Greenslade to Howley: "Final Report – Planning Project PI-71-A: Utilization of Muny Light in Best Interests of [the Company]." [Note: The year given in file is 1959, the correct date is most likely 1969].

"using CEI's advertising dollars to subvert the media"

PTX 1040, 17 June 1970, CEI Memo King to Howley: "WJW-TV and Radio will air editorial advocating the sale of Muny Light."

PTX 1037, 1 July 1971, CEI Memo, Herrick to Howley "Attached copy of a TV Radio editorial urging the sale of Muny Light system."

PTX 1039, undated, Letters to Newspapers: Letters to the editors of the *Press* and *PD* concerning the Muny Light department.

PTX 1043, 4 February 1972, CEI Memo Bridges to Howley: Asks if Howley wants to talk to "... editorial writer of the *Plain Dealer*, to give him undated information on Muny Light." [Sensitive environmental issues, dealing with air and water pollution, were covered from CEI's perspective, according to Bridges, as was Muny Light.]

"what Steve's firing meant"

"The Spectre of 1984," 18 November 1971, Dennis Kucinich speech to Cleveland Council.

Scoop-Journal, 18 November 1971, "Kucinich Sees 'Spectre of 1984', Firing of radio newsman draws councilman's wrath."

"A Valentine for CEI," 14 February 1972, Kucinich speech to Cleveland City Council.

11. ANOTHER CHRISTMAS BLACKOUT

"a path toward economic prosperity for the city"

City of Cleveland, City Planning Commission, April, 1972, "An Expanded Electric Power System for the City of Cleveland." A Proposal to Acquire Cleveland Electric Illuminating Company's Facilities Within the City of Cleveland. A Supplement to the 1973-78 Capital Improvements Program.

City of Cleveland, City Planning Commission, April, 1972, "An Expanded Electric Power System for the City of Cleveland." A Proposal to Acquire Cleveland Electric Illuminating Company's Facilities Within the City of Cleveland. A Supplement to the 1973-78 Capital Improvements Program.

Plain Dealer, 26 April 1972, Page One, "Planners Urge CEI Acquisition by City

System," by William D. McCann

Plain Dealer, 27 April 1972, "City to Consider Takeover of CEI, Council Committee Plans Hearing."

"amid continual blackouts"

PTX 1536, *Cleveland Press*, 21 February 1972, "Muny Light Users Lose Power Again."

PTX 1955, 1972 Muny Light Report: "Muny Light major outages, 1972."

"CEI continued to feign cooperation"

PTX 831, 10 January 1972, Letter from City of Cleveland Law Director Richard Hollington to CEI's Lee Howley: "Hollington accuses CEI of giving only 'lip service' to the idea of a tie-in between the City and CEI." [As a result of continuing reliance on CEI for purchased power, Muny Light still owed CEI $750,000.]

PTX 1537, 28 February 1972, Letter, Hinchee to Nassikad: "Summary of enclosed proposed draft re interconnection."

PTX 1538, undated, CEI Memo, Williams: Report deals with proper interconnection with MELP.

PTX 1545, 3 March 1972, *Plain Dealer*: "Engineer Opposes Instant Muny Tie-In."

PTX 1539, 16 March 1972, Letter, Hollington to Hauser: Suggests CEI discuss cost of interconnection with Warren Hinchee.

PTX 1546, 30 March 1972, CEI Memo, System Planning Engineer: "Background, work required and schedule re 138 CEI-MELP synchronous interconnection."

PTX 1547, 30 March 1972, CEI Memo, System Planning Engineer: "Background, work required and schedule re: temporary CEI-MELP emergency non parallel interconnection."

PTX 2694, 11 April 1972, Letter Howley to Hollington: "Discussion of 69kV non-synchronous interconnection and City's reimbursement to CEI for costs incurred…" "…suggests initiation of enabling legislation and preparation of contract of temporary load transfer service beyond May 17 expiration date and for permanent 138kV interconnection; suggests some question that municipality can participate in Davis-Besse plant under Ohio law; reiterates CEI happy to work with City on above mentioned matters and emphasizes importance of receiving contract from City to reimburse CEI for its costs."

PTX 1550, 5 May 1972, City Memo, Department of Public Utilities, Kudukis, Hinchee, Labas: "Lists reasons why pole line inter-tie with CEI will be halted (copies of progress schedule enclosed)."

PTX 1552, 12 May 1972, Letter Hauser to Hollington: "Explanation of attached license agreement for right of way for 69kV temporary emergency transmission line across CEI's Lake Shore plant property."

PTX 2532, (Undated), City Memo, Labas to Kudukis: "Update re CEI's inability to provide either 69kV, sync, or non sync to the City, in direct testimony before the FPC; Appendix A- 138kV permanent sync. Muny-CEI-interconnection capital requirements included."

PTX 3048, 21 June 1972, City Ordinance 642-72 : "Emergency Ordinance authorizing and directing Director of Public Utilities to enter into contract without competitive bidding with CEI for necessary items of labor and material to be provided by CEI - - the construction of the temporary emergency interconnection between CEI and MELP as ordered by FPC."

PTX 1557, 30 June 1972, CEI Memo, Sener to Davidson: "Information relative to 6/27/72 *Plain Dealer* article re: engineering and construction requirements for the CEI-MELP tie line." See also City of Cleveland vs. Cleveland Electric Illuminating Company (CEI) (1975-1984), Case Summary by William B. Norris of Hahn Loeser, attorney for city in antitrust case, describing significance of CEI secret sponsorship of taxpayer's lawsuit to block the interconnection; Norris' personal papers, 24 October 1997.

"he huddled with CEI executives"

PTX 390, 19 May 1972, CEI Memo, attached statement by Councilman Gaul: "City Council is holding hearings on the future of MELP. MELP saved the city $900,000 - $1 million in street lighting in 1970"… CEI also included in this memo attachments to Gaul's statement: "MELP net income and (showing steadily declining profits until 1969 and then steadily increasing losses through 1972); MELP Changes in Cost per kWh; MELP Power Plant Maintenance expense; MELP total Customers (down from about 58,000 in 1963 to about 53,000 in 1970); Estimate of 1971 and 1972 Net Income."

PTX 2102, *"Statement by Gaul to the Utilities*

Committee concerning the Municipal Light Plant," 18 May 1972, Speech, Chairman Francis E. Gaul: Exhibits attached showing MELP's Profit and Loss, Changes in Cost per kWh, newspaper editorials, maintenance expense, total number of customers, estimate of 1971 and 1972 income.

PTX 391, 25 May 1972, CEI Memo: "Cleveland City Council passed an emergency ordinance to issue $3 million in notes in anticipation of issuance of bonds for improving the street lighting system. Councilman Gaul attempted to amend the ordinance to require MELP to pay principal and interest on all obligations bonds issued for capital improvement of street lighting or for expansion of MELP plant."

"Hinchee...staunchly defended Muny Light"

PTX 2104, 29 June 1972, Warren Hinchee: "Report to the Council Committee on Public Utilities," responding to the Gaul statement of 18 May 1972.

Exhibits include: an April, 1972 Proposal to Acquire CEI's facilities within the City of Cleveland; a supplement to a, "Review of Citizens League Report - - Sept. 1964" by Vincent DeMelto dated 23 March 1965; a history of the Cleveland Muny Light Plant, a special report for the Mayor's Task Force, prepared by Warren Hinchee dated 10 November 1971; a CEI Memo regarding the Budget Planning Report for the year 1971 by the Public Information Department; a City Memo regarding the Operations, Finances and Problems of the Division of Light and Power, dated 18 November 1970; a preliminary report concerning financing requirements for the Division of Light and Power, prepared by C. M. Bednar; CEI Tables regarding Sales of Electricity by Various Communities; a draft of an Emergency Ordinance to require use of Municipal Utilities at Urban Renewal and Public Housing Sites; a page from Moody's Public Utility Manual about CEI; a newspaper article headlined "CEI Reported Weighing Move to Suburban Headquarters" dated 29 April 1972.

PTX 2103, 20 July 1972, Report, Warren Hinchee: "A Supplemental Report to the Council Committee on Public Utilities," supplementing the original report of 29 June 1972. Exhibits include: a comparative Balance Sheet for MELP for 1967 and 1968, a condensed Income Statement, Projections regarding Future Load Characteristics, Memo re Craft Rates Negotiations, and Job Descriptions.

"he tried to knock Hinchee out"

Plain Dealer, 27 November 1972, "Gaul's charges called blow to Muny" [Note: Hinchee was subsequently cleared of any conflict.]

"U.S. Senator Lee Metcalfe of Montana"

Overcharge, by U.S. Senator Lee Metcalfe and Vic Rienemer, "How Electric Utilities Exploit and Mislead the Public and What You Can Do About It." D. McKay Co., 1967.

PTX 1647, (undated), pamphlet, Senator Metcalfe: "Summary of costs of electricity and how overcharges can be reduced." A pamphlet about the unfair pricing, and sharp practices of utility monopolies.

"People have a right to own an electric system"

PTX 2422, City Document: Showing the number of MELP Customers from 1961 through 1978. [Less CEI customers through a government-owned utility meant lower rates, significant because over 2000 publicly-owned electric systems in America were providing power at rates lower than nearby investor-owned utilities.]

"Forbes and I may have been destined"

Cleveland Press, 22 August 1967, "Young Foe of Forbes Backs Council Cut," by Norm Mlachak.

Cleveland Press, 22 August 1967, City Hall Beat, by Norm Mlachak. "From the Mouths of Babes…" "Forbes blundered into a debate with the college boy candidate, during Legislation Committee hearings, provided him with a forum he would not otherwise have had and ended up literally talking to himself."

"Sell it. Now. Yes. Double 'yes'"

Plain Dealer, 7 March 1972, Page One, "Council Against Light Plant Sale." "…most vociferous against the sale was Dennis J. Kucinich, D-7, who said, 'Unlike some of my colleagues who have joined the Lee C. Howley-for-lunch-bunch, I am unalterably opposed to selling the plant. I will not see it given away to privileged business interests…' On the other end of the spectrum of opinion is George L. Forbes, D-20, the council majority leader. 'Sell it now,' he said. 'Yes, double yes. I am opposed to keeping it. It is unprofitable.'"

12. THE GREAT WHITE FATHER

"the Growth Association's pet project"

Cleveland Magazine, November, 1972, Jetport: "Dammit, Air and Water Will Mix."

13. CAMPAIGNING TO END THE WAR

"unjustly fired by WERE for his on-air criticisms of CEI"

Cleveland Press, 24 July 1972, "Steve Clark wins suit against *WERE* Radio."

Plain Dealer, 25 July 1972, "Clark Winner in Arbitration."

14. CITY HALL AND THE MOB

"police were involved in corruption"

Plain Dealer, 7 March 1974, Page One, "City Police Tied to Burglary Ring," by I-Team.

Cleveland Press, 7 March 1974, "$900 in soggy bills found in police car after robbery."

Cleveland Press, 8 March 1974, "Says police demanded payoffs."

Plain Dealer, 9 March 1974, Page One, "Police Drinking After Bar Hours," by I-Team.

Plain Dealer, 18 March 1974, Page One, "Bar Payoff to Police Charged: 'Paid $200 a week' says owner," by I-Team.

Cleveland Press, 13 March 1974, Page One, "Rademaker denies Perk transferred vice unit officer."

Plain Dealer, 13 March 1974, Page One, "Perk thwarted vice clampdown; Reassigned sergeant to traffic unit," by I-Team.

Plain Dealer, 16 March 1974, "Perk, Rini deny role in officer's transfer."

Plain Dealer, 17 March 1974, Page One, "Court Payoffs are Disclosed," by I-Team.

"the godfatherly elder would bid them"

Interview with Jack Schulman, Law Director City of Cleveland, 1977-1979.

"police...protect prostitution and high stakes gambling"

Plain Dealer, 10 March 1974, Page One, "Police Shut Eyes to Prostitution," by I-Team.

Plain Dealer, 11 March 1974, Page One, "Thefts, Drinking, Pay-offs for protection; Patrolmen cite Police Vice," by I-Team.

Plain Dealer, 12 March 1974, Page One, "Vice Officer Named in Payoff; Accused of protecting prostitution," by I-Team.

Cleveland Press, 13 March 1974, "Payoff Charge jars policeman, he denies it."

Plain Dealer, 16 March 1974, "Prostitutes apartment rent being paid by policeman."

"I often raised questions"

"*Kucinich Vice Study*," 5 April 1974, Statement by Councilman Dennis J. Kucinich.

Plain Dealer, 6 April 1974, Page One, "Kucinich demands Perk fire Rademaker,"by Tom Brazaitis.

"The city moved to shut down places ... pornographic movies"

Plain Dealer, 24 March 1974, "City vows to shut smut shows; Prosecutor launches campaign."

"clergymen to investigate police corruption"

Plain Dealer, 15 March 1974, Page One, "Perk Picks Clergy for Police Probe," by Joseph L. Wagner.

Plain Dealer, 24 March 1974, Page One, "U.S. funds for 'God Squad' lets Perk laugh at its critics," by Harry Stainer.

"legislation to deal with police corruption"

Ord. No. 506-74. By Councilman Kucinich, An emergency ordinance repealing Section 1.4776 of the Codified Ordinances of the City of Cleveland and enacting new sections 1.477601 – 1.447618 inclusive, establishing a Commission on Ethics and Corruption Control.

Personal notes of Dennis Kucinich, 20 May 1974.

Letter from Lockwood Thompson, Chairman of Board of Ethics of City of Cleveland, to Councilman Dennis Kucinich, 3 April 1975.

Plain Dealer, 25 January 1977, "Forbes to propose an end to Ethics Board," Pg A-8.

"Rini... [Kucinich] 'might get roughed up'"

Plain Dealer, Today by Judy Sammon, Column. [Note: "The mayor's labor advisor, Michael P. Rini, and Councilman Dennis Kucinich D-7, are what some call 'incompatible.' Rini, who feels he is constantly being blamed for everything that goes wrong at the Hall, is so fearful that Kucinich might get roughed up that he mused recently about hiring two bodyguards for the bantam-weight councilman."]

"Perk...called upon citizens to dump their garbage in public parks"

Plain Dealer, 28 April 1974, Page One, "Mayor names dump sites amid councilmen's cries."

Cleveland Press, 29 April 1974, Page One, "Council refuses to act as garbage piles up," by Jim Marino."

Cleveland Press, 29 April 1974, Page One, "Council urged to end strike," by Jim Marino.

Plain Dealer, 1 May 1974, Page One, "Councilmen to seek order halting use of park dumps," by Robert G. McGruder.

Plain Dealer, 1 May 1974, Perk goes to court to defend mini-dumps, by W. James Van Vliet. [Note: "City Health Director Jack C. Robertson told the judge that a health emergency does exist... He said garbage is piling up in the city at a rate of three million pounds per day, and he estimated that the city has accumulated 45 million pounds of garbage since the strike began."]

Plain Dealer, 2 May 1974, Page One, "Teamsters OK city pact, ending 17-day trash strike," by John Nussbaum and Joseph L. Wagner.

Cleveland Press 2 May 1974, Page One, "Garbage pickups begin," by Brent Larkin.

"blackout[s] caused Muny Light customers to switch"

PTX 2165, Cleveland Financial Report, 1973: "Department of Public Utilities, Division of Utilities Fiscal Control, Light and Power Financial Report."

PTX 2519, 1973 Annual Report: "CEI Annual Report for 1973." Muny continued to experience outages the previous year.

PTX 1956, 1973 Muny Light Report: Muny Light major outages, 1973.

PTX 1957, 1974 Muny Light Report: Muny Light major outages, 1974.

PTX 63, 10 January 1973, CEI Memo/Report: Statistical appendix CEI replacing Muny customers, 271 in 1972 and 174 in 1971; CEI replacing Muny, estimated annual earnings, 1972, $268,856; 1971 $207,550.

PTX 400, 6 May 1974, CEI Memo: "The rate gap." The average residential customer paid 12.6% lower rates than CEI.

PTX 177, 27 February 1974, CEI Memo: "The rate differential between Muny and CEI has not been reduced to an insignificant amount."

PTX 2462, (Undated), Table: "Entitled "CEI and MELP Residential Bills winter and summer months by amount of monthly electric use - - 1972 – 1979."

"The ... (FPC) finally ordered CEI to proceed with the interconnect"

PTX 1569, 11 January 1973, FPC Opinion and Order: "City of Cleveland vs. CEI before FPC; Opinion and Order in Interconnection Proceeding."

PTX 1570, 18 January 1973, CEI is "in agreement" to comply.

PTX 1575, 9 March 1973, FPC Opinion and Order: "Recommendations re CEI-MELP before FPC opinion and Order denying rehearing and stay."

"warning its customers"

PTX 288, July 1970 and 18 August 1971, Letters, CEI to Villa Angela Academy: "Your alternative choice is a public power system which has sustained increasingly more frequent power failures due to equipment and system breakdowns in recent years." [After several efforts to try to dissuade officials at Villa Angela, CEI decided on a new approach - - it would go directly to 'top officials in the [Catholic] Diocesan hierarchy' to discuss 'non-economic' advantage of CEI.]

PTX 305, CEI Memo 3 April 1973, "... they stated that they decided to stay with CEI because of 'service reliability' and other customer services even though the rates may be slightly higher."

"the company pursued its nuclear ambitions,"

PTX 1883, 22 July 1974, "Construction Agreement: 'Construction agreement between CEI, DL, OE, PP and TE re Perry Units Nos. 1 and 2." [applied for a license to construct two units of the Perry Nuclear Power plant.]

"[CEI] blocked $9.8 million ... to repair Muny's generators"

PTX 2384, 10 May 1974, Official [CEI] Statement: "Concerning the issuance of $9.8 million in temporary electric light and power plant and system subordinate mortgage revenue bonds City of Cleveland."

[Note: Comments section of PTX index says "Hauser ($9.8 Million proffer)." The city brought forward the bond issue but needed the approval of City Council.]

PTX 2951, 11 July 1974, City Ordinance No. 2104-72: Ordinance to issue and sell temporary electric light and power plant and systems subordinate mortgage revenue bonds of City in sum of $9,800,000....

For further reference see:

Plain Dealer, 1 September 1975, Page One, "Perk's Promises," by Joseph L. Wagner. "... The city has run up a $5 million debt by purchasing power from CEI. Perk and [Finance Director] Campanella blame the decline on Council's failure to approve $9.8 million in capital improvements bond issue for 18 months. Once the issue was authorized, however, investors could not be found."

15. BLOOD

"A bombshell"

Cleveland Press, 25 February 1975, Page One, "CEI doesn't want Muny Light Plant," by Brent Larkin.

Plain Dealer, 26 February 1975, "Kudukis Fears Ploy; CEI Turns Chilly to Muny Light Deal," CEI's Lee Howley quoted: "We have no designs on the Municipal Light Plant. We don't think there is anything to buy."

"investigating CEI for possible antitrust violations"

PTX 1880, 26 December 1968, Construction Agreement: "Construction agreement between TE and CEI re Davis-Besse Unit No. 1."

As part of the application process, CEI was required to submit to an antitrust review by the Atomic Safety and Licensing Board of the Nuclear Regulatory Commission (NRC). The NRC, created by the Energy Re-organization Act of 1974, was formerly known as the Atomic Energy Commission.

PTX 3035, 10 April 1974, "Excerpt from PUCO Direct Examination of Karl Rudolph."

PTX 1276, Information in Support of Application for construction of Davis-Besse Power Plant. Information requested by the Attorney General from Antitrust review. Submitted by TE (Toledo Edison), DL (Dayton Light), CEI (Cleveland Electric Illuminating), OE (Ohio Edison) and PP (Pennsylvania Power) pertaining to an application to build and operate the Davis-Besse power plant.

"Muny Light is losing money"

Plain Dealer, 2 April 1975, Page One, "2nd Group dealing for Muny Light; Foes of sale report profit at Plant," by Andrew M. Juniewicz. "The generator, which was destroyed by what experts believe was sabotage in 1973, produces 50 megawatts."

PTX 2165, 1973 Cleveland Financial Report: Department of Public Utilities, Division of Utilities Fiscal Co and Control, Light and Power Financial Report.

PTX 2997: Cleveland Financial Report, 1974.

PTX 2166, 1975 Cleveland Financial Report: Department of Public Utilities, Division of Utilities Fiscal Control, Light and Power Financial Report.

"intensified its media advertising and its political expenditures"

PTX 2457, 25 January 1974, Official Response of CEI to PUCO: "CEI's response to the Public Utilities Commission of Ohio." Entry re: Total dollars spent for advertising, and a description of all types of advertising.

PTX 1839, 30 April 1976, and 27 September 1976, CEI Conference Reports: Conference reports deal with CEI advertising. Attached report is titled 'CEI, Public Relations Advertising Program, 1975;' [and political expenditures, to set the stage for an all-out attack on Muny Light.]

PTX 1846, CEI Study: List of expenditures for civic, political and miscellaneous activities, Account 426-4, 1974 to 1977.

"Muny's greatest peril was the blackouts"

PTX 1958, 1975 Muny Light Report: 'Muny Light major outages, 1975.'

PTX 3012, 'Types of Outages Reported in Major Outage Reports.'

PTX 2402, MELP major outage reports, Jan-December, 1975: 'Reports re major outages January through December, 1975.'

"FPC dug in, and finally ordered"

Plain Dealer, 10 April 1975, "City, CEI Sign Agreement for System," page 6-B

PTX 1631, Agreement, 17 April 1975, CEI-Cleveland agreement for installation of 138kV synchronous interconnection. [the 138kv tie-in would replace a temporary tie, in poor condition.]

"Gaul declared, threatening a taxpayer's suit"

Cleveland Press, 17 April 1975, "Gaul Plans to Block $13 million for Muny Light Repairs" by Walter Johns, Jr.

"Kudukis fretted, because a lawsuit by Gaul"

Plain Dealer, 3 April 1975, An Editorial: "Muny Light Still a Disaster."

"the FPC also ordered CEI"

Cleveland Press, 21 May 1975, "Cheaper N.Y. Power is Closer for Muny."

"CEI sought yet another rate increase"

Cleveland Press, 13 June 1975, "Jolt from CEI." [Note: In their calculations of the value of their system as a basis for a rate increase request, CEI used a formula called RCN [LD], "reconstruction cost new minus depreciation," which let CEI cost out all of their capital assets, no matter when they were built, at the present day cost of replacing them, as if new. If CEI acquired Muny Light under this formula, CEI customers would have to pay for Muny as if it were newly constructed, even if CEI bought it from the city for a sharply discounted price.]

Cleveland Press, 13 June 1975, "Cleveland electric rates are the sixth highest in the nation."

"a $330 million antitrust damage suit"

City of Cleveland vs. The Cleveland Electric Illuminating Company, No C75-560 (N.D. Ohio, filed July 1, 1975.)

[Note: Duquesne Light, Ohio Edison, Pennsylvania Power and Toledo Edison were also named in the lawsuit, as having prevented Muny from getting the benefits of coordinated operations.]

See also communication between attorney William B. Norris, of the firm of Hahn Loeser (representing the City of Cleveland) and Dr. Harold H. Wein, consulting economist for the antitrust case, who calculated the damages done by CEI to Muny Light.

Noteworthy from Dr. Wein, "CEI refused to provide a permanent synchronous interconnection to MELP until May, 1975. Instead, during the period from February, 1970 to at least December, 1972, CEI provided only a load transfer service which had the following characteristics:

(a) CEI required MELP to use all of its own generating capacity before power would be made available through the load transfer points;

(b) Power was provided at the load transfer points by means of a dead load transfer, which meant that an outage occurred each time MELP took power from CEI and each time that service of MELP customers was returned to MELP..." (16 July 1979, case correspondence.)

16. THE GOLDEN CITY

"As the city's debt obligations soared"

[Gary] *'Kucinich Report on the Sale of City Assets,"* 7 July 1977, by Gary J. Kucinich.

"Four years later it was $369 million"

Cleveland City Record, 1972, "City's debt $323.7 million in January, 1972." [The Government Research Institute reported that Mayor Perk had added $46 million to the city's debt, which now totaled $369 million. Instead of going to the voters to approve new financing, Perk was borrowing without voter approval.]

Cleveland City Record, 1975, [City's debt $369 million in January 1975.]

Plain Dealer, 5 April 1975, Page One, "Perk Offers Slim Budget on Capital Improvements," by Joseph L. Wagner. "...funds such as the $33 million from the sale of the sewer system, which could have been used for capital improvements were spent, instead, for operating expenses"

Cleveland Press, 8 April 1975, Council President Forbes quoted: "When Perk leaves office, I pity his successor. Our indebtedness is so high we may never pay it off."

"the city's financial experts pronounced ... Cleveland financially sound"

Plain Dealer, 12 July 1975, Page One, "City is financially sound, study finds," by Thomas W. Gerdel. [See also: Greater Cleveland Growth Association report: 4 September 1975.]

Plain Dealer, 5 December 1975, "Expert rates city fiscally sound," by John E. Bryan, Financial Editor, page 7-C.

"Brookings Institution study raised doubts"

Plain Dealer, 2 December 1975, "Experts say city near fiscal crisis," by Robert Crater. [Brookings Institution study on economic conditions in selected American cities.]

Cleveland Press, 10 December 1975, [Harries said that a Brookings Institution study showed Cleveland's central city to be worst after Newark NJ, in income, housing, jobs and other economic factors.] "City Finances," a study by Professor John Burke and Professor Edric Weld.

See also: *Plain Dealer*, 28 September 1978, "Study says city lost half its stores from '50 to '74," by William F. Miller. "Much of the problem was a result of merchants abandoning the downtown and neighborhoods for the suburbs...."

Cleveland Magazine, 1 January 1976, "Mayor Ralph J. Perk and the Politics of Decay," by Edward P. Whelan, notes "there are problems looming in the future, when the city will have to convert all its short-term notes into long term bonds, - - in essence, extending its loan payments."

"Wall Street ratings agencies"

Wall Street Journal, 28 November 1975, "Credit Rating Firms Did an Inadequate Job, Sen. Eagleton Claims Moody's and Standard and Poors Overlooked NY's Shaky Finances." [Senator Thomas Eagleton commented: It is "close to a crime that Congress has continued to allow municipal bonds and securities to be marketed like cars..."]

"America's Bombing Capitol"

Plain Dealer, 6 February 1977, "Cleveland's Bombing Capitol: Rackets and labor bombings here highest in U.S."

Plain Dealer, 27 February 1977, "Study says imaginary crime hurts downtown Cleveland," by William F Miller, page 17

Cleveland Press, Page One, 18 May 1977, "2 Men Hunted in Nardi Bombing."

Cleveland Press, 18 May 1977, "Nardi Bomb Linked to Power Struggle," page A-4.

Plain Dealer, 19 May 1977, "Cleveland Bomb City Reputation Unwanted," Editorial, page A-20.

17. LAW FIRM DOUBLE DEALS CITY

"virtually a shadow government"

Cleveland Magazine, 1 June 1975, "Big Law Firms: Faceless Men with a Lock on the City," by Edward P. Whelan. "Some say that this law firm, in fact, functions almost as an unelected shadow government, particularly in its influence upon municipal bonding, a highly technical area of law in which Squire, Sanders enjoys a virtual monopoly in Ohio...referred to in the Ohio House of Representatives as "Squire, Sanders & God." Its power flows largely from its "municipal law department" ... directly involved in organizing and counseling the efforts of state and local government." Squire Sanders "is also counsel to CEI, earning a total of $357,580 from the company last year." [Two top lawyers John Lansdale, Jr. and Ralph M. Besse - - are members of CEI's board of directors, and Besse is a former president of the power company.]

"...about three years ago when the [city] decided to issue $9.8 million in bonds for repair of Muny Light facilities, John B. Brueckel, a senior bond specialist at Squire, Sanders, drafted the necessary city legislation for the bonds, according to former Councilman Francis E. Gaul, then chairman of council's utilities committee."

"In the view of Herbert R. Whiting, who was then Cleveland law director and is now a domestic relations judge, Squire Sanders' involvement in the Muny bond project was ethically unsound. He was 'quite disturbed' because of the firm's longstanding ties to Muny's competitor, Cleveland Electric Illuminating Company."

"...sources in the city's utilities department charge privately that the Squire, Sanders-written legislation severely hampered efforts by the city to sell the Muny bonds. None of them has yet been sold."

Cleveland Press, 18 February 1976, State Representative Arthur Wilkowski of Toledo, "because they are calling the shots on the sale of bonds... I think they have it within their power to stop a bond sale, a perfectly legitimate bond sale."

"trying to knock Squire Sanders out of the case"

City moves to disqualify Squire Sanders as counsel before 20 November 1975. [Note: NRC hearings commenced on 8 December 1975.]

"Squire Sanders had a conflict of interest"

Nuclear Regulatory Commission, Atomic Safety and Licensing Board, In the Matter of ... The Cleveland Electric Illuminating Company. Docket Nos. 50-440A, 50-441A, Memorandum and Order of the Board Suspending Counsel from Further Participation as Attorney in these Proceedings." P. 12

Cleveland Press, 20 January 1976, "Licensing Board suspends Squire Sanders."

Plain Dealer, 21 January 1976, Page One, "Squire Sanders Accused of Conflict in CEI Case," by George P. Rasanen. By a 2-1 vote, the Licensing Board of the NRC suspended Squire Sanders from representing CEI. Squire Sanders "told CEI of financial advice given the city in a 1972-1973 bond issue affecting Muny Light...Since 1965 information supplied by city officials to Squire Sanders lawyers had been made available to members of Squire Sanders who represented CEI....For nearly 60 years all city financial documents, including budget information, bond issue status, debt retirement, ability to repay debts, tax receipts information, accounts receivable and accounts payable were in control of and monitored daily by Squire Sanders which had control over all matters effecting the issuance and the renewal and the refinancing of all municipal bonds."

[Note: Also on Page One of the *Plain Dealer* on that day: "$40 Million Plan to Expand the [Cleveland Zoo]."

"Davis has declared war"

Testimony of Cleveland Law Director James B. Davis before the Atomic Safety and Licensing Board of the NRC. In the matter of ...The Cleveland Electric Illuminating Company, et al. Docket Nos 50-440A, 50-441A.

NRC Transcripts 4334, James B. Davis: "We have lawyers here who had the broadest kind of financial understanding of all the city's affairs... Their total awareness, their exclusive handling of the bond financing gives them knowledge and insight about that city's affairs that we feel is entirely relevant to these proceedings."

NRC Transcripts, page 4436, James B. Davis: "They handled not just the 1972 financing of the light plant, but a 1968 light plant financing, prior light plant financing, street lighting finances that have an obvious impact on the general fund and MELP... [Squire Sanders] ... "the financial counselors on all but a very few bond issues down through the years, including the entire finances of the city light plant."

NRC Transcripts, page 4438, James B. Davis: "Squire Sanders having had the background of the financing, knows the entire details. We are talking about a law firm of 180 lawyers. They are now representing our main competitors against us with all the knowledge they have gleaned over all their years of representation of the city."

NRC Transcripts, page 4453, James B. Davis: "Yes. But we have to guess at that. Let's turn to page 26. I'm reading from the Squire Sanders brief on page 26. The city argues in its supplemental brief that Squire Sanders, in the person of John Lansdale, has provided CEI with legal advice adverse to the interest of the Muny electric light plant and particularly that he has provided legal advice on antitrust and competitive parties..."

NRC Transcripts, page 4456, James B. Davis: "I will not restrict it to one isolated thing. The handling of the bond issue through 1972 and 1973 by Mr. Brueckel on the one hand for the City of Cleveland, and here in 1973 is Mr. Lansdale voting to deny us PASNY power which has a direct bearing upon the future of the light plant, the salability of those bonds."

NRC Transcripts, page 4458, James B. Davis: "It is not Mr. Brueckel's work for us in the 1972 bond issue alone. It is not any single one of the matters that were felt significant by the prior panel. It is the totality of their representation, their vast sweep of our affairs, the many lawyers that have been involved in our financial affairs in the light plant and in our general fund accounts..." "We have every reason to believe they sabotaged that bond issue."

NRC Transcripts, page 4467: Mr. Reilley, [Question by Commissioner] "How would those things relate to the bond work this firm was doing for the city?" Mr. Davis: [Response] "In the sense that because they had access to the finances of the MELP they knew how certain actions could damage the city; how certain restrictions place in the 1972 bond issue, first selling it on the outside market, would destroy the bond issue and deny the city the use of capital funds that were needed. That is what happened. Those bonds Mr. Brueckel prepared never sold. The city was never given the use of the $9.8 million. Yes, we are suspicious they were sabotaged...They should have disclosed to us that they were writing opinions to CEI that were justifying such things as the refusal to give us an interconnection, the refusal to permit us into CAPCO, the refusal to, their insistence of raising our rates, which were actions which served to damage the city's position."

[Note on April 21, 1976, its Staff urged the Appeal Board to suspend Squire Sanders: "The prior panel found at least there were major issues dealing with the city's financial ability to purchase nuclear power, the city's financial ability to enter into CAPCO arrangements, the city's financial responsibility in becoming a member of CAPCO, the city's financial ability to purchase firm power to name only those enumerated by the board in its opinion."]

"He dismissed Squire Sanders as the city's bond counsel"

Cleveland Press, 23 January 1976, "City Hires NY Counsel - - drops Squire Sanders." "For the last five years or so the Law Department hasn't even kept files on the notes and the bonds," Davis said. "The work went directly to Squire Sanders."

"A stunning reversal occurred"

Plain Dealer, 26 January 1976, Page One, "City Conflict US Clears CEI law firm."

"Law Director Davis"

Cleveland Press, 15 March 1976, Page One, "Talks may bring sale of Muny Light to CEI." [Gaul, ever ready to be Muny Light's pall bearer,]

Cleveland Press, 11 May 1976, "Gaul Pronounces Muny Light 'Kaput.'"

"CEI was making record profits"

CEI Company Reports, 24 January 1976, "CEI reported record revenues in its fourth quarter of 1975 of $124 million, with net income of $15,811,376, or seventy-five cents a share." [Profits were driven by higher fuel costs passed to consumers, an extra rate increase granted by the PUCO and increased sales.]

18. STEALING MUNY LIGHT

"It was a total capitulation"

Plain Dealer, 16 March 1976, Page One, "Tentative OK reached in suit, Transfer of Muny Light to CEI near," by Robert J. McAuley.

"Who Killed Muny Light?"

Cleveland Press, 12 May 1976, "Who Killed Muny Light, Muny Light is Bled White," by Julian Griffin and Norman Mlachak, page C-8. [In keeping with the public burial of Muny Light.]

PTX 517, 13 December 1967, "[What to do with MELP after acquisition."]

PTX 519, 15 December 1967, ["What to do with MELP after acquisition."] Mentions integrating Muny generators into CEI system.

PTX 526, 1 February 1968, [First year impact on CEI of the acquisition of MELP. Rate equalization and increases in CEI's earning per share discussed, 10% growth rate, image of a company on the move, eliminating of competition.]

PTX 541, 23 June 1969, [Discussions of logistics, Muny Light acquisition "inevitable."]

"The unpaid light bill was another trap"

Cleveland Press and *United Press International,* 16 December 1975, "Court is asked to order city to pay CEI bill."

"Forbes Reversed Field"

Plain Dealer, 11 May 1976, "Council escalates attack against CEI."

Cleveland Press, 11 May 1976, "CEI tab is put at $300 million," by Brent Larkin. "A 1972 report put the value of CEI in the city at $300 million, an amount which the city could finance through mortgage retirement revenue bonds and retire the bond in 30 years, with a net profit of $165 million."

Cleveland Press, 11 May 1976, "Forbes became CEI's implacable foe."

Cleveland Press, 11 May 1976, "To CEI Go the Spoils."

"In a moment of self-reflection"

Plain Dealer, 3 March 1976, Pre-budget maneuvers include Forbes' threat," by Joseph L. Wagner, page 4.

"an allocation of hydroelectric power"

Cleveland Press, 21 May 1976, Power from Niagara River costs 1.18 cents per kilowatt hour vs. 2.0 to 3.50 cents a kilowatt hour for Muny to produce. [This is to be compared with what CEI was charging the city: 4.3 cents a kilowatt hour.]

[Note: The *Cleveland Press* earlier reprinted a *Wall Street Journal* story (via *UPI* 16 December 1975) which quoted an engineer saying that his home electricity bill for two months from the city owned Seattle Power (hydro power access) was $24 whereas the same energy from investor-owned Con Ed in New York would have cost eight times as much, $196 for the same time period.]

"The US Justice Department filed its brief"

U.S. Justice Department Brief, 23 August 1976, before the NRC, In the Matter of The Cleveland Electric Illuminating Company, et al, Docket Nos. 50-440-A, 50-441A, 23 August 1976: "Individually and collectively, they have; 1. sought to eliminate actual and potential competition within the relevant markets; 2. by agreeing and conspiring in restraint of trade; 3. by denying the benefits of coordinated operation and development to their competitors, and; 4. by acquiring competing systems within their individual service areas. According to the Justice Department, evidence presented at the NRC hearings showed: "In large portions of Pennsylvania and Ohio there has existed and continues to exist a situation inconsistent with the antitrust laws," (page 44) Citing Section 2 of the Sherman Act: "willful acquisition or maintenance of that power as distinguished from growth or development of a superior product, business acumen or historic accident."

Cite*:* U.S. vs. Grinnell "Coupled with Monopoly Power in relevant market, in economic terms, the power to fix prices or to exclude competition"... Inferred from predominant share of market." Justice Department brief elaborating on competition: [It] "can be of great value in helping to achieve the very goals for which regulatory agencies were established by Congress and the states. A) A stimulus to efficiency and innovation that no regulator can mandate. B) No regulatory staff can supervise or regulate every aspect of the regulated business." See also:

PTX 3051: "Re-examination of the Monopoly Market Structure for Electric Utilities," by Walter Primeaux.

PTX 3052: "Some Problems with Natural Monopoly," by Walter Primeaux.

"Forbes revolved again"

Cleveland Press, 8 September 1976, "Forbes to back Muny Sale," Pg, A-4.

"the end of Muny Light"

Cleveland Press, 8 September 1976, "Perk, CEI OK Muny Light Deal," by Brent Larkin.

"Plain Dealer echoed Muny's demise"

Plain Dealer, 9 September 1976, Page One, "$158 Million Sale of Muny Light to CEI Tentatively Approved." [The sale agreement called for the acquisition of Muny's generating equipment, control of its lakefront property, the transmission and distribution system, and several power substations, the rolling stock of Muny Light and the 46,000 Muny Light accounts.]

Cleveland Press, 8 September 1976, Forbes to back Muny Light sale. page A-4.

"Lights out for Muny"

Cleveland Press, 9 September 1976, "Lights Out for Muny," Editorial.

Plain Dealer, 9 September 1976, "OK Muny Light sale." Editorial.

"If the city chooses to sell its electric plant"

Letter, 7 October 1976, Greenslade of CEI to the ASLB of the NRC: "It is true that, if the proposed sale is accomplished, certain of the findings and conclusions proposed by the opposing parties with respect to both past and prospective relations between the Illuminating Company and the City of Cleveland would essentially become academic."

"diminishing hopes of Muny Light"

The US Justice Department before the ASLB of the NRC, docket 50-440, 12 October 1976, "...The anti-competitive market structure and practices of CEI and the other applicants have finally driven Cleveland to the wall."

"legislation authorizing the sale"

Plain Dealer, 12 October 1976, "City Council's road show takes on Muny Light sale." Also in news, via Associated Press: "Electric Bills Increase 7.4%."

Cleveland: The Best Kept Secret, by George Condon, MSL Academic Endeavors, Cleveland, 1967.

My Story, by Cleveland Mayor Tom Johnson, edited by Elizabeth J. Hauser, B.W. Huebsch, NY, 1911.

"for increased street lighting charges"

PTX 2110, Graph: 'Monies saved by the [City of Cleveland] General Fund due to Low Light and Power Street Lighting Rates, 1960-1975." "CEI customers' rates could go up to pay for the acquisition."

PTX 797, 7 August 1974, CEI Memo Kemper to Moore: "CEI estimate of the RCNLD value as of June 30, 1974 for the MELP facilities is $98,336,000."

[Note: CEI internal calculation had determined that the replacement value of Muny Light's physical plant, its transmission and distribution system was $98.3 million. This is the amount of increased cost which could be figured into CEI's rate base, according to the accounting rules of the Public Utility Commission of Ohio. The actual value of Muny Light for sales purposes was much higher, per Hinchee's calculations. The value of 46,000 Muny Light customers, paying an extra $25 million in rates annually was not taken into account. In any event, CEI's customers would pay for the acquisition of Muny Light through higher utility rates.]

"one of the biggest swindles"

Cleveland Press, 8 November 1976, by Brent Larkin, [Kucinich] "Muny Light Sale...so crooked that if it ever passes into law some people in business and government will go to jail for trying to bilk the public out of hundreds of millions [of dollars]."

"A Cleveland Press editorial belittled"

Cleveland Press, 10 November 1976, Editorial, "Muny Light: What, Again?" page A-10, "Kucinich, who likes to make shocking statements...The plant has outlived its usefulness and the city should just get the best deal it can."

Plain Dealer, 10 November 1976, Editorial, "Get Rid of the Light Plant."

19. THE PLAN IS SET IN MOTION

"AMP-Ohio's offer circulated at City Hall"

Cleveland Press, 9 November 1976, Page One, "Group eyes Muny Light." "System has an immense potential. No one up there seems to realize what this could mean."...Powers Luse. Mentions Kucinich letter to Mayor Perk: "The facts make it clear that the Perk Administration has no business selling Muny Light outright to CEI."

Plain Dealer, 9 November 1976, Page One, "2nd group dealing for Muny Light," by Andrew M. Juniewicz. Letter to city asks that sale be held up so, "AMP-Ohio may also enter into purchase negotiations and make a competitive offer for purchase." [This opened up the potential of a legal attack that the system's proposed sale was not subject to competitive bidding.]

"a letter to Mayor Perk"

Kucinich letter to Mayor Perk, 9 November 1976, asking him to delay the sale.

"Muny Light is making a profit"

Plain Dealer, 11 November 1976, Page One, "Profit-making Muny Light is seen by study," by Andrew Juniewicz, "Turnaround resulted from Muny Light being a power generator to a power distributor." Hinchee describes an optimistic forecast.

"a third bidder appeared"

Cleveland Press, 11 November 1976, Page One, "City says local firm better's CEI's Muny bid," by Brent Larkin.

"traced back to the Mayor's labor adviser"

Plain Dealer, 13 November 1976, Page One, "Perk aide tied to firm seeking Muny Light deal," by Amos Kermisch.

Cleveland Press, 13 November 1976, "Perk aides back Muny firm."

"Kudukis broke ranks"

Plain Dealer, 13 November 1976, ibid.

"New offer for Muny splits directors"

Plain Dealer, 14 November 1976, Page One, "Disposal Firm can't afford Muny plant, Kudukis says," by Harry Stainer.

"falsely claiming financing"

Cleveland Press, 15 November 1976, Page One, "Muny Light bidder gave some false data," by Roy Meyers and Brent Larkin.

"bid was certain to fall apart"

Plain Dealer, 16 November 1976, "Recycling firm bid for Muny Light spurned."

Cleveland Press, 16 November 1976, Page One, "Criminal Charges eyed by city in false Muny bid," by Brent Larkin and Roy Meyers.

Plain Dealer, 16 November 1976, "Muny Light appraisal plan stalls in council," by Andrew M. Juniewicz.

Cleveland Press, 17 November 1976, Editorial, "Muny's odd bidder," page 8-A.

Plain Dealer, 18 November 1976, Editorial, "Light Plant Appraisal," Pg 28-A.

"A $300,000 profit in the third quarter"

Cleveland Press, 8 November 1976, [Note: Muny Light's revenue exceeded its expenditures by nearly $300,000 in the third quarter, due to a new power-purchase contract with CEI, which reduced the cost of power from 35 mills per kilowatt hour to 20 mills.]

"Muny's financial position would improve even further"

Plain Dealer, 9 November 1976, [Note: The new power purchase contract went into effect July 1. Muny Light is buying power from CEI 40-50% cheaper. Muny Light showed profit of $200,000 in month of September, notwithstanding claims it was losing money.]

"The sale was totally tainted"

Cleveland Press, 10 November 1976, "Kucinich to seek ban on sale of Muny Light. Wants Voter Role in Muny Sale," by Brent Larkin. Three hundred volunteers to begin circulating petitions.

West Side News, 11 November 1976, "Kucinich Hits Terms of Muny Light Sale."

"council would not budge"

Plain Dealer, 11 November 1976, "Temper shorted. Irate Kudukis calls for a decision on sale of Muny Light," by Andrew M. Juniewicz. Muny Light request for $15 million in upgrades continued to be held up in council, much to the dismay of Utilities Director Kudukis, "I have to go over on bended knee for every screw and every bolt. You can't run it that way."

"An uproar ensued"

Cleveland Press, 20 November 1976, "Kucinich to sue on Muny sale," page B-3.

Plain Dealer, 18 November 1976, "Kucinich leads Muny Light rally, 200 pledge to keep plant public; volunteers enlisted," by Andrew M. Juniewicz, page 6-A.

Cleveland Press, 19 November 1976, "Kucinich to sue on Muny sale," by Brent Larkin, page B-3.

Cleveland Press, 19 November 1976, "Kucinich tells Perk to cancel Muny Light sale."

Plain Dealer, 20 November 1976, Page One, "Muny Light sale splits planners."

Plain Dealer, 21 November 1976, "Our Puny Muny, Similar electrical systems prospering elsewhere while only a faint hope remains flickering here," by Amos Kermisch.

Cleveland Press, 22 November 1976, "Muny Light appraisal expected to be okayed," by Brent Larkin, page A-9.

Plain Dealer, 23 November 1976, "Kucinich and allies unleash attacks on Muny Light sale." page 5-A.

Cleveland Press, 23 November 1976, "Perk appraiser to show CEI bid for Muny is too high," by Brent Larkin.

Plain Dealer, 24 November 1976 Editorial, "Light plant goof."

Cleveland Press, 25 November 1976, Editorial Cartoon, 'Anyone wanna buy a turkey?"

Cleveland Press, 30 November 1976, "Forbes chastises foes of Muny Light sale."

Plain Dealer, 30 November 1976, Page One, "CEI offer to buy Muny Light ends," by Joseph Wagner.

West Side Sun, 25 November 1976, "Sliwa backs seeking new Muny appraiser," by Brian Hyps, page C-5.

Plain Dealer, 1 December 1976, "CEI keeps a string on Muny Light deal," by Joseph L. Wagner.

Cleveland Press, 1 December 1976, Editorial, "Politics and the Light Plant," page A-8. "It is irrelevant that other cities are making a go of providing power. The fact is that in Cleveland a succession of administrations has mismanaged the plant so that it is deeply in debt..."

Scoop Journal, 2 December 1976, Page One, "Kucinich talks down Muny sale at NCC," by Frank Kuznik.

Plain Dealer, 3 December 1976, "Earnings estimate from Muny Light is refused by CEI," by Amos Kermisch. "The Cleveland Electric Illuminating Co. yesterday refused to reveal how much additional the company anticipates earning if it purchases the Municipal Light Plant."

Cleveland Press, 9 December 1976, "2 city officials criticize data on Muny Light."

Plain Dealer, 9 December 1976, "Report cuts net from Muny sale to $28 million," by Andrew M. Juniewicz, page 23-A.

Plain Dealer, 13 December 1976, "Unpaid city bills cited in light plant dispute," by Richard M. Peery. "Dennis J. Kucinich, municipal court clerk, charged yesterday that City Hall is trying to force the sale of the Municipal Light Plant by not letting other city divisions pay their electric bills to the troubled plant."

Cleveland Press, 14 December 1976, "Hearings open on sale of Muny Light," by Brent Larkin.

Cleveland Press, 14 December 1976, "Study fails to support Muny Light sale," by Brent Larkin.

Plain Dealer, 15 December 1976, "View in council strongly against Muny Light sale," by Andrew M. Juniewicz, page 8-A.

Plain Dealer, 19 December 1976, Page One, "Murky outlook for Muny Light, Skeptics fight CEI's partisans over sale," by Andrew M. Juniewicz.

Plain Dealer, 21 December 1976, Editorial, "Push Light Plant sale," page 4-B.

Cleveland Press, 21 December 1976, "Muny Light study shows a dim future," by Brent Larkin.

Plain Dealer, 22 December 1976, Page One, "New offer lights up Muny future," by Andrew M. Juniewicz. "American Municipal Power of Ohio Inc. offered yesterday to manage or lease the Cleveland Municipal Light Plant in an attempt to prevent sale to the Cleveland Electric Illuminating Co."

Plain Dealer, 23 December 1976, Editorial, "Muny's future still dim."

Cleveland Press, 29 December 1976, "City considers closing Muny Light pending sale," by Brent Larkin.

Plain Dealer, 31 December 1976, "Hinchee details proposal for Muny Light takeover."

Cleveland Press, 1 January 1977, "Bidder warns Muny sale may raise rates," by Peter Phipps.

Plain Dealer, 4 January 1977, "Massive city layoffs loom over CEI tab," by Andrew M. Juniewicz. "Layoff notices may go out to more than 1,000 Cleveland employees next week ... If the Municipal Light Plant is sold to CEI within the next two weeks, the layoffs could be averted, [Finance Director] Riebe said.

Plain Dealer, 5 January 1977, Editorial, "Light plant debt crunch," page 6-B.

Cleveland Press, 5 January 1977, "Perk upset at plan, will close light plant," by Brent Larkin.

Plain Dealer, 5 January 1977, "CEI waits for city to make a move on its $9.5 million debt," by Andrew M. Juniewicz. "We have here an administration dedicated to destroying its own light plant and a giant monopoly dedicated to stealing the light plant. They work very well together," Kucinich said.

Cleveland Press, 5 January 1977, Editorial, "The Muny Light scare," page B-6.

Plain Dealer, 6 January 1977, Page One, "City Council is leaning toward Muny Light sale," by Andrew M. Juniewicz.

20. ETHICS, I THOUGHT YOU MEANT ETHNICS

"The tax abatement law"

City of Cleveland Ordinance No. 2374-76.

"Is this an ethical problem"

Transcript of City Council meeting 13 December 1976; U.S. Court of Appeals brief of Appellee Gary Kucinich vs. George L. Forbes and 12 January 1977, Plaintiff's brief, Kucinich vs. Forbes.

"I raised a question whether it was proper"

Plain Dealer, 14 December 1976, Gary Kucinich is Suspended; Questioned Ethics of Council Taking Gift," by Andrew M. Juniewicz

Cleveland Press, 14 December 1976, "Gary Kucinich is 2nd Council suspension; Gary Kucinich is Suspended."

Cleveland Press, 7 January 1977,"Suspension ruling is due for Gary Kucinich Jan. 19."

21. LOVE AND DEATH

"Someone took a shot at you"

Cleveland Press, 5 January 1977, "Police Guard Kucinich after bullets pierce home."

22. CEI DELIBERATELY CAUSED BLACKOUTS

"Muny Light had another massive outage"

Cleveland Press, 6 January, 1977, "Muny Dark, Many Shiver."

"The Perk administration blamed the weather"

Plain Dealer 7, January 1977, page 10-A, "Power failure blamed on moisture buildup."

Plain Dealer, 6 January 1977, Page One, "City Council is leaning toward Muny Light sale," by Andrew M. Juniewicz.

Plain Dealer, 6 January 1977, page 6-A, "UAW panel objects to Muny Light sale," by Joseph L. Wagner.

"Later that same day, in Washington, D.C.,"

The Atomic Safety and Licensing Board of the Nuclear Regulatory Commission (NRC/ASLB) Initial Decision (Antitrust). In the matter of Toledo Edison, The Cleveland Electric Illuminating Company (Davis-Besse Nuclear Power Station Units 1, 2 and 3).

Docket Nos 50-346A, 50-500A and 50-501A. The Cleveland Electric Illuminating Company, et al. (Perry Nuclear Power Plant, Units 1 and 2.) 6 January 1977.

"charged CEI with deliberately causing"

ASLB/NRC Initial Decision (Antitrust), pp. 70-71, Section 47, "When Cleveland needed power from CEI, the load transfer was operated in such a way at to cause an outage on MELP's system." Titas, DJ 564, pp. 90-93; Mayben, C 161, p. 10; C 82; App. 134; App. 159 Tr. 10649-10651; Tr. 2626; Tr. 2665; Tr. 2761-2773. From an operational viewpoint, no outage need have occurred. See Firestone, DJ 575, p. 54. The load transfer points (five in number) were electrical connections with substation feeders that could be switched either to Cleveland's system or the CEI system, but could not be served by both systems, Tr. 2523-2524.

"As an expert witness"

Dr. Harold H. Wein, consulting economist, to attorney William B. Norris representing the City of Cleveland, 16 July 1979, pages 3 and 4 re: City of Cleveland v. The Cleveland Electric Illuminating, Company, et al, Case C75-560, United States District Court for the Northern District of Ohio.

"CEI then prolonged the blackouts"

ASLB/NRC Initial Decision (Antitrust), page 71, Section 47, "CEI imposed severe operating problems, unnecessary restrictions and administrative delays on MELP before it could use the [power] transfer system. Tr. 2526-2761."

ASLB/NRC Initial Decision (Antitrust), page 72, Section 47, "CEI's load transfer procedures were arbitrary, cumbersome and not in keeping with modern prudent engineering practices. Tr. 2565"

ASLB/NRC Initial Decision (Antitrust), page 72, Section 47, "CEI was aware that MELP outages resulted in a conversion of customers from Cleveland to CEI, DJ 344-350; DJ 352; DJ 559, p.60; DJ 560, pp. 132-133; DJ 563, pp 36-371 DJ 566, p. 62; DJ 569, pp. 24, 94-95; C 11-12; C 14-15; C 19; C 159, page 59, and solicited the affected MELP customers after these outages, DJ 352; Tr. 2691-2695."

"It was revealed that in December 1972"

ASLB/NRC Initial Decision (Antitrust),page 61, Section 38, "CEI's attempt to fix MELP's rates and street lighting charges in exchange for interconnection constitutes a per se violation of the antitrust laws."

"Donald Hauser, CEI's corporate attorney"

ASLB/NRC Initial Decision (Antitrust), page 72, Section 47, "CEI required the approval of each load transfer by its legal officer, Mr. Hauser. This requirement obviously caused delays, at times as much as two hours, DJ 564, pp 52-62."

ASLB/NRC Initial Decision (Antitrust), page 73, Section 48, "It would seem that not every CEI's declination to supply Cleveland with power was on the grounds that it lacked power. At least on one occasion Mr. Hauser requested CEI's operating people to come up with justification for terminating service at a load transfer point, C 79."

ASLB/NRC Initial Decision (Antitrust), page 74, Section 52, "MELP's system would experience brownouts, blackouts, or voltage reductions while awaiting CEI approval of a requires for power over the 69kV tie, Tr. 2669-2670."

"The NRC termed as destructive competition"

ASLB/NRC Initial Decision (Antitrust), page. 62, Section 39, "CEI's attempt to forestall MELP's expansion is a form of destructive competition for had the plan been effected, CEI would have preempted Cleveland's opportunities to increase its productive capacity to supply final markets." DJ 587, pp. 32-34.

ASLB/NRC Initial Decision (Antitrust), page 76, Section 56, "The extremely limited coordination provided for in this agreement effectively denies Cleveland the full benefits of coordinated operation and development." DJ 450, pp. 45-46; NRC 205, pp. 50-57.

ASLB/NRC Initial Decision (Antitrust), page 76, Section 56, "CEI and Cleveland reached an agreement for a permanent interconnection, NRC 204, only after over five years of negotiation..."

"CEI engaged in 'cutthroat competition'"

ASLB/NRC, Initial Decision, Antitrust, page, 59, Section 32. To counter MELP's advantage of lower rates CEI provided promotional considerations such as free internal wiring or free upgrading of electric facilities in areas where it is in competition with MELP while not giving such allowances in areas where there is no competition, OJ 558, pp. 16·17; Tr. 10,323·10,325. Such practice is a form of cutthroat competition, Wein, Tr. 6622·6623.

"CEI blocked a permanent interconnect for five years"

ASLB/NRC, Initial Decision, Antitrust, page 76, Section 56. "CEI and Cleveland reached an agreement for a permanent interconnection, NRC 204, only after over five years of negotiation under "Phase III". of the plan adopted in January of I 970."

CEI publicly "yes" to interconnect, privately, "NO !!!" However, it was CEI's private intention' to avoid a permanent parallel interconnection, C 82; DJ 334.65

ASLB/NRC, Initial Decision, Antitrust, page 60, Section 34. "MELP having its service area completely surrounded by CEI is electrically isolated from utilities other than CEI, Tr. 2726-2727. Access to power supply sources outside its own system is possible only over CEI's transmission system. Similarly disposition of any excess capacity is possible only through the use of CEI's transmission system. See NRC Staff ff 1.094."

ASLB/NRC, Initial Decision, Antitrust, page 60, Section 35. "CEI was aware that a parallel interconnection between CEI and MELP would improve the reliability of the MELP system and make it more competitive. Rudolph, DJ 558, p. 177; Lindseth, DJ 568, p. 62; Gould, DJ 569, p. 24. CEI also knew that MELP could not feasibly interconnect with any other utility, DJ 295.

"Price Fixing"

ASLB/NRC, Initial Decision, Antitrust, page 60, Section 36. "Earlier, in the 1960's CEI did offer to interconnect with MELP but only on the condition that MELP would fix its rates at the level of rates set by CEI and that Cleveland would reduce its charges to the City for street lighting service. Lindseth, DJ 568, p. 14; DJ 293; DJ 294; DJ 295; DJ 330.56 ...nonetheless, its larger motivation was clear. [CEI] required rate-fixing as a precondition to interconnection. DJ 330; DJ 568, p. 61. 82. No action was taken until the holiday season of December 1969; when Cleveland experienced a major generating outage. Hauser Tr. 10,539.62 In January of 1970, CEI and Cleveland agreed to participate in a three phase plan in which the first two phases related to a load transfer service and the third phase would provide a permanent parallel tie in, NRC 195; App.198.64

ASLB/NRC, Initial Decision, Antitrust, page 61, Section 38. "CEI's attempt to fix MELP's rates and street lighting charges in exchange for interconnection constitutes a per se violation of the antitrust laws."

ASLB/NRC, Initial Decision, Antitrust, page 61, Section 37. CEI also believed that if MELP would fix its rates at CEI's level, this not only would eliminate the major reason for customers leaving CEI to take service from MELP, DJ 558, pp. 128-130;DJ 560, p. 132; DJ 565, p. 67; DJ 569, p. 97; ... but also would result in customers switching from MELP to CEI, DJ 560, p.22.

ASLB/NRC, Initial Decision, Antitrust, page 83, Section 62. "These present conditions to nuclear access are "an outrageous affront to the policies underlying the antitrust laws."

"The ASLB/NRC initial antitrust decision"

The Atomic Safety and Licensing Board of the Nuclear Regulatory Commission (NRC/ASLB) Initial Decision (Antitrust), et seq. Pp. 256-264. Licensing conditions 1-10, inclusive.

"All eyes turned to City Hall"

Plain Dealer, 7 January 1977, Page One, "Muny Light wins access to CEI's nuclear power," by George Rasanen, "We believe it (the decision) will prevent CEI from withdrawing from the original agreement [to buy Muny Light]," Perk said.

"Local media reports, ignored the gravity"

Plain Dealer, 7 January 1977, "Muny Light Wins Access to CEI's Nuclear Power." [The Plain Dealer's coverage downplayed the criminal attack on Muny, focusing instead on Muny gaining access to nuclear power, only one of six major directives by the NRC.]

Cleveland Press, 12 January 1977, "Ruling says CEI has violated antitrust laws." [The story was buried on page D-7. In a later edition that day, the headline was changed to "Antitrust Act cited in ruling for Muny Light.]

Also in the *Cleveland Press* that day: Cold and Shut-off Utilities Kill 2 in Mansfield [Ohio].

Cleveland Press, 7 January 1977, Editorial Cartoon, "Anybody wanna buy a light plant?"

Cleveland Press, 7 January 1977, "Dennis Kucinich outlines program to save Muny," by Brent Larkin.

"Only one individual - - Jim Cox"

Author's interview with Jim Cox, July, 2012.

"Roldo Bartimole, independent journalist"

Point of View, an independent publication, written and edited by Roldo Bartimole.

"Prior to his planned probe of CEI"

Jim Cox was fired by WJW-TV on May 27, 1977. He went on to create his own public relations firm.

"I pulled a document from the box"

"Proposed Findings of Fact and Conclusions of Law and Brief in Support Thereof of the City of Cleveland,"

"engaging in cutthroat and destructive competition, including price-fixing"

Proposed Findings of Fact: pp. 43-45, at Section 29.02: The ASLB cited CEI for "cutthroat competition" ibid at Section 29.02, page 46; rate-fixing, ibid at Section 29.02, page 45; price-fixing, "Imposition of price fixing as a condition in exchange for an interconnection is a form of cutthroat competition, ibid, page 45; destructive competition ..."Forestalling, attempted by CEI, with regard to the expansion of Cleveland's generating plant, is a form of destructive competition," ibid at Section 30.02; attempting to undermine Muny's financial position ibid, page 46 at Section 31.01.

"created blackouts by transferring power... in such a way to shut down the Muny system"

Proposed Findings of Fact, pp.. 52-54, Sections 33.01 – 34.01, The technical explanation: "The load transfer service was actuated by connecting a CEI distributing cable to a City distribution cable at a city distribution substation. Each load transfer resulted in an outage to a customer."

"Hauser personally ordered delays... causing...blackouts"

Proposed Findings of Fact, page 52, Section 30.01. NRC/ASLB Transcripts, Hauser at pp. 2660-61, "Operating problems with the load transfer service were very severe and imposed customer outages from 5 minutes to 30 minutes which were not necessary for load switching."

Proposed Finding of Fact, page 52, Section 33.01, Hinchee, NRC/ASLB Transcripts, page, 2626, pp. 2662-67. "The load transfers could have been operated more efficiently with only a 3 – 5 second outage caused by switching. The longer delays were administrative delays caused by CEI's internal requirements."

Proposed Findings of Fact: 33.01. CEI put the load transfer responsibility in the hands of a top company attorney who had no experience operating an electric system, but plenty of experience in frustrating the city's efforts.

Proposed Findings of Fact, pp. 52-56 at Section 33.01 The method of operating the load transfer points was tied directly to CEI's use of its superior reliability to obtain the City's customers.

Proposed Findings of Fact, page 54, Section 33.01, C-79. Mr. Hauser requested the Company's operating people to come up with justification for terminating service at a load transfer point...The load transfer arrangement required that a block of load be transferred at one time. This imposed an economic penalty on the City.

"CEI refused to provide [emergency power]"

Proposed Findings of Fact, page 55, Section 3401, NRC/ASLB Transcripts, Hauser at 10,572-73. "Mr. Hauser admitted that in December of 1972, CEI refused to sell emergency power to the City over the 69kV tie unless the City also agreed to a tie-in sale by executing a contract for the purchase of street lighting service as well."

See also: PTX 572, 15 August 1972, CEI Memo Re the 69kV tie: "[T] he CEI terminal is not to be tagged open and not energized without specific clearance from Don Hauser, Legal. MELP should not, under any circumstances, synchronize any generators, or combustion turbines to this tied system."

See also PTX 584, 14 June 1974, CEI Memo 'Dispatchers are notified that whenever MELP requests service through the 69KV tie Don Hauser, Legal, will make the decision to tie or not to tie."

See also PTX 1939 2 December 1974, Letter, DL to Arthur, Schaffer: 'Forwards letters of 11/11/74, Schaffer, Hauser to Goldberg and reply of 11/19/74, Goldberg to Hauser; City has urgent need for interconnection agreements; queries CEI's delay in response; Hauser explains pressing duties have delayed forwarding of drafts of Participation, Operating and Facilities Agreements - - which meant that pains were being taken to avoid even the occasion of an interconnect and that CEI could impose operational problems on Muny and, instead of talking to engineers, CEI personnel had to contact their legal department, whose dedication was to put Muny Light out of business.

"subverting the FPC [interconnect] order"

Proposed Findings of Fact, page 54 at Section 33.01 "...the City experienced delays and difficulties in constructing the interconnection."

Proposed Findings of Fact, page 55 at Section 33.01. "Although the 69kV line was built for operation as a synchronous interconnection, CEI required that it be operated as an additional load transfer point. Much worse delays were occasioned in obtaining permission to operate the 69kV tie than to operate the 11kV transfer points. On occasion it took as much as ½ day to energize the 69kV line.

Proposed Findings of Fact, page 55, at Section 33.01, ASLB/NRC Hinchee Tr. 2669-71. "The City system would experience brownouts, blackouts or voltage reductions while awaiting CEI approval of a request for power over the 69kV tie. The attorney, Donald Hauser, had said his oversight related to existing litigation, daily contact with the city, making sure FPC criteria was followed, determined that the city actually needed help, and was up on paying its bill."

"Milt and I became engrossed"

Brief of the City of Cleveland in Support of Proposed Findings of Fact and Conclusions of Law: Re: The Christmas season blackout. page 132, Paragraph 5. 'On December 21, 1969, the City experienced a forced outage of [a boiler] which was the source of steam to its 85mW turbine generator unit. The City had no emergency interconnection and the loss of the 85mW unit caused system shutdown."

"A month before the blackout"

PTX 547, 31 November 1969, CEI Memo. In the event MELP needs assistance in catastrophic situation. "Please note that all items of this conceptual plan would be treated as radial. CEI loads - - no parallel operation." The "parallel operation" CEI refers to is the synchronous interconnection which the city was seeking. 'Loads' meant transferring one block of power at a time which kept Muny Light at the mercy of CEI operations, even in an emergency.

"It had publicly promised a tie-in"

PTX 54, 29 December 1969, CEI Memo: "...a permanent underground tie to be avoided like the plague." See also PTX 546, 30 December 1969, Letter SSD [Squire Sanders] to CEI.

[Note: A few days after the Christmas blackout, Squire Sanders sent a letter to the President of CEI, expressing the legal opinion that the FPC could compel an interconnection, so a negotiated settlement, short of an interconnect, was desirable.]

Even the heat of federal action was not sufficient to cause CEI management to stop from dragging their feet. They forestalled the interconnect and, with Squire Sanders' help, adroitly delayed FPC action, going to work on the council, of which I was a new member.

" Following the 1969 Christmas season blackout,"

PTX 560, 7 January 1970, CEI Memo: "Advantages to the City of Cleveland if MELP were sold." MELP has an outstanding debt of approximately $25 million. [Note the timing. This was after the blackout and at the beginning of the new council.]

PTX "Comments" Section states this 'position paper' was 'apparently prepared for use with City Council and the news media arguing that MELP should be sold to CEI.

"On the other hand, by acquiring Muny,"

PTX 525, CEI Memo, 1 February 1968, "First year impact on CEI of acquisition of MELP... Increases of CEI's earning per share would be $2.723. Although results are presented in terms of earnings per share, there are other investor considerations such as the impact of a greater than 10% growth in one year, the image of a company on the move and the elimination of a competitive threat."

"Milt and I continued to review documents"

PTX 707, CEI Memo, 9 October 1970, "Action" d: "A consciousness of the importance of good timing, when to move in and how far, when to drop back; when to act and when to wait."

"Here, they're trying to 'keep a jump"

PTX 5, CEI Memo (Four Company Discussion) 20 August 1967, "Discussion among the participants whether the Memo of Understanding must be submitted to the FPC....Besse said his company was on notice that the City of Cleveland will ask for an interconnection. We must do something voluntarily 'to keep a jump ahead of the sheriff.'"

"They are even going after Painesville's"

PTX 601, CEI Memo, 3 March 1961; PTX628 CEI Memo, 29 July 1960;

"Since 1965, Ohio Edison"

ASLB/NRC, Proposed Findings of Fact, page 34, Section 20.01.

"I studied the scored lines"

PTX 628, CEI Memo, 29 July 1960, "The sale of limited amounts of firm power may contribute to ultimate acquisition [of Muny Light]. There is no precedent for the acquisition of a municipal system as large as Cleveland... because of this a victory for the Company might well be a real contribution to continued private ownership of the electric power business and therefore worth an extreme effort and sacrifice."

Tr. 10,323-10,325. Such practice is a form of cutthroat competition, Wein, Tr. 6622-6623.

23. DUPLI-CITY

"The Plain Dealer boiled the pot "

Plain Dealer, 13 January 1977, "Muny Light Sale a Mess," An Editorial, page 22-A.

"a speech at the prestigious City Club"

Plain Dealer, 8 January 1977, page A-10, "Kucinich barrages CEI, Perk over Muny Light," by Andrew M. Juniewicz. "It is a matter of fact that CEI has waged an intensive behind-the-scenes campaign to steal Muny Light from the people of Cleveland," Kucinich said.

Cleveland Press, 8 January 1977, "Kucinich's smokescreen," An Editorial: ". . .the smokescreen he threw up should not blind Council. A decision by Council to approve sale of the old light plant would be in the best interest of all Clevelanders."

Plain Dealer, 12 January 1977, page 4-A, "11th hour fight expected today by opponents of Muny Light sale," by Andrew M. Juniewicz.

"As details of the NRC ruling began to surface"

Cleveland Press, 10 January 1977, "Muny Light tops Council's agenda," by Brent Larkin. "Many Muny Light observers feel the NRC ruling is a sign the city could win its $325 million anti-trust suit against CEI if it decided to pursue the lawsuit rather than sell the plant."

Plain Dealer, 13 January 1977, page 14-A, "Private meeting preceded votes on light plant sale."

"Unexpectedly...the committees rejected the sale"

Plain Dealer, 13 January 1977, Page One, "4 council committees reject sale of Muny Light," by Andrew M. Juniewicz. "Prior to that ruling, 'We would have sold the light plant,' Council President Forbes told the *Plain Dealer* last night."

Cleveland Press, 13 January 1977, "Council rejects Muny Light sale," by Brent Larkin, pageA-5. "In a seven-hour meeting yesterday, four Council committees voted 19-2 to reject the Perk administration's proposed sale of the Municipal Light Plant to CEI."

Cleveland Press, 14 January 1976, "City seeking to delay $9.5 million bill to CEI." "Rudolph called City Council's decision to reject the proposed sale of Muny Light to CEI 'unfortunate'"

Plain Dealer, 14 January 1977, Page One, "CEI demands city pay $17.5 million now," by Andrew M. Juniewicz.

Call-Post, 15 January 1977, "Muny Short-Circuit." An Editorial.

Plain Dealer, 21 January 1977, Editorial, "Muny Light: A loser."

Cleveland Press, 22 January 1977, Guest Editorial, "The Muny Light deal is bad,"by Councilwoman Mary C. Zunt. "The deal was put together in the private offices of Squire Sanders and Dempsey, where representatives of CEI and the Perk administration molded the sale."

"CEI went to court, demanding $9.5 million"

Plain Dealer, 14 January 1977, "CEI demands city pay $17.5 [sic] million now," by Andrew M. Juniewicz, page 10-A.

Cleveland Press, 14 January 1977, "CEI seeks court permission to seize city assets. Perk, Forbes, vow to inform Clevelanders of NRC ruling."

Cleveland Press, 14 January 1977, Editorial, "Muny on Council's back."

Plain Dealer, 25 January 1977, "Muny Light sale plan is saved for next week," by Andrew M. Juniewicz, page 8-A.

Plain Dealer, 25 January 1977, "CEI debt ignored in city's balanced budget," page 8-A.

Plain Dealer, 26 January 1977, "CEI asks judge to force city to take steps to pay light bill," by Robert J. McAuley, page 10-A.

Plain Dealer, 27 January 1977, Page One, "City Threat of Condemnation Spikes CEI Attachment Plan," by Andrew M. Juniewicz.

Cleveland Press, 26 January 1977, Editorial, "The city's debt to CEI," page B-4.

Plain Dealer, 28 January 1977, "Muny Light rate hike heads for council," by Andrew M. Juniewicz.

"Forbes and Perk again spoke of a city takeover of CEI"

Cleveland Press, 27 January 1977, "Perk, Forbes Planned Air War Against CEI," by Brent Larkin. [Note Page One refer: "A secret smear campaign by Perk-Forbes forces got CEI to wait for its money," Brent Larkin reports. page B-1.]

Plain Dealer, 16 January 1977, Section One – 6, "City to shut down generating unit at Muny Light plant," by Harry Stainer. "The city generates only about 15% to 20% of the power it sells. It buys the rest from CEI."

Plain Dealer, 15 January 1977, "Power hookup to Niagara Falls planned by Muny." "This would allow Muny Light to increase profits and help it become solvent again," - - Muny Light Commissioner Ray K. Miller.

"Even the moribund Cleveland media"

Cleveland Press, 26 January 1977, "U.S. Charges CEI Caused Muny Outages."

"A few days later, in a sidebar"

Plain Dealer, 30 January 1977, "Who Turned Off Muny Light?" by Amos Kermisch.

"The NRC 's findings were now widely published"

Cleveland Press, 31 January 1977, "Council Expected to Reject Muny Sale."

"Changing his position for a fourth time"

Plain Dealer, 31 January 1977, "Muny Light decision is unlikely tonight," page 6-A.

Cleveland Press, 31 January 1977, "Forbes Is Seen as Having Votes for Muny sale," by Brent Larkin.

Cleveland Press, 9 February 1977, "17 in Council to OK sale of Muny Light," by Brent Larkin.

"He had held CEI in check"

Plain Dealer, 1 February 1977, Page One, "Forbes wants more for Muny Light sale," by Andrew M. Juniewicz.

Cleveland Press, 1 February 1977, "Perk Lauds Forbes in Muny Deal," by Brent Larkin, page B-1. "Privately labeling City Council President George Forbes as "the greatest Council president in Cleveland's history, …Mayor Perk is now confident his six-month crusade to sell the Municipal Light Plant will succeed."

Cleveland Press, 2 February 1977, "Cleveland's finance picture calls for straight talk. An Editorial, page B-6. " [Forbes told council] "… the Perk Administration has not been crying 'wolf,' and that the failure to sell Muny Light would put Cleveland in a disastrous financial position."

"Can any additional insight be gained"

Cleveland Magazine, February 1975, "Hey Whitey! Does George Forbes Want You for his Valentine? /Black is Beautiful, But George Forbes Is Something Else," pp. 66-77.

"Presidents and officers of international corporations"

Plain Dealer, 4 February 1977, "Muny Light Foreclosure in Looming Forbes Says," by Andrew M. Juniewicz, page 1-B.

Plain Dealer, 5 February 1977, page 3-A, "150 Trudge Through Snow to Get News City Has Problems," by Joseph L. Wagner, page 3-A.

Cleveland Press, 4 February 1977, "Leaders Urge Sale of Muny Light Plant," by Roy Meyers, page B-9.

See also: *Plain Dealer*, 2 February 1977, "City has 15 days to give judge plan to pay Muny debt."

See also: *Plain Dealer*, 13 April 1977, Outmigration of powerful discussed, page B-3.

"A Plain Dealer editor wrote"

Plain Dealer 5 February 1977, "Forbes' better idea," An Editorial, page A-14.

"Have you ever heard of someone selling"

Plain Dealer, 16 February 1977, "City Has No Plan to Pay CEI Except to Sell Muny," by Andrew M. Juniewicz, page 14-A. [This is what Perk Administration told the federal judge overseeing the antitrust case, that it would otherwise have to lay off 1,938 employees to pay the $9.8 million debt.]

Cleveland Press, 16 February 1977, "City argues for Muny Light sale," by Roy Meyers.

Plain Dealer, 17 February 1977, "Muny Light Sale is City's Debt Solution," by Robert J. McAuley. Muny Light former Commissioner Hinchee, estimated the value of Muny Light at ten times annual sales, $25,000,000 x 10 equals

$250,000,000.

Plain Dealer, 9 December 1976, "Report cuts net from Muny sale to $28 million."

"Let's get on with it"

Cleveland Press, 7 February 1977, "Sell Muny Light Plant," An Editorial: "...we are convinced that through the years CEI has contributed to the Muny Light's plant plight. But it has sifted down to a question choosing the lesser of two evils. The city's solvency is paramount and the sale of the plant will ease, not solve some financial problems. Let's get on with it."

"How do we perform an efficient"

Plain Dealer, 8 February 1977, "City is accused of destroying utilities records," by Joseph L. Wagner, page 2-A. "How do we perform an efficient and accurate audit with poorly organized records that are not fully reconciled according to generally accepted accounting principles?" - - Donald R. Lesiak, state examiner.

24. SOMETHING WICKER THIS WAY COMES (WITH APOLOGIES TO RAY BRADBURY).

"A mixture of handball and lacrosse,"

Wikipedia, Jai alai: A mixture of handball and lacrosse. The Basque Government promotes jai alai as "the fastest sport in the world because of the balls."

"City fathers envisioned a revenue stream"

Cleveland Press, 7 February 1977, Page One, "Perk wants jai alai legalized statewide."

Cleveland Press, 8 February 1977, "Legislators Back Perk Jai Alai Palace," page A-2.

"As Muny Light and jai alai consumed passions"

11 February 1977, "U.S. Court Rules Gary Kucinich had Rights Violated," U.S. District Court for Northern District of Ohio, Eastern Division, Kucinich v. Forbes, Case No. C76-1317, 10 February 1977, Order of Judge John Manos. Borrowing from the U.S. Supreme Court case in Powell v. McCormack 395 U.S. 486, 547 (1969), "A fundamental principle of our representative democracy is, in Hamilton's words, 'that the people should choose whom they please to govern them. . . it is this Court's firm belief that neither the average citizen of Cleveland, nor a councilman in Council chambers can be punished for criticizing or impugning the motives of Cleveland politicians... In our system of government only the electorate in Gary Kucinich's ward are permitted to judge him and punish him for his expression of ideas and opinions. The defendants are hereby permanently enjoined from enforcing the December 13, 1976 order suspending Gary Kucinich."

"Our Save Muny Light Committee"

Cleveland Press, 14 February 1977, Page One Bulletin, "Hearing asked on Muny Light," re: Kucinich letter to FPC to block sale.

Plain Dealer, 15 February 1977, "FPC hearing asked on Muny Light sale."

West Side Sun, 17 February 1977, "Protesters Opposed to Light Plant Sale," by Brian Hyps.

Cleveland Press, 22 February 1977, "Coalition Urges City to Retain Muny Light Plant," by Peter Phipps.

Cleveland Press, 25 February 1977, "City officials say Muny Light can be saved," by Peter Phipps. [Officials not named.]

"Forbes, fearing the referendum"

Cleveland Press, 17 February 1977, "City to Ask Five Mills for Muny," by Peter Phipps, page A-8.

Plain Dealer, 18 February 1977, "Election Sought on Pay Formula, Muny Light Issue," by Andrew M. Juniewicz.

Plain Dealer, 19 February 1977, Page One, "Muny Light, Pay Plan, Up to Voters," by Andrew M. Juniewicz.

Cleveland Press, 21 February 1977, "Debate rages over proposed tax to save Municipal Light," by Peter Phipps, page D-8.

"Press editors celebrated Forbes' ploy"

Cleveland Press, 22 February 1977, "No On Muny Light Levy, Yes on 3% pay repeal," An Editorial, page A-6. "It is too late to wring one's hands anymore at what has happened to Muny Light. Mayor Perk decided the city had to cut its losses and sell the plant to the highest bidder. We agree with that."

Plain Dealer, 25 February 1977, "Judge scolds

city, demands plan for paying debt to CEI."

Plain Dealer, 4 March 1977, "UAW Council to Oppose Proposed Muny Light Levy."

Cleveland Press, 7 March 1977, "Perk Wants 20% Muny Light Rate Hike," by Brent Larkin.

"Muny Light attracted national notice"

New York Times, 17 March 1977, "Cleveland Publicly Owned Power is Losing Out to a Private Utility," by Reginald Stuart.

"The property tax levy failed"

Cleveland Press, 16 April 1977, "Call it Muny Dark," by Brent Larkin. "Last Monday all six of the plant's boilers were shut down, perhaps permanently."

Scoop Journal, 21 April 1977, "Kucinich Urges 'no' on 5-mill tax."

Cleveland Press, 23 April 1977, "Will they pull the plug on Muny?" by Peter Phipps. "A tax levy supported by no one and opposed by everyone will fail."

Plain Dealer, 25 April 1977, Page One, "City Power on the Line," by Andrew M. Juniewicz.

Cleveland Press, 25 April 1977, An Editorial, "Vote is tomorrow: Yes on No. 1, No on No. 2," page A-6. "...The strategy is for the issue to go down and for that defeat to be a signal to Council that the people do not want Muny Light. This is transparent, and perhaps cynical, but it is the only way to get this millstone from around the city's neck, so be it."

Cleveland Press, 27 April 1977, "Muny Light Sale Appears Imminent After Levy Defeat."

Plain Dealer, 27 April 1977, Page One, "Muny Light Takes Step Closer to Sale," by Joseph D. Rice. "Mayor Ralph J. Perk and City Council President George Forbes, D-20, interpreted the levy's defeat as a mandate to sell Muny Light."

Plain Dealer, 27 April 1977, "Forbes is viewed as big winner in election," by Joseph D. Rice, page 10-A.

Cleveland Press, 27 April 1977, "Voters Pull Plug on Muny," by Brent Larkin "Cleveland's 60 year venture into the municipal power business appeared near an end today after voters slaughtered a property tax allegedly designed to save the city's light system... "As of now, the deal to sell Muny Light is off," said Forbes.

Plain Dealer, 27 April 1977, "Voters' Good Judgment," An Editorial, page 18-A. "... Muny Light is outdated, inefficient and ought to be sold."

Cleveland Press, 27 April 1977, "Sell the smudge pot," An Editorial.

Plain Dealer, 29 April 1977, "Judge denies city pleas for stay of judgment covering CEI debt," by Robert J. McAuley.

"I answered Forbes"

Plain Dealer, 1 May 1977, "Election Dispels a Power Myth and Costs Kucinich an Issue," by Joseph D. Rice. "Kucinich's protests notwithstanding, Cleveland's Municipal Light Plant appears dead as an issue in this year's mayor's race."

West Side Sun, 5 May 1977, "Muny Light sale appears imminent after levy defeat," by Brian Hyps.

"George Forbes, knowing he had delivered"

Cleveland Press, 29 April 1977, "Muny Must Share CEI A-Plant Power."

"The timing of Forbes' hold-up of the sale"

Plain Dealer, 27 April 1977, "CEI Promotes Rudolph, Ginn Becomes President at Stormy Meeting."

Plain Dealer, 30 April 1977, "CEI asks to sell 2.4 million shares to pay loans, for construction." (further reference: *Cleveland Press*, 23 April 1977 "CEI Profit Climbs").

"A month passed, CEI's difficulties mounted"

Cleveland Press, 13 May 1977, "Rate hikes won't stop customers, CEI says," by Bob Modic, page A-15.

Plain Dealer, 15 May 1977, "High-voltage ploy hiked CEI profits, former aide says," by Thomas J. Brazaitis.

Cleveland Press, 16 May 1977, "Agency will represent consumers vs. utilities," by Bob Modic.

"CEI apparently discovered"

Plain Dealer, 18 May 1977, An Editorial: "Don't Just Sit There, Sell," page 20-A.

Cleveland Press, 23 May 1977, An Editorial: "Quit Stalling on Muny Light." "Shed a tear, if you like, because Muny Light was a great idea that went wrong. But reality must be faced. Council should quit stalling and decide to sell Muny Light - - the sooner the better."

Plain Dealer, 29 April 1977, "Judge Denies City Plea for Stay of Judgment," by Robert J. McAuley. Judge Krupansky said Muny Light "is virtually, if not actually, bankrupt," and threatened to appoint a receiver as he denied the city's request for a stay of judgment on the debt.

Cleveland Press, 9 April 1977, "High Court says city owes CEI $547,115."

Plain Dealer, 24 May 1977, Page One, "Council on Muny: Sell. Close 18-15 Vote on the Light Plant Final in 40 Days," by Andrew M. Juniewicz. ["Muny Light is sold," pronounced Forbes, gaveling the meeting.]

Cleveland Press, 24 May 1977, "How they voted on Muny Light." For the sale of Muny Light: Thomas Keane, Richard Harmody, Lonnie Burten, Robert McCall, Ralph Perk, Jr., David Collier, James Boyd, Basil Russo, George Forbes, Mildred Madison, E.T. Caviness, Albert Ballew, Ceasar Moss, Walter Cox, Jr., Earle Turner, John Barnes, Emil Golub and Mary Zunt. Against the sale of Muny Light: James Bell, William Franklin, Robert Getz, Joseph Kowalski, Gary Kucinich, Mary Ann Lecate, John Lynch, David Trenton, Mary Zone, Thomas Campbell, Joseph Cannon, Benny Bonanno and David Strand.

"The next day, 24 May 1977"

Cleveland Press, Page One, 24 May 1977, "Council Sells Muny Light and Gets a Fishing Pier," by Peter Phipps. "a $250,000 fishing pier on Lake Erie - - that's really the only concession the Illuminating Co. (CEI) yielded after nine months of haggling with Cleveland Council over the purchase of the Municipal Light Plant. Headline on inside continuation of story: "Kucinich plans to bar sale of Municipal Light."

Cleveland Press, 24 May 1977, Page One, "Muny Light vote shadows Council races," by Brent Larkin. "The Municipal Light Plant will be owned by the Illuminating Co. by early July, but it will still be an issue..."

Plain Dealer, 25 May 1977, "Council's right decision," An Editorial.

Cleveland Press, 25 May 1977, "Study shows competition lowers electricity rates," by Bob Modic.

PTX 1965 1 June 1977 City Ordinance No. 2351-76: 'Emergency Ordinance authorizing and directing Mayor and the Director of Public Utilities to enter into an agreement between the City and CEI providing for the sale or lease of all assets of the Division of Light and Power."

See also PTX 1964 Memorandum of Understanding between City and CEI: Unsigned Memorandum of Understanding between City and CEI. [Note: CEI went to Wall Street with a new offering: *Wall Street Journal*, 25 May 1977, "Cleveland Electric's New Common Offered at Indicated 8% Yield."]

Plain Dealer, 26 May 1977, "CEI raises cash to buy Muny Light," page D-10. See also: *Plain Dealer*, 28 May 1977, "CEI seeking Saudi loans," page B-7.

"The city ought to be strengthening Muny Light"

Cleveland Press, 13 June 1977, "Perk's Porn War," page A-8, editorial.

"A week later, Chief Garey"

Plain Dealer, 25 May 1977, Page One, "Garey forfeits 1000 hours of overtime pay."

Cleveland Press, 25 May 1977, "Council strips Garey of overtime pay," page A-8.

Cleveland Press 28 May 1977 "Chief Lloyd Gary Fired." Also see: *Cleveland Press*, 19 April 1977, "Vice unit busts Cleveland's biggest numbers house," page A-7.

Plain Dealer, 3 July 1979, "Forbes used office for gain, jury told," by Robert McAuley and Leslie Kay. "Forbes entered into the scheme in mid-1974, Nugent charged when he threatened to pass legislation to prevent Sebring Exhibit and Supply Co. from operating any carnivals in Cleveland."

West Side Sun, 9 June 1977, "Garey firing, Muny Light moves said political 'deal'," by Brian Hyps.

Plain Dealer 19 April 1977, "Numbers spot netting $25,000 a day raided."

Plain Dealer, 17 January 1978, Page One, "Forbes took carnival raid gripes to Perk," by Daniel R. Biddle.

"I objected, since such conduct"

Plain Dealer, 19 June 1977, "Kucinich Protests Open Muny Books for CEI," Section One-15.

"I called a news conference"

Plain Dealer, 25 May 1977, "Kucinich Starts Push for Referendum on Sale of Muny Light," by Andrew M. Juniewicz. "To get the issue on the ballot, Kucinich will have to gather almost 18,500 valid signatures."

Plain Dealer, 26 May 1977, "Preserve Muny Light Plant site for the public," by William F. Miller.

Scoop Journal, 26 May 1977, "Attempts to Block Sale are Underway."

Scoop Journal, 26 May 1977, "Muny operation could be run profitably, says former commissioner [Stephen Suhajcik]."

Plain Dealer, 3 June 1977, "Kucinich Starts Drive to Force Referendum on Sale of Muny Light."

"The Cleveland Press, doing the bidding of CEI"

Cleveland Press 26 May 1977, An Editorial: "Muny Light is Gone." "The reality is that Council had no choice other than getting rid of Muny Light. No one should let Kucinich's political smoke screen obscure that fact."

"This was not a good season for a private utility"

[Note: 14 January 1977 Sixty miles south of Cleveland, in Mansfield, Ohio, a 74 year old retired factory worker named Eugene Kuhn struggled to pay his $18.38 monthly electric bill, only to have his power shut off by Ohio Edison as the mercury hovered around ten degrees. Eight days later he was found frozen to death in his bed.]

Cleveland Press, 25 May 1977, "Study shows competition lowers electricity rates," by Bob Modic.

Plain Dealer, 14 June 1977, "In a year, price of electricity leaps 23% here," by William R. Diem.
[Note: The bill for 500 kilowatt hours [average monthly use per residential customer from CEI was $24.63 in April, contrast with ten cities in Pacific Northwest which average $12.42 [hydropower].]

"The U.S. Conference of Mayors"

Plain Dealer 13 June 1977, "Mayors May Back City Owned Utilities." Plain Dealer Special. "Tuscon - - "The continued existence and viability of city-owned utilities, such as Cleveland's Municipal Light Plant, is among issues in the package of energy recommendations being considered by the U.S. Conference of Mayors."

"Bill Casstevens, Regional Director"

Plain Dealer, 27 May 1977, "UAW to Fight Muny Light Sale," by Andrew M. Juniewicz.

Plain Dealer, 29 May 1977, "They're Electrocuting the Muny Light Plant," by George E. Condon. "CEI," vowed Kucinich after the fateful meeting of City Council, "will never own Muny Light."

Cleveland Press, 10 June 1977, "Blacks should questions Muny Light sale," by George Anthony Moore. "And the nastiest rumor is that whoever negotiated this sale to CEI will receive a tidy reward."

See also: Plain Dealer, 14 June 1977, "In a year, price of electricity leaps 23% here," by William Diem.

"Councilman David Strand"

West Side Sun, 2 June 1977, Page One, "2 Say Muny Light Profit Was Hidden," by Brian Hyps. "Strand obtained an inter-office memo...two weeks ago which showed Muny Light receipts will be $4 million more than anticipated during 1977."

Cleveland Press, 23 June 1977, "Prune stew: Kucinich dines with senior citizens in campaign to save Muny Light," by Peter Phipps, page A-12.

"Markets recognize that the city is in sound financial status"

West Side Sun, 30 June 1977, "City Bond Sale Unaffected by Muny Light Deal, so far," by Brian Hyps. "We're not going to have Muny Light either way. Either we sell it and get money for it or the court sells it and we don't get money for it." - - Cleveland Finance Director Warren Riebe. Contrast with: *Wall Street Journal*, 22 June 1977, "Wall Street Is Forcing Cities to Disclose More When Floating Bonds."

Plain Dealer, 23 June 1977, "$25.58 million sale of bonds shows city in brighter position," by

Andrew M. Juniewicz.

Scoop Journal, 30 June 1977, "Kucinich will file Muny Light petitions tomorrow."

"On July 1, 1977, the day before the sale"

Cleveland Press, "Kucinich Petitions Stall Sale of Muny," by Brent Larkin. page A-6. "Kucinich, who has campaigned against the sale for nearly a year, gathered the 30,000 signatures in less than one month."

Plain Dealer, 1 July 1977, "Kucinich Files Petitions for Vote on Muny Sale." page B-4. [Re: Ordinance No. 2351-76]

"Mayor Perk, sensing complications"

Plain Dealer, 2 July 1977, "Perk Calls Muny Light Petition Drive a 'Hoax.'"

Cleveland Press, 2 July 1977, "Perk-Kucinich dispute CEI antitrust suit," page 7-A.

Plain Dealer, 4 July 1977, "CEI Deadline Spells Legal Trouble Perk Says," by Harry Stainer, page 6-A.

West Side Sun News, 14 July 1977, "Perk Assails Kucinich Push to Recall Muny Light's Sale."

25. I RUN FOR MAYOR

July 7, 1977. "The excitement," Original document, 7 July 1977, Kucinich Announcement Speech for Mayor of Cleveland.

"Clerk of Council Mercedes Cotner notified"

Cleveland Press, 12 July 1977, "Kucinich Wins Round in Muny Light Fight." [Clerk of Council certifies sufficient signatures.]

"After feasting on pork dumplings"

Cleveland Press, 19 July 1977, "Kucinich Threatens Suit on Council's Muny Vote."

Plain Dealer, 19 July 1977, Page One, "Muny Light Sale Put on Oct. 4 ballot."

"Then Forbes sent to the Elections Board"

Plain Dealer, 14 July 1977, "Muny Light Petitions May be Illegal," page 7-A.

Cleveland Press, 19 July 1977, "Vote on Muny clouded as panel gets petitions."

Plain Dealer, 6 July 1977, An Editorial. "Politics and the Light Plant." "The fact is that almost anyone with organizational ability could secure 30,000 signatures on petitions covering almost anything imaginable." See also: *Cleveland Press*, 3 July 1977, An Editorial supporting a 35-room mansion for Cleveland's mayor.

"In the previous eight months,"

Cleveland Press, 17 November, 1976, An Editorial: "We think the light plant should be sold."

Plain Dealer, 18 November 1976, An Editorial: "...sale of the light plant would be in the city's best interests."

Plain Dealer, 24 November 1976, An Editorial: "The Perk Administration should not be censured for its decision to sell the Muny Light Plant."

Cleveland Press, 25 November 1976, An Editorial Cartoon: "Anyone want to buy a turkey?"

Cleveland Press, 1 December 1976, An Editorial: Maybe some politicians think they are making points with Clevelanders by talking about preserving the plant. But in opposing the sale they are whipping a dead horse."

Plain Dealer, 12 December 1976, Page One, "Murky Outlook for Muny Light."

Plain Dealer, 21 December 1976, An Editorial: "Push Light Plant Sale."

Plain Dealer, 23 December 1976, An Editorial: "Muny's future dim."

Plain Dealer, 5 January 1977, An Editorial: "... The only real offer to buy the light plant has come from CEI..."

Cleveland Press, 5 January 1977, An Editorial: "This newspaper has said several times that the debt-ridden Muny Light Plant ought to be sold...A child could understand the basic facts about Muny Light."

Cleveland Press, 7 January 1977, An Editorial Cartoon: "Anyone wanna buy a light plant."

Plain Dealer, 13 January 1977, An Editorial: "Muny Light."

Cleveland Press, 14 January 1977, An Editorial: "Muny on Council's back."

Plain Dealer, 14 January 1977, An Editorial Cartoon: "Muny Dark."

Call and Post, 15 January 1977, An Editorial: "Muny, except for its brightest and newest years, has been a born loser. Nobody, with the exception of some unthinking councilmen, loves a loser."

Plain Dealer, 21 January 1977, An Editorial: "Muny Light: A loser. The loser should be sold."

Cleveland Press, 7 February 1977, An Editorial: "Sell Muny Light Plant....And we are convinced that through the years CEI has contributed to the Muny Light Plant's harm."

Call and Post, 19 February 1977, An Editorial: "All the evidence points to the practicability of selling the plant."

Cleveland Press, 22 February 1977, An Editorial: "It is too late to wring one's hands anymore at what has happened to Muny Light."

Plain Dealer, 27 April 1977, An Editorial: "... City Council should proceed with hearings aimed at the eventual sale of that utility to the Cleveland Electric Illuminating Co..."

Cleveland Press, 27 April 1977, An Editorial: "Sell the Smudge Pot."

Plain Dealer, 18 May 1977, An Editorial: "Don't just sit there, sell."

Cleveland Press, 23 May 1977, An Editorial: "Quit stalling on Muny Light. ...Shed a tear, if you like, because Muny Light was a great idea that went wrong."

Plain Dealer, 25 May 1977, "The municipal utility is in a condition of wreck and ruin..."

Cleveland Press, 26 May 1977, An Editorial: "Muny Light is gone. No one should let Kucinich's smoke screen obscure that fact."

Plain Dealer, 5 June 1977, An Editorial Cartoon: "Muny Light Sale: All candles half off."

Plain Dealer, 6 July 1977, An Editorial: "There was no other way out of the Muny Light mess then, there is no other way out of it now, but to close the sale."

Cleveland Press, 30 August 1977, An Editorial: "Enough of Muny Light...Frankly, we are getting tired of the Muny Light issue, and believe most Clevelanders feel the same way. Let's hear about some of the other, more important issues, Dennis."

"The sale loomed despite"

Plain Dealer, 3 August 1977, "Council Clerk Moves to Block Muny Light Vote."

Plain Dealer, 4 August 1977, "Muny Light Sale Protest Hearing Set," by William Carlson

Cleveland Press, 5 August 1977, "Kucinich Files Protest on Sale of Muny Light.

Plain Dealer, 5 August 1977, "Kucinich Requests FPC to Block Sale of Muny," page A-8.

Cleveland Press, 5 August 1977, "Kucinich Requests FPC [to block sale]," page 6-B

Plain Dealer, 24 August 1977, "Muny Light Petition's Wording Stirs Protest," by William Carlson. page A-24.

Cleveland Press, 29 August 1977, Page One, "Muny Light Sale Ruled Off Ballot," by Brent Larkin."

Plain Dealer, 30 August 1977, "Court Will Decide Fate of Municipal Light Vote," by William Carlson.
[Note: Cuyahoga County Court of Appeals Judge John V. Corrigan granted a temporary restraining order stopping the Board of Elections from taking the referendum off the ballot.]

Cleveland Press, 31 August 1977, "Court Sets Hearing on Muny Light Issue."

Plain Dealer, 10 September 1977, "Growth Association endorses Muny Light sale," page 11-A.

"Vice was a sensitive matter"

Cleveland Press, 22 September 1977, "Seawright hits media, backs Perk," by Walt Bogdanich. "Accused numbers figure William H. Seawright saying he is campaigning for Mayor Perk "right now," has attacked newspaper articles that raised questions about the propriety of his numerous heavy equipment contracts with the city... Seawright is currently under a six-count indictment for illegal numbers activity in the black community."

Cleveland Press, 27 July 1977, "Seawright asks help at City Hall," by Tony Natale. "Suspected gambling figure William Seawright sought the help of top City Hall officials, including a former police chief, to reclaim adding machines captured by police in a gambling raid. Seawright asked Mickey Rini...to intercede for him..."

"With less than two months"

Plain Dealer, 21 July 1977, Page One, "Heat wave blamed for power failure."

Cleveland Press, 21 July 1977, "Muny cable break leaves 6,000 West Siders without service," page 18-A.

27. A MAYOR IS BORN

"Three weeks before Mayor Perk's term came to a close,"

Plain Dealer, 14 October 1977, Page One, "City to cut tax; extra millions found in fund," by Harry Stainer. "Perk is expected to disclose a $4.5 million surplus in the city's debt service fund."

"A surprise endorsement came from The Plain Dealer"

Plain Dealer, 19 October 1977, An Editorial: "City must prepare to sell Muny Light," page 4-B.

Plain Dealer, 30 October 1977, An Editorial: "Kucinich for Mayor"

Plain Dealer, 3 November 1977, "Next Mayor gets 16 days to solve CEI debt problem," page 18-A.

"Dennis J. Kucinich defeated Edward F. Feighan"

Plain Dealer, 9 November 1977, Page One, "Kucinich Beats Feighan, Youngest big-city mayor wins by 3,000 votes," by Joseph D. Rice.

"Six days after the election"

Cleveland Press, 14 November 1977, Page One. "Kucinich Pledges Period of Renewal," by Brent Larkin.

See also: *Call and Post*, 12 November 1977, Page One, "Kucinich Pledges Effort to Unite Cleveland," by Ellen S. Freilich.

28. CITY HELL

"The sale of Muny Light"

Plain Dealer, 13 November 1977, Page One, "Data in Muny Light suit reported missing," by Mairy Jayn Woge.

"I gathered my staff members"

Plain Dealer, 13 November 1977, Page One, "Kucinich's cabinet: Young, forceful," by Joseph L. Wagner.

Cleveland Press, 14 November 1977, "The Cabinet. New guard at City Hall to learn on the job," by Peter Phipps.

29. LIEN ON ME.

"Tony's Diner was the great equalizer"

Plain Dealer, 8 December 1977, "Sweet talk and a mailed fist, Mayor offers CEI peace or a hard fight," by Joseph L. Wagner.

"Law Director Jack Schulman entered"

Plain Dealer, 24 November 1977, "CEI files against city to recover debt," by William Carlson and W. James Van Vliet, page 2-B. [Seeking $13.5 million.]

Cleveland Press, 23 November 1977, "Muny Light lien is sought to ensure payment to CEI," by Walt Bogdanich.

Cleveland Press, 3 December 1977, "CEI is determined to push for the debt owed by the city."

"The Bible says that it is easier"

WKYC-TV3, 9 November 1977, Interview with Joe Mosbrook, Transcript:

Kucinich: "I don't believe in tax abatement, because the people of Cleveland, the residential property owners, are paying tremendous property taxes. Property taxes are going up for homeowners in this community. Big business wants their taxes cut...big business isn't paying its fair share."

[Note: Tax abatements enabled the city's largest commercial property owners to avoid property taxation on the improved value of their property, creating a shift of the burden of taxation onto homeowners.]

For further discussion: The Cleveland school system had been long dependent upon property tax revenues for its financial support. There were several threats to this base. A court case in 1970, Park Investment, determined commercial and industrial property were to be assessed at the same rate as residential property. This shifted the burden of property taxation onto homeowners, who increasingly rejected school levies. Second, the value of prime commercial and industrial properties owned by banks, utilities and real estate trusts were under-assessed by over $200 million. The Cleveland schools appealed, yet businesses still received $20 million in reductions while homeowners taxes went up over $84 million. Ohio voters approved a state lottery in 1974, ostensibly to fund education. Instead the $165 million in revenue the lottery raised since 1974, found other uses including building new prisons.

"Bishop Burt discovered"

Plain Dealer 12 November 1977, "Kucinich will ask council to reject tax abatements."

Cleveland Press 12 December 1977 "Kucinich vetoes tax abatements."

Plain Dealer, 18 December 1977, "Save the Sohio project," An Editorial.

See also: *Cleveland Press*, 12 July 1977, "New Sohio building may cost taxpayers."

Cleveland Press, 28 July 1978, Page One, "City Seeking Tenant to Save Sohio Tower," by Dick Pergler and Ron Kovach.

"National City Bank had received $14 million"

Plain Dealer, 8 January 1978, Page One, "Bishop vs. businessman; National City chief quits church," by Darrell Holland.

"Cleveland's school system"

Cleveland Press, 12 December 1977, "Kucinich vetoes tax abatements."

Cleveland Press, 13 December 1977, Page One, "Schools must make cuts in $50 million deficit."

Plain Dealer, 21 December 1977, "Schools must make loans or switch funds for payroll," by Peter Almond.

Cleveland Press, 20 December 1977, Page One, "Mayor won't OK tax break deals," by Peter Phipps.

Plain Dealer, 22 December 1977, Page One, "Council overrides Kucinich vetoes; Vote overwhelming; tax abatements get OK; jobs spur cited," by William Carlson.

Plain Dealer, 22 December 1977, Page One, "Troubles mounting for city schools; $45 million deficit seen; Master's fee is $456,428; Officials told to buy buses," by Thomas H. Gaumer.

Plain Dealer, 22 December 1978, Schools borrow from Peter to meet Paul's payroll," by Thomas Gaumer, page 5-A.

Cleveland Press, 30 December 1977, Page One, "School Pay In Peril, Tax Levy is Proposed," by Peter Almond.

See also: *Cleveland Press*, 9 February 1978, "New payroll crisis threatens schools," by Bud Weidenthal.

Plain Dealer, 28 March 1978, "4 major banks refuse loans for city schools."The banks were Cleveland Trust, National City Bank, Central National Bank and Society National Bank.

PART II: THE MAYOR WHO SAID "NO"

31. STILL ANOTHER CHRISTMAS BLACKOUT

"Blackout! Muny Light went dark and Christmas disappeared"

Plain Dealer, 22 December 1977, Page One, "Muny Light outage, 45,000 in dark for 4 hrs."

Cleveland Press, 22 December 1977, Page One, "45,000 without power for 4 hrs."

Plain Dealer, 22 December 1977, "Mayor puts part of blame for power blackout on CEI."

"No question in my mind, CEI had precipitated this holiday-season blackout"

Plain Dealer, 23 December 1977, "Muny Light restores power, CEI denies Kucinich charges," page 8-A.

Cleveland Press, 22 December 1977, Page One, "Blackout. CEI denies it was able to prevent Muny crisis."

Cleveland Press, 22 December 1977, Page One, "Blackout. Homes got power before businesses."

Plain Dealer, 23 December 1977, "Sparks begin to fly, now that power is on," by William R. Diem, page 8-A.

"The NRC had already documented blackouts"

Federal Energy Regulatory Commission, 6 December 1977, "CEI v. Cleveland Electric Illuminating Co. Docket Nos E-7631 and E-7633 and E-7712."

"Although we failed to disqualify Squire Sanders"

Plain Dealer, 18 January 1978, Page One, "City adds two law firms to battle CEI," by Robert H. Holden.

"We pressed CEI for access"

Cleveland Press, 30 December 1977, "City to ask shutdown of Davis-Besse plant."

"CEI and other Ohio private utilities"

Plain Dealer, 6 December 1977, "Right Image for Utilities Costs Millions," by Robert H. Holden.

Cleveland Press, 10 January 1978, "Customers hold the bag as utilities skip taxes."

Cleveland Press, 16 December 1977, "Stockholders OK CEI's 3 for 2 split."

Plain Dealer, 21 January 1978, "No moratorium on gas, electric cutoffs," followed by: *Cleveland Press*, 23 January 1978, CEI construction to cost $363 million.

[Note: At the end of 1977, CEI sold $659,290,000 worth of electricity and had a net income of $111,720,000. CEI 1978 annual report.]

"CEI again struck at Muny Light"

WEWS-TV5, 23 February 1978, "Federal Marshals Tag City to Pay CEI Bill,"
Transcript:
Dave Patterson: "Today the long fight through the courts over that debt took a new turn. The federal judge on the case sent U.S. Marshals out to put tags on city property at the Muny Light plant and at City Hall, in effect, attaching that property. And it must be auctioned off if the debt is not paid in the next few weeks."

"Cleveland City Council then met today and they voted to try to issue some special bonds to pay the bill. They recognized this idea might not be legal, and intend to get clearance from the state Supreme Court before the trial."

WEWS-TV5 Anchor Ted Henry: "Dave, the action by the federal marshals today has triggered an immediate response from the mayor's office."

"Dennis Kucinich has come out swinging at CEI, an arch-foe of his for quite some time. The mayor said it is unheard of for any company to take such action against an entire city."

WEWS-TV5 Reporter Tappy Phillips: "Federal marshals went around today tagging furniture, equipment, vehicles, property and other Cleveland assets, putting the pressure on to get the city to pay a $20 million debts it owes to CEI."

"That debt is for power bought by Muny Light, and until it's paid, the city won't be able to sell any of the tagged items, but not among them police or fire equipment," said Phillips.

Plain Dealer, 23 February 1978, Page One, "CEI to wait some more; Action to seize city property is frozen," by Robert H. Holden.

Cleveland Press, 23 February 1978, "CEI frozen in attempt to attach assets."

Plain Dealer 24 February 1978, "Kucinich blasts CEI's move to attach assets over Muny bill," page A-5.

Plain Dealer, 26 February 1978, "CEI helps Kucinich; PR blunder seen in utility's claim action," by Joseph D. Rice, page 2-B.

Cleveland Press, 24 February 1978, "Muny Light debt may strain budget," by Peter Phipps.

See also: *Plain Dealer*, 24 February 1978, Page One, "Angry Judge grills lawyers on CEI debt," by Robert H. Holden. Judge threatens Kucinich administration leaders with contempt charge. "The city, Krupansky said, has ignored his April 27, 1977 order that City Council put enough money in the budget to satisfy the debt and appropriate the money not later than May 21, 1977."

"Then his tone changed"

Attorney Brad Norris, document, 26 February 1978 "Kucinich Action Plan for Muny Light." Kucinich archives.

32. THE 100 MPH BLIZZARD

"We do not have the plows"

Cleveland Press, 10 January 1978, "Snowplow trucks ordered by city fail to show up."

33. THE CHIEF

"As Hongisto arrived, an epidemic of "blue flu"

Plain Dealer, 14 December 1977, Page One, "New city police chief named; Controversial California sheriff to succeed Ahrens."

Plain Dealer, 15 December 1977, Page One, "Day One. Police chief vows active department," by William Carlson and Donald Leander Bean.

Cleveland Press, 15 December 1977, Page One, "90% of Patrolmen Fail to Show for Duty."

Cleveland Press, 15 December 1977,"Hongisto starts off with a crisis," page A-4.

Cleveland Press, 15 December 1977, "Hongisto draws faith and doubt," by Jim Marino.

Cleveland Press, 16 December 1977, Page One, "Work Tonight or Face Firing, Kucinich Warns."

Cleveland Press, 16 December 1977, "Patrol group tells callers strike could go on for weeks," by Jim Marino. "McNea said yesterday's sick call was the 'spontaneous reaction' of city policemen for months of misrepresentations..."

Plain Dealer, 16 December 1977, Page One, "City passes 1st flu day well, safely," by Donald Leander Bean and William Carlson.

Cleveland Press, 16 December 1977, Page One, "Kucinich Rebuffs Police; 'Won't negotiate with lawbreakers.'"

Cleveland Press, 16 December 1977, Page One, "Mayor scorns 'sick' patrolmen."

Cleveland Press, 16 December 1977, Page One,"City-police feud 'almost war.'"

Plain Dealer, 17 December 1978, Page One, "Police End 'Blue Flu' Walkout."

Cleveland Press, 20 December 1977, "Kucinich vs. cops," by Don Robertson, Press Columnist.

34. PAPER BAGS, PAPER CASH

"For more than three years"

Plain Dealer, 12 January 1978, Page One, "Forbes admits taking money from carnival gambling firm; used funds to help ward club, charities, he says."

Plain Dealer, 12 January 1978, Page One, "Forbes' bodyguard, Watkins, provides security for carnivals," by Daniel R. Biddle.

Plain Dealer, 12 January 1978, "Carnival brings show to town every season," by Daniel R. Biddle, page 8-A.

Cleveland Press, 12 January 1978, "County will probe Forbes carnival cash."

Cleveland Press, 13 January 1978, "FBI figure is linked to Carnival here," by Brent Larkin and Jerry Kvet, page A-8.

Plain Dealer, 13 January 1978, Page One, "FBI, Corrigan, police checking Forbes' ties," by Daniel R. Biddle. "This may be "legally wrong," Forbes conceded, but he insisted that all the money ultimately went to charity, and that therefore it is morally right."

Plain Dealer, 14 January 1978, "Prosecutor subpoenas city records connected with Sebring carnivals," by Daniel R. Biddle, page 3-A.

Cleveland Press, 14 January 1978, Page One, "Seven speak out for Forbes."

Cleveland Press, 16 January 1978, "Carnival reportedly paid 9."

Plain Dealer, 17 January 1978, Page One, "Forbes took carnival gripes to Perk; Garey says complaints were trigger for firing," by Daniel R. Biddle. "City Council President George L. Forbes, once asked Mayor Ralph J. Perk to discourage police action against illegal gambling at Sebring Exhibit & Supply carnivals here."

Cleveland Press, 17 January 1978, "Council's role in carnivals studied."

Cleveland Press, 18 January 1978, "Council and the carnivals." An Editorial. "One trouble is that no records were kept on most of the transactions. The money changed hands in envelopes, paper bags or just in wads of bills. Another trouble is that the money involved was raised form illegal gambling."

Cleveland Press, 18 January 1978, "9 on Council face Grand Jury probe," by Jim Marino.

Plain Dealer, 18 January 1978, Page One, "City Hall no longer to seek councilmen's approval of carnivals," by Daniel R. Biddle.

West Side Sun News, 18 January 1978, FBI and police launch probe into allegations," by Brian Hyps.

Plain Dealer, 20 January 1978, "Council's carnival caper." An Editorial. "It is left to the joint investigation by the FBI, the Cuyahoga County prosecutor's office and the Cleveland police intelligence unit to determine if any wrongdoing has occurred."

Call-Post, 21 January 1978, Page One,"News Media Leading Assault on Forbes, Six Councilmen."

Call-Post, 21 January 1978, "Carlton Rush Says Everyone Did It."

Plain Dealer, 19 April 1978, Carnival licensing may be lost to council."

"The county prosecutor"

Cleveland Press, 2 February 1978, Page One, "Councilmen's Records Sought on Carnivals," by Brent Larkin.

Plain Dealer, 3 February 1978, Page One, "7

Councilmen are called in carnival probe," by Daniel R. Biddle.

"We were gearing up"

Plain Dealer, 25 November 1977, "New unit to fight organized crime," by Mairy Jayn Woge.

"Jack Schulman was challenging"

Cleveland Press, 31 January 1978, Page One, "Loans to bars ignored," by Walt Bogdanich and Walter Johns Jr.

Cleveland Press, 31 January 1978, "Kucinich seeks law to ban tavern loans," by Peter Phipps.

See Also: *Cleveland Press*, 26 January 1978, Page One, "How Charity Dollars Help Bankroll the Mob," by Walt Bogdanich and Walter Johns, Jr.

Cleveland Press, 27 January 1978, Page One, "Charity-backed firm aids mob," by Walt Bogdanich and Walter Johns, Jr.

Cleveland Press, 27 January 1978, "Charity trustees surprised at loan firm's link to mobsters."

"A Cleveland Press investigation"

Cleveland Press, 30 January 1978, Page One, "Seaway Puts Secret Grip on Tavern Industry Here," by Walt Bogdanich and Walter Johns Jr.

"When we began to crack down"

Cleveland Press, 24 April 1978, "Kucinich proposes law to regulate vending machines," by Walt Bogdanich.

Cleveland Press, 1 February 1978, Page One, "Loan Firm is Winner at Bingo for Billions," by Walt Bogdanich and Walter Johns, Jr.

Cleveland Press, 8 February 1978, Page One, "How 'Mr. Charity' avoided court," by Walt Bogdanich and Walter Johns, Jr.

Cleveland Press, 20 April 1979, "Schulman reveals vending threats," by Peter Phipps.

"Ten days later"

Plain Dealer, 13 March 1978, "Carnival gambling inquiry going well, probers say."

Cleveland Press 23 March 1978, ". . . under investigation by police, the FBI and the county prosecutor for their alleged ties to the carnival operator, Sebring Exhibit and Supply Co."

"The briefest review of the public record"

Cleveland Press, 23 March 1978, "What Hongisto Charges: Pressured to curtail an investigation."

"After reading the published charges"

Plain Dealer, 24 March 1978, Page One, "Chief suspended, he'll be watched. Spell out your complaints, Kucinich tells Hongisto," by Daniel Biddle.

Cleveland Press, 24 March 1978, "Councilmen, police cry: Keep Hongisto."

"I went live on the Six O'Clock News"

Plain Dealer, 25 March 1978, Page One, "Fired Hongisto blasts the mayor; 'Kucinich wants to be president,'" by Daniel R. Biddle and W. Joseph Campbell.

Plain Dealer, 25 March 1978, "Mayor faults Hongisto on the truth," by W. Joseph Campbell and Daniel R. Biddle, page 4-A.

Plain Dealer, 25 March 1978, Kucinich on the defensive. Mayor tries to talk his way out of pro-Hongisto outcry," by Joseph D. Rice.

Plain Dealer, 25 March 1978, "Hongisto's charges," by Richard Hongisto.

Cleveland Press, 25 March 1978, Page One, "Fired police chief comes out shooting," by Peter Phipps.

Cleveland Press, 25 March 1978, "Kucinich, fastest gun, gets nicked," by Brent Larkin, page A-7.

Plain Dealer, 26 March 1978, Page One, "'Why I fired Hongisto' Chief did not accept the mayor as his superior, Kucinich states," by Daniel R. Biddle.

Plain Dealer, 26 March 1978, "Kucinich responds," by Dennis Kucinich.

35. EASTER SHOTGUN SUNDAY

"The 6:00 O'Clock News on TV8"

WJW-TV8 News Report, 27 March 1978, Transcript: "Police say Mayor target of gunman."

37. RECALL MADNESS.

"The city was at the brink of a financial crisis"

Plain Dealer, 2 February 1978, Page One, "City's money is running out," by Joseph L. Wagner.

Cleveland Press, 1 March 1978, Page One, "City faces cutbacks to pay debt to CEI," by Meg Algren.

Plain Dealer, 4 March 1978, Page One, "City must pay CEI debt this year; Order to hand over $18 million may cause financial crisis," by Joseph L. Wagner.

Plain Dealer, 5 March 1978, Page One, "Massive city layoffs loom to pay CEI, save Muny Light," by Harry Stainer.

Cleveland Press, 6 March 1978, "City has a plan on CEI - - a secret," by Peter Phipps.

Plain Dealer, 7 March 1978, "Councilmen fail push for light plant sale," by William Carlson, page 10-A.

Cleveland Press, 7 March 1977, "City studies land sale to pay CEI," by Peter Phipps.

Plain Dealer, 8 March 1978, "City officials to disclose plan for paying CEI debt," by Robert H. Holden, page 9-A.

Plain Dealer, 9 March 1978, Page One, "City may sell land to pay debt," by Joseph L. Wagner.

Cleveland Press, 9 March 1978, "City says CEI blocks Muny debt payment."

Plain Dealer, 9 March 1978, "CEI presses to collect other city debts," by Robert H Holden, page 14-A.

Cleveland Press, 11 March 1978, Page One, "Plan to save Muny is disclosed," by Meg Algren.

Plain Dealer, 19 April 1978, Page One, "September Song: City Might be Broke," by Joseph L. Wagner.

"While editorialists pointed out"

Cleveland Press, 27 April 1978, "New downtown tower to begin this year," by Meg Algren.

Cleveland Press, 17 April 1978, "It's opening night for 25-cent dog," by Peter Phipps.

Plain Dealer, 1 April 1978, "Quit criticizing my son." Letter to the Editor.

39. BANK SHOT

"It was clear Cleveland Trust was preparing"

"*Staff Study on City of Cleveland Financing,*" June 1979, page 33, by the Subcommittee on Financing Institutions Supervision, Regulation and Insurance of the U.S. House of Representatives Committee on Banking, Finance and Urban Affairs.

"The credit downgrade"

Cleveland Press, 9 June 1978, Rating drop could cost city $50,000."

"Save the city, sell Muny"

[Re: NRC orders, January 6. 1977 *Plain Dealer,* 30 June 1978, "CEI violating deal with Muny to transmit power, U.S. claims,"]

WEWS-TV5, 1 July 1978, Transcript:

Roger Morris: "Well, Bill, the latest...belongs to Muny Light. The Nuclear Regulatory Commission has issued a notice of violation against the Cleveland Electric Illuminating Company. What it amounts to is this: Muny Light claimed that when they tried to purchase power from out of state at low rates, CEI tried to set an unreasonable contract on them. They wanted the contract based on a year or so. Well, the Nuclear Regulatory Commission agreed with Muny Light, saying that they should be allowed to have a contract for a week or whatever to transmit across CEI's lines to bring cheap power into the city. This seems to back up claims by City Hall that Muny Light is being tried to put out of business by CEI. Now, CEI could face a fine or other penalties unless they respond within twenty days and have some kind of a way to turn this over."

"Meanwhile, our effort to issue $20 million"

WJW-TV8, 5 July 1978, "City cannot use judgment bonds to pay off Muny Light Debt to CEI," transcript:

Tim Taylor: "A major setback for the city of Cleveland today. Susan Howard is live with the City Cam with this late breaking report. Susan?"

Susan Howard: "At five-thirty this afternoon, that's just a half hour ago, the Ohio Supreme Court ruled that the city of Cleveland may not issue judgment bonds to pay off its debt to the Cleveland Electric Illuminating Company that's owed by Muny Light. Ever since he began to campaign for mayor, Mayor Kucinich pledged to keep Muny. All right, now that the Supreme Court has thrown a monkey wrench into those plans, what now? Well there are two options: Sell Muny Light, as Mayor Perk has said was necessary all along or watch Cleveland just go broke just like the City of New York. Cleveland already has a deficit of $17 million, now with this, we're $37 million in the red. Just a few minutes ago, the mayor said he does have a new plan, but he won't divulge what that is, he says, until some time next week. However, he did say the plan is going to require some help from City Council. We all know he hasn't had an easy time, and he probably won't have an easy time getting that."

WKYC-TV3, 6 July 1978, transcript:

Doug Adair: "As you are probably aware, the city of Cleveland had wanted to issue $20 million in bonds to pay off a big debt to CEI. Yesterday the Supreme Court said: 'You cannot do that. That is against the law.' Well Roger Wolfe right now is with Mayor Kucinich out on the steps leading to City Hall. The city says that they have another answer, and we'll find out if the mayor wants to talk to us right now."

Roger Wolfe: "Thank you, Doug, Mayor Kucinich, is there any way that the city can now afford to hold on to the Muny Light plant after the court's ruling yesterday?"

Kucinich: "Well, first it has to be stated that Muny Light is making a profit. At the end of this year we'll have $1 million profit. That's compared to the statements last year which said it couldn't make any money at all. We will pay the Muny Light debt. The Ohio Supreme Court has ruled against the payment plan that we offered, but we have been searching for alternatives and we do have alternatives. About a week from now, I'll have a plan to present to the people of Cleveland and to the City Council. I'll need the public's cooperation and Council's support to enable us to save Muny Light and to straighten out all the city's financial problems. This isn't anything that can be done alone, but I've proved that Muny Light can make money, and so I'm very certain that as the people of Cleveland find out that it is a resource they will not want to give it up, specifically when they need to keep it to hold the line on utility rates."

WJW-TV8 Report, 7 July 1978, transcript:

Anchor Tim Taylor: "Now that the Ohio Supreme Court has said no to Dennis Kucinich's plan to pay its multi-million dollar CEI bill, the next move seems to be up to CEI. Mayor Kucinich is telling a news conference this morning he's working on another plan to keep Muny Light and he'll reveal it within a week. But the question is, what if the Illuminating Company acts before then?"

Kucinich: "CEI has no right to close down the City of Cleveland, and there are some serious questions as to how far they could go in their attempt to get their money right away."

Taylor: "And CEI told us today they expect the city to pay its bill just like any other customer. No word on the next legal steps."

WJW-TV8, "Muny Light and Recall Issue," 6 July, 1978, transcript:

Anchor Tim Taylor: "Meanwhile, a leader of the movement to recall the Mayor, had a reaction to the latest Muny Light developments:

Ballew: I do think that taking it to the state Supreme Court has some merit Because now the question has been settled by the court. They can no longer speculate on it, but I think all it does is heighten the hoax that the mayor has played on the city about what he was going to do about saving Muny Light."

Cleveland Press, 6 July 1978, "Mayor has plan despite Muny ruling," by Peter Phipps.

"Nationally, investor-owned utilities"

Wall Street Journal, 7 December 1977, "Cities Protest Electric Rate Differences Charged by Investor-Owned Utilities."

"Led by CEI, private utilities"

Cleveland Press, 15 March 1978, "CEI hikes bills 3% despite lower oil use."

Cleveland Press, 22 March 1978, "Power costs rise as utilities buy, sell among selves".

Plain Dealer, 28 March 1978, Page One, "Power bills the 'catastrophe;' Coal strike blackouts, layoffs averted while consumer cost skyrocketed," by Robert H. Holden.

Plain Dealer, 31 March 1978, Page One, "CEI resold its excess purchased power at a profit," by Robert H. Holden.

See also: Plain Dealer, 30 January 1978, Page One, "Power cut is part of CEI plan."

CEI calling for "a gradual reduction of electric service as coal supplies dwindle."

"At its annual meeting, CEI's"

Plain Dealer, 26 April 1978, Page One,"Elderly pay in pennies as CEI profits decline 41%," by Thomas W. Gerdel.

Cleveland Press, 26 April 1978, "Seniors are turned off by CEI rates," by Charles Tracy.

"Ohio's Consumers Counsel"

Cleveland Press, 25 April 1978, "$50 million refund is sought from CEI."

Plain Dealer, 11 May 1978, "U.S. will probe electric utilities' coal strike deals," by Robert H. Holden.

Plain Dealer, 12 May 1978, "Utility overcharge of $100 million in coal strike claimed," by Thomas J. Brazaitis.

Cleveland Press, 12 May 1978, "CEI 'welcomes' U.S. probe for overcharges."

Plain Dealer, 31 March 1978, "CEI resold its excess purchased power at a profit."

Plain Dealer, 24 May 1978, "Consumers' counsel calls utility profits excessive."

"Whenever comparing itself to Muny Light"

Plain Dealer 7 May 1978, Page One, "Customers billed $72 million for $3 million in CEI taxes," by Amos Kermisch.

Plain Dealer, 10 June 1977, Letter-to-the-Editor, "Who threw a switch," by Christopher J. Aquila.

"CEI's attempts to keep its new Davis-Besse"

Cleveland Press, 24 June 1978, "Davis-Besse shut down 30% of time."

Plain Dealer, 1 July 1978, "CEI to face big penalty for flaws in Perry plant."

"CEI and other state utilities"

Plain Dealer, 7 September 1978, "PUCO rules utilities can continue to pass ad costs to customers," by Robert H. Holden

Plain Dealer, 23 June 1978, "Forbes weighing Rhodes' offer of a seat on PUCO," by Joseph D. Rice.

"Finances became more prominent"

Cleveland Press, 28 June 1978, "City 'discovers' a deficit of $17 million," by Peter Phipps.

Plain Dealer, 30 June 1978, "Kucinich money switching banned by worried council," by David T. Abbott.

Plain Dealer, 6 July 1978, "Scraping bottom. Concern rises over city cash shortage," by Frederick E. Freeman.

Cleveland Press, 7 July 1978, Page One, "Question: Is Cleveland Broke? Russo says city deep in debt; Tegreene says it's temporary," by Peter Phipps.

Plain Dealer, 7 July 1978, "Save city, sell Muny." An Editorial. "A municipal light plant worth 10 times the pile of dirty bricks north of E. Memorial Shoreway could never be worth more than the city's fiscal integrity."

"The city's credit rating was downgraded"

Plain Dealer, 9 June 1978, Page One, "City's credit rating cut, schools' is too," by Joseph L. Wagner.

Plain Dealer, 10 June 1978, Page One, "Tegreene blasts Moody's for cut in credit rating," by Joseph L. Wagner and Frederick E. Freeman.

Cleveland Press, 14 July 1978, "Mayor's plan lacks support," by Peter Phipps.

Plain Dealer, 11 July 1978, Page One, "City's bond rating suspended; S&P doubts financial stability," by Frederick E. Freeman.

Cleveland Press, 11 July 1978, "City loses bond rating, is likened to New York," by Peter Phipps.

Plain Dealer, 18 July 1978, "Cleveland's fall like New York's."

"We devised a new plan to pay CEI"

Plain Dealer, 18 July 1978, "Light's dim for Muny; Sale of city assets alone just won't yield enough," by Frederick E. Freeman, page 1-C.

"The state auditor"

Plain Dealer, 25 July 1978, Page One, "Books 'a mess;' State reports Cleveland is inauditable." "The condition inherited by Mayor Dennis J. Kucinich's administration..."

See also: *Plain Dealer*, 3 August 1978, Page One, "Cleveland on the Brink: Tense drama unfolds in money juggling act," by Thomas J. Brazaitis and George P. Rasenen.

"We have to wear the jacket for Perk's policy of using bond money to meet general fund obligations, Council President George L. Forbes, D-20, said in an interview. "Council could have forced the issue and told Perk, 'You don't do it.' We could have brought the city to a halt then instead of today."

40. RECALL MADNESS II

"When Schulman presented his conclusions"

Plain Dealer, 4 July 1978, Page One,"Kucinich fires salvo at dock lease; Port authority lawyer criticizes stand, points to steel needs," by David T. Abbott and Stephen A. Blossom.

"I will not be silenced, Mr. Chairman"

Plain Dealer, 11 July 1978, Page One, "Kucinich, cabinet walk out on council," by David T. Abbott.

Cleveland Press, 11 July 1978, Page One, "City Hall crisis; Kucinich storms out, Bond rating held up, Dock lease approved," by Peter Phipps.

See also: *Cleveland Press*, 5 September 1978, Page One, "We've Got a Deal' to Build Ore Dock," by Peter Phipps.

Plain Dealer, 24 October 1978, "Lorain's Ore Dock prospects brighter; Congress fails to OK deepening of harbor here," by Thomas W. Gerdel, page 1-C.

"Prior to adjourning the meeting"

Cleveland Press, 18 July 1978, "Kucinich expected to veto carnival coin machine law," by Peter Phipps.

Cleveland Press, 20 July 1978, 'The Penny Fall game." An Editorial.

"I was in the Public Auditorium"

Plain Dealer, 21 July 1978, "Steelworkers leave Kucinich speech to protest dock delay," by Jacqueline V. Jones and Joseph D. Rice.

"The police returned to work"

Plain Dealer, 15 July 1978, Page One, "Strike Ends; City Police on Job; Fired 13 get arbitration; heavy-fine threat works."

41. "WE COULD LOSE"

"A few days before the election, another nightmare"

Plain Dealer, 10 August 1978, "Mechanics' walkout ends," by David T. Abbott.

West Side Sun News, 10 August 1978, "Council tells mayor no to mechanics pay raises, by Brian Hyps."

42. PROPHETS OF POISON

"At the kitchen table"

Plain Dealer, 11 August 1978, Page One, "Sell Muny Light or risk takeover, Cleveland's financial adviser says," by Frederick E. Freeman and Joseph L. Wagner.

"Another headline read"

Plain Dealer, 11 August 1978, Page One, "City to run out of cash for payrolls," by Frederick E. Freeman and Joseph L. Wagner.

"A third front-page story"

Plain Dealer, 11 August 1978, Page One, "Service worse under mayor, poll shows," by Joseph D. Rice.

"The recall was fait accompli"

Plain Dealer, 11 August, 1978, Page One, "Hagan's choice: Mayor Feighan."

"A shiver went through me"

Plain Dealer, 26 May 1978, "Who will be new crime chief? Who wants to?" page 14-A. "James T. (Jack White) Licavoli, reputed head of Cleveland's organized crime family, was found innocent yesterday of involvement in the murder last Oct. 6, of Daniel J. Greene."

43. THEY WILL KILL YOU

Plain Dealer, 24 August 1978, Page One, "Kucinich, Forbes to chew steak, grits, city peace at Tony's."

Cleveland Press, 22 August 1978, Page One, "Council Set to Defeat Saving of Muny Light," by Brent Larkin.

Plain Dealer, 23 August 1978, Page One, "Council refuses to OK land deal; Forbes demands sale of Muny," by Joseph L. Wagner and Frederick Freeman.

Also on that day: *Plain Dealer*, 23 August 1978, "Perk, police brass testify for carnival jury," by Daniel S. Biddle.

44. NOT BANKING ON CLEVELAND

"I chose a live radio show"

Cleveland Press, 15 September 1978, Page One,

"Kucinich aims at new target - - city's banks."

Cleveland Press, 17 August 1978, "City turning to big banks to help out," by Peter Phipps.

Cleveland Press, 18 September 1978, "Mayor Threatens to Lead Uprising Against Banks," by Peter Phipps, page A-9.

Plain Dealer, 19 September 1978, "Kucinich threatens to lead drive against banks in city," by David T. Abbott.

Further reading: *Plain Dealer*, 4 September 1978, "Business problem: Kucinich won't heel," by Thomas S. Andrzejewski.

"The Plain Dealer responded"

Plain Dealer, 19 September 1978, An Editorial: "Kucinich vs. Banks."

Cleveland Press, 20 September 1978, An Editorial: "Mayor vs. the banks," page A-18, "The mayor flayed the banks for refusing to buy city notes. The truth is, though, that the Kucinich administration could not provide the detailed financial information requested nor produce any data at all to back up the mayor's claim that Muny Light is making money, a key factor in any sale of notes."

"The Chairman of the local Democratic Party"

Cleveland Press, 19 September 1978, "Dem Chief Blames Mayor, Not Banks," by Peter Phipps. "Democratic Party Chairman Tim Hagan today accused Mayor Kucinich of trying to make the city's banks a scapegoat for his own inability to govern...Kucinich's statement sounded like an attack against this country's free enterprise system."

"I spoke to our Commissioner of Economic"

Cleveland Press, 27 September 1978, "City is contemplating running its own bank."

Plain Dealer, 29 September 1978, "Forget bank, 13 councilmen tell mayor."

"One immediate justification"

Plain Dealer, 25 May 1979, "National City once targeted by city on redlining law," by Thomas S. Andrzejewski.

Cleveland Press, 2 August 1979, "NOACA says banks, S&Ls export money; County shortchanged; Loans go out of area; Economy here hurt," by Betty Klaric, page B-7. "Banks and savings and loans associations based in Cuyahoga County may be shortchanging the county's minority and integrated neighborhoods, according to the Cuyahoga Plan."

Plain Dealer, 2 August 1979, Page One, "NOACA: S&Ls, banks invest in faraway homes," by Thomas S. Andrzejewski. "The Cleveland Planning Commission issued a report that said the study had two inescapable conclusions: "The city of Cleveland has not been receiving a reasonable share of the area's conventional mortgage funds and a high percentage of local depositors' money is being used to finance residential lending in other parts of the country."

45. DEATH RIDES THE FERRIS WHEEL

"An investigation revealed"

Plain Dealer, 21 August 1978, "Carnival Operator is called on the carpet by City; Ride from which child fell was run without OK,"

Cleveland Press, 23 August 1978, "Ride That Hurt Girl Not OK'd City told."

Plain Dealer, 24 August 1978, "Girl dies of fall; city bans ride operator."

Plain Dealer, 25 August 1978, "Act in child's death."

Cleveland Press, 25 August 1978, "Death Haunts carnivals."

"The same day as the Ferris wheel"

Cleveland Press, 23 August 1978, "Jury quizzes in secrecy on carnivals."

Cleveland Press, 25 August 1978,"Carnival probe; Detectives to tell grand jurors about Sebring firm's operation"

Plain Dealer, 23 August 1978, "Perk, police brass testify for carnival jury."

Plain Dealer, 25 August 1978, "Carnival Probe Detectives to Tell Grand Jurors About Sebring Firms Operation."

"Cheryl Winiarz' mother and father"

Plain Dealer, 24 August 1978, Girl dies of fall; city bans ride operator.

46. BLOODY HELL

"Forbes was out for blood"

Plain Dealer, 3 October 1978, "Forbes is at Kucinich's Throat Again."

West Side Sun News, 5 October 1978, "Forbes calls mayor's talk communist; advises change." For further reference:

Cleveland Press, 3 October 1978, "Kucinich defines 'urban populism' speech to the National Press Club," Washington, D.C., full text, page A-9, by Dennis J. Kucinich

"The new theme became"

Cleveland Press, Centennial Edition, Page One, 2 November 1978, "Crisis Seen, Payless Paydays, Debt Defaults Loom in City, Prediction, Sale of Muny Light is called Way Out," by Peter Phipps.

47. THE MURDER PLOT

"I stepped away"

Plain Dealer, 24 October 1978, Page One, "Outsider Fox is new police chief. Council hiring lawyer to challenge selection of a non-policeman," by David T. Abbott and Donald Leander Bean.

Cleveland Press, 24 October 1978, "Police are split over new chief, by Ron Kovach.

Note: For a report on the peaceful implementation of court-ordered desegregation in Cleveland schools, see *Plain Dealer,* 11 September 1979, Page One, "First day's busing goes peacefully," by Stephen P. Adams and Christopher Jensen

"There is a plot to murder you"

U.S. Senate Subcommittee Investigation, 9 October 1978. According to the Maryland State Police, the hit man visited Cleveland during the week of October 9, 1978 to meet with those who wanted the Mayor killed. He met during that week at a Cleveland bar with an organized crime figure named Tommy, who offered to pay him $25,000 to kill the Mayor. The murder contract was arranged for that week.

Plain Dealer, 15 October 1978, Page One, "Kucinich hospitalized with stomach ailment."

48. YOU'VE GOT YOUR PROBLEMS, WE'VE GOT OURS

"Forbes used Chief Fox's appointment"

Plain Dealer, 25 October 1978, "City safety forces told they might go payless."

Cleveland Press, 25 October 1978, "Police Pay Crisis Looms; Forbes is holding up funds," by Peter Phipps. "I am fully aware this means the city could miss a police payroll, but the figures I have just been presented by the administration show the city has run up a $16 million deficit this year," Forbes said.

Cleveland Press, 27 October 1978, "Police Chief Fox tells of fight with alcohol; I'm leading a beautiful life - - sober, functioning well," by Ron Kovach, page A-5.

See also: *Plain Dealer,* 31 October 1978, "Kucinich surfaces. Absentee ballot is cast by mayor who is departing for a 'secret' spot," by David T. Abbott, page 1-B. "Since he went into the hospital [Oct. 14}...a new police chief has been appointed..."

"The tempest over the new chief receded"

Plain Dealer, 28 October 1978, "Marbles Led to Tumble. It All Started When A Man Lost $160 on a Carnival Game," by Daniel R. Biddle. Forbes [charged with] one count of intimidation, one count of extortion, four counts of theft in office, seven counts of bribery and one count of engaging in organized crime.

Plain Dealer, 28 October 1978, "Largest number of public officials ever to be indicted in a single investigation in Ohio." [Note: 498 counts against 6 councilmen, two former and 10 others.]

"I was not going to associate with the investigation"

Cleveland Press, 30 October 1978, Page One, "$100,00 is Defense Goal in Council Kickback Scandal," by Peter Phipps. "[Councilman Terrence] Copeland blamed the Kucinich Administration for instigating and promoting the carnival probe."

Plain Dealer, 31 October 1978, Page One, "Throng cheers for indicted 8," by David T. Abbott and Joseph L. Wagner. "Of the 18 persons indicted in the carnival investigation, eight are white. Most of the whites are carnival employees. The councilmen accused Mayor Dennis J. Kucinich of encouraging the investigation by putting Sgt. John E. Joyce on the case."

See also: *Plain Dealer,* 31 October 1978, Page One, "Council holds up police payroll," by Joseph L. Wagner and Frederick E. Freeman.

Plain Dealer, 2 November 1978, "Forbes, 4 others Plead Innocent to 48 Charges," by W. James Van Vliet.

"Former building commissioner Carlton Rush, now an executive of the Cleveland Electric Illuminating Company, pleaded innocent to three counts of engaging in organized crime and four counts of theft in office. He was released on $500 personal bond.

"Once under indictment"

Plain Dealer, 3 November 1978, "Police Get Paid Minutes After Council OKs Fund."

The *Cleveland Press*, Centennial Edition, 2 November 1978, "Payless Paydays, Debt Defaults Loom in City. Prediction. Sale of Muny Light is Called Way Out. Officials are Shaken. Russo and White Assail Tegreene, Say He is a 'Bold-faced Liar,'" by Peter Phipps.

"The City of Cleveland"

Plain Dealer 3 November 1978, Page One, "Council Holding Bond Issue Hostage. New Demand for sale of Muny Light," by Joseph L. Wagner and Frederick E. Freeman. Forbes quote: "I don't know what we are going to do, but I think the administration should be prepared to talk about the Muny Light Plant," said Council President George Forbes before today's hearings."

Plain Dealer, 2 November 1978, Page One, "$34 Million Deficit Predicted Without New City Fiscal Plan," by Frederick E. Freeman and Joseph L. Wagner.

"Salomon Brothers"

Cleveland Press, 6 October 1978, "City Plans Loan of $50 million to Pay Its Debt," page D-3

"I may have been convalescing 1,000 miles away"

Cleveland Press, 3 November 1978, Page One, "'I'll Risk Default'. Kucinich Warns Council on Muny," by Peter Phipps.

"The next day, things were Cleveland-normal"

Cleveland Press, November 1978, "Hear Ye, Hear Ye," by Herb Kamm. Further reference:

Plain Dealer, 23 June 1978, "Ad drive will push highlights of city. 'We are going to tell the world about its greatness, loud and clear.'" "The New Cleveland Campaign, a $4.3 million fund-raising drive to finance a marketing and communications program designed to tell Clevelanders and the rest of the nation about the positive virtues of the city, was announced today."

49. CLEVELAND DREAM

"Someone wanted to kill me"

Cleveland Press, 20 November 1978, "Mayor Feels Great."

Plain Dealer, 20 November 1978 "Mayor Feels Terrific, Juniewicz Reports."

"Tonight, News Center Eight's Bob Franken"

WJW-TV8, 15 November 1978, Report by WJW News Reporter Bob Franken.

SDX Ethics Committee Report, 19 September, 1979.

"Juniewicz put another tape into the VCR"

WJW-TV8, 17 November 1978, "Retraction," by *WJW-TV8* News Director.

"Bob Franken resigned"

Bob Franken, personal interview, 2012.

51. WE DON'T WANT YOUR MONEY

"No plan to save Muny Light was so good"

Plain Dealer, 1 November 1978, "CEI is paid $3 million on Muny Light debt."

Cleveland Press, 17 November 1978, "Utilities delay Ohio A-Plants."

"Then CEI made another claim"

Cleveland Press, 19 October 1978, "CEI given OK to foreclose on city assets."

Plain Dealer, 26 October 1978, "Court asked to block seizure of Muny."

Plain Dealer, 31 October 1978, "City ordered to pay another bill to CEI," by W. James Van Vliet.

"Forbes opposed the land transfer"

Cleveland Press, 28 November 1978, "Council Ignores Land Sale."

"Then, with tax abatement legislation"

WJW-TV8 Report, 11 December 1978, Transcript: "Council did override the mayor's veto of legislation extending tax abatement to the Tower City project."

"Judge Krupansky is threatening"

Cleveland Press, 30 November 1978, Judge warns the city: Pay Debt to CEI, or - -

"Moody's was downgrading our credit"

Plain Dealer, 1 December 1978, "City's Bond Rating Drops One More Notch."

"As we were preparing"

Plain Dealer, 6 December 1978, "Image Builders," by Mary Strassmeyer, page 9. "Speaking of the Growth Association, I understand there were people willing to work on a Christmas parade for the city even though Sandy Kucinich bowed out...."

52. FOREIGN-OWNED CITY

"Word leaked to the media"

Plain Dealer, 7 December 1978, Page One, "City Discusses Loan With Germans; Shaker man is contact to bank offering up to $50 million," by Frederick E. Freeman and Joseph L. Wagner. "I'm caught in an irreconcilable dilemma," said George Forbes. "We are used to an open policy in American public financing as opposed to the European business concept of secret negotiations."

Cleveland Press, 7 December 1978, "Bank in Germany makes offer to city - - deal 'unlikely.'"

Plain Dealer, 7 December 1978, "City Discusses Loan with Germans."

Plain Dealer, 8 December 1978, An Editorial, "A New light at Muny." "The decision by City Council to ask the courts to order Mayor Kucinich to sell the Municipal Light plant, appears to offer the mayor a fine chance to save face while ridding the city of one of its major liabilities."

"Not all of Forbes' efforts to peddle

WKYC-TV3, News Report, 12 December 1978, Transcript:

Amanda Arnold: "And another ongoing struggle, the fight to sell the Muny Light plant. The ball is now back in George Forbes' lap tonight. Late this afternoon, the city filed a motion to dismiss Forbes' request for a court order that would force Mayor Kucinich to sell the plant, under a May, 1977 law. The city's lawyer, Brad Norris, argued that Forbes failed to order the law director to comply with that law before filing his present action, so Norris said that invalidates the whole thing. The appeals court gave Forbes' lawyers until Monday to say why their action should not be thrown out of court."

WJW-TV News, 11 December 1978, transcript:

Tim Taylor: "Mayor Dennis Kucinich has been ordered to either sell Muny Light or show why he should not be forced to sell the utility. The Ohio Eighth District Court of Appeals set 3:00 p.m. Wednesday for a hearing, the same day the Cleveland banks decide whether to extend the city's $15.5 million credit line and avoid default on Friday."

"Milt Schulman was intent"

Plain Dealer, 12 December 1978, "Councilman Floors Lawyer."

Cleveland Press, 12 December 1978, "Schulman charges he was punched."

"Adding to the circus"

WKYC-TV3, 12 December 1978, transcript:

Amanda Arnold: "FBI agents, Federal Alcohol, Tobacco and Firearms people search files, confiscated thousands of records in the building and housing divisions of the community development department in a twenty-month-long investigation of arson for profit. The agents were looking for records of groups of homes and businesses owned by the same person; buildings that have been burned in arson fires."

"Only the NBC affiliate, WKYC"

WKYC-TV, 12 December 1978, transcript:

Kucinich: "If this plan fails, we could find the City of Cleveland losing its water system, losing what's left of its sewer system, losing its Municipal Light System, losing a $325 million antitrust damage suit, and a drastic reduction in city services. The city will have no capacity for any kind of capital improvements whatsoever. On the other hand, if the plan succeeds, there will be no reduction of service and we'll be able to continue our capital improvement program."

Cleveland Press, 11 December 1978, "Kucinich Tells US TV5, 8 are Unfit to Hold Licenses." I protested to the FCC, since the stations had an obligation to serve in the "public interest, convenience and necessity" according to the FCC Act of 1934 which then regulated broadcast media.

WEWS-TV5, News Report, 12 December 1978, transcript: "The mayor has turned us and Channel 8 into the FCC saying that we were unfit because we wouldn't let him on TV."

Plain Dealer, 12 December 1978, "Mayor creates static on lack of TV coverage for city finance speech."

"Councilman Russo said Muny Light"

WJW-TV8, 12 December 1978, transcript:

Reporter Susan Howard: "Still, other councilmen, Basil Russo and Bill Sullivan told me selling Muny Light should be an issue before any tax increase is recommended."

WJW-TV8, 13 December 1978, News Editorial transcript: "Mayor Kucinich has now asked for a 50% increase in the city's income tax. It has been painfully clear for a long time that Cleveland needs more money to operate. The mayor is one of the last to recognize that fact. In our opinion he can start by selling the albatross in the city's sea of financial problems, the Muny Light Plant...."

"Former Mayor Perk responded"

WKYC-TV3, 13 December 1978, transcript: Anchor, Doug Adair: "We are live right now with former Cleveland Mayor, Ralph Perk. Last night, Mayor Kucinich, here on TV3, blamed the city's financial problems on the misspending and overspending of the Perk Administration. Ralph, you are saying that Dennis is lying. Mayor Perk: "Now that he is caught with his finger in the till, he is looking around to blame someone else. Dennis is a pathological liar...he had so much money in the treasury when those kids came into City Hall, they began a wild spending spree beyond anything the city has ever known."

"I invited members of the city council"

WJW-TV8 News, December 13, 1978, transcript:

Jeff Maynor: "Well, council has voted informally 14-13 against calling a special election on the mayor's income tax increase proposal. And the mayor, in a news conference just concluded, said if council does not vote to put the tax issue on the ballot, the city will default on Friday, the day after tomorrow. Now the mayor needs 22 votes in council. He's nine short. Most importantly in that straw vote, City Council President George Forbes voted "no". And most people believe that without Forbes's support, the mayor's tax plan will die in council...."

WKYC-TV3, 13 December 1978, transcript:

Anchor Doug Adair: "Good evening everyone, Mayor Dennis Kucinich this afternoon asking City Council to support his plan to avoid default this Friday, but just a few minutes ago, council voted 14-13 to reject the mayor's plan.

NBC Network News, 13 December 1978, transcript: "...His city is in the midst of a financial crisis, and the local banks and taxpayers can help. What he must sell is a proposal to raise the city income tax by 1/2 of 1%. That is what he was doing this afternoon, meeting with the city council and the money people."

"Images of default flashed"

WEWS-TV5 News, 14 December 1978, from the transcript. Tappy Phillips.

"If Cleveland goes bankrupt"

WEWS-TV5, circa 14 December 1978, from the transcript. Dorothy Fuldheim.

53. PROPAGANDA OR TRUTH?

ABC National News, 14 December 1978, report on Cleveland.

"NBC's national anchorman, Tom Brokaw"

NBC National News, The Today Show, 14 December 1978, transcript, excerpts:

Anchor: "Leaders of the Cleveland City Council have gone on record against Mayor Dennis Kucinich's plan to boost the city's income tax by 50% just to keep that city from going broke. If Cleveland cannot renegotiate some short term notes tomorrow, it will become the first big city to default on its obligations since the Depression of the thirties. Mayor Kucinich will be questioned by Tom Brokaw...

Brokaw: The city of Cleveland is in trouble, big trouble. In just five years, from 1970 to 1975, the city's population declined by more than 15% to just over 600,000 people. Industries, for instance, employing 17,000 people moved out, many of them to the sunbelt. One family out of five in Cleveland began getting help from the government's aid to families with dependent children, they were on welfare. Tomorrow, Cleveland may go bankrupt, it may go broke, the first major city to do so in this country since the Depression... "Mr. Mayor, welcome...

Kucinich: "We've been working with individuals involved in Cleveland's financial community, and we're hoping that we'll be able to get an extension. We're hoping that the banks will recognize that this community includes not only themselves, but the people of Cleveland and all the other institutions who depend on city government, and I think that we've been successful in establishing a spirit of mutual cooperation. So, I'm optimistic that we'll be able to avoid default on those notes which are due tomorrow."

"The default story percolated"

WEWS-TV5, 14 December 1978, transcript:

Dave Patterson: "Mayor Kucinich waited for a meeting with city council, but none materialized. So he talked with reporters, repeating no matter what, he will not sell Muny Light..."

WJW-TV8, 14 December 1978, transcript:

Susan Howard: "...very late today, I learned the councilmen are now even arguing amongst themselves. Apparently, some want to let the voters vote on both the tax increase and the sale of Muny Light. Others say Muny Light should be sold first, and still others feel Muny shouldn't even be tied to a tax vote..."

WJW-TV8, 14 December 1978, transcript:

Virgil Dominic: "We believe that city council should vote to let the people of Cleveland decide for themselves whether they want their taxes increased. The time for debate and disagreement over this critical issue has already passed. In fewer than twenty-four hours, Cleveland will go into default unless dramatic action is taken..."

WEWS-TV5, 14 December 1978, transcript:

Dave Patterson: "John Lathe is here with us live on one of our Actioncams. John, what is the association saying? What are you planning to do?"

Lathe: "The Growth Association encourages the Cleveland City Council to support Mayor Kucinich's plan to put a city income tax increase on the ballot at a special election in February, but only if it should be combined with a referendum on the sale of the Municipal Electric Light system...we strongly believe that the Muny Light plant should be sold, because of the drain that it has on the city finances..."

WEWS-TV5, 14 December 1978, transcript:

Tappy Phillips: "Cleveland may not be first in many respects, but if we don't come up with $15.5 million by tomorrow, we're going to be the first major American city to default since the Great Depression...[and] abysmal credit rating..."

"The city's default is really the same thing as if you or I didn't pay back a loan. There are several solutions. One is the ½% tax increase the mayor offered us. Another is to sell what some are calling Cleveland's Alamo, the Muny Light plant."

NBC-TV, 14 December 1978, excerpts from transcript:

Tom Brokaw: "...debts worth some $15 million in bank loans that come due tomorrow. Matt Quinn reports on the mood in the Cleveland area as the deadline approaches..."

Matt Quinn: "The city councilmen would like to make the Mayor back down. They would like a little revenge. The issue, and the price for cooperation, is the sale of this municipally-owned light company. The councilmen say that the sale would solve the city's problems. The Mayor refuses to sell."

Kucinich: "I'll never sell my soul to the devil. Next question?"

WKYC-TV3, 14 December 1978, transcript:

Dick Feagler: "This is the eve of Cleveland's D-Day and you can pick your "D". Default is the "D" on everybody's mind, and tomorrow is Default Day..."

"The reporter watched as the cabbie looked"

WKYC-TV3, 14 December 1978, transcript:

Attending the meeting at the Investment Plaza, the outstanding notes were held by Cleveland Trust ($5 million), National City Bank ($4 million), Central National Bank ($1 million), Euclid National Bank, ($1 million), Society National Bank ($500,000), Capital National

Bank ($500,000). The Treasury Investment Account of the city held $1.45 million.

54. JUDGMENT DAY: "PAY UP!"

"Sandy went downstairs"

Plain Dealer, 15 December 1978, "Cleveland Trust: Pay Up. Bank would relent if Muny Light were sold," Forbes believes.

"7:20 am. My face felt frozen"

ABC News, 15 December 1978, Good Morning America, David Hartman, Matt Quinn, "Will Cleveland Default?" (From the transcript.)

56. CITY LIGHT

"I spoke with Juniewicz about a new report"

Plain Dealer, December 15, 1978, "Muny Light in black, study says," by David T. Abbott, page 10-A.

Cleveland Press, 15 December 1978, "$1 million sum called loss, not Muny profit," page A-6. R.W. Beck Report, 15 December 1978.

Other sources establishing Muny Light's profitability:

PTX 2168, 1977, City of Cleveland Financial Report: "Department of Public Utilities, Division of Utilities Fiscal Control Light and Power Financial Report." [Comparative]

PTX 2523, 1977 Annual Report: "CEI Annual Report for 1977."

PTX 2169, 1978, City of Cleveland Financial Report: "Department of Public Utilities, Division of Utilities Fiscal Control Light and Power Financial Report."

PTX 2662, Table: "Indicates MELP retained earnings 1915-1979."

"10:30 am The Mayor's Press Office"

Cleveland Press, 15 December 1978, "Council Ultimatum. Sell Muny Light or the City Defaults Today. Cleveland Trust Pushes Sale."

"Bruce Akers, Cleveland Trust Vice President"

Cleveland Press, 15 December 1978, "Default time here as nation watches," page A-4. "Bruce Akers, Cleveland Trust vice president for public relations and a one-time aide to former Mayor Ralph Perk explained that his bank would be willing to reconsider its position if Kucinich accepted something like Council's proposal to couple the tax increase with the sale of Muny Light."

See also in the same article: "Top officials at Cleveland Trust have assured us they will re-finance the notes if we pass our resolution and the mayor then sells the light plant," said Council Majority Leader Basil Russo.

57. "THE BANKERS WILL RUN THIS DAMN COUNTRY!"

"Councilman Leonard Danilowicz"

Cleveland Press, 15 December 1978.

WKYC-TV3 News, transcript:

58. PUTTING 'THE CROOK' ON THE DEAL

"Brock Weir told the eleven board directors"

Minutes of the meeting of CEI's Board of Directors, December 15, 1978. Congressional Staff report on default.

"Sunlight streamed through"

My Story by Tom Johnson, Copyright 1911, Columbian Sterling Publishing Co., USA.

59. ANY TIME NOW

"The Chief of Police"

US Senate Subcommittee Report on Organized Crime.

60. LIVE ON THE SIX O'CLOCK NEWS - BLACKMAIL

WKYC-TV3, Six O'Clock News, 15 December 1978, transcript (in the body of the chapter): Network news story followed:

NBC News with Tom Brokaw: "...the $15.5 million the city owes them, while Cleveland politicians fought and argued their way toward a possible compromise solution. Here's Jim Scott.

Councilman Leonard Danilowicz: "Somebody tells me about the disastrous results of default. What are the disastrous results of loss of freedom?"

Scott: "It was a day of high emotion...A snag

developed when Cleveland Trust, one of the banks holding city notes, did not approve of a Kucinich plan to head off default. It called for asking voters to approve a ½ of 1% income tax increase, but it did not include provisions for the sale of the debt ridden municipal power plant. So instead of approving the Kucinich plan, the city council acted on one of its own. It includes the sale [of Muny Light], a move that councilmen believe will satisfied all of the banks holding city notes..." "Later in the day, Kucinich offered a compromise. He said he would not be blackmailed into selling the plant but would agree to appoint a control board to operate it..." (transcript excerpts).

"I returned to City Hall"

WEWS-TV5, 15 December 1978, transcript:

"Andy then brought up Channel 8"

WJW-TV8 News, 15 December 1978, transcript:

TV3, TV5, TV8, 6 O'Clock News, 15 December 1978, Council Majority Leader Basil Russo recites Cleveland Trust call for sale of Muny Light.

"Andy handed me the final edition"

Cleveland Press, 15 December 1978, "Default Time Arrives as the Nation Watches," by Peter Phipps and Brent Larkin.

"News reporter Dave Patterson"

WEWS-TV5, 15 December 1978, transcript:

[Note: CEI was the sponsor of the 11 O'Clock News on *WEWS-TV5* TV, Channel 5. *WEWS-TV5* was owned by the Scripps-Howard Broadcasting Company. Scripps' fifth largest stockholder, through a nominee, was Cleveland Trust. Slogan: 'The 11 O'Clock News, is brought to you live by the Cleveland Electric Illuminating Company."]

Broadcast continues:

Anchor Dave Patterson: "Attorney John Climaco, who represents council, has been given permission to speak, and Roger Morris is down on the floor. Roger, what's Climaco talking about?"

Morris: "Well, Dave, the attorney is rendering a legal opinion on the city's charter [lengthy legal explanation...] Back to you Dave." [Transcript excerpts. Highly relevant text in *The Division of Light and Power.*]

"I had a long talk tonight"

WEWS-TV5 News, Patterson, continued: "...if the mayor would agree to sell Muny Light, and if there was some assurance of tighter financial controls in the city, Brock Weir personally said that he would lead an effort to sell $50 million dollars in Cleveland city bonds..."

"The bankers are here at City Hall tonight"

WJW-TV8, 15 December 1978, transcript:

Reporter Jeff Maynor: "Well, it was about 6:00 p.m. tonight that Basil Russo came in talking with us about some good news he felt, at least from council's viewpoint having to do with response of the banks to the situation. Let's listen to part of that..."

Russo: "...council that his bank will purchase $50 million worth of city bonds provided that sound fiscal controls are implemented. This will permanently end the city's financial crisis..."

WKYC-TV3, 15 December 1978, transcript:

Amanda Arnold: "Moody's investor service has again downgraded the city's bond rating, the fourth time since July they've done that. The rating today was dropped from B to Caa which is three notches below the lowest investor grade rating on their scale. So the clock will soon strike twelve, we've yet to hear from the mayor what happens next, and I imagine that depends on what council is doing right now..."

61. NOT FOR SALE

"Let me make a confession"

WJW-TV8, 15 December 1978, 11:45 p.m. from City Council Chambers. Mayor Kucinich addresses City Council (transcript):

Anchor Tim Taylor: "Let's go back now to the city council meeting for a live report from our City cam reporter, Jeff Maynor.

Maynor: "The Mayor has just begun to speak to city council."

Kucinich: "...there has been no interest in compromise. The clock is ticking away, and what we got was filibuster.

Now Mr. Chairman, to the members of council, I pose this to you. There was an offer made covered in the media that $50 million in assistance from Cleveland Trust if the council and the administration will dispose of the

Municipal Electric System. And I'm wondering, if Cleveland Trust, if they're so corrupt that they're trying to buy off an entire city? Because the offer of $50 million, under these conditions, I think, is an insult to the people of this city, and it's a totally dishonest device which reveals Cleveland Trust's underlying assumption that everyone has a price. Everyone has a price. Now that's the kind of psychology upon which people are sent into slavery. Everyone has a price. That's why legislatures and governments, entire governments, are bought and sold overnight, with the poor people paying the freight charges. Everyone has a price. Well maybe they can have that carry them anywhere in the world, but it isn't going to carry them through the gates of City Hall, because not everyone in this city has a price. And if Cleveland is to go into default, at least we will not have sold our souls.

Mr. Chairman and members of Council, I don't believe the City of Cleveland should be made available to the highest bidder and we have to ask if this offer of money is really enough, who is the beneficiary of all this? Are our mortgage rates really going to be lower in Cleveland? Will redlining be eliminated? No. They've offered to give us $50 million of help if we sell our electric system. Sell at a discount. They'll give us $50 million is we sell Muny Light, but they won't extend our credit $5 million. I want the members of council to be fully aware of what the impact will be if this legislation fails to pass.

Now I do not want this to be interpreted as any kind of threat because I must inform you of what the consequences will be if council fails to act tonight, so no one can say that they did not know what would happen. We are in a situation right now that if the city does not produce a plan, and we have a plan to stabilize this city's finances, and put us on a road to solvency, that there will be a run of creditors on this city's assets, and that the city can expect to be in court, and we can expect to have our income tax receipts attached, and therefore we will not have money to meet the payroll to provide the services for the people. And what this means precisely is this, we don't have all the details worked out, but we're pretty sure on the general impact. It will mean that as of Monday, I am going to be, and I don't want to, but if we don't have the money, if we can't present a plan that can indicate stabilization of this city's finances, I will have no choice but to order the layoffs of about half of the police department, of about half of the fire department, that's 1,000 policemen, 500 firemen, one half of the waste collectors, that means that the garbage would be picked up once every two or three weeks. Half of the snow removal crews. We would not be able to have any major street repairs. We would not be able to guarantee that we would be able to repair even serious chuck holes. Now Mr. Chairman, we would not be able to give preferred coverage to the downtown area, which is usually expected. And I would have to say that Cleveland's neighborhoods will be given the first priority with whatever services we have left, but they won't be much, they won't be much. And what happens next? Is that just the end? No. You cannot avoid, members of council, your responsibility to put this on the ballot. You're really going to have to consider doing this tonight, if you will. But the only way that you cannot put this on the ballot at one time or another is if the members would choose to resign because you must ask this same question again and again every week.

Now let's assume that within thirty days you've heard such a public outcry that the council recognizes it made a mistake if this isn't passed tonight. At that point, ladies and gentlemen, the city is in default and there is no sure way back. We are about a sixty day waiting period once you take action so that the issue can be voted on, and at that time the service curtailments would have to be continued until we can actually guarantee there will be some kind of a cash flow so that we can meet our payroll.

I want it understood that I offered a compromise today with great reluctance. But if that compromise could have effected a successful conclusion to this evening, it would have been worth it. But if that compromise is not accepted this evening, I have to notify you that I am withdrawing it. Because I will have no incentive to agree to a compromise after today because you will have to put the tax increase on the ballot anyway to save yourselves from the wrath of your constituents. So Mr. Chairman, three months or more from today, the tax will be enacted. But when the revenue begins to come in it won't be immediately available, because we're going to have to complete paying off the default.

This means that we're going to face six months of chaos in this city for one evening of shame.

Besides having our credit ruined for five years and having the city's reputation smeared for the next decade. It's interesting, ladies and gentlemen of council, that the business establishment of Cleveland, including Cleveland Trust and CEI, have raised $4 million to promote the image of Cleveland nationally; $4 million to promote Cleveland, but they didn't lift a finger to get the $5 million in credit we needed at home with Cleveland Trust. I would like to publicly thank National City Bank, Central National Bank, Euclid National, Banc Ohio and Society for having worked with the city and risen to the occasion, and for trying to help us to persuade Cleveland Trust to help the city. I want to thank the members of council, who have tried to assist to help the city avert default, and I want to thank the people of Cleveland for their response to our efforts to avoid this fiscal disaster.

Mr. Chairman, Cleveland Trust has never suggested that the revenue raised by my plan or the mechanisms of it are inadequate. They never said that we needed more money to make the plan viable. The never questioned if the plan was workable. They tried to use their economic power to dictate a political decision. Perhaps they could do that in other countries, but they're not going to do that here. I would like to conclude, Mr. Chairman, and I say with regret, it's unfortunate that the chair dispensed with the prayer tonight, because maybe we need that more than anything in this city, with a story from the Book of Daniel which tells about King Nebucchadenezzar who made an image of gold. He sent a herald to proclaim to all the people that they should "fall down and worship the image of gold that Nebuchadenezzar the King had set up. (And the King decreed that) whoever does not fall down and worship will, at the same moment, be thrown into the fiery furnace." Three administrators of Babylon, Chadrak, Meshach and Abednego didn't obey.

The King summoned them, threatened them with death if they did not fall down and worship an image of gold. And they responded to the King: "Let it be known to you, O King, that your gods are not the ones we are serving, and the image of gold that you have set up we will not worship."

Mr. Chairman and members of council, ultimately the history of Cleveland will reveal that Cleveland Trust and CEI and some members of City Council brought shame to this city and besmirched its history. But it will also show that there were people who recognized wrong when they saw it and condemned it for what it was."

"Six hundred citizens"

Plain Dealer, 16 December 1978, "As clock runs out." "...five persons in the decidedly pro-Kucinich crowd jumped up with a green bed sheet sign that read: 'Say No to the Banker-CEI Attack on the People of Cleveland.' Forbes told them to put the sign down, but they refused. Most of the 600 or so spectators were in no mood to take orders from Forbes..."

"Saturday morning, The Plain Dealer"

Plain Dealer, 16 December 1978, "CEI, Bank Boards Overlap; 7 of Utilities 11 Directors also serve city's lenders."

For further reference: *Columbia Journalism Review* (CJR), May/June 1979, "Pressured by Reporters, Prints a Story It Stifled. Leading Daily Probes Chief Target of Populist Mayor's Wrath; Public Swings His Way; 'There's a Revolution Over There,'" by Ellen S. Freilich. [Note: The CJR analysis covered several instances of *Plain Dealer* reporters pushing editors to publish stories.]

"A few years ago"

Personal letter from former New York City Council President Paul O'Dwyer to Mayor Kucinich, December, 1978.

62. $ GIVE ME IT ALL - - OR DIE!

"We were...destabilized, yet still in business"

Kucinich Study, November, 1977, "Perk Going Out of Business Contracts."

Plain Dealer, 14 October 1977, Page One, "City to cut tax; extra millions found in fund," by Harry Stainer. "Perk is expected to disclose a $4.5 million surplus in the city's debt service fund."

"Later that day, the national media recounted"

World News Tonight, with Walter Cronkite, 18 December 1978, transcript: "Mayor's Brother Robs Bank."

Plain Dealer, 19 December 1978, "A settling of accounts. Mayor leaves CleveTrust," by Terry E. Johnson.

See also: *Plain Dealer,* 19 December 1978, Page One. "Mayor's brother charged following bank robbery."

63. THE DIVISION OF LIGHT AND POWER

"Reality Inverted"

Plain Dealer, 22 December 1978, Page One, "CEI withdraws offer to buy Muny Light; both sides hurl charges," by Joseph L. Wagner.

"Cleveland Trust Vice President"

Cleveland Press, 15 December 1978, Page One, "Default Time Arrives," by Brent Larkin and Peter Phipps. [Reference to Akers on page 4.]

Federal Reserve Staff Report, 13 March 1979, Regarding Bruce Akers' change of position, page 26.

"On December 15th at 6:00 p.m."

TV3, TV5, TV8, 6 O'Clock News, 15 December 1978, Council Majority Leader Basil Russo with a communication from the Chairman of Cleveland Trust, calling for the sale of Muny Light.

Plain Dealer, 3 January 1979, Page One, "Kucinich laying off 275 policemen," by David T. Abbott and John P. Coyne, [story continues to page 5 with this quote: "Kucinich repeated his assertion that Cleveland Trust Chairman M. Brock Weir told him on the morning of Dec. 15 that the bank would refinance the notes and stave off default if Kucinich agreed to sell Muny Light. Council President George L. Forbes and Majority Leader Basil M. Russo also told reporters before the default that Cleveland Trust wanted Muny Light sold.]

Plain Dealer, 22 January 1979, Page One, "Kucinich takes bank fight to D.C. Seeks Probe of role in city fiscal crisis." "City Councilman Basil M. Russo, D-19, said on television that if the mayor would sign an agreement to sell Muny Light, 'the chairman of the Cleveland Trust bank has informed the council that his bank will purchase $50 million worth of city bonds.' Russo later said that he was wrong...."

Plain Dealer, 17 February 1979, "CEI plotted for years to ruin Muny Light, mayor tells City Club," by David T. Abbott, page 10-A. "Russo said last night that his remarks on TV Dec. 15 were based on what Forbes told him had occurred at a breakfast meeting that morning. Russo said Weir didn't demand the sale of Muny Light but simply agreed to go along with Forbes' plan to link the sale to council approval of a special referendum on a tax increase."

Federal Reserve Staff Report, 13 March 1979, Regarding Basil Russo's change of position, page 26.

"Forbes explained Russo's dilemma"

Plain Dealer, 25 February 1978, "Calm before the Debate. Page One and Special Section 6. On page 125: "When asked why Majority Leader Basil M. Russo, D-19, told reporters that day that Weir had offered the city $50 million in loans if Kucinich would sell the plant, Forbes said Russo misunderstood him, and Russo may have been dazed by the glare of television lights."

"My good friend Maury Saltzman"

Cleveland Press, 18 December 1978, "Kucinich Wouldn't Yield - - Why Saltzman Gave Up," by Mark Hopwood. "Brock was nice," Saltzman said. "He said, 'Look Dennis, get this (Muny Light) out of the way. Sell the building, we'll roll over the notes, and I personally will help with the $50 million in bonds.'"

"Saltzman said Weir promised Kucinich that Cleveland Trust would buy $50 million of the $90 million in bonds the city was planning to sell next year."

Federal Reserve Staff Report, 13 March 1978. Regarding Maurice Saltzman's change of position, page 26. [Note: *Cleveland Press*, 12 July 1977, "Bobbie Brooks gets redressed," (via *Women's Wear Daily*,) "but the giant eventually began to ail, and Saltzman knew it in the six months ended Oct. 31, 1976, Bobbie Brooks lost $1,700,000 on sales of $91,400,000. In the next quarter, the firm posted losses of $18,897,000 on sales of $24,696,000, compared with earnings of $71,000 for the corresponding quarter of the preceding year."]

"Forbes' December 15th Legislation"

The Council of the City of Cleveland, 15 December 1978, by Mr. Forbes, "An emergency resolution to establish a fiscal policy for the stabilization of the City of Cleveland's finances during the calendar year 1979 and thereafter, which requires the sale of the Municipal Light Plant and an increase in the municipal income tax."

Paragraph four reads: "Whereas local banks have indicated a willingness to consider renewing outstanding notes of the City in the amount of $15,500,000 if both the above actions are accomplished...."

See also:

Plain Dealer, 15 December 1978, "Cleveland

Trust: Pay Up. Bank would relent if Muny Light were sold, Forbes believes."

Cleveland Press, 15 December 1978, "Council Ultimatum. Sell Muny Light or the City Defaults Today. Cleveland Trust Pushes Sale."

Federal Reserve Staff Report, 13 March 1978,

See Staff Report characterizing Forbes' position, with this introduction: "With reference to the newspaper articles, staff offers no explanation, but believes the following comments are appropriate…"

"I'm authorizing additional security"

Cleveland Police Department, Departmental Information, 29 January 1979, "Information Regarding Conspiracy to Kill The Mayor," by A. Vanyo and E. Kovacic, Lieutenants, BCI Intelligence. [Confidential "As a result of a series of phone calls, Lieutenants Vanyo and Kovacic met with a source of the information. A working relationship was established and problems arising from this association were overcome…]

"With Sandy's Encouragement"

Plain Dealer, 20 December 1978, Page One, "Mayor OK's Muny vote," by David T. Abbott.

Cleveland Press, 23 December 1978, Page One, "Muny on ballot; Mayor predicts defeat of light plant sale,"by Peter Phipps.

"Shortly after the special election"

Committee on Banking, Finance and Urban Affairs of the United States House of Representatives, 10 July 1979, "Role of Commercial Banks in the Financing of the Debt of the City of Cleveland," page 33, Appendix 7: "…On December 26, 1978, however, CTC's Trust Investment Committee (consisting of trust department officers) approved a change in the coding to indicate that the stock was considered attractive for purchase. As a consequence, trust department holdings of CEI stock increased from 691,568 shares, as of December 26, 1978, to 782,798 shares as of February 7, 1979, an increase of 91,230 shares or 13%."

"There is a new hit planned"

Cleveland Police Department, Departmental Information, 29 January 1979, "Information Regarding Conspiracy to Kill The Mayor," by A. Vanyo and E. Kovacic, Lieutenants, BCI Intelligence. "It was decided by Chief Fox, with concurrence by Inspectors Nagorski and Gallagher, that to obtain the assistance of additional personnel it would be necessary to inform certain other members of BCI intelligence about the attempt by Sinito to hire someone to kill the Mayor. Detectives Berkey, McNally, and Roth were so informed.

"We complied with Judge Krupansky's order"

Plain Dealer, 27 December 1978, Cleveland pays CEI $2.6 million, vows full payment."

Plain Dealer, 30 December 1978, "Judge removes CEI's hold on city property."

"I opened the Plain Dealer"

Plain Dealer, 31 December 1978 and 1 January 1979, "Why has Cleveland Trust taken a strong stand on the City's Financial Crisis?" An advertisement.

See also: *Fort Lauderdale News*, 2 January 1979, "Cleveland: Banks Seeking Power and Plant," by Nicholas Von Hoffman. "...the bankers are making the city choose between access to credit and public ownership of an electric light company. Beyond the smoke and steam given off in the clash of personality, the outline of great issues can just be perceived."

64. THE COURAGEOUS BOB HOLDEN

"The polls on Muny Light"

Plain Dealer, 23 January 1979, Page One, "2 Issues take lead; Pollster finds sizable margins for tax hike, Muny Light sale," by Joseph D. Rice. "The *Plain Dealer* learned the poll showed that: Raising the income tax from 1% to 1½% was favored 65% to 35%. Selling Muny Light was favored 70% to 30%... The poll was done by Robert Dykes, who has done numerous polls in Cleveland."

See also: *Cleveland Press*, 29 March 1978, "One-half in poll say: 'Keep Muny Light," by Brent Larkin. "The survey [conducted by the *Cleveland Press*] …produced the following results: Keep it - - 48.7%. Sell it - - 51.3%."

"Jeff Moats, a member of our mayoral staff "

Cleveland Press, 19 February 1979, "Censorship by Channels 5, 8, charged by mayor," by Peter Phipps.

WEWS-TV5, 19 February 1979, transcript:

Kucinich: "I'm saying if they have a right to

freedom of speech, so do we."

Anchor John Hambrick: "Mayor Kucinich is hopping mad because two Cleveland TV stations are refusing to show one of his save Muny Light commercials. The commercial in question levels strong charges at CEI and implies its executives are guilty of criminal conduct. TV8 and TV5 flatly refused to broadcast the commercial. Channel 3 hasn't made a final decision yet."

WKYC-TV3, 19 February, 1979, transcript:

Amanda Arnold: "Well, tonight...we've got... ... the mayor showing a commercial, and in it, CEI executives are accused of price fixing. A wanted poster charges the company with what are being called crimes, such as price manipulation and the announcer says that CEI is planning to steal the Muny Light plant. Well, Channels 5 and 8 refuse to run the ad, both stations saying that it is potentially libelous, and the mayor calls that censorship."

Kucinich: "Channel 5 and Channel 8 have censored our ads to protect CEI. We know they've allowed the other side to run ads which suggest among other things that Muny Light pollutes the air, which all of you must know is false, since there are no generators. But since they're permitting absolutely false advertising to run, they are denying us an opportunity to tell our side of the story."

"William Hickey, the TV-Radio critic"

Plain Dealer, 20 February 1979, "Mayor has media down for the count," by William Hickey, page 4-B.

Plain Dealer, 20 February 1979, Page One, "Hot and cold on Muny. Sparks fly when two TV stations refuse to air on of Kucinich's ads," by David T. Abbott.

Plain Dealer, 22 February 1979, "Those 'censored' ads."

Cleveland Press, 20 February 1979, An Editorial: Callers want anti-CEI ad on TV. Addendum:

See also: *WKYC-TV3*, 8 February 1979, transcript:

Anchor Doug Adair: "The list of groups and people opposed to the sale of Muny Light has grown a little longer tonight. The latest words of support for the city holding onto the light plant came from several east and west side neighborhood groups, in particular the groups were highly critical of the commercials running on TV that label the Muny system a clunker and a lemon."

Paul Ryder, activist: "In Cleveland's neighborhoods, these TV ads are a little bit puzzling. We'd like to know if Muny Light is such a clunker, why is CEI trying so hard to get it? ...What's important to us is that it distributes electricity at cheaper rates than CEI does. That competition keeps CEI's rates down, and that's why we're voting against the sale of Muny."

"In Washington, D.C., Nader and me"

Plain Dealer, 19 January 1979, "Nader cheers Kucinich War."

Cleveland Press, 19 January 1979, "Kucinich's 'struggle' hailed by Nader."

Washington Post, 22 January 1979, "Kucinich coming to Ask Probe of Bank in Cleveland's Crisis," by Larry Kramer.

Washington Post, 23 January 1979, "Kucinich Attacks on Banks Impresses House Probers," by Larry Kramer.

"Word from the City Room"

Cleveland Press, 13 January 1979, "Reporter reassigned - - Guild to picket *PD*." *PD* Utilities Reporter Bob Holden: "The reason [for removal from utilities beat] given to me is that 'upper management' thought I would be unfair to CEI in my coverage."

Cleveland Press, 13 January 1979, "Reporter reassigned - - Guild to picket *PD*."

Cleveland Press, 16 January 1979, "Reporters refuse by-lines as PD moves utility writer."

Cleveland Press, 18 January 1978, "*PD* and Guild resolve dispute."

"Holden's resignation triggered"

Cleveland Press, 23 January 1979, "PD newsman protest flares anew," by Peter Almond. "But Holden, who charged that CEI has complained without being specific, because 'they just don't like balanced coverage.' Said he has personal knowledge that CEI Vice President John W. Fenker has been in regular contact with *PD* management about him since last spring."

Cleveland Press, 27 January 1979, "*PD* reporter resigns in fuss over CEI." "Holden, a reporter on environmental subjects, said that the *Plain Dealer* management told him on January 10 that he was being pulled off a series about CEI and the Municipal Light Plant, and was being forbidden to write again about CEI or Muny Light because he 'would be unfair'. No evidence was ever presented of past bias in his stories, Holden said."

Plain Dealer, 27 January 1979, "PD reporter resigns in fuss over CEI."

Plain Dealer, 17 May 1979, "Ex-Reporter for PD to probe utilities for city." Our Administration engaged Holden's expertise on utilities.

Further reference on Holden case: *Columbia Journalism Review*, May/June 1979, "Pressured by Reporters, Prints a Story It Stifled. Leading Daily Probes Chief Target of Populist Mayor's Wrath; Public Swings His Way; 'There's a Revolution Over There,'" by Ellen S. Freilich, 19 September 1979, page 6.

"Biddle and Abbott"

Plain Dealer, 11 February 1979, Page One, "CEI Objective: Snuff Out Muny Light," by Daniel R. Biddle and David T. Abbott

65. THE OTHER 'CITY HALL'

Ties between CEI and CleveTrust Corporation, by James Harkins, Department of Law and Dan Marschall, Department of Economic Development, 1 February 1979. Also, Study by Dan Marschall, Cleveland Economic Development Department, 15 December 1978 – 21 June 1979.

[Note: Cleveland Trust had a total of 24 direct interlocks between the bank and major Cleveland corporations....Thirty two of the nation's top 100 industrial corporations were located in Cleveland – northeast Ohio, in 1978, with a combined net income of over $1.5 billion. The corporations had assets of over $26 billion and employed over 53,000 residents.]

See also *Fortune Magazine*, 7 May 1979, and 18 June 1979.

"Because this is war"

Cleveland Press, 15 January 1979, "Weir sees no hope of reconciling city."

Cleveland Press 16 January 1979, "Weir's blunt words." An Editorial.

Cleveland Press, 19 January 1979, "Nader cheers Kucinich war."

Plain Dealer, 28, January 1979, Page One, "Nader seeks to debate Weir on role in city money mess," by Thomas J. Brazaitis.

Washington Star, 3 March 1979, "Pocketbook Issue in Cleveland Vote," by Ralph Nader.

"As I read the Harkins-Marschall study"

Commercial Banks and Their Trust Activities: Emerging Influence on the American Economy. Volume I Staff Report for the Subcommittee on Domestic Finance Committee on Banking and Currency. House of Representatives. 90th Congress. 2d session. The report noted that "Cleveland Trust potential for seriously restraining competition within a particular industry because of its interests in competing companies is quite clear. Cleveland Trust was one of CEI's top stockholders The bank's trust department has $27.5 million worth of CEI securities in fiduciary accounts administered by the bank, including 782,798 shares of CEI common stock. Its stock holdings in its name, together with the holdings the bank listed under other names, made Cleveland Trust the CEI's top stockholder.

Harkins-Marschall's initial research At the time of default, three men who sat on the Board of Directors of CEI were also directors of the CleveTrust corporation, the holding company for Cleveland Trust. When one of the three interlocking directors retired, he was replaced by another interlocking director on January 1, 1979. In addition, Standard Oil of Ohio and Republic Steel each have representatives, albeit different individuals, on the boards of both CEI and Cleveland Trust....Everett Ware Smith, the Chairman of CleveTrust until his retirement in the fall of 1978, was also a director of the North American Coal Company. CEI has underwritten $64 million in loans to two subsidiary coal companies of North American, and has a long-term purchase agreement with one of its subsidiaries.... CAPCO is a power pool made up of CEI and four other utilities. CAPCO and Cleveland Trust have the same law firm, Jones, Day, Reavis and Pogue. A partner in the law firm, Richard Pogue, is also a Cleveland Trust director. Another partner, H. Chapman Rose, is an Advisory Director of Cleveland Trust. (For a discussion of bank and utility financial relationships), see Global Reach, pp 241-245 "The Latin-Americanization of the United States."

Also of interest pp 436 – 437: "Notes for text and tables: "... Banks derive two forms of income streams from these operations. First, a high-income stream from interest on the loans extended to these firms which are needed for continued capitalization available only from external - - i.e. bank - - sources, not from retained earnings. Retained earnings are low because of the second type of income: namely, through their voting control the banks promote a high dividend-payout policy. High dividends accomplish both continued dependency of the firm on the bank for investment capital and increase in the value and investment leverage of its trust assets. The House report on the Penn Central failure provides the data for quantifying these two advantages."

"We were on the threshold"

Plain Dealer, 1 February 1979, "Coalition forming to find candidate to face mayor," by Joseph D. Rice.

"Leading bankers brought a Democratic campaign consultant"

Plain Dealer, 2 February 1979, "Leaders huddle, mute on dump-Kucinich plan," by Joseph D. Rice. [Note: Others attending the meeting included CEI board member and Higbee Company President Herbert Strawbridge, John Gelbach, board chair of Central National Bank, Claude Blair, board chair of National City Bank; James C. Davis, former managing partner of Squire Sanders.]

"After the meeting of the bankers"

WKYC-TV3, 2 February 1979, Corporate leaders flee cameras. Reporting by Joe Mosbrook, coverage of corporate Cleveland's political meeting. Also:

Cleveland Press, 20 February 1979, "New Secret meeting is held."

Cleveland Press, 20 February 1979, "Business leaders discuss the trial of Forbes, others," by Norman Mlachak.

"U.S. Representative Benjamin Rosenthal"

Plain Dealer, 27 January 1979, "SEC will look into bank's Muny stand," by George Rasanen and Thomas J. Brazaitis.

"The special election drew near"

Plain Dealer, 19 February 1979, "Nader joins Muny Light TV ad fight," by Karen R. Long. Also "Residents of Fort Wayne, Ind., voted to sell their city light plant and their bills rose 40% in 18 months, he [Nader] warns."

"I received a call from"

Plain Dealer, 9 February 1979, "CEI asks wholesale rate hike; could force Muny into increase." Full Kucinich quote: "I'm not prepared to accept that scenario...There is a cure for the city's dilemma. Buy power from a company that has a conscience, not one that has a cash register for a brain. This should be a signal to all Clevelanders that CEI is addicted to utility rate hikes and their addiction is satisfied with a quick fix from the PUCO.... Their latest rate hike plan underscores the need for competition and underscores the need for the continuance of Muny Light."

See also: Correspondence from William N. Bingham, Principal Rate Engineer, The Cleveland Electric Illuminating Company, to George S. Pofok, Systems Engineer, Dept. of Public Utilities, City of Cleveland, 8 February 1979, [Notification of rate increase]. "We believe the application will seek an approximate 25% increase in the rate for firm power service." - - Bingham.

"It took Larry Kramer"

Washington Post, 13 February 1979, "'People Power' vs. 'Shadow Government,'" by Larry Kramer, with graphic by Milton Clipper.

"Armed plainclothesmen sat in the audience"

Kucinich Speech to the City Club, 16 February 1979, "Muny Light."

"Cigarette smoke drifted up"

Findings of the Atomic Safety and Licensing Board of the Nuclear Regulatory Commission, 6 January 1977, regarding the application of the Cleveland Electric Illuminating Company for a license to operate a nuclear power plant.

"A video projector summoned"

Cleveland Press, 17 February 1979, "Kucinich goes to big screen at City Club to sell his stand." Re: TV3, TV5, TV8, 6 O'Clock News.

15 December 1978, Council Majority Leader Basil Russo recites Cleveland Trust call for sale of Muny Light.

"Then there was George Forbes"

Plain Dealer, 6 February 1979, "Mayor persecuting police, Forbes says," by Joseph L. Wagner.

Cleveland Press, 10 February 1979, "Kucinich's

police unit called gestapo by Forbes," by Tony Natale.

Plain Dealer, 10 February 1979, "Forbes blasts reign by Kucinich 'cult'... A group as dangerous as Jim Jones in Guyana," by Joseph D. Rice.

Cleveland Press, 10 February 1979, "Mayor heads cult Forbes tells Forum," by Brent Larkin.

66. REDS

Wall Street Journal, 28 December 1978, "Bond Markets: 'High-Yield Cleveland Issues Sell Quickly To Speculators Professing Faith in City,'" by Phil Hawkins, page 13.

Post-Gazette, 29 December 1978, "Speculators Snap Up Cleveland Bonds," page 16.

Columbia Journalism Review, May/June 1979, "Pressured by Reporters, Prints a Story It Stifled. Leading Daily Probes Chief Target of Populist Mayor's Wrath; Public Swings His Way; 'There's a Revolution Over There,'" by Ellen S. Freilich [Includes reference to discussion between Hopcraft and *Plain Dealer* reporters.]

"While denying the city any chance to repay"

Cleveland Press, 12 April 1979, "CleveTrust posts record earnings."

"We aren't talking about recovering $5 million"

Financier Magazine, April, 1979.

In U.S. District Court, Judge Krupansky

Plain Dealer, 28 January 1979, Page One, "Judge derails antitrust suit in city vs. CEI."

67. A MAYOR AND HIS PEOPLE

"A soft sunlight bathed the congregation"

Kucinich, 25 February 1979, "Speech to St. Paul's Church."

"Some people can't understand"

Plain Dealer, 25 February 1979, "CEI annual revenues, profit set records."

"The people in this church"

Plain Dealer, 26 February 1979, An Editorial: "Vote to Save Cleveland," [Adjacent to sample ballot.]

"Kucinich, who often quotes the Bible"

Plain Dealer, 25 February 1979, "Kucinich-Forbes: Gentle jousting, some hard shots," by Terry E. Johnson, page 30.

"As I debated and brought our closing argument"

ABC News, 26 February 1979, Cleveland's Special Election, Matt Quinn reporting, transcript: Also: *WJW-TV8* February 1979.

Anchor John Hambrick: "We've been hearing the debate over what to do with Muny Light for years now, but one part of this story we've never heard. News Center 8's Jeff Maynor has the report."

Maynor: "Most of us know that Muny Light is just a great big sub station. They don't generate power anymore, they buy it from CEI and resell it to their 46,000 customers. To most of us, Muny Light is this great big old red brick building along the shoreway. But Muny is also acres and acres of land, millions of dollars in lines and equipment, and about 200 employees, people who will likely lose their jobs if the plant is sold."

Worker: I have seventeen years myself here. And here's your pension. And I went to CEI and CEI offered me sweeping the floor, the ground, the concrete, and I'm the leading lineman at the time. That's what they offered me, so how are we supposed to feel?"

WKYC-TV3, February 1979, transcript:

Anchor Doug Adair: "The mayor's fight to save Muny Light has added some support tonight, and it comes from thirteen councilmen who say that their decisions have nothing at all to do with the positions that have been taken by the mayor or Council President George Forbes on Muny. Councilman James Rokakis says that the group will urge residents to vote "no" on the sale because they are the people who could be most hurt if Muny Light is sold."

Rokakis: "In the event of a sale, present Muny customers should prepare for a 6% - 9% increase in the utility bills to equalized rates with those of CEI. Electric bills will rise 7% - 12% for all electric power consumers in Cleveland after the PUCO rules on CEI's request for a rate hike."

Adair: "And the councilmen say that one of the main reasons that they're fighting the Muny Light sale is because they feel that the $12 - $14 million that the city could get for the plant this year still would not be enough."

"The light shines in the darkness"

Kucinich speech, special election night.

Plain Dealer, 28 February 1979, Page One, "Voters reject Muny Sale, approve income tax hike; Kucinich claims a personal victory," by Joseph D. Rice.

"You have to see this"

Washington Post, 1 March 1979, "Signaling a New Era of Urban Populism," by Larry Kramer.

"Members of Council"

Kucinich, Statement to City Council Finance Committee Hearings, 6 March 1979.

FERC News Release, 27 April 1979: FERC Law Judge Finds.

See also, PTX 2958, 21 June 1979, Pofok Report: "Data re: Census tracts in and adjacent to City where MELP does business or could do business in future which represents reasonable market expansion potentials for MELP with attached exhibits," and;

PTX 2956, 1960-1980, "History of MELP-related ordinances."

"Council balked at approving"

Kucinich letter to Council President Forbes, 13 March 1979. Re: Community Development Block Grant funds, 3/13/79.

"Cleveland Trust and Forbes"

Council of City of Cleveland, 15 March 1979. An Emergency Ordinance, Mandating the separation and segregation of City Income Tax Receipts for payment of Defaulted Notes and other purposes. By Mr. Forbes. Statement by Mayor Kucinich, 16 March 1979, "Bank Preference Ordinance."

San Francisco Bay Guardian, 22 March 1979, "The Cleveland Alternative," by Bruce B. Brugman, page 4.

68. CEI CORRUPTION GOES NUCLEAR

"I received a detailed study of nuclear safety"

Eckhart Report, 22 February 1979, A comprehensive report on outages at the Davis-Besse Nuclear Power Plant, Number 1.

Plain Dealer, 12 March 1979, "Davis-Besse operated only 6 months in 1978," by Jim Lawless. "The plant ranks near the bottom in efficiency among 66 other U.S. plants during 1978."

Chronicle-Telegram, 13 March 1979, "Davis-Besse's woes cost the consumer," by Earel Newkirk. "CEI treasurer Clement T. Loshing admitted in testimony [to the PUCO] Saturday that the Port Clinton (Davis-Besse) nuclear plant had 'caused a severe cash drain' for the Cleveland utility."

"On Wednesday, March 28, 1979"

Plain Dealer, 29 March 1979, Page One, "Nuclear accident emits radiation."

"According to the Plain Dealer"

Plain Dealer, 31 March 1979, "Davis-Besse, leaking reactor have similar systems," by Daniel R. Biddle, page 10-A. "The Davis-Besse nuclear power plant, on Lake Erie 21 miles west of Toledo, uses a heating and cooling system very similar to the one that failed this week at a nuclear plant near Harrisburg, Pa."

Plain Dealer, 4 April 1979, NRC found Davis-Besse operation unsafe in '77-'78," by George P. Rasanen, page 12-A.

Cleveland Press, 12 April 1979, "Davis-Besse; Ohio would evacuate 2-mile area in case of accident," by Bob Modic.

Cleveland Press, 19 April 1979, Page One, "Davis Besse Gets Low Rating," by *United Press International*. "Because of its many safety problems, the Davis-Besse nuclear power panel near Port Clinton - - built by the same company that build the trouble Three Mile Island, Pa., facility - - was given a "C" (or poor) rating by nuclear officials Nuclear Regulatory Commission transcripts show."

Plain Dealer, 27 April 1979, Page One, 250 march at Perry at anniversary of Chernobyl disaster," by Jim Lawless.

"Mindful of the deficiencies"

Kucinich Statement, 2 April 1979, "Requesting the PUCO shut down the Davis-Besse Nuclear Power Plant."

Plain Dealer, 11 April 1979, "City asks PUCO to

prevent the reopening of Davis-Besse."

"The Chronicle-Telegram of Elyria, Ohio"

Chronicle-Telegram, 11 May 1979, Page One, "Flirting with the 'Syndrome'; Davis-Besse cooling pumps were out almost two days," by Earel Newkirk. "The scenario could have led to the feared "China Syndrome" where the reactor, out of control without coolant, melts down and sinks into the ground spewing radioactivity over an immense area."

Cleveland Press, 23 August 1979, "Reactor inspector says NRC ignored warnings," by Edward Roby, *United Press International*, Washington Bureau, page C-6.

"Adding to questions about its ability"

Plain Dealer, 25 May 1979, "CEI is accused of hiding geology info on Perry plant," by Gary R. Clark and Daniel R. Biddle.

"The troubled Davis-Besse plant"

Cleveland Press, 2 May 1979, "$60 million hike approved for CEI," by Ted Virostko. "The increase will mean a 9.2% increase for the utility's 698,000 customers in nine northeastern counties."

Cleveland Press, 2 May 1979, "Davis-Besse power called too costly," by Bob Modic.

Plain Dealer, 1 June 1979, Page One, "CEI to seek $80 million hike for '80," by James Lawless. "The increase comes less than a month after the company received a $60.4 million increase from the Public Utilities Commission of Ohio."

Cleveland Press, 1 June 1979, Page One, "CEI rate bid stuns consumer groups."

Plain Dealer, 1 June 1979, "Kucinich says pact near for cheap non-CEI power," by David T. Abbott.

Plain Dealer, 2 June 1979, "CEI plans stock sale to raise $75 - $80 million."

Further reading: *Plain Dealer*, 26 February 1979, "CEI annual revenues, profit set records."

Cleveland Press, 6 July 1979, "Reopening of Davis-Besse plant is expected soon - - foes shocked."

Cleveland Press, 7 July 1979, "Davis-Besse plant gets start-up OK," by Ron Kovach, page A-5.

Plain Dealer, 7 July 1979, "Rating firm cuts grade give some CEI bonds, stock."

Plain Dealer, 12 July 1978, "Davis-Besse operating after a restart fails," by Gary R. Clark, page 13-A.

Further reading: *Cleveland Press*, 22 August 1978, "A-plant outages are costly to CEI," by Bob Modic. "Much of the additional cost is then passed along to customers through the fuel adjustment charge which is added to electricity rates."

Plain Dealer, 26 February 1979, "CEI annual revenues, profit set records."

Plain Dealer, 14 February 1985, "CEI nuclear costs to jolt bills $200, group says," by Jim Lawless.

Plain Dealer, 27 April 1987, Page One, 250 march at Perry at anniversary of Chernobyl disaster," by Jim Lawless. "Former Cleveland Mayor, Dennis J. Kucinich, said American nuclear industry officials criticized Russian plants as poorly built. He said that made little sense when the whole American defense industry is based on Russian technological superiority in weapons systems."

"The great irony"

Cleveland Press, 28 June 1979, "CEI has enough power without A-plant," by Bob Modic, page B-6.

Further reading: *Wall Street Journal*, 15 February 1977, Page One, "Utilities are Accused of Altering Figures On Nuclear Capacity."

Plain Dealer, 29 June 1979, "CEI sues uranium supplier over pricing," by Mairy Jayn Woge.

69. CONGRESS INVESTIGATES DEFAULT

"Prior to the release of the Fed report"

Plain Dealer, 13 March 1979, "Fed to clear CEI, Cleveland Trust. No collusion found; banks to be chided for leniency to city," by Frederick E. Freeman and Joseph L. Wagner.

Cleveland Press, 14 March 1979, "Why Fed clears bank, Weir, CEI," by Alan Thompson.

"Rep. Rosenthal's summary of key provisions"

Plain Dealer, 15 March 1979, "Kucinich pooh-poohs Fed probe report. Says it still doesn't clear CleveTrust, CEI of collusion," by David

T. Abbott, page 8. "The Fed report, released Tuesday, was done in response to a request from Rep. Benjamin S. Rosenthal, D-N.Y. Rosenthal said the report did not disprove Kucinich's allegations and in many ways supports them."

Plain Dealer, 15 March 1978, "Second House report due on default this month, by the *Plain Dealer* Washington Bureau," page 8. "The Fed report has been criticized by Rep. Benjamin S. Rosenthal, D-N.Y., chairman of another banking subcommittee, as failing to disprove Kucinich's charges."

"The Plain Dealer carried"

Plain Dealer, 14 March 1979, "Report attacked, clears CEI, CleveTrust."

"Cleveland Trust and CEI"

Plain Dealer, 15 March 1979, An Editorial: "Banks in the clear."

Cleveland Press, 15 March 1979, An Editorial: "Kucinich vs. the banks: a 'conspiracy' deflated."

Cleveland Press, 15 March 1979, "Mayor hits Federal Reserve Board report. Says conclusions are unjustified. Critical of media interpretation of it. CEI says study gives it 'clean bill,'" by Ron Kovach.

Kucinich analysis of Federal Reserve Report, 14 March 1979. [Authors note: The thrust of Rep. Rosenthal's rebuke rested on explosive passages in the Fed Report, mentioning Weir's $50 million offer, which went unreported by either paper: "Mr. Weir made a comment to the effect that if agreement between council and the Administration could be reached, he would volunteer to help raise up to $50 million for the City." This was an abridged version of the conversation I had with Weir in the boardroom the morning of December 15th and corresponded to what Forbes, Russo, Akers and Saltzman unanimously asserted, then unanimously denied, despite voluminous reports in print, radio and television to the contrary.]

Reference: Federal Reserve Report, page 24, Paragraph 1.

Further reference: *Plain Dealer,* 15 December 1978, Page One, "Cleveland Trust: Pay Up. Bank would relent if Muny Light were sold, Forbes believes," and,

TV3, TV5, TV8 6 O'Clock News, December 15, 1978, re: Basil Russo's announcement concerning Cleveland Trust, and,

Cleveland Press, 15 December 1978, Page One. "Council Ultimatum. Sell Muny Light or the City Defaults Today. Cleveland Trust Pushes Sale." [Akers and Saltzman cited.] The Federal Reserve Report, page 25, paragraph 2.

Cleveland Press, 10 May 1979, "CleveTrust changing name to AmeriTrust," by Jules Wagman. "...plans to shed its 'provincial' Cleveland name."

"The Cleveland banking community"

Staff Study on City of Cleveland Financing, June 1979, report to the Subcommittee on Financial Institutions Supervision, Regulation and Insurance, Fernand St. Germaine, Chairman.

Cleveland Press, 10 July 1979, Page One, "Mayor, Weir Square Off at House Default Probe," by Barry M Horstman.

"The gavel dropped with a sharp crack"

Role of Commercial Banks in the Financing of the Debt of the City of Cleveland. Hearing before the Subcommittee on Financial Institutions, Supervision, Regulation and Insurance of the Committee on Banking, Finance and Urban Affairs, Ninety-Sixth Congress, First Session, July 10, 1979. Serial 96-61, page 1. Fernand St. Germaine, Chairman of Subcommittee.

"He paused, looked at me"

Kucinich testimony before the subcommittee, pages 5 – 47.

"The real issue is"

Brock Weir testimony before the subcommittee, pages 51- 66.

"Congressman John J. Cavanaugh"

Congressman John J. Cavanaugh, Nebraska, questions of Brock Weir, before the subcommittee, page 567, in series of questions including pages 563-572.

"After Congressman Cavanaugh finished"

Chairman Fernand St. Germaine, Congressman from Rhode Island, statement to the subcommittee, pages 572-573.

"One week after the subcommittee hearings"

Washington Post, 17 July 1979, Page One, "Cleveland Default Linked to Effort to Unseat Mayor," by Larry Kramer.

"The second default was fabricated"

Wall Street Journal, 4 September 1979, "Cleveland Defaults for the Second Time; May and City Council Are in Standoff," by Ronald Alsop, page 28. "Mayor Dennis J. Kucinich pinned the blame for the second default on city council for not passing legislation that would have allowed the notes in the waterworks fund to be rolled over."

Washington Post, 25 September 1979, "Cleveland's Mayor, Banks Still at Odds," by Larry Kramer. "Further, the council would not approve another technical switch of funds from one city account to another that would have allowed the city to begin paying off the banks on the earlier default. And it appeared that such a waiver would not occur until after the election."

"second default"

Cleveland Press, 6 October 1978, "Council avoids default. Renews $14 million in notes held by city treasury."

See also: *Plain Dealer*, 10 May 1979, "Bank here threatens city with foreclosure," by Joseph L. Wagner and Joseph D. Rice. "Central National Bank warned the city yesterday it plans to foreclose on its $3 million defaulted loan, overdue since Dec. 15, because the city has not provided it with financial information or a repayment plan."

Plain Dealer, 10 May 1979, Page One, "Bank here threatens city with foreclosure," by Joseph L. Wagner and Joseph D. Rice.

Cleveland Press, 17 May 1979, "Pay up! National City bank joins in threat to sue city if its notes aren't repaid."

Plain Dealer, 2 June 1979, Page One, "2 banks reject city payment plan," by Joseph L. Wagner. "Cleveland Trust and Central National Bank have made their announcement in letters to city officials."

70. THAT'S POLITICS

"Forbes appeared on a local television show"

George Forbes on Kamm's Corners, Herb Kamm Show, 26 July 1979, transcript.

71. CITIZEN KUCINICH

The day after I left the Mayor's office, Cleveland Trust, established in 1893, changed its name to AmeriTrust, November 13, 1979. For further information on mergers which resulted in the extinction of AmeriTrust go to www.usbanks.landoffree.com

"Scheer had written lengthy articles"

Playboy Magazine, June 1979 Issue, "Playboy Interview: Dennis Kucinich. A candid conversation with the controversial young mayor of Cleveland about civic greed and corruption - - and his feisty new brand of politics," by Robert Scheer, pp. 81-112.

"WKYC News Anchor Doug Adair"

WKYC-TV3 Investigative Report, January, 1980, by Mel Martin.

Further Reading: *Washingtonian Magazine*, August, 1984 edition re: the assassination plot.

See also: the *Slavic Village Voice*, 4 August 1984, "Exclusive! Mob Hired Undercover Cop to 'Hit' Kucinich."

73. WHAT GOES AROUND

"The Cleveland Press reported the sensational confession"

Cleveland Press, 3 September 1980, "CEI Admits Trying to Force Muny Light to Close Down," by John Funk.

"Seven weeks into the trial"

Cleveland Press, 20 November 1980, "CEI jurors vent tears, anger." 'The city produced enough evidence that CEI did all it could to cause the downfall of Muny Light,' by John Funk.

Cleveland Press, 20 November 1980, "CEI president hopes for retrial, " by Ron Kovach. See also City of Cleveland vs. Cleveland Electric Illuminating Company (CEI) (1975-1984), Case Summary by William B. Norris of Hahn Loeser, attorney for city in antitrust case, describing significance of CEI secret sponsorship of taxpayer's lawsuit to block the interconnection, re: "The Miller Stipulations." Norris' personal papers, 24 October 1997.

Plain Dealer, 7 December 1984, Page One."CEI sues city for return of $24 million," by W.C. Miller. "A key in the city's appeal in that case was another taxpayer's suit filed by Cleveland lawyer, Charles R. Miller, but secretly sponsored by CEI. CEI paid for the 1972 suit through an outside firm to prevent construction of a vital electrical connection that would make Muny more reliable."

"Were all the legal battles for naught?"

Letter, former Cleveland Law Director, James B. Davis to William B. Norris, 14 March 1985, concerning, among other matters, the antitrust case which Norris prosecuted on behalf of the city. Personal papers of William B. Norris.

"When I left the Mayor's Office"

WKYC-TV3 Investigative Report, January, 1980, by Mel Martin.

"Four Years Later"

"U.S. Senate Permanent Subcommittee on Investigations, Hearings on Profile of Organized Crime: Great Lakes Region," 25 January 1984, Testimony of John F. Sopko, Assistant Counsel to the Minority Staff of the Subcommittee, pp 52-53.

"During the hearing"

Plain Dealer, 15 July 1982, "Past revisited. He [Sopko] had no idea that he would be the prosecutor who would help finally convict Licavoli," by James Neff.

"The visitor got to the point"

Plain Dealer, 8 August 1984, "This cow may never get out to pasture," by Brent Larkin, page 28. "When about two weeks ago the framework for an agreement with CEI began to take shape, concern over the politics of an agreement heightened. One worry obviously centered around Kucinich, now a councilman, and the prospect of a "Save Muny Light" campaign catapulting the former mayor back into the public spotlight.

"On the afternoon of July 26, an unlikely visitor showed up at Kucinich's Lansing Avenue home to discuss the ongoing negotiations. It was there, in the backyard, that Council President George L. Forbes provided Kucinich with a thumbnail sketch of the details. Five days later, Forbes and Kucinich spoke again. Forbes, not a direct participant in the CEI—city talks, came away with the impression that Kucinich would oppose any agreement, but was uncertain as to how much of a fuss the former mayor would make."

"My God! Voinovich ought to be afraid"

Plain Dealer, 17 August 1979, "Voinovich pledges to keep Muny Light." page 18-A. "He said one reason for his announcement ws to discourage any speculation that he might sell the plant."

Cleveland Press, 17 August 1979, "Voinovich promising to protect light plant." "Lt. Governor George Voinovich stood in front of the Municipal Light plant and told reporters that, if elected mayor, he would do a better job of protecting the plant as a city asset than the Kucinich administration has done."

"While the behind-the-scenes"

Plain Dealer, 20 July 1984, "Council to hire lawyers in Muny dispute." page 9-A. "Richards [Ed Richards, executive assistant to Mayor Voinovich] who confirmed rumors months ago that such negotiations sere underway, said yesterday it 'would be beneficial if both sides, and I emphasize both, could exist in peace.'"

Plain Dealer, 14 June 1984, "Power body honors Muny's improvements."

"I told George I disagreed with his decision"

Plain Dealer, 20 August 1984, "Why CEI's Deal was Rejected." City of Cleveland advertisement page 17. "The failure of the Cleveland Electric Illuminating Co. and Cleveland Public Power (Muny Light) to reach an agreement on the proposed sale of Muny Light to CEI has been controversial. ['We are going to sell.'] Because of the protest that backers of the sale have raised, it is important to review why we stopped negotiation. ['We are not going to sell.']

"The Plain Dealer described major elements"

Plain Dealer, 3 August 1984, Page One, "City, CEI near monopoly power pact," by James Lawless.

Plain Dealer, 12 August 1984, "CEI offer for Muny: Room for debate," by Gary R. Clark, page 26-A. "Little has been made public about the proposed agreement between Cleveland Electric Illuminating Co. and the city over the sale to CEI of Cleveland Public Power's transmission and distribution systems."

Plain Dealer, 12 August 1984, from Page One, "How Mayor, CEI split on Muny Light." "The more than four months of secret negotiations between CEI and the city, which led to the proposal and Voinovich's rejection of it, was authorized by Voinovich early this year during a discussion with CEI chairman Robert M. Ginn."

"If Voinovich thought he had clearly stated that Muny would not be sold, his message apparently got lost in the negotiations, which started in late March."

Plain Dealer, 12 August 1984, from Page One, "How Mayor, CEI split over deal." "Voinovich claims he never fully realized that the draft agreement developed during those negotiations included the sale of Muny's transmission and distribution systems." Also page 27.

"Voinovich said he first read the final draft agreement after he returned from vacation July 27 '...So then, it was a sale. The issue was, is it a fair deal?'" [Voinovich said.]

Slavic Village Voice, 28 August 1984, "Is Mayor Hiding Muny-CEI "deal?" "Publicly, Mayor Voinovich maintained a position FOR Muny Light. Privately, his representatives were with CEI, mapping out an elaborate agreement which would snuff out Muny Light. The negotiations were reportedly initiated by Mayor Voinovich."

"I'm glad it is working out for Cleveland"

Plain Dealer, Page One, 19 May 1993, "Kucinich always knew he was right for saving Muny Light," by Benjamin Marrison.

Plain Dealer, 8 June 1993, "Bond sale approved for City Power expansion," by Benjamin Marrison.

"On the fifteenth anniversary of default"

WJW TV News, 15 December 1993, "Fifteen years later - - Kucinich proven right on Muny Light" *WJW-TV8* News report, Tim Taylor, Denise Dufala, anchors; City Hall Reporter Bob Cerminara interviewing.

Transcript of 6 O'Clock News, TV8, WJW-TV, December 15, 1993: Anchor Denise Dufala:

"Do you remember what you were doing 15 years ago, today? What if I reminded you that it was one of the darkest days in Cleveland's history? The day the city fell into default. The players were Dennis Kucinich, the Mayor; Council President George Forbes and the Cleveland Trust bank. The kitty was the Muny Light Plant. And as the hand played out the city was brought to its financial knees. But when the game was over it was the city and its residents who ended up the winners.

Co-Anchor Tim Taylor: "News Center Eight City Hall Reporter Bob Cerminara was covering the Hall back then. Bob, I remember moderating that default debate between then-Mayor Kucinich and Council President Forbes on state-wide television. This was a big story." Bob Cerminara:

"It really was, one of the biggest in the country. Tim it was actually hectic. As many of us all know, Cleveland has been in the national and the international spotlight for various things: Mayor Ralph Perk setting his hair on fire; the Cuyahoga River ablaze. And now, the nation's youngest elected Mayor at the helm of a major American city, steering a course that made Cleveland the first city to go into default since the Great Depression."

Man on Street # 1: "I think it is terrible. I think it is a shame. I think the Mayor should be impeached."

Man on the Street #2: "As far as Dennis goes, Kucinich, he's a pretty good man. I think he is doing a good job."

Cerminara: "Headlines throughout the media broadcast the battle between the Kucinich Administration and privately-owned CEI over who would own the city's municipal power plant. While Muny was the issue, it was Cleveland's banking community that applied heavy pressure on 31 year old Mayor Dennis Kucinich to sell the power plant or they wouldn't refinance the city's outstanding bond debt. Much of the fighting was waged on the floor of Cleveland City Council:"

Mayor Kucinich: "Then we'll see if Cleveland Trust is ready to destroy this city in the interest of CEI.

Councilman Leonard Danilowicz: "But doggone it, somebody tells me about the disastrous results of default, what are the disastrous results of loss of freedom? And that's what's at stake here."

Cerminara: "It wasn't unusual for reporters to cover two and sometimes three news conferences a day. Tensions were mounting. The Mayor was threatening to layoff 1,000 police and 500 firemen. Everything was building to a crucial vote by Council, with then-Council President George Forbes in favor of the sale.

(Roll Call: Danilowicz, NO; Forbes, YES)

Councilman Benny Bonanno: "Mr. Chairman, if you can sleep with that, God bless you." Crowd chanting: " You can't trust Cleveland Trust, close your account now."

Cerminara: "But Kucinich applied some pressure of his own. Known as the people's mayor, Kucinich rallied hundreds of people to join him in withdrawing his savings from Cleveland Trust."

Kucinich: "This bank is trying to destroy this city government through blackmail and intimidation. I'm taking my money out because I don't want clean money in a bank which is dirty."

Cerminara: "But even that couldn't save the city. At 12:01,the morning of December 16th, the city fell into its darkest hour. Time for another news conference, where Kucinich unveiled his latest plan: 'Take it to the people.'

Mayor Kucinich: "The Kucinich administration will sponsor a Charter Amendment on the question of Muny Light to give the people of Cleveland a choice."

Council President Forbes: "I'm surprised. I'm basically surprised. The concept is sound."

Cerminara: "The rest is history. The people voted to keep their power plant, while it cost their mayor his political career."

Cerminara to former Mayor Kucinich: "Knowing what you know now, and maturing the way you have, do you think you might take the same stand?"

Former Mayor Kucinich: "Principles don't change with time. It is really a matter of what is inside of you. I did what was right for the people at the time. And if people today say

I was right, I'm glad they do feel that way.

I would do the same thing all over again. I wouldn't hesitate to stand up for the people."

Cerminara: "And fifteen years later, how do the people of Cleveland feel about Kucinich's stand?

Man on the Street: #1: "He had his faults but now he is getting some stuff that he was right."

Man on the Street #2: "Smart Move." Cerminara: "Why?"

Man on the Street #2: "Because if the City of Cleveland wouldn't have no competition, which it is, the prices would have naturally gone much higher."

Woman on the Street: #1: "He had the guts to do it. Good."

Cerminara: Do you think he made the right decision?

Woman on the Street #2: "Well, yes. I'd say yes."

Cerminara: "So with CPP rates about 30% lower than CEI's it's hard to find anybody except maybe a few people at CEI, who would say that Kucinich was wrong. Now, whether he knew 15 years ago that his stand would have ended this way, is hard to say. CPP is alive and well and is expanded into all parts of the city. And one thing for those of us who can't take advantage of CPP, try to imagine where there rates would be if Cleveland Public Power wasn't here.

Co-Anchor Tim Taylor: "And a few years later, former Council President George Forbes aid, Dennis was right."

Cerminara: "He agreed with him." Denise Dufala: "Thank you, Bob." (Transcript.)

"George Forbes was quoted as saying, 'Dennis was right.'"

WJW TV News, 15 December 1993, "Fifteen Years later - - Kucinich proven right on Muny Light."

Co-Anchor Tim Taylor: "and a few years later, former Council President George Forbes said Dennis was right." (See previous end note for complete transcript.)

"He [Forbes] said the default never had to happen"

Teaching Cleveland Digital - 21 August 2013, www.teachingcleveland.org - Brent Larkin interview with former Council President George Forbes, Part Five: Cleveland Goes into Default:

Forbes: "I never thought we had to go into default. If I had to do it again I probably, I probably would have done it differently… Could have done something else to make sure we didn't do that... The finances were not as bad as we made it out to be. I probably would have done it a little differently. I had the political capital to have done it."

INDEX

A

B

C

D

E

G

H

I

J

K

L

M

N

O

P

Q

R

S

T

U

V

W

Y

Z

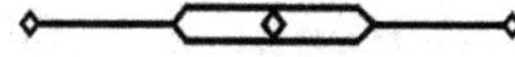

"This is an engrossing narrative of city politics, corruption, intransigence and cowardliness as few books before it. Lincoln Steffens, not being an insider, tried to get close, and he did, but not like Kucinich, whose courage comes through without chest-thumping."

- - Ralph Nader

"The epic struggle of a youthful mayor against a predatory utility company is a real-life municipal thriller. Dennis Kucinich's tale of political violence and intrigue is a cross between The Godfather and Mr. Smith Goes to Washington. He took on the fat cats on behalf of the City of Cleveland. He stared them down and won one for the good guys."

- - Geraldo Rivera

"Skillfully written, emotionally nuanced page-turner. Kucinich ultimately gives power to the people!"

- - Kenneth A. Carlson - Filmmaker

"The Division of Light and Power offers the inside story of historic events, while also implicitly taking us to the real time of the present; there is no more relevant book to read in 2021. Dennis Kucinich has written a vivid page-turner that's a political barn-burner. It reads like a novel, but it's not based on a true story - - it is a true story - - with meticulous devotion to facts, real political paradigms, and the human heart.

- - Norman Soloman - Executive Director,
Institute for Public Accuracy

"A real life, David vs. Goliath story, of one man taking on powerful corporations and political interests... An engaging and powerful read that today is more relevant than ever."

- - Joe Trippi - Noted Presidential Campaign Adviser

CPSIA information can be obtained
at www.ICGtesting.com
Printed in the USA
BVHW030844110621
609091BV00019B/2

9 781638 772347